STORMS OVER
THE MEKONG

Number 164
Williams-Ford Texas A&M University
Military History Series

STORMS OVER THE MEKONG

Major Battles of the Vietnam War

William P. Head

TEXAS A&M UNIVERSITY PRESS
COLLEGE STATION

This paper meets the requirements of ANSI/NISO Z39.48–1992
(Permanence of Paper).
Binding materials have been chosen for durability.
Manufactured in the United States of America

Library of Congress Cataloging-in-Publication Data
Names: Head, William P., 1949– author.
Title: Storms over the Mekong : Major Battles of the Vietnam War / William
    P. Head.
Other titles: Williams-Ford Texas A&M University military history series ;
    no. 164.
Identifiers: LCCN 2019052252 | ISBN 9781623498351 (cloth) | ISBN
    9781623498368 (ebook)
Subjects: LCSH: Vietnam War, 1961-1975—Campaigns. | Vietnam War,
    1961-1975—Campaigns—Mekong River Delta (Vietnam and Cambodia) |
    Vietnam War, 1961-1975—United States.
Classification: LCC DS557.7 .H43 2020 | DDC 959.704/34—dc23
LC record available at https://lccn.loc.gov/2019052252

Front Cover
Many historians, analysts, and former service members have described the
Vietnam War as the "helicopter" war. Clearly, air mobility was a key component
of US tactics throughout the conflict. Military artist James Balletto captures
this theme on the cover. Working from Blue Herron Studios in Warner Robins,
Georgia, Balletto has produced some of the most important works in military
aviation art and numerous other subjects. The author is honored by Jim's
willingness to produce such a representative painting for this book.

This work is dedicated to my wife, my comrade, my friend, and muse, Randee. She is the only thing worth living for.

Contents

Preface

When I was in graduate school, earning first my master's and then my doctorate, I published my initial articles in learned journals. As those of us who have had a professional career as historians will recall, in our early days we published and presented papers to build a résumé and make ourselves more marketable to institutions of higher learning. Much of my early work was done as a matter of opportunity, and most of what I published was not about subjects I felt passionately about. But when I went to work for the US Air Force, I discovered a myriad of original sources not only at the nearby Air Force Historic Research Agency at Maxwell Air Force Base, Alabama, but also in my own archives at Robins Air Force Base, Georgia. Since we had B-52s stationed on the other side of Robins until the mid-1980s, I discovered that my predecessors in the history office had received numerous official histories and studies about the Vietnam War. In addition, they had gathered a mass of documents and special studies relating to aircraft systems that had flown in the war.

Armed with this much material, I simply could not pass up the opportunity to write books and articles on a subject that had interested me since I entered college in 1967. I suspect my interest stemmed from the fact that the conflict was so personal. I always seemed on the verge of being drafted while many of my closest friends did serve; some never came home. Nearly every night Walter Cronkite or Huntley Brinkley reminded us of the war and its death toll. They also interviewed those who tried to convince us that it was a necessary evil.

Once I began writing about Vietnam, I developed a need to understand and explain every aspect of my beloved nation's involvement. As a result, over the past thirty-plus years I have written and published nearly a dozen articles and three books directly or indirectly related to the conflict. In recent years an increasing number of friends and colleagues have suggested I gather my articles and turn them into a book so students and researchers could read them all in one place. Finally, a couple of years ago I decided to take up the task. I soon discovered that some holes remained in telling a complete story, so I added new chapters and began revising the existing ones. The result is this book. It does not intend to cover every aspect of the war like George Herring or Mark Atwood Lawrence have done elsewhere. Instead, it focuses on what I believe are the most significant and game-changing combat events. This is not intended to demean the sacrifices soldiers on either side made in other battles and operations in Southeast Asia. Rather, by examining the opinions of reputable participants, scholars, and analysts, the consensus indicated that the battles discussed herein were the most momentous. I am sure not everyone will agree. That is okay since it is not my intention to change opinions but to start people thinking again about a traumatic period in the history of the United States and the world. Given recent events in the Persian Gulf and Middle East, Vietnam begs many questions as to why America did what it did. One may also wonder why, knowing what we thought we knew about Vietnam, the United States would repeat so many of the same mistakes and waste more lives and resources.

Some of the chapters in this book have appeared in other places in earlier forms. Most have been revised to include the most current data and historical information. Journal editors like Dan Metraux of the *Virginia Review of Asian Studies*, Richard Wolf of *Air Power History*, and Gary Kline of the *Journal of Global South Studies* allowed me to retain copyright on all the pieces they published so I might rework them into book chapters at some point. Other chapters, such as those on the Easter Offensive and Rolling Thunder, were crafted just for this book.

In executing a project of this magnitude no author completes it alone. I want to thank several close friends and colleagues, including Drs. Earl Tilford, Dennis Mills, Marc Gilbert, Gary Kline, Richard Wolf, and Dan Metraux, who read parts of the manuscript and provided sage advice as to edits and modifications. As usual I want to thank my wife, Randee, who spent far too much of her precious time editing and discussing the entire text. Last, and most importantly, I want to recognize the men and women who participated in these battles and struggled for what they believed was right and good. It is important to remember that those who went through these harrowing events were not numbers on a page or characters in a movie—they were living, breathing humans with many of the same hopes and desires we all have. Far too many, indeed millions of them, had their lives turned upside down and their dreams and futures snuffed out in a struggle to determine the course of human history across the world.

I hope the reader will find this book useful and most of all thought provoking. In the end, when humans question leaders, especially those who think it would be a good idea to have a war, fewer people suffer. Soldiers, sailors, airmen, and marines know this better than anyone since they are the ones we ask to go in harm's way. So often they are sent to some far corner of the world full of poor, downtrodden people who are sick with poverty and have nothing to lose. Perhaps Gen. Dwight D. Eisenhower described modern war best when he said, "Every gun that is made, every warship launched, every rocket fired, signifies in the final sense a theft from those who hunger and are not fed, those who are cold and are not clothed."

Reburying the victims of the Hue Massacre

The old mandarin stood by the large holes that held the bodies of several members of his city. Most had their hands tied behind them and a bullet wound in the back of their head. Some had been buried while still alive. He seemed to be in a daze and did not make a sound, just staring. Finally, he seemed to recognize one of the victims. Tears silently streamed down his cheeks and fell to the ground. As I watched him, the skies darkened and, at length, opened up with large raindrops that pounded the earth at my feet. Time passed, slowly it appeared, but finally, without a sound, my companions and I shouldered our rifles and gradually made our way from the life-changing scene. It was then that I noticed the tears in my own eyes. Were they for the old mandarin? Were they for those who died needlessly? Were they for me? Were they for the world and all the millions who suffer? As we walked on, the monsoon rains continued seemingly without end, like tears from heaven.

Abbreviations

AAA	antiaircraft artillery
APC	armored personnel carrier
ARVN	Army of the Republic of Vietnam (South Vietnam)
BUF	Big Ugly Fellow (nickname for the B-52)
CAS	close air support
CHECO	Contemporary Historical Examination of Current Operations
CIA	Central Intelligence Agency
CINCPAC	Commander in Chief, Pacific
COSVN	Central Office for South Vietnam
DMZ	Demilitarized Zone
DRV	Democratic Republic of Vietnam (North Vietnam)
JCS	Joint Chiefs of Staff
KSCB	Khe Sanh Combat Base
MACV	Military Assistance Command, Vietnam
NLF	National Liberation Front
NVA	North Vietnamese Army
NVAF	North Vietnamese Air Force

PAVN	People's Army of Vietnam
POL	petroleum, oil, and lubricant
RVNAF	Republic of Vietnam (South Vietnam) Air Force
SAC	Strategic Air Command
SAM	surface-to-air missile
USAF	US Air Force
USMC	US Marine Corps
USN	US Navy
VC	Viet Cong

STORMS OVER
THE MEKONG

Introduction

Iconic Battles of the Vietnam War

As the World War II and Korean War generations age and pass on, US Vietnam War veterans are becoming the largest group of survivors from any American war. A review of the statistics from the war make it clear how influential that generation now is, or should be, on the national culture. While 16 million Americans served in World War II, more than 9 million served on active duty from August 1964 through March 1973, with 3.4 million serving in the Southeast Asian theater of operations. Of that number 2.6 million served within the borders of Vietnam, with 1.5 million seeing combat. Peak troop strength in Vietnam reached 543,482 on 30 April 1969. In short, more than 9.7 percent of that generation of Americans were Vietnam veterans.[1]

It is well known that the United States lost 58,000 combatants, with 47,378 killed in action and 10,800 suffering nonhostile deaths. More than 300,000 others were injured, with 150,000 hospitalized and 75,000 severely wounded. Roughly 25,000 of these were declared totally disabled, while 5,000 lost at least one limb. This is particularly important since this number was, per capita, 300 percent higher than in World War II and 70 percent higher than in Korea. Of those who served, 88 percent were Caucasian and 10.6 percent were African American. More than 86 percent of the dead were white, and 12.5 percent were black. All totaled, 25 percent of all American forces during this period comprised draftees, while 30 percent of those killed in Vietnam were drafted. A total of 170,000 Hispanics served in Vietnam, and 3,070 died. In addition, 64 percent of all those killed were Protestant, 29 percent Roman Catholic, and 7 percent other religions or none at all. Of those counted as killed in action, 76 percent were from lower-middle-class or working-class families. Significantly, 79 percent had at least a high school diploma as compared to 63 percent in Korea and 45 percent during World War II. The highest number of participants and battle deaths came from the southeastern United States and the fewest from the Northeast. By the early twenty-first century, more than 90 percent of Vietnam veterans were proud to have served and believed they were now held in high public esteem. Considering that 16 million Americans participated in World War II, of whom 400,000 died and 670,000 were wounded in the most devastating conflict in world history, the numbers from the Vietnam War are, in many ways, equally significant.[2]

These numbers are only for the United States. More than 300,000 Army of the Republic of Vietnam (ARVN) troops also died along with 400,000 South Vietnamese civilians. At least twice as many were wounded, and nearly all those in the South were displaced, in some way, by the war. The North Vietnamese Army (NVA) and Viet Cong (VC) lost well over 1 million soldiers and 65,000 civilians. Another 300,000 people died in Laos and 200,000 in Cambodia. After 1975, the Pathet Lao and Khmer Rouge killed or starved millions more civilians deemed ideologically impure. In short, between 1964 and 1975, millions of humans lost their lives and homes to determine what direction Vietnam, Laos, and Cambodia would take both politically and socially. In the process of North and South Vietnam becoming the Socialist Republic of Vietnam in 1976, several large, bloody, and game-changing battles swept across the landscape and over the skies of mainland Southeast Asia. This book recounts some of those battles.[3]

Before someone decides I am wrong about my selections, let me emphasize that these are *my* selections based on a general consensus as to which battles were the most significant and supported by my research and expertise. While some who read this book may disagree on some of these actions, most are probably on everyone's list of iconic ground battles and air operations. I also realize these engagements did not take place in isolation but often in relation to negotiations and political maneuverings during America's long involvement in Vietnam. The purpose of this book is to analyze and reevaluate each of these battles in one publication to facilitate the study of the US–Vietnamese struggle.

The War on the Ground

The first ground engagement that altered the course of the conflict only peripherally involved the United States. Americans primarily served as advisers supporting ARVN units in a major battle near the village of Ap Bac in January 1963. By this time, most senior leaders in Washington believed that the South Vietnamese government of Ngo Dien Diem was gaining strength and might soon completely defeat the National Liberation Front (NLF), whose military forces still did not appear strong enough to threaten the Saigon regime. As it turned out, in one day, an outgunned VC unit inflicted so much death and destruction on a larger ARVN force that many American officials in Vietnam and in the States soon concluded not only that Diem's government was incapable of running the country but also that only a major infusion of US forces might preserve a noncommunist South Vietnam. This, combined with the Gulf of Tonkin incident in the late summer of 1964, provided the logic and rationale for the administration of Pres. Lyndon Baines Johnson to initiate a major air campaign against Hanoi and to send large numbers of US ground forces to fight the VC.

The first significant engagement involving substantial American troops was the Battle of Ia Drang Valley. After nearly a year of building up their forces, the NVA and the Americans engaged each other for the first time. US air-cavalry units, deployed by helicopter gunships, soon found themselves ambushed by a large force of mostly People's Army of Vietnam (PAVN) who had been hiding in a large tunnel complex near the designated landing zone (LZ). The battle proved not only iconic but also introduced the use of helicopters and search-and-destroy tactics that became the standard operating procedure for the remainder of the decade. Gen. William C. Westmoreland, commander of Military Assistance Command, Vietnam (MACV), believed the resulting stalemate in November 1965 validated his tactical concept of "search-and-destroy" operations. But as one North Vietnamese character in the movie *We Were Soldiers* (2002) comments at the end of the battle, though the Americans will think they have won, the outcome will be only that the fighting will go on longer and more will die. While this statement was no doubt apocryphal, the point proved to be correct.

Between Ia Drang Valley and the beginning of the Tet Offensive, these supposedly successful tactics were employed by the Americans. They inserted ground forces into hostile territory to hunt down and destroy enemy troops, materiel, weapons, and sanctuaries. As soon as the commanders decided they had won, the troops were withdrawn. During operations such as Junction City and Attleboro, helicopters and air-cavalry units became the core of this antiguerrilla method of fighting. Success was measured not by taking and holding ground, but by upping the body count.

By the end of 1967, Westmoreland and President Johnson, believing victory was at hand, began a public-relations campaign to prove this to the American people. In early 1968 the entire plan began to unravel when the VC and NVA began the Tet Offensive. In what many historians have argued was the beginning of the end for the US commitment to South Vietnam, allied forces were initially caught by surprise and bloodied by attacks throughout the South. Even though allied troops summarily defeated the communists in the field and retook all of the major cities, the political effect on American leaders and citizens proved profound: Johnson decided not to run for reelection, limited the air attacks on the North, and eventually initiated peace negotiations. All this led to the US withdrawal from South Vietnam.

Simultaneously, one of the greatest defensive battles of the war unfolded on a hilltop near Khe Sanh. This iconic siege, which played out on network television, began when Johnson determined not to suffer an American Dien Bien Phu (referring to the catastrophic French defeat in May 1954). At first the 5,000 US Marines posted in the area to block Route 9 into Quang Tri Province and to draw the PAVN into a set-piece battle actively patrolled the vicinity, seeking contact with the enemy. Sr. Gen. Vo Nguyen Giap viewed his role at Khe Sanh as one of diversion for the more important Tet Offensive. He wanted to draw the US forces to the border regions while the communists infiltrated the urban areas defended by less capable ARVN forces. During the early weeks of 1968, American marines, soldiers, and airmen beat back dozens of attacks to finally secure this isolated bastion only to abandon it later under a different policy, instituted by the new MACV commander, Gen. Creighton Abrams, that emphasized defense over offense. In many ways this policy change was the end of the Westmoreland and Johnson years.

The next great land battle took place after Pres. Richard M. Nixon took office. The May 1969 struggle between US and PAVN regulars for Hill 937, or "Hamburger Hill," took place near the Laotian border. In fact, even though the position was of little strategic value, US leadership ordered a bloody frontal assault to take the hill. No sooner was it taken then it was abandoned. This created a public outrage in the United States that ultimately led Nixon to initiate a withdrawal of American ground forces under the tenets of his "Vietnamization" policy. In many respects Hamburger Hill was one of those "big battles" for which the post–World War II US Army had trained and expected to fight on the open plains of Europe.

During the spring of 1972, the communist Nguyen Hue, or Easter, Offensive again introduced conventional combat to the Vietnam War. This and the air campaigns of 1971 and 1972 were the last great military actions of the war in which the United States played a direct role. While the PAVN offensive of 1972 was obviously a land campaign, in many ways it was also an air campaign since it was the basis for the US initiation of Linebacker I.

The final iconic land battle was one in which the United States did not participate: the desperate struggle for Xuan Loc, the last principal ARVN position defending Saigon from a PAVN conquest. Part of the long campaign to take South Vietnam after the American withdrawal, Xuan Loc became a heroic ARVN stand, culminating with the famous photograph of communist tanks breaking through the gates of the Independence (or Presidential) Palace in Saigon. It was, in fact, the end of South Vietnam and of the Vietnam War.

The War in the Air

In many ways the first major US involvement in Vietnam began in March 1965, when LBJ initiated Operation Rolling Thunder. While the naval engagement in the Gulf of Tonkin between US and Northern ships drew America into the war, the ultimate US reaction was to strike at Hanoi and other targets in the Democratic Republic of Vietnam (DRV). My examination of the air war, in which I treat major air operations as "battles," begins with a history of Rolling Thunder and then transitions to other subsequent operations such as Commando Hunt, Menu, Arc Light, Linebacker I, and Linebacker II. While there were other aerial strikes in Laos and elsewhere, these campaigns proved to be the largest. The use of airpower began as an effort to avoid substantial US ground casualties. Each operation had some component designed to force the enemy to the negotiation table but was restricted by policies in Washington, which limited their effectiveness.

Rolling Thunder began as an effort, executed by mostly fighter and fighter-bomber aircraft, to cause a strategic political solution to what was expanding into a major land war. With Johnson's decision not to run for reelection in 1968, Rolling Thunder ended. Commando Hunt then began as seven separate operations aimed at curbing the North's constant infiltration down the Ho Chi Minh Trail to augment and resupply NVA and VC troops. Instead of cutting the flow of men and materiel, intermittent and protracted interruptions in the bombing during each campaign allowed Hanoi the time to rebuild and resupply their forces. It also tempered the potential damage the Americans might have inflicted.

The introduction of B-52 strategic bombers in July 1965 led to a continuous, if also interrupted, effort to provide allied troops with close air support (CAS) in South Vietnam. These missions, better known as Operation Arc Light, not only included bombing insurgent units in the South and PAVN units near Khe Sanh but also involved attacks on targets around the Demilitarized Zone (DMZ) and in major cities such as Hanoi and Haiphong in the early 1970s.

Operation Menu comprised a series of secret B-52 raids in supposedly neutral Cambodia to eliminate enemy sanctuaries used to marshal forces invading South Vietnam. Crews risked their lives and reputations in support of sorties authorized by President Nixon but in violation of international protocols.

Linebacker I in many ways repeated Rolling Thunder. Initiated in response to the Nguyen Hue (Easter) Offensive, it began amid Nixon's withdrawal of US forces and led to some of the most extensive bombing of the war. Beginning as CAS missions against enemy attacks in South Vietnam, the effort quickly expanded into North Vietnam. While numerous kinds of aircraft were used, the most spectacular strikes were executed by B-52s. While this was part of the air war, there is also a chapter on the Easter ground campaign.

Last, but certainly not least, this work includes an examination of Linebacker II, perhaps better known as the "Christmas Bombings," in December 1972. For the first time in the war, US strategic bombers were used for a specifically strategic purpose. While the B-52s did not—and were never intended to—win the war, at this late phase their eventual effectiveness forced the North to sign the Paris Peace Accords on 27 January 1973.

Why These Battles?

As noted earlier, I have no doubt there will be those who will ask why I analyzed these battles and not others. It is my belief these are the most well-known, significant, and "iconic" engagements of Vietnam War. It is not my intention to slight, or ignore, oceanic or riverine naval actions, search-and-destroy sweeps, the fighting in Laos or Cambodia, or any other event. In an effort to keep this book a reasonable length, I limited it to those battles examined herein.

One of the things my research and the newsreel footage has reminded me of is all of those left weeping over the bodies of their loved ones during the long years of the war, whether it occurred as they dug up the bodies from the mass graves around Hue or following US or communist sweeps though villages. I am also compelled to recall that one of the major factors influencing the conflict was the natural environment—mountains, dense jungles, and subtropical weather. Monsoons constantly affected the timing of air or ground attacks; Operation Commando Hunt was specifically planned to avoid these heavy rains. Nevertheless, so much grieving and death happened even as the downpours drenched soldiers and civilians throughout Vietnam.

1

The March to Oblivion

The ARVN Defeat at Ap Bac and
the Americanization of the Vietnam War

While most Americans have never heard of the Battle of Ap Bac, it was nonetheless one of the key battles of the Vietnam War and a major reason the United States chose to take over the management and fighting of the war. The battle was fought on 2 January 1963, thirty-five miles southwest of Saigon in the Mekong delta around Ap Bac and Ap Tan, Thoi hamlets in what was then Dinh Tuong (today Tien Giang) Province in the Republic of Vietnam (South). It was fought between elements of the Army of the Republic of Vietnam and units of the insurgent National Liberation Front better known as the Viet Cong (VC).[1]

How Did It Come to This?

As most readers are aware, the defeat at Dien Bien Phu led to France's withdrawal from Indochina and into the Geneva peace talks, which brought about the division of Vietnam at the seventeenth parallel north. From the beginning of this new arrangement, rebel forces in the South, at this point only loosely tied to Ho Chi Minh's communist nationalists, the Viet Minh, were already organizing both politically and militarily to topple the Southern government. When Pres. Ngo Dinh Diem, a Roman Catholic, replaced Emperor Bao Dai as the Southern leader in 1956, many communists, leftists, and even democrats who opposed his authoritarian regime formed the NLF. By 1957, this group realized that a peaceful replacement of Diem's government was unlikely. Gradually, the hard core of the NLF began to organize what became the VC. To counteract VC guerrilla actions, Diem initiated an anticommunist campaign to eliminate what he called "Viet Minh personnel that had been left behind to foment an uprising."[2]

Meanwhile, Ho's regime in Hanoi, under the provisions of the Geneva Accords, pushed for a national election to reunify the nation under communist leadership. Fearing this, Sec. of State John Foster Dulles and Pres. Dwight D. Eisenhower directed aid to the Diem regime's efforts to avoid the elections until a strong alternative could be found to oppose the communists. While the United States tried to avoid combat, the situation was building toward open war.[3]

Considering what would happen in the future, the sobering part of this story is that Diem's anticommunist crusade in the early 1960s, through programs such as the Rural Revolutionary Development and Chieu Hoi Programs, designed to convince VC fighters to desert and join the ARVN, proved relatively successful. When the VC tried to counter this with guerrilla tactics, they often failed. They soon begged Hanoi for material support. Initially, the North Vietnamese, fearing American intervention, declined. This forced the VC to withdraw into isolated hideouts in the hills and jungles. It appeared Diem was on the verge of victory, but at this key juncture his forces failed to seize the moment. This gave the communists time to establish enclaves throughout South Vietnam.[4]

With the election of John F. Kennedy in 1960, America's commitment increased but not to the full-scale level it would reach in the middle to late 1960s. Most of the first American "advisers" to arrive were from the US Army's Special Forces. They brought with them a new weapon that changed the very nature of the war—helicopters. This seemed to provide the ARVN with a huge advantage since troops could be rapidly deployed to nearly every area of South Vietnam, allowing them to confront the enemy before they could organize or withdraw. During much of the dry season of 1961 and 1962, these new attack forces became progressively successful in beating back the VC. These tactics, mixed with the simultaneous introduction of M113/114 armored personnel carriers (APCs), took a heavy toll on unseasoned enemy fighters, who were lightly armed and had no weapons capable of stopping the APCs. When confronting these vehicles their only plan was to hit and run, with an emphasis on run. Other tactics led to heavy casualties, which communist forces could not afford—at least not at this time.[5]

The ARVN Forces

Unfortunately for the South Vietnamese and the Americans, short-sighted policies in both nations and internal rivalries in Saigon robbed them of any real chance of victory. The ARVN's most effective unit was the 7th Infantry Division, commanded by Col. Huynh Van Cao. At least part of its success was due to the dedicated support of US adviser Lt. Col. John Paul Vann and his tactical planner, Capt. Richard Ziegler. During the previous eighteen to twenty months, the 7th had bloodied the VC in its anticommunist pacification campaigns, killing or isolating thousands of them with ease.[6]

Despite the success, there were problems. As Vann often reported, ARVN leaders did not like to risk too many losses since Diem demoted officers

Figure 1.1. Lt. Col. John Paul Vann in his Saigon office

who did. Accordingly, Cao often acted cautiously even when his men were in a good position to annihilate large numbers of VC, frequently allowing the enemy to escape. At first such behavior puzzled Vann since Cao was otherwise an excellent commander. As he came to understand the nuances of the president's governing methods, Vann realized Diem was more interested in employing his soldiers to protect his regime against internal political opponents than in destroying the VC. Roger Hilsman, Kennedy's director of the Bureau of Intelligence and Research, noted in one report, Cao "was not the hard-fighting general he appeared to be, nor was he a particularly able military commander. In actuality, he is one of President Diem's political appointees, given command of the prestigious 7th Division because he was loyal to Diem and because of his background and religion—like Diem he was a Catholic from Hue."[7]

Throughout his tenure as president, Diem appointed his friends and coreligionists to key ARVN posts. Fellow Catholics like Cao, Le Quang Tung, and Ton That Dinh held high military positions not because they had military ability or experience, but because they were politically loyal and would prevent a coup. As Vann recalled, following a minor skirmish on a highway resulting in a small number of ARVN casualties and the loss of some vehicles, Diem summoned Cao to Saigon for a tongue lashing. When the division commander returned, Vann and his group of advisers were told there would be no more joint planning sessions, even though these had led to so many successful raids against the VC. Instead, Cao used the excellent military-intelligence network the Americans had developed to find areas devoid of enemy forces. In doing so he claimed to be increasing the operational tempo while decreasing ARVN casualties. In fact, many of these reported clashes never happened. This made Diem happy but allowed the NLF and VC breathing room to reconstitute their forces during this critical time.[8]

Unclear to most Americans at the time, Diem's political maneuvering sabotaged efforts to finish off the VC. This problem was exacerbated when he reorganized ARVN troop deployments by dividing the command of the region south of Saigon into two new corps areas. The original III Corps units had their zone of responsibility reduced, with the newly created IV Corps taking over responsibilities for the area west and southwest of the capital. Diem promoted Cao to general and placed him in command of this new IV Corps Tactical Zone. It included the area of operations for the 7th Infantry Division, now commanded by Cao's former chief of staff, Col. Bui

Dinh Dam. Having doubts about his own military abilities when the promotion was first proposed, Dam set aside his self-doubt out of loyalty to Cao and assumed the position. Sensing a need for support from someone with military ability, he invited Vann and the other US advisers back into the planning efforts. Even so, the same problems continued to confront the Americans with the 7th Infantry Division.[9]

While US advisers were increasingly concerned over the lack of aggressiveness among ARVN commanders, in Saigon senior leadership was convinced the VC presented a diminishing threat. There, Gen. Paul Harkins, the first senior US military representative in Saigon (as commander of the Military Assistance and Advisory Group), was convinced the ARVN could finish off the VC if only the communists would fight a conventional battle. Within Harkins's staff, American hubris was in full bloom, and why not—the general himself described the VC as "raggedy-ass little bastards." It was a view Vann and his cohorts did not share. Perhaps had Harkins gone into the field to investigate the situation himself, he might have had a different attitude.[10]

To the smattering of US military personnel sent to train and advise the ARVN, this was serious business, and they needed all hands on deck to defeat these "troublesome" rebels. Western Dinh Toung Province, which the advisers dubbed "Injun Country," was particularly vexing since it was the home of the 514th VC Regimental Battalion and was swarming with VC and NLF sympathizers. Hilsman explained: "It was an area where villages were fortified with well-prepared foxholes and bomb shelters. This was where the 7th Division's ranger platoon had been ambushed, and G-2 [intelligence] evidence was firm that about 100 men of the 514th were resting in the general vicinity of the village of Ap Bac." He concluded, "This presented the ARVN with an excellent opportunity to pin down a VC unit and destroy it by using all its advantages of mobility, firepower and armor."[11]

By November 1962, with ARVN military activities almost nonexistent, officials in VC Military Region II directed the 261st Battalion and the 1st Company of the 514th Battalion, headquartered in Dinh Tuong Province, to destroy the strategic hamlets in their region and to block ARVN sweeping operations. During 28–30 December, multiple aerial-reconnaissance sorties by US aircraft with eavesdropping capabilities picked up VC radio transmissions. The intercepted signals came from Ap Tan Thoi hamlet in Dinh Tuong near the 7th Infantry Division's headquarters. To Vann's intelligence officer, James Drummond, this data proved very unsettling since it indicated the enemy was using Ap Tan Thoi as a center of operations. Both ARVN and US intelligence analysts believed VC leaders had deployed only a reinforced company of about 120 men to protect the transmitter. This estimate would prove to be woefully small. Convinced of their superior numbers, the 7th Infantry Division was ordered to attack Ap Tan Thoi. The ARVN went into battle overconfident and unprepared for the fierce resistance awaiting them.[12]

Captain Ziegler drafted operational plan "Duc Thang I," aimed at assaulting a small enemy formation. Once completed, he presented it to Dam and his command staff. The plan called for ARVN units to attack from three directions. Three rifle companies of the 11th Infantry Regiment were to move from the north, the Dinh Tuong Civil Guards Regiment would attack from the south, and a group of thirteen M113s, carrying an infantry company, would engage from the southwest. The APCs and infantry would act as both a mobile reserve and a reaction force, positioned so they could move in if the VC began to retreat. One final aspect of the plan called for Dam to deploy two rifle companies to Tan Hiep Airfield using US Army 93rd Transportation Company CH-21 Shawnee and UH-1 Iroquois helicopters, the former known as the "Flying Banana" and the latter soon to be renowned as the Huey. The UH-1s were gunships armed with 7.62-mm machine guns and 2.75-inch rockets. Not only were their weapons state of the art at that time but also their gunners were well trained and very accurate.[13]

The poorly trained Civil Guard troops were divided into three task forces for the operation against Ap Tan Thoi. The first, Task Force A, was formed around the 174th, 842nd, and 892nd Companies. Task Force B was made up of the 171st, 172nd, and 839th Companies. Finally, the 173rd and 175th Companies constituted Task Force C, tasked with blocking the far western part of the battlefield. Task Force C was halfhearted about the operation from the start.[14]

The VC Forces

This was not the first time intelligence operatives had located VC radio transmitters. On most occasions the sets were moved before the ARVN could attack. This time, however, the VC were prepared to stand and fight. They had 300–350 of their best soldiers present, with the 261st dug in at Ap Bac and the 514th at Ap Tan Thoi, separated by less than a mile. They were supported by 30–40 local fighters from Chau Thanh District who were used as scouts, ammunition bearers, litter carriers, and emergency replacements. All were commanded by Col. Hai Hoang.[15]

As the 261st Battalion was formed, command alternated between Hoang and Tu Khue, a South Vietnamese revolutionary and North Vietnamese native who had returned to the South in 1954. Khue was not very well liked or respected because of his excessively strict and sometimes harsh treatment of the Southern cadres. Nonetheless, he carefully prepared every detail before the engagement. By contrast, Hoang led by example, which gave the men great confidence. His combat skills were the best of any VC commander in the area. For these reasons, leadership put him in charge of all forces around Ap Bac. Unlike previous engagements, where the VC fighters were poorly armed, this time they possessed captured US-made arms, including M1 carbines, Browning Automatic Rifles, .30-cal. machine guns, and one 60-mm mortar. While this was not much by later standards, at the time it was the most robustly equipped communist unit yet assembled in South Vietnam.[16]

One big advantage the VC enjoyed was intelligence. Their operatives, dressed as villagers, were able to obtain and pass along critical data. Prior to the battle, Hoang received nearly constant news that led him to conclude the ARVN forces were planning a major attack. Not only did his agents in Dinh Tuong inform him that, among other things, seventy-one truckloads of ammunition and other supplies had arrived from Saigon, but vital reports also arrived from Pham Xuan An, an influential journalist and, as it turned out, a VC agent in Saigon. An spent time in the United States in the 1950s and returned to South Vietnam in 1959, where he worked for *Time* magazine and Reuters.[17]

In preparation for the engagement, the VC trained to deal with the ARVN helicopters and APCs by studying captured US and ARVN manuals. They also built defensive positions just north of Ap Tan Thoi along a tree-lined creek. In Ap Bac they set up south of the hamlet in positions obscured by trees and shrubs, making them nearly impossible to spot from the air. In the area just south and west of Ap Bac, they dug several foxholes in front of an irrigation dike, which afforded them an unobstructed field of fire into the surrounding rice paddies. The entrenchments proved to be deep enough either for one man to stand up or to accommodate a two-man machine-gun crew. Behind the foxhole line, the irrigation dike enabled units to communicate with each other. In short, the VC enjoyed a great terrain advantage.[18]

The Battle Begins

In the early morning hours of 2 January 1963, VC reconnaissance units near Ap Bac and Ap Tan Thoi returned to their command center to report hearing trucks. With all in place, Hoang ordered his men to assume their defensive positions. Expecting a large engagement, the VC moved the vast majority of the women, children, and old men living in both hamlets into hiding places in the nearby brush and swamps.[19]

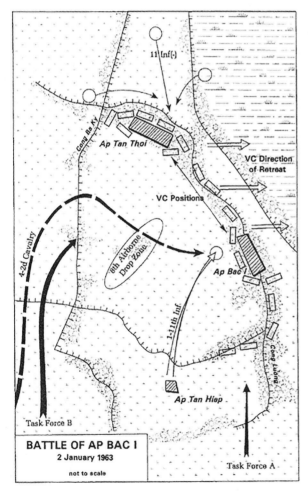

Figure 1.2. The Battle of Ap Bac, 2 January 1963

ARVN forces needed thirty CH-21 airlift sorties to ferry the 1st Battalion, 11th Infantry Regiment to the anticipated combat area. Since they only had ten choppers, each helicopter had to make three trips to deploy all the ARVN soldiers, meaning Colonel Dam could only send in one company at a time. The first wave landed at 0700 to secure the LZ until the rest of the battalion arrived. This delay had an unintended effect on the other troops involved in the assault, the greatest being felt by the Civil Guard units of Task Forces A and B, commanded by Maj. Lam Quang Tho, the Dinh Tuong provincial chief. Instead of the ready support they expected from the regular ARVN units, they had to face the well-trained VC by themselves.[20]

As the first Civil Guard troops of Task Force A advanced north toward Ap Bac, Hoang moved his units into position to ambush them. For the first time in the war, the VC had good internal command-and-control capabilities. Their radio personnel, operating captured American-made communications equipment, kept abreast of Tho's troops by monitoring ARVN frequencies. The communists were spoiling for a fight. Around 0800, as Task Force A's lead units came within one hundred feet of Ap Bac's southern entrance, the VC cut loose, killing the forward company's commander and severely wounding the task-force commander. Instead of moving ahead,

Figure 1.3. A CH-21 Shawnee (or Flying Banana) on static display at the National Museum of the US Air Force, Dayton, OH

the inexperienced troops of the Civil Guard ran for cover behind a dike. The surviving officers finally rallied their terrified men, who spent the next several hours unsuccessfully attempting to outflank the VC. They called in artillery support, but their forward observers were so scared they refused to position themselves where they could adequately observe the effects of the shelling. As a result the artillery fire was inaccurate, with nearly every round hitting behind the enemy positions. One would imagine that at some point Major Tho would have sent Task Force B to A's rescue—he did not. At 1000, with the battalion commander wounded, all maneuvering stopped.[21]

Simultaneously, just north of Ap Tan Thoi, the three companies of the 11th Infantry Regiment were also bogged down. Marching south in three separate columns, they ran into heavy fire from troops of the 514th VC Battalion. Over the next five hours, the ARVN soldiers made three attacks but failed to break through. At 0930, Dam's final reserve companies arrived at Tan Hiep, about two hours late. The venerable old CH-21s had antiquated bad-weather radar equipment and could not risk a landing in the heavy fog that socked in the airfield. With the combat situation worsening, Dam decided to force the VC to extend their lines by attacking the enemy positions from both east and west.[22]

With his forces now in danger, Dam contacted Vann, who was observing the battlefield from a Cessna O-1/L-19 Bird Dog single-engine reconnaissance aircraft. The colonel asked him to find LZs to the east and west of Ap Bac so he could insert fresh assault troops. Vann instructed his pilot to make low passes over the tree-covered areas near the hamlet. Even though he could not see the VC positions, Vann reasoned they must be well fortified along the southern end due to the concentration of enemy fire on the Civil Guards. The communists proved to be clever foes: as the plane flew over the western tree line, they held their fire to conceal their positions. The ruse worked. The American, although suspicious, decided this side of Ap Bac made for a better LZ due to the lack of heavy fighting in the area.[23]

At this point Vann contacted the other L-19, which was directing the CH-21s and UH-1s on their airlift operations. He instructed the chopper pilots to land their next wave of ARVN troops about 1,000 feet from the western and southern tree lines covering Ap Bac; he expected this to lessen the effect of the VC's .30-cal. machine guns. Unfortunately for everyone on the allied side, the pilots ignored these instructions. During this early period of American involvement in the Vietnam War, command relationships between US military units were not as formal as they became later. Thus, US aircrews tended to disregard the directives from advisors, especially Vann, who was considered overbearing. The pilots decided to come in as previously planned, with disastrous results. Flying in from the north, they saw and heard the fighting. Hoping to save the situation, the pilots mistakenly determined that the main VC positions were all located in the southern treeline and landed along the creek only 200 yards west of Ap Bac. There, heavy fire from VC light arms hit them. The Hueys strafed the enemy positions without effect since the fighters were in their foxholes under the trees and shielded from the helicopters' fire.[24]

Things went from bad to worse for the ARVN forces and their US advisers. Having deposited their troops, the CH-21s withdrew, but one was severely damaged and remained on the ground. The Americans decided not to leave its crew with the ARVN ground forces and sent another CH-21 to extricate them. This chopper was also heavily damaged. With two of their ten Shawnees downed, commanders ordered a UH-1 in to pick up the crews. As it hovered over the LZ, it too took enemy fire, which struck the main rotor, flipping it over. As if this were not enough, slightly to the north a third CH-21 had to crash-land. With ARVN forces pinned down and fearful of risking any more of their precious helicopter assets, the situation became dire. By 1030, all ARVN units were on the ground and under heavy fire from hidden VC positions. Most of the South Vietnamese refused to move. Their officers, mindful of directives from President Diem about preserving troops, ignored the US adviser's instructions to attack.[25]

Committing the APCs

With so many injured from the helicopter crashes and very little medical care available, it was left to the downed crews to improvise. In one case Sgt. Arnold Bowers, who had been on the first chopper to go down, went all over the crash area pulling his comrades to safety. When the second CH-21 crashed, he repeated the process. After making sure everyone was being cared for, he took over a field radio from a petrified ARVN operator and called in artillery and airstrikes. Soon two A-1H Skyraiders swooped in to bomb Ap Bac's thatched shacks with conventional ordnance and napalm. Believing they had been saved, several ARVN soldiers stood up to cheer and to see if the VC were retreating—they were not. Instead, they poured rounds into the exposed troops, killing several. An irate Vann, watching the catastrophe below, radioed Capt. James B. Scanlon, senior adviser to the ARVN 2nd Armored Cavalry Regiment. The lieutenant colonel directed him to get his ARVN counterpart, Capt. Ly Tong Ba, commander of the 4th Mechanized Rifle Squadron, 2nd Armored Cavalry Regiment, into action to rescue the trapped South Vietnamese company and the US helicopter crews.[26]

Captain Ba refused to take directions from any Americans and believed sending his thirteen M113 APCs through the Cong Ba Ky Canal would allow the VC to escape. Eventually, Vann joined in the argument and, when he could not get satisfaction, radioed Ziegler at the command post at Tan Hiep to contact Colonel Dam and have him order Ba to advance. In due time Ziegler got Dam's order for Ba to get his M113s moving toward the smoke rising from the burning hamlet. Vann believed Ba's M113s could save the day. They had on previous occasions, the VC having fled when the APCs appeared on the battlefield. But this time was different. Prior to the battle, Hoang had explained to his soldiers that their only avenue of escape was through the adjacent muddy rice fields—to retreat was to die. His men

Figure 1.4. APC crossing the Cong Ba Ky Canal

clearly were willing risk death, but preferred to do so while fighting, not running.[27]

Things started out well for the ARVN unit. The M113s easily crossed the streams and rivers typical of the Mekong delta. Yet when they reached the Cong Ba Ky Canal, the ten-ton vehicles bogged down. The M113 crews and the infantrymen riding on the APCs had to cut down brush and trees to fill the canal until it was shallow enough to cross, which slowed the column to a crawl. Ba exacerbated this when he attempted to get proper authorization to continue the advance from the canal. Vann urged him to speed things up. Again the stubborn ARVN captain refused to obey orders from an American adviser. Ba finally moved when Vann threatened to have him shot, though only very slowly, undoubtedly demonstrating his defiance.[28]

As this drama played out, the Americans sent a fourth CH-21 to Ap Bac to attempt a rescue of the downed helicopter crews. It had no more success than the others and was also forced to crash-land in a muddy rice field. This was a great victory for the VC since they had never before downed even a single helicopter in this way, much less five in a matter of a few hours.[29]

Around 1330, the M113 formation closed in on the helicopter-crash site from the western side of Ap Bac. For some reason known only to Captain Ba, the APCs approached the LZ in single file instead of in attack formation. They immediately drew heavy fire from the concealed enemy forces. With the vehicles in single file, the VC could concentrate all their fire on one target at a time. In addition, the M113 gunners were exposed from the waist up and became easy targets for snipers, with fourteen ARVN crewmen being killed. Despite the heavy fire, the two lead APCs soon came abreast of the downed helicopters. In the process one driver was killed because he had his head outside of the hatch while, for good or bad, Ba was knocked unconscious inside his APC.[30]

With the M113s close by, Captain Scanlon and Sergeant Bowers helped the wounded into the vehicles. With the downed crews aboard, the APCs withdrew, their .50-cal. machine guns spraying covering fire at no particular target. At some point during this retreat, Ba regained his senses and ordered a frontal assault on the enemy's foxhole line. Even as ARVN forces seemed to have victory in their grasp, a VC squad leader tossed several grenades at the lead M113s. Within seconds his men mimicked his actions, causing the cohesion of the formation to break up and ARVN morale to disintegrate. In several cases the South Vietnamese sergeants, who were both commanders and machine gunners on the APCs, were killed and replaced by less-experienced men.[31]

Finally, Ba decided to send an M113 with a flamethrower to a position only 300 feet from the VC defenses in the western tree line. Since its normal range was 660 feet, this appeared to be a workable solution. Yet when the crew commenced firing, the flame only reached about 100 feet; a later investigation revealed that the crew had improperly mixed the jelling agent with the gasoline. At 1430 the attack ended, and the APCs withdrew.[32]

Problems Elsewhere

Throughout the battlefield nothing seemed to go as planned. Vann was not only frustrated by the failures with the APC attacks but also upset that the Civil Guard troops of Task Force B had been reluctant to march to the sound of the guns. Although their comrades of Task Force A were pinned down, they seemed in no hurry to reach Ap Bac, instead slowly searching each house as they marched along the southwestern flank of the combat area.[33]

With the entire operation on the verge of total failure, Vann landed at Tan Hiep and asked General Cao to deploy an airborne battalion to the eastern side of Ap Bac, the most logical VC retreat route. By doing so he hoped to trap the enemy forces inside the hamlets by blocking them on all sides. Once surrounded, Vann intended to wipe them out by employing an elite ARVN paratroop battalion. Cao would have none of it and completely opposed the plan. He instead proposed to drop an airborne battalion behind the M113 formation on the western side of the combat zone. The irate American accused the general of wanting to let the VC escape in order to keep his casualty numbers down. Cao responded that an encircled and well-entrenched enemy would fight more fiercely than a retreating one. Furthermore, he claimed that he wanted the VC inside Ap Bac and Ap Tan Thoi to flee through the eastern side of the battlefield, exposing them to artillery and air attacks. The plan seemed at least plausible.[34]

By this time Cao no longer trusted Vann. Privately he was upset the advisor had risked the lives of his ARVN soldiers to save those of a handful of Americans. Also present during this argument between Vann and Cao was Maj. Gen. Tran Thien Khiem, chief of the ARVN Joint General Staff. He sat passively through most of the discussion and in the end agreed with Cao's plan since it was consistent with Diem's general objective to minimize Vietnamese casualties. Cao was the commander of these forces and Vann had no actual authority, so the division commander got his way.[35]

Airborne Troops to the Rescue?

Realizing he was getting nowhere, Vann accepted Cao's plan, got back in his plane, and left. That entire afternoon he pressed the general to deploy his airborne units as quickly as possible. By now the American was afraid the ARVN forces might lose the most important battle they had fought up to this point against the VC. Cao continued to say he was going to deploy the second Civil Guard battalion, which had just arrived on the southwestern flank of Ap Bac, and to drop the ARVN 8th Airborne Battalion at the rear of the APCs at 1600.

Finally, with nightfall closing in, several C-123 Provider aircraft, with 300 paratroopers of the 8th Airborne Battalion on board, arrived overhead. As they approached their intended drop area, the VC opened up with machine guns. To avoid this fire, the C-123 pilots altered their course, but either the ARVN jumpmaster or the US flight leader failed to compensate for this change in wind direction and altitude. As a result the paratroops missed the drop zone and landed directly in front of the enemy trenches. There they were cut to pieces, some while descending, others after becoming stuck in the trees. Those who survived the drop rapidly organized and made several unsuccessful assaults. Sporadic fighting continued until sundown. When it was over, the 8th had lost nineteen men killed and thirty-three wounded. In addition, US advisers Capt. Fletcher Ware and Sgt. Russell Kopti, who parachuted with the ARVN forces, were wounded.[36]

As darkness fell, Hoang began his withdrawal. The colonel realized the ARVN soldiers were moving in on his defensive perimeter, albeit slowly, from three directions. His troops were low on ammunition and completely exhausted. With the eastern accesses still clear, he now ordered both the 261st and 514th Battalions to assemble at the southern end of Ap Tan Thoi and evacuate through the rice fields, taking their dead and wounded with them.[37]

Vann proposed calling in a C-47 flare ship to drop flares over the retreating VC and light up the rice fields to the east of the hamlets, after which artillery would fire several hundred rounds along their path of retreat. Cao opposed the plan for fear of revealing his airborne battalion's position and instead ordered the artillery batteries to fire exactly 100 rounds at a rate of four shells each hour. It could not have been better for the VC. A couple of hours before midnight, Hoang led his men out of Ap Tan Thoi toward their base camp near the Plain of Reeds. Concurrently, the local-force units departed in different directions to their sanctuaries in the surrounding area. The survivors of 1st Company, 261st Battalion led the march, followed by litter carriers transporting the dead and wounded. Soldiers of 1st Company, 514th Battalion covered the rear of the column, with one of their platoons acting as rear guard. Upon reaching the canal just east of Ap Tan Thoi, they placed the wounded into sampans. The remaining VC units marched to their destination, arriving at 0700 on 3 January. The communists had won a decisive and, in many respects, textbook victory. While it had major effects on the morale of both sides, perhaps most importantly the battle prompted American decision makers to determine that the ARVN could not defeat the VC without increased—and direct— US military involvement.[38]

Aftermath and Analysis

Not surprisingly, the two sides reported differing casualty numbers. The United States claimed between 150 and 200 ARVN troops were killed and wounded, as well as eleven American casualties, with five helicopters destroyed. The communists reported 450 ARVN casualties, nineteen Americans killed, and eight helicopters downed. The VC declared victory. The US response was divided. Individuals like General Harkins and US Army chief of staff Gen. Earle C. Wheeler, while admitting the battle had not gone perfectly, declared that the "situation was not as bad as it had been depicted."[39] Senior advisers around President Kennedy were able to convince him to "stick with Diem."[40]

On the other hand, many in the press, such as *Washington Post* reporter Neil Sheehan, quickly picked up on the recrimination toward the South Vietnamese coming from people like Vann. In the aftermath Vann publically called some ARVN officers "cowards."[41] He honed in on Captain Ba, who had refused to follow his directives to support pinned-down ARVN troops at Ap Bac. The lieutenant colonel publically concluded: "It was a miserable damn performance, just like it always is. These people won't listen. They make the same mistake over and over again in the same way."[42]

For his part Sheehan, along with many other journalists like David Halberstam, declared the American public was not "getting the facts." On 7 January the *Washington Post* published a front-page article by Sheehan that stated "angry United States military advisers charged today that Vietnamese infantry personnel refused direct orders to advance during Wednesday's battle at Ap Bac and that an American Army captain was killed while out front pleading with them to attack." This was followed eight days later by a State Department analysis of national media reaction to the battle: "since Ap Bac the complaint has been increasingly heard that the American public is not 'getting the facts' on the situation in Vietnam, even at this time when American casualties are mounting."[43]

While there were differences of opinion over the success or failure of the ARVN forces, this was indisputably a volatile period in the war. Prior to Ap Bac most citizens and political leaders had been relatively apathetic about this little brushfire war on the other side of the world. Most military leaders assumed the ARVN forces, since they outnumbered the VC four or five to one and possessed superior military hardware, could not lose. Besides, the strategic-hamlet program had set up 3,500 secure villages all over South Vietnam, and the people of the nation seemed to be supporting the government in Saigon. But with the defeat at Ap Bac, all these notions had to be reassessed.[44]

The reevaluation began almost immediately when, on 3 January, US advisers brought Western journalists to devastated Ap Bac hamlet to inspect the battlefield. During the tour, Sheehan asked Brig. Gen. Robert York to recount what had happened. York replied: "What the hell's it look like happened, boy. They got away, that's what happened." The meaning of this remark was not lost on any of the reporters, nor was the fact that, after the VC had left, the ARVN artillery barrage Vann had requested obliterated the hamlet—several hours too late. The terrible targeting of the ARVN artillery crews killed five of their own soldiers and wounded fourteen more.[45]

No one who has examined the battle can lay all of the blame at the feet of the ARVN. After all, Ziegler created the operational plan, to which Vann made several alterations as well as exercised critical judgments during the early phases of the battle. Yet Vann remained adamant. When he resigned in disgust some months later, he accused President Diem of seeking to keep the war going on endlessly in order to get US aid. He also chided Washington leadership, saying they had a "tendency to play down the real picture."[46]

While Sheehan's book on Vann has all but deified the lieutenant colonel to the millions who read it, in many ways those who have reexamined the battle in recent years have argued that, by condemning the ARVN for the defeat, Vann wanted to cover up inaccurate US intelligence, especially on the number of VC in the area, and the often frenetic leadership he provided. Vann's disrespectful attitude toward all of his Vietnamese charges created much of the problem. Although a brave and knowledgeable tactical commander, he often demonstrated cultural and ethnic ignorance when it came to the Vietnamese. His heavy-handed criticisms and overt anger toward their military decisions caused them to lose face, which only made it more difficult to get them to accept the American's commands and instructions. In addition, it is clear his criticism also had an ulterior motive. Since many of the ARVN officers were anxious to please their US allies, Vann sought to take advantage of this attitude in hopes that if he presented his points passionately enough then, they would accept any future demands.[47]

In a memorandum to Kennedy signed by Harkins, the general made every effort to convince US senior leaders that the operation was basically successful since the VC had retreated and left their positions, leaving Ap Bac and Ap Tan Thoi to the ARVN. His basic argument, based on classic military precepts derived from World War II, was that since the ARVN had taken the battlefield, they had won. From the standpoint of conventional set-piece combat employing combined arms, the objective was the control of ground. Of course, this was never the goal of the VC fighters. Their objective was to undermine the credibility of the Diem regime and gather followers who would stand with them during the next phases of the people's war. Ultimately, overly positive evaluation of these encounters harmed the stability of the ARVN. Instead of constructive criticism that might have strengthened it, Harkins whitewashed the entire affair and left in place the same chronic ARVN flaws. He also undermined US advisers. Due to his misguided report, no one in the allied military learned any important lessons from the battle at Ap Bac.[48]

To demonstrate the deep-seeded distain most journalists had for Harkins and his evaluation of the situation at Ap Bac, one need only examine Sheehan's and Halberstam's descriptions of him. Sheehan said he was "an American General with a swagger stick and cigarette holder who would not deign to soil his suntans and street shoes in a rice paddy to find out that what was going on was prattling about having trapped the Viet Cong."

During a Fourth of July celebration at the US Embassy in Saigon, Halberstam refused to shake the commander's hand. During the obligatory toasts to the general, Halberstam shouted, "Paul D. Harkins should be court martialed and shot!"[49]

If Harkins had been the only senior leader to see Ap Bac in a positive light, the reality might have eventually set in. But almost all those in Saigon and in Washington also put an encouraging spin on the battle, putting reality on hold. Adm. Harold Felt, US Pacific Fleet commander, also argued that since the ARVN forces had taken the battlefield, they had won. All of this only aggravated the growing rift between the military and the press. While soldiers, many veterans of World War II, expected the press to be supportive of their viewpoints, this new group of journalists had gained increased influence from television and were determined to tell the public the "truth." Moreover, President Kennedy was not inclined to censor the press, which was generally in his corner domestically. In one indicative incident just after the battle, Associated Press reporter Peter Arnett asked Felt a hard question. The admiral lashed back, "Get on the team!"[50]

Of course, this was not an American battle but a Vietnamese battle. It was, for that time, a relatively big engagement and one that dearly cost the ARVN. The official casualty count by the Americans claimed 83 ARVN troops killed and another 108 wounded. As for the US advisers and helicopter crews who participated, they reported three dead and eight wounded. Of the fifteen US choppers participating in the battle, nine were damaged, five destroyed, and only one came through unscathed.[51]

In spite of the rosy view of some, over a half century later it is clear the VC won a major victory at Ap Bac. For the first time in the conflict, they stood toe to toe with the ARVN and inflicted severe damage, even though they were outnumbered five to one by a force supported by massed artillery, armored units, and US transport and CAS. According to official NLF records, they lost 18 soldiers killed and 39 wounded, this despite the ARVN forces firing more than 600 rounds of artillery and thirteen American aircraft dropping napalm and other ordnance—this in addition to the constant support provided by the five UH-1 gunships.[52]

Consequences: Intended and Unintended

Historian Frances Fitzgerald in her book *Fire in the Lake* declared that the battle at Ap Bac "showed a group of unbelieving American advisers that

[NLF] guerilla forces could stand up against a multi-battalion ARVN operation supported by US helicopters and artillery." She further asserted: "This military achievement was not an isolated phenomenon. By late 1962, the VC had a presence in some 80 percent of the rural communities in South Vietnam."[53] Few on the allied side seemed to grasp that the war was changing, and they needed to act decisively or risk defeat. In short, their actions had consequences.

Looking back, this single battle had compelling results for the VC. It proved to be a watershed event for its fighters, leading them to believe in their ability to defeat ARVN units no matter how well equipped they were. Accordingly, the confidence of their commanders and soldiers grew exponentially. After Ap Bac, where they had defeated "unpopular dictator" Diem's soldiers, both the VC 261st and 514th Battalions became heroes to many in the areas they controlled, much like Jesse James in the American West or Robin Hood in medieval England. Recruiting and VC activities increased significantly because of this victory.[54]

On the South Vietnamese side, the battle had a decidedly negative consequence for pacification of the rural areas. Despite the early success of the Strategic Hamlet Program and military operations in 1962, nearly all of this progress was lost in twenty-four hours to a "rag tag" force of three hundred communist fighters. Worse, the defeat increased the pressure on the president's regime to demonstrate it could still recover and subdue this VC resurgence, especially in the Mekong River valley. In the end Diem could not. In fact, he was never given a chance, due to American frustration and his own heavy-handedness.[55]

In many ways the most damaging and long-lasting consequence was as yet undefined—the future of the South Vietnamese government and US involvement in Vietnam. Some military officers, politicians, and analysts believed Ap Bac should have been a wakeup call that the United States would have to take over the fight. This was the path American leaders chose twenty months later. To do this they eventually abandoned Diem to a military coup that took his life. By the end of the 1960s, 568,000 American service personnel were committed to a war many already realized was unwinnable. Worse, the Americans never did find a really stable government to replace Diem's. Ultimately, the United States would withdraw in 1973 after losing the lives of 58,000 of its young people, sidetracking the Great Society and diverting the nation's own socioeconomic growth.

At least one Vietnamese scholar-diplomat possessed the logic and wisdom to see the tragic path down which South Vietnam would head once the United States took over the war effort. Former South Vietnamese ambassador to the United States Bui Diem in retrospect realized that when the Americans took over, the war was all but lost: "The Americanization of the Vietnam War, which took place so abruptly and imperiously in the spring of 1965, had a long, significant history. It was a history of the perennial failure of American diplomacy to foster a vital South Vietnamese democracy capable of handling its own affairs." He concluded: "The first eleven years of the United States' relationship with an independent South Vietnam set a deadly pattern. The Americans first watched the rise and fall of civilian and military dictatorships without attempting to use their influence decisively for something better." It was Ap Bac where the beginning of the end of President Diem began as well as the US assumption of war. It was a conflict that circumstances dictated the Americans could not win. To quote Ambassador Diem, following the disasters of 1963, the US leaders, "horrified by the resulting mess, took the whole ball of wax into their hands, intervening with massive military might. They did this suddenly and unilaterally, without consulting their ally in any meaningful way. In effect, they had worked themselves into a corner from which they could only escape—or so they thought—by making the war American."[56] Thus, the greatest consequence of the Battle of Ap Bac was to draw the United States into a war it would lose, one that would bring about the end of South Vietnam.

2

Too Much Rolling and Not Enough Thunder

Operation Rolling Thunder, 1965–1968

The first noteworthy American engagement of the Vietnam War was the air campaign better known as Operation Rolling Thunder. It was a measured and prolonged battle originally executed by the 2nd Air Division and later by the 7th Air Force of the US Air Force (USAF), Task Force 77 of the US Navy (USN), and the Republic of Vietnam Air Force (RVNAF). The main targets were lesser ones south of the nineteenth parallel and subsequently the limited urban and industrial targets of the DRV. Officially it lasted from 2 March 1965 to 1 November 1968. When it ended the United States had lost 938 aircraft and 1,084 airmen killed, captured, or missing. The estimate of Northern civilian casualties varies widely, with some reports claiming 52,000 killed and others as many as 182,000 killed. The DRV lost between 120 and 150 aircraft.

The USAF had dispatched advisory personnel to South Vietnam in 1961 and partaken in ARVN combat missions, including Ap Bac. Rolling Thunder became the first major engagement between American air units and the North Vietnamese. The operation was brought on by the North Vietnamese Navy's extraneous attack on American ships in the Tonkin Gulf in August 1964. This led to retaliatory raids by USN aircraft. The air force flew its first strikes against North Vietnam on 8 February 1965 in response to a VC attack against Pleiku Air Base, South Vietnam.[1]

Preliminary Reasoning, Causes, and Planning

Rolling Thunder was, in many ways, a result of the events of the late 1950s and early 1960s that entangled the United States progressively deeper into the Vietnam War. In response to President Diem's revocation of the 1956 reunification election and suppression of communist political elements in the South during the late 1950s, leaders in Hanoi began sending arms and materiel to the guerrilla forces of the NLF fighting an insurgency war to topple the US-supported government in Saigon. To combat the VC and to shore up Diem's government, the United States initially delivered monetary aid, military advisors, and supplies. Between 1957 and 1963, America found itself committed, through its acceptance of the policy of containment motivated by the domino theory, to defending Diem's regime from what US officials saw as expansive communist aggression. Publically, the Kennedy and Johnson administrations, through the State Department, defended their policy of increasing involvement in Vietnam by stating, "South Vietnam was fighting for its life against a brutal campaign of terror and armed attacks, inspired, directed, supplied, and controlled by the communist regime in Hanoi."[2]

The United States also became entangled in the cobweb of internal South Vietnamese politics, which led President Kennedy, Amb. Henry Cabot Lodge, and the State Department to give tacit approval to the coup against Diem in October 1963. Ironically, Diem's downfall came on the heels of persistent US declarations that the Saigon regime was becoming more democratic and more capable of winning the war. Instead, the Republic of Vietnam did not get better government due to the political anarchy and instability fomented after Diem's murder—no less than seven regimes came and went during 1964 alone. With US leaders increasingly concerned that South Vietnam would collapse, military planners examined ways to employ airstrikes to force the North to negotiate a political settlement. In turn, President Johnson decided no further commitment would take place without tangible proof of the regime's survivability.[3]

Doing a 180

When the United States began expanding its involvement in Vietnam, American airpower doctrine centered on the primary role of strategic bombing, which most airmen believed from the beginning of military aviation. In the USAF of 1964, this doctrine maintained that any and every future American war should be waged to destroy the enemy's ability to fight a modern industrial and high-technology war. The reality was, and it only later came to be understood, that North Vietnam was not a modern industrial state. From the outset most US political and military leaders believed the country's main objective should be to confront the DRV with enough pain and destruction to compel Hanoi's leaders to stop supporting VC forces inside South Vietnam.[4]

In the initial phases of the full US military commitment, leaders determined the least perilous policy called for the limited use of aerial bombing. "The resulting aerial campaign, Rolling Thunder," as Air University doctrine expert Col. Dennis Drew wrote, "was a far cry from that envisioned in plans developed before the American intervention. A campaign of graduated pressure intended to signal 'resolve' to the North Vietnamese, Rolling Thunder failed to persuade the North Vietnamese and it failed to destroy their ability to prosecute their war in South Vietnam." Drew further argues that, at this critical moment in the war, "American airpower doctrine developed in a manner incompatible with the employment required over North Vietnam and [shows] how even the best military advice can be ignored if it does not conform to the objectives of the civilian leadership."[5]

At this time US policymakers viewed Vietnam as one "part of a larger Communist effort to change the 'correlation of forces' to a position more favorable to the so-called Communist Bloc." In 1961 an internal State Department study reasoned, "While attention is diverted elsewhere—to Berlin, to negotiations over Laos, to turmoil in the Congo, to the United Nations itself, as well as to dozens of other problems—the communist program to seize South Viet-Nam moves ahead relentlessly."[6] This general concept permeated both the Kennedy and Johnson administrations, the idea being that the issues in Southeast Asia were small but important aspects of a much larger worldwide struggle with China and the Soviet Union. This view formed a major component of the validation for initiating Rolling Thunder in 1965.

American Fears and Objectives

Based on the belief that Vietnam was part of an international competition, senior government officials were fearful military actions might get out of hand and escalate into another world war. They reasoned that since the major problems on mainland Southeast Asia derived from North Vietnam's political ambitions, and the regime survived due to support from the Soviet Union and China, then military intensification could result in a nuclear-superpower confrontation much like the Cuban Missile Crisis of 1962. Drew notes that General Westmoreland later recalled in his book, *A Soldier Reports* (1980), "'an almost paranoid fear of nuclear confrontation with the Soviet Union' that influenced many of the decisions made in Washington about the conduct of the war." Many military leaders believed such a concern was excessive and argued that such an event could happen only due to the most extreme actions by either side. A most reasonable concern was that the People's Republic of China, much as it had during the Korean War a decade earlier, might intervene if the United States invaded North Vietnam.[7]

Steps toward Rolling Thunder

In July 1964 US intelligence operatives provided allied analysts with the first clear-cut evidence exposing the direct participation by the NVA in the war in the South. The numbers of Northern regulars in South Vietnam grew so much that "by the end of the year," US leaders though, "the situation was approaching crisis proportions." Westmoreland believed the enemy was "capitalizing on the political disorder which afflicted the Saigon government, upon the weakness of government administration throughout the country and upon deteriorating morale in the Vietnamese Armed Forces; the North Vietnamese and their southern affiliates were moving in for the kill."[8]

With such dire circumstances facing them, US leaders settled on airpower as an alternative to possibly losing South Vietnam to communism or a full-scale military commitment. Planners reasoned that bombing the DRV would bring the war home to its population and political leaders, influencing what the Americans considered the enemy's center of gravity—the central leadership in Hanoi. It also avoided the commitment of large numbers of troops in a land war in Asia. Bombing appeared to allow the United States to fight the war both remotely and relatively inexpensively. It was a politically palatable plan the American public could stomach. Most policymakers believed the risk of potential aircraft losses was acceptable even if an all-out air war was joined with the North. Measured against the costs of losing South Vietnam, this program seemed to be a bargain. But even if the air campaign failed to obtain its objectives, they reasoned, "the value of the effort seems . . . to exceed its cost."[9]

Planners began preparations as early as March 1964 for air operations over the North. With the South Vietnamese position rapidly deteriorating, they had to move quickly. Ultimately, they with the USN's Commander in Chief, Pacific (CINCPAC) headquarters developed Operations Plan 37-64. Set to unfold in three phases, the air campaign would strike at targets in Laos, Cambodia, and North Vietnam. The central component of the plan was the so-called 94 Target List. Planners selected each site based of three criteria: 1) degrading North Vietnamese assistance to insurgent operations in Laos and South Vietnam; 2) limiting Hanoi's ability to directly act in Laos and South Vietnam; and 3) destroy the North's limited industry.[10]

As the year wore on, communist forces began to attack US installations and armed forces, leading to an increase in American troop levels. As noted, in August 1964 the USN reported that Northern patrol boats attacked the destroyer USS *Maddox* in the Gulf of Tonkin on two separate occasions; only one instance was confirmed. This occasioned the Gulf of Tonkin Resolution, by which "Congress essentially authorized the president to take all actions he deemed necessary," as well as the first retaliatory airstrikes against North Vietnam. These raids did little to end enemy forays. Instead, occasional strikes against US facilities and personnel continued through the end of the year. Following an enemy assault on Bien Hoa Air Base on 1 November 1964, the Joint Chiefs of Staff (JCS) advised the initiation of B-52 raids on, among other places, Phuc Yen airfield near Hanoi. These kinds of raids would not take place until June 1965, and then only in South Vietnam (until Linebacker I). They also recommended "strikes against other airfields and major POL (petroleum, oil, and lubricant) facilities in the Hanoi/Haiphong area, . . . armed reconnaissance against infiltration routes in Laos, air strikes against infiltration routes and targets in North Vietnam, and progressive PACOM (Pacific Command) and SAC (Strategic Air Command) strikes against remaining military and industrial targets on the 94 Target List."[11]

Given the JCS plan and the method of determining which of the vetted targets to strike, military leaders in Washington evidently wanted "a classic strategic bombing campaign and a complementary interdiction campaign. . . . [P]lanners selected targets whose destruction would impair the enemy's ability 'to continue as an industrially viable state.'" Blueprints called for the United States "to first gain air superiority with attacks on the principal enemy airfields." With control of the skies, the next step called for strikes against POL sites, followed by the methodical degradation of the North's industrial network. Concurrently, they wanted to interdict troops and war materials in route to the South along the Ho Chi Minh Trail's infiltration roads. The JCS sought to adapt a World War II–style bombing campaign into an intensive campaign against North Vietnam.[12]

Despite these military plans, President Johnson's objective was not to destroy or even impede Vietnam's continued modernization and industrial growth. Instead, the administration's goal was to convince communist leadership in Hanoi that their military efforts at unification were futile. Besides, the president did not want an intense bombing campaign for fear it might draw the Chinese into the war. Johnson was not ready to adopt the JCS vision for air operations over the DRV. To him, bombing was a political tool to be used judiciously: "our planes and our bombs could be used as carrots for the South, strengthening the morale of the South Vietnamese and pushing them to clean up their corrupt house, by demonstrating the depth of our commitment to the war."[13] Johnson believed US "bombs could be used as sticks against the North, pressuring North Vietnam to stop its

Figure 2.1. Secretary of State Dean Rusk, President Lyndon B. Johnson, and Secretary of Defense Robert McNamara during a meeting in the Cabinet Room

aggression against the South." He further supposed: "By keeping a lid on all the designated targets, I knew I could keep the control of the war in my own hands. If China reacted to our slow escalation by threatening to retaliate, we'd have plenty of time to ease off the bombing. But this control—so essential for preventing World War III—would be lost the moment we unleashed a total assault on the North—for that would be rape rather than seduction—and then there would be no turning back. The Chinese reaction would be instant and total."[14]

On 29 November 1964, an interagency working group, chaired by Assistant Secretary of State William Bundy, recommended moderation in aerial bombardment, suggesting the United States apply pressure on North Vietnam, including airstrikes, "designed to signal US determination, to boost morale in the South and to increase the costs and strains upon the North." The members of the JCS disagreed, "preferring their own earlier recommendation for a short, sharp, and violent campaign against North Vietnam." Bundy attached a note to this report explaining "the JCS believed that their intensive bombing campaign 'could be suspended short of full destruction of the DRV if our objectives were earlier achieved.'"[15]

Despite the pressure brought to bear for a massive bombing campaign, Johnson refused to back down. But when NVA and VC troops attacked the US airbase at Pleiku on 7 February 1965, he had no choice but to retaliate. The next day the president ordered an air raid, designated Flaming Dart I. Previously, US "reaction to enemy provocations had been limited to quid-pro-quo reprisal raids."[16] Following the Pleiku attack, however, the president's assistant for national security, McGeorge Bundy, suggested a policy revision. In his subsequent report he declared, "We believe that the best available way of increasing our chance of success in Vietnam is the development and execution of a policy of sustained reprisal against North Vietnam." The US position would then be that "air and naval action against the North is justified by and related to the whole Viet Cong campaign of violence and terror in the South."[17]

As Bundy envisioned it, such a "reprisal policy should begin at a low level. Its level of force and pressure should be increased only gradually . . . [and] should be decreased if VC terror visibly decreases. The object would not be to 'win' an air war against Hanoi, but rather to influence the course of the struggle in the South." He continued: "We believe, indeed, that it is of great importance that the level of reprisal be adjusted rapidly and visibly to both upward and downward shifts in the level of Viet Cong offenses. We want to keep before Hanoi the carrot of our desisting as well as the stick of continued pressure. We also need to conduct the application of the force so that there is always a prospect of worse to come."[18]

With this narrative as a basis for debate, administration and military officials discussed what course of action might best achieve these aims. The JCS advocated the aforementioned three-phased bombing campaign they believed would, over the course of eleven weeks, destroy "the bulk of the targets on the 94 Target List." Gen. John P. McConnell, the USAF chief of staff, "favored an even more intense 28-day bombing program to destroy the 94 targets quickly."[19]

Johnson Approves Rolling Thunder

In the midst of this, the communists attacked the US camp at Qui Nhon on 10 February 1965. This resulted in another retaliatory strike, designated Flaming Dart II, launch the following day. In justifying this action, the administration cited a long list of North Vietnamese offenses occurring in South Vietnam rather than the attack on Qui Nhon specifically. Since the retaliatory raids had not had the desired effect of convincing DRV leaders to cease their support of VC forces in the South, two days later a frustrated Johnson authorized a campaign of sustained but graduated bombing against North Vietnam closely resembling the earlier proposals of McGeorge Bundy. The campaign would be called Rolling Thunder.[20]

Soon, officials finished planning Operation Rolling Thunder, formulating it to be a sustained bombing campaign that would interdict supplies flowing to communist forces in the South by destroying transportation routes in the southern part of North Vietnam. Those in the White House believed this campaign would slow or end the movement of communist personnel and supplies into South Vietnam. Plans called for "an amalgam of the objectives suggested by William Bundy, McGeorge Bundy, and, to a lesser extent, the Joint Chiefs of Staff." Subsequently, Asst. Secretary of Defense John T. McNaughton sent a memo to the Department of Defense and the White House summarizing US goals as

> (1) To reduce DRV/VC activities by affecting DRV will [to fight].
>
> (2) To improve the GVN [government of Vietnam]/VC relative balance of morale.

(3) To provide the US/GVN with a bargaining counter.

(4) To reduce DRV infiltration of men and materiel.

(5) To show the world the lengths to which US will go for a friend.[21]

With policies in place to govern Rolling Thunder, officials scheduled the first mission for 20 February. But the chaotic political situation in Saigon caused US embassy officials to strongly advise a delay. Rolling Thunder thus began on 2 March, when 104 USAF aircraft (mostly tactical fighters) attacked the Xom Bang ammunition depot 370 miles southeast of Hanoi just across the DMZ, while nineteen propeller-driven RVNAF planes attacked a naval base at Quang Khe, 65 miles farther north. Both were considered minor targets. While several USAF commanders believed this would be the first of many successive raids, Rolling Thunder soon became "more of an isolated series of thunderclaps." Instead of around-the-clock assaults, it took nearly two weeks before Johnson authorized a second strike. On 15 March a group of aircraft, similar in numbers and makeup to the first raid, attacked Tiger Island, off the North Vietnamese coast, and another ammunition depot just north of the DMZ.[22]

The president declared he had started the air campaign to thwart the North's goal of conquering the South and extending communism in Asia. He concluded, "Our power, therefore, is a very vital shield. If we are driven from the field in Vietnam, then no nation can ever again have the same confidence in America's promise of protection. We did not choose to be the guardians at the gate, but there is no one else."[23]

The entire operation ignored the enemy's real strength in and around Hanoi and Haiphong. The lack of consequence from the raids was amplified by the two-week lull before the next mission took place, again directed against insignificant targets just above the DMZ. Over the next three and one-half years, air operations expanded to include North Vietnamese ammunition dumps and oil-storage facilities in 1966, then power plants, factories, and airfields in the Hanoi-Haiphong area in 1967.[24]

From the outset, a White House policy of gradual escalation hindered Rolling Thunder by taking away the effectiveness of airstrikes and providing the DRV time to recover and adjust. Johnson, fearful of a triggering incident with the Soviet Union or China, placed a plethora of restrictions on planners and crews—for example, pilots could not attack surface-to-air-missile (SAM) sites unless they were attacked first. In short, the president implemented a policy that dropped a lot of bombs but did little, if anything, to threaten the Northern regime. In fact, government buildings and other facilities in downtown Hanoi were never attacked.[25]

The overall air campaign was tightly controlled by the White House, and at times targets were personally selected by Johnson and his advisers. By the time it came to an end on 1 November 1968, US aircraft had dropped 643,000 tons of bombs on the North at a cost of $900 million. US forces lost 938 aircraft and 1,084 airmen killed, wounded, or captured. Due to the restrictions on the raids, the Johnson administration gained precious little in terms of destroying the will of the DRV or the VC. Rolling Thunder began primarily as a diplomatic signal to impress Hanoi with America's determination, essentially a warning that the violence would escalate until Ho Chi Minh "blinked," punishing the North without provoking their Soviet and Chinese protectors. Secondarily, it attempted to bolster the sagging morale of the South Vietnamese.[26]

When Rolling Thunder began, American leaders hoped to provide a morale boost to South Vietnamese forces, interdict the flow of supplies going south, and discourage North Vietnamese aggression. Flying from bases in South Vietnam and Thailand, the USAF started hitting sites near the DMZ. By advancing the target areas northward across North Vietnam, planners intended to apply gradual pressure coupled with bombing halts as incentives to negotiate. In the view of USAF leaders, the campaign had no clear-cut objective nor did its authors have any real estimate of the cost of lives and aircraft. These officers and others argued that military targets, rather than the enemy's resolve, should be attacked, and the blows should be rapid and sharp, with the results felt immediately on the battlefield as well as by the political leadership in Hanoi.[27]

Intelligence operatives and analysts in Saigon believed the VC could not prevail without support from the North. Planners proposed that US air-power annihilate the industrial targets in Hanoi and the storage facilities in the port of Haiphong, thus increasing the quotient of pain. They also argued in favor of cutting infiltration routes into South Vietnam, depriving the VC of men and supplies. Even though he had retired on 1 February 1965, Gen. Curtis LeMay contended that, by using the latest airpower, the allies could blast North Vietnam "back to the Stone Age." Others pointed out that area bombing raids on civilian populations during World War II had limited success and advocated bombing only selected targets, such as military bases

Figure 2.2. F-105 Thunderchiefs, or Thuds, preparing to take off during Rolling Thunder

and fuel depots, and increasing the number and value of these targets over time in order to force the communists to negotiate a settlement.[28]

Interestingly enough, only three months after being elected president, Johnson approved Rolling Thunder. USAF leaders hoped it would be an escalation from earlier bombing raid in August 1964 and during Flaming Dart II. They wanted to destroy enough of the DRV's infrastructure and economy to be effective. The president and his advisers wanted to force the enemy to stop helping communist fighters in the South and negotiate a settlement. Ultimately, Rolling Thunder, designed to be a temporary campaign, lasted more than three years.[29]

One collateral aspect was, as bombing increased, guerrilla units in the South focused their attacks on US airbases. This led Westmoreland to request an increase in his 23,000-man base-defense force. In response, 3,500 US Marines went ashore on 8 March 1965, the first "official" combat troops sent to South Vietnam. To contain negative public reaction, this escalation in the US military commitment was described by leaders as a short-term measure. A public-opinion poll from late 1965 showed that nearly 80 percent of Americans supported the Rolling Thunder bombing raids as well as sending these combat troops to South Vietnam.[30]

Throughout 1964 and early 1965, events in Vietnam outraced US policy, especially with regard to supporting Southern leaders following Diem's death. A strong case can be made that American policy in Vietnam had been a terrible failure. By early 1965, it was clear that without full-scale action and intervention by the United States, South Vietnam could not survive. This led American leaders to seek the most convenient method to deal with the VC insurgency. Civilians and military advisers alike urged Johnson to use strategic aerial bombardment to one degree or another. Many reasoned that a small nation like the DRV, with a limited industrial base after emerging from a protracted war with France, probably would be reluctant to risk its newfound economic viability to support the communists in the South. This proved to be completely wrong.[31]

American policymakers feared that either the Soviet Union or China might increase aid to the DRV or intervene. Facing this restraining concern, Johnson's civilian consultants advocated bombing to affect Hanoi's behavior, while US military leaders were mainly concerned with breaking the enemy's will. The initial example of this division followed the August 1964 Gulf of Tonkin incident. In the aftermath the president commanded US air forces to initiate Operation Pierce Arrow, consisting of retaliatory airstrikes against North Vietnam. Limited in both scope and intensity, it failed to placate military leaders, who recommended a wider and more aggressive campaign.[32]

Bombs Away

As noted earlier, by 1965 the JCS had created a list of 94 targets to be destroyed as part of a coordinated, eight-week air campaign against North Vietnam's transportation network, including bridges, railyards, docks, barracks, and supply dumps. But the president's fears of direct Chinese or Soviet intervention made him oppose such an all-out policy. Strongly backed by Secretary of Defense Robert McNamara, Johnson dug in his heals in favor of a much more limited effort. From January to the end of February 1965, he initiated only retaliatory raids against southern portions of the DRV. Planners designed Rolling Thunder to be an eight-week air campaign consistent with the restrictions Johnson and McNamara imposed.[33] In short, if the insurgency in the South continued unabated "with DRV support, strikes against the DRV would be extended with intensified efforts against targets north of the 19th parallel."[34]

Many in the administration believed selective pressure, controlled by Washington and combined with diplomatic overtures, would prevail and force Hanoi to end its "aggression." Military leaders were still not satisfied, however, since for the time being the bombing campaign was limited to targets below the nineteenth parallel, each of which required clearance by Johnson and McNamara. Ultimately, these retaliatory strikes proved less than effective, leading to the beefed-up aerial campaign.[35] Some advisors were not sold on the idea this operation would succeed at all, however, but reasoned that, even if costly, it was "an acceptable risk, especially when considered against the alternative of introducing US combat troops."[36]

As mentioned, the first Rolling Thunder mission took place on 2 March with a USAF attack on an ammunition-storage area near Xom Bang, supported by nineteen RVNAF A-1 Skyraiders striking the North Vietnamese naval base at Quang Khe. The Americans lost six aircraft during the mission, five of the downed crewmen being rescued by exceptional US search-and-rescue forces. Even so, officials were left in a state of shock at the numbers of aircraft lost. What they did not realize was this would become a pattern.[37]

Nearly from the outset, both military and many civilian leaders and advisors argued the operation was too sporadic and directed against insignificant targets—which it was. Protests aside, Johnson remained resolute in retaining tight personal control of the action. The president did not really trust generals who, he thought viewed the war solely as a military problem ignoring the political factors. But privately Johnson believed these generals loved the war and wanted to expand it at all costs: "It's hard to be a military hero without a war. Heroes need battles and bombs and bullets in order to be heroic. That's why I am suspicious of the military. They're always so narrow in their appraisal of everything. They see everything in military terms."[38] Years later, though, he stated that at one point in the discussions prior to Rolling Thunder, "Suddenly I realized that doing nothing was more dangerous than doing something."[39]

Thus began a process of managing the bombing campaign that left Johnson in total control. Throughout, military commanders in Vietnam submitted their suggested targets to CINCPAC, Adm. Ulysses Simpson Grant Sharp, in Honolulu, Hawaii. The admiral's staff then weighed the "virtues" of these proposals, then put together a coordinated program that they sent to the Pentagon. There, military staff again evaluated the strike program to determine each target's strategic value. After this, area experts in the State Department measured the international political ramifications of attacking each target. This filtering process complete, the "scrubbed down" target list was sent to the White House for final approval.[40]

The entire torturous procedure proved to be a formula for failure. In the vast majority of cases, the targets selected were those military leaders and experts justifiably believed were inadequate to accomplish their vision of the purpose of Rolling Thunder. They also considered the rules of engagement far too restrictive for anything resembling an effective military operation. Johnson and his closest advisors specified the exact size of the attacking force, the munitions used, and the precise time of each strike. The efficacy of these early assaults proved minimal. After the 15 March raid, under increasing pressure from the Pentagon, the president removed some operational restrictions. While targets were selected from weeklong packages, the exact timing of the sorties were left to the local commanders, with approved alternates available if weather or other factors obscured the primary targets.[41]

As aerial operations evolved, targeting devolved into two categories. The first included the fixed or numbered targets that were part of the 94 Targets List and required individual authorization from the president. The second list included traditional strategic targets like power plants and industrial facilities, which did not always require approval from Washington. Intelligence experts designated these as part of North Vietnam's "modern industrial sector," which was minimal, even by Asian standards of the time. Industry produced only about 12 percent of the DRV's annual 1965 gross national product of $1.6 billion. According to the JCS, there were only eight industrial installations worth targeting, and they contributed little to the NVA's military capabilities. Nearly all of its military equipment, and all of the heavier and technical assets, were imported from China and the Soviet Union. Given the lack of high-value targets in the North, the geographic restrictions on the bombing campaign—with Hanoi and the surrounding area, Haiphong and its environs, and a wide swath along the border with China off limits—made the campaign's potential effectiveness even more difficult to achieve.[42]

To make matters worse, even executing these early attacks proved difficult, and subsequent bomb-damage appraisals indicated poor results. Of these initial 267 sorties aimed at 491 buildings, only 47 structures were destroyed and 22 damaged. These results prompted McNamara to send a scathing message to the JCS: "Our primary objective, of course, was to communicate our political resolve. . . . Future communications of resolve, however, will carry a hollow ring unless we accomplish more military damage than we have to date."[43]

Later analysis determined that much of the problem resulted from poor training. While fighter-bomber crews proved skilled in the necessary techniques for dropping nuclear weapons, they were less proficient in delivering conventional munitions. At the onset of Rolling Thunder, US aircrews' average probable-circular error—"the radius of a circle centered on the target within which half of the bombs will fall"—was nearly 750 feet. It took months of retraining to improve accuracy and cut this error average to 365 feet. While being 750 feet off target did not matter when using nuclear weapons, it was quite significant when placing conventional bombs and rockets on specific targets like a building or a bridge.[44]

Low-level air attacks dispersed napalm, sowed mines, or dropped delayed-fuse bombs. Hard targets requiring 500- or 750-pound bombs required a 45-degree dive from 10,000–15,000 feet to release ordnance at 6,000 feet to assure a pullout at 3,000 feet and avoiding enemy ground fire. Accuracy was measured in hundreds of feet. The development of precision-guided munitions was still in its infancy during the Vietnam War, especially in 1965.[45]

One of the more complex and controversial aspects of Rolling Thunder was the periodic attacks on bridges in North Vietnam and the measurable success of these attacks. As air operations over the DRV stretched into months and years, leaders in Washington, especially in the White House, sought an accurate assessment of the results. It fell to members of the Central Intelligence Agency (CIA) and Defense Intelligence Agency to make independent studies of the bomb damage by employing aerial photographs. The most difficult damage to accurately pinpoint was that to bridges. To quote one CIA report, "Although the extent of damage and the cost of repair are the principal topics . . . , the White House was equally concerned to find out how much time would be needed to restore lines of communication (LOCs)."[46]

As we have seen, Rolling Thunder's main focus became slowing "the flow of men and supplies from North Vietnam to South Vietnam. Although a number of different target systems were taken under attack, the Rolling Thunder campaign was essentially and at times almost exclusively an interdiction program. A standard bombing strategy to achieve such a goal was to stop or slow military traffic in rear areas by interdicting critical choke points along heavily used LOC's [ ]. Bridges of course qualify as such, and during Rolling Thunder more attack sorties were flown against bridge targets than against any other fixed target system."[47]

As operations progressed, the issue of the numbers being reported became a problem. In 1966 this turned into a public embarrassment when the famed journalist Art Buchwald penned an article wondering how the United States had seemingly "destroyed all of the bridges in North Vietnam many times over." The only possible explanation he could see was the Americans "were dropping our own bridges on North Vietnam and then bombing them." Depending on the source, the number of bridges destroyed ranged from 657 to 7,000—a remarkable variance. Clearly, an accurate intelligence assessment was needed. Personnel in the CIA's Construction Branch of the Office of Economic Research tried to provide it.[48]

These specialists, working with their counterparts in the Defense Intelligence Agency, realized that the main source of the "bridge kill" exaggerations were pilot reports. Reassessing the photos and gun-camera footage, they realized that it was "very difficult for a pilot to assess accurately the results of a strike while traveling at high speed and when the target area is obscured by smoke and dust." As a result of this more intense scrutiny, they reported "216 bridges actually had been destroyed during the first year of the interdiction campaign." This number totaled 541 bridges by the end of Rolling Thunder. Photo-scanning personnel examined "all photographic missions looking for damaged bridges. Each bridge crossing was measured and cataloged, and a photograph of each was prepared for later analysis. . . . During the three years of bombing, personnel in the Construction Branch analyzed and filed over 2,500 prints covering some 600 bridges." This vast quantity of images "provided the basic input for answering many questions posed by the Department of Defense and the White House on the effectiveness of the interdiction campaign."[49]

Another aspect of this study was to define "bridge." It was ridiculous to put a "10 or 20 foot water crossing in the same category as the 1,000 foot bridge at Viet Tri or the mile-long Paul Doumer Bridge crossing the Red River near Hanoi." Many smaller spans were nothing more than "culverts, causeways, or simply improved fords." CIA professionals also had to define the meaning of "destroyed" or "damaged." They concluded, "cratering of bridge approaches or 'near misses' in adjacent rice paddies could not be counted as damage serious enough to interdict a water crossing." Instead, they developed the term "severe damage occurrence" to describe "damage sufficiently severe to deny a crossing to users until a significant amount of repairs had been performed, requiring considerable time, materials, and labor." This included "a dropped span, a destroyed pier, or a destroyed abutment." One examination of forty-six JCS-targeted bridges disclosed "there were 249 hits out of 11,744 bombs dropped, for an average of one hit for every 47 bombs dropped in other words, slightly over 2 percent."[50]

The cost of repairing the bridges was also significant. The CIA concluded this came to $700 per linear foot. The estimated cost to restore all bridges damaged or destroyed was $10 million after Rolling Thunder's first year and $30 million total by the end of the campaign. As for wooden bridges, the price of reconstruction "averaged $50 per lineal foot and required 30 men for each 20 feet of bridge under construction." During all of Rolling Thunder, "292 temporary wooden bypass bridges were built at an estimated cost of $10,000,000."[51]

One of the most creative solutions to downed bridges developed by the North was to build bypasses, such as "pontoon bridges, causeways, ferry slips, and fords, at a cost of approximately $3,000,000." In fact, the need for

Figure 2.3. The Paul Doumer, later Long Bien, Bridge near Hanoi, 1940

manpower proved the greatest challenge to the North, the CIA estimating that "72,000 full time and nearly 200,000 part time workers were required to keep the LOC's open. . . . [T]here were several Chinese engineer battalions totaling more than 20,000 troops working on the roads and railroads north of Hanoi." In addition to these solutions, the communists employed ferries and temporary bridges to circumvent the destruction. All of this proved incredibly effective and, in many ways, was brilliant in its simplicity. The CIA reported: "The North Vietnamese preoccupation with the construction of bypasses was a well-conceived response to the bombing campaign. In effect, they dispersed their LOC chokepoints just as they had dispersed their POL storage facilities and other targets which gave their system a built-in redundancy that greatly lessened its vulnerability to effective air attack." The result was, "where it may have taken one raid to interdict a crossing during the early days of the bombing program, in later periods it took two or three raids to interdict the same crossing."[52]

One of the most sobering facts about the bombing of river and waterway crossings during Rolling Thunder has to be the results of attacks on the Long Bien (formerly Paul Doumer) Bridge, spanning the Red River at Hanoi. Considered "the most important rail/highway crossing in North Vietnam," it was the only connection over the river between Hanoi and the main DRV port at Haiphong. In 1967 the first attack, by twenty F-105 fighter-bombers, felled the center span of the bridge. The follow-up CIA assessment found that the bombing had not done much to interrupt cross-river traffic. Later examinations indicated Northern engineers eventually built twenty pontoon bridges to bypass the damaged structure, allowing traffic to flow at a higher rate than it had previously. From this and other examples, analysts logically concluded, "multiple bypasses thus increased the probability that at least one crossing at a site would always remain serviceable." Further, "because it normally took as much ordnance to interdict a bypass as to interdict the original bridge, the cost of bombing a water crossing in North Vietnam increased much faster than the cost of repairing it with cheap local materials." Lastly, American aircraft faced "the same risks when attacking bypasses as when attacking the original bridge." The first use of laser-guided, or "smart," bombs took place in late 1968 and early 1969. Despite their improved accuracy, they were only used about 3 percent of the time. The North Vietnamese eventually rebuilt the Long Bien Bridge. In May 1972 it was finally effectively destroyed by laser-guided bombs.[53]

Figure 2.4. F-4C dropping a laser-guided bomb on the Long Bien Bridge

Yet by then it was too late to make any difference. The opportunities for consequential airstrikes had long since passed, and the only meaningful result in 1972 was that America could now force through a peace settlement that would let its military go home.

From Johnson's viewpoint, if they were going to follow a doctrine of "gradualism," then having the ability to destroy a target was more important and better demonstrated American resolve than did the actual destruction. In essence, they planned to hold important targets "hostage" by bombing trivial ones and then increasing the quotient of pain as circumstances warranted. This is why White House officials wanted to dictate which targets would be struck, the day and hour of the raid, sometimes even the direction of the attack, and the number and types of aircraft, the tonnages carried, and the types of ordnance utilized.[54]

Most of these decisions were made during Tuesday luncheons hosted by President Johnson at the White House in a very casual atmosphere. The attendees usually included the press secretary, Secretary McNamara, Secretary of State Dean Rusk, the special assistant for international security affairs, and sometimes Gen. Earle Wheeler, chair of the JCS. In his seminal work on the Vietnam air war, former USAF historian Earl H. Tilford Jr. argued: "Targeting bore little resemblance to reality in that the sequence of attacks was uncoordinated and the targets were approved randomly—even illogically. The North's airfields, which, according to any rational targeting policy, should have been hit first in the campaign, were also off-limits."[55]

In fairness, as Rolling Thunder continued, some restrictions were eased or rescinded altogether. Even so, the president and secretary of defense kept a tight rein on the campaign, a fact that exasperated US military leaders, conservatives in Congress, and even members of the administration itself.[56] From the military point of view, one of the main objectives of Rolling Thunder should have been the closure of Haiphong Harbor and other ports by aerial mining, thereby retarding or stopping the flow of seaborne supplies from the Communist Bloc. President Johnson would not take such a provocative step. Ironically, this was exactly what his successor, President Nixon, did in 1972 with some success. Perhaps the most intolerable practice was Johnson's lack of consultation with his military chiefs during the target-selection process. Even General Wheeler was not present for most of the deliberations in 1965—and thereafter took part only occasionally.[57]

Standard Operating Procedures

Most Rolling Thunder airstrikes were launched from four airbases located in Thailand: Korat, Takhli, Ubon, and Udorn Royal Thai Air Force Bases. In addition, one South Vietnamese–based squadron, stationed in Da Nang, took part in the missions over the DRV. Standard operations called for the aircraft to conduct aerial refueling over Laos before striking their targets in the North. After their bomb runs, the warplanes refueled and returned directly to Thailand or flew out over the relatively safe waters of the Gulf of Tonkin. Early on, in order to limit airspace conflicts between USAF and naval strike forces, officials divided North Vietnam into six target areas designated "route packages." Each route package was assigned to either the USAF or the USN, from which the other was excluded. Naval attacks were launched from the aircraft carriers of Task Force 77, located just off the North Vietnamese coast in an area known as Yankee Station. The naval aircraft had shorter ranges and carried lighter bomb loads. They approached their targets from seaward, with the majority of their strikes flown against coastal sites. In many ways this explains why the USN suffered fewer losses during the campaign: Navy pilots had to look out for antiaircraft artillery

(AAA), SAMs, and fighter attacks in only a 90-degree arc to their front. If an aircraft went down, search-and-rescue operations were flown closer to their home base.[58]

After nearly a month of frustration, on 3 April 1965 JCS leaders persuaded McNamara and Johnson to launch a four-week series of attacks on Northern transportation and lines of communication in an effort to isolate the DRV from its overland sources of supply in the Soviet Union and China. Roughly one-third of North Vietnam's imports came down the northeast railroad from China, while the remaining two-thirds came by sea via Haiphong and other ports. For the first time during Rolling Thunder, officials selected targets for their military, rather than their psychological, importance.[59]

During these four weeks, twenty-six bridges and seven ferries were destroyed. Other targets included the extensive North Vietnamese radar system, barracks, and ammunition depots. Concurrently, missions were flown against targets in the panhandle of the southern DRV. All totaled, in April the USAF flew 3,600 sorties and 4,000 more in May. Throughout the remainder of the year, operations gradually shifted away from the destruction of fixed targets to "armed reconnaissance" activities, in which small formations of aircraft patrolled highways, railroads, and rivers searching for targets of opportunity. These missions increased from 2 to 200 sorties per week by the end of 1965. Ultimately, armed reconnaissance missions constituted 75 percent of the total bombing effort in part because the system through which fixed targets were requested, chosen, and sanctioned proved too cumbersome.[60]

From the American perspective, much changed after 8 March, when 3,500 US Marines landed near Da Nang, ostensibly to defend the South Vietnamese airfields to be used for Rolling Thunder operations. Almost from the outset their mission increased to active combat operations marked by increased troop deployments and the escalation of ground operations in the South.[61]

American leaders were shocked the North fought back so hard once air operations commenced. On 3 April NVAF MiG-17s attacked US aircraft for first time. Five days later Pham Van Dong, the DRV premier, declared his government could only begin negotiations if the United States stopped the bombing campaign and withdrew all of its forces from South Vietnam. He also demanded the Saigon government to acknowledge all the NLF's stipulations for peace and agree to the reunification of Vietnam by the Vietnamese themselves. Only the day before, at Johns Hopkins University, Johnson had publicly offered both South and North Vietnam a billion-dollar regional postwar-development assistance program. While the North's leadership summarily spurned the offer, in mid-May the United States suspended Rolling Thunder missions for five days to allow Hanoi to reconsider without "losing face." The five-day bombing pause produced no political results, and the aerial campaign resumed on 18 May.[62]

By then, Rolling Thunder had become a much larger air campaign. Sorties against JCS targets increased from only a couple to ten to twelve per week. The weekly number of sorties against all targets increased four to five times. eventually numbering 900 by July 1965. In turn, the interdiction campaign began affecting the DRV's transportation and infiltration system. The attack zone now extended just beyond the twentieth parallel. Still, the North maintained its support for insurgent forces in South Vietnam, apparently more defiant than ever. As Rolling Thunder dragged on, the rationale and targeting emphasis shifted from the initial purpose—destroying the North Vietnamese will—to convincing Northern leaders to stop supporting the VC and to accept a settlement. In short, the US aim became "strategic" in nature, even if its target selection was not. By July 1965, the campaign began to focus on destroying "bridges, tunnels, rail lines, river and canal transportation, and other perceived transportation chokepoints."[63]

On 1 July McNamara prepared a memorandum advocating the complete quarantine of Haiphong harbor by mining it in order to halt the flow of war materials into South Vietnam by sea, canal, rail, highway, and even footpath. The rationale was, by stopping seaborne supplies from China to Hanoi, they might increase the quotient of pain on Hanoi. Throughout July, a heated debate took place in Washington raged over escalating US involvement in the war by sending more troops to South Vietnam. The JCS proposed going a step further by destroying "the 'war making' supplies and facilities of NVN [North Vietnam], especially POL." This reflected a return to their original concept of a full-scale air offensive that included strategic and interdiction attacks.[64]

Facing such an important policy shift, Johnson dispatched McNamara to Vietnam to assess the situation. By the time he returned to Washington, McNamara's position had softened, and on 20 July he amended his 1 July proposals by recanting his desire to mine North Vietnamese harbors and supporting current operations. Specifically, "he called for a continuation of the slowly intensifying Rolling Thunder program, now centered on interdiction, while avoiding any population and industrial targets not directly related to North Vietnam's support of the Viet Cong." This abrupt reversal remains perplexing. Even so, the future pattern of Rolling Thunder was now in place. The air war would not quickly escalate, nor would strategic targets in and around Hanoi-Haiphong come under attack. Instead, a gradual expansion of operations would take place to place increasing pressure on Hanoi to negotiate a settlement. Apparently, Johnson and McNamara wanted to structure the campaign to instill in Northern leaders the belief that an increasing intensity and extent of bombing operations could be avoided only by their agreeing to serious negotiations.[65]

Despite McNamara's cave in, military leaders pressed for a more aggressive air campaign. Concurrently, the administration wondered if a "pause" in the bombing might encourage officials in Hanoi to start peace talks. Those in favor of this argued that, "even if the pause did not result in negotiations, it would 'clear the decks' politically for a far more aggressive bombing program." Johnson finally agreed, and a pause to the bombing campaign commenced on 24 December 1965. It lasted thirty-seven days but did not result in negotiations or any reduction in DRV support for the VC. By this time the various US air forces had undertaken an enormous operation over North Vietnam to no avail. "Even with the reins held tightly in Washington, Rolling Thunder in 1965 amassed 55,000 total sorties, which dropped 33,000 tons of bombs on 158 fixed targets and a far larger number of 'targets of opportunity.'" But negotiations with the North were no nearer, and communist fighters and materiel continued to flow into South Vietnam without any significant reduction. While the bombing operations boosted morale in South Vietnam, this lift in spirits came at the loss of 171 aircraft and many among their crews. Yet as large as this part of the campaign was, it was nothing compared to what was to come.[66]

Expansion in 1966

On 24 December 1965, when the extended bombing lull began, the United States had already lost 180 aircraft: 85 from the air force, 94 from the navy, and 1 from the marines. The RVNAF had lost 8 warplanes. These numbers included combat loses, ground and midair accidents, mechanical failures, and unknown reasons (some of these probably due to bad weather). USAF aircrews had flown 25,971 sorties and dropped 32,063 tons of bombs. Naval aviators (including the marines) had flown 28,168 sorties and dropped 11,144 tons. The RVNAF had contributed 682 missions. These were significant numbers, and yet it was only the first year in an operation that lasted three more years.[67]

While the Americans waited for what they hoped would be an indication the North would come to the negotiating table, combat in Vietnam continued. On 5 April 1966 a US reconnaissance flight pinpointed a group of NVA troops constructing what could only have been a SAM site. Rather than bringing about peace, the bombing pause had provided the enemy time to construct air defenses that would cost the allies more lost aircraft and aircrew lives. Together, USAF and USN leaders quickly sent a joint appeal to the Defense Department for approval to attack these sites. The request was denied since the SAMs were positioned near urban areas. Not surprisingly, on 24 July an F-105 was shot down by an SA-2 missile. On the twenty-seventh Washington officials approved a onetime bombing raid aimed at the two offending missile sites. These, however, proved part of an elaborate enemy rouse. When US aircraft attacked, the pilots discovered the SAM "batteries" were actually dummies surrounded by AAA defenses. As one described the resulting situation, the entire scene "looked like the end of the world." At the end of the fiasco, the Americans had lost six attack aircraft, with two pilots killed, one missing, two captured, and one rescued.[68]

Throughout the spring and into the summer of 1966, Rolling Thunder meandered along with no apparent goal or aim. Long interruptions were followed by major raids against key infrastructure and economic targets. In June 1966 the White House approved long-requested JCS airstrikes against the North's POL storage areas. This came after months of urging by US military leaders since the inception of Rolling Thunder. Strike advocates assumed the destruction of the DRV's POL would cause the NVA's ground operations to grind to a halt. Air attacks began on the 29 June and at first appeared successful, destroying tank farms near Hanoi and Haiphong. CIA operatives and analysts estimated 70 percent of North Vietnam's oil facilities destroyed at a cost of forty-three aircraft lost. But their success proved limited. As it turned out, leaders in Hanoi had anticipated such a campaign and had dispersed most of their POL stocks in 50-gallon drums throughout the country. Moreover, the DRV and China had begun building pipelines from China into northern parts of North Vietnam to keep the supplies of

POL flowing. On 4 September, when the POL attacks ended, allied intelligence admitted there was "no evidence yet of any shortages of POL in North Vietnam."[69]

Throughout, Rolling Thunder operations revealed interservice issues in many areas, especially the command-and-control organizational layout existent in Southeast Asia. Officially, at first the USAF's 2nd Air Division, replaced by the Seventh Air Force on 1 April 1966, was responsible for directing all aerial operations over North and South Vietnam. Under the chain of command in Southeast Asia, the commanders of the 2nd Air Division and the Seventh Air Force were subordinate to General Westmoreland, who had his hands full fighting the VC and, increasingly, PAVN ground forces in the South. As a result, USAF units based in Thailand and the Philippines had to bomb Rolling Thunder targets in North Vietnam as well as support ground forces in the South, leaving them with not only a dual role in the war but also a dual command structure. The command-and-control intricacies became increasingly complex when leaders divided responsibilities for the aerial bombing sorties into four competing operational areas: South Vietnam, the DRV, and northern and southern Laos.[70]

To add to the complexity, Task Force 77 received its orders through the Seventh Fleet from Admiral Sharp, headquartered at Pearl Harbor. Sharp's primary air-power subordinate was the commander of the USAF's Pacific Air Forces. While USAF leaders, based on their theory and doctrine, advocated a single air commander and integrated air operations, the navy refused to integrate its air operations over the DRV. The initial Seventh Air Force commander, Gen. William "Spike" Momyer, believed that CINCPAC and Pacific Air Forces wished to keep the Thai-based aircraft out of his hands: "By denying Momyer, they were really denying Westmoreland and keeping air operations against the DRV under their control." To make matters worse, Graham Martin, US ambassador to Thailand, and William H. Sullivan, US ambassador to Laos, constantly exerted influence over operational and command arrangements. This created such a mess that leaders transferred Route Package I, the area nearest the DMZ, to Westmoreland as an extended battlefield.[71]

Such a command structure went against every USAF premise in every manual and doctrine in existence. Worse, it violated the basic precept that in combat there should always be a single air manager determining what every aircraft does and coordinating all air assets within a combat theater.

It was an arrangement that irritated airmen in both Washington and Vietnam and convinced them the war was headed in the wrong direction.[72]

If this command-and-control issue was a strange, the way targets were selected was even more bizarre. As noted before, requests for airstrikes originated with the 2nd Air Division and Task Force 77 in Vietnam, then proceeded to CINCPAC, which, in turn, reported to superiors at the JCS and Defense Department. Then followed the vetting of targets by Defense and State experts and finally Johnson's "Tuesday Cabinet" luncheon review for authorization discussed earlier. It was micromanagement of the worst sort, leaving combat crews and commanders in Vietnam to fight with one arm tied behind their backs.[73]

Another problem during not only Rolling Thunder but also throughout the war was that the USAF had been trained to fight a strategic, perhaps even nuclear war, with the Soviet Union in Europe, not a localized, conventional war. Most of the flight crews were neither trained nor equipped for the operations they were being asked to fly in 1965. Many air force leaders were upset that the navy was better prepared for this mission. It possessed the new A-6 Intruder, the only all-weather aircraft in the US inventory except for the B-52, which the air force sought to save for its primary strategic role. The navy also led the way in the development of the F-4 Phantom fighter-bomber, which became one of the most iconic symbols of the entire Vietnam War. USAF dogfighting skills had diminished since its pilots had racked up a significant kill ratio during the Korean War. The air force and navy F-4s both used USN-developed AIM-9 Sidewinder and AIM-7 Sparrow air-to-air missiles, not the USAF AIM-4 Falcons. Worse, the F-4 was not equipped with a gun for air-to-air combat. (It was not until 1968 that gun systems were built into USAF F-4s.) Most USAF leaders were opposed to adapting their aircraft to the war in Southeast Asia, convinced that the conflict was an aberration that would be quickly resolved. Once this little regional spat ended, they planned to return their attention to the main threat—the Soviet Union.[74]

The USAF did have an all-weather-capable aircraft with radar-guided bombing equipment and awe-inspiring destructive potential. That was the B-52 Stratofortress. In the beginning, the Johnson administration determined not to use this awesome weapon against the North, fearing it would signal too big of an escalation. Besides, General McConnell opposed sending the SAC's "Big Ugly Fellows" (BUFs), as the bombers where sometimes called, at all. The B-52 was a major component of America's strategic nuclear triad whose primary mission was to fly low-level single-integrated-operational-plan missions. Airmen balked at the notion of turning their most powerful weapon over to an army general (Westmoreland) for CAS, ground support, and air-defense missions in South Vietnam. While some later Arc Light raids, as these intial B-52 missions were designated, were flown slightly above the DMZ in Route Package I, this also irritated airmen since the targets were selected by a navy admiral in Hawaii (CINCPAC). Not only was this a matter of pride, but most airmen believed the B-52s were being ill used.[75]

The first Arc Light mission took place on 18 June 1965, when thirty B-52Fs launched for an attack on a VC regional headquarters ten miles north of Saigon. They took off from Andersen Air Base, Guam, at 0100, scheduled to execute an aerial refueling over the South China Sea at 0330. Two aircraft collided in midair and crashed, killing eight crewmembers. Another bomber had to make an emergency landing due to a broken hydraulic pump and faulty radar. The remaining twenty-seven BUFs reached their target three hours later and dropped 1,300 bombs in a one-by-two-mile target box. On the return trip one plane had to land at Clark Air Base in the Philippines. Thirteen hours after departure, twenty-six aircraft landed in Guam. Subsequent recce (reconnaissance) revealed the raid had scored only 50 percent hits and destroyed very little. One report compared it to a "house wife using a sledgehammer to kill house flies." Later it was discovered that a VC operative concealed in an ARVN unit alerted enemy forces to the aerial raid. Even though Westmoreland praised the effort, USAF analysts decried how difficult it was going to be for B-52s to hit mobile VC troops hiding under triple-canopy jungles. While the Arc Light raids improved and, at the end of Rolling Thunder, B-52 raids expanded north, most airmen remained frustrated with such employment of the BUFs.[76]

Yet another problem arose involving the one-year rotation policy adopted by the Pentagon. The first aircrews to arrive in theater were professional, experienced, and among the best pilots and crewmembers of their generation. But as Rolling Thunder constantly expanded due to the increasing operations tempo and ever-expanding length of the campaign, the air component in Vietnam required more and more personnel. As time passed and the best crews rotated home, the replacement aircrews were increasingly inexperienced. Added to this problem was a USAF policy that decreed universal pilot training while prohibiting compulsory second combat tours. These combined circumstances had the effect of rotating personnel to different aircraft. For example, an experienced F-4 pilot could end up flying forward-air-control missions in an O-2 Skymaster observation aircraft during a second or third tour. In turn, a SAC bomber pilot or a Military Airlift Command pilot might find themselves flying an F-4.[77]

By the end of Rolling Thunder, the USAF was short of experienced fighter pilots. Provisions preventing immediate multiple tours, combined with the 100-mission requirement, rapidly ran through the first wave of the most experienced pilots. Leadership at both SAC and the Military Airlift Command were concerned their aircrews were falling behind in promotions and sought to make flying their aircraft competitive. As noted, this put transport and bomber pilots in high-performance fighters flying tactically demanding missions into the world's heaviest concentration of air defenses. Predictably, this led to the death of a lot of these airmen. By 1968, top graduates from pilot schools were sent to F-4C/D and RF-4 Reinforcement Training Unit before being sent to Southeast Asia. An examination of the number of first lieutenants killed and whose bodies were not returned between 1968 and 1972 was staggering. Some sources recorded the number to be as high as 600 men.[78]

As for the Arc Light operations, by 3 January 1967, overall pilot shortages required USAF leaders to recall 2,300 older pilots and crewmembers while instituting a new, shorter, and more intense training program to prepare 3,247 new B-52 pilots and crewmembers each year. Since in the States it required fewer crewmembers on base to perform the same jobs as it did in Southeast Asia, SAC units drew on crews from all across the region, including those engaged in Rolling Thunder, to fill their needs. One method SAC officials initiated to deal with this shortage was to order hundreds of personnel to 179-day temporary-duty assignments; the program failed. The shortages increased (while the airmen's divorce rate skyrocketed). It was a problem that continued to affect Rolling Thunder, while it lasted, and Arc Light throughout the war.[79]

As for the USN, its policies tended to keep its aircrews within the same aircraft community for the duration of their careers, thereby not only retaining their expertise but also incurring greater losses among experienced crews who served during multiple combat tours.[80]

Weather in the theater of operations was another issue that hampered Rolling Thunder and, for that matter, every other extended air campaign during the war. The monsoon patterns made regular flight operations nearly impossible from late September to early May, when rain and fog tended to make target acquisition very difficult. Lack of adequate all-weather and night-bombing capabilities forced the majority of US missions to be conducted during daylight hours, thereby easing the burden on Northern air-defense forces.[81]

This also led to a mechanical pattern that fit the managerial mindset that dominated air-force conceptualization following World War II. USAF leaders conducted bombing missions in Southeast Asia to increase sortie rates to prove that the overall operation was making adequate progress. Historian Earl Tilford eloquently analyzed the problem with this approach: "The term 'Dr. Pepper War' accurately described the production line method by which strike packages were assembled and dispatched. Dr. Pepper advertisements touted, '10, 2 and 4' as good times to enjoy the beverage. Because of the way strike packages were generated, attacks on North Vietnam followed a predictable routine. Usually, there was a big effort at about ten o'clock in the morning. A second strike would take place in the early afternoon, around two, with a smaller effort coming just before dark. All this may have been but it was not very "[82]

Initially, these standardized operations worked well enough, and there was a good reason for choosing the times they did. Aircrews preferred to attack "after the sun had fully risen to avoid visual misperceptions more common in the half-light of dawn or dusk." And if it were to happen, it was better to go down early in the day, providing the aviators a better chance of rescue and lessening the risk of spending the night in the jungle. But these USAF attack schedules became so predictable the enemy soon adapted their movements and air defenses accordingly. After a while they were waiting each day for the Americans to make an appearance—far too often they shot down several US aircraft.[83]

Northern Air Defenses and Rolling Thunder, 1967–1968

Even while US officials began planning for Rolling Thunder, leaders in Hanoi anticipated the United States might make some bold move. In February 1965 they directed their military and civilian population to "maintain communication and transportation and to expect the complete destruction of the entire country, including Hanoi and Haiphong."[84] They also proclaimed that "in a people's war against the air war of destruction . . . , each citizen is a soldier, each village, street, and plant a fortress on the anti-American battlefront." In preparation for the bombing campaign, they expected everyone except those deemed "truly indispensable to the life of the capital" to be evacuated to the countryside. By early 1967, Hanoi's population had been cut in half.[85]

Of course, wresting general air superiority from US air forces was not a practical plan, so the North resolved to make access to their skies as difficult as possible. When Rolling Thunder began, the DRV had nearly 1,500 mostly light 37-mm and 57-mm AAA guns. By early 1966, US intelligence sources estimated the number had grown to almost 5,000 AAA guns, which now included 85-mm and 100-mm radar-directed weapons obtained from the Soviet Union and China. By early 1967, this number had increased to a high of 7,000 units, only to be reduced to as low as 1,000 by early 1972. This lower number was likely the result of the NVA moving their AAA from around Hanoi after Rolling Thunder ended in 1968 to positions near the Ho Chi Minh Trail once the Commando Hunt operations began in 1968.

Figure 2.5. MiG-21 Fishbeds in flight

Besides, by 1971 and 1972, the primary defenses around the larger cities in the North were SAMs, not AAA. Significantly, during Rolling Thunder, 80 percent of US aircraft losses came from AAA fire.[86]

Initially, the North Vietnamese Air Force (NVAF) only consisted of fifty-three MiG-17 Fresco fighters. While they were, by the standards of the day, considered antiquated compared to US supersonic jets, the NVAF turned the apparent limitations of the MiGs into advantages since they were just fast enough to carry out hit-and-run ambush operations. They proved to be very maneuverable, which allowed them to stun US fighter crews by shooting down more sophisticated F-8 Crusaders and F-105 Thunderchiefs during the initial stages of Rolling Thunder.[87]

The F-105 was the largest and heaviest fighter-bomber every built for the USAF. It was originally designed in the early Cold War to deliver nuclear weapons against Soviet forces in Eastern Europe. Like so many of America's air weapons in the mid-1960s, this aircraft was not really what was needed for Rolling Thunder. If a MiG attacked these heavy fighter-bombers, pilots often jettisoned their bombloads to engage in air combat or to flee. Between August and December 1966, enemy fighters intercepted 192 US aircraft. Of this number 107, or 56 percent, jettisoned their bombloads. It proved to be a shocking fact that US airpower was not winning this fight.[88]

As Rolling Thunder unfolded, the United States increasingly employed its new missile-armed F-4 Phantom IIs. This aircraft had advantages over the others, but soon the NVAF also had a newer airborne weapons system. In 1966 the North added small numbers of more modern, Soviet-built MiG-21 Fishbeds, roughly equal in quality to US fighters, to their inventory. By 1967, the NVAF was able to maintain a total interceptor force of 100 aircraft, 22 being MiG-21s. Many of the warplanes were based at Chinese airfields and thus out of reach of American air attacks.[89]

To make bombing more difficult, Northern leaders decentralized their country's large factories. These immense structures, originally located in the heavily populated Red River delta, were broken down and rebuilt in caves and small villages scattered across the countryside. In the more heavily bombed southern panhandle, entire villages moved into underground tunnel complexes. This had the effect of bringing on widespread food shortages in North Vietnam, especially in the urban areas, as rice farmers went into the military or volunteered for service repairing bomb damage.[90] What one must realize is Northern leaders were not concerned about the privations their people had to suffer since they believed their peoples' war was a struggle to the death. They were willing to sacrifice thousands of lives in order to reach their goal of a unified, communist Vietnam. It was an attitude many of the people in the North also accepted.

Finding a way around the bombing became one of the NVAs most successful efforts. For example, when the DRV's transportation system was attacked, thousands of "volunteers" would rush to repair rail lines and rebuild bridges. Where repairs were difficult, they simply replaced the river crossing with dirt fords, ferries, and/or underwater or pontoon spans. The resulting alternative system of transportation proved to be durable, well built, easily repaired, and practically impossible to shut down.[91]

In all of this, the North's greatest asset was its people. During 1965, 97,000 North Vietnamese "offered" to work fulltime repairing bomb damage; another 370,000–500,000 worked part time. When the US turned its attention to bombing the Northern logistics-and-communications network, the authorities divided the supply trains and the truck convoys into smaller elements that traveled only at night. Civilians supported this logistical initiative by using sampans, driving carts, pushing wheelbarrows, or hauling supplies on their backs to keep the war effort going. To keep up their resolve, they repeated propaganda slogans like "Each kilogram of goods . . . is a bullet shot into the head of the American pirates."[92]

As daunting as the interceptors and AAA fire were, North Vietnam's acquisition of Soviet-built SAMs and their increasing deployment around Hanoi confronted US pilots with some of the deadliest weapons they faced. In order to make their bomb runs, they had to decide whether or not to approach targets at higher altitudes in order to evade AAA but be vulnerable to the SAMs, or fly lower to dodge the missiles but become an easier target for AAA gunners. To deal with this threat, the Americans developed strike packages employing different kinds of aircraft to confront the various threats. These tactical changes, combined with the increased use of electronic-warfare radar-jamming systems, helped reduce the number of SAM kills. During 1967 and 1968, the SAM success rate fell from one kill per thirty launches to less than one per fifty. In some ways this did not matter since the Communist Bloc nations constantly resupplied the North with plenty of missiles, which became a major advantage.[93]

Because the Johnson White House had chosen to escalate Rolling Thunder gradually, planners in Hanoi had time to adapt to each new situation.

By 1967, North Vietnam had activated approximately twenty-five SAM battalions, with six missile launchers each, that rotated among 150 sites. On average it took four hours to install a SAM battery and two more hours to make it an operational site. With the support of the Soviet Union, the North Vietnamese also integrated an early warning radar system housed in more than 200 facilities. This network covered the entire nation in order to track incoming strike formation and coordinate SAMs, AAA batteries, and MiG fighters to attack them. It proved to be a very effective system. During 1967 alone, the United States lost 248 aircraft, with 145 belonging to the USAF, 102 to the USN, and 1 to the US Marine Corps (USMC).[94]

US Countermeasures

In order to survive in such a deadly air-defense zone, the Americans had to adopt new and more specialized tactics. The USAF and USN adapted new, large-scale strikes, known as force packages in the air force and multicarrier "Alpha strikes" in the navy. These formations were assigned numerous support aircraft to protect the fighter-bombers. The first to strike the target areas were specialized Iron Hand flak-suppression aircraft, normally consisting of F-105 Wild Weasel hunter-killer teams configured with sophisticated electronic equipment to detect and locate the emissions associated with SAM guidance-and-control radars. The Wild Weasels also carried electronic-countermeasures (ECM) equipment to protect themselves. Each aircraft made flak-suppression strikes using USN-produced AGM-45 Shrike antiradiation missiles to home in on the SAM radar systems and destroy them. The SA-2 had greater range than the AGM-45, but if the Shrike was launched and the radar operator stayed on the air, the American missile would lock on to the signal and destroy the source. A sophisticated game of chicken thus ensued between North Vietnamese radar operators and the Wild Weasel pilots. The navy utilized different aircraft in a similar role. Regardless, these antiradar aircraft were followed by the fighter-bombers carrying mostly 500-pound or 750-pound iron bombs. The strike planes were protected by escort fighters and electronic-jamming aircraft to degrade any remaining enemy radar capabilities. The air force and navy had hurriedly attached new ECM devices to their aircraft to protect them from missile attacks. At first these units experienced numerous breakdowns due to environmental conditions in Southeast Asia. USAF KC-135 Stratotanker aerial-refueling aircraft as well as search-

and-rescue helicopters protected by A-1 Skyraider escorts were also part of the package.[95]

The entire process became increasingly expensive and controversial. While the aerial-combat kill ratio was still 2.3:1 in favor of the Americans, nearly every US pilot shot down crashed in North Vietnam, and despite the excellent search-and-rescue crews, his chances of rescue were about one in six. In addition, American aircraft were very expensive, especially in comparison to the smaller MiGs. By October 1968, according to Alain C. Enthoven, a USAF deputy controller and assistant secretary of defense for systems analysis, Rolling Thunder inflicted $600 million in damage on the DRV. This was at the cost, however, of "more than 800 dead and captured airmen and $6 billion in projected replacement costs for the more than 900 aircraft lost."[96]

Even as the bloodletting continued, President Johnson, from mid-1966 to the end of 1967, continued to approve a few problematic targets to placate his air commanders and generals while also pandering to antiwar members of Congress and his own administration with periodic cutbacks and halfhearted peace initiatives. It proved to be an erratic policy course that satisfied no one and did little to alter the course of the war. The whole affair, especially the nature of the targets and the risk of bombing and rebombing them, resembled a rather macabre comedy. It also took a toll on the men flying the missions. In September 1966 David McDonald, chief of naval operations, traveled to South Vietnam to review the situation. In his report he explained that the aircrews were frustrated by the targeting process and angered by a campaign they believed was full of "guidelines requiring repetitive air programs that seemed more than anything else to benefit enemy gunners." As if to verify how bad things had become, during 1967, the second full year of Rolling Thunder operations, 362 US aircraft were lost over North Vietnam—208 air force, 142 navy, and 12 marine. Even so, the worst was yet to come.[97]

Air-to-Air Combat

Rolling Thunder reached its pinnacle in 1967. Then as gradually as it expanded, it slowly began to recede. The campaign reached the last stage of its operational evolution between late 1967 and November 1968 even as its missions changed into strikes moving farther north into the route packages of North Vietnam. Bit by bit, its tasks evolved into interdicting

Figure 2.6. "Wolfpack" aviators of the 8th Tactical Fighter Wing carry their commanding officer, Col. Robin Olds, following his return from his last combat mission over North Vietnam.

the flow of supplies and equipment as well as the destruction of those segments of the DRV's infrastructure supporting the PAVN's military effort. While AAA fire inflicted most American aircraft losses, air force F-105s and navy A-4s were increasingly confronted with SAM and MiG attacks. NVAF interceptors also became a particular problem because of the lack of radar coverage in the Red River delta, which provided the MiGs the opportunity to ambush the strike forces. US airborne early warning aircraft had difficulty detecting the enemy fighters at low altitudes, which were often difficult to pick up visually. While F-105s did score twenty-seven air-to-air victories during the war, the overall kill ratio was roughly one for one.[98]

Figure 2.7. Robin Olds's F-4C, "SCAT XXVII," on display at the National Museum of the Air Force, Canton, Ohio

Operation Bolo

One of the most successful USAF operations of the war took place on 2 January 1967. Since the White House refused to target North Vietnamese airfields until April 1967, the air force had to find another way to reduce the lethality of the airspace over North Vietnamese targets. In this effort to lessen the number of aerial losses, especially of F-105s, Col. Robin Olds and his F-4 crews planned a deception for the NVAF MiG-21s. Under normal circumstances, the US strike packages included refueling aircraft, F-105 fighter-bombers at low altitudes, and F-4s at higher altitudes. In what was designated Operation Bolo, the F-4s imitated the F-105s, using their call signs and ECM emissions, attack patterns, and communications in order to fool enemy ground controllers into sending MiG-21 interceptors to meet what they thought were bomb-laden F-105s; instead, the interceptors faced F-4s, locked and loaded for action. To maximize coverage over Hanoi and prevent the MiGs from escaping into China, the plan called for four-teen flights to converge over the city. The two units involved were Olds's 8th Tactical Fighter Wing, based at Ubon Royal Thai Air Base, Thailand, and the 366th Tactical Fighter Wing, located at Da Nang, South Vietnam.[99]

The day of the mission dawned with marginal weather, which delayed operations until the afternoon and limited the number of F-4s to only three flights. Olds, 8th Tactical Fighter Wing commander, led the first flight, designated "Olds"; Col. Daniel "Chappie" James led the second flight, designated "Ford"; and Capt. John Stone led the third flight, designated "Rambler." Olds's aircraft flew over the Phuc Yen airfield twice before the MiGs broke through the clouds. There ensued an intense dogfight that lasted less than fifteen minutes. Even so, it proved to be the largest single air clash of its kind in the entire war. The twelve F-4s shot down seven MiG-21s and probably two others. None of the Americans went down. More than 25 percent of the NVAFs most modern interceptors were destroyed that day. The North was reluctant to risk such losses in the future, thus making Operation Bolo a complete success by achieving its primary objective—reducing US air losses.[100]

Other Operations

Later that same year, the president, frustrated by the lack of movement toward negotiation, authorized the USAF to launch its most intense and sustained attempt to force North Vietnam into peace talks. Nearly all of the original 94 Target List sites, and roughly 300 more, were approved for attack, including airfields previously off limits; only central Hanoi, Haiphong, and the Chinese-border area remained prohibited. Airmen made a concerted effort to isolate Northern urban areas by destroying bridges and other lines of communication. In some of the most dangerous missions of the entire war, USAF pilots, again led by Colonel Olds, flew daring low-level attacks, destroying the Thai Nguyen steel complex, thermal and electrical power plants, ship and rail repair facilities, and warehouses. Reluctantly, NVAF MiGs reentered the air battle to defend the capital. As a result, the kill ratio increased to two MiG kills for each US aircraft downed in aerial combat. In 1968, MiG interceptors accounted for 22 percent of the 184 American aircraft lost over the North: seventy-five air force, fifty-nine navy, and five marine warplanes. Johnson, who previously had only allowed limited attacks against airfields, at last opened them to full-scale raids.[101]

Success or Failure?

Despite all of the efforts by US airmen, Rolling Thunder's flaws undercut its chances for success. On 30 January 1968, VC and PAVN units launched a massive series of attacks throughout South Vietnam during the lunar New Year holiday, known as the Tet Offensive. Even though it ended in military disaster for North Vietnam and its allies in the South, it had a negative influence on US public opinion and President Johnson's will to continue the war. While opinion polls in early 1968 indicated Americans still supported the war effort, they were upset by constant assurances from military and civilian leaders that victory was just around the corner. Tet made it clear to the Johnson administration the public wanted a victory soon or an end to the open-ended commitment of US resources and manpower.[102]

Tet became the beginning of the end for Rolling Thunder and for Johnson's presidency. To some bombing advocates, the only solution was to play the US trump card and move B-52 operations from the South and DMZ into the North. Yet even supporters such as McConnell feared risking the loss of even one BUF, the only US aircraft capable of delivering a lot of bombs in bad weather. Without the B-52s, however, there was little that could be done over the North in response to Tet: bad weather minimized fighter operations until the beginning of April, and by then Johnson had announced he would not seek reelection and would end the bombing campaign in an effort to initiate peace negotiations.[103]

The Beginning of the End

After the war Secretary McNamara maintained that, by the spring of 1967, he and other civilians in the administration were convinced that both Rolling Thunder and the ground war in South Vietnam had failed. He claimed he and others consistently opposed most JCS recommendations for an amplified bombing tempo and the loosening of target restrictions.[104] American military leaders eventually found themselves on the horns of a dilemma of their own making. Throughout, they had proclaimed the air offensive was working, and yet, simultaneously, they were demanding additional resources and greater latitude in order to help operations succeed. In retrospect, it is clear the airmen could not back down. This was their opportunity to show the essential nature of their service, and to back down would be not only humiliating personally but might also be the basis for losing future roles and having their budgets cut. It took two more years before a few officials in the Department of Defense and the White House realized the incompatibility of Johnson's limited foreign-policy goals and the military's focus on total victory. With this as the baseline for discussion, the great conundrum became "how to defeat North Vietnam without defeating North Vietnam."[105]

On 9 August 1967, members of the Senate Armed Services Committee began hearings on Rolling Thunder due to objections from military officials that had piqued the interest of many of the most vocal prowar political leaders on Capitol Hill. The military chiefs testified before the committee, grousing about the gradual nature of the air war and its civilian-imposed restrictions. It was obvious McNamara, the only civilian subpoenaed and the last to testify, was to be the scapegoat. He focused his counterarguments on what he described as a random air war and successfully rebutted the military chiefs' criticism.[106] He also bluntly declared there was "no basis to believe that any bombing campaign . . . would by itself force Ho Chi Minh's regime into submission short, that is, of the virtual annihilation of North Vietnam and its people."[107]

By 1968, with Tet well underway and Johnson under increasing pressure, the president concluded that McNamara was a political liability. Accordingly, in February 1968 McNamara resigned and was replaced as secretary of defense by Clark Clifford, who was selected mainly due to his personal friendship with Johnson and his previous opposition to suggestions that the number of troops in the South Vietnam be stabilized and Rolling Thunder ended. Yet almost immediately Secretary of State Rusk adopted McNamara's old position, even though he had been a hardcore proponent of bombing operations in the past. Rusk called for restricting the campaign, without preconditions, to the North Vietnamese panhandle and waiting to see how Hanoi reacted.[108]

Ironically, as he notes in his memoirs, it took only six weeks for Clifford to change his course and slowly adopt his predecessor's views. He gradually came to believe that the United States had to withdraw from an open-ended commitment to the war. Crestfallen by what he viewed as political defeats at home and desperately hoping leaders in Hanoi would begin negotiations, on 2 February 1968 Johnson announced a stop to all bombing north of the nineteenth parallel and his decision not to seek reelection, hoping these actions would spur the North toward peace.[109]

Facing this new reality, the navy and air force began to pour all the ordnance they had previously spread all over the DRV into an area between the seventeenth and nineteenth parallels. USAF planners doubled the number of sorties sent into Route Package I to more than 6,000 per month, with the campaign concentrated on interdiction chokepoints, road closing, and truck hunting. Once again military leaders were faced with the same old dilemma of justifying this policy change. They publically proclaimed the new approach had a lot of merit, especially when considering the alternative of not bombing. DRV officials responded by doubling the AAA batteries in the panhandle while leaving most of their SAM batteries around Hanoi and Haiphong.[110]

Those in Hanoi had always specified they would not consider negotiations as long as the air campaign continued. Once the bombing did end, they agreed to meet with US representatives for preliminary talks in Paris. On 1 November 1968, just prior to the US presidential election, Johnson declared that bombing would end completely throughout all parts of North Vietnam. Members of the JCS remained skeptical that he would ever reopen bombing under any circumstances. They were correct. Rolling Thunder was over.[111]

Drawing Conclusions and Learning Lessons

Between March 1965 and November 1968, USAF crews flew 153,784 attack sorties against North Vietnam, while the USN and USMC flew an additional 152,399. As early as 31 December 1967, Defense Department officials announced US forces had dropped 864,000 tons of bombs on the DRV during Rolling Thunder, an astonishing total compared with 653,000 tons dropped during the entire Korean War and 503,000 tons in the Pacific theater during World War II. By October 1968, official reports stated that Rolling Thunder attacks had destroyed 77 percent of all ammunition depots, more than 60 percent of all POL storage facilities, nearly 60 percent of North Vietnamese power plants, over 50 percent of all major bridges, and 40 percent of all railroads. Defense also reported US airstrikes had destroyed 12,500 vessels, 10,000 vehicles, and 2,000 railroad cars and engines.[112]

In a report dated 1 January 1968, CIA analysts estimated the damage inflicted on North Vietnam at $370 million in physical destruction, including $164 million worth of damage to capital assets such as factories, bridges, and power plants. Agency experts estimated that nearly 1,000 people per week were casualties among the North Vietnamese population—about 90,000 during the entire forty-four-month period—with 72,000 being civilians. All totaled, over or near North Vietnam, the USAF had lost 506 aircraft, the USN 397, and the USMC 19. Within these planes fell 745 crewmen. USAF records indicated that 145 were rescued, 255 were killed, 222 were captured (of whom 23 died in captivity), and 123 were declared missing. The navy and marines indicated that 454 naval aviators were killed, captured, or missing during operations over North Vietnam and Laos. The United States flew 304,000 fighter-bomber sorties and 2,380 B-52 sorties over the North, losing 938 aircraft.[113]

Given the magnitude of the campaign and the lack of positive results, USAF historian Tilford asks, "How could one of the longest bombing campaigns in the history of aerial warfare, during which a million sorties were flown and around three quarters of a million tons of bombs dropped, fail so totally?" He provides two primary reasons. "First," he notes, "in their pride, American civilian and military planners did not—probably could not—imagine that North Vietnam would endure American aerial attacks." To this end, "too many people believed too strongly in the efficacy and applicability of military power." In addition, "civilian policymakers did not understand airpower well enough to know that their policies might be crippling its potential effectiveness." Moreover, "military leaders, for their part, were victims of a doctrine that they could not, or would not, believe had little applicability in a limited war." The second cause was that "military leaders failed to develop and propose a strategy appropriate to the war at hand. Bombing strategic targets in the North and the unconventional war going on in the South had little direct interconnection." On top of all of this, "even after they realized that the constraints imposed by civilian policymakers would not be completely removed, the generals and admirals never devised a strategy applicable to the war as it was defined for them."[114]

Clearly, Rolling Thunder began as an operation aimed at psychological and strategic persuasion. It rapidly changed into a tactical mission focused on interdiction. Ultimately, it failed because civilian and military leaders could never conceive that the North Vietnamese would endure the aerial devastation unleashed upon them. Moreover, civilian authorities never understood how their policies undermined the application of airpower. Lastly, most US military leaders failed to develop or adapt an appropriate strategy for the war. Throughout, Rolling Thunder fell prey to the same dysfunctional managerial attitude as did the general military effort in Southeast Asia. The process became an end unto itself. Sortie generation became the standard by which progress was measured. Sortie rates and the number of bombs dropped, however, equaled efficiency, not effectiveness. In the end it was not even efficient in many cases since, in an effort to enhance the sortie rate, eight planes were sent with small bombloads when one or two planes could have accomplished the same mission.[115]

Despite these problems, there were positive results. In the beginning those in the US fighter community were stunned to discover aged, subsonic MiG-17s inflicting losses on the F-105 Thunderchief, the fastest and most sophisticated strike fighter then in the USAF. Eventually, aircraft designers and mission planners had to radically reconsider air combat and aircraft design. Air combat had, since the end of World War II, been focused on the delivery of nuclear weapons in Europe and missile interception. The initial solution was to employ the F-4 Phantom II as both the USAF and USN air-superiority fighter during the last half of the Vietnam War. Originally armed with missiles for dogfighting, eventually the USAF's F-4E was fitted with maneuvering slats and an internal gun. The USN so appreciated the F-4 that it cancelled a new fighter version of the General Dynamics/ Grumman F-111B in favor of more Phantoms. Beginning in the 1970s and throughout the 1980s, the air force and navy developed a new generation of fighters that were optimized for visual-range dogfights. These included the so-called "teen" fighters, the F-14, F-15, F-16, and F-18.[116]

Finally yet importantly, both the USN and USAF learned important lessons with regard to air-to-air combat. With the kill ratio having dropped dramatically from the Korean War, airpower leaders analyzed reports and statistics to help rectify this problem. As a result, the navy developed the Top Gun training program at Miramar Naval Air Station, California, while the air force instituted its Red Flag program at Nellis Air Force Base, Nevada, to improve the dogfighting skills of their pilots. In the navy program, F-5 Tigers and A-4 Skyhawks simulated small subsonic and supersonic MiG fighters to examine the hidden threats they presented. Although the first of the new generation of fighters did not enter service soon enough to cover the US withdrawal from Vietnam, they would dominate future air battles, serving well into the twenty-first century. Many remain in service as do the dogfighting skills US pilots continue to perfect.[117]

3

A Reassessment of the Battle of Ia Drang Valley, 1965

The Role of Airpower, Heroic Soldiers, and the Wrong Lessons

Just prior to the release of the movie starring Mel Gibson, I was invited to a preview showing of the movie along with family and friends of many of the main characters depicted on screen and from the source book by Joe Galloway and Lt. Gen. Hal Moore. I sat near the middle of a very large theater with a group of colleagues and friends. Just before the movie began, a man and woman sat down directly in front of me; I remember being grateful she was not too tall so I could see over her. At one of the more dramatic moments in the movie a significant player in the story is shot and killed boarding a helicopter. The woman in front of me gasped and began to sob uncontrollably. I learned later that it was her father's death being recreated in the movie. As we left the theater, not one of the 200 people attending the showing said a word—they were overcome with emotion.

As poignant and impressive as the film and book from which it came are, they provide only part of a much larger story. Naturally, Moore and Galloway wrote about what they knew and had experienced at LZ X-Ray. But there were other aspects of the much larger military campaign in the Ia

Drang Valley, which began after a VC attack on the US Army Special Forces camp at Plei Me in late October and ended on 28 November 1965. The operation was designated "Silver Bayonet" and included most of the troops in the 1st Cavalry Division as well as a sustained airpower effort and ARVN participation. It also involved an entire division of PAVN regulars as well as VC units.[1]

While this chapter examines the more well-known combat at LZ X-Ray, it also discusses the ambush at LZ Albany, the massive use of airpower to save US forces on the ground, and the misinterpretation of events by senior US leadership. It also examines the significance of the Battle of Ia Drang Valley as a turning point in the war. In a February 2009 CBS News report, correspondent Mary-Jayne McKay opened by saying, "Of all the battles fought in Vietnam, the one fought in the Ia Drang River [ ] Valley in 1965 stands out as a pivotal moment that may have helped escalate the American involvement in that war."[2] Of this there can be no doubt. But there were other reasons the battle was significant and compelling.

From the time the first reports reached US news-media outlets in November 1965 and the public first heard about a battle in the Ia Drang Valley, the name has caused a strong reaction, especially from those who experienced the bloodletting between the US Army and the People's Army of Vietnam. Even so, the battles during the Tet Offensive and for Khe Sanh a little more than two years later were more costly and had more consequence on the outcome of the conflict. Perhaps this is because many people then and now argued the key to a military victory in the Second Indochina War was the control of South Vietnam's (Republic of Vietnam) Central Highlands. If so, then this was only the first of many struggles for this part of Indochina.

The Battle of Ia Drang Valley was certainly the first of its kind. It was the first time US Army units and PAVN regulars fought each other in a set-piece battle. In most respects it was a conventional engagement unlike the guerrilla or low-intensity conflict that had previously been the norm in Vietnam. The outcome deluded General Westmoreland and MACV into believing they had found the tactical imperative for victory—search out enemy forces, engage them in open combat with superior firepower, and kill large numbers of enemy troops. This, he was certain, would force the communists to sue for peace. In hindsight it proved to be a substantially flawed concept that eventually led to stalemate.

There was another first during this campaign. While B-52 Arc Light bombing raids had been taking place since 27 July 1965, it was the first time the BUFs had flown support strikes for ground forces in a major land battle—not just in Vietnam but ever. Besides the big bombers, propeller-driven and jet fighter aircraft, flare ships, transports, and observation aircraft proved to be critical to the salvation of US forces on the ground at both LZs X-Ray and Albany. Neither Moore nor Galloway were part of the ambush at LZ Albany or witnessed the B-52 raids, thus the role of airpower is sparsely covered in their book. Yet in the first extended news story about the battle, CBS News correspondent Morley Safer reported that airstrikes had kept the men on the ground alive. This chapter seeks to explore not only the role of airpower but also the clash at LZ Albany, which could and should have provided a logical argument for ending the US military presence in Vietnam.[3]

Background

The Ia Drang Valley is located about thirty-two miles southwest of Pleiku in the Central Highlands of Vietnam. The word "ia" comes from the "Montagnard," or Nguoi Thuong, people's word for "river" (thus, River Drang). While this region of Vietnam was strategically important throughout the history of mainland Southeast Asia, especially during the First Indochina War (1946–54), the valley itself remained anonymous to most Americans prior to 14 November 1965.

Figure 3.1. Lt. Col. Hal Moore during the Battle of Ia Drang Valley

On that morning a forty-three-year-old West Point graduate (class of 1945), Lt. Col. Harold G. Moore from Bardstown, Kentucky, received orders to take 457 men of the 1st Battalion, 7th Cavalry Regiment (1/7) into the valley on an air mobility search-and-destroy mission against what American intelligence reported to be a regiment of irregular enemy troops. As it turned out, Moore was leading his men into a hornets' nest. Later analysis revealed the communists had the equivalent of a division of their best light infantry waiting to annihilate the Americans. Moore's 1/7 was supposed to have 765 troopers but was well short of this due to illness (mostly from malaria) and end-of-tour departures.[4]

Prior to the insertion of his forces, Moore made an aerial reconnaissance of the area, deciding to land his men in a football field-sized clearing at the foot of the Chu Pong Massif, a 2,400-foot mountain that stretched just beyond the Cambodian border. His troopers were flown in on UH-1 helicopters and deposited in the clearing, designated LZ X-Ray. Requiring numerous sorties to bring in the entire battalion, not all of Moore's men had arrived when, just after noon, NVA units struck. This phase of Operation Silver Bayonet continued at LZ X-Ray and across the valley for the next four days. Afterward, senior leaders on both sides declared victory, although those who fought and died did not see it that way. Recalling their comrades bleeding and dying all around them, the veterans described their experience as "tragic" and "terrible." For some, it was an experience that haunted their dreams for the rest of their lives.

Silver Bayonet was the deepest penetration American forces had ever made into the communist-held jungles of the Central Highlands. Here, the Ia Drang flowed into Cambodia, made a dramatic turn, and joined the Mekong River, which then rushed back into Vietnam far to the south. The sweeping Ia Drang Valley, or the "valley of death" as the French called it, was seventeen miles from a lone red-clay road that traversed to Plei Me. In the aftermath of the upcoming battle, the US death toll at LZs X-Ray and, later, Albany shook the Johnson administration as well as the American military establishment to its very core. US forces had lost relatively few soldiers up to this point in the war. The casualty numbers from Ia Drang shocked the American public out of their apathy over this little war halfway around the world. From the moment the battle began, leaders on both sides realized the war had taken a dramatic turn.[5]

While Moore's role in the engagement has been well documented in word and on film, it should be noted that almost all of the 3rd Brigade, 1st Cavalry Division was involved, including the 1/7 and the 2/7 as well as the 2nd Battalion, 5th Cavalry Regiment (2/5). Facing them were 2,000–2,400 troops of the PAVN's B3 Front, 304th Division and some of the best VC available. In addition to the ground engagement, the battle would witness intense close air support by US aircraft, including the bombing strike by B-52s. The first communist attacks came against Moore's forces at LZ X-Ray and were beaten back after three days and two nights of heavy fighting. But the ensuing PAVN ambush of the 2/7 on 17 November became one of the worse disasters in US Army history. Roughly 60 percent of the 250 Americans killed during the thirty-five days of Operation Silver Bayonet died on that one day at LZ Albany.[6] Had it not been for airstrikes, artillery barrages, and ground reinforcements, the outcome might have been more like the US defeat at the Little Bighorn in 1876 or the British annihilation at Isandlwana in 1879.

Prior to Ia Drang Valley, the Republic of Vietnam had experienced several military and political setbacks. Despite increased material support from the United States, the ARVN refused to risk its forces in open combat against the VC. South Vietnamese president Ngo Dinh Diem, a Roman Catholic, maintained tight control over ARVN forces, most of which were led by Buddhists. This allowed the VC to buildup, train, and supply their forces in relative peace. This and other issues led the United States to secretly seek an alternative to Diem.

One of the biggest challenges Diem brought upon himself with his heavy-handed treatment of South Vietnamese Buddhists. This on top of his disagreements with the Americans on how to conduct the anticommunist war created a volatile situation. On 20 August 1963 Diem's brother, Ngo Dinh Nhu, head of South Vietnamese security forces, led a raid on the Xa Loi pagoda in Saigon while dressed in an ARVN uniform, taking 400 monks into custody in Saigon and thousands of others throughout the country. Afterward, Diem asked to discuss the situation with US ambassador Henry Cabot Lodge Jr., who refused. Having learned that ARVN generals, led by Gen. Duong Van Minh and backed by the CIA, were planning a coup, Lodge assured the rebel officers the United States would not interfere.[7]

On 1 November the conspirators overthrew the South Vietnamese government, promising to allow Diem to go into exile. The deposed president
escaped through an underground passage only to be captured the next
morning. Under orders from General Minh, Capt. Nguyen Van Nhung murdered both Diem and Nhu in the back of an APC. Diem was buried in an
unmarked grave in a cemetery next to the house of the US ambassador.[8]

Ultimately, the action proved to be a mistake since the South Vietnamese were never able to build a strong or stable government again. The communists were delighted. Ho Chi Minh supposedly remarked, "I can scarcely
believe the Americans would be so stupid."[9]

Less than a month later, on 22 November 1963, President Kennedy was
killed in Dallas. Leadership passed to Vice President Johnson. From the outset, Johnson and his advisers concluded that only US intervention could
bring the conflict in South Vietnam to a successful conclusion. Five days
after the USS *Maddox* received fire from three North Vietnamese gunboats
in international waters in the Gulf of Tonkin on 2 August 1964, the president took advantage of what later proved to be an exaggerated report to
ram through Congress the Gulf of Tonkin Resolution. The measure gave
Johnson free rein to send US troops into South Vietnam in large numbers.[10]

By early 1965, General Westmoreland had assurances of receiving in
excess of 200,000 US regulars. As these forces arrived during the spring and
summer, he moved them into place in preparation for combat operations
in Vietnam rather than continue to rely only on the ARVN for such missions. By this time, Hanoi had begun sending hundreds of thousands of
its best forces south to support the VC. One of the main destinations for
the Northern troops was the Central Highlands, northeast of Saigon. It was
there Westmoreland determined to test his new air mobile units of the 1st
Cavalry Division. He believed by utilizing their UH-1 Huey helicopters, his
new troops could be swiftly airlifted into hot combat sites throughout the
region, thus overcoming the rugged terrain.

In October the enemy launched what seemed to be a typical—and
unsuccessful—attack on the Army Special Forces camp at Plei Me. The
ease with which they were beaten back and their swift retreat should have
alerted the Americans something was afoot, a fact only partially considered. Instead, Westmoreland ordered Col. Thomas Brown, commander
of the 3rd Brigade, 1st Cavalry Division, to move his forces from Pleiku
and find, engage, and destroy the enemy. While Brown did not locate the

communist attackers, Westmoreland instructed him to continue toward the Cambodian border. As he drew near the border, the colonel received word there were enemy troops near the Chu Pong Massif. At this point in early November, Brown instructed Lieutenant Colonel Moore to conduct a reconnaissance in force with his men from the 1/7. It was this action that initiated the Battle of Ia Drang Valley.[11]

Prior to their deployment to Vietnam, all new units had their designations changed. In what seemed a supreme irony to Moore, his battalion now held the same 1/7 designation as Lt. Col. George Armstrong Custer's doomed command in 1876. His men were also about to go into "the valley of death." They understood the situation and affectionately called their commander "Old Yellow Hair." Throughout his tour, Moore was constantly aware of the dubious honor of following in the footsteps of the men who had died at the Little Bighorn. The lieutenant colonel was determined to prevent his men being similarly massacred, so he read as much as he could about infantry tactics in circumstances similar to those he might face in Vietnam. More importantly, he studied French reports of their experiences against this same foe. Nevertheless, he was painfully aware he could only control his own actions and not necessarily his situation. If his superiors set him up to fail, he might indeed be leading his battalion into another Custer-style defeat. As it turned out, it was not the men of the 1/7 but their comrades in the 2/7 who would suffer near annihilation.[12]

Brown directed Moore not to climb the nearby mountains but instead to land in one of several landing areas, specifically LZ X-Ray, Albany, Columbus, Tango, Yankee, Whiskey, or Victor. Moore selected X-Ray, a flat, clear area surrounded by low trees near the base of Chu Pong Massif, bordered by a dry creek bed to the west and the Ia Drang about a mile to the northwest. He was to receive artillery support from Firebase Falcon about four miles to the northeast. The LZ was just large enough for eight to ten Hueys to land at one time. As was normal for that time, the 1/7 had three rifle companies—A, B, and (C)—and a heavy-weapons company, D. As the operation began, the battalion had 457 troopers and sixteen helicopters to transport them into battle, with each ship carrying 10–12 men. This meant they could airlift about one full company, with each trip taking thirty to forty-five minutes. As the operation began, Moore led B Company in first along with his command team; they were followed by A, C, and D Companies. The initial plan was to move B and A Companies to the northwest beyond the creek bed and C Company south toward the mountain. D Company, with its mortars and heavy machine guns, was to act as a battlefield reserve. Moore's command post was at the center of the LZ near a six-foot-tall termite mound.[13]

The Battle Begins

Action on the fourteenth began at 1017 hours with a thirty-minute artillery barrage and airstrikes. At 1048 hours B Company, led by Capt. John Herren, touched down at LZ X-Ray. He was accompanied by Moore and his command group, which included World War II and Korean War veteran Sgt. Maj. Basil L. Plumley. Known as "Old Iron Jaw," he proved to be one of the most important leaders during the battle. It is important to understand the entire brigade was made up mostly of young men, the vast majority of whom had not seen combat. The steady hand of veterans like Plumley and others proved critical to their survival. By the same token, the bravery of these young men must also be acknowledged. At first the company stayed near the center of the LZ while smaller units were sent out to reconnoiter the surrounding area.

Figure 3.2. Sgt. Maj. Basil L. Plumley seated during a lull in the fighting in the Ia Drang Valley

Figure 3.3. The first men of Bravo Company, 1/7, 1st Cavalry Division unload at LZ X-Ray

Lieutenant Colonel Moore was agonizingly aware, when he landed, that he had only ninety men with which to hold the LZ, with no reinforcement for at least forty-five minutes. But luck was with him—and he needed it. Just minutes after they arrived, a squad under Sgt. John Mingo captured an unarmed prisoner from the 33rd PAVN Regiment. The frightened private told them that three communist regiments were on the mountain and anxious to kill as many Americans as possible. This news sent chills down everyone's back. Fortunately, within an hour the second group of the 1/7 arrived and still the enemy had not attacked. Before the communists finally did, Moore had enough men to hold the LZ for the present.

What Moore did not know was the NVA had 2,000–2,400 troops nearby under the expert command of veteran Lt. Col. Nguyen Huu An. They also had built a series of interconnecting underground tunnels and rooms to allow them to pop out in force at various spots all around LZ X-Ray. These soldiers were well trained, well armed, dedicated, and anxious to prove their ability to their new enemy. Lieutenant Colonel An had brought with him a new tactic described as "grabbing hold of the enemy's belt buckle." This entailed getting his troops so close to the Americans they would not dare employ their artillery or airstrikes for fear of hitting their own men. It was a tactic that had some success, though not as much as expected, mainly due the precision of US artillery and especially close air support.[14]

At 1120 hours the second airlift set down, bringing the remainder of B Company and one platoon of A Company, commanded by Capt. Tony Nadal. Fifty minutes later the third group arrived, consisting of most of A

Figure 3.4. Lt. Gen. Nguyen Huu An, who, as a lieutenant colonel, commanded NVA forces at Ia Drang Valley

Company. The troops immediately moved into position at the rear and left flank of B Company, along the dry creek bed, and to the west and to the south, facing perpendicular down the creek bed.[15]

At 1230 B Company took the first shots as its three platoons patrolled the undergrowth northwest of the creek bed. Captain Herren directed his 1st Platoon, under Lt. Al Devney, and his 2nd Platoon, under Lt. Henry Herrick, to form up abreast of one another, while the 3rd Platoon, under Lt. Dennis Deal, was to follow in reserve. As they advanced Devney's platoon took the lead, 100 yards west of the creek bed, with Herrick's troopers just to his rear and off his right flank. At 1330 Devney was attacked on both flanks by dozens of communist soldiers. Several troopers fell, and within minutes the entire platoon was pinned down. Soon after, Herrick reported his unit coming under intense fire from their right flank. He also radioed that he was in hot pursuit of what appeared to be a squad of enemy soldiers moving away from him to his right. Herrick acted aggressively and soon was far ahead of the rest of the company. As the enemy fire increased, Devney and Deal's platoons sought cover.

As the 2nd Platoon chased the PAVN troops on the right, the men became spread out over a wide area and advanced ahead of the rest of the battalion by 300–500 feet. Herrick soon realized he was not in contact with the rest of the company and feared his unit might be cut off from the battalion if he tried to skirt the clearing just ahead. As the running firefight grew more intense, it appeared his men were inflicting heavy losses on the enemy, who poured out from behind the surrounding trees. Yet after only five minutes Herrick radioed Herren to tell him the PAVN soldiers were constricting the area around his left and right flanks. Herren ordered Herrick to make an effort to link up with Devney's 1st Platoon.

This soon became impossible, and Herrick reported that a large force stood between his men and the 1st Platoon. Things soon went from bad to worse, and the 2nd Platoon began taking significant casualties. The lieutenant directed his men to form a defensive perimeter on a small knoll in the clearing. Within minutes, five members of the 2nd were killed and Herrick was mortally wounded; his last orders were for Sgt. Carl Palmer to take command and for everyone to destroy all vital records and their signal codes. In short order Palmer and Sgt. Robert Stokes were also killed, and Sgt. 1st Class Mac McHenry officially took command. But McHenry was pinned down away from the radio, and so Sgt. Ernie Savage effectively assumed command for the time being. Savage quickly called in repeated artillery barrages on his own position to prevent it from being overrun. At this point eight men had been killed and thirteen wounded. The 2nd Platoon, now isolated, was in constant danger of being overrun.[16]

As this action was underway, troops at the LZ and command post successfully defended the area around the termite hill while the remainder of B Company beat back attacks at the creek bed. At 1520 the last members of the battalion arrived, and Lieutenant Colonel Moore swiftly established a 360-degree perimeter around X-Ray. Ever mindful of having promised his men he would never leave any of them behind, Moore was keen to rescue his isolated platoon. At 1545 he ordered A and B Companies forward toward the clearing. Heavy enemy fire halted the advance. Of note were the actions of Lt. Walter "Joe" Marm, who singlehandedly captured a PAVN machine-gun position during the aborted advance, which earned him the Medal of Honor.[17]

As for the men of the 2nd Platoon, things seemed to become more hopeless as the sun set around 1915 hours. Yet several things did work in their favor. First, there was the outstanding leadership of Sergeant Savage, who kept his composure throughout the fighting. On numerous occasions he called in artillery strikes—even nighttime airstrikes—on top of his own position. Second was the expert care the wounded received from the platoon's medic, Charles Lose. Third was the vital air cover provided by US aircraft. As Moore later wrote in his after-action report: "The man who ended up on the radio was a Sergeant E-5 squad leader. He could not get to the ranking man (a Staff Sergeant), since any move he made drew immediate enemy rifle fire." Indeed, the communists made "three separate attacks . . . during the night," each time with about fifty men. These were beaten back by small-arms and artillery fire. Some of the wounded continued to fight. The largest enemy assault was the second one, taking place "at approximately 0345 hours" and "preceded by bugle calls around the platoon and up on the mountain . . . above the platoon." With his men facing dire circumstances, Moore "requested and received a TAC [Tactical Air Command] Air strike in the area above the platoon. It was conducted under Air Force C-123 flare ship illumination. It was right on target and greatly assisted in breaking up the second attack on the surrounded platoon."[18]

A similar account came from a USAF Project Contemporary Historical Examination of Current Operations (CHECO) Southeast Asia report written in February 1966. According to the author, "One platoon of this company [B Company] was cut off from the battalion, practically in the shadow of the Chu Pong slopes." As night fell they were in serious trouble and called in an AC-47 Spooky gunship—a modified C-47 Skytrain transport—which fired "12,000 rounds at the high ground to the west of the platoon's position." Around 0345 hours on the fifteenth, a relief unit "launched a heavy probe from the southwest." The enemy attacked again, forcing the members of B Company to again call for tactical air support. This time "a flight of A-1Es scrambled from Plieku at 0450," and after receiving detailed instructions from ground reconnaissance and the airborne forward air controller in the C-123 Provider flare ship, the A-1E Skyraiders dropped twelve 500-pound and twelve 100-pound general-purpose bombs within a few dozen feet of the platoon's perimeter; four of the 100-pound bombs contained white phosphorus. By 0600, the enemy probe had been halted. As the sun rose, the platoon's survivors could breathe a sigh of relief—they would be okay for now. The CHECO and other reports later confirmed a body count of enemy dead to be seventy. Airpower had saved B Company that night. The next day it would do the same for the entire battalion.[19]

One can only imagine the waking nightmare these Americans faced during the night. In the aftermath Spec. Galen Bungum declared: "We gathered up all the full magazines we could find and stacked them up in front of us. There was no way we could dig a foxhole. The handle was blown off my entrenching tool and one of my canteens had a hole blown through it. The fire was so heavy that if you tried to raise up to dig you were dead. There was death and destruction all around."[20] Savage was naturally focused on the repeated PAVN assaults: "It seemed like they didn't care how many of them were killed. Some of them were stumbling, walking right into us. Some had their guns slung and were charging barehanded. I didn't run out of ammo—had about thirty magazines in my pack. And, no problems with the M16. An hour before dark three men walked up on the perimeter. I killed all three of them 15 feet away."[21]

Around 1330 on the fourteenth, C Company, commanded by Capt. Robert Edwards, arrived and assumed a position on the LZ X-Ray defensive perimeter south and southwest, facing the mountain. At the same time Moore contacted his airborne-operations officer, Capt. Matthew Dillon, requesting artillery, aerial rocket artillery, and airstrikes on Chu Pong to prevent another PAVN attack.

While this action unfolded, along the creek bed, Lt. Robert Taft and the men of the 3rd Platoon, A Company were attacked by 150 PAVN fighters approaching from the south down the length and sides of the dry bed. Taft's men were ordered to drop their packs and counterattack. It was disaster. Within minutes the lieutenant was cut down and command passed to Sgt. Lorenzo Nathan, who quickly ordered the decimated platoon back to its original defensive positions. A hardened veteran of the Korean War, his quick thinking forced the enemy to attempt a frontal attack, which the Americans defeated. Blocked by the 3rd Platoon's withering fire, the communists swung their attack to the right in an effort to flank B Company. This maneuver was stopped by the men of 2nd Platoon, A Company, led by the aforementioned Lieutenant Marm. These troopers were only present because Moore had ordered Captain Nadal to send one of his platoons to help Herren fight through to Herrick's position. Marm's unit killed seventy-nine enemy soldiers. As the surviving PAVN forces retired down the creek bed, many were cut down by fire from the rest of A Company. After Taft's dog tags were found on the body of an enemy soldier, an outraged Nadal, recalling Moore's promise not to leave anyone behind, went forward to find the lieutenant's body. Under heavy fire and accompanied by his radio operator, Sgt. Jack Gell, and others, Nadal returned not only with Taft but also the other Americans killed in the 3rd Platoon's attack.[22]

As the day progressed, Moore realized he was up against an extremely large enemy force. Accordingly, he shored up his defensive perimeter to fight them off and to be able to call in more artillery, aerial rocket artillery, and airstrikes without suffering friendly fire casualties. At 1430 hours the remaining troops in C Company touched down along with the lead elements of D Company, commanded by Capt. Raymond Lefebvre. With enemy fire increasing, this insertion proved to be the most difficult yet. Still, the helicopter crews, led by Maj. Bruce Crandall (later a lieutenant colonel), never flinched in their support of their brothers on the ground. Crandall, better known by his call sign "Ancient Serpent Six" or by his nicknames "Old Snake" or "Snake Shit," personally flew nearly two dozen sorties on the first day alone, often landing in complete darkness; he only stopped when Moore ordered him to. Even as they landed C Company, the UH-1 crews suffered several casualties. Immediately, Moore sent the lead elements of D Company to take up positions on A Company's left flank. All of C Company moved in to the south and southwest of the growing defensive ring, arriving just in time to confront a frontal assault by 175–200 PAVN troops.[23]

Since Edwards had a clear line of sight over this part of the battlefield, he was able to ask for and adjust artillery support with exacting precision. The enemy suffered heavy losses; these were made worse when, after the first barrage temporarily halted, several of the survivors tried to escape, only to be burned alive by a second barrage. At about 1530 the attack ended, and the NVA and VC main-force units withdrew.

Concurrently, A Company and lead elements of D Company on the perimeter near the creek bed were hit by an enemy attack. On the vital left flank were two A Company machine-gun crews, posted seventy-five yards southwest of the company's main position. The first was manned by Spec. Theron Ladner and his assistant gunner, Pfc. Rodriguez Rivera, and the second by Spec. 4 Russell Adams and his gunner, Spec. 4 Bill Beck. They placed their guns ten yards apart and poured heavy fire into the communist attackers as they tried to drive between C and A Companies. Moore credited these teams with preventing the enemy from rolling up the flank and dividing the two companies. Adams and Rivera were severely wounded and carried back to the battalion's collection point near Moore's command post to await aerial evacuation. Beck and Ladner, now supported by Pfc. Edward Dougherty, continued their suppression fire until the attack finally petered out. Beck later declared: "When Doc Nall was there with me, working on Russell, fear, real fear, hit me. Fear like I had never known before. Fear comes, and once you recognize it and accept it, it passes just as fast as it comes, and you don't really think about it anymore. You just do what you have to do, but you learn the real meaning of fear and life and death. For the next two hours I was alone on that gun, shooting at the enemy."[24]

During these concurrent skirmishes, each American unit involved suffered losses. D Company's commander, Lefebvre, was wounded not long after he arrived, as was Lt. Raul Taboada, one of his platoon leaders. This left SSgt. George Gonzales in command, even though he too was wounded, unknown to Lefebvre. Standard operating procedure called for medical evacuation or medevac helicopters to extract the growing number of injured. But these unarmed choppers were just too vulnerable to enemy fire, so under the circumstances all but two of the wounded were evacuated by assault Hueys, after ferrying troops to the LZ. During one evacuation, injured battalion intelligence officer Capt. Tom Metsker was killed while assisting his wounded fellow officer Lefebvre on board one of the blood-soaked UH-1s.

Figure 3.5. Evacuating the wounded from LZ X-Ray. *Courtesy Joseph L. Galloway*

Throughout the battle, Major Crandall flew in no matter how much fire his Huey took or how dark the landing area was. He and his comrades literally became the lifeline for the 1/7. As the story goes, when he heard that medevac units could not fly in, Crandall turned to his men and declared: "Screw these guys. I'm going back. Who is coming with me?" His wingman, Big Ed Freeman (who stood six feet, six inches tall), stepped forward, and together they and other UH-1 crews flew in and out of LZ X-Ray twenty-two times. Crandall won the Distinguished Flying Cross and eventually, in 2007, the Medal of Honor; Freeman won the Medal of Honor in 2001.[25]

At 1530 the last of the battalion's forces arrived, including Lt. Lawrence Litton, who assumed command of D Company. During this trip, one of the Hueys came in too high and was force to crash-land outside of the perimeter not far from the battalion command post; thanks to quick action by members of the post, those on board were rescued. With D Company's weapons teams on the ground, Moore ordered their mortar units massed with the rest of the battalion in a single location to support A and B Companies. D Company's reconnaissance platoon, commanded by Lt. James Rackstraw, took up position along the north and east sectors of the LZ. At last, the 360-degree perimeter around X-Ray was fully manned. Thankfully for Moore, the PAVN leaders never realized that the northern defenses were only now being filled in. Had they attacked that point in force, it might have resulted in the massacre of US forces that Moore had feared.

Once his men were in place and the wounded airlifted out of the LZ, Moore returned his attention to the isolated 2nd Platoon, B Company. At this point on the first day, Moore directed A and B Companies to try a second time to relieve Herrick's men. As noted, they did so with little success due to an entrenched enemy machine-gun position at a large termite mound. They tried everything to eliminate the threat, including firing a light antitank weapon at the position; it had little effect. This compelled Marm to singlehandedly charge the position, eventually destroying it with hand grenades and rifle fire. He killed twelve enemy soldiers but was wounded in the neck and jaw. Additional heavy fire from the PAVN finally halted the advance after it had moved forward seventy-five yards. With night coming on and the skirmish having deteriorated into a stalemate, Nadal and Herren radioed the battalion commander to recommend they withdraw into the defensive perimeter until the next morning. Moore reluctantly agreed.

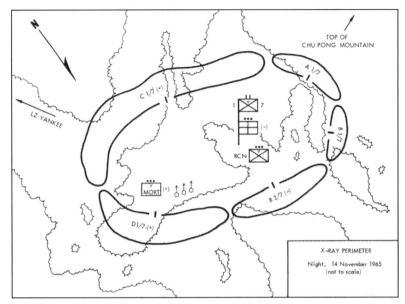

Figure 3.6. LZ X-Ray defensive perimeter, night of 14 November 1965

Early in the battle, Moore had asked Colonel Brown to send him more men. Unlike the Little Bighorn, where Custer's note for help was ignored by Capt. Frederick William Benteen, Brown responded to Moore's request. Late that afternoon lead elements of B Company, 2/7 arrived. Moore immediately ordered its commander, Capt. Myron Diduryk to move his platoons between the 1/7's B and D Companies on the northeast perimeter. The men of 2nd Platoon, B Company, 2/7 reinforced C Company, 1/7, which was stretched thin. By nightfall, B Company, 1/7 had suffered forty-seven casualties, and A Company thirty-four casualties. C Company had been lucky (at least for now), having only four casualties.

Throughout the night, the men remained on full alert. Even with a nearly full moon overhead to light the area, enemy troops probed every inch of the perimeter except near D Company. Moore directed his troopers to restrain their response, specifically ordering the M60 machine-gun crews not to fire to conceal them for what he was sure would be a major attack in the morning. Moore's greatest concern continued to be the welfare of his isolated platoon. Despite three assaults, they survived the night without further casualties.[26]

The Second Day

The reinforced defenders of LZ X-Ray were all able to get through the overnight hours, even though most did not get much sleep. Just before the dawn, around 0620, Moore sent out patrols to search for PAVN positions. What the weary Americans did not know was the communist probes from the night before were about to evolve into the largest attack of the battle. Lieutenant Colonel An had decided to make his major assault against C Company's section of the perimeter.

Around 0700, C Company patrols from its 1st Platoon, commanded by Lt. Neil Kroger, and 2nd Platoon, commanded by Lt. John Geoghegan, were about 150 yards from the perimeter when they ran into a group of NVA soldiers, sparking a firefight. The patrols made their way back to the perimeter. No sooner had they reached their lines when more than two hundred enemy troops hurled themselves into the 1st and 2nd Platoons' defenses on the south side of the perimeter. Despite US artillery support, within moments the PAVN soldiers were within 75 yards of the American lines. Their fire ripped through C Company's positions and into the command post. The men of 1st and 2nd Platoons suffered heavy losses, including both Kroger and Geoghegan; Lieutenant Geoghegan died trying to rescue Pfc. Willie Godboldt, who died of his own wounds soon after. Only the efforts of two M60 crews, one manned by Spec. James Comer and Spec. 4 Clinton Poley and the other by Spec. 4s Nathaniel Byrd and George Foxe, kept the communist assault from overrunning the two platoons. No sooner had this action died down than another enemy attack hit C Company's 3rd Platoon. Captain Edwards was wounded, so Lt. John Arrington assumed command of the company; Arrington was also wounded in the ensuing chaos.[27]

As it turned out, these attacks were just a prelude. Every time a PAVN assault was beaten back, another unit joined the fight, seemingly from a slightly different place. Around 0745, C Company's lines were ready to break, and Moore asked Lt. Charles W. Hastings, his USAF forward-air-control liaison, what he could see from his position while also telling him to call in an airstrike. At this point Hastings made critical decision. Using his knowledge of USAF guidelines for the situation and with Moore's approval, he radioed the code phrase "Broken Arrow," announcing to every US listening site that an American combat unit was in danger of being overrun. This overrode all other communications and directed every available combat aircraft in the region to hasten to the imperiled unit's support. In the meantime C Company's survivors fell back, the enemy troops wading through the fallen Americans along the broken lines, killing the wounded and stripping them of weapons and ammunition.[28]

What seemed like an eternity was only ten minutes before Moore ordered the men in his crumbling defenses to throw colored-smoke grenades over the lines to identify their perimeter. The CAS then came in at treetop level, dropping their loads only yards from the Americans. It proved very effective. Aircraft from A-1s to F-100 fighters dropped iron bombs and napalm, engulfing an enemy who only a moment before was near victory. But this successful airstrike did not come without a price. In a demonstration of why CAS is so difficult, Moore's command post experienced a friendly fire catastrophe. With the combat lines on the ground tangled and smoke obscuring the target, two F-100s swooped in for a bomb run. The first one inadvertently dropped napalm on both American and NVA troops. In horror Hastings frantically radioed for the second jet to change course, but it was too late. Several Americans were killed or wounded in this incident.

Joseph Galloway was the only reporter to make it to LZ X-Ray, hopping a ride with one of Crandall's helicopters in anticipation of scooping all his colleagues. What he found was more than he bargained for. Since Galloway was at the command post when the napalm hit, he carried one of the badly

Figure 3.7. Young Joseph L. Galloway just before the Battle of Ia Drang Valley

Figure 3.8. F-100 dropping napalm

burned Americans to an aid station. As he tried to pick him up, the man's charred skin peeled off. The injured soldier was James "Jimmy" Nakayama of Rigby, Idaho, a second lieutenant from the Idaho National Guard. Despite Galloway's efforts, Nakayama died two days later. The entire battle was seared in the journalist's mind forever, recalling later, "at LZ X-Ray 79 men died and 121 were wounded, many of them terribly."[29]

As if in an old Hollywood western, at 0910 the first elements of A Company, 2/7, led by Capt. Joel Sugdinis, arrived to reinforce what was left of Company C's lines. An hour later, with order restored, the firefight subsided, and the NVA survivors began to withdraw. C Company had been savaged by the communists, but they had given as good as they got. The resulting body count of the assaults totaled forty-three NVA killed and twenty wounded. Lt. Richard Rescorla of B Company later recalled of his policing the battlefield: "There were American and PAVN bodies everywhere. My area was where Lieutenant Geoghegan's platoon had been. There were several dead PAVN around his platoon CP [command post]. One dead trooper was locked in contact with a dead PAVN, hands around the enemy's throat. There were two troopers—one black, one Hispanic—linked tight together. It looked like they had died trying to help each other."[30]

In his own after-action report, Moore noted: "PAVN body fragments, and PAVN weapons and equipment were littered in profusion around the edge and forward of the perimeter. Numerous body fragments were seen. There was massive evidence e.g. bloody trails, bandages, etc. of many other PAVN being dragged away from the area. Some of the enemy dead were found stacked behind anthills. Artillery and TAC Air was placed on all wooded areas nearby into which trails disappeared. Numerous enemy weapons were collected along with other armament. Two prisoners were taken and evacuated. Friendly dead and wounded were also collected."[31]

Even with this lull, US commanders were still concerned for the security of LZ X-Ray. As a result, they dispatched other units of the 1st Cavalry Division to relieve Moore, specifically the companies of 2/5, commanded by Lt. Col. Robert Tully. They flew into LZ Victor, located roughly two and one-quarter miles east-southeast of LZ X-Ray, arriving there around 0800. From Victor they quickly organized their formations and made the four-hour march to LZ X-Ray, during which they received only minor small-arms fire. As the 2/5 was on the way, at about 1000 hours, 800 yards east of LZ X-Ray men of the 2/7's A Company reported taking light fire from concealed posi-

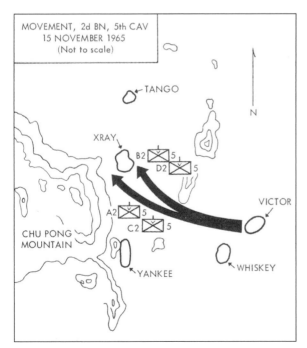

Figure 3.9. Relief of LZ X-Ray, 15 November 1965

tions, though no assaults followed. To the delight of everyone at LZ X-Ray, at 1205 Tully's forces arrived to bolster the defense line and eventually replace Moore's men, who were to be airlifted out.

With his position strengthened and the enemy bloodied, Moore devised a plan to rescue B Company's still-isolated 2nd Platoon. Elements of several units of the 7th and 5th Cavalry, preceded by significant support fire, gradually advanced toward the knoll without encountering any enemy resistance. Finally, the survivors of 2nd Platoon were saved. Of the original twenty-nine men, nine were killed and thirteen wounded. Around 1530, as the Americans fell back to the LZ perimeter, they received sniper fire, but no one was hit. With their expanded force, Moore and Tully dug in for the night even as their wounded and dead were being airlifted out.[32]

If the Americans thought the fight was over, they were mistaken. From sunset until about 0400 the next morning, there were more enemy probes—then all hell broke loose. Late the previous afternoon, men in Captain Diduryk's Company B had placed grenade booby traps and trip flares all along their defensive lines. At 0422 explosions occurred all along the front, followed by a maniacal assault by about three hundred NVA troops. The intensity of US fire from behind their new barriers as well as the precise artillery fire called in by forward observer Lt. William Lund proved decisive. Lund called on four separate batteries, organizing their fire into different enemy concentrations all along the Americans' front. With the battlefield illuminated by a C-123 flare ship, the enemy advance was cut to pieces in about thirty minutes. As a second attack against B Company subsided around 0500, a third assault slammed into Diduryk's forces. No sooner had these attackers been beaten back than another unit struck around 0630. Once again Lund ordered artillery fire that decimated the PAVN forces. Dozens of enemy troops died in these assaults, but only six Americans were wounded.[33]

Day Three

With the attacks repulsed during the early morning hours of 16 November, plans now called for the 1/7 to be evacuated as soon as possible. At around 1030 Colonel Brown ordered Moore out. Using the remaining UH-1s, his men relocated to LZ Falcon and then to Camp Holloway at Pleiku for two days of rest. Before they left, the men made one final sweep of the area to their front to make sure none of their comrades, dead or alive, was left behind. Moore reported, "By 1830 hours all elements had left LZ Falcon by air and closed into Camp Holloway."[34]

The lieutenant colonel was the last man in his unit to depart in a Huey piloted by Major Crandall and Jon Mills. When the 1/7 finally reached Camp Holloway, Moore made an immediate check of each company to be sure everyone had returned, dead or alive. He also made sure the wounded received proper care and everyone else got whatever they needed. Moore then asked the UH-1 pilots, "Where can we get a drink around here?" Crandall and Mills pointed to the nearby officers' club. Once inside, all three ordered a gin and tonic only to have the bartender refuse them service because Moore was too "dirty." The lieutenant colonel placed his M16 on the bar and declared through clenched teeth, "You've got exactly 30 seconds to get some drinks on this bar or I'm going to clean house." Crandall and Mills were standing next to him with their .38-cal. pistols drawn. The drinks arrived in a shaking hand and were quickly downed. Within a couple of minutes, most of those in the club realized who these guys were, after which "they drank for free." Galloway later observed: "To this point, the Ia Drang Campaign had been a magnificent feat for the cavalry. But before the fighting ended another 155 Americans would die in the Ia Drang Valley."[35]

From the American point of view, the battle was over. The enemy had suffered hundreds of casualties and appeared no longer capable of offensive action. Moore's forces had suffered 79 killed and 121 injured, with LZ X-Ray reinforced to levels that allowed them to depart. Given the situation, there was no reason for the US forces to stay in the field, apparently having successfully completed their mission. Still, Colonel Brown was concerned about reports that additional NVA units were moving into the area from across the Cambodian border. Once the battered 1/7 had returned to the LZ, he had planned to evacuate the other units. But General Westmoreland ordered the 2/7 and 2/5 to stay at X-Ray to avoid the appearance of a retreat.[36]

Recipe for Disaster

On 17 November, after a suitable face-saving delay, the other two battalions departed LZ X-Ray to begin a tactical relocation to new LZs. Tully and the 2/5 moved toward LZ Columbus, just over 2.5 miles to the northeast. The 2/7, led by Lt. Col. Robert McDade, marched toward LZ Albany, about the same distance to the north-northeast. Part of the reason for the withdrawal was planners had prepared a massive airstrike near X-Ray using eighteen B-52s. Stationed at Andersen Air Base in Guam, the bombers had a long way to fly, and once begun they were locked into the mission. These aircraft, also known as "aluminum overcast," were to drop their loads of 500- and 750-pound iron bombs on Chu Pong Massif. Senior officers concerned for the safety of the units still at LZ X-Ray ordered them to withdraw outside a two-mile safety zone by midmorning. Tully's forces departed at 0900, followed fifteen minutes later by McDade's men.[37]

At first things went peacefully enough. Then McDade's point squad of the reconnaissance platoon, led by SSgt. Donald J. Slovak, identified sandaled footprints, bamboo arrows on the ground pointing north, and remnants of rice grains. After the two main units, still within sight of each other, reached roughly the halfway point in their march, the 2/7 headed northwest, while the 2/5 proceeded toward LZ Columbus. Not long afterward, troopers of A Company, 2/7 came upon a group of thatched-grass huts, which they were told to burn. At 1138 hours Tully's battalion arrived at LZ Columbus. What none of the Americans fully realized at this point was the NVA still had a very large force nearby, consisting of the 8th Battalion, 66th Regiment; the 1st Battalion, 33rd Regiment; and elements of the 3rd Battalion, 33rd Regiment. Even though the 33rd Regiment was under-strength due to the casualties it had taken during the earlier attack on the US Special Forces Plei Me camp, the 8th, under Gen. Chu Huy Man, was a fresh and fully manned unit.[38]

As Tully arrived near LZ Columbus, he radioed McDade and said he would have his artillery specialist send the correct coordinates to cover him on the way into LZ Albany. The recently assigned lieutenant colonel mulled over the offer and then turned it down. As McDade's battalion moved forward, A Company marched in a wedge formation, which presented the enemy with a formidable target. But just behind this force, especially farther to the rear, the men straggled along in single file. Near the end of their journey, Captain Sugdinis of A Company realized his normal air cover was missing and he could not immediately locate his commander. He did hear the earthshaking distant explosions of the B-52 bomb runs against the Chu Pong Massif. The BUFs dropped 344 tons of general-purpose bombs on the southeast slope, with considerable effect on enemy forces there. But as they continued marching, all of a sudden Lt. D. P. "Pat" Payne, the leader of the reconnaissance platoon, swung around a gathering of termite hills and saw an enemy soldier resting on the ground, swiftly pinning the man to the ground and taking him prisoner. At nearly the same moment, some dozen yards away, his platoon sergeant captured a second enemy soldier.[39]

The soldiers of the 8th Battalion had been taking a midday break and were strewn all over the area, resting. Their scouts soon reported to the officers that the Americans were on their way. The Vietnamese now prepared for an attack on the US column. When he received word of the dual captures, McDade ordered a halt to the march so he could move up to personally question the prisoners. Payne's platoon was roughly hundred yards from the southwestern edge of a clearing designated LZ Albany. At noon McDade notified division headquarters in Pleiku of his circumstances.[40]

Over the next twenty minutes, McDade attempted to reorganize his force. He called his company commanders, accompanied by their radio operators, forward for a conference. A Company then moved ahead to LZ Albany along with McDade and his command group. D Company, next in the column, was to follow A Company but held their place temporarily so C Company could catch up with them. Next in line were the members of the Battalion Headquarters Company, followed by A Company of the 1/5, which was at the rear of the column. The Americans were stationary, unprepared, in open terrain, and strung out in a 550-yard line. It was as if they were asking to be attacked.[41]

McDade's men put out flank security. But the men were worn out from the four-hour march after having only very little sleep over the previous sixty hours. To make matters worse, the surrounding elephant grass was so high no one could see very far. And with all the radio operators forward with McDade, no one farther back could call for air or artillery support if needed. About an hour after the Americans had taken the NVA prisoners, McDade and the lead unit made it to LZ Albany. The lieutenant colonel and his group crossed the main clearing into a clump of trees, leaving the remainder of the battalion spread out to the east. At this point the battalion sergeant major, James Scott, and Sgt. Charles Bass once again questioned the prisoners. As they did, Bass heard other Vietnamese voices, which the interpreter confirmed were from enemy soldiers. The members of A Company had been in the LZ about five minutes when all hell broke loose.[42]

The NVA Strikes

As it turned out, Lieutenant Payne's reconnaissance platoon had stumbled into the headquarters of the 3rd Battalion, 33rd Regiment, with the 550-man strong 8th Battalion, 66th Regiment resting just northeast of the US unit. The twenty minutes McDade had taken to get his bearings proved disastrous. It gave the enemy commander time to organize an ambush that began around 1315, with combat lasting nearly sixteen hours. The actual assault was preceded by a brief series of mortar shells that landed with devastating effectiveness. The first unit to feel the sting of battle was 2/5. The NVA's L-shaped ambush struck the battalion's point and rapidly worked its way down the right, or east, side of the column. It was a slaughter.[43]

The CHECO report described the Vietnamese tactics: "Snipers in trees kept the friendlies pinned down as the enemy drove a wedge between the two perimeter positions to keep them from re-enforcing each other." At the high point of the combat, the fighting evolved into "hand-to-hand fighting." Worse, the enemy enjoyed numerical and fire superiority, which caused "heavy casualties, especially on the most forward of the two perimeters."[44]

As the enemy worked its way down the length of the column, some small units broke off to directly attack the surprised and outnumbered Americans. Unlike most engagements during the war, this one experienced intense and brutal close-in, hand-to-hand combat. As the fight began, McDade's forward group was in the clump of trees, where they took cover from rifle and mortar fire near termite hills. At first the recon platoon and A Company's 1st Platoon provided defense at the position. Within thirty minutes, they had been cut off from the remainder of the column and surrounded by a swarm of communists. Their only hope was to call in air support. As they waited for the warplanes, the Americans fended off several assaults. The enemy was winning the battle. Within minutes, the Vietnamese were searching the high grass for wounded Americans, killing and stripping them of weapons, ammunition, and other valuable items.[45]

Throughout, pockets of US soldiers held on by their fingernails. The 2/7 was forced into a small perimeter at LZ Albany. These survivors were made up of A Company, the recon platoon, survivors from C and D Companies, and the command group. In addition, there was a smaller perimeter at the rear of the column, about 500–700 yards to the south. These men consisted of Capt. George Forrest's A Company, 1/5. When the fight began, Forrest ran the gauntlet of enemy fire all the way from McDade's conference site back to his company. C Company suffered 45 killed and 52 wounded, the largest casualty numbers of the battle at LZ Albany.

It must have seemed like an eternity, but within minutes USAF A-1 Sky-raiders arrived. The warplanes had been called in by Capt. Joe Pirie, the army forward ground observer who, in spite of being in constant danger, was able to direct the strikes with exacting precision. The CHECO report said: "The [A-1] fighters worked the VC [NVA] back steadily with 20 mm fire until they had sufficient room to drop napalm and GP [general-purpose bombs]. Unfortunately, with the two forces intertwined, the attacks no doubt caused at least some US casualties."[46]

In the end the napalm canisters fell "so close that a few Americans troops got singed, but the consensus was that the very close-in fighter strikes had saved many lives, even though a calculated risk of injury to friendly person-nel was taken."[47]

5th Cavalry to the Rescue

As soon as word arrived of the ambush at division headquarters, troops from the 5th Cavalry were ordered from LZ Columbus to reinforce the belea-guered troops at LZ Albany. Troops of B Company, 1/5, under Capt. Buse Tully departed at 1455 hours and headed for the rear of the 2/7's defensive position. After a two-mile march, they contacted remnants of A Company under Captain Forrest. At that point the troops created a secure one-helicopter landing zone and evacuated the wounded. With this accom-plished, Tully's forces pushed toward the remainder of their ambushed comrades. Enemy units blocked their advance, however, with heavy fire from a wood line. Tully's men held off PAVN attacks, and at 1825 head-quarters ordered them to fashion a two-company perimeter for the night. Plans called for the 1/5 to continue the advance the next morning.[48]

That same afternoon, division leadership decided to add weight to the relief effort and at around 1600 deployed Captain Diduryk's B Company, 2/7, veterans of the fight at LZ X-Ray. At 1845 the first helicopters landed in a clearing at LZ Albany. Lieutenant Rescorla, the only remaining platoon leader in B Company, led his men to bolster the Albany perimeter. The remaining wounded were airlifted out around 2230 that evening, the heli-copters subjected to intense enemy ground fire as they landed and took off.[49]

After a restless evening, Friday, 18 November, dawned on the previous day's battlefield, and the Americans began recovering their dead and wounded. With the enemy having pulled back, the task was less tense but no less horrific. Nevertheless, the recovery took them nearly the entire day. Bodies from both sides covered the field. Rescorla described the scene as "a long, bloody traffic accident in the jungle."[50] At one point the lieutenant found a dying NVA soldier clinging to an old French bugle. Although the man received care, he did not survive, and Rescorla took possession of the relic. On 19 November the Americans left LZ Albany for LZ Crooks, about six miles away. This part of the Battle of Ia Drang Valley had resulted in 155 Americans being killed and 124 wounded. In one final supreme irony, on 24 November a wounded US survivor, Toby Braveboy, flagged down an H-13 scout helicopter, which rescued him. He was the last American to leave Ia Drang Valley.[51]

The Conclusion of Operation Silver Bayonet

As US forces withdrew, Silver Bayonet continued. Late on 18 November, ARVN paratroopers of the 3rd Airborne Battalion were airlifted into LZ Gulf, three miles from the Cambodian border. They were to sweep west to the border and then south across the Ia Drang Valley and onto the Chu Pong foothills just east of Cambodia. With the Americans still holding LZs Crook and Columbus in a semicircle defensive ring, the ARVN units began their movement on the twentieth. Fighting was sporadic, and only twelve air-support sorties were requested. As the CHECO report noted, "From this point until the termination of the operation, the enemy seemed less inclined to mass, or to meet friendly operational units in strength." It went on to state: "The intensity and frequency of the actions declined and the scale of the battle diminished. At 1710 hours, 28 November, Operation Silver Bayonet was officially terminated."[52]

Thus concluded the "longest continuously fought operation since the struggle in Vietnam began." It had been "bitterly fought and closely engaged." From the US standpoint, "casualties in Silver Bayonet were by far the heaviest suffered in a like period during the war." This included 240 killed and 247 wounded. Enemy losses, based on the total body count, came to 1,295 killed. American leaders believed the "PAVN/VC forces defended Chu Pong and the Ia Drang valley with a dedication bordering on the fanatic, in the face of massive and at times overwhelming firepower."

Subsequent prisoner interrogations revealed that prior to the battle PAVN troops believed the Americans were poor fighters who would turn tail and run—this they learned was not true. The second thing the interrogations discovered was enemy soldiers had been "demoralized by the constant bombing more than any other single factor."[53]

Indeed, the role of airpower in preserving the US defensive positions throughout the battles in the valley cannot be overstated. To quote the concluding section of the CHECO report, "Tactical fighter strikes during the battles on the 14th through the 17th of November involving the 1st and 2nd Battalions of the 7th Regiment, contributed directly in keeping the cost [in lives] from mounting." Furthermore, "Without airpower in its entirety; close air support and interdiction, the B-52 strategic bombers-turned-tactical, the FACs [forward air controllers], and the overall coordination and response within the Tactical Air Control System, the cost would have been much higher."[54]

Honor, Recognition, and Vivid Memories

While in most cases the brave deeds of the Americans involved in the battle took a long time to be recognized, several of the heroes of Ia Drang did receive medals. The most immediate decoration was presented to 2nd Lieutenant Marm, who received the Medal of Honor on 15 February 1967 for his actions during the three-day action at LZ X-Ray. Big Ed Freeman and Snake Crandall did not get their Medals of Honor until 16 July 2001 and 26 February 2007, respectively. Sergeant Savage's work with the precise placement of artillery near his isolated platoon won him the Distinguished Service Cross. Lieutenant Colonel Moore also won the Distinguished Service Cross for his cool handling of a crisis and his "leadership by example." And Joe Galloway became the only civilian awarded the Bronze Star during the Vietnam War for his help with the wounded while under fire.[55]

One person who deserved a medal but never received one was Julia Compton Moore, the lieutenant colonel's wife. Since casualty notifications had only been mostly about individual deaths, US Army hierarchy in late 1965 had failed to establish a casualty-notification system. The notification telegrams at this time were handed over to taxi-cab drivers for delivery to the next of kin. The trauma to both the taxi driver and the next of kin when dozens of telegrams began arriving at Fort Benning was awful. Mrs. Moore had the cab company give her the telegrams, and she, along with other

military wives, delivered the terrible news to the families living in the housing complex on post. Concurrently, she tried to comfort the grieving wives
and children. When the caskets came home, she attended the funerals of
all the men killed under her husband's command who were buried at Fort
Benning. The wife of the battalion's executive officer, Mrs. Frank Henry, and
Mrs. James Scott, wife of the battalion command sergeant major, delivered
the telegrams to the families of those killed from the 2/7. Later, Julia Moore
contacted army officials about the notifications procedures. Realizing
their oversight, officials soon established a process whereby two-person
teams, consisting of an officer and a chaplain, delivered the devastating
telegrams.[56]

As for Hal Moore, he and Galloway have undoubtedly become the most
famous survivors of the battle, mostly due to the book they wrote and
the subsequent movie adaptation. During the intervening years, General
Moore traveled widely to remind those of later generations about the sacrifices his troopers made. Prior to the opening of Gibson's movie, he returned
to West Point with his wife and the actors from *We Were Soldiers*. More than
2,000 cadets came to hear the general speak and to see the film. Afterward,
one cadet asked what his generation should know about the battle. Moore
replied: "The most important thing that Americans should know about this
battle is, 'Hate war. Love the American warrior.' Got that?"[57]

This was not the only trip he made. In 1993, in an amazing turn of
events, he and other veterans from both sides of the conflict arranged for
the Americans to return to Vietnam and visit the site of the bloodshed. As
Moore put it:

> My unending thirst for peace and unity drove me to return to the
> "Valley of Death" in 1993. Some of my men accompanied me to meet
> with the man, along with a few of his soldiers, who had once endeav-
> ored to kill us all. Lieutenant General Nguyen Huu An and I came fact-
> to-face. Instead of charging one another with bayonets, we mutually
> offered open arms. I invited all to form a circle with arms extended
> around each other's shoulders and bowed our heads. With prayer and
> tears, we shared our painful memories. Although we did not under-
> stand each other's language, we quickly saw that the soul requires no
> interpreter.[58]

In the Aftermath

While the battle at LZ X-Ray was important and proved the courage and bravery of the men of the US Army, the ambush at LZ Albany should have made US leaders aware of the difficulty of winning anything approaching a victory in Vietnam. Ironically, at least in one case, we now know that a senior official had figured it out. Unfortunately, for the rest of the 58,000 Americans who would die over the next eight years, the lessons of Ia Drang were ignored.

According to Galloway, Richard Merron, an Associated Press photographer, and Vo Nguyen, a Vietnamese television-network cameraman, hitched "a ride on a helicopter going into [LZ] Albany on the morning of November 18." Having seen the carnage firsthand, the stunned Merron soon took "another chopper going back to Camp Holloway, and the word spread quickly that a battalion of Americans had been massacred in the valley."[59]

When word of the slaughter at LZ Albany filtered back to Washington, President Johnson directed Secretary of Defense McNamara, then in Europe, to return home by Saigon in order to discover the actual details of what had happened in the Ia Drang Valley. From the outset, military leaders in Vietnam worked to put a positive spin on the events at Albany. Late on 18 November Brig. Gen. Richard T. Knowles, deputy commander, 1st Air Cavalry, convened a news conference in a tent at Camp Holloway. He explained to the dozens of swarming reporters there had been no ambush at LZ Albany. He described the action as "a meeting engagement" and said the casualties were "light to moderate." He also told the gathered throng he could speak with authority since he "had just returned from Albany." Galloway, having made his way from LZ X-Ray to Holloway, stood up and declared, "That's bullshit, sir, and you know it!" After a pregnant pause, the general ended the meeting amid "a chorus of angry shouting."[60]

When McNamara reached Saigon, he met with Ambassador Lodge and received more or less the same rosy appraisal army leaders were providing. After this meeting he flew to An Khe, the 1st Cavalry Division's base camp. There, he was briefed by the division commander, Maj. Gen. Harry W. O. Kinnard, and by Lieutenant Colonel Moore himself. Unlike Lodge and Westmoreland, Kinnard was less upbeat, and Moore was as straightforward and blunt as possible. On 30 November, as he flew back home, McNamara penned a top-secret memorandum to the president that summed up the situation in Vietnam.

In brief, McNamara concluded the United States was at a crossroads that appeared to provide only two options. First, the administration could devise a diplomatic excuse to immediately leave Vietnam, or second, they provide Westmoreland the 200,000 troops he was asking for. McNamara added that all the second option would achieve was a military stalemate at a much higher level of violence, which he reasoned would mean a full-scale war in which thousands of Americans would die.[61]

The secretary declared in his situational overview, "Pacification is thoroughly stalled, with no guarantee that security anywhere is permanent and no indications that able and willing leadership will emerge in the absence of that permanent security." He continued: "The dramatic recent changes in the situation are on the military side. They are the increased infiltration from the North and the increased willingness of the Communist forces to stand and fight, even in large-scale engagements," pointing out that "the Ia Drang River [ ] Campaign of early November is an example." He then delivered a sobering assessment of what American forces would be up against: "The Communists appear to have decided to increase their forces in South Vietnam both by heavy recruitment in the South (especially in the Delta) and by infiltration of regular North Vietnamese forces from the North. Nine regular North Vietnamese regiments (27 infantry battalions) have been infiltrated in the past year, joining the estimated 83 VC battalions in the South."[62]

McNamara then went on to describe how this would probably change during the coming year:

> The rate of infiltration has increased from three battalion equivalents a month in late 1964 to a high of 9 or 12 during one month this past fall. General Westmoreland estimates that through 1966 North Vietnam will have the capability to expand its armed forces in order to infiltrate three regiments (nine battalion equivalents, or 4,500 men) a month, and that the VC in South Vietnam can train seven new battalion equivalents a month—together adding 16 battalion equivalents a month to the enemy forces. Communist casualties and desertions can be expected to go up if my recommendations for increased US, South Vietnamese and third country forces are accepted. Nevertheless, the enemy can be expected to enlarge his present strength of 110 battalion equivalents to

more than 150 battalion equivalents by the end of calendar 1966, when hopefully his losses can be made to equal his input.[63]

The secretary continued: "To meet this possible—and in my view likely—Communist build-up, the presently contemplated Phase I forces will not be enough. Phase I forces, almost all in place by the end of this year, involve 130 South Vietnamese, 9 Korean, 1 Australian and 34 US combat battalions (approximately 220,000 Americans). Bearing in mind the nature of the war, the expected weighted combat force ratio of less than 2-to-1 will not be good enough." He concluded that the "contemplated Phase II addition of 28 more US battalions (112,000 men) [may not] be enough. . . . Indeed, it is estimated that, with the contemplated Phase II addition of 28 US battalions, we would be able only to hold our present geographical positions."[64]

As for what America's military options might be, McNamara opined: "We have but two options, it seems to me. One is to go now for a compromise solution (something substantially less than the 'favorable outcome' I described in my memorandum of November 3) and hold further deployments to a minimum." Option two was "to stick with our stated objectives and with the war, and provide what it takes in men and materiel. . . . (Recommend up to 74 battalions by end-66: total to approx. 400,000 by end-66. And it should be understood that further deployments (perhaps exceeding 200,000) may be needed in 1967)."[65]

The most sobering part of the memo is the final paragraph, titled "Evaluation." In it McNamara warned: "We should be aware that deployments of the kind I have recommended will not guarantee success. US killed-in-action can be expected to reach 1,000 a month, and the odds are even that we will be faced in early 1967 with a 'no-decision' at an even higher level."[66]

In hindsight this memo seems so logical and prophetic. On 15 December 1965 Johnson convened a meeting of his "council of 'wise old men,'" which included such foreign-policy luminaries as Clark Clifford, Abe Fortas, Averell Harriman, George Ball, and Dean Acheson. Also at this meeting was Secretary McNamara. According to Galloway: "As the president walked into the room, he was holding McNamara's November 30 memo in his hand. Shaking it at the defense secretary, he said, 'You mean to tell me no matter what I do I can't win in Vietnam?' McNamara nodded yes." Amazingly, the assembled group spent two days discussing the alternatives but never really seriously considered departing Vietnam. In the end they "voted unanimously in favor of further escalation of the war."[67]

Apparently, Westmoreland was always confident the war would go on. His examination of the numbers from the battle led him to see only the kill ratio of twelve communists killed for each American. As British general Alexander Haig (better known as the "Butcher") had in World War I, Westmoreland decided he would follow a strategy of attrition and bleed the enemy white. Galloway later noted: "One of Westmoreland's brighter young aides later would write, 'a strategy of attrition is proof that you have no strategy at all.'" But there was one fact that neither Westmoreland or anyone else considered: "In no year of that long war did the North Vietnamese death toll even come close to equaling the natural birth rate increase of the population. In other words, every year reaching out far into the future there were more babies born in the north than NVA we were killing in the south, so each year a new crop of draftees arrived as replacements for the dead."[68]

As for Ho Chi Minh's appraisal of the battle, he was now nearly certain he could win the war. His worker/peasant forces had stood toe to toe with the Americans, had withstood their maelstrom of firepower, and had held their own. He believed if they could demonstrate the same patience and perseverance they had maintained against the French, they could wear down the Americans' will to fight as well. General Giap also analyzed the Battle of Ia Drang Valley correctly, noting that the use of helicopters was the "biggest threat and biggest change in warfare that the Americans brought to the battlefield." Years later he would muse: "We thought that the Americans must have a strategy. We did. We had a strategy of people's war. You had tactics, and it takes very decisive tactics to win a strategic victory. . . . If we could defeat your tactics—your helicopters—then we could defeat your strategy. Our goal was to win the war."[69]

Another lesson the North Vietnamese general learned was that American military leaders had to ask permission to pursue Northern forces into their sanctuaries inside Cambodia and were told under no circumstances to cross international borders. As Galloway shrewdly noted, in this regard "the United States ceded the strategic initiative for much of the rest of the war to General Giap. From that point forward, Giap would decide where and when the battles would be fought, and when they would end."[70]

Analysis and Conclusion

In the movie *We Were Soldiers*, following the engagement at LZ X-Ray, Colonel An exclaims: "Such a tragedy. They will think this was their victory. So this will become an American war. And, in the end the outcome will be the same . . . except for the numbers who will die before we get there." While it is doubtful An, no matter how skilled a commander he was, had the foresight to predict so accurately what the future would hold, the quote draws the correct conclusion. The US buildup in 1965 and the so-called "victory" at Ia Drang Valley led to Westmoreland's commitment to similar search-and-destroy actions during the next three years of the war.

On a broader scale the entire operation created a blueprint for the tactics both sides would use in the future. Westmoreland, convinced that Silver Bayonet had been a great victory, decided that the employment of air mobility, artillery fire, and CAS could and would obtain all future battlefield objectives. As for the PAVN, they concluded that they could neutralize the US advantage in firepower by rapid and close-range engagements to prevent the Americans and their allies from using artillery and CAS. In his after-action directives from the battle at LZ X-Ray, used in his orders for LZ Albany, General An instructed his troops to "move inside the [Americans'] column, grab them by the belt, and thus avoid casualties from the artillery and air."[71]

Those at MACV headquarters supported their claims of victory with numbers they asserted proved their point. In what was one of the few set-piece battles of the war until 1972, US leaders began to popularize the concept of body counts to measure success. In this case they reported a 12-to-1 kill ratio to the press. In truth this was much inflated, even for the official casualty numbers, since the US losses for LZ X-Ray totaled 79 killed and 121 wounded and 155 killed and 124 wounded at LZ Albany. Estimates for NVA casualties were around 800 killed at X-Ray and 500 killed at Albany. So often enemy numbers were estimated and determined by some technocratic formula that seemed logical but never took into account the numerous variables present in combat. Whatever the actual numbers, what is clear is the fighting in the Ia Drang Valley was the opening salvo in a protracted conflict that still had eight years to unfold.[72]

In retrospect, even though both sides saw Ia Drang Valley as a formula for victory, the reality was for Giap and his forces that the fighting, while costly in numbers of troops lost, bolstered his belief in ultimate victory. While there can be no doubt the bravery of US service personnel was demonstrated at Ia Drang Valley, as was the viability of CAS, tactical airpower, and air mobility, "the cost of such 'victories' was clearly unsustainable, even then."[73]

Ultimately, the Battle of Ia Drang Valley provided several military lessons and historic imperatives. As Secretary McNamara realized, victory against such a determined enemy could only be attained by a large and protracted commitment similar to the one America made during World War II; it was one he believed was not worthwhile. Sadly, few others in the Johnson administration had the courage to draw the same appropriate conclusions. In the battle itself, both the US and PAVN soldiers fought well. The tactics and firepower of the Americans proved to be a key to preventing a defeat. A sustained airpower presence proved essential in containing the communist assaults and in preserving the unit integrity of US ground forces. While artillery was significant, as many have declared, airpower was the decisive and critical factor for any success the United States experienced in this battle. One classified report (now declassified) by a cryptologic unit involved in the battle observed: "Tactically, the battle had illustrated the limitations of the helicopter. Despite its mobility, landing zones were predictable, and the PAVN units managed at least twice to ambush units as they were landing. Often at a tactical disadvantage, American units had to rely on firepower in the form of massive air strikes to bail them out."[74]

While Westmoreland concluded he had won a victory using a new airmobility tactic, his concept of victory was flawed since it had no clear formula for success or a strategic goal with which to undergird it. Finally, while the heroic fight at LZ X-Ray has become justifiably well known due to the writings of Moore and Galloway and an epic movie, this aspect of the battle was not the one that should have been the lesson learned by US military leaders in late 1965. Instead, the true lessons were taught at LZ Albany. They were lessons McNamara wrote down in his 30 November memo to Johnson. But they were lessons that were not learned.

Perhaps the most poignant thoughts about the many western wars in Vietnam were penned by General Giap in the late 1940s: "The enemy will pass slowly from the offensive to the defensive. The blitzkrieg will transform itself into a war of long duration. Thus, the enemy will be caught in a dilemma: He has to drag out the war in order to win it and does not possess, on the other hand, the psychological and political means to fight a long-drawn-out war."[75]

The struggle in the Ia Drang Valley in 1965 should have demonstrated these realities. Then again, American leaders would have had only to read Giap's writings or even those of the defeated French commanders. They did neither. US leaders could have listened to McNamara's words or to the logic of Lieutenant Colonel Moore's briefings. Again, they did not. For all of these reasons, the Battle of Ia Drang Valley can only be viewed as a missed opportunity to avert a larger disaster.

4

Bloodshed and Bitterness

The Battle for Khe Sanh—Diversion or a Second Dien Bien Phu?

One of the most important battles of the Vietnam War took place just prior to and during the general communist uprising of 1968. It focused on a US outpost in South Vietnam near the border with Laos known to history as Khe Sanh. According to Peter Brush, one of the preeminent experts on the battle, late in 1967, when Generals Westmoreland and Giap brought their forces into contact, their "tactical and strategic goals, combined with their perception of one another's intentions, led them into combat at this particular time and place."[1]

Westmoreland believed Giap was trying to repeat his victory over the French at Dien Bien Phu, while Giap claimed Khe Sanh was a diversion to draw US forces away from the populated areas of South Vietnam. Ironically, "both sides claimed victory at Khe Sanh, fueling a debate that continues today—was Khe Sanh a territorial imperative or bait and switch?"[2]

The Tet Offensive

No one can understand the battle for Khe Sanh without examining the concurrent events comprising the Tet Offensive. In what proved to be the eventual turning point of the American war in Vietnam, the PAVN joined forces with the VC in the South to formulate surprise attacks on the major cities and towns in the Republic of Vietnam on 31 January 1968, during the customary ceasefire that accompanied the Vietnamese New Year.

The offensive was conceived as a joint military, political, and diplomatic campaign called "Tet Mau Thanh or General Offensive, General Uprising" to regain the initiative in the war and start a popular uprising to topple the South Vietnamese government. It featured the suspension of the guerrilla war in the countryside in favor of a sustained assault on the urban centers of the South, including its capital, Saigon. This daring change of strategy sent a torrent of improved weapons and PAVN troops down infiltration routes into the South to bolster the VC.

In October and November 1967, PAVN regular forces attacked the Con Thien marine base near the DMZ, specifically the towns of Loc Ninh and Song Be near Saigon, and Dak To in the Central Highlands. US troops repelled these attacks, but the enemy succeeded in luring American and South Vietnamese forces away from Southern cities. According to Giap, this was all part of a broader strategy to distract and divert US forces while his own assault forces moved into their assault positions.

At the same time, President Johnson, in an effort to strengthen sagging public support for the war, asked his ever-confident commander in the field, General Westmoreland, to make a series of public appearances reassuring the public of the inevitability of a US victory. Westmoreland told Congress, "We have reached an important point where the end begins to come into view." Both Westmoreland and Johnson believed the enemy might launch an attack during Tet, but the general produced enemy casualty figures, whose accuracy has since been disputed, that appeared to prove the NVA was incapable of doing much damage.

At 0245 hours on 31 January 1968 (Washington time), a suicide squad of nineteen VC sappers blasted their way into the US embassy compound in Saigon, holding their positions for over six hours before being overpowered at 0915 hours. All totaled, the Southern capital, twenty-seven of forty-four provincial capitals, five of six autonomous cities, 58 of 245 district towns, and over fifty major hamlets came under enemy attack. Over the next two and a half months, US and ARVN troops steadily recovered the lost ground, though US leaders were forced to commit large numbers of tanks, aircraft, and artillery to the counteroffensive. Casualties were heavy on both sides.

The most ferocious battle was for the ancient imperial capital of Hue, a historic city filled with Buddhist shrines, which was all but razed during the fighting. Roughly 8,000 enemy troops attacked Hue, capturing the Citadel, the heart of the city. While attackers in most cities were quickly defeated after the initial assault, Hue proved an exception. It took three bloody weeks to retake the city. US and ARVN troops lost nearly 500 killed and the communists almost 5,000 killed. Thousands of refugees clogged exit roads attempting to flee the holocaust. In the aftermath 2,800 bodies, mostly civilians, many of them government officials, were found in mass graves in and around the city, the product of enemy executions.[3] Later, special ARVN political units entered the city and conducted their own liquidation of suspected communists.

By the close of the initial fighting, US forces had suffered 1,100 killed, ARVN losses were 2,300 killed, and the civilian dead numbered 12,500. The final phase, in October–November 1968, proved to be the costliest two months of the war for the United States. During this same period, US-estimated communist casualty figures were 160,000–175,000 killed or wounded. To the embarrassment of many US officials, it soon became clear these numbers exceeded the actual number of PAVN and VC forces committed to the fight. The NLF's Southern guerrilla forces were crippled, however, and from then on, the PAVN did most of the fighting. This development also reflected the post-Tet shift in the enemy strategy of insurgent units supported by conventional forces to conventional forces supported by insurgents.

After the Tet Offensive, US troops began their withdrawal from Vietnam, rendering the NLF's guerrilla strategy—designed to sap the will of American fighting forces—no longer important. The communists had not caused the fall of the Saigon regime, nor had they ignited an uprising among the people in the South, but they had forced US leaders to reevaluate their continued commitment to the conflict. Tet shifted the war, for the first time, from the countryside to South Vietnam's supposedly impregnable urban areas and discredited US leaders' claims of near victory. Middle America soured on the war and began to question the ability of the United States to establish a stable government in Saigon. This created a feeling of uncertainty and defeat within the Washington power structure. By March, Johnson's 24-percent approval rating was reflected in his near defeat to a write-in antiwar candidate, Eugene McCarthy, in the New Hampshire primary.

Before 1968, most military leaders had been a willing part of the effort to convince the American public and Congress that "victory was just around the corner." Tet proved this was wrong and that more troops, more casualties, more expense, and more resolve were necessary to "win" the war, even though few really seemed able to specifically define what "win" meant. Washington unwittingly created the shock of Tet with Westmoreland's victory tour, which fostered a rosy mood of public confidence and, despite a certain dose of skepticism in some quarters, left most leaders believing a major enemy offensive could not occur. And then in late January 1968, Tet exploded on every American's television screen. A month later, on 27 February, Walter Cronkite concluded his CBS News special "Report from Vietnam" by asserting the war was a stalemate that should be ended through negotiations in which US leaders would act "not as victors but as an honorable people who lived up to their pledge to defend democracy and did the best they could."[4] In retrospect, this was the turning point. Johnson reportedly told advisers, "If I've lost Cronkite, I've lost middle America." But Westmoreland still believed that "the enemy had delivered himself into the hands of the Allied troops."[5] Conversely, columnist Art Buchwald compared the so-called victory to "General Custer having the Sioux on the run."[6]

By 18 March, Johnson had sunk into a state of despair. South Vietnamese ambassador Bui Diem later recalled of a private meeting with Johnson at this time, "I can say for sure that . . . , when I met with President Johnson, even though he did not mention anything about stopping the war, I felt in my heart that to US leaders the entire course of the war had changed."[7]

As public support for the war waned, congressional opposition increased, even among former supporters. Advisors like Dean Rusk, McGeorge Bundy, and especially the new secretary of defense, Clark Clifford, began raising doubts about US involvement in Vietnam.

In late March Westmoreland asked for 200,000 more troops to "cut the Ho Chi Minh trail, to invade enemy sanctuaries in Cambodia, and carry out an 'Inchon-type' landing in North Vietnam, encircling the enemy troops at the DMZ." It was what he always wanted, and now with the Tet "victory" he believed Johnson would accept. The president, confronted with the possibility of calling up inactive reserves amid growing unrest, turned to his "wise old men" to analyze the request. The group, which included respected former generals like Omar Bradley as well as Washington insiders from both

parties, rejected the proposal and recommended a cessation of the bombing of North Vietnam and the initiation of negotiations. Thus, Johnson
rejected Westmoreland's request, sending only 13,500 men to confront the
continuing emergency. Then on 31 March, on national television, Johnson
not only announced a cessation of the bombing campaign and attempts
to start negotiations but also, in order to concentrate on peace efforts, that
he would not seek the Democrats' presidential nomination. He thus "had
become the latest and best known casualty of the Tet Offensive."[8]

Khe Sanh

In late December 1967, even before Tet unfolded, intelligence data convinced Westmoreland that Giap was planning a Dien Bien Phu–style attack
on Khe Sanh, an isolated fire-support base near the border with Laos. With
Giap's commitment of two crack PAVN divisions totaling 30,000 men,
Westmoreland sent 6,000 US Marines to defend the outpost. Eventually,
the US commitment to Khe Sanh would include massive B-52 raids, which
dropped thousands of tons of bombs on a five-square-mile battlefield,
some within 300 yards of the US perimeter; and hundreds of CAS sorties.
The battle became such an obsession for President Johnson that he had
a terrain map set up in the basement of the White House. Officially, the
battle began on 21 January 1968 and ended on 9 April, when elements of
the US 1st Air Cavalry Division, fighting their way up Route 9, linked up
with the defenders. Enemy casualties were in the thousands, but the siege
was also costly for US and allied forces. And, as perhaps intended by Giap,
it prevented many US units from responding to the Tet assaults.[9]

The Camp at Khe Sanh

The firebase that US Marines occupied early in 1968 was located near the
village of Khe Sanh, the government seat of the Huong Hoa District. The
camp was located on Route 9, the northernmost transverse road into South
Vietnam, near several Hmong and Montagnard (native peoples) settlements
and coffee plantations, roughly seven miles from the Laotian frontier. The
roadway, which was in poor condition, ran from the coastal region, through
the Central Highlands, and into Laos. In the summer of 1962, the Americans established an Army Special Forces (Green Berets) base and airfield
near an old French fortification. The troops posted there watched for any
infiltration by NVA forces into South Vietnam.[10]

Robert Pisor has provided perhaps the best description of the area:

> From the height of Hill 881 one could see the bone-shaped scar of an Army Special Forces camp at Lang Vei, the church steeple of Khe Sanh Village, the smoky hamlets of the mountain tribes known as Bru [Hmong], the air strip and bunkers of Khe Sanh Combat Base—and even thick-walled villas of French planters where wrinkled, brown women sorted coffee beans and gracious ladies served crème de menthe on the patio.
> All around lay a phantasmagorical landscape, the kind of place where trolls might live. An awesome, sheer-sided mountain of stone called Co Roc guarded the gateway to Laos, the land of mystery and green mountains that flowed gently around [Hill 881S] to the South. Tiger Peak loomed large in the hazy far distance, a barrier near the boundary of North Vietnam. Down on the plateau, confusing tangles of thorn and vine and low brush gave way to incredibly dense stands of twelve-foot-high elephant grass. Plummeting mountain streams frothed white against house-sized boulders on the hillside. Across the valleys silent waterfalls flashed like sunlit diamonds in the deep, green, velvet lushness of the jungle.[11]

This description also provides a glimpse into the strategic significance of the region: "It was Indochina's geography that made Khe Sanh important." Indeed, from the time of the Viet Minh's struggle against the French (1946–54), what eventually became known as the Ho Chi Minh Trail was used as a supply and interaction network between communist forces in North and South Vietnam. By 1968, the trail had evolved into a succession of roads, trails, and footpaths that originated in North Vietnam and led into Laos through passes in Ban Kari, Nape, Mu Gia, and Ban Raving Mountains, after which the route went either into South Vietnam or Cambodia. The trail and these passes were so important that the North dedicated 200,000 troops and volunteers to keeping them open, while the United States later sent thousands of bombing sorties against these networks during a four-year series of campaigns dubbed Commando Hunt I–VII. With Khe Sanh overseeing the conjunction of North Vietnam, South Vietnam, and Laos, an area serving as the primary NVA entry point into the South, US leaders believed that having an American military presence at Khe Sanh was critical.[12]

In July 1962, as the Green Berets took up their positions near the village, an ARVN engineer unit began construction of the first airstrip. Over the next two years, US Marine Corps helicopter units deployed to the area to support the Special Forces and ARVN. In addition, in April 1964 the marines sent an intelligence unit to the area to monitor enemy radio communications. Not long afterward, Westmoreland paid his first visit Khe Sanh.[13]

It was during this visit the general began to believe in the "critical importance" of Khe Sanh: "It would serve as a patrol base for the interdiction of enemy personnel and supplies coming down the Ho Chi Minh Trail from Laos into northern South Vietnam; a base for covert operations to harass the communists along the Trail; an airstrip for aerial reconnaissance of the Trail; the western terminus for the defensive line along the Demilitarized Zone (DMZ) separating North and South Vietnam; and a jump-off point for invading Laos by land in order to cut the Ho Chi Minh Trail."[14]

As time went by, the question of whether to maintain such a detached station had to be answered. As early as the spring of 1964, Westmoreland concluded that "abandoning the US military presence at Khe Sanh would allow the PAVN the ability to carry the fight into the populated coastal regions of Northern South Vietnam."[15]

He also believed the base could be used to harass enemy units infiltrating from Laos. That November, Green Berets moved their base camp to the Xom Cham plateau, and soon afterward other US personnel from the super-secret MACV Studies and Observations Group moved their operations first into the village and then into the old French fort. It was from these locations that reconnaissance teams went into Laos to gather intelligence on the NVA.[16]

By early 1966, Westmoreland was conceiving a plan to invade Laos itself. To this end, Khe Sanh would act as his jump-off point and base of operations. He confided to other senior officers in Vietnam that he believed Khe Sanh was a vital strategic base to be held at all cost. That September he ordered his staff to begin detailed planning for invading Laos. Coincidentally, in October construction crews completed the airfield at Khe Sanh.[17]

As the new year dawned, USMC units began to occupy the plateau camp, establishing their headquarters immediately next to the airstrip. Westmoreland intended for this fortified camp to act as the westernmost tactical anchor for the five northernmost provinces of South Vietnam, known as the I Corps Tactical Zone. Late the previous year, Special Forces troops had departed from the plateau and constructed a smaller camp at Lang Vei, on Route 9, halfway between the marine camp and the Laotian border. This

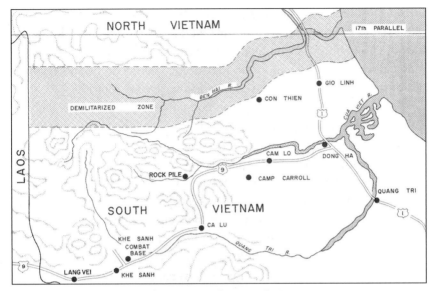

Figure 4.1. I Corps Zone near the DMZ: Northern South Vietnam, 1968

was designed to support the marines' positions, which stretched below the DMZ and along Route 9 from the coast to Khe Sanh.[18]

Throughout 1967, the communists attacked US and ARVN sites across the DMZ. Unlike previous hit-and-run raids, the enemy made sustained assaults with regimental- and later battalion-size forces that included artillery support; much of the shelling was aimed at Con Thien and other targets in Quang Tri Province. To counter these incursions, Westmoreland used airstrikes for seven weeks, dropping 40,000 tons of bombs on enemy positions.

The intensity and frequency of these enemy forays increased throughout October and November 1967, featuring attacks on an ARVN battalion at Song Be, a Special Forces camp near Loc Ninh in Binh Long Province, and Dak To in the Central Highlands province of Kontum. This latter engagement lasted twenty-two days and involved 1,500 NVA troops and major elements of the US 4th Infantry Division and 173rd Airborne Brigade as well as elite ARVN airborne units. The fighting was costly for both sides. At the time, US intelligence was puzzled by the attacks, which were made to divert allied attention away from preparations for the Tet incursions.[19]

Meanwhile, after months of building up marine forces at Khe Sanh, Westmoreland decided to reduce their numbers in order to face enemy threats elsewhere. The general's concerns about a potential invasion across the DMZ, coupled with his reasoning that if the enemy attacked Khe Sanh it would probably be surrounded and have to be resupplied by air anyway, motivated him to reduce troop strength there. This had to concern Giap if, as he later claimed, Khe Sanh was only meant as a diversion.[20]

As early as March 1967, only one company of marines defended the Khe Sanh base. Lacking their own aerial assets, adequate troop strength, or logistical support to maneuver, they maintained a fixed position. Periodically, the marines conducted patrols to locate enemy infiltration routes. Once they spotted enemy forces, they called in airstrikes, artillery barrages, or a reconnaissance-in-force, often with mixed results. During the intervening weeks, the PAVN ratcheted up their offensive activity against the marines. Soon, enemy sappers and demolition teams cut the overland supply route into the base along Route 9. In turn, an NVA regiment surrounded the base while another unit launched diversionary 1,200-round rocket, artillery, and mortar barrages at marine fire-support bases and helicopter facilities throughout I Corps Zone.[21]

On 24 April 1967 a patrol from B Company engaged in a firefight with an enemy force of unknown size north of Hill 861. This action prematurely triggered an NVA attack on Khe Sanh in an effort to take high ground before launching a full assault. The units of the 3rd Marine Regiment, commanded by Col. John P. Lanigan, quickly reinforced the Khe Sanh Combat Base (KSCB). Once they had stabilized the area, Lanigan's men began pushing the North Vietnamese off Hills 861, 881N (or North), and 881S (or South). The marines suffered 155 killed and 425 wounded, while the enemy suffered 940 casualties. It was at this point the Americans maintained a presence on the hills surrounding the KSCB. By June, there was a lull in NVA activity near Khe Sanh, and marine forces were reduced again, from two battalions to one. Concurrently, Lt. Gen. Robert E. Cushman Jr. became commander of III Marine Amphibious Force.[22]

The Fighting Expands

No sooner had Cushman arrived than the communists launched a frontal assault aimed at overrunning the KSCB and airfield; they also assaulted the nearby Special Forces camp at Lang Vei. To avert complete disaster, the Americans sent two marine battalions to the besieged area. After nearly a week of bitter fighting, the US defenders finally beat back the PAVN attack.

As soon as the immediate threat abated, Westmoreland pulled the reinforcements out and restored the previous defensive status quo. As for the NVA, this stalemate left them in a difficult situation. Economic woes, the increasing devastation of American bombing of Northern urban centers, and the reduction of resupply efforts were all taking a toll on their war effort. Communist purists in Hanoi finally realized that a rural struggle alone was insufficient to defeat the Americans. Northern leaders correctly feared the United States was planning an invasion of North Vietnam. As a result, they decided that a different strategy was in order. At the center of this new plan was an effort to disrupt the successful US pacification program, "expand their [communist] control in the countryside, end any US plans to invade the North, destroy US faith in its ability to achieve a military victory, and nudge the Americans in the direction of negotiations. They sought to take the war, for the first time, to the cities of South Vietnam." This was the beginning of the Tet Offensive.[23]

In October 1967 Giap ordered men and material down the Ho Chi Minh Trail. These included the 304th Division, the first large regular formation of PAVN soldiers to enter South Vietnam. The 304th had fought at Dien Bien Phu and came to Khe Sanh supported by attached artillery and antiaircraft units. The other major units were the 325-C and 320th Divisions. CIA analysts concluded that the communists had enough supplies to support their main assault force of 22,000 troops for roughly seventy days. Giap also had a supporting force of 35,000–40,000 in nearby Laos and the central DMZ. Concurrently, one USMC infantry battalion, reinforced with marine and army artillery and tanks, defended the outpost at Khe Sanh. Intelligence gathered on enemy movements in December caused allied leaders to airlift three more marine battalions and one ARVN Ranger battalion to Khe Sanh. Peter Brush observed, "By the time the US build-up at the Khe Sanh Combat Base and surrounding fortified hill positions was complete on January 27 [1968], allied strength numbered 6,053—a reinforced regiment."[24]

From the outset, US commanders determined that keeping control of the prominent terrain features (the high ground) to the north and northwest of the combat base was essential. They deployed about half of the defenders (mostly marines) outside the base perimeter to Hills 64, 558, 861, 861A (or Alpha), 881N, 881S, and 950—each named for its height in meters. Engineers had built the base itself on a gentle plateau, with the hills affording the ability to detect NVA/VC infiltration routes from the northwest and west. They fortified each height with infantry, light artillery, mortars, recoilless rifles, and tracked antitank weapons.[25]

Sporadic skirmishes began at 0830 on 2 January 1968, when reconnaissance personnel spotted six NVA soldiers on a slope near the base's outer defenses. When marines hailed the six without response, they opened fire, killing five. The dead were originally identified as enemy officers. News of the incident convinced Westmoreland that there must be several thousand communist soldiers near Khe Sanh and Giap was planning a massive attack. He believed that after three years of chasing the enemy across South Vietnam, they were finally coming to him.

The general deployed veteran army units north into I Corps Zone to counter the NVA buildup. He placed troops of the 1st Cavalry Division and the 101st Airborne Division, as well as other US and ARVN units, within striking distance of the base just in case they were needed. In retrospect, while controversy still swirls around Giap's later assertion he meant to affect this buildup to draw American forces away from the populated coastal areas, this initial deployment seems to verify his claim—at least in part. American leaders responded to this PAVN deployment just south of the DMZ by dispatching 50 percent of its maneuver battalions in Vietnam to the region, even though they realized this might jeopardize their ability to meet threats against other sites. They were so certain of the severity of the threat to the KSCB they were willing to risk being without tactical reserves just to secure the base.[26]

By December 1967, intelligence had confirmed the presence of the NVA's 325-C Division as well as two additional divisions, believed to be the 324th, positioned in the DMZ roughly ten miles north of Khe Sanh, and the 320th, which was about the same distance to the northeast. These forces were being supplied by units sending logistics down the nearby Ho Chi Minh Trail. This report only reinforced Westmoreland's decision to send the 1st Battalion, 9th Marine Regiment (1/9) to the KSCB to reinforce the position.[27]

In addition to troop dispositions, Giap located artillery, rocket, and mortar emplacements west of Hill 881s and north of Co Roc, a ridge across the border in Laos. From these positions the NVA could fire independently on the base or provide support to its assault troops. They were assisted in their deployment efforts by the continuing bad weather from the winter monsoon, which kept most US aerial-reconnaissance flights grounded.[28]

The official history of the NVA claimed that by December 1967, Giap had deployed the 304th, 320th, 324th, and 325th Infantry Divisions; the independent 270th Infantry Regiment; the 16th, 45th, 84th, 204th, and 675th Artillery Regiments; the 208th, 214th, and 228th Antiaircraft Regiments; four tank companies; one engineer regiment; one independent engineer battalion; one signal battalion; and a number of local militia units. The NVA artillery included 152-mm artillery pieces, with a range of ten and a half miles, and 130-mm guns, introduced later in the battle, with a range of nineteen miles. The heaviest USMC ordnance at Khe Sanh was the 155-mm gun, which had a range of only nine miles. While the enemy used this range discrepancy to avoid counterbattery fire, what they could not avert were air attacks, which the marines could call in with impunity.[29]

The Match to Light the Fire

Clearly, the 2 January incident with the six NVA men just outside the KSCB's defensive wire was the spark that began the fight. Even though there are various versions of the story, what is clear is that when they failed to respond to the warning challenge, five were shot and killed while the sixth, although wounded, escaped. According to John Prados and Ray Stubbe, two of the most knowledgeable experts on Khe Sanh, several myths have proliferated regarding this incident. At first it was reported the dead men were wearing USMC uniforms and were a regimental commander and his staff on a reconnaissance. One dispatch went so far as to say they were all identified by name and rank. All this was supposed to be based on examinations of the bodies and the documents they were carrying by US intelligence. None of this was actually totally verified. Even so, the incident led General Cushman to reinforce Col. David E. Lownds, overall marine commander at Khe Sanh, with the rest of the 2nd Battalion, 26th Marines (2/26), which marked the first time that all three battalions of that regiment had operated together in combat since the landings at Iwo Jima during World War II. The F, G, H, and I Companies of the 2/26 deployed to Hill 558 to cover a defilade near the Rao Quan River, while E Company occupied Hill 861A.[30]

On 20 January La Thanh Tonc, an NVA senior lieutenant of the 14th Antiaircraft Company, 325th Division, defected to the marines at that KSCB and subsequently provided them with detailed plans for all the upcoming attacks. When Hills 881S, 861, and the main base were assaulted simultaneously early the next day, the marines were prepared. Even so, enemy infantry penetrated the defensive perimeter and had to be repulsed with close-quarters combat.[31]

This infantry assault was followed by a mortar-and-rocket attack on the main base, which destroyed most of the aboveground structures. One shell hit the main ammunition dump, hurling artillery and mortar rounds into the air, most of which exploded as they hit the ground. Later, another shell hit a cache of CS tear gas, covering the entire base with gas fumes. The smoldering fires left by this attack ignited new explosions that caused more damage. With chaos all around the KSCB, the NVA failed to exploit this opportunity with another ground attack.[32]

Instead of assaulting the base, the enemy attacked Khe Sanh itself. This large village was defended by 160 local troops and fifteen American advisers supported by heavy artillery from the KSCB. These defenders now faced a 300-man NVA battalion. The Americans immediately sent reinforcements aboard nine UH-1 helicopters, but they were overrun, as was a small

Figure 4.2. NVA artillery makes a direct hit on the ammunition dump at KSCB

ground-rescue force sent to assist. The survivors evacuated to the safety of
the KSCB. NVA forces finally captured the village on 28 January.[33]

On the night of 23 January, three NVA battalions, with seven Soviet-built
tanks in the lead, attacked Laotian Battalion BV-33 at Ban Houei Sane,
near Route 9 in Laos. The Laotians were quickly overrun, with the survivors fleeing to the Special Forces camp at Lang Vei. It was the first time in
the war that PAVN units had used armor in a battle. NVA heavy artillery
made its debut the following day with a bombardment by 152-mm guns on
Hill 881S, Hill 861, and then the KSCB. The marines and the ARVN soldiers
hunkered down, hoping the approaching Tet truce (scheduled from 29–31
January) would provide some respite. But on 29 January 3rd Marine Division headquarters notified the KSCB that the truce had been canceled.[34]

Fall of Lang Vei

As the Khe Sanh battle intensified, the enemy launched the Tet Mau Thanh
campaign on 30–31 January. It did not divert Westmoreland's attention
from Khe Sanh. A press release prepared the following day (but never
issued) at the height of Tet read: "The enemy is attempting to confuse the
issue. . . . I suspect he is also trying to draw everyone's attention away from
the greatest area of threat, the northern part of I Corps. Let me caution
everyone not to be confused."[35]

Meantime, there had been a lull in fighting around the nearby Special
Forces Camp at Lang Vei. About a week later, on the morning of 7 February,
the enemy attacked the Green Berets of Detachment A-101 and their four
companies of local tribal units. While they had some warning, especially the
noise of the NVA tanks, few Americans believed they could move near Khe
Sanh without being seen. Thus, when enemy forces struck the camp, led by
twelve Soviet-built PT-76 amphibious tanks of the 203rd NVA Armored Regiment, they were stunned. The armored units were supported by infantry of
the 7th Battalion, 66th Regiment and the 4th Battalion, 24th Regiment, both
elements of the 304th Division. These troops were equipped with satchel
charges, tear gas, and flamethrowers. Although the camp's main defenses
were overrun in only thirteen minutes, the fighting lasted several hours,
during which the defenders were able to destroy five tanks.[36]

The marines had a plan that called for sending a ground relief force to
save Lang Vei. But based on past disasters involving Lang Vei and other
nearby camps as well as his reading of recent intelligence, Colonel Lownds

decided not to implement the plan. He feared the attack was designed to be a diversion that would lead to an ambush once he sent marines to the rescue. He also rejected a suggestion to send helicopters to extract the survivors. Both Westmoreland and Cushman approved Lownds's decision. According to Jack Schulimson, USMC historian, Lt. Col. Jonathan Ladd, commander of the army's 5th Special Forces Group, later admitted to being "astounded that the Marines, who prided themselves on leaving no man behind, were willing to write off all of the Green Berets and simply ignore the fall of Lang Vei."[37]

The Main Engagement Begins

With the fall of Lang Vei and the village of Khe Sanh, the marines at the KSCB were now surrounded by 40,000 NVA troops. Recognizing the threat, the Americans dug in as much as they could in anticipation of the inevitable attack. Most official histories mark 21 or 27 January as the beginning of the battle. But the entire process had been unfolding since the previous October. As for the US Marines at the base itself, combat had intensified on 17 January, when enemy troops had ambushed a reconnaissance patrol near Hill 881S. When communications with those marines broke off near daybreak on 20 January, I Company, 3/26, under the command of Capt. William H. Dabney, was sent to locate the ambush site, rescue survivors, recover bodies, and regain possession of classified communications information.

At 0530 Dabney and 185 men slowly moved between Hills 881S and 881N. While such patrols were commonplace, the captain sensed he would make contact that day and requested additional support. Lownds sent 200 men to support Dabney, who divided his command, sending one platoon up one hill and two platoons up the other. As they climbed, they were preceded by a World War I–style rolling artillery barrage. The captain hoped the communists would respond and give away their positions. Instead, they waited until Lt. Thomas Brindley's platoon came within range and fired automatic rifles, machine guns, and rocket-propelled grenades at them. The point man was killed immediately, and several others were hit soon after.[38]

Dabney sent a second platoon to flank the enemy position, while Brindley called for artillery fire on his own position. The lieutenant ordered his men to make a dash for the hilltop. Even though Brindley was killed at the summit and dozens of others were wounded, with the support of fighter-bombers dropping napalm, the marines eventually took the hill. Dabney soon realized he had come upon a heavily fortified enemy defensive line constructed along an east–west axis. The fighting lasted for several hours until Colonel Lownds, "fearing an enemy attack on the entire base, ordered the marines to return to their positions on Hill 881 South."[39]

Lownds had assumed command of the 26th Marine Regiment the previous August. As mentioned, from the outset there had been sporadic actions in the vicinity of Khe Sanh, with the most alarming being the ambush of a supply convoy on Route 9. In fact, this brought to an end allied efforts to resupply the firebase by land until the following March. During December and early January, allied units sighted several NVA troops near Khe Sanh, but the sector remained relatively quiet until Dabney's skirmish on the twentieth. What became clear later was that the NVA units had crossed into South Vietnam from Laos and had coalesced northwest of KSCB. They were supported by an armored regiment and two artillery regiments.[40]

After the action of the twentieth, Lownds began to prepare for a large PAVN attack he was certain would ensue. The marines had lost seven killed and thirty-five wounded during Dabney's firefight. By nightfall, the captain's troops were back on Hill 881S, and the entire base was on maximum alert. Lownds had 3,000 men at the main base and 3,000 more on the various hill positions. That night the marines received information from Lieutenant Tonc that a big attack was planned on Hills 881S and 861 at 2330 hours on the twenty-first. The marines brought up several special weapons, including two Ontos assault vehicles capable of firing Flechette rounds containing 10,000 steel darts. The men also strung out razor-sharp concertina wire and placed hundreds of claymore mines and trip flares along the perimeter.[41]

PAVN forces attacked Hill 861, on schedule, using Bangalore torpedoes to break through the defenses. The marines' initial position was overrun, but at 0500, supported by mortars, they counterattacked and drove the enemy off. That afternoon six C-130 Hercules cargo planes arrived despite heavy damage to the landing strip. They carried twenty-four tons of mostly artillery shells. At this point Colonel Lownds estimated he would need sixty tons of supplies per day to hold out.[42]

Even as this action transpired, Khe Sanh village came under attack and thousands of residents sought refuge with the marines. They were not

Figure 4.3. President Johnson and his staff pour over a map of Khe Sanh at the White House

allowed in for fear of sabotage. Nearly 3,000 tried to escape down Route 9 to Dong Ha—only 1,432 made it. Despite the earlier allied setbacks at Khe Sanh village and Lang Vei, the marines at KSCB held. Back in the States, however, the ammunition-dump explosion made for spectacular head-lines, which fed public concerns about US involvement in the war. Johnson was so concerned about the situation at KSCB he had hourly reports sent to him and a room set up in the White House basement with a large board map of Khe Sanh.

The ammo-dump explosion was only part of the bad news. During the enemy mortar and rocket attacks on 21 January, several helicopters were destroyed, several trucks were riddled with shrapnel, and the base com-mander's quarters were leveled. The direct hit on the dump had resulted in the destruction of 16,000 artillery shells and a large supply of tear gas, which spread a cloud of fumes over the entire base. Five hours later a size-able quantity of C-4 plastic explosives also went off. To counter the attack, the senior artillery officer, Maj. Roger Campbell, measured the fresh artil-lery craters in order to target the distance and direction of the enemy guns so his batteries could return fire. To assure the efficient use of the remain-ing shells, Campbell dealt them out carefully, insisting that each round be fired with as much accuracy as possible. The immediate crisis was overcome as more C-123s and C-130s continued resupply efforts to make up for the lost ordnance. As the NVA guns began to effectively target the landing strip, resupply was carried out by helicopter or parachute drops. During the next forty-eight hours, the fire caused by the original barrage continued to detonate smaller ordnance explosions; the marines said it "cooked off" in the flames. As it did, the KSCB became the centerpiece for most national evening newscasts over the next several weeks. One indication of just how seriously US leaders took this battle came on 23 January, when one plane unloaded four large crates, addressed to "Fifth Graves Registration Team, Khe Sanh," filled with 4,000 body bags.[43]

Now What Do We Do?

It was at this point in the battle that US leaders had to determine whether to evacuate the base at Khe Sanh or commit more of its limited manpower from I Corps Zone, which contained only nine battalions for the entire area.[44] General Westmoreland maintained his position that "Khe Sanh could serve as a patrol base for blocking enemy infiltration from Laos along Route 9; as a base for native Laotian forces to harass the enemy in Laos; as an airstrip for reconnaissance planes surveying the Ho Chi Minh Trail; as the western anchor for defenses south of the DMZ; and as an eventual jump-off point for ground operations to cut the Ho Chi Minh Trail."[45]

Westmoreland had been building operational plans for an invasion of Laos since 1966. The initial plan was designated Operation Full Cry, which called for a three-division invasion, but was replaced in early 1967 with two less ambitious contingency plans labeled Southpaw and High Port. Even as Khe Sanh was unfolding, the general concocted another invasion scheme, dubbed Operation El Paso, which resurrected the three-division idea. Before he departed as MACV commander, Westmoreland had begun to formulate yet another proposal (York) that envisaged the use of larger forces.[46]

While many senior military leaders in Vietnam publically supported Westmoreland, others were opposed to such a plan. For example, Lieutenant General Cushman, desperately trying to repair the broken relationship between the US Army and USMC, tolerated Westmoreland's plan at least to a point. Other marine officers argued, with good evidence, that the primary threat to the viability of I Corps Zone came from a potential vulnerability to Quang Tri City and other urban areas. They believed that defending Khe Sanh was a futile gesture since NVA troops could easily bypass this remote firebase near Laos and find another way into South Vietnam. The communists had been finding different ways into the South for years and would continue to do so until the end of the war. Many officers believed the KSCB was seriously isolated and the marine forces there did not have "the helicopter resources, the troops, nor the logistical bases for such operations." Weather conditions were another detriment "because the poor visibility and low overcasts attendant to the monsoon season made such operations hazardous to say the least."[47]

Perhaps the most outspoken opponent was the deputy commander of the 3rd Marine Division, Brig. Gen. Lowell English, who thought that defending this isolated outpost was "ludicrous." He went on to say: "When you're at Khe Sanh, you're not really anywhere. You could lose it and you really haven't lost a damn thing." Despite such objections, Westmoreland remained determined to preserve the outpost so he could know when the NVA had amassed large-enough numbers of troops to start a set-piece battle. He found the prospect of a combat base in a desolate area where US firepower and airpower could be fully applied without worrying about collateral civilian casualties exciting. To him, Khe Sanh presented the opportunity to engage and obliterate a previously elusive enemy by maneuvering them into fixed positions, offering the possibility of an unprecedented victory. The North Vietnamese were well aware of the general's thinking, however, since he had expressed it to the media many times.[48]

Dien Bien Phu Again or Diversion?

So why did Giap initiate the battle for Khe Sanh in the first place? Were the NVA troops attempting to repeat the Viet Minh success at Dien Bien Phu more than a decade earlier? Was it, as Giap would later contended, a diversion to turn US attention away from the urban centers of South Vietnam in preparation for the full force of the Tet Offensive? Dozens of historians, participants, and analysts have expressed their opinion. Westmoreland had no doubt that, due to the large NVA buildup near Khe Sanh and the DMZ, it had to be an effort to repeat their victory over the French. He believed a diversion would have been more logically staged in some other location and with fewer troops. The general contended it was more likely Giap was "concentrating on creating something like Dien Bien Phu at Khe Sanh and seizing the two northern provinces [of South Vietnam]."[49] Maj. Gen. Philip B. Davidson, Westmoreland's intelligence officer, later called the diversion theory a "myth . . . with no factual basis."[50]

In hindsight, only Giap knew what he intended. What we do know is that Westmoreland viewed the NVA attack as an opportunity and shifted his assets to Khe Sanh to defend the combat base. Because in earlier battles it seemed the VC were "adept at slithering away," perhaps the MACV commander believed Khe Sanh presented a location with great potential and little risk of collateral damage or civilian casualties; besides, there were no South Vietnamese government facilities nearby, which eliminated the need to consult their seemingly fainthearted allies. Moreover, the NVA seemed to be spoiling for a fight. If all his plans worked, the general US advantages in firepower and air cover could create the perfect killing zone.[51]

Maj. Mirza Baig, the KSCB's target-selection officer, explained it this way: "Our entire philosophy [is] to allow the enemy to surround us closely, to mass about us, to reveal his troop and logistic routes, to establish his dumps and assembly areas, and to prepare his siege works as energetically as he desires. The result [will be] an enormous quantity of targets . . . ideal for heavy bombers." In short, US military commanders planned to use the marines at Khe Sanh as bait, or as Peter Brush put it, "chum liberally spread around the Khe Sanh tactical area to entice large military forces of North Vietnam from the depths of their sanctuaries to the exposed shallows of America's high technology killing machine."[52]

While this appeared to be an unusual tactic for dealing with an enemy, this concept had been employed in previous wars and would be again during the later phases of this one. In late 1950, when communist forces surrounded the US Marines at the Chosen Reservoir in Korea, USMC general Chesty Puller was credited with saying: "We've been looking for the enemy for some time now. We've finally found him. We're surrounded. That simplifies things." While the subsequent fighting at Chosen was a tactical defeat, the "breakout" from that apparent trap succeeded.[53] Of course, during the NVA's Spring Offensive in 1972, the communists' decision to surround and fight ARVN units in fire-support bases left their own troops out in the open and vulnerable to B-52 attacks, which devastated their ranks.

At Khe Sanh the marines did not much appreciate the role they were delegated by their US Army superiors. They were concerned that the KSCB was too isolated and too hard to support. Maj. Gen. Rathvon M. "Two-Star"

"Tommy" Tompkins, the 3rd Marine Division commander, privately believed General Westmoreland had become especially interested in Khe Sanh since the nearby Special Forces camp at Lang Vei had been overrun for the first time in 1967. (As mentioned above, it was overrun again during the fighting around Khe Sanh in 1968.)[54]

From the communist side of things, if one buys the notion Khe Sanh was designed to divert US military assets away from the populated areas in South Vietnam, then this means North Vietnam must have been willing to commit an entire army corps to keeping a single marine battalion occupied. If so, both sides were baiting each other by their very presence in and around the village. Considering that, up to this point in the entire course of the Second Indochina War, these forces represented the largest military concentration on a single battlefield for either side, it is questionable that the operation was just a deception by the NVA. This makes sense if one

Figure 4.4. Gen. Wallace Greene, USMC commandant; Lt. Gen. Robert E. Cushman, III Marine Amphibious Force commander; and Gen. William C. Westmoreland, MACV commander

accepts historian Cecil Currey's argument in his biography of Giap in which he stated the general told him he was more a student of Prussian soldier-scholar Carl von Clausewitz than Sun Tzu. One need only recall that, prior to becoming a revolutionary, Giap had taught classes on Napoleon and the French Revolution. Like most great strategists, he was a student and teacher of history.[55]

If this actually was Giap's attempt at a second Dien Bien Phu, it is understandable why the upcoming battle was fought with such commitment and ferocity. It is worth recalling the 2 January 1968 incident when KSCB marines confronted the six enemy soldiers. If one of the five killed was a PAVN regimental commander, why would the NVA risk exposing such a senior officer for anything less than a major attack—certainly not for a diversionary action.[56]

The kind of troops used by the enemy during Khe Sanh and Tet is important. The vast majority of communist military forces fighting in Hue and other cities during Tet 1968 were from the VC, the military arm of the NLF. Only in I Corps Zone did North Vietnam commit large numbers of regular NVA troops. Logically, such a commitment of their best units indicates that leaders like Giap were especially determined to inflict a severe and permanent military defeat upon the Americans in the northern provinces. If Khe Sanh was only a ruse, why continue the all-out attacks once the diversion had been realized?[57]

BUFs Fly CAS

As Major Baig recalled, one of the critical aspects of Westmoreland's plan was the employment of B-52 bombers to pummel the concentration of enemy units as they massed near the KSCB. As the battle unfolded, the general ordered in CAS operations, which employed nearly every kind of air asset available—especially the big bombers. The most spectacular attacks were by the B-52D Stratofortress bombers, known to the men as BUFs. By late January, they were bombing targets in three-aircraft cells every three hours. From that point until 31 March, they dropped 15,000 tons of bombs. In addition, US fighter-bombers flew an average of 300 sorties a day. NVA command-center caves in Laos were attacked by B-52s as were artillery positions, staging areas, and storage centers. At times the B-52s dropped bombs within 300 yards of the Khe Sanh defensive perimeter, even though the marines were unable to see the high-flying bombers.[58]

Figure 4.5. B-52D Stratofortress flying an Arc Light mission near Khe Sanh

These missions were part of what were known as Arc Light raids, which had begun in June 1965. "Arc Light" was a general term and codename for B-52 operations flown out of Guam (Andersen Air Force Base) and Thailand (U-Tapao Air Base) from 18 June 1965 to 15 August 1973. Officially, these were missions flown at high altitudes (above 20,000 feet) in South Vietnam and Laos in support of ground forces or to interdict Northern infiltration. They were conventional tactical missions (until the Linebacker I/II operations) flown by the flower of SAC's bomber fleet. Employing 500- and 750-pound iron bombs, most of the sorties were flown first by B-52Fs and later by modified B-52Ds, known as "Big Bellies" because their bombload capacity had been increased by thirty tons. Arc Light operations were most often CAS carpet-bombing raids on enemy basecamps, troop concentrations, or supply lines. Raids by F models carried fifty-one 750-pound bombs, twenty-seven internally and twenty-four externally on the wings. The need for greater payloads led to the initiation of the "Big Belly" program for the B-52Ds. These modifications increased their internal 500-pound-bomb capacity from twenty-seven to eighty-four and 750-pound capacity from twenty-seven to forty-two. In addition, the Ds still carried twenty-four 500-pound or 750-pound bombs externally.[59]

These high-altitude raids were welcomed by the ground forces, who dubbed them "aerial excavations." Their support of the marines at KSCB in 1968 proved vital to saving the firebase from being overrun. These operations began in late January 1968, and even though the siege ended in early April, B-52s continued to pound areas in northern South Vietnam throughout the year. Targets of particular importance were the A Shau Valley, Kontum, Dak To triborder area, and the NVA/VC infiltration area in southeastern War Zone C—the Cambodian border region nearest Saigon. During Khe Sanh, aircrews used ground-based radar to direct their ships to the targets. The attacks on the NVA proved to be very successful.[60]

During the war, SAC scheduled 126,663 B-52 combat sorties, of which 126,615 were launched. Of these, 125,479 reached the target and 124,532 released their bombs. Over 55 percent of these sorties were flown over South Vietnam, 27 percent over Laos, 12 percent over Cambodia, and 6 percent over North Vietnam. Altogether, the USAF lost thirty-one B-52s, eighteen to enemy fire over North Vietnam during Linebacker II, and thirteen due to operations problems.[61]

Why Fight at Khe Sanh?

One of the most interesting events that took place just before the battle started was the capture of the previously mentioned deserter, Sr. Lt. La Thanh Tonc, commander of the PAVN 14th Antiaircraft Company, 325-C Division. An examination of this event explains much about the fight for Khe Sanh. On the morning of 20 January, marines at the eastern end of the airstrip at KSCB were just taking up their positions when they were alerted to enemy activity. They were stunned to see what appeared to be an NVA soldier approaching their position and prominently holding a white flag. The guards demanded that the intruder halt. They then sent word to their superior officers, who dispatched a marine fire team to accept the soldier's surrender. Their prisoner proved to be the enigmatic Lieutenant Tonc. Unlike most enemy captives, Tonc proved to be forthcoming with all kinds of information. His willingness to "tell all" made his interrogators suspicious. But Colonel Lownds believed that his information was real. While such deception was common for the NVA, allied intelligence reports supported much of what he was saying, and if his additional information was legitimate, it would be the biggest intelligence coup of the war. As such, "Tonc was too important to be ignored."[62]

As the interview of Tonc progressed, he disclosed that he had decided to surrender because he was passed over for promotion and lied to by his superiors. He also claimed to be despondent over the high number of casualties the US forces were inflicting on his troops. Finally, he disclosed what the Americans most wanted to hear. The PAVN were planning an attack that would begin that very evening, beginning with an infantry assault on Hill 861. Once it was overrun, two NVA regiments would strike the main firebase from the northeast and south, intent on destroying heavy-weapon positions and the airstrip. They also planned to interdict US helicopters as they came to resupply the marines. Tonc further revealed that the NVA had tanks in reserve north of the DMZ designated to support the attack. He claimed this was to be their most important effort yet and was aimed at obtaining bargaining leverage at the negotiating table. The ultimate goal was to seize US bases along the DMZ and eventually "liberate" Quang Tri Province. He noted that General Giap was in personal command.[63]

What seemed to confirm Tonc's story was a top-secret report by Robert Brewer, senior CIA officer in Quang Tri. In late 1967 he had obtained a communist-party document from a North Vietnamese double agent that described an attack on Khe Sanh and other bases in Quang Tri scheduled to commence in early 1968. Besides this data, US radio operators had intercepted transmissions indicating that an assault was imminent. To this end, the marines at Khe Sanh were on high alert. The skirmish of the twentieth only intensified this situation. Then all hell broke loose just after midnight on 21 January, when hundreds of enemy rockets, mortar rounds, and rocket-propelled grenades pounded Hill 861. This was followed by an attack by roughly 250 enemy soldiers on Hill 861. At this point it was clear that Tonc had been telling the truth.[64]

Once again, it is evident that Giap had succeeded in luring US military assets away from the populated coastal regions to northern I Corps Zone. But it is also clear he had committed such a large force, specifically three infantry divisions, a support division, tanks, and artillery, with the intent of overrunning Khe Sanh as he had Dien Bien Phu. While there were similarities, there were also many differences in the two battles. At Dien Bien Phu the French had made the mistake of basing their defenses on previous victories in battles such as Na San, employing "Hedge Hog" tactics that depended largely on superior artillery capabilities. The French became victims of their own success and the hubris they had developed toward the Viet Minh. At Dien Bien Phu Giap held all the high ground and, to the shock of the French, had superior artillery numbers and targeting. In the end the Viet Minh whittled away at the French outposts that surrounded the main firebase, effectively isolating and eventually overrunning it.[65]

At Dien Bien Phu and Khe Sanh, the communists undertook classic siege tactics by trying to take the high ground, cut lines of communication, and later commencing massed multibattalion attacks against surrounding outposts. The big differences were that the marines held much of the high ground, they had superior artillery, and they could call in much better airpower capabilities than the French had at Dien Bien Phu. To add to this, the Americans seeded the area surrounding KSCB with remote sensors that tracked enemy movements. American artillery and aircraft used the targeting data from these sensors and from reconnaissance patrols to decimate attacking NVA formations. Last but not least, General Giap was confronted by one particular reality he did not encounter at Dien Bien Phu: The marines' hill defenses around Khe Sanh were simply too strong to fall to small- or medium-sized PAVN units. To achieve success, the NVA had to amass large forces to overwhelm American units. But when they did this, the sensors picked up the movements, and the massed troops became "rich targets" for US artillery and bombers.

The best example of this took place in late February 1968 along Route 9. Late one evening the sensors along the road between the firebase and the Laotian border began whistling numerous signals to the monitors at KSCB. Experts soon computed the size and location of the massed enemy column, and Colonel Lownds called in an Arc Light raid. The subsequent bombing left only one company of this NVA regiment capable of reaching its attack position; they were annihilated by an ARVN Ranger battalion at the southeast corner of the base perimeter.[66]

Davidson believed that, at some point in these early days of the battle, Giap's primary objective of taking the KSCB changed due to the realities confronting him. Whatever his main goal had been when the attacks began in January, by late February, Giap had given up his dream of making Khe Sanh another Dien Bien Phu. Davidson later contended that at Dien Bien Phu Giap had established his headquarters nearby from which he directed all operations. He appeared to have repeated this at Khe Sanh since US intelligence reported that the general was not seen in Hanoi between September 2, 1967, and February 5, 1968. Davidson's "best guess" was that Giap was at a forward headquarters facility during the battle.[67]

Not every expert agrees. Peter McDonald, in his biography of Giap, believed he was not onsite since he could not have risked being away from Hanoi, which was the NVA's command-and-control nexus. Robert J. O'Neill's biography of the general agrees, arguing that Giap would no more have directed a tactical operation than Westmoreland. He believed there were issues of reputation involved, and if the NVA suffered a defeat, it would have significantly damaged Giap's reputation. Whatever the case, the cave headquarters where the general might have been was repeatedly bombed by the USAF. Over time, its tactical importance diminished.[68]

The Battle Grinds On

Just as Tonc had warned, the NVA rocket attacks began on the twenty-first and continued nearly unabated for days on end. It made life for those on the plateau both difficult and dangerous. Hygiene and psychological stress soon became major immediate problems—and for some, long-term demons. Sniper duels broke out on a regular basis, evolving into what resembled, in the twenty-first century, macabre video games of life and death. In some cases, if the enemy sniper was a poor shot, the marines made sure he stayed alive, fearing his replacement might be more accurate. Despite these tensions, morale at Khe Sanh remained high throughout.

Between 21 January and 5 February, several small attacks took place against USMC positions on Hills 861A and 64, near what became known as the "Quarry." On the fifth the NVA overran a portion of Hill 861, killing seven marines. But their success was short lived since the Americans retook the position, using tear gas, CAS, and artillery support. In addition, mortar crews on Hill 881S fired 1,100 rounds into the enemy positions. In the last phases of this struggle, the fighting devolved into hand-to-hand combat.

Even as these initial attacks were unfolding, VC and NVA assaults were occurring all over South Vietnam. In Hue, the old imperial capital of the nation and an important Vietnamese cultural and political center, the communists committed large numbers of their regular-army forces to capturing the city during the Tet Offensive of 1968. On 30 January ten VC and PAVN battalions struck Hue in an effort to destroy the Saigon authority there, establish a revolutionary administration, and hold the city for as long as possible. The battle became one of the bloodiest of the war, one that the leaders in Hanoi desperately wanted to win. To this end, on 10 February they sent several thousand troops from Khe Sanh to Hue. This shift of forces could be viewed as supporting the idea that, at least by this stage, enemy leaders had adjusted the priorities from capturing KSCB to diversion. After weeks of bitter fighting, the communists were unable to hold Hue and by 25 February had either fled or been killed.

While this would seem indicate that overrunning the KSCB was no longer a priority, it does not explain the NVA assault during the night of 29 February. A regimental-size attack, it was their largest on the base to that time and was stopped only by overwhelming US firepower. An effort of this size does not lend itself to the idea of the communists only using Khe Sanh as a diversion. Likewise, neither can Giap's shift of five infantry battalions from Khe Sanh be seen as a major redeployment of forces since they were not decisive in the struggle for Hue. As Davidson stated, "In effect, Giap left too few troops at Khe Sanh to overrun it, and shifted too few troops from Khe Sanh to Hue to affect the outcome of the fighting there," concluding that the 29 February assault was "useless."[69]

The Battle Enters a New Phase

During February, the combat intensity ratcheted up, and the NVA dug trenches within yards of the KSCB. This seemed to mirror tactics used at Dien Bien Phu, where the Viet Minh constructed trenches to within a few yards of the French positions. On 25 February a US aerial observer reported seeing an enemy trench running only a dozen yards from the base perimeter. This meant that in one night the PAVN added significantly to their trench network. To counter this effort, the Americans dropped napalm and 500- and 750-pound iron bombs as well as employed almost continuous artillery fire. This reaction shocked NVA commanders, who had observed in battles such as Ia Drang and Con Thien that if they used the tactic of "hugging the belts" of the Americans, they would be reluctant to use their massive firepower for fear of causing friendly fire casualties. At Ia Drang, for example, one infamous US aerial napalm attack killed and wounded more than a dozen Americans—but it also helped save the unit from being overrun. At Con Thien, in contrast, the American CAS did not come so close to their own positions, which nearly lead to disaster. US combat leaders at Khe Sanh were not so squeamish. They were willing to attack close-proximity targets with any and every available weapon, including B-52s. Clearly, the fact that the NVA was willing to build trenches up to the edge of the combat base does not seem to be consistent with a diversion.[70]

The number and size of the NVA attacks increased during the month. In mid-February the marines on Hill 64 were overrun, with twenty-one killed and twenty-six wounded. The same day the extremely close trench was reported, the marine commander sent out a twenty-nine-man patrol to search for an enemy mortar position. Instead of the mortar unit, the marines ran into a heavily defended NVA bunker. Colonel Lownds was unable to send support and ordered them to extricate themselves as best as they could. Ultimately, they were overwhelmed, and only three men escaped. Worse, the dead marines lay on the field for another month until the battle ended.

After all the attacks and all the bloodshed, on 6 March the NVA gave up. On the ninth Westmoreland reported to President Johnson that enemy forces in the vicinity of Khe Sanh had shrunk to between 6,000 and 8,000 men. The next day surveillance units reported that the enemy had ceased maintenance of their trench system. The exchanges of fire began to taper off, and American leadership was left to wonder why the NVA would leave the battlefield at that particular time. Eventually, 1 April would become the official end of Operation Scotland, the military designation for the battle for the KSCB itself. That same day allied units began Operation Pegasus to reopen Route 9 toward the base. A week later, on the eighth, they linked up with the marines defending Khe Sanh. The next day was the first since 21 January that no enemy shells hit the KSCB.[71]

The Nuclear Option

In looking back Davidson believed that one possible motive for the NVA withdrawal might have been the fear of the United States using tactical nuclear weapons. What researchers know now is that senior US officers had been examining how Khe Sanh compared to Dien Bien Phu. At one point General Wheeler, the chair of the Joint Chiefs of Staff, asked Westmoreland if there were targets near Khe Sanh that lent themselves to nuclear strikes and if contingency nuclear planning would be appropriate. According to several sources, Westmoreland replied that if the situation altered signifi-cantly, he could "visualize that either tactical nuclear weapons or chemical agents should be active candidates for employment." Davidson suspected that the discussion of using nuclear weapons was leaked to the press, which also published reports that the MACV commander had requested permission to employ them at Khe Sanh.[72]

There is at least some evidence that General Westmoreland had advocated using nuclear or chemical weapons if the situation became too dire at KSCB. This notion was presented in a 106-page top-secret report (now declassified), "The Air Force in Southeast Asia: Toward a Bombing Halt, 1968," produced by the Office of Air Force History in 1970. According to the report, Westmoreland's comments "prompted Air Force chief of staff, General John McConnell, to press, although unsuccessfully, for JCS authority to request Pacific Command to prepare a plan for using low-yield nuclear weapons to prevent a catastrophic loss of the US Marine base."[73]

In addition, Secretary McNamara sent a secret memo dated 19 February 1968 (declassified in 2005) to President Johnson that advised him not to consider the use of nuclear weapons, especially inside South Vietnam. Fearing the effects on US forces near an area so close to them, the secretary concluded, "Because of terrain and other conditions peculiar to our operations in South Vietnam, it is inconceivable that the use of nuclear weapons would be recommended there against either Viet Cong or North Vietnamese forces."[74]

Davidson believed Giap knew about the nuclear option, having been well aware fourteen years earlier that some US leaders had advocated using nuclear weapons against Viet Minh forces besieging Dien Bien Phu. Surely, the general must have reasoned that, if the Americans had contemplated employing its tactical nuclear ordnance to save their French allies, the possibility of using them to save US Marines had to be exponentially greater at Khe Sanh. One can only imagine that even the mere consideration of such an action must have alarmed not only the North Vietnamese but also Soviet and Chinese leaders.[75]

Many others have disagreed with this argument, contending that Davidson's reasoning goes over the top and has little actual evidence to support it. They argue it is one thing to discuss doing something and another thing to do it. In fact, at no time did Presidents Eisenhower or Johnson consider using nuclear weapons to save Dien Bien Phu, Khe Sanh, or any other base or unit in Indochina. Risking a general nuclear war between the superpowers was of such concern to Johnson that he refused to mine North Vietnamese ports, strike at lines of communication near the

Vietnam-China border, or bomb North Vietnamese population centers for fear of risking a confrontation with the Soviet Union or China. The president believed Khe Sanh could be saved with conventional weapons. As Peter Brush noted, "certainly the use of nuclear weapons in Vietnam would be viewed as a greater provocation by the Russians and Chinese than the other actions which President Johnson was unwilling to implement."[76]

Tactical Options Unfold during February and March 1968

While many experts, including General Davidson, initially believed there was not sufficient evidence to explain North Vietnamese tactics at Khe Sanh, most now agree that sometime during February 1968, Giap decided that seizing KSCB was too costly. But it is worth noting that on 23 February, the firebase was hit by 1,307 rocket, artillery, and mortar rounds, setting a single-day record.[77] While this may seem to contradict the original opinion, Brush convincingly explained it as a logistical matter: "PAVN forces had gone to considerable efforts to stockpile these munitions in the Khe Sanh area. By 23 February, the diversion had been accomplished and attempts to seize the base had proved unsuccessful. Rather than move this ammunition back into Laos under the constant threat of US airstrikes, the communists chose to fire it at the Marine positions."[78]

Of course, another event that seemed to be hard for Davidson and others to reconcile was the multibattalion attack of 29 February. The assault force was not large enough to succeed and took place, apparently, after the NVA began its drawdown. Some analysts believe it was designed to exploit media coverage, coming only two days after CBS anchorman Walter Cronkite had said Khe Sanh would fall.[79] Nonetheless, if one accepts the notion that Giap was a student of Clausewitz, then this action was a classic case of attempting to shake the enemy's will.

In the 1990s Thomas L. Cubbage II, a Vietnam-era US Army intelligence analyst, maintained that the data he had seen at that time confirmed that the NVA attack on Khe Sanh was aimed at realizing a decisive victory like Dien Bien Phu: "the Tet Offensive failed because the attack on Khe Sanh failed and . . . because the Dien Bien Phu model was out of date." In support of this he wrote that new military technology had provided the United States with a vast firepower advantages that the French did not enjoy in 1954. He went on to contend that the taking of Khe Sanh was at the core of Hanoi's plan for Tet Mau Thanh. The operation against KSCB was initiated roughly two weeks before Tet and sought to clear the way for NVA forces to move rapidly from the DMZ to the coastal plain. Had the communists attained their goal, Hue would have fallen and Da Nang's fate would have hung by a thread. In short, the attack against Khe Sanh was Giap's blueprint for the realization of another Dien Bien Phu. As for Westmoreland, Cubbage asserted that due to excellent intelligence, he knew about Giap's designs, thus his plans were focused on the broader picture and not just KSCB. Cubbage judged Khe Sanh as such an important strategic position that its fall might well have permitted the DRV to achieve its goals and force the United States to exit Vietnam.[80]

While there are those who agree with Cubbage and believe that had the NVA won the United States would have left Vietnam much sooner, the North Vietnamese military ability to prevailed in an operation such as Khe Sanh had never been clearly demonstrated. In this regard, this potential for a supposedly decisive victory was problematic at best. According to Brush, who was at Khe Sanh, the PAVN "never realized the means by which this could have been achieved."[81]

The Key Issue of Logistics

Obviously, the main issue facing the marines at Khe Sanh was being resupplied. In mid-January Lownds estimated that his forces required 60 tons per day. Once the battle began in earnest, this figure increased to 185 tons per day. Once the enemy closed Route 9 and the winter monsoons began, the resupply effort became a daunting proposition. From mid-January to early March, low-lying clouds and fog covered the area from daybreak until midday. Even without the fog, the cloud cover seldom rose above 2,000 feet, closing the airfield to all but the most intrepid pilots. To make matters worse, resupply aircraft that did get through the weather and attempted to land soon became the target of NVA antiaircraft fire. Once on the ground, the aircraft were continually shelled by enemy artillery or mortar crews. The ordeal was repeated in reverse as they departed. One of the more famous incidents occurred on 10 February, when a USMC KC-130F attempting to land was hit by an incoming round. As the crew scrambled out of the damaged tanker, the onboard fuel bladders caught fire, and the airframe was slowly consumed on the main airstrip. Moving the wreck proved impossible, and throughout the remainder of the battle, it was yet another obstacle to resupply operations.[82]

With such a degree of difficulty, it is not surprising that, ultimately, 65 percent of all logistical items had to be delivered by paradrop from C-130 aircraft. One of the main reasons USAF crews bore the brunt of this duty was that they had significantly more experience in airdrop tactics than USMC aircrews. By early April, the air force had delivered 14,356 tons of supplies to Khe Sanh, 8,120 tons of that by paradrop. According to the official reports by the 1st Marine Air Wing, that unit conveyed an additional 4,661 tons of cargo into the KSCB. The most dangerous delivery tactic employed there proved to be the low-altitude parachute extraction system. Cargo aircraft (mostly C-130s) touched down but did not brake. As they continued to roll down the runway, supplies tied to pallets were pulled out of the cargo bay using an attached parachute. Once out of the plane, the pallet slid to a halt on the airstrip. With the ejection process completed, the aircraft opened up its engines and flew out of the area. One mistake could spell disaster. Nevertheless, during the battle, this proved a highly successful tactic.[83]

Supplying the main base was one thing, but getting items to the isolated hill outposts was fraught with similar and additional perils. The primary means were helicopters, of which NVA guns took a heavy toll. Ultimately, the most successful tactic developed by the defenders was the "Super Gaggle" concept, which had twelve to fifteen A-4 Skyhawk fighter-bombers fly flak-suppression sorties while massed flights of twelve to sixteen helicopters swooped in to resupply the hill defenders. They adopted this tactic in late February, and it proved to be a turning point in the resupply effort. Marine helicopters flew in 465 tons of supplies during the rest of that month, and as the weather cleared in March, that number increased to 40 tons per day.[84]

Another key logistical aspect proved to be artillery support. As the number of infantrymen at the KSCB increased, so did artillery reinforcements and the need for ordnance. By January, the defenders were receiving fire support from forty-six artillery pieces of various calibers, five tanks armed with 90-mm guns, and ninety-two single or Ontos-mounted 106-mm recoilless rifles. The base also received fire support from US Army 175-mm guns located at Camp Carrol, east of Khe Sanh. During the battle, marine artillerymen fired 158,891 mixed rounds. By comparison, official USMC reports estimated that enemy gunners fired 10,908 artillery, mortar, and rocket rounds at marine positions.[85]

Not only was resupply a priority for the defenders but it was also prominent at most meetings with President Johnson. Throughout the siege, Johnson and his key advisers remained concerned about the marines' survival and their ability to hold Khe Sanh. He and all his top military and intelligence advisers, including members of the National Security Council, were briefed regularly on matters at Khe Sanh. Johnson had a tabletop map set up in the White House basement with the current situation updated on a regular basis. He agonized over the fate of the Americans undertaking this heroic and, he hoped, decisive action, not only because he cared about their safety but also because he was convinced his own historical legacy lay in the balance. At one National Security Council meeting, the president made his attitude clear when he looked at those in the room and declared, "I don't want any damn Dinbinphoo."[86] To allay the Johnson's worries, Generals Wheeler and Westmoreland both guaranteed him that Khe Sanh was well defended and could be resupplied. Logistics support for KSCB took priority over every other operation in Vietnam.[87]

Supplying the camp would have been a massive and complicated operation under the best of circumstances. But this was no ordinary airlift. The fact that roughly 40 percent of the time visibility was below minimum requirements for airfield operations cannot be overstated, nor can the enemy's AAA fire, which was very effective and reduced the amount of provisions reaching the marines.[88]

At first, as nerve-racking as it was, most supply aircraft got through. But after the 10 February C-130 crash, the Khe Sanh airstrip became something akin to a runway obstacle course. Not only was this aircraft destroyed but the fire from it also damaged other aircraft already on the ground. This increased the danger of operations, and the cluttered landing area forced a temporary suspension of C-130 landings, forcing parachute drops. While on the surface this seemed eerily similar to what happened at Dien Bien Phu, the abundance of US aircraft tipped the balance in favor of the Americans, and the parachute drops worked well enough. While this was okay for supplying rations and ammunition, things like bringing in replacement personnel, conducting medical evacuations, and replenishing medical supplies could only be done by aircraft that landed.[89]

During the battle, the marines faced a lack of food and, worse, water. For example, a hot meal was officially defined as a heated C-ration. In reality the men went days without hot meals. Most only had two meals per day, and some less than that. Water was an even more daunting problem. Chaplain Ray Stubbe and Peter Brush, both of whom were at Khe Sanh, later wrote: "One company commander on Hill 861, located about two miles northwest of the combat base, reported his men were forced to go for days with little water. Another reported that his water ration was one half canteen cup of water per day, which had to suffice for drinking, shaving, and brushing teeth."[90]

One major problem with water was how hard it was to deliver since it was heavy, unwieldy, and had to be carried in special containers that could not be used for other liquids. These containers were not only vulnerable to even spent bullets and artillery shrapnel but also easily broken open if dropped from even a low level. In one case a helicopter crew delivering water to Hill 861 became unnerved by enemy fire and released its cargo from a height of two hundred feet. To quote Brush, "The parched Marines watched the water containers burst apart in mid-air."[91]

The water-supply situation could have been even worse. Somehow, the NVA failed to realize just how exposed the KSCB's water supply was. While the marines who were positioned on the hilltops received water from helicopters of the 3rd Marine Division Forward base at Dong Ha, the main base only received water in this manner during the early days of the battle. Eventually, the firebase got its water from the small Rao Quan River, which flowed through hills into an area to the north occupied by the communists. The primary water point itself was located roughly five hundred feet outside the northern base perimeter. One after-action report noted that a small hill and tall grass obscured visual contact with the water point. The water was drawn ninety feet over an eight-hundred-foot span by pumps and into a six-foot-deep reservoir created by a dirt dam eighty-two-feet wide. In the fall of 1967, intense rain ruptured the dam, and USN Equipment Operator 1st Class Rulon V. Rees led a repair unit. They blasted a hole in the riverbed about thirty feet in front of the dam to act as a reservoir in case the river level fell, then placed scrapped Marston matting from the Khe Sanh airstrip on the face of the dam. During the battle, water was pumped inside the perimeter into a large black-rubber water tower. While it was often punctured by stray rounds, which caused temporary water shortages, it was rapidly repaired.[92]

One of the great mysteries of the battle remains the question of why the PAVN never cut off the KSCB's water supply by either diverting or fouling the river. Most Dien Bien Phu experts point to the fact that General Giap won that battle, in large measure, due to his careful battlefield planning. Khe Sanh seemed to be more improvisational. There, neither Giap nor any of his onsite commanders realized how exposed the marines' water supply was. Indeed, General Westmoreland also failed to understand the potential water problem until after the base was surrounded and evacuation was no longer an option. The enemy perhaps did not poison the river out of kindness or humanity. Pursuant to the Geneva Protocol of 1925, which the North Vietnamese ratified in 1957, the fouling of a stream was permitted as long as its water was only used by military personnel. Since the Rao Quon was not used by civilians, legally, it could have been poisoned.[93]

An ancillary aspect of getting supplies into the KSCB was the possibility that the marines might have to be evacuated, a sobering thought to be sure. The idea of a ground withdrawal by a USMC regiment fighting through 40,000 of the enemy's best troops was so daunting, Westmoreland was reluctant to even discuss it. This was why, in retrospect, the water-supply issue was so important. Afterward, General Tompkins declared that had the communists succeeded in interdicting KSCB's water supply, it might well have been impossible to resupply it with water along with its other logistics requirements. At the time, however, General Davidson claimed he had received a letter from Tompkins saying that water could be added to the provisions already being airlifted to the firebase. The only way to determine the veracity of these two conflicting statements is to examine the USMC resupply requirements and US logistical capabilities.[94]

According to the supply records of the III Marine Amphibious Force, Khe Sanh's official requirements were 235 tons per day. Given the situation, trying to reach that level was problematic at best, especially once the enemy effectively closed the airstrip. During February, the KSCB experienced a shortfall of 1,037 tons of supplies. The ability of C-130s to land had all but ended on the tenth, after which only smaller C-123 cargo aircraft, each having much less capacity, could be used to ferry in materials and personnel. Each aircraft thus had to fly more sorties, which increased the chances it might get shot down. Indeed, ground-repair personnel for one C-123 at Da Nang counted 242 holes after one mission. In the first month of the fight, four aircraft were lost to enemy fire. The worst incident took place on 6 March, when communist AAA fire downed a C-123 transport near Khe Sanh, killing forty-eight Americans.[95]

With the risk to these valuable fixed-wing assets increasing, the United States began to use helicopters more often. As noted earlier, one of their benefits was that they could get to and land on the small hilltop positions. According to official records, the outposts' daily supply requirements totaled 32,000 pounds. Officials initially placed the helicopters at the KSCB to facilitate their use. Yet on the ground, the soon became so susceptible to enemy artillery fire the choppers had to be constantly in flight, even if they did not have a mission. Even this tactic proved futile, and at the height of the combat, helicopters were being lost at a rate higher than they could be replaced. Losses became so great, they finally had to be moved away from Khe Sanh. By the end of the battle, thirty-three had been lost.[96]

All of this had a direct effect on continuous water delivery. At the time, the US Army field manual on supply declared, "The water supply requirement for drinking, personal hygiene, food preparation, laundry, and medical treatment is six pounds of water per man per day." At this level the marines had enough water to face constant combat operations for a protracted time. To attain this requirement at Khe Sanh, though, required an additional 158 tons per day, or an increase of 67 percent in supplies even without water. As noted before, supply units could pack on pallets and parachute ammunition and food without the need for special containers, while water was not only difficult to stockpile but also nearly impossible to deliver when enemy fire or weather restricted landings. Despite the initial optimism of US commanders in overcoming all of these logistical challenges, the reality was that resupplying water under the existing tactical conditions was a nightmare, something all leaders should have made it their business to know and understand.[97]

And the Fighting Continued

As February waned, the combat went on. The same night Lang Vei fell, three companies from the NVA 101-D Regiment took up attack positions near advanced outpost Alpha-1. This position was immediately outside KSCB and manned by sixty-six men of the 9th Marines. Supported by a mortar barrage, the PAVN troops breached the perimeter and pushed the remaining Americans into a pocket at the southwestern portion of their defenses.

It seemed all was lost, but for some reason the enemy halted their advance, which allowed a relief force from the KSCB to push them out of their hard-won position. As the assaulting troops retreated, they were pummeled with supporting tank and artillery fire. For all their efforts, the NVA soldiers had achieved nothing.[98]

Among the final engagements, one should recall that on 23 February, the marines at KSCB suffered the most intense artillery assault of the entire siege. The enemy fired 1,307 rounds of 130-mm (used for the first time on the battlefield) and 152-mm artillery pieces located in Laos, inflicting casualties of ten killed and fifty-one wounded. Two days later the first NVA trenches appeared, coming within eighty-two feet of the KSCB's perimeter. That same day a forty-one-man patrol platoon from B Company, 1/26 was ambushed during a short patrol beyond the wire to examine the strength of NVA units. The marines spotted and chased three enemy scouts, who led them into the ambush. After a three-hour firefight, the Americans suffered thirty-one killed and one taken prisoner, while only nine were able to make it back to base.[99]

Soon after this disaster, US intelligence reported that the 66th Regiment, 304th NVA Division was deploying to attack the 37th ARVN Ranger Battalion on the eastern perimeter. To counter this possibility, during the night of 28 February, the Americans unleashed artillery and airstrikes on the predicted NVA staging areas. At 2130 the enemy assault began but was decisively beaten back by the Rangers, with the support of thousands of artillery rounds and dozens of airstrikes. The communists launched two more attacks the next morning before withdrawing. During early March, the PAVN attacked this sector five more times, with similar results. By the middle of the month, intelligence began to note the aforementioned NVA withdrawal. The much reduced 325-C Division headquarters units left first, followed by the 95-C and 101-D Regiments, which moved west. Concurrently, the 304th Division withdrew to the southwest. While the number of enemy forces shrank, the fighting did not end. On 22 March the NVA fired more than 1,000 rounds at the KSCB, once again hitting the ammo dump with spectacular results.[100]

With a lull in the action, on 30 March B Company, 1/26 sent a large force toward the location of the ambush that had claimed so many of their comrades on 25 February. After a rolling barrage by nine artillery batteries, the marines attacked through two NVA trench systems but never found the bodies of those killed during the patrol. US after-action reports counted 115 North Vietnamese killed and put American killed at ten, with one hundred wounded and two missing. At 0800 the next day, higher headquarters terminated Operation Scotland, and operational control of Khe Sanh passed to the US Army's 1st Air Cavalry Division until the end of Operation Pegasus.[101]

It is worth noting that at this point that Operation Scotland, which began on 1 November 1967, officially saw 205 Americans killed in action, 1,668 wounded, and 25 missing and presumed dead. This does not include the troops at Lang Vei, Khe Sanh village, or the aircrews. Official MACV records counted 1,602 NVA bodies but estimated that between 10,000 and 15,000 had been killed, which totaled 60–90 percent of the enemy's assault force of 17,200 men. As with other battles, the US figures must be questioned since nearly all estimates were mostly gathered by sensor readings, sightings of secondary explosions, reports of defectors or prisoners of war, and inference or extrapolation. Years later, researchers discovered that the PAVN reported losses of 2,500 killed, roughly 14 percent of the attacking force, which is a large number of killed in any case. The earlier numbers would suggest that Giap sacrificed his main veteran army wantonly and with no regard for their welfare or with the remote possibility of victory. No one who has studied the general would believe he was that stupid; thus, the original numbers are less than reliable.[102]

Relief at Last: Operation Pegasus,
1–14 April 1968

With all the bloodshed and bitterness faced by the marines at Khe Sanh, one might wonder when a relief force finally arrived. Planning for a ground-relief operation began on 25 January 1968, when General Westmoreland directed Maj. Gen. John J. Tolson, commander of the 1st Air Cavalry Division, to create an operational plan to save the KSCB marines. This proved to be a daunting task since Route 9, the only viable overland road from the east, was in terrible disrepair and mostly under the control of the NVA. Tolson did not want this assignment, believing that the best plan was to use his division to attack the enemy in the A Shau Valley. But the relief of Khe Sanh was only the first part of Westmoreland's overall scheme. He envisioned moving into the post and using it as the jumping-off point for a "hot pursuit" of enemy forces into Laos and, eventually, even an invasion of the North.

By 2 March, Tolson had created Operation Pegasus. This called for the 2nd Battalion, 1st Marine Regiment (2/1) and the 2nd Battalion, 3rd Marine Regiment (2/3) to commence an armored assault from Ca Lu, ten miles east of Khe Sanh, and roll west on Route 9. The 1st, 2nd, and 3rd Brigades of the 1st Air Cavalry Division were to employ air-assault tactics at vital spots along Route 9 to form fire-support bases and cover the marine advance. Planners called for these units to be supported by 102 pieces of artillery. The 11th Engineer Battalion would accompany the marines to repair the road as they moved forward. Later revisions added the 1st Battalion, 1st Marine Regiment (1/1) and elements of the 3rd ARVN Airborne Task Force to the operation.[103]

Privately, the marines, who never wanted to hold Khe Sanh and who had been criticized for the manner in which it had been defended, hated the plan. They consistently maintained that the battle was not a siege and they had never been really isolated. General Cushman expressed his ire at the "implication of a rescue or breaking of the siege by outside forces." All of this notwithstanding, the operation began on 1 April. As it turned out, enemy resistance was light, and the main issue proved to be heavy morning cloud cover that kept the helicopters grounded until later in the day. As the relief effort progressed, the marines at KSCB left their positions and began to patrol farther out. The most intense engagement took place on 6 April, when units of the 1st Air Cavalry Division ran into an NVA blocking force and fought a daylong engagement. The next day other units of the 1st Air Cavalry captured the old French fort near Khe Sanh village. On 8 April at 0800, members of the relief force and the marines at KSCB finally linked up. Three days later the commander of the 11th Engineers officially opened Route 9 to traffic.[104]

That same day, his part in the plan complete, General Tolson directed his forces to undertake immediate actions to initiate Operation Delaware, an air assault into the A Shau Valley. At 0800 on 15 April, US leadership officially ended the relief operation. They had lost 92 killed and had 667 wounded, with 5 missing. A total of 33 South Vietnamese soldiers were killed and 187 wounded. Official estimates put NVA casualties at 1,100 killed and 13 captured.[105]

Also, on 15 April began Operation Scotland II, which involved the marines at the combat base attacking the NVA forces outside the camp. The killing and the dying had not ended near Khe Sanh. The following day a marine company began a patrol near Hill 689 in some tall vegetation, only to be ambushed and massacred by concealed NVA soldiers. Soon, two more companies were sent to support them, but they too were hammered by the enemy troops and forced to retreated back to the KSCB, having 41 men killed and 32 wounded. Two of 15 missing marines were later rescued by helicopters. The battalion commander was relieved of duty.[106]

The 1st Air Cavalry Division and its 400 helicopters also conducted airmobile operations deep into enemy territory. The fighting was heavy throughout this period, and, by the end of June 1968 during Scotland II, 413 more marines were killed. This operation continued until the end of the year, resulting in 72 additional USMC deaths. Despite this, none of these casualties were included in the official body count. US casualties during the ten weeks of Operation Pegasus were more than twice the casualties officially reported during the "siege."[107]

After the KSCB's initial relief, Colonel Lownds and the 26th Marines left their camp and relinquished defense of the base to the 1st Marine Regiment. On 23 May Lownds and his regimental sergeant major received a Presidential Unit Citation from President Johnson on behalf of their regiment. Westmoreland continued to believe the firebase should be maintained until he left Vietnam on 11 June 1968. Gen. Creighton W. Abrams, his successor, waited one week, out of courtesy, and then began Operation Charlie, the evacuation and destruction of KSCB. US forces finished this task on 6 July.[108]

Work on closing the base began in earnest on 19 June, as the remaining marines packed up all salvageable materials and demolished everything else. Throughout, the enemy continued shelling the base, and on 1 July they even made a company-sized infantry assault against the base perimeter; two marines died in the attack. On 5 July, in a brief ceremony, senior base officers formally closed the KSCB. That same day, in one more cruel tragedy, five marines were killed in fighting near the base camp. Finally, the next night the last marines left. Their egress was temporally halted for several hours when an NVA artillery round severely damaged a bridge on Route 9. After several hours' delay as engineers repaired the bridge, this somber gathering completed its journey east down Route 9.[109]

Even after most of the marines departed, some remained in the area in an effort to recover the bodies of their fallen brothers. On 10 July Pfc. Robert Hernandez of A Company, 1/1 was manning an M60 machine-gun position when it took a direct hit from an enemy mortar. He was killed. Hernandez became the last of ten marines and eighty-nine NVA soldiers who died in July, none of whom were included in the official US body count. On 12 July the last Americans left the Khe Sanh area. Mercifully, the battle for was finally over.[110]

The NVA saw things differently. The official history of the 304th Division stated that on "9 July 1968, the liberation flag was waving from the flag pole at Ta Con [Khe Sanh] airfield." Four days later Ho Chi Minh sent a message to NVA forces in the area lauding "our victory at Khe Sanh."[111] The official history stated: "On June 26, 1968, the enemy announced he was withdrawing from Khe Sanh. Our armed forces rapidly tightened their siege ring, mounted shelling attacks, suppressed the enemy's efforts to transport troops by helicopter, and conducted fierce attacks to block the overland route, forcing the enemy to prolong his withdrawal. On July 15, 1968, our soldiers were in complete control of Khe Sanh."[112]

The North Vietnamese claimed the siege continued well into late July, and when it ended in a great victory, they had killed 1,300 US troops and shot down thirty-four aircraft. Despite this obvious exaggeration, no one can deny the KSCB and the entire area were in the hands of the NVA. After six months of bloody fighting, the US had abandoned what at one point was supposed to be the key to a military victory in Indochina. Now, like a dagger at the heart of South Vietnam, it was a jumping-off point for deeper penetration into the Republic of Vietnam.[113]

News of the closure of the KCSB opened the door to the US press to ask why it was vacated. They demanded to know if it had been so vital in January, what had happened in six months to lead to its closing. US officials in Saigon explained that "the enemy had changed his tactics and reduced his forces; that NVA had carved out new infiltration routes; that the Marines now had enough troops and helicopters to carry out mobile operations; [and] that a fixed base was no longer necessary." While there may be truth to this, it would soon become a moot point since, within a year, "Vietnamization" had become the cornerstone of President Nixon's policy, and "US military participation in the war would soon be relegated to a defensive stance."[114]

Khe Sanh by the Numbers

In late March the communists had begun their draw down. By April, the USMC regiment withdrew down the reopened Route 9. After three months of bitter bloodshed, it was over. The US goal at Khe Sanh had been to kill large numbers of NVA soldiers. To this end, they seemed to have been very successful. The official enemy body count totaled 1,602 troops, while leaders at MACV placed the number of enemy dead at 10,000–15,000. In addition, these same commanders allowed that around 200 US Marines had died defending KSCB. But this does not count all those who fought around Khe Sanh during the relief effort or during the two months after the battle was declared over. If we add the numbers of US service personnel killed (that Peter Brush so painstaking calculated for more than thirty years after the battle), this number should total between 900 and 1,000.[115] Thus, in a war that focused on kill ratios and body counts as a measure of success, Khe Sanh was considered a victory by the American military. In later years Captain Dabney, who saw so much of battle up close, asserted: "Most body counts were pure, unadulterated bullshit. Generals manipulated a 'good kill' by flip-flopping numbers, and a certain kind of dishonesty was bred."[116]

Was It a Ruse or a Potential Dien Bien Phu 2?

While there are clear comparisons between the sieges at Dien Bien Phu and Khe Sanh, it is important to note there were also important differences. To be sure, both the US Marines at Khe Sanh and the French paratroopers at Dien Bien Phu were stationed at their precise locations so they would act as "bait" for the Vietnamese communist forces. In both cases the French commander, Gen. Henri Navarre, and MACV commander, General Westmoreland, hoped to draw General Giap into a conventional battle in order to destroy the Viet Minh and the NVA main forces, respectively. In the case of Dien Bien Phu, the French could not have selected a poorer position. Their belief in the inferiority of their enemy and its leaders led them to pick low ground and fail to take the high ground around their position. In addition, the French troops were outnumbered and had less artillery support. Superior airpower might have overcome this problem, but their air assets were limited and their aircraft relatively old.[117]

Unfortunately for the French, Western hubris convinced them they could not lose. One US observer at Dien Bien Phu reported that the French base could "withstand any kind of attack the Viet Minh are capable of launching." Indeed, General Navarre, in spite of the concerns of his subordinates, was completely confident his forces would win because of their superior firepower and their ability to resupply the firebase using an old Japanese airfield nearby. But once the Viet Minh shut down the airstrip, resupply became tenuous, and the enemy's superior artillery and troop numbers forced the French to surrender on 7 May 1954. The defeat at Dien Bien Phu led the French to withdraw from Indochina.[118]

As for Khe Sanh, American forces held the high ground, had better artillery coverage, and could rely on superior air assets, both in terms of aerial resupply and CAS. While Giap, the "Clausewitzian," made the Americans sweat, in retrospect, he had little chance of another Dien Bien Phu. While Tet would eventually lead to Johnson's departure from office and America's withdrawal four years later, the fighting in 1968 did not lead to an immediate communist victory. It forced them to pull back, reconsider their tactics, and lick their wounds from the loss of so many resources.[119]

In what scholars and journalists have come to describe as the "Riddle of Khe Sanh," the question remains as to whether the NVA attack on the KSCB was a diversion or an attempt at replicating Dien Bien Phu. Neither answer seems to adequately explain the events that transpired in this small but strategically significant corner of South Vietnam. Ironically, if Giap's priority was to capture the base, he would not have needed the 22,000 men he sent to Khe Sanh in the fall of 1967. He could have overwhelmed the few hundred American defenders with only a fraction of that number.[120]

If he had access to sufficient intelligence, Giap should have concluded the Americans likely would reinforce the base in response to a massive buildup of PAVN forces, pulling men from other areas of Vietnam. What he may not have known was the disagreement between the US Army and the USMC regarding the value of sending large numbers of reinforcements to Khe Sanh. But even if the general had had intelligence regarding this, he had no way of knowing what the outcome of this internal dispute. If the marine position against sending reinforcements and advocating abandonment of the base prevailed, Khe Sanh would have been but lightly garrisoned or abandoned when Giap's units arrived, and his strategy would have been for naught. His army, instead of creating a diversion, would have diverted only itself, since the Americans would not have sent troops to a base they planned to abandon.[121]

One reasonable explanation may be that Giap's primary motivation at Khe Sanh was to do both. In seeking to divert large numbers of US forces away from the populated coastal areas, he was successful. But achieving a significant victory over the marines must have also been a major consideration. Giap's forces tenaciously remained in the fight too long, fought too hard, and sustained too many casualties to believe the creation of a diversion was the only motive in attacking the KSCB. Indeed, one explanation has to be that the North was fighting a "total war" designed to annihilate the ARVN and eliminate the Southern government in order to reunite the country under its leadership. To this end, Northern leaders were willing to suffer enormous casualties. Against the Americans, however, the North sought to fight a more limited war that would inflict enough losses and convince US leaders that continuing the contest was simply no longer worthwhile, much as the Americans had done to the British during their own revolution. Ultimately, the Northern political and military leaders were willing to accept heavy losses while the United States was not.

Even with the claim of victory by the MACV at Khe Sanh and during the Tet 1968 fighting in general, the psychological victory of the Vietnamese communists during this period led to the beginning of the end for the United States in Southeast Asia. It was during the Tet Offensive that opposition in the States to the ongoing war, in terms of US involvement as a mistake, first rose above 50 percent and exceeded the level of support. Approximately one-fourth of all the televised reports on the evening-news programs during February and March 1968 were devoted to the situation at Khe Sanh.[122]

In truth, only Giap can say for sure what his ultimate goal was at Khe Sanh. Of course, ever since the battle he has claimed it was only diversion, a claim that preserves his reputation. Surely, the government in Hanoi knew about the anxiety and concern US leaders and citizens had over Khe Sanh and must have made the general aware of this. Thus, having achieved his diversion by early February, Giap had little to lose by seeking a victory. One need only recall that during the battle, President Johnson declared, "The eyes of the nation and the eyes of the entire world—the eyes of all of history itself—are on that little brave band of defenders who hold the pass at Khe Sanh." With such knowledge in hand, Giap must have reasoned that a US defeat at Khe Sanh might cause history to unfold as it had after Dien Bien Phu. With nothing to lose (except the lives of his men), Giap pursued the goal of overrunning the KSCB as long as it seemed remotely possible. Once it did not, he withdrew.[123]

Was It Worth It?

As previously mentioned, in April 1968 the US Marines at Khe Sanh departed and were deployed elsewhere in I Corps Zone. Two months later the new leadership at MACV opted to abandon the KSCB. Engineers bulldozed the camp and the airstrip so that it appeared that no one had ever been there. The Americans did this to prevent the communists from taking propaganda pictures of the combat base. In July the last marine departed Khe Sanh. In the aftermath both sides claimed victory and passed out medals. In the light of history, it is clear neither adversary won a definitive victory. While the NVA occupied the area for a while, even they abandoned it to fight battles in other parts of I Corps Zone. In one respect Khe Sanh, which had been such a desperate fight, proved in the end to have been really unimportant. The magnitude of the battle cannot be realized by examining the battle by itself but only as a part of the larger Tet Offensive, which was, in turn, a component of the yearlong communist winter–spring offensive.

For many American leaders, the battle appeared to provide the best chance to draw the enemy into a conventional engagement and annihilate NVA forces at a rate above which they could be replaced. At Khe Sanh the Americans seemingly attained the best enemy body counts and kill ratios of the war—or so they reported, Westmoreland believing that the PAVN had lost between 10,000 and 15,000 soldiers. (Again, the official NVA body count was 1,602.) Yet the outspoken General Tompkins observed that the Americans had collected only 117 individual and 39 crew-served weapons and from this surmised that the US-reported body count was "false."[124]

The official US casualty figures were placed at 205 killed, 1,668 wounded, and 1 missing. In the forty-five years since the battle, no reputable researcher has accepted these numbers. In the immediate aftermath, Chaplin Stubbe put the killed at 476. He also was clear to point out this did not account for other combat deaths, which over the intervening years have been calculated by experts like Peter Brush to include 219 killed at Lang Vei, 25 at Khe Sanh village, 125 during the relief of Khe Sanh, and 52 in plane crashes, ambushes, and other such events. All totaled, allied casualties were approximately 1,000 killed and 4,500 wounded.[125]

Another determinant worth noting has to be the use of material resources. No matter what the number of enemy casualties might have been, one thing is clear: the US expended massive quantities of firepower against enemy forces. The artillery units at the KSCB alone fired 158,891 rounds in direct support of marine forces. They certainly met the Fire Support Coordination Center's motto—"Be Generous."[126]

Seventh Air Force fighter-bombers flew 9,691 sorties, dropping 14,223 tons of bombs and rockets. USMC aircraft executed 7,078 sorties and expended 17,015 tons of ordnance, while USN aviators flew 5,337 sorties and dropped 7,491 tons of bombs. Added to this were the 2,548 sorties flown by B-52s, which released an incredible 59,542 tons of munitions around Khe Sanh. These Arc Light raids delivered the equivalent of a 1.3-kiloton nuclear device every day of the siege. Putting PAVN force estimates at around 30,000 troops, the United States expended over 5 tons of artillery and aerial munitions for every NVA soldier at Khe Sanh.[127]

In the end what is most sobering is that, in many ways, the massive amounts of ordnance used and the apparently large number of enemy killed did not really matter. From the moment that Ho Chi Minh and General Giap began their fight with the French until the day the NVA took Saigon in 1975, what was demonstrated repeatedly was that body counts, even if close to reality, made little, if any, difference. To quote Brush, "Leaders of the Vietnamese communists were willing to absorb losses of this magnitude in order to continue, and win, their struggle."[128]

Thus, in retrospect, it cannot be overstated to say that if the struggle for Khe Sanh was supposed to be a NVA "ruse," it was a successful one since significant amounts of US military assets were diverted to this isolated area of South Vietnam. Nevertheless, in a strictly military sense, this diversion had little effect on the outcome of the fighting during the Tet Offensive. Ironically, the biggest communist victory in 1968 was the psychological damage Khe Sanh and Tet overall did to the US public and the US political psyche—all an unintended consequence. If Khe Sanh was meant to be another Dien Bien Phu, it can only be called a NVA strategic failure. Tragically, for the most part, the battle for Khe Sanh affected the military outcome of the war very little. In this regard it was generally a setback for both sides.

Perhaps the most reveling evidence of the communist perspective on Khe Sanh is on a masonry monument erected by the Vietnamese well after the fact. The text specifically alludes to Khe Sanh as another Dien Bien Phu and surely indicates that they deemed the battle a victory that enabled them to win the war.[129]

> Liberated base monument the area of Tacon Pont [ ] base built by US and Sai Gon puppet. Built 1967. Air field and well-constructed defense system. Co Luong [town] dong ha [county] Quang Tri [province]. US and army puppets used to monitor the movement and tried to stop assistance from the north into the battle of indo china (3 countries). After 170 days and nights of attack by the surrounding liberation army, Tacon (Khe Sanh) was completely liberated. The liberation army destroyed the defense system for the battle of indo china. 112,000 US and puppet troops killed and captured. 197 airplanes shot down. Much war material was captured and destroyed. Khe Sanh also another Dien Bien Phu for the US.[130]

In the spring of 1994, *New York Times* journalist Malcom W. Browne traveled to the former combat base at Khe Sanh, where he found seventy-two communist graveyards for NVA troops who fell in Quang Tri Province alone. At one point during the visit, a Khe Sanh Village People's Committee official, after gazing at the vast meadow covered with tombstones, turned to Browne and observed, "We paid dearly for this land." As Brush later commented, "Of that there can be no doubt."[131]

Final Thoughts

If we accept the concept that war is an extension of diplomacy, then regardless of who won the combat at Khe Sanh, the effects of the battle led to America's eventual withdrawal and a communist victory. Thus, while there is truth in the US claim of victory at Khe Sanh and during the Tet Offensive, the unintended psychological victory of the Vietnamese communists during this period led to the beginning of the end for the American presence in Vietnam. Indeed, during and after Tet, public opposition to US involvement first grew to more than 50 percent. This would continue to grow over the next few months as the average American now joined young protesters in demanding a US withdrawal. Yet as bad as this may have been, it could have been much worse. One is left to speculate on the outcome had the NVA interdicted the KSCB water supply, forcing the marines to evacuate and no doubt to suffer heavy casualties in the process. Would Khe Sanh have been America's Dien Bien Phu?[132]

Only days after the marines left KSCB, Westmoreland requested 200,000 more men to, as he put it, "finish off the Commies." Secretary of Defense Clifford, with the approval of President Johnson, turned down the request. Khe Sanh in particular and Tet in general, had disheartened the US public that now questioned the cost and worth of Vietnam to America. By 1969, despite the relative US military success during the Tet Offensive, Nixon began Vietnamization, a policy that would culminate in American withdrawal in January 1973.[133]

5

The Battles for Saigon and Hue during the Tet Offensive, 1968

Tet, or the Lunar New Year, is one of the most important holidays of the year in Vietnam, if not the most important. One custom practiced during this celebration is giving yellow chrysanthemums to close friends and relatives. In particular, the traditional flower is part of the custom Tao Mo, when family members visit the graves of their ancestors on the last day of every lunar year to clean and decorate them so their ancestors can help welcome the new year. With the dawn of Tet, the Vietnamese decorate their homes with the yellow chrysanthemums, providing a vivid hue and gentle fragrance. Since the chrysanthemum is symbolic of a composed and unpretentious lifestyle, they arrange the flowers in vases and pots at the front door to welcome the new year to let everyone know a harmonious and happy family lives in the home. The bright yellow clusters represent confidence and hope for a happy year to come. A chrysanthemum vase put in the house provides a cozy feeling to the family.

Each generation has taken time from daily activities to celebrate Tet and to pay homage to their ancestors and their traditions. Even in times of war and pestilence, they still follow these ancient customs. As the Tet holiday of 1968 drew near, the leaders of both North and South Vietnam indicated they would respect a ceasefire to honor this important holiday. But this truce was torn asunder by a series of battles that collectively became known as the "Tet Offensive." Instead of pristine yellow mums spread across cities like Saigon and Hue, the flowers were spattered with blood and tears. The war in Vietnam had taken a new turn, leading to seven more years of carnage and eventually the fall of South Vietnam.

Many analysts believe the Tet Offensive caused one of the deepest and most permanent tears in the fabric of US public unity, so much so that it became the turning point in America's war in Indochina. Some believe it was the defining moment when the United States seized defeat from the jaws of victory, while to others it was the wakeup call that convinced American leaders and citizens the war was unwinnable. Normally, such events possess the redeeming virtue of eventually leading to a general synthesis that awaits even the most heated of historical debates. Such were the political stakes and personal passions swirling around this aspect of the Vietnam War that the integration of the competing interpretations of Tet has proven elusive. Was Tet a turning point because of the military actions of the VC and PAVN, or was it a case of US politicians and media throwing away the fruits of a battlefield victory? To answer this question, it is necessary to reexamine this great battle, which changed the war materially.

Defining the Tet Offensive

The foreword to the US Army Center of Military History's account of the Tet Offensive provides a good summation of the event: "The offensive itself, an all-out effort by Viet Cong and North Vietnamese forces to overrun the major cities of South Vietnam, marked the turning point of the Vietnam War. Although the attacks were costly failures in military terms, they set the United States on a path of disengagement from the war that ultimately led to the fall of Saigon some seven years later."[1]

As the spring of 1967 faded, the cost of the Vietnam War continued to grow for both sides, with no clear or final military victory in sight. Leaders in Hanoi decided to initiate a general offensive in the countryside and a popular uprising in the main urban centers of South Vietnam. Their primary goals were to subvert the regime in Saigon and compel the United States to agree to a procommunist settlement. The main planner for the campaign was General Giap, who had taken over as the primary strategist when Gen. Nguyen Chi Thanh was killed. In later years Giap claimed he had opposed the offensive plan but went forward with it "reluctantly under duress from the Le Duan dominated Politburo." He had always advocated using guerrilla tactics against allied forces, whereas Thanh promoted regular offensive action. Even so, Northern political officials decided the time was ripe for a major conventional offensive. They believed the South Vietnamese government and the US presence were so unpopular in the South that a widespread attack would spark a spontaneous popular uprising by the Southern population, allowing the NVA to conclude a swift and final victory.[2]

Accordingly, communist planners created a strategy calling for PAVN units to first assault South Vietnam's border regions to divert US attention. Once engaged, they planned on direct VC attacks against all the South's major population centers. This they anticipated would initiate the disintegration of the Saigon government and instigate full-blown popular revolt that would then force the United States to leave the country or face decisive attacks by VC and PAVN forces.[3]

In October 1967 the communists initiated the first phase of what became the Tet Offensive with a series of small raids against isolated border areas designed to draw American and the ARVN forces away from the cities. The PAVN infiltration rate grew to 20,000 troops per month during the last three months of the year. As intelligence reports warned of this increase, senior officers at MACV in Saigon came to expect a major enemy incursion as early as January 1968. Leaders believed that forces in the area around the DMZ would be able to hold out against the most determined communist attack. Thus, US units deployed to bolster these northern border positions, while ARVN forces were repositioned to defend the Saigon area.[4]

On 23 October 1967 the JCS sent a memorandum to Secretary McNamara declaring their opposition "to any stand-down during Christmas, New Year's or the Tet period." They concluded, "In the past, these stand-downs have resulted in increased casualties to US and allied forces."[5] Even with this warning, local troops were in a holiday mood and not as vigilant as they should have been. Perhaps only with the benefit of hindsight it seems all too obvious Tet was a perfect time for a large assault. Even with adequate time and intelligence to prepare for the enemy uprising, in the days just before the Tet Offensive, neither the ARVN nor its US allies seemed terribly concerned about an attack. Looking back, it seems South Vietnamese officials did not believe an offensive would happen during such a revered Vietnamese holiday. By mid-January 1968, more than one-half of ARVN forces were on leave to celebrate Tet. Concurrently, leaders in Hanoi had announced plans to observe a seven-day truce from 27 January to 3 February in honor

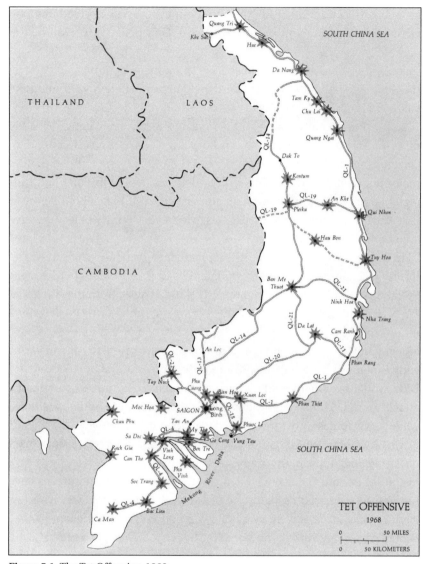

Figure 5.1. The Tet Offensive, 1968

of the holiday. As a result, leaders in Saigon granted most of their remaining troops leave.[6]

The Communists Strike

In the early morning darkness of 30 January 1968, the PAVN and VC struck towns and cities across South Vietnam. It was a new twist. American forces had been in Vietnam for three years, and the vast majority of the combat they had encountered took the form of small guerrilla-style skirmishes in the countryside. Although the United States had more and better weapons as well as hundreds of thousands of trained soldiers, they were bogged down in a stalemate with the communists. The Americans had only begun to comprehend the enemy's low-intensity combat tactics and that their own traditional set-piece tactics were not working, a lesson they should have learned from the failures of their French predecessors. Even though US and ARVN intelligence predicted an impending enemy assault and the PAVN had already launched what appeared to be a diversionary attack against the US Marine outpost at Khe Sanh on 21 January, allied leaders and positioned forces seemed surprised by the size and scale of the assaults. Not only did the coordinated campaign break the traditional agreed-upon ceasefire, its breadth staggered the allies.[7]

The all-out offensive began on the thirty-first, with simultaneous attacks on five major cities, thirty-six provincial capitals, sixty-four district capitals, and numerous important villages. The attack in Saigon was particularly shocking. Around 0130, suicide squads assaulted, in order, President Thieu's home at the Independence Palace, the main radio station, the ARVN's Joint General Staff compound, Tan Son Nhut airfield, and the US embassy, causing extensive damage and sending the city into a state of panic. Estimates of the communist forces varied. Senior ARVN leaders estimated they totaled 323,000 throughout the South, including 130,000 PAVN regulars and 160,000 VC main-force troops. Experts at MACV projected the numbers were around 330,000 total, while the CIA and US State Department hypothesized them at between 435,000 and 595,000. Most of the attacks were broken within a few days, most often due to US aerial bombing and artillery attacks. As much damage as this caused the enemy, it also caused terrible destruction to South Vietnam's urban infrastructure.[8]

On 15 December 1967, Americans relinquished defense of Saigon to the ARVN. As a result, on the night of 30 January 1968, with the Tet truce having been cancelled only recently, four South Vietnamese police posts made up the outer line of defense for the US embassy. Two men from the 716th Military Police (MP) Battalion, 18th MP Brigade were on guard at the embassy's vehicle entrance on Mac Dinh Chi Street. Meantime, inside the Chancery itself, two US Marine security guards were at their guard post, with another marine on the roof. Shortly after midnight on the thirty-first, nineteen VC sappers from the C-10 Sapper Battalion gathered at a VC safe house at an auto-repair facility at 59 Phan Thanh Gian Street in preparation for an attack on the embassy. As they rode a small truck and a taxi into central Saigon, South Vietnamese police spotted them with their vehicle lights off. Instead of stopping them, the police hid.[9]

As the vehicles turned onto Thong Nhut Boulevard, they opened fire on the two MPs at the night gate. Spec. 4 Charles L Daniel and Pfc. William E Sebast, fired back, then closed and locked the steel gate before radioing for help. Simultaneously, Sgt. Ronald W. Harper, USMC, hearing shooting from the rear of the compound, rushed back through the Chancery past LCpl. George B Zahuranic, USMC, who was also calling for help. Harper pulled the Vietnamese night watchman inside the building and bolted the heavy teak doors. Only a few moments later, at 0247 hours, the VC blew a small hole in the outside wall along Thong Nhut.

The first two sappers who came through the hole were killed by Daniel and Sebast. The specialists then contacted their headquarters: "They're coming in! They're coming in! Help me! Help me!" The radio went dead as both MPs were killed by the intruders.

Meantime on the roof, Sgt. Rudy A. Soto Jr., USMC, fired on the VC with his twelve-gauge shotgun and his .38-cal. revolver, with little success. Inside the embassy, the sappers fired their T-56 assault rifles and B-40 rocket-propelled grenades at the Chancery, piercing the walls, injuring Corporal Zahuranic, and destroying the two radio sets in the guard post. Since Soto could not contact Harper or Zahuranic, he assumed they were dead and called for support. At present, Col. George Jacobson, mission coordinator, awoke to the sound of gunshots and immediately began looking for a weapon—all he could locate was an M26 grenade.[10]

An MP jeep patrol, composed of Sgt. Johnnie B. Thomas and Sgt. 1st Class Owen E. Mebust, rushed to the aide of Daniel and Sebast. When they reached the embassy, the sergeants met incoming automatic-weapons fire, and both were killed. By this point, there were three marines, two Vietnamese, and six American civilians inside the Chancery building. They armed themselves with .38-cal. revolvers, M12 Beretta submachine guns, and a shotgun to confront the assailants.[11]

During the initial firefight, Bay Tuyen and Ut Nho, the two officers leading the enemy unit, were killed. Probably for this reason the remaining guerrillas milled about aimlessly. Even though they had enough C-4 explosives to blast their way into the Chancery, they decided not to press their attack and awaited further orders, taking up positions in or near the circular planters nearby. They fired at the increasing numbers of US personnel arriving and engaging them. At the marine guards' living quarters five blocks from the embassy, Capt. Robert J. O'Brien organized the remaining USMC security guards together and rushed to the embassy. They found the side gate locked and began receiving fire from the VC inside the grounds. Taking up defensive positions, they began to return fire.[12]

About 0400 hours, Amb. Ellsworth Bunker, through an aide, contacted the head of Saigon police, Lt. Nguyen Van Luan, requesting police reinforcements. Instead, not only did the First Precinct police director refuse to move his men in darkness but also insisted that US forces escort his men to the compound.[13]

Twenty minutes later, at 0420, General Westmoreland directed the 716th MP Battalion to immediately clear the embassy. This proved to be difficult since they did not have armored vehicles or helicopters. At first the MPs cordoned off the embassy, uncertain of the situation due to darkness and the poor communications between those inside the Chancery and their brethren outside the walls. Harper and his group inside the Chancery communicated with those outside by telephone, while Soto used a radio. In an effort to help his comrades, Cpl. James C. Marshall, USMC, climbed to the roof of a small building in the compound and fired on the enemy forces, even after he was wounded by shrapnel from a rocket. Eventually, the VC killed him, making Marshall the last American killed at the embassy.[14]

At 0500 hours members of the 101st Airborne Division were airlifted in by helicopters. When they tried to land on the rooftop helipad, the VC drove them away. Finally, at 0615 hours, with the VC now short of ammunition, a medevac helicopter landed on the roof to evacuate Corporal Zahuranic and drop off three cases of ammunition for M16 rifles, even though those inside did not have any M16s. As dawn broke, the troops outside found the hole the sappers had blown in the compound wall. At the same time, embassy guards had finally managed to shoot off the locks of the front gate, ramming it open with a jeep. The MPs and marines then charged through and quickly dispatched the remaining VC. Simultaneously, the helicopter carrying troops from the 101st finally landed on the roof and proceeded to sweep the Chancery building, finding no enemy personnel inside. By 0900, American troops had retaken the compound, having killed all of the attackers.[15]

The Attacks Widen

Thus began a bloody series of clashes throughout South Vietnam that would devastate many of the larger cities in the Republic of Vietnam and, in the United States, bring into question both the efficacy of and the requirement for an American presence in Vietnam. The combined VC and PAVN forces attacked nearly one hundred major cities and towns all across the South. The allies were particularly surprised by the scope and ferocity of the fighting. The two major battles of the offensive occurred in the cities of Saigon and Hue. While the siege of the US Marine base at Khe Sanh took place at roughly the same time, it was a separate battle designed to divert American attention away from the urban battles and to protect communist supply lines.

It took more than two weeks for ARVN and US forces to reestablish control of Saigon and nearly a month to retake the city of Hue. From a military viewpoint, the United States defeated the communists, who did not take control of any part of South Vietnam. The enemy also suffered severe losses, from 45,000 to 50,000 killed and twice as many wounded. Yet whether on purpose or coincidentally, the Tet Offensive shattered American faith in ultimate victory and caused many in the States to question why their young men should be fighting and dying in Southeast Asia. The shock and surprise caused by the attacks led to a major US reassessment that eventually led to an American withdrawal.

So how had the war come to this? Why did the communists decide to act at this point? What was their goal? Western historians and analysts interpret Tet in one of two ways. Many like Westmoreland believed the offensive had intended political consequences designed to discourage prolonged US participation in the war.[16] While in hindsight this appears logical, as James J. Wirtz has noted in his work on Tet, it "fails to account for any realistic North Vietnamese military objectives, the logical prerequisite for an effort to influence American opinion."[17] The alternative thesis, which in the aftermath of the Vietnam War is supported by communist documents, argued the goal of Tet Mau Thanh was the overthrow of the government in Saigon, the creation of a coalition government in the South, or the seizure of large portions of Southern territory.[18] What is clear is the seeds for the bloody struggles of early 1968 were sown in the fall of 1967.

The Events of 1967 and the Lead in to Tet Mau Thanh, the Tet Offensive

In mid-1967, with the US general election coming up just beyond the horizon in November 1968, Johnson became increasingly immersed in successfully concluding the Vietnam War. Westmoreland had developed a strategic theory that postulated if the allies could reach a point where the number of enemy personnel killed or captured during military operations exceeded their ability to recruit replacements, the United States would win the war. He was convinced his numbers proved his plan was working. This was a reality that the CIA disputed, a fact demonstrated in September when MACV intelligence services and the CIA met to prepare a "Special National Intelligence Estimate" the Johnson administration had ordered to determine the war's success.[19]

Figure 5.2. Gen. William C. Westmoreland, MACV commander, during a press briefing

The Americans should have had a significant advantage since they had obtained a glut of intelligence data on VC planning during Operations Cedar Falls and Junction City. With these materials in hand, the CIA and other analysts had determined there might be as many as 400,000 enemy guerrillas, irregulars, and cadre in South Vietnam poised for some kind of major action. Concurrently, MACV's Combined Intelligence Center informed Westmoreland there were only 300,000 in the South. Even at 300,000 Westmoreland knew that in the recent past reporters had been constantly told the numbers were much lower.

The general feared these new numbers might change American public attitudes about an imminent US victory in a war that had already lasted longer than most citizens had anticipated.[20] Gen. Joseph A. McChristian, MACV's chief of intelligence, expressed such concerns when he privately admitted the new figures "would create a political bombshell" since they were positive proof the enemy "had the capability and the will to continue a protracted war of attrition."[21]

Through the early summer of 1967, MACV and CIA intelligence analysts continued arguing both the enemy's numbers and intent. MACV claimed VC militias were in no way a real fighting force but "low level fifth columnists used for information collection." Their CIA counterparts contended this was absolute nonsense because VC militia forces had been directly responsible for half of the casualties inflicted on US forces. It fell to the CIA's deputy director for Vietnamese affairs, George Carver, to reconcile the disagreement. By September, Carver, under pressure from his boss, CIA director Richard Helms, settled on a politically motivated compromise. The CIA agreed that the irregulars should not be counted as part of enemy forces and included an addendum explaining this position. It was a ridiculous choice and one that would contribute to future problems for US forces during Tet.[22]

While US intelligence groups squabbled with each other from June to December 1967, the Johnson administration, with a national election only a year away, became concerned about the increasing internal and external criticism of its Vietnam policies. Public-opinion polls indicated the percentage of Americans who opposed the deployment of US troops to Vietnam had grown from 25 percent in 1965 to 45 percent by December 1967. The main reasons for this change were growing casualty figures, rising taxes, and a belief there was no end in sight.[23]

It must also be noted that many within the administration, including Secretary of Defense McNamara, Undersecretary of State Nicholas Katzenbach, Assistant Secretary for Far Eastern Affairs William Bundy, Ambassador Lodge, General Abrams, and Lt. Gen. Frederick C. Weyand, II Corps field commander, all urged a strategic change.[24] As Weyand later revealed, the president refused to accept the CIA's or the Pentagon's "negative analysis." Instead, he embraced the "optimistic reports from General Westmoreland." In retrospect, the policy that evolved came from what Johnson wanted to believe, not reality.[25]

A November 1967 poll indicated 55 percent of Americans wanted a tougher war policy. According to Stanley Karnow, this was based on a popular belief that "it was an error for us to have gotten involved in Vietnam in the first place. But now that we're there, let's win—or get out."[26] Instead of bending to public desires, Johnson initiated what became known as the "Success Offensive." This was a rigorous effort to change the pervasive public perception the war had reached an impasse and to persuade the public that his strategy was working. Led by Walter W. Rostow, the White House national security advisor, the program flooded the news media with hundreds of stories and reports implying an imminent and positive outcome to the war. Every statistical gage of progress, from "kill ratios" and "body counts" to village pacification, was crammed down the throats of the press and Congress. In mid-November Vice Pres. Hubert H. Humphrey told NBC's *Today Show* hosts: "We are beginning to win this struggle! We are on the offensive. Territory is being gained. We are making steady progress."[27]

This public-relations ploy reached a climax in late November 1967, when the president ordered General Westmoreland and Ambassador Bunker to Washington for a "high level policy review." The two men spent most of their time explaining to the media just how successful Johnson's Vietnam policies were. In Saigon, Pacification Chief Robert Komer told reporters the Civil Operations and Revolutionary Development Support pacification program in rural South Vietnam had proven incredibly successful, with 68 percent of the Southern population loyal to the Saigon regime and only 17 percent to the VC. Gen. Bruce Palmer Jr., one of the three American field-force commanders, publically declared "the Viet Cong have been defeated" since "he can't get food and he can't get recruits. He has been forced to change his strategy from trying to control the people on the coast to trying to survive in the mountains."[28]

Westmoreland went even further. In his speech to the National Press Club on 21 November 1967, he announced that by the end of 1967, the enemy would be "unable to mount a major offensive. . . . I am absolutely certain that whereas in 1965 the enemy was winning, today he is certainly losing. . . . We have reached an important point when the end begins to come into view."[29]

Even so, in early January 1968 a Gallup poll showed 47 percent of the US public still disapproved of the president's handling of the war. What Johnson's snow job had done was create an untenable situation. On the one hand, the citizenry was "more confused than convinced, more doubtful than despairing and had adopted a 'wait and see attitude.'"[30] On the other hand, they also expected Johnson to tell the truth. If he did not, they were prepared to dump his policy and perhaps his administration. The icing on the cake was an interview by Westmoreland with *Time* magazine in which he challenged the communists to attack, saying, "I hope they try something, because we are looking for a fight."[31]

Plotting and Planning in Hanoi

In the meantime, communist planners in North and South Vietnam spent from early 1967 to early 1968 conceiving their 1968 winter-spring offensive. According to official Vietnamese sources, Tet Mau Thanh, or the General Offensive General Uprising, was the product of a perceived US failure to win the war quickly, the failure of the American bombing campaign against North Vietnam, and the growing American antiwar sentiment. It was also the culmination of an acrimonious, decade-long debate among the leaders of the Vietnamese Communist Party. The moderate faction, led by party theoretician Truong Chinh and Defense Minister Giap, who supported the Soviet's policy of peaceful coexistence, advocated assuring the economic viability of North Vietnam before becoming involved in a massive conventional conflict in South Vietnam. The radicals, led by Vietnamese Communist Party first secretary Le Duan and Le Duc Tho, supported the foreign-policy concepts of the People's Republic of China, which promoted reunification by military means without negotiations with the United States. Since the early 1960s, the radicals had shaped the direction of the war in South Vietnam mainly through the efforts of Gen. Nguyen Chi Thanh, the chief of the Central Office for South Vietnam. They centered their strategies on large-scale, main-force actions rather than the protracted guerrilla war espoused by Mao Zedong.[32]

The radicals' strategic predominance faded between 1966 and 1967 due to their heavy losses, the battlefield stalemate, and the disintegration of the Northern economy caused by US bombing during Operation Rolling Thunder. Some leaders in Hanoi feared that if these trends continued, they soon would be unable to win a military victory in the South even with the multiplying infiltration routes, growing stockpiles of supplies and numbers of troops, and growing number of pipelines. Throughout 1967, the battlefield situation was so bad that Le Duan encouraged Thanh to revert to protracted guerrilla warfare. With these concerns facing the Politburo, increasing numbers of members called for negotiations and a revision of the existing strategy. They argued that a return to guerrilla tactics fit the situation better since, as constituted, they could not win a conventional war against the United States. The moderates argued the appropriate strategy called for resiliency, wearing down the Americans in a war of wills that could best be described as "fighting while talking."[33]

At this point a new centrist group evolved, led by Pres. Ho Chi Minh, Le Duc Tho, and Foreign Minister Nguyen Duy Trinh, advocating negotiations. While Ho's health was failing and his actual role in party and national leadership had dwindled since 1963, his name and reputation still carried great influence. From October 1966 through April 1967, Thanh and his main military rival, General Giap, carried on a very public debate over military strategy both in the newspapers and on the radio. Giap called for a defensive, primarily guerrilla strategy against the United States and South Vietnam, while Thanh scolded Giap and his supporters for persisting with outdated tactics and policies from the First Indochina War.[34] Thanh accused them of being too cautious and conservative because they were bogged down in "old methods and past experience . . . mechanically repeating the past."[35]

These debates also had a political component. Each side was heavily influenced by loyalties or beliefs in the attitudes held either in the Soviet Union or China. This was in large measure based on the fact that North Vietnam was totally dependent on outside military and economic aid from one or the other of their communist brethren. By late 1967, leaders in Beijing pushed their North Vietnamese counterparts to conduct a pro-

Figure 5.3. Gen. Hoang
Van Thai, leader of the VC
and senior operational
commander during the Tet
Offensive

tracted war on the Maoist model, fearing a conventional struggle might draw China into this conflict as it had during the Korean War. They also opposed negotiations with the Americans and/or the South Vietnamese. Moscow recommended negotiations but concurrently sent large amounts of military equipment to North Vietnam, which it needed for conventional operations on the Soviet model. Hanoi's leaders devised their own synthesis from the several concepts to formulate a critical balance between war dogma, internal and external policies, and foreign allies with "self-serving agendas."[36]

Fearing their internal political opponents might take power and thwart their planned Tet Mau Thanh uprising, on 27 July 1967 the radicals had several hundred pro-Soviet members, party moderates, military officers, and intelligentsia arrested. Dubbed the Revisionist Anti-Party Affair, those arrested were all those who opposed the Politburo's tactics and strategy for the proposed general offensive. This action galvanized the militants' strategy, which rejected negotiations, forsook protracted warfare, and focused on attacks in the towns and cities of South Vietnam. More arrests occurred in November and December.[37]

The Kick Off of Tet Mau Thanh

The operational plan for Tet Mau Thanh evolved from an April 1967 "proposal" by the Central Office for South Vietnam (COSVN) sent to Hanoi from General Thanh's headquarters in South Vietnam. Northern leaders, in turn, instructed Thanh to come to Hanoi to present his plan in detail to the Military Central Commission. Subsequently, the general presented the plan to the Politburo, which accepted it and instructed him to initiate preparations without delay. To celebrate the decision, on the evening of 6 July, communist leaders gathered for a party, with Thanh as the guest of honor. According to Vietnamese sources, while drinking a toast, Thanh, who had been drinking heavily, grabbed his chest and fell to the floor dead of a heart attack. Most Western sources believed the general actually died from wounds received during a US bombing raid. Whatever the case, Thanh's death did not slow preparations for the offensive.[38]

Now in control of the Vietnamese Communist Party, the radicals pushed forward with planning for Tet Mau Thanh, a major conventional offensive to break the military deadlock. Senior officials determined the South Vietnamese government and the US presence were very unpopular among the people of the South and that a widespread attack would spark a spontaneous popular uprising. Combined with the expected success of the offensive, the communists would then sweep to a quick and decisive victory. They based this on the notion that the ARVN's combat effectiveness was gone and the fall 1967 presidential election, putting Nguyen Van Thieu and Nguyen Cao Ky in power with only 24 percent of the popular vote, had established a disliked government. This belief stemmed from the Buddhist upheavals of 1963 and 1966, the antiwar demonstrations in Saigon, and repeated disparagement of the Thieu government by the Southern news media.[39] According to historian Lien-Hang T. Nguyen, militant leaders believed the Tet Offensive finally would put an end to what they called "dovish calls for talks, criticism of military strategy, Chinese diatribes of Soviet perfidy, and Soviet pressure to negotiate—all of which needed to be silenced."[40]

In October 1967 Politburo members decided to initiate the attacks during the Tet holiday, a decision they reaffirmed during their December meet-

Figure 5.4. Sr. Gen. Vo
Nguyen Giap, North
Vietnamese defense
minister

ing and formalized at the Fourteenth Plenary Session of the Party Central
Committee in January 1968. During this conference, the militants pushed
through Resolution 14, which for the time being ended any domestic opposition or "foreign obstruction." Their stated goal was "a spontaneous uprising in order to win a decisive victory in the shortest time possible." While
the radicals made some concessions to the centrists concerning possible
negotiations, they had set Tet Mau Thanh in motion.[41]

Although Vietnamese writers are critical of Western scholars who claim
Giap had little to do with planning or leading the Tet Offensive, both sides
of this debate agree Thanh's operational plan was expanded by a party committee led by Pham Hung, Thanh's principle subordinate, and then more-or-
less amended by Giap. Some have suggested the arrests and imprisonment
of several members of Giap's staff during the Revisionist Anti-Party Affair
caused him to support the plan "reluctantly, under duress." Being a survivor
of many years of internal intrigue within the communist movement, Giap
knew when to be accommodating. With the radical Politburo having made
its decision, his job was to make the plan work. The general, considered by
some as the "red Napoleon," melded low-intensity tactics into what basi-

cally was a conventional military offensive and placed the burden of starting the popular uprising on the VC. He reasoned that if it worked, everyone involved would be hailed as heroes. If the plan failed, the blame would fall on the party militants. Regardless, the brunt of suffering would fall on the VC, not the PAVN. In the aftermath the moderates and centrists would then be able seek negotiations, resulting in a possible end to US bombing of the North. On the eve of Tet Mau Thanh, only the militants were all in. The less extreme members of the Politburo were willing to settle for much less.[42]

The operational plan called for a preliminary phase, during which communist forces would make diversionary attacks along the border areas of South Vietnam to divert US attention and units away from the targeted urban centers. In the next phase the "General Offensive General Uprising" would begin with concurrent assaults on major allied bases and nearly every Southern city, with the main focus on Saigon and Hue. At the same time, the NVA would attack the US Marine combat base at Khe Sanh, meaning that PAVN forces would not be part of the urban assaults. According to Giap, this was necessary to protect his supply lines and divert US attention to the north. To him, assaults against other US forces were secondary since his main objective was to destabilize or destroy the ARVN and the Southern government through the anticipated popular uprising. If this were the case, then the main purpose of Tet Mau Thanh was to undermine public support in South Vietnam, not in the United States. In retrospect, contradictory evidence exists as to whether, or to what extent, Tet was supposed to affect either the March primaries or the November presidential election in the United States. William Duiker and Clark Clifford later argued that Tet was aimed at US public opinion, while Stanley Karnow disagreed.[43]

When Thanh died, Gen. Tran Van Tra assumed command as the military leader of COSVN. With Tet already in the preparatory phase, it fell to him to ensure its success. Years later he wrote there were to be three distinct phases. The first, to be executed primarily by VC forces beginning on 30 January 1968, involved nationwide attacks on as many Southern cities as possible. Concomitantly, fifth-column operatives would spread propaganda throughout the South to persuade ARVN soldiers to desert and the population to rise up against the government. While many did not believe this would achieve a quick victory, these activities could lead to the creation of a coalition government and the withdrawal of US forces. If this failed, Phase II follow-on operations were scheduled for 5 May, which they believed would prompt a negotiated resolution. If not, they planned a third phase for 17 August.[44]

The troop and supply buildup began in the late summer of 1967. By January 1968, they had gathered 81,000 tons of supplies in hidden depots all over South Vietnam. In turn, seven infantry regiments and twenty independent battalions traversed the Ho Chi Minh Trail, bringing to 200,000 the total number of communist troops in the South. VC soldiers were rearmed with new AK-47 assault rifles and B-40 rocket-propelled grenades. By the time Tet began, they actually had more firepower than their ARVN counterparts. In order to create a smokescreen to obscure this buildup of forces, Northern leaders began a diplomatic offensive on 30 December 1967, when Foreign Minister Trinh announced they would be willing to start negotiations with the United States designed to end Operation Rolling Thunder. Despite the scramble by American leaders to take the North up on this proposal, it amounted to nothing more than a diversion.[45]

Allied Intelligence Issues

Even as the new year began, the aforementioned intelligence reports began to reach the desks of ARVN and MACV leadership. They estimated that there were 130,000 NVA, 160,000 VC, and 33,000 service-and-support troops in South Vietnam. These 323,000 enemy forces were organized into nine divisions composed of thirty-five infantry and twenty artillery or AAA regiments, which were, in turn, composed of 230 infantry and six sapper battalions. This evidence should have raised concerns among the allies, but instead it had only a limited effect.[46]

During late 1967, allied intelligence continued to digest clues indicating a major change in communist strategic planning. By mid-December 1967, this data convinced many in Washington and Saigon something big was underway. From October to December, allied intelligence agencies observed signs of an extensive enemy military buildup. In addition to captured documents, such as a copy of Resolution 13, firsthand observations of VC and PAVN logistical movements made it clear they were going to make an assault somewhere. In October operatives reported the number of enemy trucks moving south along the Ho Chí Minh Trail had grown from the previous monthly average of 480 to 1,116. At the end of November, this number had reached 3,823 and in December, 6,315 vehicles.[47] In response, on 20 December Westmoreland cabled Washington that he expected the communists "to undertake an intensified countrywide effort, perhaps a maximum effort, over a relatively short period of time."[48]

Even though the allies had significant warning that something big was in the works, once it actually happened, the size and extent of the Tet Offensive proved to be a surprise. Col. Hoang Ngoc Lung of the ARVN, in his book on the General Offensives of 1968–69, later placed the blame on the tendency of allied intelligence to approximate the communist's most plausible course of action based on their abilities, not their intentions. The Americans believed such a broad offensive was foolish and something the North certainly would not undertake. They did not realize the plan was not based on cautious logic but rather on ideological enthusiasm for a bold stroke. US and Southern intelligence analysts determined the enemy did not have the resources to initiate such an ambitious scheme. As Lung put it, "There was little possibility that the enemy could initiate a general offensive, regardless of his intentions."[49]

Yet another reason for the confusion rests with the lack of collaboration between the various and often rival US and South Vietnamese information-gathering groups. Army and CIA analysts constantly disagreed with one another and jealously protected their turf. Similar issues existed prior to the Japanese attack on Pearl Harbor, the German attack that initiated the Battle of the Bulge, and, of course, the suspicions that facilitated the attacks of 9/11. Then again, sometimes even if an adversary's plans are known, it is difficult to believe them. In the case of Tet, the US assessment followed a similar pattern. As one MACV intelligence specialist remarked: "If we'd gotten the whole battle plan, it wouldn't have been believed. It wouldn't have been credible to us."[50]

Tet Mau Thanh, the Preface

Between April and October 1967, American leaders in Saigon became increasingly puzzled by the numerous, seemingly unconnected engagements launched by the VC and PAVN along the border regions. On 24 April a Marine Corps reconnaissance patrol stumbled on a sizeable PAVN force preparing to attack the airstrip and combat base at Khe Sanh, the US western defensive position in Quang Tri Province. When the enemy withdrew on 9 May, 940 NVA troops and 155 marines were dead. Then, throughout most of September and October, PAVN artillery units fired 100–150 rounds per day at the US Marine outpost at Con Thien, located near the DMZ.

This led General Westmoreland to initiate Operation Neutralize, an aerial-bombing campaign that sent 4,000 sorties against the NVA artillery sites just north of the DMZ. In retrospect it should have been clear that all of this was a diversion in preparation of something important. The allies failed to grasp this warning.[51]

On 27 October a NVA regiment assaulted an ARVN battalion at Song Be, the capital of Phuoc Long Province, and two days later another enemy regiment struck an American Special Forces outpost at Loc Ninh in Binh Long Province. The second attack initiated a ten-day battle that included elements of the elite ARVN 18th Division and the US 1st Infantry Division and cost the communists 800 killed. The most intense engagement of what became known as the "Border Battles" commenced in early November in and around Dak To in Kontum Province. This time the NVA committed four regiments of their 1st Division. The Americans committed the 4th Infantry Division and the 173rd Airborne Brigade, while the ARVN also sent in infantry and airborne elements in to a battle that last twenty-two days. The enemy gained nothing and lost 1,500 killed; the Americans lost 262 killed. When Westmoreland asked his intelligence experts what this all meant, they could not definitively pinpoint the PAVN motives for these series of large-scale actions in remote regions where US firepower and aerial superiority could operate with impunity. According to MACV analysts, they made no sense either tactically or strategically. But this was the first stage of the North Vietnamese operational plan for the Tet Offensive. They had fixed the allies' attention on the borders and drawn the bulk of US forces away from the heavily populated coastal lowlands and cities.[52]

The most significant diversion began on 21 January 1968, at the KSCB, where 40,000 NVA attacked and surrounded the defending US Marines until 9 July. Westmoreland and MACV intelligence officials were certain the enemy was focused on overrunning the base in order to take control of the two northernmost provinces of South Vietnam. With this concern foremost in his mind, the general sent a quarter of a million men, including half of MACV's US maneuver battalions, to the I Corps Tactical Zone.[53]

The commander of the III Corps Tactical Zone and the Capital Military District, Lt. Gen. Frederick Weyand, was deeply concerned by Westmoreland's redeployment of troops. Perhaps his instincts as a former intelligence officer caused him to distrust the communists' action. Whatever his reasons, Weyand contacted Westmoreland on 10 January to urge him to alter repositioning so many troops. Fortunately, Westmoreland agreed and instructed his staff to bring fifteen battalions back from their positions near the Cambodian border to the suburbs of Saigon. This later proved to be a fortuitous action since twenty-seven allied battalions defended the capital and its surrounding area when the enemy struck. In many ways this decision was one of the most important tactical choices of the war.[54]

In early January 1968 America had 331,098 army personnel and 78,013 marines in nine divisions, an armored cavalry regiment, and two separate brigades inside the borders of South Vietnam. The allies also had the 1st Australian Task Force, one Royal Thai regiment, two South Korean infantry divisions, and one Korean Marine Corps brigade. The ARVN had 350,000 men serving. There were also 151,000 South Vietnamese Regional Forces troops and 149,000 South Vietnamese Popular Forces—that is, regional and local militias.[55] Despite a million military personnel, Weyand's adept analysis just prior to Tet was that the allies remained ill prepared. Perhaps this was because in October, with assurances from leaders in Hanoi that they would observe a seven-day Tet holiday truce between 27 January and 3 February, Southern leaders had allowed roughly half of their troops to take leave. But now with his suspicions peaked, Westmoreland cancelled leave in I Corps Zone and asked President Thieu to do the same elsewhere. Thieu reduced the Southern observance of the ceasefire to thirty-six hours but went no further, declaring it might harm troop morale and affirm communist propaganda.[56]

On 28 January ARVN patrols captured eleven VC cadres in the city of Qui Nhon. They had two prerecorded audiotapes with an impassioned communication entreating the inhabitants in Saigon, Hue, and Da Nang to rise up against the puppet regime in Saigon. The next afternoon the chief of the ARVN Joint General Staff, Gen. Cao Van Vien, directed his four corps commanders to put their troops on high alert. Despite this, no one, not even Westmoreland, acted with any sense of urgency. If the American truly understood what a dangerous situation the allies were in, he did not make this clear to any of his subordinates. During the evening of 30 January, 200 American officers, all on the MACV intelligence staff, went to a pool party at their quarters in Saigon.[57] One attendee, James Meecham, an analyst at the Combined Intelligence Center, recalled: "I had no conception Tet was coming, absolutely zero. . . . Of the 200-odd officers present, no one I talked to knew Tet was coming, without exception."[58]

Perhaps worst of all, Westmoreland failed to alert leaders in Washington to any concerns he may have harbored. Even though he informed Johnson as early as 25 January that there was a significant chance of "widespread" communist attacks, the administration rested comfortably on the general's optimism expressed during his November visit.[59] Yet in fairness to the MACV commander, one has to admit an attack on the embassy by nineteen sappers was in no way a big event. His calm demeanor demonstrated leadership in the face of fire. Even so, Westmoreland probably realized US forces had been caught with their pants down. He would soon realize to what extent.

"Crack the Sky, Shake the Earth"

Depending on the source, the initial assaults began either on purpose or by accident just after midnight on 30 January 1968.[60] Almost simultaneously, enemy units struck targets in all five provincial capitals in II Corps and I Corps Zones as well as the major city of Da Nang. Over the years, some experts have argued these first attacks commenced prematurely due to misunderstanding over the change in the calendar date by communist units. Leaders in Hanoi chose to arbitrarily shift the holiday forward in an effort to provide the people of North Vietnam a breather from what they were certain would be retaliatory airstrikes. Whether this is true or not, what is clear is all of the eight attacks that took place on the first day were supervised by the PAVN headquarters in Military Region V.

The first assault struck Nha Trang, the headquarters of the US I Field Force, followed shortly by attacks on Ban Me Thuot, Kontum, Hoi An, Tuy Hoa, Da Nang, Qui Nhon, and Pleiku. Each began with a rocket and/or mortar barrage, followed closely by a massed infantry onslaught carried out by battalion-sized groups of VC, often supported by NVA regulars. Frequently, indigenous cadres acted as guides, leading these troops to the local ARVN headquarters and the radio stations in an effort to eliminate senior leadership and communications. As shocking as the assaults were, locally, they were not well coordinated.

By dawn the next day, nearly all communist forces had been denied their objectives. The new MACV chief of intelligence, Major General Davidson, contacted Westmoreland and warned, "This is going to happen in the rest of the country tonight and tomorrow morning." Literally within minutes, the entire US military had been contacted and placed on maximum alert.

The same orders were dispatched to all ARVN units. Even then, allied units moved slowly, some disregarding orders cancelling leave.[61]

By the end of the thirtieth, the first wave of attacks had died down. Allied forces and South Vietnamese citizens hoped the worst had passed. It had only just begun. Around 0300 on 31 January, enemy forces struck again. In the Capital Military District they attacked Saigon, Cholon, and Gia Dinh. Simultaneously, units assaulted Hue, Quang Tin, Tam Ky, and Quang Ngai as well as American bases at Phu Bai and Chu Lai in I Corps Zone. They also struck Phan Thiet, Bong Son, and An Khe in II Corps Zone, and Can Tho and Vinh Long in IV Corps Zone. Finally, they assaulted Tuy Hoa and Quang Tri again. The following day the communists attacked Bien Hoa, Long Thanh, and Binh Duong in III Corps Zone and Kien Hoa, Dinh Tuong, Go Cong, Kien Giang, Vinh Binh, Ben Tre, and Kien Tuong in IV Corps. The final assault of this initial operation was launched against Bac Lieu in IV Corps on 10 February. More than 84,000 enemy troops took part in Tet, with thousands more standing by as reinforcements or blocking forces. Communist forces also mortared or rocketed every major allied airfield and attacked sixty-four district capitals and scores of smaller towns.[62]

On the first day of Tet Mau Thanh, CIA intelligence analysts penned a top-secret intelligence memorandum for senior leaders and other intelligence personnel, providing an initial evaluation. They argued, "The current series of coordinated enemy attacks in South Vietnam appears designed for maximum psychological impact and to demonstrate the communists' continued power despite the presence of strong US forces." The document went on to assert: "The communists clearly have made careful preparations for the offensive. These preparations point to a major assault in the Khe Sanh area possibly in conjunction with a drive throughout the northern portion of the I Corps area, and widespread attacks against US installations may be preparatory to or in support of such action." The analysts concluded: "The enemy probably hopes to score some major battlefield successes during their campaign. Their military actions appear related to Hanoi's recent offer to open talks, but it is questionable that the communists are making a final desperate bid before suing for peace."[63]

In most cases South Vietnamese forces were able to repel the enemy within a few hours—at worst in two or three days. Still, heavy fighting continued for a week or more at places like Kontum, Ban Me Thuot, Phan Thiet, Can Tho, and Ben Tre. According to Westmoreland, the outcome was normally a decisive ARVN victory led by some "excellent local command-ers." Of note was the fact that throughout the Tet battles, no South Viet-namese unit broke or was defected. The general later said he responded to the news of the offensive with "optimism," both in media presenta-tions and in his reports to Washington.[64] While this might well be how Westmoreland remembered it, others who observed his actions asserted he was "stunned that the communists had been able to coordinate so many attacks in such secrecy" and was "dispirited and deeply shaken."[65] Defense Secretary Clifford later recalled at the time of the initial attacks, the reaction of the US military leadership "approached panic."[66] Even if one accepts Westmoreland's version, one aspect on which he miscalcu-lated was his conviction that KSCB was the real enemy objective and that 155 separate attacks by 84,000 troops was a diversion. It was an argument he would make until mid-February, when the size and intensity of the Tet Offensive made it impossible to ignore reality.[67] Peter Braestrup, a reporter for the *Washington Post*, remarked, "How could any effort against Saigon, especially downtown Saigon, be a diversion?"[68]

In Saigon, which was the main focus of the Tet Offensive, the enemy's primary goals were all in the downtown district. They included the Joint General Staff headquarters, located at Tan Son Nhut Air Base; the US embassy; the Independence Palace; the Long Binh Naval Base; and the national radio station. Each target location was attacked by small compo-nents of the local C-10 Sapper Battalion. On the outskirts of Saigon, ten VC Local Force battalions attacked the central police station, the Artillery Command, and the Armored Command headquarters, the last two located at Go Vap. Their tactical plan called for these units to capture and hold their positions for at least forty-eight hours, by which time reinforcements were expected to arrive.[69] It was an extraordinarily complex and risky plan, with numerous prospects for failure.

It was left to the ARVN to defend the Capital Military District. When the Tet Offensive began there were eight ARVN infantry battalions supported by the local police force in Saigon. Within four days, five ARVN Ranger battalions, five Marine Corps battalions, and five ARVN airborne battal-ions had joined them. In addition, the US Army's 716th MP Battalion, six infantry battalions, one mechanized battalion, and six artillery battalions participated in the capital's defense.[70]

As the conflict unfolded, one of the key enemy targets was the Armored Command and Artillery Command headquarters on the northern edge of the city. The communists planned to surprise the defenders and seize the tanks they believed were stored there, then use them along with captured artillery against US and ARVN forces. In fact, the tanks had been moved to another base two months earlier, while the artillery pieces' breech blocks had been removed, rendering them unusable. Another vital target was the national radio station. VC storm troopers were supposed to capture it and then transmit a tape recording of Ho Chi Minh proclaiming the liberation of Saigon and calling for a general uprising against the Thieu government. While the VC forces were able to take the building and hold it for six hours, they were not able to make broadcasts because the audio lines stretching from the main studio to the transmitting tower had been severed soon after the communists took the facility.[71]

The most significant incident of the battle in Saigon had taken place at the US embassy. Many Americans back home had viewed television scenes of the massive six-story stone building, completed only the previous September, sitting in the middle of a four-acre compound. As noted, at 0245 on the thirty-first, nineteen VC sappers blew a hole in the eight-foot-high wall surrounding the main building. They charged in but failed to take the building and, with their officers dead, were forced to take up positions in the Chancery grounds. They fought for six hours, resisting to the bitter end. Eventually, all nineteen were either killed or captured by US reinforcements that landed on the roof of the main building. By 0900 allied personnel had secured the embassy and grounds, having lost five Americans killed.[72]

As the drama played out, small squads of VC dispersed throughout the city, attacking the homes and billets of ARVN officers and enlisted men as well as district police stations. They possessed hit lists bearing the names of military officers and civil servants. Where they could, the marauding VC squads rounded up and executed as many on the list as possible. As the ARVN beat back these groups, they retaliated against any VC they captured. In one of the most iconic photographs of the war, on 1 February Gen. Nguyen Ngoc Loan, chief of the National Police, is shown personally executing a VC officer named Nguyen Van Lem (also known as Bay Lap/Hop), who had been arrested wearing civilian clothes. Famed Associated Press photographer Eddie Adams took the photo, while NBC's Vu Suu recorded

Figure 5.5. Gen. Nguyen Ngoc Loan executes VC soldier Nguyen Van Lem on a street in Saigon

a film of the event. Within days the photo had appeared in nearly every major newspaper or magazine in the world, including *Life* and the *New York Times*; the video appeared on NBC. This event proved to be a public-relations nightmare for the United States, with world leaders condemning the act. Ironically, Loan's actions were legally justified under the Law of Armed Conflict. As for Lem, his VC unit had just massacred the family of one of Loan's best friends and had earlier executed dozens of other ARVN members.[73]

Just outside the city, two VC battalions attacked the US logistics and headquarters complex at Long Binh, while a PAVN battalion struck Bien Hoa Air Base. Nearby, the ARVN III Corps headquarters was assaulted by another battalion, and Tan Son Nhut Air Base was targeted by three other enemy battalions. In the latter action, a battalion of ARVN paratroopers were waiting to be transported to Da Nang. When the VC struck, the airborne troops hurled them back.[74]

The enemy committed thirty-five battalions, many of which contained covert operatives who had lived and worked inside the city for years. Even as the initial attacks were quelled, new fighting erupted in the Chinese neighborhood of Cholon near the Phu Tho racetrack, located southwest of Saigon, which the PAVN was employing as a staging area and command-and-control center. The battle in this area was a bitter and destructive building-to-building engagement. On 4 February allied officials instructed local civilians to depart their homes, thus turning the area into a free-fire zone. The struggle there did not subside until 7 March, with both ARVN Ranger units and PAVN forces suffering heavy casualties.[75]

This phase of the Tet Offensive officially ended on 8 April. It cost the PAVN and VC forces perhaps as many as 45,000 killed. While many historians have been skeptical of this number, representing more than half of the enemy troops engaged, Stanley Karnow claimed in 1981 to have confirmed this number while in Hanoi.[76] Westmoreland's staff estimated the allies had killed 32,000 enemy combatants and captured 5,800 others. Official Defense Department numbers claimed the ARVN suffered 2,788 killed, 8,299 wounded, and 587 missing in action, while the Americans and other allies lost 1,536 killed, 7,764 wounded, and 11 missing.[77]

The Battle for Hue

While the initial phase of the Tet Offensive had been a tactical nightmare for the VC and NVA, the struggle for the ancient imperial capital of Hue not only proved to be one of the bloodiest battles of the Vietnam War but also one whose images proved to have a major influence on US public opinion about the war. Hue is the capital of Thua Thien Province in the central portion of Vietnam. It is the country's third-largest city, with a population of about 150,000. According to an ancient Buddhist legend, Hue first came into existence as a lotus flower sprouting from a puddle of mud. By the 1960s, the city was separated into two sections by the Perfume (Hoang) River. The north was highlighted by a fortified three-square-mile section known as the Citadel, its esthetic structure modeled after the Forbidden City in Beijing. Surrounded by a moat and a massive earthwork, this masonry fortress had been built at the beginning of the nineteenth century by the Annamese emperor Gia Long. Its massive walls formed a diamond-shaped fortress, with the four corners pointing toward the cardinal directions of the compass. The Citadel surrounded the old city and was, in turn, encircled by a water-filled moat. The old Imperial Palace was in the southeastern corner.[78]

In 1968 the more modern part of the city lay south of the river, consisting mostly of French-style homes along with the city's university and former

French provincial-capital buildings. This area, about half the size of the Citadel, was an active commercial center where the main hospital, jail, and treasury were located. Hue had long been the cultural, spiritual, and educational center of Vietnam. Most of its residents attempted to remain aloof from the war, while city intellectual and religious leaders emphasized traditional values and distrusted both the Hanoi and Saigon governments.[79]

Erik Villard, who wrote an account of the battle for the US Army's Center for Military History, described Hue as follows:

> Befitting the royal prerogative of an imperial city, the residents of Hue enjoyed a tradition of civic independence that dated back several hundred years. The Buddhist monks who dominated the religious and political life of Hue viewed the struggle between North and South with aloof disdain. Few felt any attachment to the government in Saigon. Indeed, the monks were fundamentally at odds with President Thieu; they demanded an immediate end to the war and a program of national reconciliation that would give the communists a prominent role in a new coalition government. Their political views sometimes went beyond mere words. In the spring of 1966, the monks had engineered a popular revolt in Hue and other cities to protest the succession of generals who had ruled since 1963 and to demand free national elections and a negotiated end to the war. South Vietnamese troops quickly crushed the uprisings in other cities, prompting the Buddhist leaders to end the protest movement before Hue was affected. The city had been stable since that time, with few indications that politics or even the war would disturb the calm.[80]

For such an important city, Hue was poorly defended. Just before Tet, there were only 1,000 ARVN troops present, and many of them were on leave at the time celebrating the holiday. According to Villard: "The American presence in the city was minimal, with only about two hundred troops on assignment there at any given time. Approximately one hundred US Army advisers and administrative personnel, as well as a few Marine guards, were headquartered in a lightly defended compound a block and a half south of the Perfume River on the east side of Highway 1, just across from the University."[81]

What neither the South Vietnamese nor the Americans realized was the communists had shifted several regiments from Quang Tri City and Khe

Sanh to Hue. These were battle-tested PAVN units armed with 122-mm rockets, 82-mm mortars, 75-mm recoilless rifles, heavy machine guns, and rocket-propelled grenades. "By the eve of Tet, the enemy had quietly assembled a strike force near Hue equivalent to at least fourteen battalions."[82]

Enemy operatives had spent weeks in and around Hue evaluating its defenses. They created a logistics and administrative zone, designated the "Hue City Front," and formed a combat headquarters staffed with senior military officers, party members, and political officials. Communist forces spent most of December 1967 and January 1968 preparing for the attack by scouting the ground and obtaining the most current tactical intelligence available. In mid-January they launched several small, diversionary assaults. Eventually, they divided the Hue City Front into a northern wing and a southern wing for simultaneous strikes on the city and its surroundings. The main target was the ancient Citadel. Communist political officers exhorted the troops to a maximum effort, explaining that "such opportunities came only once in a thousand years. If all went as planned, they predicted that the war would be over in the near future." They called the fighters liberators and patriots. The PAVN soldiers wore their best uniforms on the day of the assault, anticipating they would be hailed as they "marched through the city streets," serenaded by a chorus of cheers from the crowds in the liberated city.[83]

Despite these careful preparations, as was the case in at least a dozen other cities, communist forces began their attacks prematurely. This gave the Americans and the South Vietnamese clear warning that more attacks were eminent. At 0945 on 30 January, President Thieu ended the Tet cease-fire and ordered all troops to return to their units as soon as possible. In Hue ARVN 1st Division commander Brig. Gen. Ngo Quang Truong had difficulty notifying his troops, most of whom were at home celebrating the holidays in the southern half of the city. He sent three platoons to protect the provincial headquarters, the power station, and the prison on the south bank of the Perfume River. He sent his remaining forces to augment security at the Citadel and around Tay Loc airfield. As for US forces, MACV's senior adviser in the city, Col. George O. Adkisson, had posted extra guards and had recently run a practice drill simulating a sapper attack. That evening he received orders to "take special measures to protect the compound." Still, the allies had no notion of the magnitude of what was about to hit them.[84]

Villard noted: "At 0333, a signal flare burst over Hue. Viet Cong Saboteurs in the old city cut the telephone lines leading into General Truong's head-quarters. A few seconds later, four sappers dressed as South Vietnamese soldiers approached the sentries inside the closed Chanh Tay Gate, hav-ing earlier gained entry to the city through a culvert in the southeastern wall with help from a pair of agents inside Hue." The communists killed the guards before they could sound the alarm, then blew open the gate. Behind them came elements of the PAVN 800th Battalion. Within minutes, these and other units had swept into the Citadel and seized predetermined posi-tions all over the northern part of the city. They struck so fast that General Truong had no time to organize the city's defenders.

At 0340—ten minutes behind schedule—on this foggy 31 January morn-ing, mortar and rocket rounds from the PAVN 6th Regiment struck allied defensive positions north of the Perfume River. In short order two battal-ions of this same regiment attacked. They drove quickly toward the head-quarters of the ARVN 1st Division, located in the Citadel and enveloped by a complex of palaces, parks, and residences. Led by General Truong, the outnumbered ARVN defenders, known as the "Black Panthers," fought des-perately even as the surrounding parts of the Citadel fell to the commu-nists. At 0800 North Vietnamese troops raised the VC banner, red-and-blue with a gold star, over the Citadel's flag tower.[85]

Truong was one of the few leaders who sensed the impending attack. His own intelligence staff told him the enemy did not have the ability to launch such a major assault. Still, he was well aware of how vulnerable Hue was, exacerbated by the fact most of his tough and battle-hardened sol-diers were spread across the surrounding area searching for enemy troops; others were training in the Van Thanh center. The general's subordinates assured him that even if Hue was attacked, there were ARVN forces near Quang Tri City and US Marines and air-mobile units in Phu Bai not far to the south. Still, these units also were not expecting action. Addition-ally, helicopter units were low on reserve materiel, leaving any troops who might be deployed to carry their equipment in trucks or on their backs.[86]

In other parts of the city, the attacks met with different results. On the south bank of the river, the PAVN 4th Regiment attempted to seize the local MACV headquarters but was beaten back by a makeshift force of about 200 Americans. The rest of the city was overrun by enemy forces initially about 7,500 strong, later growing to as many as 12,000 soldiers in ten PAVN and six VC battalions. As both sides reinforced and resupplied their forces, few realized the struggle to take back Hue would last twenty-six days, until 25 February. The most chilling aspect of this battle would not be discovered until after the fighting was over—the "Massacre at Hue," the communists' execution of 2,000–3,000 government officials, religious leaders, police, and others the occupiers deemed "counterrevolutionaries."[87]

Once ensconced, the communists had to be rooted out by US Army troops, US Marines, and ARVN soldiers totaling 2,500 men. Given the cultural and historical significance of the city, the allies initially decided not to employ airpower or artillery to the extent they did elsewhere. Members of the 1st Marine Division, supported by numerous US Army and ARVN units, cleared out enemy resistance street by street and house by house. It was a tactic the Americans had rarely used since World War II and one in which they were not well versed; the last real urban engagement had been during the Battle of Seoul during the Korean War. Beginning on 4 February and lasting for several days, US troops slowly advanced toward the Citadel.[88]

At first US intelligence failed to grasp just how many enemy troops were in the city or just how hard it was going to be to remove them. This was exemplified by Westmoreland's message to the JCS that "the enemy has approximately three companies in the Hue Citadel and the marines have sent a battalion into the area to clear them out."[89] With so few US forces in Hue, relief had to come from Phu Bai, five miles to the southeast. In a misty drizzle the 2,500 men of the 1st Marine Division, soldiers of the ARVN 1st Division, and US Army units began the deadly business of retaking the city. While urban tactics proved difficult for US forces, at least they had studied them. The communists were even less prepared for such fighting. The house-to-house combat became such a meat grinder that US leadership decided to employ at least some artillery and CAS in the process.[90]

The Allies Fight Back

As noted, when the communists attacked Hue, USMC units in Phu Bai, a few miles to the southeast, were sent to retake the city. When first notified of the enemy attack, Colonel Adkisson sent a radio message requesting support to marine headquarters at Phu Bai. Task Force X-Ray commander Brig. Gen. Foster C. LaHue promised to send a reduced company to bolster the forces defending the advisory compound. This was all he could send since his own outposts from Hai Van Pass to Phu Bai were also being

Figure 5.6. Allied forces fighting their way into Hue

assaulted. LaHue had three marine battalions present to protect this western entrance to Hue when he should have had two fully manned regiments. But Westmoreland's obsession with Khe Sanh had led to the deployment of more troops to the KSCB. Col. Stanley S. Hughes commanded the USMC forces in Hue. He was a World War II and Korean War veteran who had received the Navy Cross and Silver Star. He would soon be awarded a second Navy Cross for heroism.[91]

On 31 January, when the enemy first assaulted Hue, they also hit the Phu Bai airstrip with rocket and mortar fire, followed by a massed infantry attack. At 0400 an NVA company struck the ARVN bridge-security detachment and adjacent Combined Action Platoon (CAP) H-8 located at the key Truoi River Bridge. Hughes ordered H Company, under Capt. G. Ronald Christmas, to relieve this embattled CAP unit. As they arrived at their destination, the marines caught the enemy departing the CAP's area of responsibility and opened fire. At this point Lt. Col. Ernest C. Cheatham Jr., 2nd Battalion, 5th Marines (2/5 Marines) commander, perceived an opportunity to trap the entire NVA force between his men and the river. He sent his own Command Group and F Company to reinforce H Company.[92]

Ultimately, Cheatham's plan took a backseat to the larger events unfolding in Hue. The next day F and G Companies disengaged and began to move toward the city. Subsequently, the NVA was able to break off the battle and also move back toward Hue. Officially, the marines killed eighteen enemy troops, took one prisoner, and recovered a significant amount of equipment and weapons, including six AK-47s, and suffered casualties of three killed and thirteen wounded. Slowly but surely, as the Americans set up defensive positions at Phu Bai, they also began to realize what was happening to the north. It became clear the main battle was in Hue, defended at that time only by ARVN units. General LaHue also received little reliable intelligence. What he knew for sure was that Truong's ARVN headquarters was under attack as was the MACV compound in the city. Due to the communist rocket and mortar fire, "the initial deployment of forces was made with limited information," LaHue later wrote, making it a complicated and uncertain move.[93]

At 1030 a second marine company left Phu Bai, joining the convoy shortly thereafter. Around noon, three ARVN M41 tanks of the 7th Cavalry also joined this gaggle ambling up Highway 1. Even with 300 US Marines and dozens of ARVN troops, it took nearly four hours to negotiate the last portion of the road to Hue. But LaHue knew that Truong and his men were in peril and urged his men on.[94]

The column carefully moved toward the embattled city. As it reached the southern suburbs of Hue, the allies came under heavy sniper fire. In one of the small villages near the road, they left their trucks and tanks to clear the houses on either side of the main street before advancing farther. This became a pattern, the main convoy halting numerous times to eliminate resistance in heavy house-to-house and street fighting. After intense combat the reinforcements reached the MACV compound even as the attackers pulled back. Lt. Col. Marcus J. Gravel met with Adkisson, and after some discussion, they deployed their forces.[95]

Gravel left A Company to defend the MACV compound and moved out with G Company, supported by the three tanks from the 3rd Tank Battalion as well tanks from the ARVN 7th Armored Squadron. This assemblage advanced toward the main bridge over the Perfume River. In part concerned that the heavy US Marine M48 tanks would crash through the bridge supports, Gravel left the armor behind on the southern bank to provide direct fire support. In addition, the ARVN M24 light-tank crews "refused" to advance without the American tanks leading the way. As the marine infantry started across, they drew heavy fire from an enemy machine gun on the other side, which killed or wounded several men. Finally, LCpl. Lester A. Tully worked his way forward to hurl a hand grenade that destroyed the machine-gun position. Tully's action, for which he later received the Silver Star, allowed two platoons to reach the other side of the bridge. Once across, they moved to their left, only to come under fire from a recoilless rifle hidden behind the Citadel wall. Stuck in an untenable situation, they had no choice but to withdraw. This process also proved very difficult as the communists' poured fire from multiple locations on the north side of the river. At this point the marines located several abandoned civilian vehicles and used them to remove the wounded. Later that night they pulled back to a defensive position near the MACV compound and established a helicopter LZ west of the Navy Landing Craft Utility ramp on the south side of the river. At the end of the first day, these two marine companies had suffered ten killed and fifty-six wounded. That night the defenders called in a helicopter to evacuate the worst cases. Unfortunately for the troops onsite, senior US leaders still had not grasped the severity of the situation in Hue.[96]

At 0700 the following morning, Gravel sent two marine companies, supported by tanks, to seize the jail and provincial-government buildings. Almost immediately they came under sniper fire, and one tank was hit by fire from a 57-mm recoilless rifle, forcing them to withdraw to the MACV compound. In northern Hue the ARVN 1st Division held its ground inside the Citadel, but the 2nd and 3rd Battalions of the ARVN 3rd Regiment could not push through the NVA defenses within the walls. Perhaps the best news came from the ARVN 2nd and 7th Airborne Battalions, which, supported by APCs and the Black Panther Company, recaptured the Tay Loc airfield.[97]

That afternoon the ARVN 1st Battalion, 3rd Regiment (1/3 ARVN) reached the ARVN 1st Division command post at the Mang Ca compound. Soon after, US Marine helicopters airlifted part of the ARVN 4th Battalion, 2nd Regiment from Dong Ha into the Citadel. The weather quickly deteriorated, however, and they were not able to bring in the entire battalion. F Company, 2/5 Marines landed in southern Hue to relieve personnel at a besieged MACV microwave-tropospheric-scatter communications facility. The location was extremely important as the primary communications link into Hue, the DMZ, and Khe Sanh. Afterward, the marines spent most of the afternoon trying to reach the isolated US Army Signal Corps 513th Signal Detachment, 337th Signal Company, 37th Signal Battalion communications site, even though it was only one and a half miles southeast

Figure 5.7. Marine 106-mm recoilless rifles like this one played a key part in retaking Hue

Figure 5.8. Marine M50 Ontos and commandeered vehicles in Hue

of the MACV compound. F Company suffered three killed and thirteen wounded.[98]

Even as these actions continued, General Cushman, overall USMC commander, notified Major General Tolson, commander of the 1st Cavalry Division, to prepare his 3rd Brigade to deploy into an area west of Hue. Tolson decided to airlift two battalions into a sector northwest of the city. The 2nd Battalion, 12th Cavalry would go in first, followed by the 1st Battalion, 7th Cavalry. By midafternoon on 2 February, the battalions had landed roughly six miles northwest of Hue and advanced on the city. Moving southeast, they cut the enemy supply lines into Hue, though the operation progressed with great difficulty.[99]

Concurrently, in southern Hue, the 1/3 ARVN finally relieved the MACV radio facility and, after a three-hour firefight, reached the Hue University campus. The previous night NVA sappers had destroyed the railroad bridge across the Perfume River west of the city but left the bridge over the Phu Cam Canal intact. About 1100, H Company, 2/5 Marines crossed the An Cuu Bridge over the canal in a "Rough Rider" armed convoy, supported by US Army trucks equipped with quad .50-cal. machine guns and two marine M50 Ontos tracked vehicles. Near the MACV compound, they faced heavy enemy machine-gun and rocket fire. Army gunners and the two Ontoses, each with six 106-mm recoilless rifles, fired back with deadly accuracy. Unfortunately, in the haze of confusion, they also fired on a USMC unit already in the city. Still, the NVA held out and even took out a supporting tank. By evening, the marines had lost two killed and thirty-four wounded, while killing 140 communist defenders.[100]

On the afternoon of 16 February, General Abrams, Westmoreland's MACV operational commander, met with South Vietnamese vice president Nguyen Cao Ky, General Cushman, and Lt. Gen. Lam Quang Thi, ARVN commander in this sector. They determined the biggest issue facing them at Hue was logistics, maximizing their own and denying the enemy's. Abrams told the gathering his intelligence staff had stated the communists had committed three more battalions to the fight in order to keep a corridor open for supplies to reach their comrades in the Citadel. To break this up, he ordered Col. Hubert S. Campbell's 3rd Brigade to be fully supplied and to seize Thon Que Chu and Thon La Chu to the northwest of Hue. Abrams believed this would break the stalemate as the VC and NVA in the Citadel would soon run out of supplies. On 21 February Campbell brought his troops into position, launching his attack the next day. It took two difficult days but the Americans finally pushed the opposing forces out of the area. Enemy troops in the Citadel now were surrounded.[101]

Victory at Last

Throughout these long weeks, as US and ARVN forces fought their way through Hue, they experienced bitter and protracted street fighting. The 1st and 5th Marine Regiments, the 7th and 12th Cavalry Regiments, and the ARVN 1st Division gradually pushed the NVA and VC out of Hue and retook the city one block at a time. None of the forces on either side had much experience in urban combat, and since the city was of religious and cultural significance, the allies initially self-limited their combat options. At first, problems with the monsoon rains and low clouds on many days limited CAS and slowed progress. As casualties increased, the policy of protecting shrines and historic buildings was eliminated. The enemy employed lots of snipers, normally hidden inside buildings or in what were called spider holes, and prepared makeshift machine-gun bunkers. They carried out night attacks, especially when the exhausted allied soldiers were sleeping. In addition, they planted a variety of booby traps, often under dead bodies, frequently those of their fallen comrades.[102]

As this drama unfolded, outside the city elements of the 101st Airborne "Screaming Eagles" Division and 1st Air Cavalry Division continued to block Hue from communist lines of supply and reinforcement. Desperate to save their deteriorating situation, at one point two NVA regiments were redeployed from the siege at Khe Sanh to Hue, only to be cut to pieces by these US blocking forces. As February wore on, US and ARVN units gradually fought their way toward the Citadel. After roughly two weeks of fighting, the allies came within reach of the old fortress. At last it had come down to the retaking the Citadel and the Imperial Palace at its center. With better weather and permission to use airpower, USMC A-4 Skyhawk aircraft swooped in and dropped bombs and napalm on the Citadel. Even so, it required four more days of intense combat before these final enemy strongholds fell.[103]

Villard described the close of the battle: "The allies crushed the last organized enemy resistance in the Citadel on 25 February. At 0300 the Vietnamese marines attacked toward the southern corner and wiped out the few enemy troops remaining there." The next day President Thieu arrived from Saigon to congratulate General Truong on his great victory. In turn, US forces spread out from the city to kill or capture as many retreating enemy troops as possible. They discovered discarded equipment and important documents left by the defeated foe.[104]

On 29 February the Imperial Palace in the center of the Citadel was secured, and troops from the elite Black Panther Company of the ARVN 1st Division, along with Task Force X-Ray, tore down the PAVN and VC flags that had flown since 31 January.[105]

The battle at Hue was the longest action of the Tet Offensive and "generated more casualties than any other single engagement of the war to that date." Villard stated that 142 marines were killed and 1,100 were wounded. The ARVN lost 333 men killed and 1,773 wounded, while Vietnamese marines lost another 88 killed and 350 wounded; the ARVN 1st Cavalry alone lost 68 killed and 453 wounded. The American 101st Airborne Division reported 6 killed and 56 wounded, while "Allied estimates of the number of enemy killed ranged from between 2,500 to 5,000."[106]

Communist forces claimed to have lost 1,042 troops. The MACV staff reported they had killed 5,133 enemy troops. The two sides also reported the communists had lost about 1,400–3,000 killed outside of the city. All totaled, allied intelligence estimated the PAVN lost 8,000 troops in the city and in fighting in the surrounding area. Thousands of civilians were also killed and wounded by both sides during the battle, and 80 percent of the city was destroyed by American airstrikes. The allies did not go unscathed; one historian stated the Americans lost 216 men and the ARVN 384 soldiers.[107] As USMC captain Myron Harrington was quoted as asking, "Did we have to destroy the town in order to save it?"[108]

The Massacre

As bitter as the fighting had been, what the allies found among the ruins of the historic city was even more shocking. Based on civilian rumors of mass executions, allied troops began a search for missing citizens. They soon discovered numerous mass graves containing the bodies of mostly South Vietnamese officials; the last one was unearthed in 1970. Forensic evidence suggested the victims had been clubbed, shot in the head, or even buried alive; many were bound or displayed signs of torture. The magnitude of the communist massacre of civilians was only gradually realized. Ultimately,

Figure 5.9. Reburying the victims of the communist massacre at Hue

2,800 bodies were found, including men, women, children, and infants, while another 2,000 persons remained missing. Added to these were the several thousands more who lost their lives when caught in the crossfire of the battle.[109]

According to famous foreign-service officer and later historian Douglas Pike, not long after PAVN forces occupied the city, they systematically rounded up dozens of key local Southern leaders, telling them they were to undergo a reeducation program. Ultimately, though, they methodically executed around 2,800 South Vietnamese civilians they believed opposed communist rule. Among those arrested were ARVN military personnel, serving or former government officials, local civil servants, teachers, policemen, and religious leaders.[110]

Historian Gunther Lewy maintained that a captured VC document he saw indicated the enemy "eliminated 1,892 administrative personnel, 38 policemen and 790 tyrants."[111] Former PAVN colonel Bui Tin, who defected to the West, later admitted that communist troops in Hue rounded up what he called "reactionary" captives for transport to the North. Yet as the battle unfolded and keeping captives became difficult, commanders on the scene decided to execute them for expediency's sake.[112] General Truong claimed the detainees had been executed by the communists to protect the identities of members of the local VC infrastructure, whose covers had been blown. The exact events leading to the murder of the victims contained in the mass graves may never be fully understood, but the overwhelming evidence from captured documents and eyewitness accounts points to communist executions.[113]

A Detailed Account of the Massacre

Over the years various publications and international agencies have estimated the death toll of the massacre at Hue was between 2,800 to 6,000 civilians and prisoners of war. Sometime after the battle the Republic of Vietnam issued a list of 4,062 victims identified as having been either murdered or abducted by communists forces there.[114]

Based on this physical evidence and eyewitness accounts, many by American and Vietnamese reporters, officials, and investigators almost immediately came to the conclusion the communists carried out large-scale atrocities during their four-week occupation of the city. These murders were part of a purge of an entire social class, including teachers, government officials, religious leaders, and especially those friendly to US forces in the region. Over time the massacre came under increasing media scrutiny, especially after reports trickled in of the activities of South Vietnamese "revenge squads" carrying out reprisals toward citizens they suspected of supporting the communist occupation.[115]

Apparently, just after the NVA and VC captured Hue on 31 January, the NLF established their own quasigovernment authority, which set about dismantling the existing governmental structure and replacing it with a "revolutionary administration." Using lists that included people VC intelligence officials designated as "cruel tyrants and reactionary elements," cadres rounded up ARVN soldiers, civil servants, members of noncommunist political parties, local religious leaders, schoolteachers, US civilians, and other international people. The cadres combed the city, stating the names on the lists over loudspeakers and ordering them to report to a local school. Those not reporting were hunted down.[116]

It Was Premeditated

The roundup came from orders issued by either the High Command and the Provisional Revolutionary Government or COSVN as part of a 3,500-page compendium released on 26 January 1968 by the Tri-Thien-Hue Political Directorate. Working with the approval of military and political leaders, these cadres were to "destroy and disorganize the RVN [Republic of Vietnam (South Vietnam)] administrative machinery 'from province and district levels to the city wards, streets, and wharves;' motivate the people of Hue to take up arms, pursue the enemy, seize power, and establish a revolutionary government; recruit local citizens for military and "security" forces . . . , transportation and supply activities, and to serve wounded soldiers.'" Further they were to "pursue to the end (and) punish 'spies, reactionaries, and tyrants' i.e., government administrators, civil servants, police, and others employed by or notable adherents of the Republic of Viet Nam; and 'maintain order and security in the city i.e., control the population.'"[117]

Among the other parts of these orders was one aimed at "Target Area 1," or the Phu Ninh Ward. It directed the VC cadres to "annihilate all spies, reactionaries, and foreign teachers (such as Americans and Germans) in the area. Break open prisons. Investigate cadre, soldiers and receptive civilians imprisoned by the enemy. Search for tyrants and reactionaries who are receiving treatment in hospitals" As for "Target Area 2," or Phu Vinh Ward, they were to "annihilate the enemy in the area. . . . Rally the Buddhist force to advance the isolation of reactionaries who exploit the Catholics of Phu Cam." The cadres sent to "Target Area 3," or the wharves along the An Cuu River and from Truong Sung to the Kho Ren Bridge, were to "search for and pursue spies, tyrants and reactionaries hiding near the wharf. . . . Motivate the people in the areas along the River to annihilate the enemy." As for "Target Area 4," or the district including Phu Cam and the Binh Anh, Truong Giang, Truong Cuu and An Lang sections, the orders were to "search for and pursue spies and reactionaries in the area. . . . Destroy the power and influence of reactionary leaders." The cadre in Area 1, Cell 3 was given the job of "annihilation of tyrants and the elimination of traitors."[118] In retrospect, the entire document was a chilling set of marching orders designed to terrorize the population and force them to support the uprising.

In June 1968 members of the US Army's 1st Cavalry found enemy documents that included a directive written two days before the battle at Hue began. These directives for the communist cadres stated: "For the purpose of a lengthy occupation of Hue, we should immediately liberate the rural areas and annihilate the wicked GVN [government of Vietnam] administrative personnel. . . . We must attack the enemy's key agencies, economic installations, and lines of communications. We must also annihilate the enemy mobile troops, reactionary elements and tyrants."[119] Once the communists seized Hue on 1 February, their troops were ordered "to wipe out all puppet administrative organs of the puppet Thieu-Ky clique at all levels in the province, city and town down to every single hamlet." NLF radio broadcasts declared: "We tell our compatriots that we are determined to topple the regime of the traitorous Thieu-Ky clique and to punish and annihilate those who have been massacring and oppressing our compatriots. . . . [W]e ask our compatriots to . . . help us arrest all the US-puppet cruel henchmen."[120]

Douglas Pike has maintained that captured enemy documents directed the communists to take members of the provincial administration out of the city and punish them for their "crimes against the Vietnamese people." South Vietnamese police were to be rounded up and held outside the city. Senior civilian and military leaders were also removed from Hue to await "the study of their individual cases." Civil servants who worked for "the Saigon enemy" out of necessity but did not oppose the communists were destined for reeducation and later employment. Low-level civil servants who had been involved at some point in paramilitary activities were to be held for reeducation but not employed. There were documented cases of individuals who were executed by the VC if they tried to hide or resisted.[121] Perhaps the best summation came from the respected author Don Oberdorfer, who said the killings as "the deliberated and planned execution of government military men, policemen, civil service and elected functionaries and those suspected of working for or collaborating with the Americans."[122]

What the Survivors Saw

The daughter of the deputy mayor of Hue, Nguyen Cong Minh, revealed that her father was seized by the VC at their home after ordering the rest of the family to flee when the communist cadres knocked on their door on the first day. Three days later they told him to report to a reeducation camp. He was never seen again nor was his body ever recovered. In her search for her father, Nguyen went to several mass graves. She stated that many of the dead had had their hands tied behind their backs and their skulls crushed.[123]

In 1971 Oberdorfer, in his book *Tet!*, recorded eyewitness accounts of the massacre. One recalled that Pham Van Tuong, a part-time janitor for the Hue government information office, was on the communist hit list. He and his family tried to hide, but Tuong was found with his three-year-old daughter, five-year-old son, and two nephews. They were all shot by the VC and their bodies left on the street for the rest of the family to see. In 1969 Oberdorfer had spent five days with Paul Vogle, an American English professor at Hue University, talking to those who survived the occupation. Vogle classified all the killings into two categories. One group was the premeditated execution of government officials, civil servants, and those friendly with the United States. The other consisted of nongovernmental civilians who tried to escape questioning, who spoke harshly about the occupation, or who the communist believed "displayed a bad attitude" toward them. This was best exemplified in Phu Cam, the Roman Catholic district of the city, where more than 400 males over fifteen years of age were taken from the cathedral and summarily murdered.[124]

Prof. Horst-Günther Krainick, Dr. Alois Alteköster, and Dr. Raimund Discher, who taught in the medical school at the German Federal Republic's Cultural Mission in Hue, along with Mrs. Horst-Günther Krainick, were arrested and executed by NVA troops in February 1968. Their bodies were discovered on 5 April in a mass grave near the city. In addition, two French priests, Fathers Urbain and Guy, were killed. Urbain was buried alive, while Guy was stripped of his cassock and forced to kneel before being shot in the back of the head. They were found in the same grave with eighteen other victims. Stephen Miller of the US Information Service was executed in a field behind a Roman Catholic seminary, and NBC International journalist Courtney Niles was killed during an attack by communist forces. Philip W. Manhard, a US senior advisor in Hue, was taken to a prison camp in the North and held until 1973. Manhard recalled that during the communists' withdrawal, they killed anyone who resisted being taken out of the city or who was too old, too young, or too frail to make the journey.[125]

After the fact, the search for those who had disappeared proved frustrating. While some graves were found in obvious places, many others were discovered by accident. For example, in one case a farmer ploughing his field tripped on a wire sticking out of the ground. As he tried to remove it, the skeleton of a hand came through the soft earth. Some burial sites were found when people noticed suspiciously green grass in sandy areas. Three VC fighters who eventually defected told allied authorities where the graves of the victims of the Da Mai Creek Massacre were located. In one instance, an ARVN soldier on patrol south of Hue noticed a wire sticking out of the ground. Thinking it was a booby trap, he very carefully worked to uncover it. He discovered the body of an old man, his hands tied together with the wire. Within two days, 130 bodies had been uncovered at the site.[126]

Confirming the Communist Massacre

While the above accounts are sufficient to implicate the enemy occupiers of Hue, communist documents taken later confirm their culpability. Many of these papers boast how they "eliminated" thousands of people and "annihilated members of various reactionary political parties, henchmen, and wicked tyrants." A single regiment claimed to have killed 1,000 people, another 2,867 civilians, and yet another of killing more than 3,000. Another document listed 2,748 executions.[127]

On 26 April 1968, when the allies announced the discovery of the mass graves, officials in Hanoi declared those who had been slain were "hooligan lackeys who had incurred blood debts of the Hue compatriots and who were annihilated by the Front's Armed Forces in the early spring of 1968."[128] In addition, 1st Air Cavalry Division troops captured an enemy diary, in which one entry read: "The entire puppet administrative system from hamlet to province was destroyed or disintegrated. More than 3,000 persons were killed. The enemy could never reorganize or make up for his failure. Although he could immediately use inexperienced elements as replacements, they were good for nothing."[129]

We Were Sort of to Blame

After years of excuses or denial, in February 1988 Vietnamese communist-party leaders admitted to their "mistakes." Still, Col. Nguyen Quoc Khanh, a senior officer at Hue, declared: "There was no case of killing civilians purposefully. . . . Those civilians who were killed were killed accidentally, in cross fire." But he admitted, "some rank and file soldiers may have committed individual mistakes."[130] This opened the door to the controversies that have followed. Adding to it was the memoir of Bui Tin, published in 2002.

While he admitted there had been civilian executions at Hue, he argued that troop discipline had fallen apart as US airstrikes intensified. He also said the "units from the north" had been "told that Hue was the stronghold of feudalism, a bed of reactionaries the breeding ground of Can Lao Party loyalists who remained true to the memory of former South Vietnamese president Ngo Dinh Diem and of Nguyen Van Thieu's Democracy Party."[131] According to Bui Tin, more than 10,000 prisoners were taken at Hue, the most important of whom were sent to North Vietnam to be incarcerated. When the US Marines' counterattack moved closer to retaking the city, communist officials ordered the troops to take these prisoners with them. Bui Tin asserted that in the "panic of retreat," the company and battalion commanders shot their prisoners "to ensure the safety of the retreat."[132]

A few Western historians, such as Marilyn B. Young, have brought into question the "official" number of executions in Hue. In her book on the Vietnam Wars, she said freelance journalist Len Ackland, who was at Hue, has estimated the number to be roughly between 300 and 400 executions.[133] Brilliant Harvard-trained and equally controversial professor Ngo Vinh Long stated in an interview, "there was a total of 710 persons killed in the Hue area, from my research, not as many as five thousand, six thousand, or whatever the Americans claimed at that time, and not as few as four hundred as people in the peace movement here claim."[134]

Villard noted that "approximately 75 percent of the houses in Hue were damaged or destroyed in the fighting." Ultimately, "some 115,000 people were left temporarily homeless. Food quickly ran short throughout the city, although enough remained available to prevent widespread starvation." Lastly, "more than 4,000 civilian deaths were confirmed," and nearly "1,200 of those fatalities came as a result of errant bombs and bullets."[135] Others have estimated that the total casualties were as high as 8,000 civilians, with many deaths resulting from US airstrikes and ARVN revenge squads, who killed dozens after the battle ended. Perhaps James Willbanks summed up the tragedy best: "We may never know what really happened at Hue, but it is clear that mass executions did occur."[136]

Tet, Phase II: Mini-Tet

This bloodletting in January and February 1968 are what many people call the Tet Offensive. But the communist offensive was far from over. Beginning on 13 May 1968, a new round of negotiations began in Paris. Even as the North began these talks, they were also planning a new series of attacks. Late in April allied intelligence estimated that, between February and May, the NVA had sent 50,000 troops down the Ho Chi Minh Trail to replace the forces lost in January and February. In fact, on 29 April, even before the talks began, there occurred some of the most bitter and protracted fighting of the war, lasting until 30 May. The combat began when 8,000 men of the PAVN 320th Division, supported by artillery stationed on the other side of the DMZ, assaulted the American logistics center at Dong Ha, in northwestern Quang Tri Province. The ensuing struggle became known as the Battle of Dai Do. In the end US Marine, US Army, and ARVN forces beat back these PAVN units, which lost 2,100 men, but at a cost of 290 allied defenders killed and 946 wounded.[137]

While it was an important victory for the allies, it was only the beginning. Early on 4 May the communists officially began the second phase of their offensive, or what the Americans called "Mini-Tet," simultaneously striking 119 targets all across South Vietnam, including Saigon. This time allied intelligence was better prepared, eliminating the element of surprise. American and ARVN screening units quickly intercepted most of the communist forces before they reached their targets. Even so, thirteen VC battalions infiltrated the cordon and once again plunged the capital into chaos. At Phu Lam it took two bloody days of fighting before the allies were able to eliminate the VC 267th Local Force Battalion around the Y-Bridge and at Tan Son Nhut. The struggle ended on 12 May, with the VC retreating and leaving more than 3,000 dead.[138]

After this the enemy pulled back, and the struggle gradually subsided. Then on 10 May two regiments of the NVA's 2nd Division attacked the last Special Forces border-surveillance camp in I Corps Zone at Kham Duc, in Quang Tin Province. The camp's 1,800 US and ARVN troops were soon surrounded and isolated. Determined not to repeat the situation that beset US Marines at Khe Sanh, leaders at MACV ordered the air evacuation of the entire contingent of allied troops, thus leaving the base area to the NVA. In retrospect, it was public-relations nightmare that provided the communists with a major propaganda victory.[139]

Two weeks later, on 25 May, enemy forces initiated another wave of attacks in Saigon. Unlike Tet Mau Thanh and Mini-Tet, this time no US installations were attacked. Instead, the VC occupied six Buddhist pagodas, believing the allies would not dare assault them with artillery or air attacks. Once again, the bloodiest engagement took place in Cholon. On 18 June 152 members of the VC Quyet Thang Regiment surrendered to ARVN forces, the largest number of communist forces to surrender during the war. When this second phase of operations ended, there had been 500 civilians killed, 4,500 wounded, and 87,000 more left homeless. The United States had had 1,161 troops killed and 3,954 wounded, while the ARVN had suffered 143 killed and 643 wounded.[140]

Tet, Phase III: The PAVN Assumes the Offensive

The third and final phase began on 17 August 1968. With the VC nearly wiped out at this point, it fell to the PAVN to execute this series of attacks in I, II, and III Corps Tactical Zones. Just prior to this phase, its troops also attacked the border towns of Tay Ninh, An Loc, and Loc Ninh in another effort to divert allied forces away from the cities. On 16 August US Marines made a preemptive strike against communist troops preparing to attack Da Nang. In turn, three PAVN regiments assaulted an Army Special Forces camp at Bu Prang, in Quang Duc Province, only a stone's throw from the Cambodian border. The intense combat lasted for two days before the enemy forces withdrew, leaving 776 NVA, 114 ARVN, and two American soldiers dead.[141]

Once again, numerous attacks hit Saigon but were less persistent and easily rebuffed. Analysts at MACV headquarters deemed the August effort a "dismal failure." As for the communists in five weeks of combat that cost them 20,000 troops, they failed to achieve a single objective or take a single town or city. In turn, the Americans suffered 700 troops killed in action. In what was supposed to be the "final and decisive phase," the enemy had spent so many lives and so much treasure for nothing. But as historian Ronald Spector has noted, "the communist failures were not final or decisive either."[142] While the allies had, by all traditional measures, won a major tactical victory, they had not finished off the communists. Moreover, the subsequent alterations in American strategic policies all but assured the enemy a respite in which to recover and reassess their own policies.

As 1968 wound down, the catastrophic casualties and the incredible suffering the communists had experienced during these continual attacks finally took its toll. It also damaged morale since there had been no obvious military gains that could justify such massive losses. But communist leaders were nothing if not adaptable. On 5 April 1969 COSVN issued Directive 55 to all of its subordinate units, which disavowed "reckless offensives." In part it read: "Never again and under no circumstances are we going to risk our entire military force for just such an offensive. On the contrary, we should endeavor to preserve our military potential for future campaigns."[143] It was a policy that saved the Northern cause and eventually led to victory.

The Results

As noted, the initial assessment of Tet Mau Thanh was that it was a major communist defeat. Leaders in Hanoi struggled to understand why their main goal of creating a general uprising had ended so disastrously. One source contended that between 85,000 and 100,000 enemy troops took part in the initial phase of the offensive and the ensuing phases of the Tet attacks; of this number, 45,267 were killed.[144] Villard's very thorough and balanced study stated, "MACV intelligence estimated that as many as 45,000 of the 84,000 enemy soldiers who participated in the offensive may have perished in the course of the battle."[145]

Why did this come to pass? North Vietnamese leaders underestimated the strategic mobility of US and ARVN troops, which consistently redeployed at a moment's notice to meet any and every threat. The communists' battle plan was excessively complex and nearly impossible to coordinate, as demonstrated by the premature and haphazard attacks of 30 January 1968. In addition, by striking everywhere at once instead of concentrating their forces on specific targets, the communists allowed their forces to be defeated piecemeal. Frequently, their troops assaulted heavily defended positions in massed attacks that ran headlong into the teeth of vastly superior firepower. The results were predictable. Lastly, they made overly optimistic assumptions about potential popular support for the uprising, the underpinning for the entire campaign.[146] In 1983 Tran Van Tra went so far as to declare, "We did not correctly evaluate the specific balance of forces between ourselves and the enemy, did not fully realize the enemy still had considerable capabilities, and that our capabilities were limited, and set requirements that were beyond our actual strength."[147]

This being said, in the countryside the VC and NVA made some progress. One State Department report asserted the VC had "made pacification virtually inoperative. In the Mekong Delta the Vietcong was stronger now than ever and in other regions the countryside belongs to the VC." General Wheeler declared the Tet Offensive had halted counterinsurgency programs, and "that to a large extent, the VC now controlled the country-side."[148] Yet by the end of 1968, this success had begun to erode. The enormous number of losses suffered by the communists reduced their ability to send cadres into the scattered villages of South Vietnam, which led to a resurgence of US and South Vietnamese support among the average people in these rural areas. It is worth noting that one of the reasons the allies were able to push back was the implementation of Abrams's new "One War" strategy, after he became the new MACV commander in June 1968, and the CIA/ARVN's Phoenix Program, which eliminated local communist leaders in the South.[149]

Tet cut the heart out of the basic structure of the VC units in South Vietnam. It had taken the communists nearly a decade to create such an effective infrastructure. In the first ten months of 1968, American estimates determined nearly 200,000 VC and NVA soldiers had been killed and many more thousands severely wounded or permanently disabled. Beginning in late 1968 and continuing until the end of the war, the North had to supplement or replace VC units with their own regular troops. William Duiker has estimated that, by the end of 1968, 85,000 of the 125,000 VC main-force personnel in South Vietnam were actually Northerners.[150] Of course, where the troops came from was ultimately irrelevant except within the overall Vietnamese-communist political world itself. According to some historians, one of the ulterior motives for the Northern push for the offensive was to liquidate Southern party members who might be competitors for power "when" they finally unified Vietnam. While hard evidence of this possibility remains inconclusive, this notion still resonates in some quarters.[151]

Turning Defeat into Victory

Even as leaders in the North wrung their hands over casualties, there evolved a means for translating such massive sacrifice into victory. The NVA commander at Hue, Gen. Tran Do, provided the following spin: "In all honesty, we didn't achieve our main objective, which was to spur uprisings throughout the South. Still, we inflicted heavy casualties on the Americans and their puppets, and this was a big gain for us. As for making an impact in the United States, it had not been our intention—but it turned out to be a fortunate result."[152] Such a strategic outcome had never been anticipated by communist officials. They never foresaw the political and psychological effect the Tet Offensive would have on US leaders and citizens. When they recognized the American reaction, the North Vietnamese began to flaunt their "victory." When negotiations began again, party leaders emphasized the diplomatic struggle as much as the military contest. The very thing the party militants feared most prior to the offensive soon took center stage along with the military struggle.[153]

Within the party itself, things took an about face on 5 May 1968, when, at the Vietnamese Communist Party Congress, Truong Chinh rebuked the radical members for a careless effort at a quick victory. His invective inspired a sober reappraisal within the leadership over which direction the war should take. The debate, which lasted well into the fall of that year, could not have taken place even ten or twelve months earlier. The greatest criticism fell upon Le Duan, the leader of the "main force war" and "quick victory" faction. That same August, Chinh submitted a report that condemned Le's faction. The party congress approved it without reservation, and the report was broadcast on Radio Hanoi. The communist vision of the war shifted 180 degrees when Chinh switched the nation's war strategy and restored himself to prominence as the party's ideological conscience. In turn, the NLF declared itself the Provisional Revolutionary Government of the Republic of South Vietnam and, backed by North Vietnamese insistence, was eventually granted a place at future peace talks. These changes, although not fully understood at the time, proved vital to the communist victory seven years later.[154]

The Devastation in South Vietnam

The Tet Offensive ravaged South Vietnam. Up to January 1968, the cities in the South had suffered little of the destruction of the war. As the communists struck, ARVN forces withdrew from the rural areas to defend the urban centers, the VC filling the void they left. The unexpected and protracted devastation felt by the civil population caused a psychological scar from which many, now homeless, found it impossible to recover. Their confidence in the Thieu government was shaken. The offensive seemed to disclose that, even with substantial US military and material support, their leaders were powerless to protect them from such violence.[155]

The cost in terms of human suffering and material loss was staggering. The Southern government estimated the 14,300 civilians were killed and 24,000 wounded. Equally alarming was the official assertion that there were 630,000 new refugees, adding to the 800,000 already displaced by the war.

Figure 5.10. Residents of Cholon going through their destroyed homes in the aftermath of the Tet Offensive

By the end of 1968, one out of every twelve South Vietnamese lived in a refugee camp. This did not help the counterinsurgency effort to win the hearts and minds of the population. One reliable assessment determined that more than 70,000 homes had been destroyed during the fighting, with 30,000 more heavily damaged. By the end of 1968, the South Vietnamese infrastructure had been all but destroyed.[156]

While the ARVN had performed relatively well—certainly better than the Americans anticipated—their overall morale suffered. Desertion rates increased from 10.5 per thousand before Tet to 16.5 per thousand by July. At that point, the year 1968 became the bloodiest year of the war for the ARVN, with 27,915 men killed.[157] While the efforts of American forces to retake the cities caused numerous casualties, they also did the same among NLF fighters in the villages of rural South Vietnam. In Long An, around-the-clock B-52 Arc Light raids left only 1,415 out of 3,448 local communist guerrillas alive by the end of June.[158]

Thieu's Apparent Opportunity

As for the government in Saigon, it now seemed an opportunity to seize the upper hand in the war. On 15 June the National Assembly approved

President Thieu's request for a general mobilization of the population and the induction of 200,000 draftees into the armed forces by the end of the year. This same bill had failed to pass just five months earlier. The increase brought ARVN troop strength to more than 900,000 men. Thieu also began anticorruption campaigns and administrative reforms, going so far as to fire three of the four ARVN corps commanders for their poor leadership, that helped win political unity. He established the National Recovery Committee to supervise food distribution, resettlement, and housing construction for the new refugees. American leaders also were heartened by what appeared to be a new resolve among even the ordinary citizens in the Republic of Vietnam. Many of those living in the cities were incensed by the communist attacks during Tet, and many who had been apathetic previously became active supporters of the Southern government. Journalists, political figures, intellectuals, religious leaders, and even Buddhists militants avowed support for the Saigon government.[159]

Figure 5.11. Pres. Nguyen Van Thieu contemplates his options

On a less altruistic note, Thieu consolidated his own personal power by undermining his only real political rival, Vice President Ky, the former RVNAF commander who had been forced by Thieu to take the vice-presidential position during the election of 1967. The president now moved to eliminate Ky supporters from the government and military. He also repressed the South Vietnamese media. Perhaps worst of all, Thieu allowed the return of the murdered President Diem's Can Lao Party by putting its members in key government and military positions. These actions quickly disillusioned the citizenry, who began to call him the "the little dictator."[160]

Thieu became highly suspicious of his US allies. Unlike most South Vietnamese, he refused to accept the notion the Americans had been caught off guard by Tet. On one occasion after the Tet Offensive ended, he asked visiting US officials, "Now that it's all over, you really knew it was coming didn't you?" President Johnson's 31 March decision not to seek reelection and to end the bombing of North Vietnam only substantiated Thieu's belief that, if given the chance, the United States would abandon South Vietnam. To the South Vietnamese president, the cessation of bombing and initiation of negotiations with the North brought not the hope for an end to the war, but "an abiding fear of peace." When he met with Johnson on 18 July in Honolulu, the US president assured him that Saigon would be a full partner in all negotiations and the United States would not "support the imposition of a coalition government, or any other form of government, on the people of South Vietnam." Thieu was mollified—at least for the time being.[161]

The Effects on the United States

Tet's strategic effect on the United States was the major outcome of the communist bid for victory. Within the Johnson White House, Tet marked the beginning of the end. Despite the enormous number of enemy combatants killed and the complete failure of their effort to create a popular uprising sweeping them into power throughout Vietnam, the Johnson public-relations staff found it nearly impossible to convince the American people they had won a major tactical victory. The administration's over-confident predictions of victory being just around the corner in late 1967 brought scorn upon the president and the military and soon expanded the growing "credibility gap" into a chasm. To make matters worse, on 18 February MACV reported the highest US casualty figures for a single week during the entire war: 543 killed and 2,547 wounded. By the end of 1968, 16,592 American soldiers had been killed in action.[162]

On 23 February the US Selective Service System announced a new draft call for 48,000 men, the second highest of the war. Five days later Secretary McNamara, the author of the escalation of US participation the war in 1965 who had eventually turned against it, resigned. Concurrently, Generals Westmoreland and Wheeler requested more US forces be sent to Vietnam above those already scheduled for deployment. The JCS chairman told Westmoreland he believed Johnson might even relax operational restraints and consent to US troops moving into Laos, Cambodia, or possibly even North Vietnam itself.[163] On 8 February the MACV commander responded he could use another division "if operations in Laos are authorized."[164] In response, Wheeler questioned Westmoreland's assessment of the situation, alluding to perceived dangers he believed his theater commander had not considered, concluding: "In summary, if you need more troops, ask for them."[165]

Apparently, Wheeler's urging was influenced by the personnel pressure felt by the US military's commitment to the war without the mobilization of its reserve forces. Throughout the buildup, members of the JCS called for a national mobilization, not only in case the war expanded but also to guarantee America's strategic reserve was not exhausted. By suggesting that Westmoreland ask for more troops, Wheeler sought to resolve two problems at once.[166]

By 12 February, when Westmoreland requested 10,500 more men, the attitude at MACV had completely changed from confidence to urgency: "I desperately need these troops. Time is of the essence."[167] The next day the airborne and marine forces requested were sent to Southeast Asia. The JCS tried to force Johnson's hand by urging the president to refuse MACV's request for division-sized reinforcements unless he also called up 1,234,001 reservists. Instead of acquiescing, on 20 February Johnson ordered Wheeler to Saigon to assess the military requirements. Both generals believed things were finally getting better. As a result, MACV would get the troops, reservists would be called up, and within eight days McNamara would be replaced by Clark Clifford, who most people in the military viewed as "hawkish." Surely this meant US forces might finally be able to widen the war and go on the offensive, though Wheeler's subsequent trip report never mentioned this. Instead, the JCS chairman mentioned how grave the situation was in Vietnam and how vital the requested 206,756 additional soldiers were. Westmoreland claimed in his memoir that Wheeler had purposely concealed the truth in order to force the issue of the strategic reserve on the president.[168]

What Wheeler and Westmoreland had overlooked in their little scheme was the economic and financial realities facing the United States. On 27 February, in one of his last official duties, McNamara met with President Johnson to discuss the proposed troop increase. They both agreed such an increase would raise America's total military strength by 400,000 men and require an added expenditure of $10 billion during fiscal year 1969 and an additional $15 billion in fiscal 1970. Of greatest concern was the fact that, in late 1967 and early 1968, the United States was facing "one of the most severe monetary crises" in some time. Johnson's efforts to fund "guns and butter" had brought the nation to the verge of bankruptcy. The government needed a tax increase and budget cuts to prevent out-of-control inflation "and the possible collapse of the monetary system."[169]

From the minute Clifford became secretary of defense, he became anxious about what the public would think of escalating the war. He asked himself, "How do we avoid creating the feeling that we are pounding troops down a rat hole?"[170] A document in the Pentagon Papers asserted, "A fork in the road had been reached and the alternatives stood out in stark reality." If the president accepted the Pentagon's request for more troops, it would mean a total US military commitment. Conversely, "to deny it, or to attempt to cut it to a size which could be sustained by the thinly stretched active forces, would just as surely signify that an upper limit to the US military commitment in South Vietnam had been reached."[171]

With this dilemma facing him, on 28 February Johnson gathered together what became known as the "Clifford Group" to consider a total policy reassessment. Advising the president were McNamara, Clifford, former ambassador Gen. Maxwell Taylor, Deputy Secretary of Defense Paul H. Nitze, Secretary of the Treasury Henry Fowler, Undersecretary of State Nicholas Katzenbach, National Security Advisor Walter Rostow, CIA Director Richard Helms, Assistant Secretary of State for Far Eastern Affairs William Bundy, the Pentagon's International Security Affairs chief Paul Warnike, and Bundy's aide Philip Habib. These were the brightest minds in the government at the time and some of the most influential advisors in the Johnson administration. Many of them contended the Tet Offensive had ended with a US victory that afforded the allies an opportunity to defeat the VC and the North Vietnamese. They argued that taking the offensive at this point meant the United States could end the war on its own terms. Others expressed the opinion that neither side could win a complete military victory and Hanoi could match any US troop increase. They went on to recommend ending the bombing of the North and a change in strategy to end the war short of military victory. These advisors believed this required determination to reach a negotiated settlement. This, they asserted, required a less aggressive strategy designed to protect the population of South Vietnam. The group failed to reach a consensus, and in a final report dated 4 March, they admitted they had "failed to seize the opportunity to change directions . . . and seemed to recommend that we continue rather haltingly down the same road."[172]

On 1 March Clifford succeeded McNamara as secretary of defense. Within one month, Clifford, an ardent supporter of the Vietnam policy and an opponent of McNamara's recent phasedown efforts, turned against the war. Clifford later wrote, "The simple truth was that the military failed to sustain a respectable argument for their position." In the wake of Tet and the meetings of the group that bore his name, the new secretary became certain a drawdown was the only sensible solution. He was increasingly convinced a troop increase would lead to a more violent stalemate. To forward his new opinion, he searched for others in the administration to help him convince Johnson to cap force levels at 550,000 men, to seek negotiations with Hanoi, and to turn responsibility for the fighting over to the ARVN. Gradually and unobtrusively, he found supporters in Nitze, Warnike, Assistant Secretary of Defense for Public Affairs George Elsey, and USAF colonel Robert E. Pursely.[173]

The military leaders saw things in a different light. Major General Davidson, MACV chief of intelligence, later described the secretary's change of heart: "Clifford's use of the Wise Men to serve his dovish ends was a consummate stroke by a master of intrigue. What happened was Johnson had fired a 'Doubting Thomas' (McNamara) only to replace him with a Judas."[174] Davidson was not alone in his bitterness toward Clifford. But considering the subterfuge General Wheeler had undertaken, one wonders if this was more a case of disappointment that the plan had failed rather than one of betrayal by Clifford, who considered his options carefully.

On 27 February Secretary of State Rusk had recommended a partial bombing halt in North Vietnam and an offer to Hanoi of an opportunity to open peace negotiations. On 4 March Rusk once again proposed a bombing halt, explaining that, during the rainy season in Vietnam, bombing was less effective and no military sacrifice would thus occur. In fact, the secretary was unveiling a thoroughly political ploy, knowing full well nothing short of a total bombing halt would convince the North Vietnamese to negotiate anything. Even if the communists did refuse the offer, it put the ball in their court of public opinion, "thus freeing our hand after a short period . . . [and] putting the monkey firmly upon Hanoi's back for what was to follow."[175]

The Media's Role

Even as the internal policy debate swirled about the White House, Westmoreland's request for more forces was leaked and published in the 10 March 1968 issue of the *New York Times*. The article also disclosed this request had led to a serious debate within the administration, during which numerous high-level officials believed any US increase would be matched by the communists and would merely maintain a stalemate, though at a higher level of violence. The article concluded there was "a widespread and deep change in attitudes, a sense that a watershed has been reached."[176] Johnson believed that Undersecretary of the Air Force Townsend Hoopes was the leak. Author Don Oberdorfer later determined the article was based on a variety of sources that the newspaper had pieced together. Another author, Herbert Schandler, surmised that the main sources were the senators Johnson had briefed on the Vietnam situation.[177]

While the *Times* article opened the door, the greatest media influence came from CBS News anchorman Walter Cronkite. Some researchers have argued the news media's reporting of Tet actually made it the apparent "turning point" of public opinion in America. On 27 February 1968 Cronkite took time near the end of his special report from Vietnam to declare: "We have been too often disappointed by the optimism of the American leaders both in Vietnam and Washington to have faith any longer in the silver linings they find in the darkest clouds. We are mired in a stalemate that could only be ended by negotiation, not victory." He concluded that US forces should withdraw from Vietnam, "not as victors but as an honorable people who lived up to their pledge to defend democracy, and did the best they could."[178] Supposedly, when he heard Cronkite's remarks, Johnson said, "If I have lost Cronkite I have lost Middle America."[179]

Changing Directions

In recent years the legitimacy of Johnson's remark has been questioned. Nonetheless, while popular memory views this declaration as the end of the American public's commitment to the war, a reexamination of public-opinion polls of the day demonstrate something far different. Instead of a loss of morale, it appeared that most Americans rallied to the side of the president. A January 1968 Gallup poll reported 56 percent of respondents considered themselves hawks on the war and 27 percent doves, with 17 percent offering no opinion. Even at the peak of the Tet Offensive in mid-February, 61 percent described themselves hawks, 23 percent doves, and 16 percent held no opinion. Given these numbers, it seemed a perfect time for the president to seize control of public opinion by making his case for continuing the fight. Instead, Johnson did not speak to the press immediately after the first phase of Tet. To many, this created an impression of indecision that then resulted in a drop in popular support. Polls at the end of February showed the president's approval rating down from 63 percent to 47 percent. Worse still, in late March the public's confidence in US military policies in Vietnam had fallen from 74 percent to 54 percent.[180]

Figure 5.12. Secretary of Defense Clark Clifford and Secretary of State Dean Rusk in the Oval Office

Once begun, this change in course moved quickly. On 22 March the president formally communicated with General Wheeler and told him to "forget the 100,000" troops. Instead, Johnson agreed to call up 62,000 reservists, 13,000 of whom would be sent to Vietnam.[181] On the twenty-fifth, the president gathered, at Secretary Clifford's recommendation, the wise men, this time former secretaries of state Arthur H. Dean and Dean Acheson, former secretary of the Treasury Douglas Dillon, Gen. Omar N. Bradley, former undersecretary of state George W. Ball, Supreme Court associate justice Abe Fortas, twice former ambassador to South Vietnam Henry Cabot Lodge, former West German high commissioner John J. McCoy, former ambassador General Taylor, Gen. Matthew B. Ridgeway, former secretary of defense Cyrus Vance, and American UN representative Arthur J. Goldberg. Not only were they all highly respected statesmen or military leaders but, with few exceptions, they also had been or were still supporters of the war. Not long after the first meeting, they were joined by Rusk, Wheeler, Bundy, Rostow, and Clifford.[182]

Clifford noted, "Few of them were thinking solely of Vietnam anymore."[183] Bradley, Fortas, Murphy, and Taylor believed the United States should disengage from the war as quickly as possible. This overwhelming disavowal of Johnson's war policy left the president "deeply shaken." The power of their opinion could not be ignored, and thus Johnson decided to curtail the bombing of North Vietnam and to seek a negotiated settlement.[184]

To make matters worse for the president, on 12 March Johnson barely bested Minnesota senator Eugene McCarthy in the New Hampshire Democratic primary 49 percent to 42 percent. While it was clear McCarthy never had the staying power to defeat the sitting president, the result was an indication that a large percentage of Democrats were not happy with America's continued participation in the Vietnam War. If this did not plummet Johnson into a state of depression, dynamic New York senator Robert F. Kennedy soon afterward declared his candidacy for the Democratic nomination.[185] While McCarthy had been an embarrassment, the former attorney general's name and cachet manifested a real threat. Kennedy was also an antiwar candidate.

With events swirling around him, Johnson scheduled a nationally televised speech focused on his Vietnam policy for 31 March. In the interim he and his staff continued to discuss both Westmoreland's troop request and the president's response to the military situation. On 28 March Clifford, who had been working diligently to convince Johnson to modify what was, at this point, a hardline speech, proposed a compromise policy that maintained force levels at their existing size and reiterated Rusk's earlier proposal to offer peace talks for a cessation of the bombing. Clifford was shocked to find that neither Rusk nor Rostow, who had previously opposed any pullback, spoke out against his proposals.[186]

On the night of 31 March, Johnson delivered the modified speech that reduced the deployment of troops to a token force of only 13,500 and unilaterally ordered a partial halt to the bombing of the North. He then stunned the nation by announcing he would not seek the Democratic nomination for a second term as president. He also promised to make every effort to bring about peace negotiations that would lead to an American troop withdrawal from Vietnam. Four days later leaders in Hanoi added to the general shock and surprise by agreeing they would join in the proposed negotiations now expected to begin on 13 May in Paris.[187]

Military leaders were not only dumbfounded but also extremely angry. They felt betrayed. Westmoreland later admitted he was "bitter" and was offended that he "had been made the scapegoat for the war."[188] While he had been at the center of the American tactical processes in Vietnam, he was not the author of foreign—or even defense—policy. Leaders like Johnson, Rostow, McNamara, and others were the ones who formulated the policies that, after Tet, they could not live with and chose to abandon.

All of this became a moot point on 9 June 1968, when Johnson replaced Westmoreland as commander of MACV with General Abrams. This was not a punishment since the command change had been agreed upon in December 1967. When Westmoreland returned to the United States, he was made US Army chief of staff. But in the popular eye, many viewed his reassignment as penance for what by then was being called the Tet debacle. The new drawdown policy was soon demonstrated when Abrams closed the "strategic" USMC base at Khe Sanh, where Westmoreland had expended so many lives, and ended the tactics of large-scale "search and destroy" operations. Under the new MACV commander, there were no more dialogues about defeating North Vietnam. The general's new "One War" policy centered on having the ARVN assume the main combat role—during the Nixon years, this became known as "Vietnamization." The new policy also focused on pacification of the countryside and the destruction of communist logistics with a series of bombing campaigns codenamed Commando Hunt.[189]

In Summary

In the 1968 elections Republican former vice president Richard M. Nixon defeated serving Democratic vice president Hubert Humphrey by a razor-thin margin. Nixon, who ran promising to end America's military role in the war during his first term, secured the Paris Peace Accords on 27 January 1973, five days after Lyndon Johnson's death. In many ways he had become the final casualty of the Tet Offensive and the American war in Vietnam.

In short, the Tet Offensive had been a tactical defeat for communist forces since they lost 30,000–40,000 troops killed and about 5,800 captured and made no real gains in the South. Still, Tet Mau Thanh made it clear to many in the Johnson administration that victory in Vietnam required a greater commitment of men and resources than the American people were willing to invest. When Johnson announced he would not seek his party's presidential nomination and declared a partial halt to the bombing over most of North Vietnam, he also urged Hanoi to open peace talks. Coincidentally, with US troop strength at 525,000 and American military leadership wanting even more men, soon thereafter Clifford refused Westmoreland's request for an additional 200,000 troops. From this time forward, American support for the war in Vietnam declined. During the next five years, US involvement slowly but steadily decreased until March 1973, when the last American troops left Vietnam.[190]

6

The Air Battles Continue after Rolling Thunder

Arc Light, Commando Hunt I–VII, Menu, the Easter Offensive, and Linebacker I and II

While none of these air campaigns was specifically or technically a "battle," each was so important to the pattern and outcome of the war that no adequate examination of combat in the Vietnam War can be completed without examining them. For one thing, nearly half of all American resources were expended on the air war. Spectacular images of aerial combat also played a major role in galvanizing the American antiwar movement. For example, when the "secret" bombing of Laos became public, many citizens, ignorant of the fact the targets were trespassing PAVN troops and supplies coming down the Ho Chi Minh Trail, became outraged over 2.5 million tons of bombs being dropped on tiny Laos. Lastly, many conservative critics of the war believed a resolute bombing of the North alone might have caused Hanoi to agree to a peace settlement that preserved the political integrity of the Republic of Vietnam.

The close of Rolling Thunder in November 1968 did not end allied bombing of either enemy troops in South Vietnam or sites in North Vietnam. There were several more aerial campaigns aimed at various enemy targets throughout mainland Southeast Asia over the next four years. Among these major operations were Arc Light, the B-52 raids that began in June 1965 and lasted until August 1973; Operations Commando Hunt I–VII, which were aerial interdiction attacks focused on stemming the tide of PAVN troops, equipment, and supplies traversing the Ho Chi Minh Trail; the secret Operation Menu, a B-52 bombing campaign carried out under orders from President Nixon against communist sanctuaries in Cambodia; Linebacker I, which bombed enemy targets in the North and South to beat back the Easter Offensive of 1972; and Linebacker II, or the strategic Christmas bombings of December 1972.

Arc Light, 1965–1968

Early in the Cold War, the USAF, through policy, doctrine, and weapons development, focused on its strategic role of delivering a nuclear strike against the Soviet Union or China. It was for this mission the B-52 Stratofortress was built and deployed during the 1950s and 1960s. These strategic bombers were stationed at bases throughout the United States during a time of massive nuclear retaliation, mutual nuclear-force buildups, and US conventional-force reductions. USAF leaders never intended to use their massive strategic weapon for nonnuclear missions. But that is what happened with the initiation of Arc Light sorties during 1965. These raids began during Rolling Thunder and ended after the signing of the Paris Peace Accords.

Even though B-52s were and are strategic bombers, Arc Light was not a strategic air campaign. Its raids were B-52 operations flown out of Guam and Thailand (as well as some from Kadena, Japan) from 18 June 1965 to 15 August 1973. They were missions flown at high altitudes over South Vietnam, Cambodia, and Laos to provide CAS to allied ground forces or to interdict Northern infiltration of troops or supplies. Up to 1968, most Arc Light sorties were flown below the seventeenth parallel, with only 141 missions flown over North Vietnam, all near the DMZ below the twentieth parallel.[1]

The first thirty B-52s arrived in Guam in February 1965. In March, as US Marines landed near Da Nang, the JCS proposed melding B-52s into the new Rolling Thunder campaign. The State Department opposed this proposal, believing it would send dangerous signals of escalation to China and the Soviet Union. Besides, many planners realized that B-52s, with 1965 technology, would have difficulty flying missions in Vietnam since the terrain provided few offset-aiming points or specific ground references to assure accurate bombing. Officials feared that the loss of even one B-52 to enemy fire would be a major blow to America's world image and to South Vietnamese morale.[2] Besides, USAF leadership was displeased the BUFs were in Southeast Asia at all. As the flagship of US strategic nuclear bomber force, senior officers at SAC worried that if too many B-52s went to Asia, they might not have enough remaining on alert to fulfill their role as part of the US strategic nuclear force.[3]

The JCS amended the Joint Strategic Capability Plan in 1964 to require that thirty B-52s be available for worldwide contingency. In April General Westmoreland, during meetings with JCS leaders in Honolulu, implored them to allow him to use B-52s against VC basecamps. The general argued that B-52s were better suited for this job than fighters and fighter-bombers since they could deliver a wide, even pattern over a large area in a short period of time.[4]

In 1965 the notion of large-scale, nonnuclear conventional bombing was inconsistent with the existing SAC mission. Additionally, B-52 crews were trained and their doctrine designed for strategic nuclear conflict. Arc Light area bombing required only a narrow spectrum of the available conventional weapons inventory, including M117 750-pound bombs, MK-82 500-pound bombs, BLU-3B and BLU-26B antipersonnel bomblets, and AN-M65A1 general-purpose and AN-M59A1 semi-armor-piercing 1,000-pound bombs. At first the standard Arc Light load for B-52s based at Guam was forty-two M117s loaded internally and twenty-four MK-82s loaded externally. B-52s in Thailand carried eighty-four MK-82s internally and twenty-four M117s externally. During the first three years of Arc Light, high-explosive bombs accounted for 97.2 percent of the total bombloads.[5]

In May the JCS approved Westmoreland's request. Bomber pilots were used to employing radar to locate ground targets, but in 1965 there was scarce radar data on Vietnam and the airmen had little experience flying over such dense three-canopy jungle. Air-force officials temporarily solved this ground-reference problem with homing and targeting beacons seeded in the target areas. Planners decided once radar files had been built up sufficiently, they would go back to radar-synchronous bombing.[6]

On 15 June 1965, VC forces were discovered near Ben Cat, a regional headquarters ten miles north of Saigon, and a raid was scheduled for the eighteenth. Johnson, fearing negative world reaction from the use of the B-52s, demanded assurances that no civilian areas would be hit during the raid.

Thus, Ambassador Taylor instructed Brig. Gen. George Simler, 2nd Air Division chief of operations, to accompany the mission in a C-123 to guarantee tight command-and-control so no bombs would accidently fall on nearby villages.[7]

Plans called for thirty B-52Fs of the 7th Bomb Wing and 320th Bomb Wing to launch from Guam at 0100; rendezvous for aerial refueling over Luzon, Philippines; and be over the target at 0730. There were ten three-aircraft cells: twenty-four planes carried 51 750-pound bombs, while six carried 1,000 armor-piercing bombs. Things started out as planned, but soon tailwinds from a typhoon in the eastern Pacific pushed the bombers ahead of schedule. When the first cell banked 360 degrees to slow for the arrival of the refuelers, they ran into the path of the second cell in the pitch-black skies over the South China Sea. Two planes collided and crashed into the ocean; eight crewmembers perished, with the four survivors and one body recovered. Only twenty-seven of the bombers refueled; the twenty-eighth bomber suffered a broken hydraulic pump and radar en route and was forced to land in Okinawa. The remaining bombers crossed the Vietnamese coast at 0630 and dropped their first bombs fifteen minutes later from about 20,000 feet. Guiding off a beacon placed in the area the night before, they bombed a one-by-two-mile target box with 1,300 bombs; about half of the bombs hit inside the box. The aircraft then flew south to avoid the Cambodian border, and near Saigon, they turned east toward Guam. One was forced to land at Clark Air Force Base, Philippines, due to electrical problems. The last bomber landed exactly thirteen hours after the first one had departed.[8]

Afterward, three US-led thirty-six-man ARVN reconnaissance teams inspected the area and found no enemy bodies and little damage to the camp area. Later, MACV discovered the VC had fled on a tip from a spy in a local ARVN unit. The raid made worldwide headlines, some terming it a "fiasco." One newspaper compared it to "swatting fleas with a sledgehammer."[9]

While the results were less than spectacular, Westmoreland told the media he now had the perfect weapon to attack a "dug-in enemy target, saturate large areas, surprise the enemy, reduce his safe havens, and encourage the timid South Vietnamese soldiers to venture into Viet Cong base areas." The air staff was not so pleased. One USAF report responded: "Of course, this would have to be balanced against the problem of fixing VC targets with enough accuracy to allow attacks on small target areas. Also, the longer reaction time of Arc Light forces does not allow for a response against transient VC targets."[10]

Altering Tactics and Weapons for Arc Light

Despite these concerns, plans went forward for more Arc Light raids. B-52s flew five missions in July and ten in August. On 2 August 1965 they returned to the use of radar-synchronous bombing. By mid-August, the thirty-bomber flights were replaced by fewer planes flying more missions. Raids no longer had to be preapproved; instead five "free bomb zones" were created and target folders prepared for short-notice missions. Two zones were just north of Saigon, two were at the southern tip of South Vietnam, and the last was just southeast of Da Nang near a suspected VC regimental head-quarters. The JCS assumed final target approval for Arc Light, while West-moreland became involved only when US troops were in the target area to avoid alerting enemy agents again. The smaller raids began on 26 August, and by October, as few as five planes flew in formations, allowing the thirty B-52Fs to carry out multiple missions.[11]

On 14 November 1st Air Cavalry Division units, having repelled an attack against the Plei Me Special Forces Camp in the Central Highlands and mop-

Figure 6.1. B-52D "Big Belly" on a bomb run during an Arc Light raid

ping up near Pleiku, uncovered a secret NVA base in the Ia Drang Valley, near the Cambodian border, defended by two regiments. The allied ground forces called in airstrikes, and eighteen B-52s hit the area two days later, dropping 344 tons of bombs. By late November, they had flown ninety-six sorties against this target and dropped 1,795 tons of bombs.[12]

Modifying the B-52 Fleet

The results of these early raids proved to USAF officials that the B-52s needed to carry more bombs. As early as the summer of 1965, the air force had approved Engineering Change Proposal 1224-7, "Hi-Density Bombing System," to modify eighty-two B-52Ds to carry eighty-four rather than twenty-seven 500-pound bombs or forty-two instead of twenty-seven 750-pound bombs internally, increasing their bombload from 38,000 to 60,000 pounds. The first D model went into modification on 16 December 1965. The following February, approval was granted to modify the remainder of the 155-bomber fleet, which was completed on 8 September 1967. B-52Ds from the 28th Bomb Wing and 484th Bomb Wing deployed to Andersen Air Force Base, Guam, in April 1966, gradually replacing F models in combat. In March 1967 B-52Ds began operating out of U-Tapao Air Base, Thailand. Deployment of the new bombers was completed in early 1968. Of these 155 aircraft, 22 were lost in Vietnam—12 to SAMs.[13]

The USAF selected the B-52Ds for modification for several reasons. There were only eighty-two B-52Fs, and they were running out of flying time. They had no reserve capability and could barely fly the ever-growing monthly sortie requirements of 1965–66. Even though the Ds were older, they were being upgraded in many other basic areas, which increased their life expectancy by 2,000 hours—double that of the Fs. The G and H models were held back for their "more significant SIOP [single integrated operational plan] role"—delivering a strategic nuclear payload. Finally, the Ds were refitted with all-weather capability, a major problem facing all US aircraft in 1965 and 1966. As one 1966 RAND Corporation report noted, "The Air Force had no (conventional weapon) capability for all-weather bombing in [Southeast Asia]."[14]

As noted, the 28th Bomb Wing and 484th Bomb Wing had the first B-52Ds to deploy to Guam in April 1966. When they arrived, however, the base lacked standard ordnance for the aircraft, and there were no MK-82 bombs left on Guam. Until these were shipped from Ellsworth Air Force Base, the Big Belly missions flew with twenty-four M65 1,000-pound bombs internally and twenty-four M117 750-pound bombs externally. The B-52s were not the only ones to suffer shortages. Naturally, in 1966–68, as the sortie rate for the BUFs went up from 100 to 1,600 per month, so did the expenditure of bombs. Soon, this began to affect Rolling Thunder missions as well. Some officers went so far as to privately suggest that US Army leadership in Vietnam was undertaking the Arc Light raids just to steal attention from what USAF leaders perceived to be the more important air campaign over North Vietnam.[15]

Arc Light Expands and Airpower Controversies Grow

By spring 1966, President Johnson had become less concerned with the B-52's negative effect on public opinion, believing they were effectively curtailing enemy infiltration and hurting enemy morale in South Vietnam. Thus, Adm. U. S. G. Sharp, CINCPAC, obtained approval for target designation. But instead of facilitating the use of the B-52s, the new policy compounded the tensions between airmen and ground commanders. To airmen, it was bad enough that army ground commanders were ordering the greatest strategic bomber ever built into a CAS role, but now to have a naval officer pick targets was simply unbearable. Of course, target restrictions and lack of target flexibility was nothing new, having always been an annoying feature of Rolling Thunder. But in those cases the restrictions and target approvals came directly from the White House, degenerating target value and delaying response time.

While Westmoreland was pleased with the new Arc Light policies, Gen. William Momyer, Seventh Air Force commander, worried openly that the entire process not only violated the basic concept of a separate strategic and tactical air force, run by airmen trained in such combat, but also that "Westmoreland's employment of the B-52s as long range artillery to suppress 'what may or may not be suspected concentrations or supply areas' was questionable and relatively ineffective."[16]

Momyer wanted to use the BUFs against specific targets, reserving just two squadrons to fly about 150 sorties a month, while using tactical aircraft to strike enemy concentrations. This disagreement came about partly because no one had any hard evidence of just how effective US air forces were since, as John Schlight has argued in his book on the air war in the

South, there were no "quantifiable assessments, each general adopted a position that fit his preconception of the role of air power."[17]

Normal USAF intelligence and data collection was all but completely absent during the Vietnam War. In previous wars the air force had kept a data catalogue for airmen to use in planning operations. This was not available in Southeast Asia until the 1968 Tet Offensive. Air officers' lack of ability to select CAS targets or how to use their assets to support ground troops also meant it was all but impossible to commit reconnaissance assets to establish the effectiveness of Arc Light or any other raids in Vietnam. Perhaps World War II hero and retired air-force lieutenant general Elwood R. Quesada put it best after returning from a special fact-finding tour in early 1966.[18] In his evaluation of the use of airpower (especially B-52s) in Vietnam, he declared: "Our effort in Vietnam . . . to me as far as air power was concerned was a little bit of what I used to refer to as operational masturbation. I have always felt that the B-52s were to a large extent bombing forests. . . . [I]t was just clear to me that tactical air power as being exercised in that theater was the product of the Army and Army thinking."[19]

There can be little doubt Vietnam was an army show. The direction of the Kennedy and Johnson defense policy, as we have seen, moved away from strategic policies and nuclear bombers toward weapons and policies (mostly ground oriented) designed to conduct guerrilla wars. In the early 1960s the buildup of US Army aviation mirrored this new direction. Eventually, helicopter gunships and transports as well as a myriad of observation aircraft fit nicely into the JCS's Publication 2, *Unified Action Armed Forces*. To the USAF, this new direction was not only a violation of assigned roles and missions but also an expensive duplication of Air Force assets and capabilities. Perhaps worst of all, Air Force Regulation 1-1, *Aerospace Doctrine: Responsibilities for Doctrine Development*, charged Tactical Air Command "to work in coordination with the Army Combat Developments Command to develop mutually agreeable joint doctrinal manuals for submission to the Joint Chiefs of Staff."[20]

In retrospect, one of the primary reasons B-52s had to do a job normally reserved for tactical fighters was the smaller warplanes were being used in large numbers during Rolling Thunder. But another reason was the lack of fighters of the kind needed to carry out CAS or other important tactical roles, especially in the South. Tactical-weapons development and fighter training had reduced the American fighter advantage in all areas, especially air-to-air combat. As Frank Futrell lamented, "It was a tragic irony that the air war in Southeast Asia would necessitate an agonizing relearning process and a hurried adaptation of weapon systems back into an arena thought to have been eliminated [conventional tactical-fighter operations]."[21]

The numbers show just how far the US fell between Korea and Vietnam. During World War II, the best figures available indicate that in Europe, 7,422 enemy fighters were shot down, while US forces lost 1,691 aircraft, a ratio of 4.4 to 1. In Korea the numbers were 874 to 122, or a ratio of 7.2 to 1. In Vietnam the enemy lost 195 fighters—139 to USAF fighters and 56 to USN fighters—while the United States lost 61 air-force fighters and 16 navy fighters, totaling 77 warplanes; the ratio was 2.53 to 1. Of course, this changed once better aircraft, antiradar jammers, and targeting systems like Teaball were employed. In 1972 the ratio reached 5 to 1, but clearly better training also made a big difference.[22]

It is also worth noting that many experts, especially airmen, believed Vietnam was a ground war run by ground commanders to the exclusion of concerns from any other service. To airmen like Momyer, not only was Westmoreland's focus totally on the ground war but army forces also became too dependent on air cover. Maj. Gen. Theodore Milton went so far as to declare, "The Army became over-dependent on air support, and air support of a kind highly vulnerable against a modern force."[23] For these reasons, the B-52 Arc Light raids became the primary support weapon, and in this regard Westmoreland was probably right.

In fact, the B-52s should have been placed directly under Momyer's command since he was in the best position to decide which targets were most valuable and how best to employ all air resources. In the end the JCS concocted a compromise by which Momyer became Westmoreland's MACV air deputy. Under the new plan, operational control was given to Momyer and his subordinate USAF officers, especially intelligence personnel, who were moved from MACV to his own staff. But much remained the same since Westmoreland still selected the targets. As Momyer put it, "as long as Westmoreland picked the targets the aircraft would continue to be used for close air support rather than for interdiction."[24]

Even with this, throughout the years of Rolling Thunder (1965–68), controversy swirled over actual control of air assets. It took Momyer months before he had something resembling a single manager for all tactical-combat aviation. This struggle for control of air assets remained a chaotic malaise of interservice rivalry until, finally, on 18 January 1968 Westmoreland proposed placing all tactical and CAS assets under the MACV deputy for air. When he revealed his plan to Maj. Gen. Norman J. Anderson, commander of the 1st Marine Air Wing, and Lieutenant General Cushman, commander of the III Marine Amphibious Force, they balked. As Westmoreland recalled, "Anderson became rather 'emotional' declaring that the Marine Air Wing belonged to the Marines and no one else."[25]

The disagreement went all the way to Washington, where USMC Commandant Gen. Leonard Chapman Jr. supported his subordinates so vehemently that the overall area commander, Admiral Sharp, decided to have Westmoreland temporarily withdraw the proposal. But the Tet Offensive soon made Westmoreland's reorganization plan a must, and as a result, on 8 March 1968 Momyer was given mission direction and the USAF was finally given overall command. It was a policy continued under General Abrams from 1968 to 1972, and as Momyer remarked years later, it was a policy that "should have been done long before." In fact, in many ways—and as Momyer believed—the turning point of the siege at Khe Sanh was the flexible air response under a single manager, which only came about in March.[26]

Later Arc Light Operations

During April 1966, B-52s bombed enemy infiltration routes through the Mu Gia Pass in North Vietnam and Laos. Among the targets were trucks, road-work crews, and air-defense sites. Westmoreland continued to rave over the results, declaring at one point, "we know, from talking to many prisoners and defectors, that the enemy troops fear B-52s." The annual report by PAVN headquarters, Military Region VII, captured by the 173rd Airborne on 14 March 1966 during Operation Silver City II, seemed to confirm the general's argument: "There was some evidence of reluctance of performing missions for fear of B-52 aircraft."[27]

While B-52 strikes caused great fear, one must question the complete efficacy of these raids. After two weeks of bombing the Mu Gia Pass, MACV requested CINCPAC allow them to continue since the traffic flow had returned to prestrike levels. The admiral replied that while interdiction operations were important, he could "not allow additional B-52 strikes because of the increased danger from antiaircraft weapons: 'Past Arc Light strikes have closed Mu Gia for relatively short periods of time. Results of future strikes probably would not improve this situation significantly. As circumstances stand now, further strikes do not appear justified unless the results can be offset by reducing the threat anticipated.'"[28] The reply not only demonstrated the potential futility of the entire interdiction effort but also demonstrated CINCPAC's justifiable concerns over antiaircraft weapons being placed along the Ho Chi Minh Trail.

In 1966 B-52s dropped an average of 8,000 bombs a month and flew a total of 5,000 bombing sorties. By contrast, US tactical aircraft flew 355,000 sorties, 74,000 of these fixed-wing missions. In March the JCS had approved Westmoreland's request to set the monthly B-52 sortie rate at 450, which he raised to 800 in the second half of the year. The previously mentioned bomb shortage kept this number to 450 until August, while the actual sorties did not reach 800 until March 1967. By late 1967, Arc Light had already cost $780 million.[29]

On 1 July 1966 the first Arc Light Quick Run operations began when six B-52s and six KC-135s of the 4252nd Strategic Wing from Kadena Air Base, Japan, began a modified alert system that reduced response time to nine

Figure 6.2. B-52D at Andersen Air Force Base, Guam

hours from notification to time-over-target. It allowed field commanders to concentrate bombing with the support of the Skyspot rapid-response targeting system, a ground-directed-bombing system in South Vietnam employing SAC mobile ground-radar units. It increased MACV targeting latitude since the selection of targets no longer depended on a nearby prominent geographical feature. B-52s could be guided to targets as long as they were within range of a Skyspot radar point. One report went so far as to say, "Accuracy soon surpassed that of any previously used radar synchronous bombing."[30] While an overstatement, Skyspot did upgrade bombing accuracy, especially regarding target location.

As the actual sortie rates grew to 1,800 in March 1968, the turnover of trained pilots and crews soon caused a problem since "the quantity of rated personnel was insufficient to fulfill SAC's dual mission role during the first three years of Arc Light." Pending separations, valid deferments, medical deferments, and other considerations kept the number of qualified crews low. Since the skills necessary to fly nuclear and conventional bombers were different, training had to be altered in many cases to meet new requirements.[31]

As early as 3 January 1967, overall USAF pilot shortages required officials to recall 2,300 older pilots while instituting new shorter and more intense training programs to qualify 3,247 new pilots per year. In addition, since operations in Southeast Asia required more personnel than continental US bases to do the same job, SAC units in theater had to draw on crews from all over Southeast Asia, thus hampering other operations, including Rolling Thunder. In one effort to solve this problem, SAC officials began allocating hundreds of men to 179-day temporary-duty assignments. Nevertheless, the shortages continued while the crewmen's divorce rate skyrocketed. Despite every effort to remedy these problems, pilot and ground-crew shortages remained a problem throughout the war.[32]

In the summer of 1967, B-52s began Arc Light operations from U-Tapao Royal Thai Air Force Base, Thailand, which meant they could fly two- to five-hour nonrefueled missions instead of the twelve- to fifteen-hour missions from Guam that included dangerous midair refueling rendezvous over the Pacific. On 13 September the final modified B-52D arrived in Guam. While crew training delayed the full use of these new large-capacity BUFs, by the end of the year, they were doubling the Arc Light bomb-delivery rate. In late 1967 B-52 units in Southeast Asia were augmented by elements of the

Figure 6.3. B-52 landing while a B-52D prepares for takeoff at U-Tapao Royal Thai Air Force Base, Thailand

22nd, 91st, 99th, 306th, 454th, and 461st Bomb Wings, allowing a further increase in the number of Arc Light raids. B-52s flew nearly 9,700 bombing sorties in 1967, twice the number flown in 1966. On 6 May 1967, B-52s flew their 10,000th sortie, having dropped a total of 190,000 tons of bombs to that point.[33]

Thus, during 1967, Arc Light was a growing enterprise. During Operation Junction City, 22 February to 14 May, B-52s flew 126 sorties and dropped 4,723 tons of bombs. Of the 2,700 enemy troops killed during the operation, 75 percent died under the rain of bombs from B-52s, including COSVN's commanding general, Nguyen Chi Thanh.[34]

Between 11 September and 31 October 1967, B-52s supported US Marine units defending Con Thien and Gio Linh just south of the DMZ. Fearing enemy attacks were the prelude to a major offensive, allied forces countered with Operation Neutralize. B-52s flew 910 sorties during around-the-clock operations against enemy artillery positions six miles north of Con Thien. All totaled, 3,000 enemy troops were killed.

In late 1967 B-52s flew 228 sorties against thirty-two targets during an engagement between the US 4th Infantry Division and the NVA 1st Division near the Special Forces camp at Dak To. They also flew 36 sorties in late November in support of US and ARVN forces fighting VC main-force units near Loc Ninh. The BUFs made their deepest penetration into North Vietnam to that point when they attacked storage areas and truck traffic 102 miles northwest of Con Thien.[35]

In September 1967 Secretary McNamara requested a report on the air war from the Jason Division, an ad hoc group of eighty-seven high-level scholars and scientists at the Institute for Defense Analyses. Based on CIA data, the group's December 1967 report "categorically rejected bombing as an effective tool." They concluded that enemy transportation, rather than being degraded, "actually had been improved because of added redundancy. Where one road had existed previously, several had [now] been built." They determined the United States was "unable to devise a bombing campaign in the North to reduce the flow of infiltrating personnel into SVN [South Vietnam]."[36]

Despite this compelling report, the JCS tenaciously clung to their belief in the success of bombing and made new proposals they believed would make the air war more effective. These included removal of all restrictions on military targets, the ability to mine all ports, and the wider use of B-52s throughout the theater. Johnson considered all opinions since he was still determined to win the war. He desperately wanted a conventional strategy to defeat the communists, but every time the JCS demanded more freedom to bomb enemy sanctuaries, the president wondered if their next request would be to "bomb targets in China." In one moment of utter frustration, he lashed out at several officers, "Bomb, bomb, bomb, that's all you know."[37]

Figure 6.4. Loading a B-52 for an Arc Light raid

One of the most significant B-52 operations occurred during the NVA's siege of the KSCB, which began in late January 1968. During Operation Niagara (14 January–31 March), B-52s flew 2,707 sorties and dropped 75,631 tons of bombs using a scheduling technique known as Bugle Note, which used ground radar and ground crews to keep aloft an unbroken stream of three to six aircraft that struck enemy targets every three hours. The three-aircraft bomber cells arrived over a previously designated interception point, then picked up by Skyspot ground radar and directed to a series of specific targets. In this way targets could be changed up to two hours prior to release of payload. These tactics also meant the BUFs, for all intents and purposes, could bomb the enemy twenty-four hours a day.[38]

At first the targets were staging areas, storage sites, and artillery positions 3,300 yards outside the marines' outer perimeter. Later, US scouting units discovered an enemy bunker complex inside the buffer zone. On 26 February B-52s and other aircraft bombed within one-sixth of a mile of the US lines. Here, the BUFs proved just how accurate they could be, inflicting no US damage during 589 close-in sorties.[39] President Johnson called the Khe Sanh air campaign "the most overwhelming, intelligent, and effective use of air power in the history of warfare." Westmoreland declared, "The thing that broke their back basically was the fire of the B-52s." A captured NVA officer estimated that 75 percent of his 1,800-man regiment was killed by a single Arc Light strike.[40]

In April B-52s flew in support of Operation Pegasus, the 1st Air Cavalry Division's spearhead to break through enemy positions on Route 9 and end the siege. Later the same month they supported Operation Delaware, a sweep of enemy positions near the Laotian border in the A Shau Valley west of Da Nang. There, B-52s flew 726 sorties and hit 123 targets. Between 19 April and 24 June, B-52s supported Operation Turnpike, an effort to impede "the infiltration of the unprecedented volume of men and material flowing into South Vietnam" since the cessation of the Tet and Khe Sanh bombing raids. The targets were truck parks, storage areas, and troop concentrations along the Laotian border. Some B-52s first cut main artery roads in order to force traffic backups, then others bombed the congested areas.[41]

The pace of the air war changed in November 1968, when President Johnson halted US bombing of the North in a move designed to start serious peace negotiations. Yet not only did regular Arc Light raids continue until 1973, but later President Nixon would sanction secret Operation

Menu missions in Cambodia during 1969 and 1970 as well as six of the seven Commando Hunt interdiction operations over Laos, which lasted from late 1968 to early 1972. For the B-52s, the coup de grâce to their continued involvement in the air war would come during the Linebacker I and II strategic missions of 1972.

Commando Hunt Operations

In the early 1950s, as they struggled to dislodge the French from Indochina, the Viet Minh built a rudimentary network of infiltration roads to supply their units to the south. After the French left and Vietnam was divided at the seventeenth parallel, the new leadership in Hanoi formed contacts with Southern factions for the purpose of reunifying the country under a communist regime. In 1957 the VC guerrillas, supported by the NVA, were established, and over the last two years of the decade, the NLF also came into being to act as the political arm of this antigovernment movement in South Vietnam. Hanoi also created the 559th Transportation Group to furnish the VC with material support from the North.[42]

By 1964, circumstances in the South were in a state of flux after the intractable Roman Catholic strongman Ngo Dinh Diem had been overthrown and killed during a coup the previous November. The focus of US aid and hopes for preserving an anticommunist Southern state, Diem's demise had left South Vietnam with a leadership void and soon near total collapse. Concurrently, a Northern mission to the South, led by Col. Bui Tin, determined "there was little hope that the insurrectionists could, at their current level of support from the north, prevail against the Republic of Vietnam, which [is] . . . the object of lavish American subsidies." Thus, Hanoi determined to up the ante and, even as Washington made plans to commit combat forces, decided to send its regular forces to fight in South Vietnam.[43]

Between April and December 1964, over 10,000 NVA, including the first tactical units, travelled south to support the VC. At the same time, Northern engineers led by Col. Dong Si Nguyen began to upgrade the road network through Laos that would become known as the Ho Chi Minh Trail. In spite of the inhospitable terrain in the Laotian panhandle (or Steel Tiger, as Americans dubbed the area) and during good or bad weather, the NVA engineers carved roads through the mountain passes from North Vietnam into Laos, across the limestone cliffs, and through mountains as high as

5,000 feet. They pushed through the jungles and bamboo forests and forded rivers, including the Xe Pon. As Stanley Karnow wrote, "The communist had added a new dimension to the struggle." In fact, the NVA men and supplies that moved down the new infiltration routes in 1964 were "a trickle compared to the numbers three years later, when they were pouring into South Vietnam at the rate of twenty thousand or more per month."[44]

By 1971, the 559th Transportation Group, now the 559th Military Region, had expanded the trail from "a fragile net of jungle footpaths" into thousands of miles of "well-tended motor roads." Hanoi subdivided southern Laos into fifteen semiautonomous military districts, or "Binh Trams," each with a commander responsible for all functions, including control of transportation, engineering, antiaircraft, liaison, and support battalions. Transportation battalions moved supplies, engineer battalions built and repaired roads and moved supplies if needed, liaison battalions managed the infiltration of personnel along trails separate from those used for supplies, and support groups provided food, shelter, medical services, and other staff functions.[45]

From 1964 on, US leaders realized these supply routes had to be closed by aerial interdiction, but until November 1968 air assets were busy with Rolling Thunder and other missions. Most American aerial efforts were aimed at Southern ground operations, where ground forces attempted to destroy Northern units and supplies once they reached South Vietnam. This is not to say Laos was not bombed, but the full brunt of US airpower would not be felt in the Laotian panhandle until after Tet revealed the full importance of the Ho Chi Minh Trail. On 31 October 1968 Johnson announced a halt to US bombing operations in North Vietnam in an effort restart negotiations in Paris. The next day Adm. John S. McCain Jr., CINCPAC, announced the halt to attacks in Southeast Asia at 2100 hours Saigon time. The last Rolling Thunder mission was flown over the panhandle area at 1930 by Maj. Frank Lenahan in an F-4C of the USAF 8th Tactical Air Wing.[46]

On 15 November Commando Hunt I became the first of seven such codenamed operations, each lasting roughly six months and alternating from the winter–spring dry season (November–April) to summer–fall wet monsoon season (May–September). Attacks concentrated on four primary kinds of targets: against trucks traveling on the Ho Chi Minh Trail, using primarily AC-119 and AC-130 gunships; against the road network, including truck parks, rest areas, and such; against terrain such as passes, river fords, and jungles; and against AAA and, later, SAM sites the enemy placed along the route. The USAF employed fighters or fighter-bombers using laser-guided bombs on the later targets as well as against bridges. The B-52s were particularly effective against the passes and stationary targets such as trucks congregated at chokepoints.[47]

The Seventh Air Force bombed using one-square-mile boxes labeled A, B, C, and D, representing the Ban Kari, Mu Gia, Ban Raving, and Nape Passes. An average of 27 B-52 sorties per day attacked these boxes, while by Commando Hunt V, tactical aircraft were averaging 125 sorties a day. The Igloo White sensor system created by Task Force Alpha at Nakhon Phanom Royal Thai Air Force Base in December 1967 guided the attacks. Originally set up to target enemy troop movements around Khe Sanh, it worked well for the Commando Hunt truck-killing campaigns. During 1968, B-52s supported this operation with 838 sorties in Laos and also flew 156 missions to support Steel Tiger South below sixteen degrees, thirty minutes north latitude. The BUFs averaged 21 sorties per day, flying twice as many during specific surge periods.[48]

While operations worked well at first, USAF schedules became too predictable, and the communists soon adapted their movements accordingly. Generally, the hours the enemy used the trail were from 0400 to 0800 and 1600 and 2000, which "coincided with shift changes at American bases and with changes in the deployment of aircraft. Fighter-bombers usually arrived on station after dawn, at around 0800."[49]

Initially, Commando Hunt operations were confined to a 1,700-square-mile sector of Laos bordering South Vietnam. Commando Hunt I deployed 40 percent of its sorties to cut the narrow roads along the Ho Chi Minh Trail, while 35 percent attacked trucks and storage areas and 10 percent attacked antiaircraft sites. The campaign ended on 30 April 1969, when analysts decided US air forces had inflicted enough damage to force the enemy to use "water routes including the Cambodian port of Kompong Som." By then, average monthly tactical sortie levels, which had been 4,700 in October 1968, had increased to 15,100 in December. The B-52 levels had begun at 273 in October and had risen to 600 by December. During 1968, B-52s flew 3,377 sorties over Laos, but as one author put it, "Notwithstanding their rising material losses, the communists doggedly continued to send a substantial flow of supplies through Laos into South Vietnam."[50]

At the outset of the southwest monsoon season in May 1969, US aircraft attacked the Laotian panhandle again, this time using B-52s to drop 500- and 750-pound bombs, which caused mudslides along the wet mountain passes and helped the rains close the roads. The communists used frequent bad-weather bombing pauses to rebuild these roads and to stage troops, trucks, and supplies along the North Vietnamese border. They also imported more and newer trucks, built a POL pipeline, and set up AAA defenses all along the trail. With bombing of the North curtailed, the enemy built up its convoys in safe havens. As the Seventh Air Force commander, Gen. George S. Brown, put it, "the enemy had a 'free ride' to the border of Laos and South Vietnam."[51]

As the next dry season dawned, the third campaign witnessed the employment of seismic and acoustic sensors to detect truck movements. These were unaffected by darkness and allowed spur-of-the-moment gunship attacks to catch the enemy exposed. From November 1969 to April 1970, B-52s supported Commando Hunt III, and during April and May 1970, they also supported ground operations in both Laos and Cambodia. But "during Commando Hunt III the tempo of air operations declined gradually." In early 1970, intelligence estimates indicated infiltration had decreased more than 50 percent. With growing domestic dissent and the ever-draining expense of what seemed to be a never-ending war to consider, Nixon cut the sortie ceiling on 26 February 1970 as Commando Hunt III wound down.[52] What most US analysts apparently failed to understand was that the North was rebuilding and waiting. In this guerrilla war the enemy required almost no logistics lines since their troops lived off the land, the people, and in this case foreign resupply of vital materials. Thus, the VC and NVA often pulled back from conventional combat or even uprisings like Tet to conserve their men and supplies while they prepared for later campaigns. Such was the case between 1970 and 1972.[53]

As Commando Hunt operations unfolded for the fourth time, B-52s were diverted to Operation Barrel Roll in northern Laos, which supported Gen. Vang Pao and his US operative forces, the native Hmong, in their ever-widening struggles with the Pathet Lao and the PAVN. In late 1970, as Commando Hunt V began, intelligence discovered vast stockpiles of supplies around Tchepone at the upper end of the Ho Chi Minh Trail—a supply hub for communist forces headed south. Leaders, fearing this was the buildup for an attack on Thua Thien and Quang Tri Provinces in northern South

Vietnam, moved to eliminate the depot using ARVN ground troops and US aircraft. Like the earlier bombing of Cambodia, this Laotian incursion was made to buy time, ensure the success of "Vietnamization," and cover the withdrawal of US forces from Vietnam.[54]

The first phase of the Laotian invasion, codenamed Lam Son 719, began on 30 October 1970 as US aircraft cleared Quang Tri and established a logistics base on the Laotian border near the Khe Sanh and Vandegrift USMC bases. They delivered 20,000 tons of supplies and over 12,000 ARVN soldiers in preparation for a ground attack. Phase two began on 8 February 1971, and by the twenty-third over 17,000 ARVN troops had entered Laos, supported by fighter-bombers and 399 B-52 sorties.

On the twenty-fifth 24,000 NVA combat troops counterattacked. This larger-than-anticipated force was supported by 120 tanks, large numbers of AAA batteries, and dozens of mortars and artillery pieces. The ARVN offensive bogged down on 3 March, and a week later another enemy counterstroke forced the South's ground commander, Lt. Gen. Hoang Xuan Lam, to order a withdrawal. The retreat soon turned into a rout. With US helicopters airlifting survivors and B-52 strikes covering the retreat, most of the ARVN troops were extracted by 24 March.

During Lam Son 719, B-52s flew 1,358 sorties and dropped 32,000 tons of bombs, while fighter-bombers flew over 8,000 sorties. Some of the bombs were used to create LZs for helicopters supporting the ground advance toward Tchepone. While these helicopter crews saved thousands of ARVN soldiers, the cost to them was high, with 108 choppers lost and 600 damaged. The United States lost 176 killed, 1,042 wounded, and 42 missing, many of them dying while saving their South Vietnamese allies. The operation officially ended on 6 April 1971, with the enemy losing an estimated 14,000 killed and 4,800 wounded as well as 20,000 tons of food and ammunition, 156,000 gallons of fuel, 1,530 trucks, 74 tanks, and 6,000 individual weapons destroyed, mostly due to airstrikes. The ARVN lost 1,519 men killed, 5,423 wounded, and 651 missing; 75 tanks; dozens of APCs; 198 crew-served weapons; and 3,000 individual weapons. During the retreat, ARVN forces also abandoned large quantities of undamaged weapons and supplies, which the communists salvaged and used.

Commando Hunt VI lasted from May to October 1971 as a diminished operation. Yet during this time, the enemy flow of traffic down the Ho Chi Minh Trail actually grew markedly. The North added 140 miles of new roads,

Figure 6.5. SAMs like this SA-2, were always a major threat to US aircraft in Southeast Asia

and by October had over 2,170 miles of single-lane roads, multilane roads, parallel routes, bypasses, and spur roads available in Laos. The communists also added 344 AAA batteries and dozens of SA-2 SAM sites most along the Laotian–North Vietnam border as well as new MiG bases in southern North Vietnam. One estimate placed 96,000 NVA troops in Laos, 63,000 in Cambodia, and 200,000 in South Vietnam. Concerned US leaders planned a final campaign.[55]

Plans for Commando Hunt VII called for US air forces to bottle up the North's transport system within Laos, employing B-52s to close the passes leading from North Vietnam into Laos and subsequently from Laos into Cambodia and South Vietnam. Planners hoped to force enemy vehicles to congregate in truck parks where they would be attacked and destroyed. Concurrently, BUFs would bomb other roads to divert traffic to specific routes where gunships and tactical bombers could attack exposed vehicles with "predictable success." That was the plan anyway.[56]

At the outset US intelligence discovered 310 additional miles of uncharted main roads as well as hundreds of miles of small backroad cutoffs and bypasses that helped keep supplies moving. In the early years the communists had built roads along "the paths of least resistance," usually near rivers or in valleys, but this made them vulnerable to flooding and mudslides.

As they gained experience and better equipment, roads began appearing at higher altitudes. Most were twelve- to fifteen-feet wide and surfaced with gravel, logs, or, where drainage was poor, bamboo. While this network could not sustain heavy traffic during the rainy season, some always could get through.[57]

Road maintenance during Commando Hunt VII required 96,000 support personnel, an increase of 35,000 from 1971. When Laotian roads were unusable during the rainy season, the enemy partially compensated by using the swollen rivers, whose powerful currents carried supply containers rapidly over long distances. The communists often used the Kong and Banhiang Rivers, whose tributaries flowed across the DMZ into Laos, locating transshipment points. where supplies were unloaded using nets and booms and stored for transport by trucks or porters, several miles apart.[58]

The North also constructed pipelines. Three ran into Laos from Vinh in the North Vietnamese panhandle, near docking facilities for Communist Bloc tankers. They continued through the Mu Gia Pass to points along the northern parts of the trail, where they serviced truck parks and other facilities in and around Ban Phanop. Another ran "through the Ban Raving Pass to a distribution point near Tchepone." From here other lines "extended to the Lao Bao Pass and the A Shau Valley, both major entrances into South Vietnam." They were made of imported Soviet plastic pipes and connected with metal couplings. Soviet-made pumps pushed through them motor oil, gasoline, diesel fuel, and kerosene. A variety of "petroleum products could be sent along the same line. Water mixed with detergent separated the shipments and prevent[ed] contamination."[59]

Of all the Commando Hunt operations, Commando Hunt VII (1 November 1971–31 March 1972) witnessed the greatest use of B-52s and employed the latest airborne technology and weaponry available. OV-10 Bronco forward-air-control aircraft directed laser-guided bombs dropped by fighters directly on their targets. Target-detection had been upgraded on most US aircraft, especially the AC-119 and AC-130 gunships and the B-57G Canberra tactical bombers. Other upgrades included lowlight-level televisions, illuminators, beacon-tracking radar, and infrared sensors. New F-4 fighters equipped with the LORAN long-range electronic-navigation position-fixing bombing systems provided all-weather bombing capabilities.[60]

Commando Hunt VII developed in three phases, with initial operations centered in the Steel Tiger areas of Laos. Phase one began when US aircraft, primarily B-52s, struck the Mu Gia, Ban Karai, and Ban Raving Passes as well as areas in the western DMZ. Concurrently, fighter-bombers carrying laser-guided bombs attacked earthmoving equipment repairing roads. As the roads dried, the B-52s struck the southern routes at the Ban Raving Pass and western DMZ to detour traffic through the northern Mu Gia and Ban Karai Passes.[61]

As planned, the B-52s bombed target boxes. The Mu Gia Pass contained the A, or Alpha, boxes, encompassing an area of thirteen by eighteen nautical miles. The Ban Karai Pass was designated with B, or Bravo, boxes that held an area of fourteen by fourteen nautical miles, while the Ben Raving Pass had C, or Charlie, boxes containing an area of twenty by twenty-one nautical miles. The Delta boxes were located in the western DMZ and measured five by twelve nautical miles. During the first three weeks, tactical aircraft and B-52s dropped 14,400 instantaneously fused 500-pound bombs, 17,100 750-pound bombs, and a few dozen 2,000-pound laser-guided bombs, MK-36 magnetic-influence mines, and cluster-bomb antipersonnel mines.[62]

The initial bombing appraisal determined that "enemy traffic had been slowed some of the time in some places." By 4 November, intelligence indicated the Mu Gia Pass roads were already being repaired, with a near-normal flow of supplies and personnel. During 10–17 November, bombing resumed with good results. Even so, the communists proceeded to build up supplies in preparation for an offensive against South Vietnam.[63]

During phase two, which began in late November, US aircraft struck enemy units as they moved south. Roads were cut by B-52s, whose bombs left large craters and created "choke points" and "blocking belts." As enemy truck traffic backed up, USAF fighters attacked with laser-guided bombs using data gathered from Task Force Alpha sensors. They also seeded the area with airdropped mines. As enemy units attempted to clear the mines or repair the roads, further attacks caught them exposed and caused great destruction.[64]

During Commando Hunt VII, three major blocking belts were created—the Tchepone belt, composed of six blocking points created from 23 November 1971 to 22 January 1972; the second belt, forty miles south of Ban Bak, with two points formed 24–26 December 1971; and the final belt near Chavane, with a point set up on 15 February 1972 and a second on 2 March. The last belt proved nearly useless since the North abandoned this route at the outset. In the Tchepone belt, three blocking points were retained effectively until 2 February, however, point 427 on highway 92C was never actually closed because the NVA ignored the other blocking points and concentrated on maintaining that one spot. Even though traffic slowed because of detours, this belt was always open. Despite the heavy bombing, neither of the Ban Bak points was closed for very long. According to Seventh Air Force analysts, "the North Vietnamese were able to keep both points breached most of the time."[65]

The final phase began in early 1972 and shifted attacks to exit points from Laos into South Vietnam and Cambodia as well as against enemy AAA batteries. Fighters and fighter-bombers flew 31,500 sorties, half by the USAF, while B-52s flew 3,176 more. The BUFs lost thirteen planes. Official reports claimed that large numbers of enemy vehicles were destroyed or damaged, with thousands of NVA troops killed and tens of thousands of tons of supplies destroyed. Officials declared the operation a success that had prevented another Tet-style offensive.[66]

On 31 March 1972 Commando Hunt came to a halt, a day after General Giap launched the Easter Offensive into South Vietnam, since "the resources of the US Air Force in Southeast Asia were insufficient, even with considerable augmentation, to continue interdiction in Laos while seeking to blunt the enemy's bold thrust."[67] Concurrently, Seventh Air Force officials proudly claimed 4,727 truck kills and that only 5,024 of the 30,947 tons of supplies sent into Laos ever reached Cambodia or South Vietnam. Yet Gen. Alton D. Slay, who directed the operation, did not agree with this evaluation. He later declared there were several factors that explained "the failure of the interdiction effort to produce a higher degree of success."[68] His deputy, Brig. Gen. Richard G. Cross, echoed this in his end-of-tour report, writing, "this interdiction effort failed to prevent the enemy from positioning sufficient supplies to initiate an all-out offensive against South Vietnam."[69]

For all the efforts of three and a half years, Commando Hunt left many questions as to its value. It probably helped buy the United States time to withdraw its ground forces and begin Vietnamization, but as Earl Tilford has pointed out, "The strongest evidence against the reputed success of Commando Hunt was North Vietnam's launching of a major invasion against South Vietnam in late March 1972." Of course, there are also those who have argued the supplies and troops used in 1972 "had been carefully husbanded and stored in Laos over a period of four years." There is no question many enemy soldiers and tons of supplies came south between the end of Tet and the start of Commando Hunt VII, but this means if that one iteration was a success, then the other Commando Hunt operations were not.[70]

Perhaps the greatest controversy comes from the vast claims of trucks destroyed since, if one follows the official indices for success in all the operations, then it should have been impossible for the communists to launch any kind of offensive. After Commando Hunt V MACV officials created a flurry of controversy when they estimated that 16,266 trucks had been destroyed and 4,700 damaged. In retort the CIA quickly pointed out such figures "more than doubled the total number estimated in all of North Vietnam and Laos."[71]

Officials claimed US aircraft overall had destroyed 11,009 trucks and damaged 8,208 others, well above the 4,727 destroyed and 5,882 damaged in Commando Hunt VII alone. In both cases the criteria for truck-damage claims were haphazard. If a vehicle was seen to be hit and stop, it was claimed. This basically proved nothing since most drivers, when attacked, abandoned their vehicles to seek shelter. Most trucks hit by gunships might have holes in them, but they still might be useable. Later tests by US vehicle units proved that unless a truck blew up or burned, it was hard to destroy. Besides, the enemy had many overhaul facilities along the Ho Chi Minh Trail, and damaged trucks were quickly repaired.[72]

Moreover, the North was importing trucks from the Communist Bloc at a rate of between 4,500 in 1968 to around 10,000 in 1972, and "even if the US Air Force destroyed 4,727 trucks during Commando Hunt VII, such losses were probably insufficient to disrupt the logistical operations of the North Vietnamese for extended periods, if at all." The Seventh Air Force estimated at the beginning of Commando Hunt that there were 2,000–3,000 trucks in service along the trail. This was an estimate probably based on how many vehicles it would normally take to operate the infiltration routes. But it ignores that others, such as Task Force Alpha, using photographic reconnaissance, had indicated the communists had "about 9,850 trucks in storage." Historian Eduard Mark has argued, "even if it be assumed that the 3,000 initially in Steel Tiger were destroyed twice over (which was not claimed), the North Vietnamese would still have been able to replace the trucks destroyed with those in reserve at the beginning of the dry season, to say nothing of those subsequently received from the Soviet Union and other communist countries."[73]

Of course, the number of trucks getting through was important mainly in regard to how much material got to communist forces in the South. Using sensors for detection, supply tonnage was derived from the number of trucks getting through—US analysts multiplied each truck by 3 tons in the dry season and by 4 tons, or the maximum capacity of these vehicles, when the roads were completely dry. Thus, the total number of estimated trucks predicted the amount of material transported starting out. In turn, this estimated starting supply total was then reduced by the number of trucks destroyed, using these same calculations, and the throughput was determined. To this end, 3 tons were subtracted for each southbound truck hit, while 1.5 tons were subtracted for each one in a truck park. An additional ton was subtracted if the truck was moving, but only a half ton if it were stopped. If the direction of the truck could not be determined, the subtraction level was divided by two. An additional two-tenths of a ton was subtracted for observed fires at storage areas and a half ton for an explosion.[74]

The entire technocratic process was generally denounced by most intelligence operations, including the CIA, which dubbed it playing the "numbers game." Based on their own sources—usually agents inside the enemy forces—CIA analysts concluded, "Communist forces in South Vietnam were only occasionally inconvenienced by interdiction." Since the sensors were vulnerable to the damp climate and later to circumvention, their reliability was (and remains) suspect. The best proof of this was that by March 1972, two hundred PAVN tanks entered South Vietnam almost entirely undetected. The theory of great material loss when a truck was disabled or damaged is also doubtful, not only because they were easily repaired but also because of the simple, but effective, precautions the communists took to save supplies, such as covering precious southbound cargoes with bags of rice. If the trucks were hit with bullets or fragments, the bags absorbed them and as long as the vehicle did not burn, even if it was inoperable, the supplies got through.[75]

Thousands of young men and women lived in work camps near the trail and quickly repaired it at night and during bad weather, also extending the road network into small auxiliary roads through the dense jungle and underbrush to diversify and actually improve it. The road system was thus too redundant and too easily repaired to be a good target. The communists also built an entire route system in western Laos that was almost uncharted and nearly devoid of sensor coverage. Worse, the years of bombing so defoliated the landscape that it "probably made it easier for the North Vietnamese to keep the passes open." B-52 bomb patterns were so evenly distributed through a target box that few bombs on average actually struck the narrow roads. Where they did, the work crews built temporary bypasses in defoliated areas, where the soil, "tilled by thousands of bombs, had become easier to work."[76]

The enemy also used waterways and coastal routes not often scrutinized or covered by US aircraft. They floated down the rivers barrels and plastic bags of supplies, which barely broached the surface and were difficult to detect from the air. Dams and channeling walls were also hard to hit and easy to repair—after bombings, one only needed to collect the scattered dam stones, piledthem back, and the repair was complete.[77]

The sensors, while effective at first, were soon discovered by NVA forces, which devised dozens of ways to circumvent or trick the units and those listening. Originally, the Commando Hunt VII sensor field consisted of 160 strings arrayed to monitor thirty-three potential target areas. Each string was to have eight sensors—five seismic and three acoustic. But Seventh Air Force experts analyzing precampaign intelligence data determined that the North had expanded its route structure, thus at the last minute commanders ordered Task Force Alpha to reduce the number of sensors in each string to five—three seismic and two acoustic. This meant a reduction in accuracy, though necessary to assure coverage.[78]

Sensors had a short lifespan of 60–160 days under normal conditions. The first strings were seeded on 8 September 1971, but Commando Hunt VII did not begin until November, thus many were not functioning. To add to the predicament, the aerial campaign was competing for sensors with Operation Island Tree, which was attempting to detect the infiltration of enemy soldiers. As the Commando Hunt operations began, Task Force Alpha units were reseeding at a rate of about nine a day. This greatly reduced the overloaded computer's data-output accuracy. The enemy soon realized that seeding aircraft dove differently than bombing aircraft, and they could fix the general location of many of the sensors by observation. Some strings were neutralized, but more often the communists opted to deceive rather than disable the sensors. To fool the Black Crow ignition-and-exhaust-detection sensors, they began to wrap their ignition systems with aluminum foil to suppress electromagnetic emanations. To counter infrared sensors, they placed layers of banana leaves and bamboo over hotspots on vehicles.[79]

The airdropped magnetic-influenced mines used by the USAF proved to be just as ineffective, having been designed to work against steel-hulled ships and thus having limited effect on wooden boats. The communists most often cleared mines that formed the blocking belts by throwing rocks tied to ropes or cords into the minefield. As they retracted the ropes, they caught the tripwires on the wide-area antipersonnel mines, causing them to explode. Sappers disarmed the pressure-sensitive gravel mines by picking them up and detonating them elsewhere. In addition, many of these mines were not functioning due to the extreme dampness of the Laotian jungles. Once through these barriers, it was easy for sappers to defuse the MK-36 magnetic-influence mines. Whenever the NVA was able to marshal such resources, they cleared blocking points in "fewer than twelve hours."[80]

During Commando Hunt VII, enemy air defenses were far more vexing than during previous campaigns. The Seventh Air Force determined the North had 345 23-mm to 57-mm guns at the outset of the campaign. This number rose to 554 during the height of operations, with six of those being 85-mm weapons and one a 100-mm gun. Task Force Alpha disputed these numbers, estimating the enemy had 600–700 guns by the end of Commando Hunt V and 1,500 at the height of Commando Hunt VII. Afterward, Pacific Air Forces reported a total of eighteen aircraft were shot down over southern Laos: nine F-4s, five OV-10s, one USN A-4, one USN A-7, one AC-130, and one A-1.[81]

One other problem was the appearance of SAMs near the target areas. During Commando Hunt V, there had been 49 launches, while during Commando Hunt VII, there were 153. On 9 November USAF intelligence sources detected SAMs at a target site, and the B-52s scheduled to make the raid stood down until the threat could be assessed. Fighters could not keep this particular route package closed because only the B-52s' bombing caused the necessary cratering. Enemy traffic surged south as the roads dried and the passes opened. The B-52s returned to bombing on the twentieth but once again were called off because a MiG-17 fired a single missile at the vulnerable old BUFs. The bombers returned on 21–22 November for the final days of phase one, but by then many convoys had escaped south.[82]

Lost sortie rates due to SAM threats continued during phase two. Their real danger was demonstrated over the Mu Gia Pass on 12 December, when an F-105 was destroyed by a Soviet-built SA-2, utilizing its twenty-four-mile effective range. Not only did the B-52s have to be cautious but so did the AC-130s. On 13 January 1972, with SAMs located near Tchepone, the lumbering gunships were withdrawn from the vital Steel Tiger region. Only after intensive fighter-bomber attacks over 11–15 January reduced the threat could the AC-130s return. Even so, on 29 March, ten miles north of Tchepone, an SA-2 brought down an AC-130, killing the crew of fourteen. Three other AC-130s and three AC-119s were damaged by AAA fire during March, which led to a stand down by gunships until the operation ended on 31 March.[83]

As phase two shifted south and west in early December 1971 to force the enemy to take longer routes, the NVA moved some of its SAM sites as well. As a result, on 7 December B-52s were withdrawn from operations around the Mu Gia and Ban Karai Passes, and neither target was attacked again during Commando Hunt VII until 9–10 March 1972, when Ban Karai was raided. Besides, enemy road building had increased so much by January 1972 that even if the B-52s had been available, it is doubtful they could have "kept pace with it."[84]

Not only were the B-52s pulled off bombing major passes and routes in Laos for extended periods of time but also the gunships, the most effective antivehicle weapon. Equally important was the USAF's expenditure of 4,066 fighter-bomber sorties in attempting to suppress enemy AAA and SAM air defenses. Since these aircraft also flew 4,209 sorties against vehicular targets, this meant that nearly half of all fighter-bomber sorties were diverted from their primary interdiction missions. Finally, while MiG-17s posed a lesser threat, their mere presence forced the USAF to plan for potential interceptor attacks, again diverting attention from the primary task.[85]

The communists also sought shelter at night, when US fighters and bombers did not usually fly. The Americans soon overcame this encumbrance by employing the AC-119K and AC-130A/E fixed-wing gunships. The AC-119K Stingers used their four 7.62-mm Gatling guns, two 20-mm cannon, and infrared sensors to run up a remarkable nighttime truck-kill ratio. Even more lethal were the AC-130s, with their two 40-mm cannon and two 20-mm cannon; later models were fitted with a 105-mm cannon in place of one of the 40-mm weapons. They too carried a wide range of sensors, such as "infrared detectors to pick up the heat of engines and exhaust, lowlight television, and ignition detectors to register the electrical emanations of operating internal combustion engines."[86]

The United States used sixteen AC-119s and eighteen AC-130, with the 130s claiming 7,335 truck kills and the 119s 940, compared to 461 by B-57s and 1,873 by fighter-bombers. Sensors made the AC-130s particularly deadly at night, but the enemy discovered these sensors were blinded by daylight, having a hard time visually fixing targets at dawn and at dusk. As Slay later noted, "we never did get a handle on the early movers at dusk and the late movers at dawn."[87]

In addition, US bombing efforts were never well coordinated since each group of attackers—gunships, night raiders (B-57Gs and A-26s), fighter-bombers, B-52s, and Task Force Alpha—all pulled in opposite directions. In typical bureaucratic fashion, during this time of withdrawal from Vietnam, each unit sought to justify its own existence and funding. Perhaps most damaging of all was the bombing halt over North Vietnam begun in late 1968. As previously noted, this gave enemy units a head start along the early part of the Ho Chi Minh Trail and staging areas from whence they fanned out all over the bypass roads of Laos.[88]

The Legacy of Aerial Interdiction

As French officers and authors had emphatically suggested in the mid-1950s, and USAF authors declared in the 1960s, aerial interdiction, especially in the jungles of Vietnam, was a very difficult task. Commando Hunt consistently experienced many of the frustrations of which these early writers had warned. Thus, even though the B-52 and tactical air raids seemed to destroy great numbers of trucks, they never seemed able to stem the flow of enemy supplies into South Vietnam. The fact that the North was able to stage vast quantities of supplies, tens of thousands of troops, and two hundred tanks in preparation for launching the Easter Offensive of 30 March 1972 indicates that even the two most ambitious operations, Commando Hunt V and VII, were only marginally successful. As noted, this was due in part to the ever-growing (96,000 by the 1970s) and well-organized repair forces stationed along the extensive and redundant paved roads, dirt trails, footpaths, and waterways that made up the Ho Chi Minh Trail. During the late 1960s and early 1970s, keeping these infiltration routes open became a national obsession in North Vietnam.[89]

Spotting well-disguised enemy movements in the dense jungles, fog-shrouded mountains, and vast, sparsely populated regions of Laos and Vietnam proved a very difficult task for American pilots. The torrents of the monsoon season also meant that the communists had periodic relief from bombing raids. Not only finding the targets but also maintaining blocking belts and chokepoints, not to mention actually destroying trucks, proved difficult. Besides, the massive resupply of vehicles from the Eastern Bloc and the growing sophistication of the massive POL pipeline complex throughout North Vietnam and Laos made it next to impossible to totally cut off communist lines into South Vietnam. Again, and it cannot be over emphasized, one of the biggest reasons for Commando Hunt's lack of success was the fact that it began after Rolling Thunder ended, leaving a gap during which the enemy took a head start down to the Ho Chi Minh Trail.[90]

The PAVN invasion of 1972 changed the air war again. With the need to resupply 200,000 combat troops, the North employed long logistics networks that soon experienced the full furry of US airpower. Linebacker I and Arc Light raids in South Vietnam would be the deciding factors in preventing the fall of the South—at least in 1972.

The Beginning of the End—the 1972 Nguyen Hue Offensive and the American Response

By 1972, Nixon, who had become president amid promises to end US involvement in Vietnam, seemed no closer to a settlement than his predecessor despite the diplomacy of Dr. Henry Kissinger and the withdrawal of nearly 500,000 US troops. On 30 March, as the president considered his next move, 120,000 communist regulars, supported by artillery and two hundred tanks, invaded South Vietnam, threatening to overrun America's ally. The invasion, the centerpiece of the Nguyen Hue, or Easter Offensive, violated the agreements reached between Washington and Hanoi when Johnson had ended the bombing of the North in 1968. While Nixon was concerned South Vietnam might fall, he now had an excuse to discard the restrictions that previously had prevented him from fully employing airpower.[91]

The Easter Offensive lasted from 30 March to 16 September 1972. The enemy named it the Nguyen Hue Offensive in honor of the Vietnamese emperor who had defeated Chinese invaders in 1789. Using the rainy season to avoid US air attacks, General Giap ultimately committed fourteen divisions and twenty-six separate regiments. One division was placed in northern Laos to protect supply lines, while four others remained on the border in North Vietnam in reserve.[92] Enemy goals were to erode flagging US public war support during an election year, to counter South Vietnamese successes in rural areas since 1969, and to win the war before Nixon's detente policy effected Soviet and Chinese material support of Hanoi.[93] What Hanoi failed to grasp was the audacity of the attack "provided Nixon with the public support necessary to retaliate."[94]

Linebacker I

American forces were not completely caught off guard this time, even though scheduled reductions in US troops to 69,000 in May 1972 and aircraft to 375 left them reeling from the initial attack. In the spring of 1971, the CIA had warned of a potential election-year attack, but they believed the enemy could not "launch a nationwide military offensive on anything approaching the scale of Tet 1968."[95] Nonetheless, the PAVN deployed two hundred tanks undetected to various staging areas in 1971–72, and as one analyst later noted, "This stealthy deployment, together with the persistent perception that the enemy's logistical system was less efficient than it was,

Figure 6.6. Le Duc Tho and Henry Kissinger at the Paris Peace Talks

deflected American intelligence analysts from a correct understanding of communist plans."[96]

The initial attack was launched by 50,000 troops coming from Laos against Quang Tri Province in Military Region I. On day two, 160 miles south of the DMZ in the Central Highlands in Military Region II, 28,000 more NVA soldiers attacked Kontum Province. The enemy opened a third front with 31,000 men attacking 375 miles south of the DMZ and 60 miles west of Saigon. Of the 200,000 enemy troops eventually involved, 130,000 were PAVN regulars and 50,000 VC main-force troops. Supported by tanks and artillery and protected by low clouds, communist units in Military Region I pushed ARVN units out of Quang Tri City by 1 May. The new ARVN commander, General Truong, retreated south to set up a defensive line on the south bank of the My Chanh River. By 14 May, PAVN units in Military Region II had overrun Dak To and placed Kontum City under siege, while in Military Region III they had destroyed an entire ARVN division, taken Loc Ninh, and surrounded An Loc by 13 April.[97]

At An Loc the VC 9th Division fought the ARVN 15th and 21st Divisions. On 11 May, with the eastern part of the city under attack, one enemy prisoner of war later recalled that B-52s struck about 0500. The BUFs pounded the eastern approaches to the city hourly for more than a day, hitting several locations more than once. Whole units were wiped out. Five days later a PAVN column, aided by twenty tanks, attacked an ARVN force just south of Kontum City on Route 14. Three cells of B-52s attacked the column and "obliterated" it. On the twenty-sixth the enemy made a last unsuccessful assault on Kontum City that was repelled by the ARVN defenders supported by B-52s.[98]

In December 1971 Nixon, concerned by the abovementioned intelligence reports, had responded with Operation Proud Deep Alpha, during which USAF fighters flew over 1,000 sorties against enemy staging areas just south of the twentieth parallel. Additional attacks took place in February 1972 but were limited during the president's trip to China. Simultaneously, the number of US aircraft in Southeast Asia increased with the dispatch of 207 USAF F-4s from 29 December 1971 to 13 May 1972, bringing the total in theater to 374 Phantoms.[99]

Nixon subsequently ordered 161 additional B-52s to Andersen Air Force Base and U-Tapao between 5 February and 23 May, creating a total force of 210 BUFs in East Asia, over half of SAC's entire strategic-bomber force. This

Figure 6.7. Pres. Richard M. Nixon briefing the nation on air operations in Cambodia

redeployment had begun under Operation Bullet Shot in February, when 30 B-52s were sent to Andersen. All totaled, between 1 April and 31 July 1972, the number of USAF strike aircraft increased from 375 to 900.[100]

By mid-April, USMC officials had deployed 40 F-4s to Da Nang and two squadrons of A-1s to Bien Hoa. Concurrently, Nixon sent the USS *Kitty Hawk* and *Constellation* to join the USS *Coral Sea* and *Hancock* in the Gulf of Tonkin. By the end of April, the USS *Midway* had also arrived, followed on 27 June by USS *Oriskany* and on 3 July by the USS *America*, which replaced the *Constellation*. By mid-July, three and a half months after the offensive began, the United States had six carriers on station, each with 60 strike aircraft, a total of over 350 USN aircraft. Altogether, US strike aircraft now totaled 1,380 in theater, up from the 495 present in March.[101]

As Nixon put it, he was now ready "to go for broke and bring the enemy to his knees." He was determined to resume bombing North Vietnam and mining Haiphong harbor. Having negotiated closer ties with both Moscow and Beijing, he now believed he could afford to be bolder with Hanoi. Gen. John W. Vogt Jr., on his way to assume command of the Seventh Air Force, met with the president and later described him as "wild-eyed."[102]

On 2 April Nixon authorized airstrikes against AAA and SAM sites as well as logistics targets 25 nautical miles north of the DMZ. But poor weather hampered operations until the fifth, when US fighters attacked supply and logistics targets south of the eighteenth parallel, 60 miles north of the DMZ, as part of Operation Freedom Train. The results were disappointing. With the major flow of enemy supplies unimpeded, the president expanded the area of operations to twenty degrees, twenty-five minutes north parallel, or 231 miles farther into North Vietnam. On 16 April, using B-52s for the first time, Nixon sent eighteen of the giant bombers from the 307th Strategic Wing, stationed at U-Tapao, to attack oil-storage facilities near Haiphong. Four similar raids took place in April, all with impressive results.[103]

Even as Nixon prepared to send Kissinger, his foreign-policy adviser, back to Paris for a 2 May negotiating session with North Vietnam's lead negotiator, Le Duc Tho, he considered a three-day series of B-52 raids against Hanoi to commence on the fifth. Kissinger, fearing domestic reaction, and General Abrams, declaring his need for the B-52s in the South to curb the enemy offensive, convinced the president against this. Instead, Nixon opted for a plan from Kissinger's military assistant, Maj. Gen. Alexander Haig, which called for sustained bombing by fighter-bombers and the mining of Haiphong and other North Vietnamese harbors. Similar in design to Rolling Thunder, this campaign's main force was to be fighter-bombers from the carriers of Task Force 77 and from the Seventh Air Force; only a handful of B-52s were to be used, and these mostly in the South. The operation, codenamed Linebacker, began on 10 May and officially ended on 15 October 1972.[104]

Planners conceived Linebacker in four phases. The first involved an attack against railroad bridges and rolling stock in and around Hanoi and to the northeast toward China. The second phase targeted primary storage areas and marshaling yards near the Northern capital. Phase three would strike at storage and transshipment points created to cope with phases one and two. Planners chose to attack these targets at the discretion of local commanders and as often as necessary to impede the shipment of supplies south. Phase four targeted associated enemy defenses, such as ground-control-intercept radar sites, command and control, MiG airfields, SAM and AAA sites, and their logistics depots and support facilities.[105]

Part two of the overall effort involved aerial mining of Northern ports and was codenamed Operation Pocket Money. On 9 May at 0800 Saigon time (Monday, 8 May, at 2000 in Washington), the president announced on national television that US warplanes would begin mining ports and harbors at 0900 local time and that these mines would be activated on 11 May at 1800. Initially, the mining achieved its goal: "from the day the mines came alive through September, no vessels are known to have entered or to have left North Vietnam's ports." At first the enemy had freighters stop twelve miles from port, where they unloaded 6,000 tons of cargo per month. American fighter attacks restricted these activities to night, thus significantly reducing the flow of materials into the North.[106]

The risks were great, since Nixon was scheduled to meet with Soviet leaders at the end of May, and there was fear among advisers that the public would react negatively. But the president's instincts told him the public would accept a failure with the Soviets over the fall of Saigon. In the end the summit was a success, and for now South Vietnam was saved, by and large, as a result of this latest air campaign.[107]

During Operation Freedom Train, April–June 1972, US forces flew 27,745 attack and support sorties, with B-52s flying 1,000 of these. The United States lost fifty-two planes total, seventeen to SAMs, eleven to AAA, three to small arms, fourteen to MiGs and seven to unknown causes. The North launched 777 SAMs in April, 429 in May, and 366 in June. At first they employed ripple-firing tactics, sending one missile high, another low, and a third in the middle, for total coverage. Early enemy successes were later offset by countermeasures, including the use of chaff, especially by the B-52s. The United States also used Iron Hand anti-SAM operations, employing F-105 Wild Weasels that used the enemy's SAM-radar rebound signals to guide laser-guided bombs to the target. "Hunter/killer" formations, with Wild Weasels spotting sites and F-4s dropping high-explosives and cluster bombs on them, also limited the effectiveness of the SAMs.[108]

The North had 4,000 23-mm to 100-mm AAA guns, half around Hanoi and Haiphong. USAF analysts decided these defenses were less dangerous than those faced during Rolling Thunder because laser-guided bombs "were dropped at a much higher, and therefore safer, altitude than unguided munitions."[109] Hanoi also had over two hundred MiG interceptors, including seventy MiG-21s; the rest were MiG-17s and MiG-19s. But the NVAF flew fewer sorties and aircraft than during Rolling Thunder, and these mostly around Hanoi and Haiphong. Only one US aircraft was lost to MiGs over the North during Freedom Train, while American pilots downed nine fighters.[110]

As the campaign unfolded, the NVAF revised its tactics, using ground-control radar to direct MiG-21s onto the tail of incoming US formations heavy with fuel and munitions, which would then launch air-to-air missiles at the vulnerable warplanes as they maneuvered on low-speed bomb runs. MiG-21s also attacked from the rear to force formations to take evasive maneuvers while a wave of MiG-19s attacked from the front. By July, enemy fighters had downed twenty-six US aircraft, losing thirty-two. The Americans reacted by using the Teaball weapons-control center in Thailand to coordinate data from airborne radars over Laos and the Gulf of Tonkin to warn their pilots of enemy aircraft locations. From 1 August to 15 October, MiG loses totaled nineteen, while US loses had dropped to five.[111]

In early June a Pacific Air Forces report on the air operations declared, "the enemy has 'shown no signs of response to the interdiction . . . ; therefore it is estimated that only a small amount of material is entering NVN via the highway system.'"[112] As fighters and fighter-bombers struck the North, most B-52s continued to support ground operations in the South. The Seventh Air Force, which was still responsible for support of defenders facing Route Package I in southern North Vietnam and the DMZ, concentrated these raids against enemy storage areas, supply transportation chokepoints, and staging areas. As the offensive slowed, their role was revised to attacks on bridges, ferries, and fords in Military Region I (northern South Vietnam), eventually moving up to Route Package I in phase two. In phase three the BUFs created chokepoints around Dong Hai in Route Package I by destroying bridges on Highways 101 and 1A. On average, B-52s flew thirty sorties per day, mostly against the bridges in Route Package I.[113]

Officials also revised campaign priorities, now listing Northern rail lines out of China, rail and road links between China and Hanoi/Haiphong moving south to the DMZ, oil and gas areas, power stations, and rolling stock and storage areas other than fuel storage as primary targets. By late June, North Vietnamese industry, mine-clearing forces, and inland waterways were added to the list. Despite this emphasis on the North, 86.6 percent of US missions were flown against road, rail, and storage targets in Military Region I and Route Package I to interdict the flow of supplies to communist troops in the South. General Momyer later noted the Seventh Air Force operated this way since there were too few planes to cover ARVN defenses in the South and attack all targets in North Vietnam. Once the ground fighting ended in late September, attacks moved north of Route Package I.[114]

As Linebacker began, air leaders were pleased by promises to lift restrictions that had hampered Rolling Thunder. While some political considerations, such as legitimate fears of Soviet or Chinese intervention, had been reduced by the cooling of East-West tensions, the United States still had no desire to incite either communist power into a rash act. Nixon understood that Vietnam, while important, was only part of a much larger chess match and that detente benefited US interests more than anything short of (what by now seemed) an unlikely victory in Vietnam. Thus, while Linebacker I generally had fewer restrictions than Rolling Thunder, it was still subject to strict guidelines. These included a no-bombing buffer on the Sino-Vietnam border as well as placing Northern dams, dikes, civilian watercraft, civilian population centers, and non-Vietnamese seaborne shipping off limits. Once again, all attacks had to be approved by the JCS first. Restrictions were especially tight from 21 May to 5 June, during Nixon's trip to Moscow. In fact, four strategically critical bridges and tunnels near the Chinese border received only minimal attention during this operation.[115]

The most effective attacks against bridges and railroads employed MK-84 ordnance, which composed over 90 percent of the laser-guided bombs used in Southeast Asia. These were 2,000-pound general-purpose bombs with a laser-seeking head, small computer, spiral tail assembly, and canard control surface. One less-effective electroguided bomb was the "Walleye" launch-and-leave glide bomb, which was guided by a computer and television camera. Its system was too often fooled by camouflage, clouds, or smoke and so was used only in daylight. Its very low 6,000-foot release point also proved to be a major drawback to its wider use.[116]

In May and June, F-4s using MK-84s destroyed the main bridges on the Sino-Vietnamese border, including the Thanh Hoa Bridge over the Song Me. The primary rail and road lines in the northwest remained interdicted through the end of June, while the northeastern passages were less effectively blocked. But nothing seemed to be very effective against less sophisticated targets such as inland water traffic. One JCS report determined this "was the most difficult system to attack." Even mining inland streams and rivers with MK-36 mines had little effect. Only armed reconnaissance or naval gunfire brought meaningful results. One major reason for this was these routes had no real chokepoints, and loading and unloading small vessels required only "a firm bank and a few planks."[117]

While mining Northern harbors seemed to end enemy shipping, the pipelines out of China were so widely dispersed that Pacific Air Forces analysts concluded that they were virtually immune to serious disruption, being "too hard to find, too hard to hit, and too easy to repair." Linebacker also failed to effectively cut highways, which also proved hard targets to destroy. They were also well-defended assets requiring large, fully escorted formations that drained US resources. Night attacks were limited due to technology lags and limited armed reconnaissance. On 28 June Pacific Air Forces admitted the "tonnage involved in shipments from China to North Vietnam could easily equate to the amounts received via North Vietnamese ports prior to US mining operations."[118] The CIA estimated that 85 percent of "North Vietnam's needs could be supplied overland in the event of a blockade."[119]

The failure of Commando Hunt to interdict enemy supplies allowed the North to preposition caches of supplies in South Vietnam. Thus, the attacking NVA had plenty of materials to draw from during the spring and early summer of 1972. As a result, the most important air operations were carried out in the South in support of ARVN defenders, where many of the battles between ARVN and communist troops were so intense, B-52s bombed within 1,000 yards of the defenders. In April–May B-52s flew 1,682 sorties in Military Region II, with 727 flown in support of defenders in An Loc. The enemy air-defense threats in the South were fewer, even though one hand-held SA-7 did shoot down the first AC-130 gunship lost in South Vietnam. The reduced threat allowed the allies to use both fixed-wing and helicopter gunships as well as other propeller-driven aircraft, including those of the RVNAF, which flew nearly 3,000 CAS sorties between April and October. Flying lower and slower, often at only 500 feet, these aircraft proved very effective in their CAS roles.[120]

Concurrently, F-4s destroyed forty-five bridges along the DMZ and eleven of twenty-three PT-76 Soviet-built light tanks that tried to outflank ARVN units at the My Chanh defense line near the South Vietnamese coastline. B-52s returned to Route Package I in July, flying 1,308 sorties by September and totally destroying 109 supply depots, truck parks, and fuel-storage sites. All totaled, during the Linebacker operations, US aircraft of all types flew over 6,000 sorties in Route Package I, making it the most heavily bombed region during the spring and summer of 1972.

The Easter Offensive slowed in May and was all but over by June. The last attack against the My Chanh line came on 25 May and was blunted by ARVN units supported by RVNAF and US air components. On 8 June ARVN units began a counteroffensive that eventually retook Quang Tri

City on 16 September. Among the key elements in the communist failure was their inability to fully employ tanks, largely due to constant allied CAS operations. The enemy suffered heavy casualties taking Quang Tri City, which delayed their original timetable and prevented them from moving on Hue. B-52 raids against advancing enemy units and their supply lines in the South also caused enormous casualties. The BUFs' constant attacks on enemy logistics and communication lines delayed the communists' advance at least two or three weeks, expending far more of the prepositioned supplies than the PAVN had planned.[121]

Linebacker I and collateral air operations (during 5 April–23 October 1972) dropped 155,548 tons of bombs on North Vietnam, or about 25 percent of what Rolling Thunder had expended. Vogt declared, "More damage was done to the North Vietnamese lines of communications during Linebacker than during all our previous efforts." He also noted that US aircraft destroyed almost all fixed oil-storage facilities and 70 percent of the electric-power-generating capacity in North Vietnam, meaning nearly all of Hanoi's portable generated power had to go to military use. In addition, the psychological effect was great since 20–40 percent of Hanoi residents were evacuated.[122] Palmer concluded, "The North Vietnamese appear to have had in South Vietnam and adjacent areas of Laos supplies sufficient to see them through their defeats, which were the accomplishments of the South Vietnamese infantry, tactical close air support, and the B-52s."[123]

Despite their losses, the communists had made important gains, holding much of the countryside in South Vietnam and still determining the tempo of the war. In fact, the PAVN had not been defeated, only delayed. The North slowed the offensive to preserve its remaining Southern forces, which it planned to rebuild during a new series of negotiations with the Americans. US airpower played a decisive role in saving the Republic of Vietnam in 1972. The enemy offensive had moved ahead full speed with its prepositioned supplies until June, when the lack of resupply due to US air raids caused it slow down. But during the ARVN offensive to retake Quang Tri City, six PAVN divisions (albeit understrength) were well supplied, especially with artillery shells, often an excellent indicator of logistics strength. In this case the enemy defenders expended 3,000 rounds per day against the three attacking ARVN divisions. Thus, as one analyst put it, "it is not likely the NVA in Military Region I were ever effectively interdicted."[124]

In turn, America's prodigious Linebacker effort meant the Laotian interdiction effort almost completely ceased, with allied air forces, even after the spring build up, insufficient to continue simultaneous operations against the Ho Chi Minh Trail and North Vietnam. Moreover, the CIA and Defense Intelligence Agency reported that the enemy still had 14,000 trucks available during the offensive and that from 55,000 to 75,000 tons of supplies per month still entered North Vietnam from China, effectively countering mining efforts. Their extensive use of inland waterways, the pipelines, and the vast numbers of trucks, heavily defended by AAA and SAM batteries and hidden at night, meant the enemy could—and did—weather Linebacker to wait for a better day.

US air forces could not afford even modest attrition rates, which meant the Seventh Air Force was reluctant to conduct armed-reconnaissance missions in the northern route packages, not because of enemy AAA and SAMs, but because to do so meant risking or diverting precious resources. They tried to compensate, in part, by using precision-guided munitions. While these proved to be very effective against bridges, structural features, and industrial targets, the North, unlike World War II Germany, was not totally dependent on such things.[125]

Linebacker II

In July Kissinger, encouraged by requests from the North Vietnamese for renewed talks, convinced Nixon to reopen negotiations in Paris. Hanoi accepted, but by now the president, flush with the success of his Moscow trip and confident going in to the November elections, no longer believed he had to have peace in Vietnam to win reelection. He believed he could gain better terms after the voting, when he would have a free hand to use more airpower. Kissinger did not agree, fearing the broad use of airpower, especially B-52s, "would cause a domestic outcry and that in any case such attacks were unnecessary." Even so, Nixon authorized B-52 and fighter-bomber attacks against storage and communications targets along the DMZ, averaging thirty sorties a day over the North through October.[126]

In the meantime, Kissinger held talks with an apparently more conciliatory Le Duc Tho from 19 July to 14 August. Still, the North Vietnamese negotiator would not give in on many of his US counterpart's demands to preserve the Republic of Vietnam. On 8 August Nixon, convinced that the communists would not settle anything before the November US elections, cabled Admiral McCain, telling him to "notify his subordinate commanders that *Linebacker* would begin to hit the North harder." US military planners subsequently made plans for forty-eight sorties per day over Route Package V and Route Package VI, with naval air focusing on VIB and the USAF on V and VIA. Periodic B-52 strikes over North Vietnam continued, but most of the missions were executed by fighter-bombers, sometimes using precision ordnance. One spectacular success for precision-guided munitions came when a single flight of F-4s dropped laser-guided bombs on the Son Tay warehouse and storage area. Three buildings—one 300 feet by 260 feet, another 260 feet by 145 feet, and last only 210 feet by 65 feet—all received direct hits that completely destroyed them.[127]

On 25 September forty-eight new all-weather F-111 "swing-wing" Aardvarks, capable of flying at night, at low altitude, and at supersonic speeds, arrived in Thailand. By 13 October, these warplanes made half of all airstrikes in the North, averaging twenty-four sorties per night. Often scheduled at random and without warning, they were an awesome new weapon that deeply affected enemy planning.[128]

As US air forces upped the ante, on 15 September Kissinger once again commenced negotiations in Paris. On 8 October Le Duc Tho seemed to make a major concession when he dropped the requirement for a coalition government. He seemed to accept Nixon's April 1972 call for a cease-fire-in-place, followed by the withdrawal of the last US combat troops. In retrospect, he could make such an apparent compromise because 150,000–200,000 PAVN troops would be left in South Vietnam by such a settlement. As a result of this "breakthrough," the president curtailed, but did not halt, US bombing.[129] As Earl Tilford has noted: "By early May it was clear that the invasion had not toppled the Saigon Government. Still, the fact that 14 new divisions of North Vietnamese troops had joined about 100,000 PAVN troops already in South Vietnam not only posed a considerable military threat but also constituted a grim political reality for the Saigon regime."[130]

One of the greatest impediments to ending US involvement in late 1972 was the 200,000 troops Hanoi argued had entered the South prior to 31 March. While the communists agreed to withdraw 100,000 troops they conceded had entered the South after March, they demanded that the other 100,000 stay. Saigon demanded they all leave. In order to end US involvement in the war, Nixon opted to ignore this issue, and the final peace allowed 100,000 PAVN forces to stay in the South.

On 19 October Thieu read the new draft agreement for the first time and was indignant over the tenets that allowed PAVN troops to remain in the South and that allowed for the creation of the National Council of Reconciliation and Concord, including communist representatives. The South Vietnamese president realized this last provision was a coalition government in disguise. He defiantly made sixty-nine revisions deemed absolutely necessary for his acquiescence. Nixon was reluctant to act without Thieu's support and so did not sign the draft agreement. He did, however, suspend air attacks above the twentieth parallel as an act of good will. While frustrated by Thieu's hesitation, Nixon sympathized and assured him no agreement would be signed without his prior approval.[131]

Hanoi leaders were outraged, and on the twenty-sixth, in an effort to force Nixon's hand, Radio Hanoi publicly revealed the heretofore secret records of the negotiations. The North condemned the US officials for "going back on their word" and demanded they sign the draft agreement immediately. Soon after, Kissinger held his first nationally televised news conference, stating that "peace was at hand," a declaration most Americans believed. While Nixon's lead in the election polls reached 25 percent, Kissinger's own popularity seemed to eclipse the president's. Many in the White House believed Kissinger was trying to take full credit for the peace, something Nixon could not tolerate. Thus, according to Kissinger, the president began to "look for ways of showing that he was in charge."[132]

In November Nixon won a decisive victory over Democratic South Dakota senator George McGovern, but the Republicans fell well short of a majority in Congress. The president now had to rethink his peace timetable. With negotiations scheduled to resume on 20 November, Nixon had to end the war before the Democratic Congress did it for him. He did not want to end US commitments to Saigon and was willing to risk the loss of public support to guarantee continued material aid for South Vietnam once US combat troops left. He also wanted to be sure he, not Kissinger, got credit for the peace. Thus, Nixon pressured Thieu to accept the best deal possible as soon as possible and pushed Hanoi to accept at least a few of Thieu's revisions. Nixon dispatched General Haig to Saigon to assure the Southern president the United States would retaliate swiftly if Hanoi broke the treaty. Nixon was willing to make a "separate agreement if Thieu delayed much past 8 December," and so he now decided to use his trump card—airpower.[133]

November negotiations were characterized by Northern "foot dragging," and so by the end of the month, Nixon ordered plans for a B-52 campaign against the North. As US military planners prepared for a three- or six-day strategic-bombing campaign, Le Duc Tho continued to wax and wane. At one point on 7 December, he seemed ready to give in on all points, but then on the thirteenth he delayed proceedings while linguists made seventeen changes in the final draft. At this point the president decided to turn up the heat. Some White House staffers like Haig wanted a repeat of Linebacker I, but Nixon decided to aim this new campaign at enemy morale.[134]

Nixon chose to use the B-52 because it was such a powerful weapon and would send a message of US resolve to end the war to both Hanoi and Saigon. As important as the actual destructive power to the president was psychological effect: since the big bombers flew above 30,000 feet, when they attacked, those on the ground neither saw nor heard the B-52s before their bombloads began exploding around them. After the war, VC minister of justice Truong Nhu Tang described a B-52 raid as follows: "It seemed, as I strained to press myself into the bunker floor, that I had been caught in the Apocalypse. The terror was complete. One lost control of bodily functions as the mind screamed incomprehensible orders to get out."[135]

Nixon wanted Northern civilians to feel the sheer terror of US airpower. The full use of the B-52s stunned the JCS. Nixon told the JCS chairman, Adm. Thomas H. Moorer, "This is your chance to use military power effectively to win this war and if you don't I'll consider you personally responsible." Plans called for a three-day, around-the-clock, all-weather campaign against Hanoi. SAC planners, who had originally designed a Linebacker I–style campaign, rewrote the operations plan to focus on the B-52s. The final draft was approved in early December and sent to the SAC commander, Gen. John C. Meyer. Moorer, on orders from Nixon, warned Meyer, "I want the people of Hanoi to hear the bombs, but minimize damage to the civilian populace."[136]

Planning Linebacker II

It was one thing to decide to use B-52s, but quite another matter to plan and execute the missions. Frank Futrell has noted, "Although B-52 strategic bombers had long been committed to the single-integrated operational plan, general war strikes against route and terminal air defenses in the Soviet Union, the problem confronting them in the Linebacker II strikes

. . . was immensely more complex."[137] In short, as in horseshoes, nuclear bombs do not have to be as precise as iron bombs in order to score. Futrell concluded: "In the case of the Soviet Union, the number of potential targets was very large, and the air defenses had to be spread over a vast area. Moreover, the Air Force were to be penetrating at low altitude and using short-range air missiles (SRAMs) to suppress SAM defenses. They were to be using nuclear weapons, so that only a single bomber would need to penetrate to destroy the target and probably much of its defenses."[138]

In August Meyer, anticipating further B-52 actions, had ordered Eighth Air Force planners to prepare an operations plan. In November its commander, Lt. Gen. Gerald Johnson, had sent the draft plan to SAC headquarters for final approval. The proposal called for extensive attacks against Hanoi and Haiphong employing multiple-bomber formations simultaneously attacking from different directions. Meyer was particularly concerned with collateral bomb damage causing large numbers of civilian casualties. Nixon had made it clear that he did not want such casualties since it might

Figure 6.8. B-52Ds in line for takeoff for strikes against Hanoi and Haiphong during Linebacker II

cause a major propaganda setback, even domestically. For this reason, Meyer did not use the Eighth Air Force plan and instead detailed his own staff to create a new plan.[139]

With few traditional strategic-bombing targets around Hanoi or Haiphong, the B-52s needed to attack in concentrated groups and several times to assure target destruction. Having only three days to work, planners formulated an inflexible scenario that sent all three waves of bombers on the same route, at the same altitude, and at the same times for the first three days. To avoid civilian casualties, crews would be required to hold to the "planned course and fly in a trail formation with cells of three aircraft." The flight was supposed to stabilize four minutes prior to bomb release to avoid midair collisions.[140] Eighth Air Force staffers were alarmed by the repetitive routing, and some feared that aircraft losses might be as high as 16–18 percent. Meyer, using the operational plan developed for attacks on the Soviet Union, instead estimated losses at 3 percent.[141]

The plan aimed the attack at "rail yards, storage areas, power plants, communications centers, and airfields located on Hanoi's periphery." In support, Seventh Air Force and USN fighters, using precision-guided munitions, were to strike targets in heavily populated areas to avoid civilian casualties. The B-52s would hit targets within ten miles of Hanoi, making night raids to force the populace to seek shelter during sleeping hours, thus increasing the psychological discomfort and reducing the threat of MiG interceptions.[142]

Linebacker II Begins

On 18 December 129 B-52Ds and Gs from U-Tapao and Andersen launched their first attack. At 1945 the first wave of 48 aircraft struck the Kinh No storage complex, the Yen Vien railyard, and three airfields on Hanoi's outskirts. Supported by thirty-nine other US aircraft, the bombers flew in formation on a west–east route near the Sino-Vietnamese border, turning southeast to make their bomb runs. Attacking in a trail formation of three-ship cells later known as an "elephant walk," the BUFs dropped their bombs with up to ten minutes of separation between the cells; pilots stabilized the flights four minutes before bomb release to assure accuracy and destruction. After dropping their bombload, the pilots turned west to avoid SAM attacks. The second wave struck at midnight, and the third at 0500. The results were good. The bombers had hit 94 percent of all targets, while losing three B-52s to SAMs, with two others severely damaged.[143]

Nixon was exuberant, extending the operation indefinitely. Even before the bombing began, he had also made overtures to Hanoi for meetings any time after the twenty-sixth based on the November draft augmented with a few negotiated changes. The president hoped his stick-and-carrot policy would force the North back to negotiations and demonstrate US resolve to Saigon.[144]

On the nineteenth ninety-three B-52s struck Thai Nguyen thermal power plant and Yen Vein railyards, employing the same tactics. Two more of the big bombers were damaged but none shot down. Now confident the North had not made a fix on the routing scenario, and realizing a change would require a long lead time, officials sent out a third strike on the twentieth. The ninety-nine B-52s attacked in the familiar three-wave pattern. Their targets were basically the same, but this time SAMs downed six B-52s and severely damaged another one.[145]

Nixon was furious and complained to senior officials that such losses would cause Linebacker II to have the opposite effect of those he desired. He "raised holy hell about the fact that [B-52s] kept going over the same targets at the same times." While Nixon later asserted he convinced the military to alter the bombing plans, in fact USAF leaders, especially Meyer, recognized how unacceptable such loses were, especially since the B-52s were the centerpiece of the US nuclear-strike force. Nevertheless, two more bombers went down on the twenty-first, while most Seventh Air Force raids that day were canceled by bad weather. On December 22 Meyer directed planners to change tactics and create plans for a new kind of raid, scheduled for the twenty-sixth.[146]

The Turning Point

During these initial raids, the North launched large numbers of SAMs to gain their kills, expending a total of 884. As historian Carl Berger wrote, they "resorted to salvoing large numbers of missiles in a shotgun pattern into the calculated path of the oncoming aircraft." It was wasteful but temporarily effective: "since all portions of Linebacker II got underway more or less concurrently, the Air Force had no opportunity to send tactical aircraft to wipe out . . . the numerous SA-2 missile sites that encircled both cities [Hanoi and Haiphong]."[147] MiG interceptors were never much of a problem

Figure 6.9. Inside the cockpit of a B-52 during a Linebacker II sortie

since Linebacker II missions were flown in darkness. The only enemy fighters to challenge them B flew aimlessly through the bomber formations, causing little damage. In fact, B-52 tail gunners shot down two MiGs.[148]

While day three proved disastrous due to the number of B-52s that went down, it also proved to be the turning point of the campaign. Upon examining aerial photos of the raid, officials discovered that none of the SAM sites had spare missiles. Meyer decided to target these sites along with SAM supply dumps to clear the skies over North Vietnam of these threats to the B-52s.[149]

The SAC commander also turned over planning responsibility to General Johnson in Guam and reduced the B-52 sortie rate to thirty per day until a new plan could be fully implemented. He also made U-Tapao the sole Linebacker II base of origin since crews there could handle the sortie rate without bombers from Andersen and would not require aerial refueling. If making SAM sites the new primary targets worked, it would reduce the lethality of Northern air defenses. The immediate tactical change would avoid Hanoi (for now) and concentrate on Haiphong.[150]

During 22–24 December, B-52s, escorted by USN planes, flew raids against railyards and storage facilities, fainting attacks against Hanoi and then turning on Haiphong. Each route and altitude was different, thus results were excellent and only one aircraft was damaged. On the twenty-second Nixon offered a new peace plan, calling for renewed meetings on 2 January 1973. As a show of goodwill, he initiated a thirty-six-hour Christmas bombing pause and guaranteed he would halt bombing above the twentieth parallel if the North would agree to renew talks. Hanoi remained silent. While many around the president urged a continuation of the pause after Christmas, Nixon decided only renewed pressure would gain the desired effect.[151]

On 26 December 120 B-52s struck ten different targets in fifteen minutes. Four waves totaling 72 bombers hit four targets in Hanoi from four different directions at the same time two other waves of 15 bombers each struck Haiphong from the east and west and 18 B-52s raided Thai Nguyen railyards north of the capital. Even though the enemy fired dozens of SAMs, only two BUFs were lost. In the largest effort of the campaign, the United States had staggered the North. Not long after, officials in Hanoi notified Washington they would accept Nixon's offer to return to the negotiations. On the twenty-eighth they also agreed to the president's demands that preliminary meetings between Le Duc Tho and Kissinger would begin on 2 January 1973 and matters already resolved in the basic agreement would not be reopened. Nixon promised to end bombing above the twentieth parallel once demands were met. But he warned that negotiations had a time limit, and the clock was ticking.[152]

As Northern leaders moved toward agreeing to Nixon's terms, on the twenty-seventh sixty B-52s attacked the Hanoi and Lang Dang railyards near the Chinese border. In a small-scale version of the previous day's attack, the bombers again struck from various directions, hitting numerous targets all at once. SAMs downed two more B-52s that day, bring the total losses to fifteen. On the twenty-eighth sixty more bombers struck concentrating on SAM sites around Hanoi. That same day Hanoi agreed to begin preliminary talks after the New Year's Day. At 1900 on 29 December, the president ended Linebacker II after a final raid. There were no enemy air defenses on that last day of the operation. As one participant, Capt. John R. Allen, declared in a subsequent interview with Lt. Col. Mark Clodfelter: "By the tenth day there were no missiles, there were no MiGs, there was no AAA—there was no threat. It was easy pickings."[153]

After Linebacker II

During Linebacker II's eleven days, B-52s flew 729 sorties against thirty-four targets north of the twentieth parallel and dropped 15,237 tons of bombs. USAF and USN fighters flew 1,216 sorties and dropped 5,000 tons. Altogether, US warplanes destroyed 383 pieces of rolling stock; made 500 rail cuts, leaving rail traffic in total disarray; totally destroyed 191 warehouses around Hanoi and Haiphong; reduced electric power generation from 115,000 kilowatts to 29,000; and reduced POL capacity by three-quarters. Perhaps of equal importance, PAVN troops in the South soon were very low on food and supplies. US sources reported civilian casualties during these raids were relatively low, even though enemy sources claimed 1,318 killed and 1,216 wounded overall, with 305 killed in Hanoi itself. As had been the US goal, morale in Hanoi suffered while little major damage was done to the city itself. A total of fifteen B-52s were lost and nine damaged during Linebacker II, all to the twenty-four SAM hits. Of the ninety-two crewmembers in the downed aircraft, twenty-six were rescued, thirty-three bailed out and were captured, twenty-nine were listed as missing, and four were killed outright.[154]

On 27 January 1973 Secretary of State William P. Rogers signed a peace agreement with Hanoi, ending America's active participation in the war. Nixon had won, but what had he won? He had earned the right to disengage the enemy, but his war aims were very limited, and the results were not the kind of victory America had originally envisioned in the 1960s. Linebacker II and the heroic efforts of US aircrews had forced a reluctant group of Northern leaders back to the negotiating table to finalize the peace accords. But while a major reason for the peace, bombing was not the only reason: "Nixon's threat of another Linebacker if the North refused to settle helped persuade the Politburo to accept terms that included some of Thieu's provisions."[155] Hanoi was also concerned about their troops in the South. Nixon's offers of a settlement, leaving them in control of major portions of the South, forced them to continue to fight a war of movement, leaving them susceptible to additional US air attacks until a final peace could be signed. General Tra observed years later: "Our cadres and men were fatigued, we had not had time to make up for our losses, all units were in disarray, there was a lack of manpower, and there were shortages of food and ammunition. . . . The troops were no longer capable of fighting."[156]

Equally important was Nixon's progress toward closer relations with China and the Soviet Union. While both continued to support Hanoi, they "sacrificed support for North Vietnam to achieve warmer relations with the United States." Not only had detente dismissed the very real menace of direct Chinese or Soviet intercession that had tormented Johnson, but it also likely prevented the North from adequately resupplying its forces at critical junctures during the summer and fall of 1972. On 17 August *Nhan Dan*, the Communist Party newspaper in Hanoi, grumbled: "Nixon's detente had saved South Vietnam from defeat. The failure of China and the Soviet Union to provide North Vietnam with adequate assistance equated to 'throwing a lifebuoy to a drowning pirate . . . in order to serve one's narrow national interests.'"[157]

Hanoi also knew that Nixon's aims, unlike Johnson's, were limited by both potential congressional constraints and US public opinion. Johnson had fought the war to ensure an independent South. Rolling Thunder, restrained by Cold War geopolitical concerns, was aimed at this long term and, as it turned out, problematic goal. Conversely, Nixon had the limited goals of ending US participation while leaving the South intact—what he called "peace with honor." With Nixon constrained by campaign promises of Vietnamization, Hanoi staked final victory on an Easter gamble, believing the president would not recommit US ground forces. While this effort to reunite Vietnam failed, the North remained committed to that goal. And with bases in the South assured by the agreement, Northern leaders had no reason not to sign the Paris Accords in January 1973.[158]

Even if those who have argued that Linebacker II provided the United States an opportunity to win the war are right about the military change in momentum: the most likely follow up to continued full-scale bombing would have been the recommitment of US ground troops to clear out the remaining enemy forces and assure Southern stability. At best that would have returned Vietnam to a stalemate much like the one that had existed in the early sixties, only this time not with only the VC in the South but with enemy forces all over Southeast Asia. Nixon would not and could not return 500,000 American boys to such an uncertain future. Like the British in 1783, the US public and polity were weary of the fight and no longer saw any real need to sacrifice its youth or its wealth. Besides, Vietnam was only one aspect of a much larger struggle. In that regard, the considerations of superpower diplomacy was as important as US military power.[159]

B-52s and Doctrine

Despite these implied influences, the overall effect of the Vietnam War on official USAF doctrine has been negligible. Undoubtedly in the case of B-52s, this lack of influence on doctrine and theory can best be explained by the confusion and disagreement caused by the effectiveness of Linebacker II and its illusion of potential victory. Some senior and junior officers, as well as civilians, have suggested that a Linebacker-style campaign begun in 1965 could have brought the war to a successful conclusion. Such an argument is, of course, not historical in nature and one that ignores a myriad of factors at work in Vietnam and internationally, factors that in the eight years of major US involvement mutated and changed totally or by degrees.[160]

The argument for an earlier Linebacker campaign also ignores the fact that the required B-52 Big Bellies were not actually available in adequate quantities until 1967. Even then, SAC officials at the time were not willing to commit the numbers Nixon committed in 1972 for fear of being unprepared to meet their strategic responsibilities. Moreover, between 1965 and 1972 the Cold War was altered by detente, making overt actions against the city of Hanoi easier. Over the same period, the nature of the war changed from a counterinsurgency campaign, primarily against Southern guerrillas, to a lull following the Tet Offensive of 1968, to a conventional war of unification fought mostly by PAVN forces beginning with the Easter invasion of 30 March 1972. The changing domestic sociopolitical attitudes of the American public, as well as the fluctuating perspectives of government and military leaders, also affected the way the war unfolded and eventually came to an end. And then there was also the significant influence that enemy strategy, tactics, and political/diplomatic manipulation had on the outcome. These are just a few of the factors that determined the outcome of the Vietnam War and might have modified collateral events, resulting in a different kind of air war.

There are still other authors, experts, and historians, both civilian and military, who suggest that, even as late as December 1972, had the United

States had the resolve to continue the Linebacker air campaign and recommit US troops, a better resolution could have been attained. Not only does this ignore the aforementioned factors but also the parameters of "limited war," constraints that Johnson seemed unable to grasp but that Nixon clearly perceived as inviolate. Besides, does any truly reasonable person believe Nixon could have recommitted troops, should have, or even wanted to?

Conclusion: The Bottom Line

Ultimately, America did not lose in Vietnam for lack of an air effort, even though one can argue the lack of a focused air effort over the North from 1965 to 1968, and the collateral damage wrought in the South due to the air campaigns, cost the allies popular support and squandered any real possibility of a military success. The facts are that from 1964 to 1973 US aircraft dropped eight million tons of bombs and lost over 2,000 aircraft, more than the United States later deployed to fight Desert Storm. Between 18 June 1965 and 15 August 1973, SAC scheduled 126,663 B-52 combat sorties, launching 126,615. Of these, 125,479 actually reached the target and 124,532 released bombs. Over 55 percent of these sorties were flown over South Vietnam, 27 percent over Laos, 12 percent over Cambodia, and 6 percent over North Vietnam. Altogether, the USAF lost thirty-one B-52s, eighteen of them to enemy fire over North Vietnam. Half of the money spent on the war by the United States, about $200 billion, went toward aerial operations.[161]

Johnson's use of airpower grew out of his own preconceptions of history and was deeply influenced by the advice he received from his closest advisers, including McNamara, McGeorge Bundy, Rusk, and others. Vietnam presented Johnson and his advisers with a war their experiences and expectations had not prepared them to fight. Thus, they had no theory of victory or political redress, no Gulf War–style coalition, and no understanding of what Edward Rice has called "Wars of the Third Kind" from which to formulate tactics or policies.[162] It left US leaders in a position where they knew what they wanted to achieve but were unable to formulate a plan to reach their goal. It also caused them to ineffectively employ airpower. Tactical planes, under heavy restrictions, flew most of the strategic missions, while B-52s flew ground-support and interdiction missions, which USAF leaders were loath to support.

The B-52s did not—and could not—win the Vietnam War because there were no sound US theories of victory and the policy derived from this malaise, especially in the 1960s, meant no weapon, no matter how powerful, could prevail. Airpower doctrine gave only brief consideration to the problem, and airmen, given these constraints, never really saw airpower as a means to victory until 1972, when it could fight a conventional bomber war.

To be sure, the Vietnam War left most airmen and airpower experts frustrated by its conclusion and caused many, with some justification, to say this is what you get when airmen do not fully control air assets and run an air war. After America's withdrawal from the conflict, these painful memories, bitter legacies, and misconceptions about the nature and conclusion of the war, as well as disagreements over the very nature of the remaining strategic role of the USAF against the Soviet Union, made it all too easy for airmen to assign their efforts in Vietnam to the trash bin of history. Many found it more comfortable to retire into the more familiar issues of nuclear warfare and the European scenario. But this is not meant to condemn these airmen; rather, it is an explanation of why they did not immediately choose to wrestle with these issues.

With this in mind, it is also worth recalling, as important as Vietnam was, it was after all only part of a much larger geopolitical struggle whose main participants were more concerned with events in other distant lands. Ultimately, one must remember the primary role of the B-52 was to act as a deterrent to a hot war with the USSR and, failing this, to evaporate the Soviets in a mushroom cloud. As a deterrent, they eventually succeeded. Even if B-52s could not win their bitter sojourn in Vietnam, they did ultimately help the United States win the larger Cold War conflict. That is another story.

7

The Battle of Hamburger Hill, 10–20 May 1969

The Beginning of the End of America's Commitment to the Republic of Vietnam

The Battle for Hill 937, which took place 10–20 May 1969, is best known by its sobriquet, "Hamburger Hill." The name portends a negative connotation as a meat grinder, or turning American troops into hamburger. Indeed, it was in the strictest terms another bloody tactical victory for the United States, but another that became a strategic defeat. Fought over by 800–900 regular troops of the NVA and 1,800 American airborne troops, Hill 937 was located in Thua Thien Province in South Vietnam. In fact, even though the hill was of little strategic value, US leadership ordered it taken by bloody frontal assaults. No sooner was it seized than it was abandoned. All of this created a public outrage in the United States, ultimately causing President Nixon to initiate the withdrawal of US ground forces, create his "Vietnamization" program, and later introduce the "Nixon Doctrine."

As one military study has said: "The Vietnam conflict wore many faces. It was at once an insurrection by indigenous guerrilla forces and an invasion by the regular army of a neighboring regime." So it was, but for the most part (until the Spring Offensive of 1972), it was not a conventional war

Figure 7.1. Hill 937, known as "Hamburger Hill"

with set-piece battles like those in the World Wars and Korea. There were some exceptions, however, like The Battle of Hamburger Hill being one of those "big battles" for which the post–World War II US Army had trained and expected to fight on the open plains of Europe.[1]

The bloodletting took place on a rugged, jungle-shrouded mountain a little more than a mile from the Laotian border named Dong Ap Bia, or Ap Bia Mountain. It is a solitary peak, unconnected to the other ridges of the Annamite range, that rises out of the western part of the A Shau Valley. It is 937 meters, or 3,074 feet, above sea level. There are also a series of other high points to the south also reaching more than 3,000 feet. The reason it was designated "Hill 937" was because of the elevation shown on US Army maps. It was, and remains, covered by triple-canopy jungles, dense thickets of bamboo, and elephant grass often taller than a man. Local tribesmen call it "the mountain of the crouching beast." In short, it was a hell of place to fight a battle.[2]

Col. Harry G. Summers opened his article on the battle with a quote about the mountain and the fighting: "'Don't mean nothin.' That was the refrain of the powerful 1987 movie about the battle for Hamburger Hill, more correctly Ap Bia Mountain or Hill 937. Many veterans of that May 1969 fight would no doubt agree, since the hill was abandoned to the enemy soon after it was taken. But the truth is that it was one of the most significant battles of the war, for it spelled the end of a major American ground combat operations in Vietnam."[3] The battle itself was part of Operation Apache Snow, the second part of a larger three-phased campaign to destroy PAVN basecamps in remote areas of the A Shau Valley. The first phase, known as Operation Massachusetts Striker, had taken place about ten weeks earlier with limited success. Even so, American leaders believed this rapid follow-on campaign would further degrade PAVN forces and set them up for a coup de grâce.[4]

The region was seized by communist forces in 1966 during a protracted struggle that witnessed the fall of significant US and South Vietnamese outposts throughout the valley. One official report described the capture of the primary outpost, a US Special Forces camp in the I Corps Tactical Zone located twenty miles from Hue and two miles from the Laotian border. It was manned by twelve American advisers, 149 Chinese Nung mercenaries, nine interpreters, and 210 Vietnamese Civilian Irregular Defense Group troops. Despite heroic efforts, during which dozens of sorties were flown by AC-47D fixed-wing gunships, A-1E ground-support fighters, C-123 transport aircraft, and B-57 tactical bombers, the communists captured the base after a battle that lasted from 9 to 11 March 1966. It was during this struggle that Maj. Bernard F. Fisher, under heavy fire, landed his A-1E and rescued a downed comrade, Maj. Dafford W. Myers. For this and other actions during the battle, Fisher won the Medal of Honor.[5]

The enemy overran the camp, with heavy casualties on both sides. One camp defender later acknowledged: "Without the air support . . . we wouldn't have lasted one day. If you hadn't flown at all, the Special Forces wouldn't have blamed you. It was suicidal, but you carried out your mission anyway."[6] This would be the pattern over the next three years as a determined enemy dedicated considerable manpower and material to taking and defending the vital logistics route into South Vietnam. It would be here that, eventually, the main event would be staged—the bloody battle of Hamburger Hill.

The A Shau Valley was critical to both sides. Without it, the PAVN could not bring troops and supplies from North Vietnam into the South. In this respect it was the final link to the Ho Chi Minh Trail and essential to Northern victory. As for the United States, shutting down this route was vital to cutting off the flow of enemy men and materials. To quote one official US Army analysis, the "key to removing this logistical superhighway was con-

Figure 7.2. Maj. Gen. Melvin Zais, commander of the 101st Airborne "Screaming Eagles" Division during the Battle of Hamburger Hill

trolling the A Shau Valley, where the Viet Cong and North Vietnamese Army had developed logistical bases following the removal of the A Shau Special Forces Camp."[7]

From 1966 to 1969, American efforts to take back the valley failed. The 1969 campaign was only the latest in a long series of attempts to neutralize the enemy presence in the A Shau, which had been a thorn in Westmoreland's side throughout his tenure; it continued to be for allied forces after General Abrams succeeded him. In the spring of 1969, the commander of the XXIV Corps, Lt. Gen. Richard G. Stilwell, assembled two infantry divisions, supported by massed artillery and CAS, to push the PAVN out of the area once and for all.[8]

Three battalions of the 101st Airborne Division, commanded by Maj. Gen. Melvin Zais, were at the core of Stilwell's units. These included the 3rd Brigade, led by Col. Joseph B. Conmy Jr.; the 3rd Battalion, 187th Infantry Regiment (3/187, the "Iron Rakkasans"), led by Lt. Col. Weldon Honeycutt; the 2nd Battalion, 501st Parachute Infantry Regiment (2/501), commanded by Lt. Col. Robert German; and the 1st Battalion, 506th Parachute Infantry Regiment (1/506, the "Currahees"), commanded by Lt. Col. John Bowers. In addition, two ARVN battalions of the 1st Division were temporarily assigned to support the 3rd Brigade. Other units included the 9th Marine Regiment; 3rd Squadron, 5th Cavalry Regiment; and the ARVN 3rd Regiment.[9]

One important point is that, under Westmoreland, the main thrust of American operations was to reduce the Vietnam War to a war of attrition. Once Abrams took over, this operational approach changed to one of "clear and hold." This meant US units were supposed to create secure areas surrounding population centers (in this case the old imperial capital of Hue) to provide time for "institutional rebuilding in South Vietnam." To this end, Zais planned to destroy the PAVN forces in the A Shau Valley and secure the area, which in his opinion would bring the United States and the ARVN "another step closer toward achieving the strategic goal in Vietnam: a stable South Vietnam free of communism." The major fallacy with this notion was that, while the enemy had more than 1,000 trucks moving supplies down the Ho Chi Minh Trail, individualized operations like Apache Snow lacked the synchronized nature necessary to "disaggregate" the PAVN's ability to move troops and supplies from the North to the South.[10]

As for the PAVN forces in A Shau, they were still recovering from a February engagement with US Marines during Operation Dewey Canyon. Leaders in Hanoi sent the 6th, 9th, and 29th Regiments into the area to bolster their surviving forces. The North Vietnamese soon took up well-defended positions on the highest points on Hill 937. The 29th Regiment would do most of the PAVN's fighting and dying in the upcoming battle.[11]

Planning the Operation

In formulating the attack, Colonel Conmy planned to airlift by helicopter five infantry battalions into the valley on 10 May 1969. Sixty-five UH-1 Hueys were to transport 1,800 men to near the base of Ap Bia, a move he and Zais called a reconnaissance in force. Each battalion would search their designated sector for PAVN forces and supplies. Marine and 5th Cavalry forces were ordered to recon toward the Laotian border. The ARVN units were supposed to occupy and divide the main road running through the base of the valley. Assuming they accomplished this, troopers of the 2/501 and the 1/506 were to contact and destroy PAVN units in their operating areas and block enemy escape routes into Laos. If one of the US battalions ran into a large enemy force, Conmy planned to send support from one of the other battalions by helicopter. The basic concept was, being a mobile force, the 101st had the ability to move its forces quickly enough to keep the PAVN from massing against any one unit. Concurrently, any US battalion confronting a significant communist unit could fix it in place until a reinforcing battalion could arrive and cut off the enemy's retreat, then together destroy it.[12]

As preparations continued, American and ARVN personnel from top to bottom knew that, throughout the previous three years, each time they had ventured into the A Shau Valley, they had encountered heavy resistance from the PAVN. Based on cursory intelligence reports, they expected the same kind of opposition this time. But most of the information was sketchy, especially regarding the number and location of communist units. Douglas Scalard noted in his official analysis of the battle, "they had little evidence as to the enemy's actual strength and dispositions." Throughout this time, the PAVN were able to camouflage virtually all their bases from aerial observation and relegated their movements to nighttime along trails hidden under triple-canopy jungle. To prevent the Americans from monitoring their communications, they performed their command-and-control activities most often using runners to eliminate any electronic signatures. As a result, in order to gather tactical information US commanders had to detail patrols to seize prisoners, documents, and equipment. This was the raw data from which they had to derive their assessment of the enemy's order of battle and dispositions.[13]

On 10 May 1969 the 3/187 set down at its LZ on Hill 937 at 0710, expecting a "hot" reception. To Honeycutt's great surprise, the entire deployment

Figure 7.3. The battle for Hamburger Hill begins

was uncontested. He would later discover that the 29th PAVN was waiting for him in heavily fortified positions on the hill. But for now, once on the ground, the Iron Rakkasans spent much of this first phase of the operation seeking intelligence on the enemy. At this early stage, however, the lack of contact continued. As the hero in the movies often says, "it was very quiet, too quiet." The Americans soon gathered captured dispatches indicating the PAVN 29th Regiment, better known as the "Pride of Ho Chi Minh," was lurking somewhere on the hill. The 29th had played a major role in the battle for Hue, during the Tet Offensive, and comprised a hardened group of veterans willing to fight to the end. Still, US commanders were convinced, like in most of the battles against the PAVN, if encountered, the communists would put up a ferocious fight for a short time and eventually withdraw. After all, they reasoned, protracted battles like Ia Drang Valley and Dak To were rare, especially once US firepower was brought to bear.[14]

As intelligence data trickled in, it became clear to Honeycutt "the enemy was looking for a big fight." He "was eager to oblige." If the PAVN followed their previous patterns of combat, the lieutenant colonel believed he would not need more troops to execute the "reconnaissance in force." He did ask that his own B Company, the brigade's reserve, be sent to support his move, which was granted. Honeycutt, a protégé of Westmoreland's and known for his aggressive personality and tactics, thus decided to spread out his forces to comb the area north and northwest of Hill 937. His men also searched the area to the west, near the Laotian border, then finally pushed up the north slope of Ap Bia itself. Here, late in the day, they encountered heavy PAVN fire. The main battle had begun.[15]

The Battle Begins

Once the 3/187 was engaged with the PAVN, Honeycutt requested support from AH-1 Cobra attack helicopters. Called "Snakes" by their crews, US Army personnel named them aerial rocket artillery. It appeared American planning was working out flawlessly, and the troops had the PAVN right where they wanted them. Things soon went terribly wrong. Unable to correctly identify friend from foe under the thick jungle foliage, the AH-1s mistakenly attacked the 3/187's command post, killing two and wounding thirty-five. This cost the Americans an early opportunity. B Company had been only a few hundred yards from the summit of the mountain. Now, with the battalion's command and control destroyed, all units pulled back to

Figure 7.4. AH-1 Cobra
attack helicopter

nighttime defensive positions. What soon followed confirmed Honeycutt's suspicions—the area to his front was thick with enemy soldiers determined to fight savagely. Of primary concern was that they were a much larger force than anticipated. Instead of "a few trail watchers," the lieutenant colonel was confronted by at least a "reinforced platoon or even a company." While his troopers could still deal with such numbers, they "would have to concentrate to do so."[16]

Concentrating his forces proved to be a difficult proposition, and it took Honeycutt two days to merge them in order to organize a planned three-company attack on the mountain peak. Not only did the craggy terrain and jungle undergrowth slow them to a crawl, but well entrenched and deftly hidden PAVN troops also ambushed the Americans on several occasions as they tried to maneuver around these natural encumbrances. In one case an ambush stopped D Company cold as it tried to descend a steep ravine, requiring five hours for the unit to move 500 yards. Scalard described their predicament: "The steep, mud-covered slopes, more than the enemy, kept this company from fulfilling Honeycutt's intent. Ultimately, they had to abandon their attack and withdraw the way they had come."[17]

During these three days, Honeycutt was left to do a great deal of reflection. Intelligence operatives had grossly underestimated the size of the enemy forces. In addition, the map references and aerial data were equally useless. On top of everything else, the lieutenant colonel's own instincts, honed by a long and "distinguished" career in Korea and Vietnam, now betrayed him as he was slow to fully grasp the miscalculations. Sticking to his original evaluation of the enemy's strength, he ordered attacks by both B and C Companies, with dreadful results. What he finally came to understand was not only were the PAVN forces larger than anticipated but also were reinforced every night with more troops from Laos. Since the PAVN commander was willing "to replace heavy losses," Honeycutt soon realized, "he intended to put up a stiff fight." That resistance would certainly be more tenacious than any US officer had anticipated.[18]

On 13 May Conmy changed things up. Since his own troops had faced only limited enemy resistance through noon, he decided to support Honeycutt's assault up the southern side of Hill 937. First, the colonel moved to cut off PAVN reinforcements from Laos, then he had helicopters take B Company to Hill 916, which the company captured on 15 May. The rest of the battalion marched the two and a half miles to the base of Hill 937. They anticipated 1/506th forces being ready to make an attack up the hill by the fifteenth. But the march through the thick jungles and elephant grass proved very difficult, so the entire battalion was not in position until 19 May. Scalard noted in his report, the "1/506 Infantry's pace was glacial. In one forty-hour period over 13–14 May, the battalion was able to cover only 1,500 of the 4,000 meters separating it from its objective on Ap Bia Mountain."[19]

As they waited for the other battalions, troopers of the 3/187 attempted several multicompany maneuver strikes on 14–15 May. Their casualty numbers again proved severe. On 16–17 May other units of the 506th made probing attacks on the south slopes of the mountain with little success. Not only did the terrain prove daunting to navigate but also the PAVN were well dug in and determined not to give up their positions. The Americans could never seem to get any forward momentum started due to concealed fire and unexpected ambushes on Hills 916, 900, and 937. Efforts to initiate helicopter airlifts or airdrops were nearly impossible due to the steep gradients and dense foliage, which limited nearby LZs.[20]

Since the landscape concealed PAVN positions, any airlift was in danger from hidden antiaircraft fire. On those occasions when US aircraft attempted drops or landings, enemy units, able to maneuver nearly at will, damaged or destroyed several helicopters with small-arms fire, rocket-propelled grenades, and crew-served weapons (mostly mortars). The communists also hit adjacent logistical-support LZs and command posts at least four times during the battle. This meant US units that might have helped in the assaults were forced to undertake security details instead. Each time a unit tried to move up the hill, they had to deploy security flankers as they maneuvered since the topography generally prevented nearby units from supporting one another. With this awkward and slow-moving American formation before them, PAVN units repeatedly smashed into the rear or flanks of ambling US forces.[21]

In short, the great strength of US forces—their ability to quickly maneuver—was nearly eliminated. They were instead forced down narrow trails that reduced their effective size at the combat point to squads or platoons. This allowed PAVN units to hit the Americans with similar-size units in prepared locations with interlocking fields of fire. Another consequence of this arrangement was that most firefights were close in with small arms, thus impeding American fire support. As a result, US forces often had to withdraw in order to call in artillery or CAS. The PAVN quickly realized that when US troops pulled back, they needed to take cover in their well-hidden and cleverly built bunkers, which even had overhead cover to withstand most aerial bombardments.[22]

From the beginning of US ground operations, American tacticians decided to employ rapid troop movement by using helicopters flying over jungles and rice paddies. They saw this as a means to improve maneuverability and avoid being ambushed on the ground, as had happened with French vehicular convoys. Even so, once on the ground, the Vietnamese terrain, as it did on top of Hill 937, impeded quick movement. In short, 150-to-160-pound soldiers lugging 80-to-90-pound packs through jungles and elephant grass in sweltering heat could shift positions only under the most difficult circumstances, and then only slowly. As one marine veteran of the A Shau Valley described it, maneuver was more like "pack mules trudging through a sauna."[23]

The Nightmare Continues

As the battle proceeded, the vegetation became stripped away, exposing some of the enemy trenches. Still, the communists had built so many that they could abandon the revealed positions and take refuge elsewhere. Some of these trenches were so well made the Americans could not destroy them with indirect fire or recoilless rifles; even napalm proved ineffective in some cases. The only real success came from small-unit actions, which proved slow and costly in terms of lives and equipment. Throughout, command of the US units was fragmented, even though Honeycutt urged his company commanders to push forward. It was not until the final attack, with units closer to each other, that he could coordinate the movement of his men and order effective fire support. Prior to this final push, artillery fire and CAS proved a risky business. There were five friendly fire events that killed seven and wounded fifty-three members of the 3/187. Four of these were accidental attacks by Cobra helicopter gunships, one of which was more than a mile from the actual target.[24]

On 17 May 1969 the Currahees pushed forward again with little progress, prompting Conmy to order a two-pronged assault by two battalions for the next morning. The 1/506 would attack from the south and the 3/187 from the north. He thus hoped he could prevent PAVN units from concentrating on either battalion. Troops of D Company, 3/187 reached within 246 feet of the summit. Throughout the attack most of the fighting was close combat; at one point the two forces fired small arms within 66 feet of each other. Both sides suffered heavy casualties; all of the 3/187's officers were either killed or wounded. Circling overhead in a light observation helicopter, Honeycutt struggled to coordinate the movements of supporting companies. Nevertheless, they were making progress. Just as it seemed the Americans might finally take the summit, a violent thunderstorm struck, cutting visibility down to zero and ending the combat. The 3/187 was forced to abandon all the ground they had so dearly won.[25]

Even as this drama played out, three converging companies of the 1/506 were groping their way up Hill 900, the southern crest of the mountain. All along their path they faced heavy opposition. Having already sustained severe casualties in earlier fighting, the high number suffered during this push led Major General Zais to consider ending the advance entirely. Besides, he had already suffered a great deal of media criticism for making the attack in the first place. Nevertheless, publicly supported by General Abrams, Zais decided to commit three fresh battalions to the battle. One of these was slated to replace the battered 3/187, which had suffered the greatest losses up to this point, with 320 killed and wounded, including 60 percent of the 450 experienced troops who had originally ventured into the valley. Two of the battalion's four company commanders and eight of twelve platoon leaders were among the casualties.[26]

Following the attack of 18 May, Lt. Col. Gene Sherron, commander of the 2nd Battalion, 506th Regiment, came to Honeycutt's command post to coordinate relief. As he arrived the 187th was airlifting its latest casualties out of the battle area. At this point Honeycutt had not been told about his unit being relieved and was not happy to hear this news. Before he could argue the point, Major General Zais landed. The lieutenant colonel instantly told him his battalion was still capable of taking their objective. Zais relented, though not before he redeployed one of Sherron's companies to Honeycutt to bolster what he hoped would be the final assault.[27]

Figure 7.5. Airlifting the wounded from Hamburger Hill

Putting an End to It: The Final Attack

On 19 May, in preparation for this final push, Zais ordered the 2/501 and the ARVN 2nd Battalion, 3rd Infantry airlifted into LZs northeast and southeast of the base of Ap Bia. They quickly moved onto the mountain to their attack positions. Plans called for this assault to begin the following morning. Meanwhile, for the third day in a row, the 506th pressed on with its effort to take Hill 900.[28]

On 20 May the final action began, with four battalions spearheading the push. These included two companies of the 3/187 reinforced by A Company, 1/506. Beginning at 0800 and lasting for two hours before the ground action began, the USAF hammered the enemy positions with every conceivable kind of attack and gunship aircraft available. The air attacks were so successful, in retrospect one has to wonder why the Americans, from the outset, did not choose to eliminate the enemy forces with several Arc Light carpet-bombing raids or, in order to penetrate into the enemy's tunnels, C-130s dropping 15,000-pound "Daisy Cutter" bombs. At 0830 the air sorties were joined by ninety minutes of preparatory artillery fire. The

Figure 7.6. Soldiers rename Hill 937

ground assault began at 1000, with the battalions simultaneously attacking. By 1130, PAVN fire slackened, and by noon, units of 3/187 had reached the crest. Once they had gained a foothold, the men cleaned out the enemy bunkers, most often without knowing if PAVN soldiers were still inside. If anyone inside was alive, they were either buried or burned alive inside. The vast majority of the PAVN defenders were killed, but a few did escape into Laos. At 1700, Hill 937 was officially secured.[29]

While the Battle for Hill 937 was primarily an American effort, the ARVN 2nd Battalion, 3rd Regiment participated in the engagement. According to General Abrams, in what are known as the "Abrams Tapes," this unit was positioned near a place where the PAVN line was lightly defended. Once in place, they sent a scout party to test the forward enemy lines earlier than the proposed assault time. Once close to the PAVN positions, these ARVN soldiers reported the communist strength as minimal. The battalion's commanding officer decided to exploit the situation and attacked before the other allied units. Thus, they reached the crest of Hamburger Hill ahead of the 3/187 but were directed to withdraw since allied artillery was about to open fire on the summit. Instead of arguing the point, the ARVN troops did as directed, and the opportunity to overrun the PAVN lines facing the 3/187 was lost. Shortly after the ARVN battalion withdrew, the 3/187 broke through the enemy defenses and occupied the summit.[30]

Figure 7.7. US troops rest after finally reaching the summit

US losses during the ten-day battle totaled 72 killed and 372 wounded. To take the position, the 101st Airborne Division eventually committed five battalions and ten batteries of artillery. In addition, the USAF flew 272 missions and expended more than 500 tons of ordnance. American forces claimed the PAVN 7th and 8th Battalions, 29th Regiment suffered 630 dead, the number of bodies found on or around the battlefield. A large number of these corpses were discovered in makeshift mortuaries located in the myriad tunnel complexes.[31]

On 5 June 1969, less than two weeks after the eleventh and final assault, Maj. Gen. John M. Wright, now in command in the area, quietly abandoned the hill. A spokesman for the 101st Airborne Division said the US troops had "completed their search of the mountain and are now continuing their reconnaissance-in-force mission throughout the A Shau Valley." A few weeks later the PAVN reoccupied the valley once and for all.[32]

The Public Outcry and the Origins of the Name "Hamburger Hill"

So the battle was over. The Americans had taken the hill—temporarily. Like Khe Sanh less than a year before, after such dedication from and bloodshed by the American troops involved, their senior commanders abandoned the battlefield. All the while these officers had argued they had to fight on despite suggested alternatives, including aerial bombing, because taking this precious ground spelled a tactical victory and would bring the enemy closer to defeat due to the heavy losses they were taking. Yet once the ground was captured and held, at great expense and loss of allied life, military planners decided the blood-soaked ground was no longer strategically valuable. These commanders have gone down in history with the ignominy due other officers who have failed to take care of the lives of their men.

At least this was the public perception, which was fueled by reports from the battlefront. On 16 May, even with the battle was still underway, Jay Sharbutt, an Associated Press reporter who was in Saigon, got word of a protracted engagement going on for Hill 937. It seemed a worthwhile news story, so he went to General Zais's headquarters to interview him about the fighting. Taking the time to answer journalists' questions and conduct a battle at the same time annoyed Zais. Depending on one's point of view, the general either "answered Sharbutt's questions politely and honestly" or was evasive. According to Scalard's account, "the journalist was not satisfied. His subsequent newspaper account of 'Hamburger Hill' stirred up a storm of controversy that swept the nation and resounded in the halls of Congress."[33]

From Sharbutt's viewpoint, he was just trying to get the real story and report it to the American public. One of the more pointed questions he asked concerned the use infantry rather than firepower as the primary offensive tool on Hill 937. This was a legitimate question that required a detailed answer, but one General Zais believed he did not have the time nor the inclination to answer. A product of the World War II army, Zais was used to supportive correspondents like Ernie Pyle, not confrontational ones like Sharbutt. As is all too often the case when officials do not or will not directly answer hard questions, reporters assume they are covering up. The resulting article or report is frequently not favorable to the official involved.[34]

As had been the case since the United States had first sent soldiers to fight in Indochina, the relationship between generals and reporters changed. Television-news anchors like Chet Huntley, David Brinkley, Howard K. Smith, and Walter Cronkite had become trusted agents for millions of Americans who spent much of their evening hours listening to what they were certain was the factual truth they needed to make informed decisions. A new kind correspondent was born at this time, the investigative reporter. Such journalists dug deep to find the "truth." They often made news as much as they reported it, and the relationship between military leaders in Vietnam and journalists was not always friendly, especially since the United States was not winning.

In the case of the battle for Hill 937, the relationship festered after Sharbutt's interview with Zias and led to two critical news articles which appeared on 20 and 21 May. Sharbutt, harkening back to the Korean War and the much-bloodier Battle of Pork Chop Hill, sought to increase public interest in his piece by coining the term "Hamburger Hill," referring to American soldiers being ground up in combat. More reporters soon arrived to cover the battle, and the term "Hamburger Hill" became widely used. Concurrent with Sharbutt's articles, other items appeared in numerous other newspapers. To veterans of World War II and Korea, like Zais, this was simply no way for the "American" media to behave—to the generals, it was all but un-American.[35] In fairness several other articles provided the army's view of the situation.[36]

In fact, the public outcry began even before the end of the battle. The furor quickly made its way into the halls of Congress. After ten days and eleven attacks, on 20 May Zais and his men could finally breathe a sigh of relief. The battle was over. They had captured their objective and won a hard-earned victory. While they had suffered roughly 350 casualties, these numbers, while significant, were far less than those incurred at either Khe Sanh, Hue, or Dak To and about the same as Ia Drang Valley. Yet back in the States, "Hamburger Hill" became a catchphrase for defeat, hard evidence America could not win the war and, and proof the time had come for Nixon to bring the troops home.[37]

On the heels of the conclusion of the struggle for Hill 937, Sen. Edward "Teddy" Kennedy (D-Massachusetts) spoke before the US Senate and declared, "I feel that it is both senseless and irresponsible to continue sending our young men to their deaths to capture hills and positions that have no relation to ending this conflict." It was a shocking statement, but one that reflected the growing public fatigue over what seemed to be a never-ending nightmare. While the president and senior members of the US Army, especially Zais, denounced these kinds of statements as disloyal to the troops in Vietnam. The fact was America was at a crossroads that would eventually see Nixon begin the withdrawal of US military personnel.[38]

Throughout the aftermath of the battle and eventually the war, General Zais spent much of his time attempting, as he put it, to make sure the "proper story" of the battle was told and the 101st Airborne's reputation, especially that of Lieutenant Colonel Honeycutt, was protected: "I didn't care about me, but I just thought that we had fought such a gallant and brilliant fight, and that Honeycutt had done well. For those men to think that it had all been a needless, suicidal attack just galled me, and that is why I was willing to talk to the television, radio and newspaper people who obviously were aware of what Senator [Edward] Kennedy said and were clamoring to talk to me."[39]

One can hardly blame Zais for defending the deserved reputation and consistent courage of his troops. They fought bravely and, given the circumstances, as well as might be expected. Despite everything, they did finally take their objective at a devastating cost to the PAVN. But a tactical effort without a strategic purpose is a futile gesture, and the blame for the public response can only be placed at the feet of senior leaders who failed to formulate a winnable definition of victory. Thus, it is quite understandable why senators like Kennedy, who were already convinced of the futility of the war, would react the way they did. In fact, in a sense, Zais and Kennedy were both concerned about the lives and welfare of the young men who fought on Hill 937. What was happening was that, as the war was being lost, the blame game was already in full flower.[40]

Soon after the battle *Time* published an article that highlighted this fact and reported on the intense fighting, claiming that 597 North Vietnamese were killed while 56 Americans were killed and 420 wounded. The piece described the combat as "bitter" and the loss of life as 'high." *Time*, being a highly respected news magazine, had a major influence on public attitudes.[41] Unfortunately, the article failed to note that the initial purpose of the operation was not to hold territory but rather to kill North Vietnamese soldiers and cut off supply routes.

In early June, when the Americans left the hill, no one could ignore what appeared to be the senseless nature of the battle. The cold hard fact was that, after American leaders asked the flower of the nation's young men to sacrifice so much against such a determined enemy, once they had achieved their goal, the soldiers had to abandon the mountain and watch the PAVN reoccupy it a month later.[42]

Perception vs. Reality

On 27 June 1969, with the controversy swirling over US battle casualties, *Life* magazine published a troubling photographic montage openly questioning what appeared to be the never-ending and senseless loss of American lives. The piece showcased the pictures of 241 US soldiers killed during "that week's combat." The effect on Nixon was direct and powerful. He immediately ordered Abrams to avoid such high-casualty engagements. Because of Hamburger Hill and other battles like it, the president would now move to replace US troops with ARVN forces and emphasize what he called "Vietnamization." From here on, South Vietnamese young men would engage in direct-combat operations, not Americans.[43]

As if to keep the public fires burning against further US involvement in Vietnam, *Harper's Weekly* published a poignant article by Neil Sheehan, entitled "Letters from Hamburger Hill," in its November 1969 issue. Done in Sheehan's masterful style, it was enough to bring tears to the eyes of most

Americans. Focusing on the loneliness and fear only a combat soldier could feel, the letters made it clear many of the men at Hamburger Hill were convinced they would never get home.[44]

In simple terms, the controversy over the conduct of the Battle of Hamburger Hill led to a reassessment of US policy and its commitment to South Vietnam. As a direct result, to reduce casualties, Abrams was forced by the president to cease his policy of "maximum pressure" against the PAVN and replace it with one of "protective reaction" for troops threatened with combat action. At the same time, Nixon announced the first troop withdrawal from South Vietnam. In short, America had had enough and was going home. In hindsight, they had also signed the death warrant for the Republic of Vietnam.[45]

Abrams himself was frustrated by the entire situation. One night, not long after the battle, he had friends over for a round of poker. He told those present he had had a visit from a congressional delegation headed by Senator Kennedy that morning who expressed displeasure over the loss of lives at Hamburger Hill. Abrams lamented to his guests, "the last time the 29th PAVN Regiment came out of North Vietnam it destroyed Hue, and I heard from every antiquarian in the world." After a short pause he continued: "This time, when they came out again, I issued orders that they were to be intercepted and defeated before they could get to Hue. We drove them back into North Vietnam, but I was criticized for the casualties that entailed." He then concluded, "If they would let me know where they would like me to fight the next battle I would be glad to do it there." At that point they dealt the cards.[46]

The real battle over Hill 937 took place in the US Senate and the national media, not on a mountain in Vietnam. As noted, in late May, soon after the Americans took the hill, the debate over Hamburger Hill came to the floor of the Senate when Senators Kennedy, George McGovern, and Stephen M. Young chastised American military leadership for a lack of concern for the lives of their troops and for repeatedly attacking an unimportant position. Most powerful was the protracted 29 May speech by Young, in which he accused US generals of knowing nothing about military history and instead "flinging our paratroopers piecemeal into frontal assaults." These, he said, were repeated attacks that were ineffective and only "killed our boys who went up Hamburger Hill."[47]

Later, when the portrait-laden 27 June issue of *Life* appeared, the name "Hamburger Hill" once again appeared front and center in the public consciousness. In retrospect, many historians saw this publication as a watershed event of negative public opinion toward the Vietnam War. In fact, only 5 of the 241 featured photos were of men killed on Hill 937. Regardless, most Americans concluded all of the featured photos were casualties of that battle.[48]

Many veterans and revisionist analysts have long contended America never lost a battle during the Vietnam War, but the politicians lost the war. But winning or losing the battles was beside the point. Harry G. Summers explained:

> The Hamburger Hill battle had run afoul of a fundamental warfighting equation. Master philosopher of war Karl von Clausewitz emphasized almost a century and a half earlier that because war is controlled by its political object, the value of this object must determine the sacrifices to be made for it both in magnitude and also in duration. He went on to say, once the expenditure of effort exceeds the value of the political object, the object must be renounced. And that's exactly what happened. The expenditure of effort at Hamburger Hill exceeded the value the American people attached to the war in Vietnam. The public had turned against the war a year and a half earlier, and it was their intense reaction to the cost of that battle in American lives, inflamed by sensationalist media reporting, that forced the Nixon administration to order the end of major tactical ground operations.[49]

In another words, winning tactical victories is only relevant if they lead to the strategic goal of contributing to attaining the policy goals of the nation. This is the definition of winning a war and realizing victory. Hamburger Hill, while another demonstration of the heroism of Americas fighting forces, failed to contribute anything to winning the war. Instead, it was like the last drop of water that causes a bucket to overflow.

8

The Nguyen Hue (Easter) Offensive, 1972

As 1972 dawned and Commando Hunt VII ended, many US leaders hoped this last and most ambitious of the seven interdiction campaigns, flown by nearly every kind of air weapon available to the United States, had slowed any communist plans for another Tet-style offensive that coming spring. As it turned out, they were wholly disappointed. On 30 March 1972 nominal commander in chief General Giap and the actual battlefield commander, PAVN chief of staff Gen. Van Tien Dung, launched the largest and most elaborate conventional assault on the South of the entire war. Known as the Nguyen Hue, or Easter, Offensive, it lasted from 30 March to 16 September 1972 (or 22 October, depending on the source). It was the largest invasion of one country by another since 300,000 Chinese had crossed the Yalu River in late 1950 during the Korean War. The North's initial goal was to seize as much territory and kill as many ARVN troops as possible in order to improve their position at the Paris peace talks. As the incursion began, many PAVN leaders began to hope a complete victory might be at hand.

Leaders in Hanoi named the campaign the Nguyen Hue Offensive to imbue it with patriotic fervor. In 1773 three brothers, all named Tay Son after their village of origin, united Vietnam following years of civil war and social turmoil. In 1788–89, the youngest brother, Nguyen Hue, defeated an invading Chinese army on the outskirts of Hanoi. Using the rainy season to avoid US air attacks, Giap ultimately committed fourteen divisions and twenty-six separate regiments. He placed one additional division in northern Laos to protect supply lines, while four others remained in reserve on the border in North Vietnam.[1] Additional aims included the erosion of flagging US public support for the war during an election year, the countering of South Vietnamese successes in rural areas since 1969, and winning the war before Nixon's detente policy affected Soviet and Chinese materiel support of Hanoi.[2] What Northern leaders failed to grasp was that the audacity of the attack "provided Nixon with the public support necessary to retaliate."[3]

When the enemy launched their offensive, Nixon, who had been elected amid promises to end US involvement in Vietnam, seemed no closer to a settlement than his predecessor, despite the diplomacy of Kissinger and the withdrawal of nearly 500,000 US troops. While considering his next move, 120,000 communist regulars, supported by artillery and 200 Soviet-built tanks invaded South Vietnam, threatening to overrun America's ally. The invasion violated the agreements reached between Washington and Hanoi when Johnson had ended the Northern bombing in 1968, and, while Nixon was concerned South Vietnam might fall, he now had an excuse to discard restrictions which prevented him from fully employing US airpower.[4]

Allied forces were not completely caught off guard even though scheduled reductions of US troops to 69,000 in May and aircraft to 375 left them reeling from the initial attack. In the spring of 1971, the CIA had warned of a potential election-year attack, but they believed the enemy could not "launch a nationwide military offensive on anything approaching the scale of Tet 1968."[5] Still, 200 PAVN tanks deployed, undetected to various staging areas in 1971–72 and as one analyst later noted, "This stealthy deployment, together with the persistent perception that the enemy's logistical system was less efficient than it was, deflected American intelligence analysts from a correct understanding of communist plans."[6]

In December 1971 Nixon concerned by these intelligence reports, had responded with Operation Proud Deep Alpha during which USAF fighters flew over 1,000 sorties against enemy staging areas just south of the twentieth parallel. Additional attacks took place, in February 1972, but were limited during the president's trip to China. Simultaneously, the number of US aircraft in Southeast Asia increased with the dispatch of 207 USAF F-4

Phantoms from 29 December 1971 to 13 May 1972, bringing the total in theater to 374.[7]

The Easter Offensive unfolded in three phases. In April the initial PAVN assaults were successful. Then for roughly a month, beginning in May and ending in June, there existed a stalemate. The final phase began in late June and early July, with ARVN counterattacks climaxing with the recapture of Quang Tri City in September.[8] As the first attacks took place, it seemed the PAVN had again caught US and ARVN forces unprepared (as during Tet in 1968). In the I Corps Tactical Zone, communist troops overwhelmed ARVN defenders in a month-long battle for Quang Tri City. After victory there, they headed south intent upon capturing Hue. The communists destroyed frontier defense forces in II Corps Tactical Zone and advanced on the provincial capital of Kontum, planning to cut South Vietnam in two. Concurrently, in the III Corps Tactical Zone north of Saigon, PAVN forces overran Loc Ninh, pushing toward An Loc, the capital of Binh Long Province.[9]

It seemed the enemy was perched on the edge of a great victory, however, their early triumphs were encumbered by excessive casualties, inept tactics, and the increasing application of US and RVNAF airpower, especially after the introduction of Operation Linebacker I. While the ARVN fought well and temporarily saved their nation, the PAVN secured vital bases inside South Vietnam from which to launch future offensives. The North also attained a better bargaining position at the Paris talks.[10]

Preliminary Events

Plans for the spring 1972 invasion began in early 1971, following the failed ARVN Lam Son 719 campaign. At this time Northern leaders gathered in Hanoi for the Nineteenth Plenum of the Central Committee of the Lao Dong, or Vietnamese Communist Party. After a protracted series of discussion, in December members of the Politburo agreed to launch a major offensive in early 1972 as soon as their forces were in place. With 1972 being an American presidential-election year and the Politburo convinced they might affect the outcome by encouraging more antiwar sentiment within the US government and public, North Vietnamese leaders simply could not pass up what they believed was a great opportunity. In addition, with the United States making major troop withdrawals, causing ARVN forces to become overextended along their 600-mile border, victory seemed a very real possibility.[11]

Communist officials came to this decision at the culmination of three years of political bickering between two factions within the North Vietnamese Politburo. The first group supported Truong Chinh, who backed a strategy advocated by the Chinese that sought to continue a low-intensity insurgent conflict while rebuilding the DRV. The other group, known as the "southern firsters," believed in a Soviet strategic path and backed Defense Minister Giap and First Party Secretary Le Duan, who called for a big offensive. While the disastrous defeat in the Tet Offensive of 1968 had diminished the Giap–Le Duan faction's influence temporarily, the 1971 successes

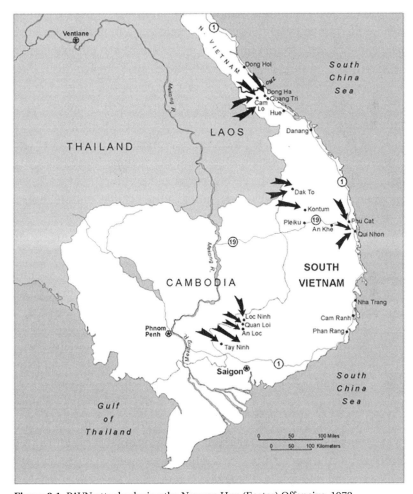

Figure 8.1. PAVN attacks during the Nguyen Hue (Easter) Offensive, 1972

against ARVN units during the Laotian incursion resurrected their strategic vision. Ultimately, Le Duan assumed the responsibility for planning the operation, while Giap dealt with logistical plans and final operational action. In turn, General Dung was entrusted with the battlefield conduct of the offensive.[12]

For more than a decade, the PAVN had used the Ho Chi Minh Trail infiltration routes, along the border regions of Laos and Cambodia, to bring supplies and manpower into South Vietnam. In late 1971 Le Duan and his planners decided this area provided them with the shortest conduit into the South and the best place to mass their forces. It also appeared to be the location where "the enemy was weakest." They believed that "violent attacks would disintegrate enemy forces . . . , making it impossible for them to have enough troops to deploy elsewhere." Communist organizers reasoned such a thrust would distract the ARVN and cause them to divert their focus and resources, even as the other two assaults—one in the Central Highlands and the other one east from Cambodia toward Saigon—would deal the death blow.[13]

As noted earlier, plans called for Hanoi to commit fourteen divisions and twenty-six regiments to this offensive. Their official goals were limited to crippling large elements of the ARVN, perhaps deposing President Thieu, and possibly persuading the United States to curtail or end continued support for the Republic of Vietnam. Northern leaders also hoped to capture a Southern provincial capital, which they could then declare to be the seat of the Provisional Revolutionary Government.[14] The party's view of things was best reflected in a 1972 article in their journal: "It doesn't matter whether the war is promptly ended or prolonged. . . . Both are opportunities to sow the seeds; all we have to do is to wait for the time to harvest the crop."[15]

As the planning phase began, Northern leaders were confident their operation would succeed. But that summer they were shocked to discover Nixon was going to make a state visit the People's Republic of China before May 1972. To mollify the DRV, Chinese leaders provided reassurances they would continue to provide military and economic aid in 1972. Soviet leaders were pleased by this perceived antagonism between China and North Vietnam, and they sought to extend the split by agreeing to send "additional aid without reimbursement" to the PAVN. While this seemed to mean the bulk of DRV aid was coming from the Soviet Union, in fact, of the nearly $1.5 billion in military aid sent to North Vietnam, almost two-thirds came from

China. Specifically, the NVA's two largest communist cousins sent a torrent of supplies and modern equipment, such as four hundred Soviet T-34 and T-54 tanks as well as a Chinese version of the T-54, or Type 59, medium tank. They also received two hundred PT-76 light amphibious tanks. Further, China and the Soviet Union supplied the North with hundreds of AAA pieces; SAMs, such as the shoulder-fired, heat-seeking SA-7 Strela; antitank missiles like the wire-guided AT-3 Sagger; and heavy-caliber, long-range artillery. To crew this new equipment, Hanoi now had 25,000 troops who had received specialized training abroad, 80 percent of them in the Soviet Union or Eastern Europe. Of note, 3,000 PAVN tank crewmen went to the Soviet armor school in Odessa.[16]

Allied Intelligence

Some authors have suggested the US and South Vietnamese were caught completely by surprise when the PAVN attacked on 30 March 1972. Yet this does not seem to be altogether true. During the last half of 1971, US and South Vietnamese intelligence analysis of future communist intentions, while uncertain in some regards, predicted an offensive. But the experts disagreed about its timing, origin, and magnitude. They did agree, though, that the Tet Offensive had been conducted mostly by the VC, and since that force had been effectively annihilated during Tet, the only way to carry out another such offensive required a major PAVN commitment. Intelligence officers were split over the communsits' ability to do this.[17]

In December things began to become clearer when reports filtered in that PAVN forces, supporting offensive operations by the Khmer Rouge in Cambodia, were relocating to staging areas near the border with South Vietnam. In addition, even as America's last Commando Hunt bombing campaign drew to a close, infiltration activities along the Ho Chi Minh Trail were growing rather than slowing, contrary to the goal of these air attacks. In Washington, administration officials, hoping to convince the public that Nixon's Vietnamization policy was working, assured everyone the enemy could not possibly initiated another Tet-style offensive. In January 1972, even though Defense Intelligence Agency specialists advised Secretary of Defense Melvin Laird that the communists would attack following the Tet holidays and employ tanks and other conventional weaponry, he remained skeptical, telling Congress, "A large communist offensive was not a serious possibility."[18]

The one group that seemed to have a handle on things was MACV. Officers in Vietnam had dispatched numerous reconnaissance teams into the areas near the Mu Gia and Ban Karai Passes to inspect the effects of Commando Hunt VII bombing. Instead, these units discovered a huge buildup of enemy troops and equipment. From this, MACV analysts predicted the PAVN was preparing for a significant offensive in the Central Highlands and the northern provinces of South Vietnam. By 20 November 1971, with the United States having withdrawn all but 27,000 troops from Southeast Asia, most of whom were support units, Abrams was convinced the enemy would launch an offensive soon after the Tet holidays of 1972. The general reported this data to the JCS chairman, Admiral Moorer, declaring the PAVN likely would attempt to "duplicate the effects of the 1968 offensive, perhaps by a limited operation aimed less at inflicting defeat on the battlefield than in influencing American public opinion."[19]

As it turned out, Abrams's prediction was early by two months, and when Tet came and went without significant enemy activity, he and his staff were ridiculed by the press. As one *Life* magazine editorial put it, "the Tet offensive didn't happen."[20] By March, allied forces, having been on high alert, began to relax. While some of these units returned to pacification efforts, Ambassador Bunker departed for Nepal, and General Abrams went to Thailand to spend the Easter holiday with his family. The advantage provided by the accuracy of the intelligence MACV had gleaned was now lost, meaning few were prepared when the Nguyen Hue Offensive did come.[21]

Waiting in the Wings

In the meantime, the ARVN forces in II Corps Zone, soon to bear the brunt of the PAVN assault, took a deep breath and settled in their fixed defensive positions. These included the 1st, 2nd, and 3rd Infantry Divisions in Quang Tri and Thua Thien Provinces, augmented by the 147th and 258th Marine Brigades, the 51st Infantry Regiment, the 1st Ranger Group, and members of Regional and Popular Forces. This South Vietnamese force totaled nearly 30,000 men. At the center of this defensive position was the 3rd Division, which had been formed in October 1971 and stationed in an arc of outposts near the DMZ, in place of departing US units. In the process, ARVN leaders had stripped the 1st Division, generally considered the South's best unit, of its 2nd Regiment, with the 11th Armored Cavalry from the I Corps reserve sent to serve as a supporting force for the division. Both the 2nd and 11th were experienced, well trained, well equipped, and well led. But the 3rd Division's other two regiments, the 56th and 57th, comprised of recaptured deserters, men released from jail, and regional and provincial forces. Worse, they were commanded by discarded officers and noncommissioned officers from other units. In many cases, the soldiers of these regiments did not trust their leaders. At a time when the Americans were leaving the war to the ARVN, far too many of its units, especially at this stage of the conflict, depended on a scarcity of US advisors, who by then served only at regimental, brigade, and divisional headquarters.[22]

Since most South Vietnamese reasoned the PAVN would not violate the demarcation line, the 3rd Division appeared to be stationed in a relatively safe area directly below the DMZ. Officials assigned recently promoted Brig. Gen. Vu Van Giai, former deputy commander of the 1st Division, to command the exposed unit. His immediate superior was Lt. Gen. Hoang Xuan Lam, the I Corps commander who in many ways typified the indecisive nature of the ARVN's officers and command structure. Lam proved to be a good administrator but left tactical decisions to his subordinate commanders. This was a workable posture as long as his division leaders did not run into any major difficulties. With US intelligence unable to reach a consensus on future PAVN actions, Lam and his American advisers mistakenly concluded the North would not violate the DMZ.[23]

As Easter weekend 1972 approached, Giai decided to transfer the 56th Regiment from near the central DMZ to a location near the Camp Carroll artillery base. In turn, he planned to move the 2nd Regiment from Camp Carroll to the 56th's old position. Having a shortage of trucks, he moved the troops concurrently, the two units becoming hopelessly intertwined and jumbled in short order. On 30 March, at 1130, the two regimental headquarters turned off their radios as they worked to complete the move. With their lines of communication disjointed and their forces entangled, the weather turned bad enough to thwart aerial operations. At this point the 3rd Division offered the massed communist troops to the north a wonderful target.[24]

The Nguyen Hue Offensive Begins

The PAVN launched the offensive around noon on 30 March 1972 with a massive barrage from 130-mm field guns against the northernmost ARVN outposts in Quang Tri Province. As the firing died down, the PAVN 304th and 308th Divisions, totaling 40,000–50,000 troops, supported by more than one hundred Soviet-built tanks, swept out of Laos and crossed the DMZ into I Corps Zone. The 308th Division and two independent regiments smashed into the "ring of steel," the arc of ARVN firebases just south of the DMZ. Pouring in from the west, the NVA's 334B Division, including an armored regiment, moved along Route 9 past Khe Sanh and into the Quang Tri River Valley.[25] Surprised of the size of the attack, and the swiftness of the advance provided the communist juggernaut "the inestimable benefit of shock effect, a crucial psychological edge over defenders who had expected something quite different."[26]

On 1 April, 160 miles south of the DMZ in the Central Highlands, 28,000 PAVN troops attacked Kontum Province. The enemy opened a third front with 31,000 men 375 miles south of the DMZ and 60 miles west of Saigon. Of the 200,000 troops eventually involved, 110,000 were PAVN regulars and 50,000 VC main-force personnel. Supported by tanks and artillery and protected by low-lying clouds, PAVN units in Military Region I pushed ARVN units out of Quang Tri City by 1 May. Afterward, the new ARVN I Corps commander, Lt. Gen. Ngo Quang Truong, approved a plan for Giai to withdraw the 3rd Division to the south and set up a tenuous defensive line on the south bank of the My Chanh River. By 14 May, enemy units in Military Region II had overrun Dak To and placed Kontum City under siege. In Military Region III the communists had destroyed an entire ARVN division, taken Loc Ninh, and surrounded An Loc by 13 April.[27]

On 1 April, when Giai ordered the withdrawal of the 3rd Division south of the Cua Viet River, he was able to make the move in good order. He reorganized his forces, and the following morning ARVN armored elements briefly withstood a PAVN assault when the crucial Highway QL-1 bridge over the Cue Viet River at Dong Ha was destroyed by Capt. John Ripley, adviser to the Vietnamese 3rd Battalion. These communist units were soon joined by the 320B and 325C Divisions, making the ARVN position tenuous. Concurrently, the PAVN's 324B Division advanced east from the A Shau Valley to attack Firebases Bastogne and Checkmate, which protected the city of Hue. With the campaign designed to coincide with the monsoon rains, USAF airstrikes proved to be limited above 500 feet. As its shock troops advanced, the NVA followed with AAA units armed with the new ZSU-57-2 tracked-weapon platforms and shoulder-fired SA-7 Grails, which made low-level bomb runs very dangerous.[28]

"Despite the weather," according to historian and former USAF intelligence officer Earl Tilford, "the SA-7 missiles and antiaircraft guns, and a confused ground situation, airpower dealt the PAVN a major setback by preventing a rout from turning into a total collapse of the northern front." Tilford further noted, "B-52s flew a total of 1,398 Arc Light sorties hitting PAVN base camps, bivouac areas, troop concentrations, and antiaircraft artillery sites throughout Quang Tri Province." These sorties helped the ARVN hang on until its units could counterattack.[29]

The ARVN Tries to Hang On

The artillery firebase at Camp Carroll, halfway between Laos and the South Vietnamese coast—a key position in the ARVN's northern and western defensive line—was the hardest obstacle for the NVA to overcome as they pushed toward Quang Tri City. On 2 April Col. Pham Van Dinh, the commander of the ARVN 56th Regiment, surrendered the camp and his 1,500 troops, having barely fired a shot. Later that same day ARVN troops abandoned their final western base at Mai Loc. This allowed enemy troops to traverse the Cam Lo Bridge, only five miles from Dong Ha, affording them nearly unopposed access to western Quang Tri Province north of the Thach Han River. Only intermittent rearguard delaying actions slowed the PAVN during the next three weeks. On 27 April communist forces launched a three-pronged attack against Dong Ha, which fell the next day. From there they pushed within a mile of Quang Tri City. On 29 April Giai ordered a general retreat to the My Chanh. To facilitate this movement, US advisors in the imperiled city radioed for an emergency helicopter extraction. On 1 May 132 survivors, including eighty Americans, were flown out.[30]

With the military gone, there followed a mass exodus of tens of thousands of civilians. As the throng of terrified people fled south down Highway 1, enemy artillery opened fire on the mass of humanity. Concurrently, communist infantry attacked the flanks of the unarmed column; no ARVN units provided defense. To the west, despite a spirited defense and B-52 bombing raids, Firebases Bastogne and Checkmate fell, with heavy casualties on both sides. On 21 April General Abrams contacted Secretary Laird: "In summary . . . the pressure is mounting and the battle has become brutal. . . . [T]he senior military leadership has begun to bend and in some cases to break. In adversity, it is losing its will and cannot be depended upon to take the measures necessary to stand and fight."[31]

Quang Tri City fell on 2 May. That same day General Lam was summoned to Saigon to meet with President Thieu, who relieved him of command of the I Corps and replaced him with Lieutenant General Truong, commander of III Corps and one of the finest ARVN generals. Truong's job was to defend Hue, stop further losses, and recapture lost territory. While Giai had inexperienced troops and was constantly overruled by his superiors, he had done a decent job. General Truong spoke up for him and advocated he keep command of the 3rd Division. Nevertheless, he became the scapegoat for the defeat and was tried for "desertion in the face of the enemy." Giai was convicted and sentenced to five years in prison. The cruel irony was Lam, in spite of his poor leadership, was promoted to position within the Ministry of Defense because of his political connections.[32]

The Struggle for Hue

At the end of April, despite their steady series of setbacks, ARVN forces had recovered and dug in, with a stalemate apparently developing on the northern front. Hoping to quickly break this impasse, Lt. Gen. Tran Van Quang, commander of the PAVN B-4 Front, sent the troops of his 324B Division on a concentrated assault out of the A Shau Valley toward Hue. While they made progress, the ARVN 1st Division defended their positions tenaciously, and soon the communist advance slowed to a crawl. On the last days of April, the PAVN 29th and 803rd Regiments overran Firebase Bastogne, which made Firebase Checkmate untenable. As a result, under cover of darkness, Southern troops withdrew, leaving Hue vulnerable to enemy capture once again. The communists took advantage of this opportunity and made a direct thrust toward the city along Route 547. Supported by units swinging to their right, the PAVN force attempted to invest Hue on 2 May.[33]

Concurrently, enemy forces pressed their attack southward, down Highway 1 and across the Thach Han, toward Hue. As they did, Truong sent the 2nd and 3rd Brigades of his Airborne Division to bolster the 1st Division and Marine Division in Hue. The ARVN forces now had three battalions, and the reorganized 1st Ranger Group, increasing their troop strength to more than 35,000. As the allies increased their defensive forces, the weather also cleared for one week. This allowed US aircraft to provide significant CAS. The combination of reinforcements and airstrikes halted the communist advance on 5 May 1972.[34]

In mid-May Truong took the offensive in a series of controlled raids and maneuvers he codenamed Song Than (or Tidal Wave). The attacks sought to confuse PAVN forces and expand the ARVN's defensive perimeter around Hue. Truong also hoped to deny the enemy time to reorganize and continue their assault. On 15 May his troops retook Firebase Bastogne and, five days later, Firebase Checkmate. This left the communists in a weakened state. Even so, the day after Checkmate's recovery, they initiated an attack on Hue itself, only to be repulsed with the loss of eighteen tanks and eight hundred men. The course of the battle was changing in favor of the ARVN.[35]

This trend continued between 25 and 29 May, when a second PAVN strike managed to cross the Perfume River, only to be driven back across. This was the communists' last major attack on Hue. Many US advisors, such as Maj. Gen. Frederick J. Kroesen, the senior American advisor in I Corps Zone, later admitted he believed the fall of Quang Tri City foreshadowed the fall of Hue.[36] As he noted, the PAVN had not made the best use of their chances and thus "failed completely to take advantage of the moment," making it yet "another great blunder of the Quang Tri campaign."[37]

In June, as the weather continued to improve, US air attacks and naval shelling increased. On 14 June Lieutenant General Truong briefed President Thieu and MACV leaders on his plan to recapture Quang Tri Province. Thieu was reticent about anything too large and preferred a less ambitious operation. Truong would not give up and finally persuaded the president by explaining how such an endeavor could work by "employing the superior firepower of our American ally." Thieu finally approved the plan, which Truong put into action with Operation Lam Son 72 on 28 June.[38]

As the main South Vietnamese ground push began, the troopers of the 1st Division moved west toward Laos while the Airborne and Marine Divisions, the 1st Ranger Group, and the 7th Armored Cavalry drove north to retake Quang Tri. Airborne troops used airmobile end runs to outflank the PAVN defenses along the way. ARVN forces soon overran them, coming within ten miles of Quang Tri City. Thieu then interceded, overriding Truong's plan to bypass the city and cross the Cua Viet River in order to cutoff any retreating PAVN defenders. In an act of stubborn pride, the president insisted Quang Tri City be recaptured since it was "a symbol" of "his authority."[39]

The primary PAVN defenders in the city were replacements and militia. One of them later described the situation: "The new recruits came in at dusk. They were dead by dawn. . . . No one had time to check where they were from, or who their commander might be." Others described the defense as a "senseless sacrifice," calling Quang Tri City "Hamburger City."[40]

On 11 July 1972, men of the ARVN Marine Division launched an assault north and east of the city that severed the last remaining land route into town. It was a bloody business for the marines, who were airlifted into position by US helicopters. The South Vietnamese lost nearly 25 percent of their 8,000 marines during the overall campaign, most during this attack. As for the communist remnants, they could only be reinforced and resupplied across the Thach Han River, making them vulnerable to airstrikes. After a ferocious three-day battle, the PAVN's 48th Regiment of the 320B Division was forced to attempt a desperate retreat.[41]

Throughout the remainder of the summer, USN, USMC, and USAF warplanes flew 5,461 fighter CAS sorties and 2,054 B-52 Arc Light raids in support of the ARVN offensive.[42] Beginning on 27 July, the ARVN Marine Division took over as the lead unit from the airborne units in Quang Tri City. Progress proved to be agonizingly slow since much of the fighting was house to house. Finally, in September the ARVN initiated the assault to capture the heavily defended citadel, which fell on the sixteenth. Afterward, South Vietnamese forces moved to the southern bank of the Thach Han, where the exhausted troops halted, unable to press on to Dong Ha.[43]

While this aspect of the Easter Offensive had petered out and Hue had been saved, ARVN forces continued battling communist forces at several other vital areas of South Vietnam. The most important were at An Loc and Kontum City.

The Assault on An Loc

While the PAVN attacked Quang Tri City and Hue, at An Loc the combined PAVN/VC 9th Division engaged the ARVN 15th and 21st Divisions. The second wave of the offensive struck on 5 April, with a communist advance from the Cambodian Base Area 708 into Binh Long Province, northeast of Saigon. Its main targets were the towns and airfields at Loc Ninh, Quan Loi, and An Loc. The assault began as a probing action into the III Corps Zone, staying close enough to the Cambodian sanctuaries so that the troops could be easily resupplied and reinforced. The initial spearhead of this strike force was the B-2 Front's 5th Division (PAVN/VC) and 203rd Armored

Regiment, which advanced down Highway 9 toward the border outpost of Loc Ninh. Defending Loc Ninh were 2,000 men of the ARVN 9th Regiment and a battalion of rangers. For three days South Vietnamese troops repelled five infantry attacks supported by tanks. Finally, on 7 April the exhausted Southern defenders fell back. The PAVN then surrounded the ARVN's 25th Division in neighboring Tay Ninh Province by attacking their forward outposts with two full regiments.[44]

As he reviewed the situation, III Corps commander Lt. Gen. Nguyen Van Minh correctly deduced the next communist target would be the provincial capital of An Loc. He quickly sent the 5th Division to defend the town, supported by two Ranger Group battalions. On 10–11 April Minh sent two additional units, including the 21st Infantry Division (which had been stationed in the Mekong delta), to Chon Thanh to join a 9th Infantry Division regiment defending the town. In an effort to coordinate the defense of the area, he placed Brig. Gen. Le Van Hung, commander of the 5th Division, in overall command. The move came none too soon. PAVN forces were moving toward An Loc, having sent the 7th Division around the town, south along Highway 13, to block any relief effort launched from Chon Thanh. Enemy leaders decided An Loc, being so close to Saigon, when captured would make the perfect capital for the Provisional Revolutionary Government.[45]

By 13 April, An Loc was surrounded. The communists poured in artillery fire and then sent in armor and infantry through a hail of rockets, bombs, and napalm from US and RVNAF aircraft and massed artillery. The ARVN troops were supported by several American advisors, who proved essential to the town's defense by helping organize CAS, artillery fire, logistics, and intelligence. The senior advisor, Col. William Miller, constantly urged Hung to initiate counterattacks. Instead, the general appeared willing to allow US airpower to defeat the PAVN and VC. Miller became so frustrated that he reported to his superiors, "He is tired—unstable—irrational—irritable—inadvisable—and unapproachable."[46] The irony was Hung was later lauded as the "Hero of An Loc." When the communists finally overran South Vietnam in April 1975, the general committed suicide rather than surrender to the PAVN.[47]

The stubborn PAVN and VC assaults finally pushed into the town itself. The communists overran the airfield and reduced the ARVN perimeter to a small pocket in the center of An Loc. On 21 April PAVN tanks temporarily broke through this ARVN defensive perimeter but were finally beaten back by antitank weapons and helicopter gunships. By late April, the communist infantry had captured most of the northern part of An Loc. Unable to finish off the Southern defenders, they dug in, sometimes right across the street from their opponents. With many of their tanks destroyed, PAVN forces could no longer attack ARVN troops, which the Southerners soon realized. They also discovered the Northern tanks were easy prey to antitank weapons. This failure of tactical skill was one of the PAVN's prime weaknesses during the offensive, one that the allies quickly exploited. The PAVN 9th Division commander's failure to take An Loc brought him an official reprimand and loss of local command, which was transferred to the senior officer of the 5th Division.[48]

Another issue facing the NVA proved to be the rain of ordnance delivered upon them by incessant airstrikes, which further reduced manpower and made resupply difficult. This was borne out by the disastrous assault on 21 April, at which point the battle for An Loc largely became a siege. Throughout, the communists pounded the ARVN defenders with 1,200–2,000 mortar, rocket, and artillery rounds per day. Surrounded and with the airfield in enemy hands, the ARVN could only be resupplied by air drops. Difficult as it was, pilots and crews of the US Army's 549th Quartermaster Air Delivery (QM AD) Rigger Company, which had been sent from Okinawa in early April, flew 448 missions and delivered 2,693 tons of food, medical supplies, and ammunition.[49]

From 22 April to 10 May 1972, both sides dug in for the next round as the tactical situation remained unchanged. The weekly news magazine *Paris Match* described the situation in the III Corps Zone as similar to "Verdun or Stalingrad."[50] Finally, on the morning of 11 May, the NVA launched another attack following an intense artillery barrage that sent more than 8,300 shells into the defensive perimeter. By day's end, the ARVN position had shrunk to an area measuring 1,000 by 1,500 yards. PAVN forces again pushed into An Loc only to be thwarted by a massive aerial attack, which cost the North Vietnamese forty tanks and over eight hundred men.[51]

Looking back at the failed attack, airpower played a key role in the victory. As one communist prisoner of war recalled, as they attacked the eastern part of the city around 0530, B-52s struck their columns. They pounded the eastern approaches to the city, every hour, on the hour, for twenty-five hours, bombing several targets more than once. Whole units were wiped out. For the next three days, each time PAVN troops assembled

Figure 8.2. Lt. Gen. Cao Van Vien (third from left), Brig. Gen. Le Van Hung (third from right), and Pres. Nguyen Van Thieu (second from right) celebrate the ARVN victory at An Loc

to resume the attack, they were bombed. Five days later, on another defensive front, a PAVN column supported by twenty tanks attacked an ARVN force just south of Kontum City on Route 14. Three cells of B-52s attacked each enemy column and "obliterated" them. On the 26th, the enemy made one last assault on Kontum City that failed because of a tenacious ARVN defense and B-52 support.[52]

Even before this dramatic defense unfolded, a relief mission was underway led by the ARVN's 21st Division. It would never make it to An Loc. For three weeks the division crept north up Highway 13, under constant delaying actions by smaller numbers of communist troops.

While it appeared to have been a failure, in retrospect, it had the inadvertent effect of diverting significant PAVN 7th Division resources. This certainly helped save the beleaguered city. If this bloodletting had not been enough for communist leaders, they hurled yet another assault at An Loc defenders on 14 May. PAVN troops stormed directly into the teeth of the ARVN defenses. As Col. Walt Ulmer, the 5th Division's senior advisor, recalled: "They were simply trying to pile on and pile on and pile on. They frittered away an awful lot of manpower."[53]

The main battle was over. Northern forces remained in the area and continued to shell An Loc until 12 June, when they began to withdraw. Simultaneously, more than 1,000 ARVN wounded were evacuated. Gradually, the decimated enemy faded away to the north and west as other communist units covered their withdrawal. On 18 June officials at III Corps headquarters declared the siege had ended. The government in Saigon announced 8,000 Southern defenders had been killed or wounded at An Loc as well as 1,000 civilians. American sources claimed 25,000 communist troops killed or wounded during the action, though many authors and researchers have since questioned those numbers.[54]

Kontum

In the third and final phase of the Easter campaign, the NVA aimed at capturing the cities of Kontum and Pleiku in an effort to control the Central Highlands. If they accomplished this, it would allow them to push to the coastal plains, thus splitting South Vietnam in two. On 5 April VC forces began this phase with a diversionary attack on Binh Dinh Province along the coast. Seeking to close Highway 1, they also sought to capture ARVN firebases and divert Southern troops away from PAVN operations to the west. These Northern units were under the direction of Lt. Gen. Hoang Minh Thao, commander of the B-3 Front, which included 50,000 men of the PAVN 320th and 2nd Divisions in the highlands and the 3rd Division in the lowlands.[55]

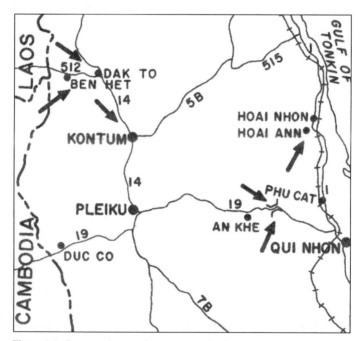

Figure 8.3. Communist attacks in Kontum Province, 1972

The ARVN troops facing them in II Corps Zone were the 22nd and 23rd Divisions, two armored cavalry squadrons, and the 2nd Airborne Brigade, all under the command of Lt. Gen. Ngo Du. As noted, as early as January many allied leaders were convinced the PAVN were preparing for an offensive in the triborder region. To deal with this possibility, dozens of B-52 Arc Light sorties were flown over the area. Southern troops also deployed toward the border in order to slow any possible PAVN advance and afford airpower a chance to destroy enemy forces, equipment, and supplies.[56]

At first the VC assault alarmed Du so much he almost fell for the enemy ruse and sent the bulk of his forces to the coast and away from the highlands. Fortunately, John Paul Vann, now a civilian and the director of the US Second Regional Assistance Group, calmed the general's fears and convinced him to keep his troops in place in order to be prepared for the main assault, which he was convinced would come from western Laos. Vann was granted the unique authority to command all US military advisors in his region, the first civilian official in US military history to hold essentially the rank equivalent of general and command US ground forces in the field.

Vann had spent more than a decade in Vietnam and had become notorious for being an outspoken critic of his superiors and American war policy there. Just prior to the enemy attack, he had worked day and night, employing his vast civilian and military contacts to direct US logistics and air support to the region.[57] Maj. Gen. John Hill, Du's senior military advisor, described Vann's efforts as remarkable: "The rest of us organized around Vann's personal efforts and concentrated on getting the resources marshalled to take advantage of the leadership he was exerting with the Vietnamese."[58]

To counter the impending attack, Vann instructed Du to deploy two regiments of the 22nd Division to the basecamps at Tan Canh and Dak To and to send two armored squadrons to Ben Het. While Du often resisted Vann's directions, he agreed enough times so that some members of the general's staff privately called him "the slave of John Paul Vann." In this case Du's decision to follow Vann's advice was fortunate.[59]

On 12 April the PAVN's 2nd Division, elements of the 203rd Tank Regiment, and several independent regiments of the B-3 Front attacked the outpost at Tan Canh and the nearby Dak To firebase. Things soon went wrong for the ARVN. As their armored units departed Ben Het to relieve Dak To, they were ambushed and annihilated. In addition, the ARVN defense force northwest of Kontum City was hammered as they left the provincial capital. At this crucial moment communist leaders inexplicably halted the advance to the south for three weeks. With the immediate crisis averted, instead of becoming increasingly confident, Du began to lose his nerve, finding it increasingly difficult to make decisions. At this point Vann cast aside any pretext of ARVN leadership and took command himself. He put the task of defending Kontum City on the shoulders of Ly Tong Ba, commander of the 23rd Division. Subsequently, he called in massive B-52 strikes to keep the NVA at arm's length and to reduce their numbers until he could incorporate more ARVN troops into his units to stabilize the situation.[60]

On 14 May communist troops reached the outskirts of Kontum City. Once in place, the PAVN's 320th Division, the 1st and 141st Regiments of the 2nd Division, and elements of the 203rd Tank Regiment assaulted the capital from the north, south, and west. Those defending the city comprised the ARVN's 23rd Division and several ranger groups. With the most intense part of the fighting in I and II Corps Zones over and a majority of the B-52s free to concentrate on the Central Highlands, the NVA troops at Kontum caught the full fury of the ARVN and American forces. Initially, during the PAVN attack on 14 May, many of the outlying ARVN positions began to crumble until a skillful B-52 Arc Light raid dropped most of its ordnance directly on the PAVN attackers at the point of the breakthrough, with spectacular results. When the ARVN troops returned to their defensive positions the next morning, they were completely unopposed. Within their cratered trenches they found four hundred bodies and seven smoldering tanks. Between 14 May and 7 June, Vann was able to get the USAF to fly more than three hundred B-52 Arc Light raids near Kontum City.[61]

As the communist campaign against III Corps unfolded, Vann contacted Thieu, demanding there be a personnel shakeup in III Corps. The president replaced Du with Maj. Gen. Nguyen Van Toan. While Toan's confident and assertive public persona was in direct contrast to Du's, many experts believed "Toan was one of South Vietnam's most undistinguished officers."[62]

The next three weeks followed the same pattern. Several times PAVN troops assaulted the ARVN defenses only to be clobbered by B-52, fighter-bomber, and helicopter-gunship attacks. Once an airstrike ended, ARVN troops counterattacked, sweeping through the remains of the attacking enemy forces. The only real enemy success came on 26 May, when four infantry regiments, supported by armored forces, broke through the defenses. The breakthrough did not last very long. Vann and ARVN officials called in airstrikes by US helicopters, which successfully fired eighty-five new BGM-71 TOW (Tube-launched, Optically tracked, Wire-guided) missiles at the advancing enemy. During the next three days, twenty-four PAVN T-54 tanks were destroyed by TOWs, and the breach was sealed.[63]

During the struggle for Kontum City, both sides suffered heavy casualties. Despite the large number of enemy forces attacking, the ARVN, with support from the USAF and RVNAF, held on to the city. The II Corps defenders also received logistics resupplies from the US Army's 549 QM AD Rigger Company, which had made the aforementioned rapid-deployment from Okinawa in early April. Early in June the NVA began to withdraw to the west, leaving behind more than 4,000 dead. American intelligence estimated that at the end of the offensive, communists casualties in the Central Highlands totaled between 30,000 and 40,000 troops.[64]

Vann never got to enjoy the victory. At the official end to the campaign on 9 June, he boarded a helicopter to return to his headquarters. Not far from his basecamp, the helicopter carrying the forty-seven-year-old Vietnam expert, along with its crew and other passengers, crashed. Vann died almost immediately. On 16 June 1972 he was buried in Section 11 at Arlington National Cemetery. Attending the funeral were General Westmoreland, Maj. Gen. Edward Lansdale, Lt. Col. Lucein Conein, Sen. Edward Kennedy, and Daniel Ellsburg.[65]

Airpower to the Rescue—
Freedom Train and Linebacker I

Even though chapter 6 details Operation Freedom Train and Linebacker I and II, it is important here to tie them into the Easter Offensive. One should recall that leadership in Hanoi had timed the Nguyen Hue Offensive to coincide with the end of the annual winter monsoon season, when low cloud cover and heavy rain provided refuge under which their forces could advance without being subjected to air attacks. At the time, all-weather combat was only in its infancy, and most airstrikes could only take place in clear daylight. But this situation was changing with the increased use of B-52 bombers with all-weather capabilities and retrofitting aircraft with radar direction finders such as the LORAN long-range electronic-navigation system, a hyperbolic radio-navigation system developed during World War II but, due to its high cost, not deployed on a wide range of aircraft until the late 1960s and early 1970s. Originally, the USAF, US Coast Guard, and USN built their own versions of this system in the 1950s, LORAN-A, B, and C. Of these the LORAN-A, or standard LORAN, became the most used version in the 1960s and 1970s. It was from this beginning that all military aircraft were able to employ all-weather radar. In Vietnam this proved fortuitous since, with these new capabilities, US aircraft could accurately deliver their ordnance through cloud cover, making them much more lethal.[66]

Aircraft and crews of Task Force 77, offshore in the South China Sea, as well as the Seventh and Thirteenth Air Forces executed the missions in South Vietnam and Thailand. While the monsoon weather continually created problems, the reduction in US forces was also an issue, resulting in fewer ground-support aircraft and maintenance crews. In the spring of 1972, the air force had only three squadrons of F-4s and one squadron of A-37 Dragonflies still in the Republic of Vietnam—seventy-six aircraft. Another 114 fighter-bombers were stationed at bases throughout Thailand, while eighty-three B-52s were stationed at U-Tapao Royal Thai Air Force Base, Thailand, and at Andersen Air Force Base, Guam. In addition, Task Force 77, which normally had four carriers, at this point in the drawdown only had two still on station, the USS *Coral Sea* and the USS *Hancock*, with 140 strike aircraft between them.[67]

To deal with this dearth of warplanes, between 7 April and 13 May, 176 F-4s and twelve F-105s were transferred from South Korea and the continental United States to Thailand as part of Operations Constant Guard II–V. From 5 February to 23 May, SAC carried out Operation Bullet Shot, sending 124 bombers to Guam and raising the total in theater to 209. Nixon also ordered a buildup of the Seventh Fleet, dispatching four more carrier groups that included the USS *Kitty Hawk*, USS *Constellation*, USS *Midway*, and USS *Saratoga*. This meant four carriers were always available at any time to conduct aerial operations over Vietnam. The RVNAF at this time constituted nine squadrons of A-1 Skyraiders (propeller driven), A-37s, and F-5 Tigers totaling 119 strike aircraft. They also had two squadrons of AC-47 and AC-119G/K fixed-wing gunships, totaling twenty-eight aircraft. These gunships had originally been part of the USAF contingent in Vietnam. But as US AC-130s assumed roles as CAS, aerial armed reconnaissance, nighttime truck killers, and interdiction weapons, these AC-47s and AC-119s were transferred to the South Vietnamese.[68]

With the start of Linebacker I operations in early May, American airpower filled two major roles. First, CAS missions were flown in the South, and second, bombing raids took place against Northern targets, much as they had done during Operation Rolling Thunder, only without the major restrictions of the earlier effort. The weather and increased number of enemy AAA made the initial stage of aerial operations very difficult. The North deployed 85-mm and 100-mm radar-directed batteries south of the DMZ. On 17 February eighty-one SA-2 SAMS were launched from the DMZ, downing three F-4s. This surprised the Americans and marked the most southerly deployment of SA-2 units so far in the war. The communist missile crews launched their SAMs high and fired their AAA low, making US aerial attacks extremely hazardous. This worsened when the enemy introduced new enhanced shoulder-fired Grail SAMs. Even so, US air operations both in North and South Vietnam during this period proved very effective in blunting not only the Nguyen Hue Offensive but also in damaging resupply efforts out of the North. Airpower temporarily thwarted Hanoi's goal of overrunning South Vietnam.[69]

Figure 8.4. Pres. Richard Nixon and National Security Advisor Henry Kissinger discuss Vietnam strategy and the Paris peace talks

Even as the air campaign unfolded, ground operations hung by a thread. The USN provided artillery support as one solution. When the firebases in I Corps Zone fell early in the offensive, naval gunfire became the main source of artillery support in the area. American officials assigned USMC gunfire observers to fly with forward air controllers to provide coordinates for shore targets. At the height of the offensive, three US cruisers and thirty-eight destroyers provided vital naval-gunfire support.[70]

While this proved significant, air attacks were still the key to beating back the communist advance. As the weather improved, so did the number of aircraft sorties. From April to June allied pilots and crews flew 18,000 CAS sorties to aid ARVN defenders. Of these, 45 percent were by the USAF, 30 percent by the USN and USMC, and 25 percent by the RVNAF. In addition to these, B-52s flew 2,724 sorties. Ten American and six RVNAF aircraft were shot down, all by SAMs or AAA.[71]

On 4 April President Nixon, deeply concerned by the ferocity of the enemy's assault, authorized tactical airstrikes, from the DMZ north to the eighteenth parallel, or within the southern panhandle of the DRV. This supply-interdiction effort was the first systematic bombing carried out in North Vietnam since the conclusion of Operation Rolling Thunder in November 1968. The next day the president approved air operations north of the twentieth parallel under the codename Operation Freedom Train. The first B-52 strikes were carried out on 10 April.[72]

With peace negotiations in Paris bogged down and the North continuing its attacks in South Vietnam, a determined Nixon increased the air campaign by zeroing in on targets in and around Hanoi and Haiphong. Between 1 May and 30 June, B-52s, fighter-bombers, and fixed-wing gunships carried out 18,000 sorties over North Vietnam, with twenty-nine aircraft lost.[73]

By 8 May 1972, the president initiated Operation Pocket Money, the aerial mining of Haiphong and other DRV ports. With Nixon conducting negotiations for a strategic-arms-limitation treaty, also known as SALT I, this action proved a major gamble. He assumed Soviet leaders were anxious enough to sue for peace that they would not have a negative reaction. His instincts proved impeccable. Officials in China also muted any overt response to the escalatory measures for the same reason. Emboldened by his diplomatic successes, the president went one step further and launched Operation Linebacker, later dubbed Linebacker I, a systematic aerial-bombing campaign against North Vietnam's transportation, storage, and air-defense systems, on 10 May. Over the next five months, aircraft from the air force, navy, and Marine Corps swept across the skies of North Vietnam, wreaking decisive damage to the limited Northern infrastructure. The price proved severe, though, with the Americans losing 134 aircraft while the RVNAF lost 54.[74]

The Results

When the ARVN counteroffensive ended, both sides were bloodied and depleted. Nevertheless, both Hanoi and Saigon claimed victory. The ARVN and the Americans also concluded their "success" had validated Nixon's Vietnamization policy.[75] General Truong noted in his official study of the Easter Offensive: "The Nguyen Hue campaign failed to accomplish its intended objectives. In exchange for some insignificant territorial gains, North Vietnam had virtually exhausted its manpower and materiel resources." Truong further argued: "Estimates placed its losses at over 100,000 casualties and at least one half of its large-caliber artillery and tanks. By the end of 1972, it became obvious that Hanoi no longer possessed the capabilities for another general offensive in South Vietnam in the immediate future." In conclusion, he asserted, "It was obvious that when planning the Easter invasion, North Vietnam's leaders had grossly underestimated two things: first, the RVNAF capability for sustained combat and capacity for endurance, especially as far as the territorial forces were concerned; and second, the extent and effectiveness of US airpower."[76]

In retrospect, while there is some truth in what Truong wrote in the late 1970s, his analysis overlooked one vital fact. What the North could not achieve militarily, they were able to accomplish through negotiations. Even as the offensive wound down in late September and early October, negotiations between Kissinger and Le Duc Tho seemed to be on the verge of finally attaining a peace treaty. Both sides had made major concessions. The United States agreed to allow 100,000 PAVN troops already in South Vietnam to stay, while Hanoi dropped its demand that Thieu resign as head of the Southern government. Thieu was appalled by the US compromise. To him, leaving enemy troops in his country was like giving it away. In the end he demanded dozens of revisions be made before he would support the final settlement. When Kissinger presented these changes to Le Duc Tho, it seemed to derail everything. Nixon, who had just won a decisive vic-

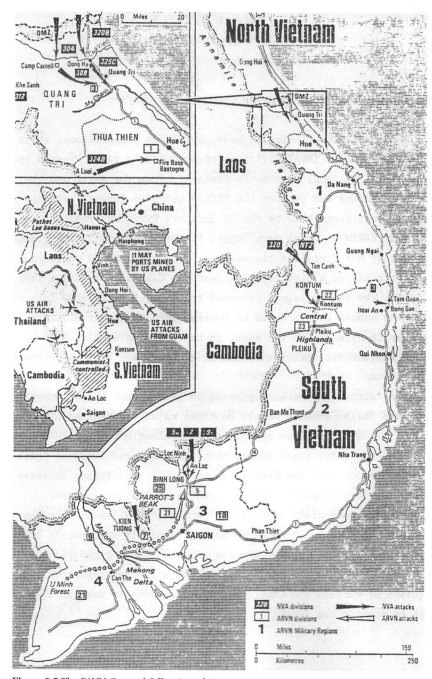

Figure 8.5 The PAVN General Offensive of 1972

tory in the 1972 presidential election, appeared to receive public support for his policies. But both houses of Congress remained Democratic, and he feared they would cut off funds to South Vietnam. To prevent this, the president sent large amounts of supplies and equipment to South Vietnam to bolster their military capability. He had Major General Haig reassure Thieu the United States would always provide military and economic support to South Vietnam. Nixon also assured him if the North ever repeated their invasion, America would come to their aid.[77]

Eventually, Thieu relented, at least in part. But Le Duc Tho, convinced he had the upper hand, remained adamantly opposed to further concessions. On 13 December he and Kissinger ended the talks, promising to "keep in touch, and went home."[78] What no one had counted on was how much things would change. During the Easter crisis, the constant ARVN internal-command-structure weaknesses were partially resolved. Yet no sooner did the fighting end than these resurfaced. This weakened the South and its future ability to defend itself. In addition, more than 25,000 South Vietnamese civilians had been killed during the offensive, and almost a million more became refugees, 600,000 of whom were desperately trying to stay alive in rudimentary camps under government care. As for the Americans, they suffered three hundred killed during all of 1972. No sooner had the offensive ended than the US troop withdrawal began again.[79]

Northern leaders had begun the year by committing virtually their entire army to the offensive. The North had suffered nearly 100,000 casualties and lost almost all the tanks committed, numbering 134 T-54s, 56 PT-76s, and 60 T-34s. But the communists had gained permanent control over 10 percent of South Vietnam, taking half of the four northernmost provinces—Quang Tri, Thua Thien, Quang Nam, and Quang Tin—as well as the western fringes of the II and III Corps Tactical Zones. As Truong reported, Northern leaders had underrated the combat capability of the ARVN, which by 1972 had become one of the best-equipped armies in the world. The communists also had failed to grasp the lethality of US airpower in conventional warfare. Tactically, PAVN field commanders had also thrown away their best-trained troops by making suicidal frontal attacks into heavy defensive fire that accomplished only massive casualties.[80]

But the communists, as they had proven time and again, were resilient. At the end of the offensive, they had begun to repair what had been damaged or destroyed and take advantage of what they had won. Rapidly, they extended logistics infiltration routes and supply corridors from Laos and Cambodia into South Vietnam. They also expanded the port facilities at the captured town of Dong Ha. Within a year, over 20 percent of the materiel destined for the battlefields of South Vietnam were flowing along supply routes, docks, and pipelines from China and the Eastern Bloc into North Vietnam and on into South Vietnam. In addition, those NVA troops who had survived and remained in the South dug in, retooled, and waited for the start of yet another offensive.[81]

With peace talks in Paris on hold, Nixon decided that one more massive air campaign might break things loose. Thus, he launched Operation Linebacker II, or the "Christmas Bombings." It was a campaign that employed America's most powerful air weapon, the B-52, and was aimed at the DRV's transport network, especially around Hanoi and Haiphong. When it ended on 29 December 1972, Northern leaders were willing to accept the previous compromises, which led to the signing of the Paris Peace Accords in January 1973. Instead of a lasting peace, the agreement provided only a brief respite that would lead to another communist assault.[82]

9

The Final Act

The Battle of Xuan Loc and the Fall of Saigon

I n all of recorded human history, there have been heroic events in which an outnumbered force of soldiers defended their people against overwhelming odds, knowing their chance for victory—or even survival—was remote. Many are familiar with the heroic defense of the pass at Thermopylae by King Leonidas and his three hundred Spartans or the valiant and defiant defense of the mountaintop fortress of Masada by a handful of Jewish rebels against the elite Roman X Legion in 73 CE. Of course, readers of this book know about the battles fought by US forces during the Vietnam War. Names such as Ia Drang, Khe Sanh, Tet, Hue, and Hamburger Hill still echo throughout the pantheon of American military deeds.

The final, desperate battle to save the Republic of Vietnam was not fought by Americans; rather, it was a heroic struggle fought against overwhelming odds by members of the ARVN at an obscure outpost only forty miles from Saigon known as Xuan Loc (or Tran Xuan Loc). After nearly thirty years of bitter conflict and bloody war, the opposing forces in the erstwhile civil war between the pseudo-republican forces of the South, recently abandoned by their American sponsors, and the Marxist/nationalist forces of the North locked horns in one final struggle to decide the ultimate fate of Vietnam. South Vietnam's final stand at Xuan Loc, despite the casualties its forces inflicted on the PAVN, ended in defeat. This in turn led to the resignation of President Thieu and the eventual fall of Saigon.

In hindsight, by the time the South Vietnamese government sent its last mobile forces to Xuan Loc, specifically the 18th Infantry Division, under Brig. Gen. Le Minh Dao, the war was already lost. Still, Thieu hoped to slow the PAVN's advance and form a defensive perimeter with these troops. Even though General Dao himself probably realized how untenable his position was, he and his troops put up a tenacious struggle between 9 and 21 April 1975, when he was ordered to withdraw and the town of Xuan Loc was occupied by the PAVN's IV Army Corps. Since this was the last defensive line of the ARVN III Corps in front of Saigon, once Xuan Loc fell, there was little between the communist forces and their final victory. Even though elements of the III Corps Armored Task Force, remnants of the 18th Infantry Division, and depleted ARVN marine, airborne, and ranger battalions continued a fighting retreat for nine days, PAVN armored columns smashed through the gates of South Vietnam's Presidential Palace on 30 April 1975, effectively ending the war.[1]

In the years since Xuan Loc fell, the battle itself has been defined by the inspirational leadership of Brigadier General Dao and the determined resistance of the ARVN 18th Division. The numbers alone, demonstrate how effective they were. On the first day of battle, the PAVN's 4th Army Corps, under Maj. Gen. Hoang Cam, lost more than 700 men. By 13 April, the death toll climbed to 2,000 without Cam having advanced a single inch. At this point, according Gen. Tran Van Tra, the communists had to alter their tactics from a standard frontal assault to a more subtle encircling action designed to wear down the 18th. Over the following week, the PAVN concentrated their forces around Xuan Loc. Despite the enemy's apparently superior position, Dao's men struck out wherever and whenever possible, hammering their opponents even though they were outnumbered four or five to one. Then Dao was ordered to fall back to Saigon, which required all of his skill to outmaneuver PAVN forces.[2]

Ultimately, the heroic defense by the 18th Division came to nothing since Saigon fell on 30 April. Even though Dao could have evacuated with other key leaders and officials, he stayed with his men, and on 9 May he surrendered to enemy forces. Dao was tried and sentenced to seventeen years in prison. He was released on 4 May 1992 and eventually migrated to the United States. Like so many South Vietnamese who had made such a devoted commitment to their nation, Dao was left to wonder how it came to this. How had he and millions of others become refugees, members of a defeated nation that after 1975 ceased to exist?

The Beginning of the End for South Vietnam

While signing the Paris Peace Accords on 27 January 1973 garnered acclaim and renown for Nixon and Kissinger and allowed the United States to withdraw from the war, it did not end the fighting in South Vietnam. Almost immediately both sides violated the tenets of the ceasefire and attempted to gain control of as much territory as possible. Both Saigon and Hanoi realized they needed to control Southern population centers to gain leverage in any future dialogues or efforts at reunification. While Thieu seemed to hold a strong position, especially since he had assurances from Nixon of continued US aid, the truth was 200,000 enemy troops were in South Vietnam with enough supplies to launch the PAVN's three-phase "Land-grabbing-and-population-nibbling" campaign, which included assaults by four division-sized units aimed at several strategically significant positions.[3]

As the year wore on, Northern leaders held critical meetings to discuss the future direction military operations would take. On the one hand, Generals Dung and Giap ardently counseled the renewal of conventional military operations, fearing a lack of action would allow the ARVN to grow stronger while the morale of their own army waned. On the other hand, Premier Pham Van Dong worried increased fighting would bleed away precious resources needed to rebuild the Northern infrastructure and economy as well as increase the constant military sacrifice and commitment by the citizens of the DRV. Some leaders feared a full-scale assault in the South might cause the United States to increase their supply of resources to Saigon and possibly recommit their forces, no matter how unlikely that appeared later.[4]

What evolved was Resolution 21, calling for "strategic raids" against ARVN units in order to retake ground they had lost since the signing of the Paris Accords. The purpose of this new tactic was to test the reaction of both South Vietnam and the United States. The initial manifestation of the new policy occurred during assaults in Quang Duc Province in March 1974 and again in November, when the PAVN attacked the ARVN at Bien Hoa. While the Southern soldiers put up a determined fight, there was nothing really new in their response. Northern leaders anxiously waited to see if the United States might initiate B-52 airstrikes. Gradually, it became clear the North had nothing to worry about. In December the PAVN once again seized the military initiative, gaining experience in combined-arms operations, depleting ARVN forces, and causing them to expend large quantities of supplies, ordnance, and manpower. Equally important, the communists found new opportunities and routes to probe deeper into South Vietnam and create staging areas and launch points for a new full-scale offensive. In short, they had found the keys to final victory.[5]

In the meantime, Thieu wrestled with the circumstances accruing from the signing of the Paris Peace Accords and a ceasefire agreement he neither agreed with nor wanted. Even before the accords were concluded, he had openly proclaimed the "Four Nos: no negotiations with the communists, no communist political activities south of the Demilitarized Zone, no coalition government, and no surrender of territory to the North Vietnamese or Provisional Revolutionary Government." Of course, the Paris Accords all but excluded these demands. While the agreement upset Thieu, he took solace in promises made by Nixon to reintroduce American airpower if any serious violations took place. He also anticipated US financial and military aid would continue, at previous levels, following the signing of the peace agreement. They did not.[6]

On 1 July 1973 the US Congress passed legislation restricting nearly all direct or indirect US aerial combat over Vietnam or in any part of Southeast Asia. On 7 November Congress overrode Nixon's veto of the War Powers Act. This caused aid to the Republic of Vietnam to shrink from $2.5 billion in 1972 and 1973 to $965 million in 1974.[7]

The president's increasing political problems, brought on by the Watergate break in and subsequent cover up, exacerbated the situation. With Democrats in charge of Congress, there was antipathy between the legislative and executive branches over nearly all of Nixon's policies, especially regarding Southeast Asia, making it increasingly difficult for the president to support South Vietnam. Meantime in Saigon, Thieu's expectations of US aid remained high. A few Southern leaders were more realistic. Gen. Dong Van Khuyen, RVNAF commander, declared later: "Our leaders continued to believe in US air intervention even after the US Congress had expressly forbidden it. . . . They deluded themselves."[8] If the reduced aid in 1974 was not bad enough, Nixon's resignation on 9 August 1974 left South Vietnamese leaders in a state of shock, confronting them with the cruel reality that their independence was in grave jeopardy.

Yet even without US supplies, Thieu took advantage of Hanoi's brief combat respite during 1974 to launch numerous assaults against PAVN forces in several locations throughout South Vietnam. While the ARVN took back most of the lands seized by the enemy during their own attacks in 1973 and nearly a quarter of the land area controlled by the communist forces at the time of the ceasefire, Thieu had stretched his own forces dangerously thin. This fact was soon recognized by the PAVN.[9]

On 27 April 1974 the ARVN initiated the Svay Rieng Campaign against enemy sanctuaries in eastern Cambodia. It began with a major push against the PAVN 5th Division by crack ARVN units. South Vietnamese Regional Force units established blocking positions on the southwestern edge of the 5th Division while the RVNAF struck its base areas. Commanded by General Thuan, the ARVN 40th Infantry Regiment and the 7th Ranger Group spearheaded the attacks against positions around Duc Hue, not far from the Cambodian border. The next day communist troops countered by smashing into eleven ARVN battalions preparing for their own assault near the Long Khot District Town. The PAVN forces were soon repelled, and on the twenty-ninth ARVN armored units drove across the Cambodian border just west of Go Dau Hau. With PAVN 5th Division headquarters in danger, the communists committed all their reserves to defend their logistics network. When ARVN actions ended on 2 May, they had severely damaged communist communication lines and logistical installations. Due to the secrecy, speed, and intensity of the operation, the ARVN lost fewer than 100 men, while the PAVN lost more than 1,500 men and large quantities of weapons and supplies.[10]

This proved to be the last major offensive operation launched by the ARVN. While these campaigns were successful, they created a feeling of overconfidence among the Southern leadership. In addition, while they lost a relatively low number of troops, the reduction in US supplies was already being felt. By the end of the year, the South Vietnamese military was experiencing shortages, while communist forces had begun to gain strength. The cruel irony was, even as the Southern forces appeared to be winning, they were actually sowing the seeds of their own defeat by expending precious resources at a high rate and compelling the PAVN to initiate countering actions to retake the momentum in this back-and-forth struggle.

By the end of October 1974, leaders in Hanoi decided on a new strategy known as the Resolution of 1975. It proclaimed the war was entering its "final stage," and Northern forces would consolidate their gains, eliminate South Vietnamese border outposts, and secure a logistics corridor in order to complete their buildup in South Vietnam. Finally, in 1976 the concluding general offensive would begin. In many ways this operational plan reflected the divergent views of Giap and Premier Dong in 1973 and the need to find conciliation in 1974. As a compromise, the overall strategy proved very conservative. Part of this came from the general staff's overestimation of the ARVN's abilities based on battles like the ones they experienced in the spring and summer of 1974. Until nearly the end of the war, most PAVN leaders erroneously believed they were outnumbered by the ARVN.[11]

In November 1974, officials in Hanoi summoned PAVN field commanders and their political officers to the capital to evaluate the new strategy. They all believed they had a chance to break the stalemate and finally win the war. The officers agreed that an attack in the Central Highlands offered the greatest chance of success. There was one voice raised in opposition— General Tra. His forces included main-force Southern guerrilla troops of the B-2 Front. He and his staff had already developed a plan for a direct assault on Saigon. General Tra proposed his forces initiate a "test" attack in Phuoc Long Province to see how well the ARVN would fight and if the United States would react with any kind of support. His plan was very appealing since it offered the potential of immense benefit with relatively low risk. Le Duan approved the operation. No sooner was the ink dry than he forewarned Tra that failure was not an option: "Go ahead and attack . . . [but] you must be sure of victory."[12]

Sizing up the Two Sides

In the spring of 1973, South Vietnam, due in large measure to the US "Enhance" and "Enhance-Plus" programs, had the fourth-largest military in the world. Their army had received new tracked armored vehicles, helicopters, combat and transport aircraft, top-of-the-line artillery pieces, and other weapons systems worth $753 million. Nevertheless, ARVN troops suffered a lack of proper training, near-total reliance on an American logistical system and dependence on a continued resupply of ordnance, spare parts, and fuel. In addition, while the ARVN outnumbered PAVN and VC forces in South Vietnam nearly 1,500,000 to 500,000, roughly 482,000 Southern forces were Regional or Popular Forces, which often were notoriously undependable. While that still left more than 1,000,000 ARVN regulars, only 250,000 of them were actual combat forces, the rest being administrative and supply personnel in support of the frontline soldiers. Ironically, the US military had too perfectly replicated its institutional structure within the ARVN organization.[13]

Yet another issue facing ARVN leaders was keeping soldiers from retiring, resigning, deserting, or finding some other way out of the army. The problem reached a peak between 1973 and 1975. In the critical year of 1974, only 65 percent of authorized manpower was present for duty at any one time. Legitimate promotions were scarce among the officer corps since many generals owed their positions to political loyalties rather than professional abilities. Among many ARVN officers, depravity, mendacity, and ineffectiveness was not just endemic, in some cases it had been raised "almost to an art form." According to retired colonel James H. Willbanks, at this time, in an effort to appease his detractors, Thieu dismissed several senior military leaders, including Generals Toan and Nguyen Van Nghi, the II and IV Corps commanders, respectively. While both Thieu loyalists were infamous for their corruption, they were proven leaders popular with their troops. They had won battles, and their absence would prove a major problem for ARVN field forces, eventually leading to Toan's reinstatement.[14]

By late 1974 and early 1975, the austere reductions in direct US aid negatively affected ARVN military operations. For example, artillery batteries that had once been allocated one hundred rounds per day were reduced to only four per day, while each Southern soldier received only eighty-five bullets per month. Fuel shortages and a lack of spare parts reduced RVNAF sortie rates for helicopters and cargo aircraft by more than half. Worse still was Thieu's order not to surrender any ground. This left his army overextended attempting to defend vast, useless terrain along a six-hundred-mile frontier. Even the nation's strategic reserve, the Airborne and Marine Divisions, were occupied in static defensive roles. Considering ARVN soldiers had been trained by US advisers in tactics focused on rapid mobility and the application of massive firepower, their inability to deliver either frustrated most of them. In 1974–75, at the worst possible moment, the South Vietnamese economy buckled from refugees pouring into the cities seeking food and protection. A spike in worldwide fuel prices caused by the Arab oil embargo of 1972 and a major reduction in rice harvests in Asia did not help this situation. On top of fighting a cleaver and dedicated enemy, Saigon now had to feed thousands more residents, some of whom were, in fact, communist operatives.[15]

As these events unfolded in the South, the PAVN was still recovering from the devastating losses suffered during the Easter Offensive of 1972. While they had to recruit or commandeer increasingly younger troops, they also were able to obtain more modern weapons and equipment from Moscow and Beijing. In 1973 alone, North Vietnam received 2.8 million metric tons of goods worth $330 million from Communist Bloc countries, or a 50-percent increase over the previous year. According to the CIA, by the following year, this had grown to 3.5 million metric tons worth $400 million. While the US cut back on assistance to South Vietnam, the Soviet Union was increasing aid to its client state. The NVA's artillery pieces rose to 430, including the latest 122- and 130-mm models, and tanks and APCs to 655. Among these were the latest BTR-152s, constructed in the Soviet Union. The enemy also created two army corps to mirror the South's I and II Corps Tactical Zones. They blended most independent PAVN infantry regiments in the South into divisional structures. Based on these actions, the American Defense Attaché Office, established in 1973 to replace MACV, reported the PAVN had increased their strategic reserve from two divisions to seven. This meant there were 70,000 more troops available to supplement the 200,000 combat and 100,000 support troops already in South Vietnam. The support troops were mostly young "volunteer students" who maintained communist resupply routes in and out of South Vietnam.[16]

By 1975, Hanoi improved its extensive logistics network throughout Vietnam and Laos to accommodate increased shipments and deployment of food, weapons, ordnance, troops, and other equipment required for the planned all-out campaign. Soon after the Paris Peace Accords were signed, the 559th Transportation Group, which managed and sustained the Truong Son Strategic Transportation Route from North Vietnam to southeastern Laos, received a directive to expand this infiltration network east of the Annamite Mountains directly into South Vietnam. Throughout 1973 and 1974, thousands of young members of the 559th labored on this ambitious project. Known as Corridor 613, the new route crossed the DMZ into South Vietnam and ran all the way to Loc Ninh. Being so tactically important, the 559th built all-weather, hard-surfaced roads to accommodate the modern mechanized army the PAVN had developed since Paris. This new pathway reduced the transport time of personnel from North Vietnam to the southernmost combat zones from four months to three weeks.[17]

Even as the road network progressed, Northern workers augmented the air defenses. This new network was focused on artillery and missile systems established in South Vietnam. By early 1975, it was composed of twenty-two PAVN regiments equipped with radar-controlled AAA systems in addition to SA-2 Guideline and SA-7 Grail shoulder-fired antiaircraft missiles. General Momyer later wrote that these new structures "posed a major deterrent to the South Vietnamese Air Force, since its aircraft were not equipped to deal with such threats."[18]

Many of the South's aircraft were older models without radar and sensor capabilities, which American crews had used on more modern aircraft but had not left behind for the South Vietnamese. For example, while the USAF gave the RVNAF AC-47 and AC-119 gunships, they did not provide AC-130s, which had more modern sensors and radar systems. Besides, even with these more modern weapons and aircraft, the United States had not defeated the PAVN.

Momyer also noted that the hundreds of aircraft the United States provided to the RVNAF were "relatively unsophisticated aircraft." They did this partly because, they reasoned, better aircraft would tempt the South Vietnamese to initiate operations over North Vietnam, and US leaders hoped this would keep "the fighting at a relatively low level," thereby enhancing the possibility of negotiations.[19] While this may be overstated, the fact was that by late 1974, RVNAF aerial interdiction of the PAVN's supply buildup had become almost impossible. Reconnaissance flights were also limited, thus restricting the South's ability to collect adequate intelligence data and estimate enemy strength or operational plans.[20]

In one ironic twist, sometimes the PAVN experienced deficiencies in armored and heavy artillery forces that were essential for attacks on heavily fortified ARVN regimental and divisional basecamps. In the later stages of the war with the French, the Viet Minh had plenty of excellent artillery. At Dien Bien Phu, for example, the abundance of superior artillery was a key factor in the communist victory.[21] But the vast expenditure of artillery ordnance during the 1972 Spring Offensive and the slowdown in Soviet and Chinese resupplies, due in part to improving relations with the United States, left leaders in Hanoi worried about what kind of an offensive plan they could formulate. General Staff planners who drew up the proposal presented to the Politburo in October 1974 were particularly focused on this issue. Many who have examined the collapse of the ARVN suggest the lack of ammunition for the South constituted a key factor. But recent research demonstrates the North also experienced similar shortages. The reduction in Soviet and Eastern Bloc resupplies also effected PAVN armored units, many in poor condition and desperately needing spare parts. Most communist units in the South were still equipped only with light mortars, single-tube rocket launchers, and recoilless rifles. Leaders in COSVN reported that in their area of operations, consisting of the southern half of the country, they had only five artillery battalions to support the 3rd, 4th, 5th, 6th, 7th, 8th, and 9th Infantry Divisions and the IV Corps headquarters. Two of the artillery battalions were mainly equipped with captured US-made weapons with little ordnance or spares.[22]

By 1974, PAVN's entire stock of heavy artillery and tank ordnance, including that for combat units and strategic reserves, totaled just 100,000 rounds. For this reason, many leaders replaced their larger weapons with obsolete 7.62-mm and 57-mm artillery pieces drawn out of storage, for which there were still ample shells. The initial notion by many US analysts that the American withdrawal gave the North an advantage in rounds of ordnance would appear to have been exaggerated. The fact is that most of the ARVN troopers were hard-bitten veterans, and they had maintained significant stores of ammunition and equipment—a fact illustrated by the large amount of American-made materiel captured by the PAVN at the end of war. The ultimate fall of the South may well have had more to do with the psychological effect of the 1974 PAVN campaign, audacious in both its planning and execution. It was well led, and the unexpected strategy dealt Thieu a shock from which he did not recover.[23]

It Begins at Phuoc Long

The first engagement in the campaign leading to Xuan Loc took place near Phuoc Long, the northernmost provincial capital in the III Corps Tactical Zone about seventy-five miles northeast of Saigon. In mid-December 1974 PAVN units deployed from their Cambodian sanctuaries to attack. The town was defended by five regional battalions, forty-eight Popular Force platoons, and four territorial artillery sections. The III Corps commander, Lt. Gen. Du Quoc Dong, headquartered in Bien Hoa, supplemented these forces with the ARVN 2nd Battalion, 7th Infantry Regiment of the 5th Division; two artillery sections; and three reconnaissance companies. The battle began on 13 December when PAVN forces moved to cut off Phuoc Long City's overland communications and then destroyed the outlying ARVN defensive positions. Once the communists surrounded the city, they initiated highly accurate artillery fire followed by concentrated armor and infantry attacks, which began on 27 December.[24]

One of the biggest problems facing the Southern defenders was they had their families with them. While this elevated their morale, it also tended to lock them in place and discourage them from moving to support other threatened positions. As the enemy closed in, many civilians began a desperate evacuation south. Every time ARVN relief columns pushed north to try to relieve Phuoc Long, they found the roads clogged with refugees. Not surprisingly, as their families left, so did many of the regional soldiers. Desertion soon became commonplace as combatants sought to find and protect their wives and children. This became a pattern repeated throughout the PAVN push toward Saigon.[25]

On 2 January 1975, with catastrophe staring them in the face, President Thieu, Lieutenant General Dong, and the Joint General Staff (JGS) met at the Independence Palace in Saigon. Dong submitted a plan to relieve Phuoc Long, but reality thwarted his proposal. Too few reserve forces were available, while the main land routes to the city were either choked with civilians or controlled by the communists. In addition, even though Southern forces held excellent defensive positions in Phuoc Long, they did not have sufficient forces to repel two enemy divisions long enough for any aid to arrive. In hopes of preserving their remaining forces, commanders gave the order to abandon the city and fall back to positions from which to defend more strategically important cities such as Tay Ninh and Hue. This seemed to be a reasonable plan, but when the fighting ended on 6 January and ARVN leaders took stock of things, the surrender of the first provincial capital had been a bigger disaster than they first realized. The South had started the battle with roughly 5,500 troops, but only 850 reached the safety of their own lines afterward. Southern forces had lost 10,000 rounds of artillery shells, and the psychological blow to the South Vietnamese government was crushing. This capture of materiel solved the artillery-ordnance issue for the PAVN, using these shells in their captured American artillery pieces.[26] General Cao said of this; "Almost gone was the hope that the

United States would forcibly punish the North Vietnamese for their brazen violations of the ceasefire agreement. . . . What more encouragement could the communists have asked for?"[27]

The news of the PAVN victory at Phuoc Long reached Hanoi during the Politburo's Twenty-Third Plenum. Le Duan proclaimed, "Never have we had military and political conditions so perfect or, a strategic advantage as great as we have now."[28] Leaders quickly began planning a follow up, affirming that, as they had postulated, America would not reenter the war. Initially, plans called for an attack on Duc Lap, a border outpost in Darlac Province in the II Corps Zone. According to General Tra, he now lobbied for a more ambitious assault on Ban Me Thout, the provincial capital. While Le Duan was reluctant to take such a risk, Le Duc Tho also favored this plan. Hanoi dispatched General Dung south to command the new offensive, known as Campaign 275.[29]

Campaign 275 in the Central Highlands

General Dung had developed an operational plan aimed at taking Ban Me Thout, which he designated "Blossoming Lotus." It circumvented the ARVN's forward positions and attacked the city itself. Thus, it would be "like a flower bud slowly opening its petals." The plan called for 70,000–80,000 PAVN troops to isolate Ban Me Thuot by occupying key points on Highways 14, 19, and 21 to block any ARVN reinforcement efforts. The PAVN 320th Division then would seize outposts in the north as well as Phuong Duc airfield. Once accomplished, the soldiers of the F-10 Division were to make the main attack on the city along Route 14.[30]

The ARVN III Corps commander was Maj. Gen. Pham Van Phu, headquartered in Pleiku. Existing documents indicate Southern intelligence sources provided him with plenty of data warning him of the PAVN attack plan. General Phu, probably fooled by an intricate series of false enemy messages, hesitated to move his troops to meet this potential threat, determining that the communist movement toward Ban Me Thout was a diversion intended to distract him from their real target, Pleiku. As a result, only one ARVN Ranger unit and some Popular Forces and Regional Force elements, totaling roughly 4,000 men, were posted to defend Ban Me Thuot. Early in March, Phu augmented this small group with elements of the ARVN 53rd Regiment of the 23rd Division.[31]

The battle itself began on 10 March and ended slightly more than a week later. The opening salvo literally came from an intense artillery barrage, after which components of the 10th Division swarmed into the city and seized the ammunition depot. That same evening the PAVN 316th Division joined the bloody fight for the heart of the city. On 13 March, with the defenders teetering on collapse, Phu sent the 44th Regiment of the 23rd Division and a battalion of the 21st Ranger Group, airlifted by helicopters, to Phuoc An, twenty miles east of Ban Me Thuot, to form a relief force to save the beleaguered city. As they advanced the ARVN troops found the roads crammed with thousands of refugees and military dependents fleeing the highlands. By the time they confronted the 10th Division, the South Vietnamese troops were so dispersed they could only avoid being overrun themselves. These men soon joined the retreat.[32]

By 18 March, PAVN units had seized Phuoc An and completely isolated Ban Me Thuot. Over the next two days, all of Darlac Province fell to the North Vietnamese, forcing the ARVN to shift positions in an effort to prevent the PAVN from moving east to take the coastal lowlands. Future examination of the battle placed the primary blame for the loss of the Central Highlands on Phu, who overanalyzed what proved to be sound intelligence and acted too slowly in correcting his misinterpretation by sending reinforcements into Ban Me Thuot.[33]

As this catastrophe befell South Vietnam, Thieu sent a delegation to Washington to ask for an augmentation of economic and military aid. Graham Martin, the US ambassador to South Vietnam, sent several messages arguing that additional aid could still save the Republic of Vietnam and eventually flew to Washington to speak personally with Pres. Gerald R. Ford. While Ford seemed inclined to act, Congress was not about to divert money from America's own economic recovery into what most Americans saw as a lost cause. They soon slashed Ford's proposed 1975 military-aid package for South Vietnam from $1.45 billion to $700 million. While he probably did not believe it, the Ford administration continued to reassure Thieu that Congress would restore the funds. Historian Arnold Isaacs called it a "pipe dream."[34]

Back in Saigon, Thieu became increasingly isolated and desperate. One of his closest advisors described him as "suspicious . . . secretive . . . and ever watchful for a *coup d'état* against him." In his paranoia Thieu no longer listened to "competent people" nor had "adequate staff work, consultation, and coordination."[35] His military decisions were carried out by the officer corps without question. As General Vien said, "Thieu made all the decisions as to how the war should be conducted."[36] Many of these decisions were wrong or poorly considered.

Even before Ban Me Thuot fell, Thieu met with his key advisors, including Generals Vien and Quang. After briefings on the military situation, the president unfolded a small-scale map of South Vietnam and reviewed the possible redeployment of the ARVN forces needed to "hold and defend only those populous and flourishing areas which were really most important."[37] Thieu then sketched on the map the areas he considered most important, which included the entire III and IV Corps Tactical Zones. He also pointed out those places then under communist control that he believed would have to be retaken. What made these territories so important was the heavy concentration of natural resources, including rice, rubber, finished goods, and other vital items. He was also convinced they had to hold the coastal areas, where oil had been discovered on the continental shelf. Thieu believed this region was to become South Vietnam's "untouchable heartland, the irreducible national stronghold."[38]

As for I and II Corps Zones, he drew a series of phase lines on the map, stating that ARVN forces should hold what they could but that they could redeploy southward as circumstances dictated. Thieu called this new strategy "Light at the top, heavy on the bottom." At the time Vien agreed with the president that redeployment was necessary. Only later did he admit he should have told Thieu it was too late to redeploy, something the South Vietnamese should have done in early 1974 or at the latest when Nixon left office. By the time Thieu decided to take this step in 1975, the PAVN had attained a numerical superiority, making it difficult to disengage and redeploy to adequate defensive positions without being constantly pressed. Vien also admitted he then realized any ARVN movements would be hampered, as they had at Ban Me Thuot, by the flight of masses of refugees. Nevertheless, no one had the courage to disagree with President Thieu.[39]

As Ban Me Thuot teetered into collapse, Thieu made his final decision at Cam Ranh Bay during a meeting with Phu. He determined to abandon Pleiku and Kontum and redeploy the troops there to retake Ban Me Thuot, which he believed was more strategically significant. Later the general recalled thinking Thieu was joking. Only when the president reemphasized his orders did Phu point out the only route possible for the redistribution of forces, given the communists' blocking actions, was little-used Interprovincial Route 7B. This, he noted, was an unkempt, narrow, rough-surfaced logging road with downed bridges all along its path. Nothing seemed to dissuade Thieu, and fearing he might be jailed, Phu set about implementing the impossible.[40]

With desperation taking hold in Saigon, General Dung advised Hanoi he was redirecting his forces to attack and overrun Kontum City and Pleiku. Le Duan urged the General Staff to take advantage of the foothold they had gained in the highlands. Two months remained before the onset of the monsoon season, when military operations would be slowed to a crawl. He argued they could still make major strategic gains if they took bold action, especially in light of Saigon's apparent weakness and the lack of any US support or action.[41]

The Final Blunder

At this point, General Phu was left to move a corps-sized column of troops, equipment, and vehicles over a generally unknown road some 160 miles through the mountains and jungles of the Central Highlands to Nha Trang for the attempted counterattack. Plans called for the force comprise one battalion of the ARVN 44th Regiment, five ranger groups, the 21st Tank Squadron, two 155-mm artillery battalions, one 175-mm artillery battalion, and Popular Forces and Regional Force troops. In support of this gaggle were the men and equipment of the 20th Combat Engineer Group and the 231st Direct Support Group. As ambitious as the plan was in the first place, Phu's undue obsession with secrecy all but doomed the endeavor from the outset. He restricted operational planning to a few trusted subordinates who either had contributed to it or knew about it. In the aftermath the II Corps chief of staff revealed not even he had been informed of the planned abandonment of Pleiku and Kontum. In turn, Phu directed the commander of the II Corps rangers to take charge of the convoy itself and his primary deputy of operations to oversee the withdrawal.[42] It was like a coach making a game plan and failing to share it with his assistant coaches and players.

Even with all of its foibles, on 16 and 17 March things began well enough. Then at Hau Bon the column, as Phu had feared, ran into a mass of refugees and was completely bogged down. To add to the difficulty, combat engineers had to build a pontoon bridge across the Ea Pa River. On the night of the seventeenth, local communist forces attacked and further impeded the mass of 200,000 troops and refugees, by now known as the "column of tears." Even though General Dung was initially surprised by the ARVN withdrawal, he acted quickly, sending the 320th Division to strike the flank of the column while coastal forces rushed to halt its forward progress. In addition, troops of the 968th Division pushed through Pleiku and struck the rear of the ARVN units, which were by then in headlong retreat.[43]

Over the next several days, the convoy met one PAVN roadblock after another. When they reached the Da Rang River, the South Vietnamese had to construct another pontoon bridge. The last few miles to Tuy Hoa were the worst, as artillery shells, mortar rounds, and rockets constantly ploughed into their ranks. Finally, on 27 March the forward units in the column reached safety in Tuy Hoa. Throughout, the RVNAF could offer only minimal air support due to extremely bad weather. While no one knew exactly how many made it through, one reliable source suggested only a third of the 60,000 ARVN and half of the 180,000 civilians who fled the highlands made it to Tuy Hoa.[44] James Willbanks has stated, "Of the estimated 400,000 civilians who had attempted to flee Kontum, Pleiku, Phu Bon, and Cheo Reo, only about 60,000–100,000 got through."[45]

Strategically, the "withdrawal" proved a complete disaster. The combat capability of II Corps had been reduced by 75–80 percent, including the loss of some of its best troops and large numbers of military vehicles and supplies. It also meant any plans to retake Ban Me Thuot had to be scrapped. As for the PAVN, their confidence level increased as their main units advanced toward the coast. Only the ARVN's 22nd Division blocked their path. While the Southern Vietnamese fought bravely and with great determination to defend the mountain passes to the coast, by the end of March, the PAVN's 3rd and 968th Divisions were in Hue and Da Nang. In an effort to save the survivors, Southern troops were ordered to withdraw to Qui Nhon to be evacuated by sea on 1 April. The withdrawal was a bloodbath as they fought their way through enemy troops the entire way. Two regimental colonels committed suicide rather than evacuate. The 47th Regiment was ambushed at Phu Cat and lost half its combat strength. Several soldiers, including the 47th's colonel, also committed suicide. When it regrouped near Vung Tau, the division had only 2,000 men left.[46]

The PAVN Turns toward Hue and Da Nang

Even as this drama unfolded, other PAVN units were moving against Hue and Da Nang. These included the crack 2nd, 304th, 324B, 325C, and 711th Divisions. The ARVN's forces in the I Corps Tactical Zone included the 1st, 2nd, and 3rd Infantry Divisions; the elite Airborne and Marine Divisions; four ranger groups; and the 1st Armored Brigade. These units were commanded by Lieutenant General Truong, one of the ARVN"s finest and most aggressive generals. At first the PAVN contented itself with trying to cut Highway 1, the main north–south line of communications between Hue, Da Nang, and Chu Lai. The PAVN massed five divisions, nine independent infantry regiments, three sapper regiments, three armored regiments, twelve AAA, and eight artillery regiments under Brig. Gen. Le Trong Tan for the effort.[47]

On 13 March, during the aforementioned meeting in Saigon, Truong and Toan, recently appointed III Corps commander, briefed President Thieu on the military situation in the north. After Thieu explained his reorganization plan, the meeting broke up, with Truong believing he had the freedom to redeploy his forces to hold the Da Nang area. Subsequently, he was stunned to find out his Airborne Division was to be redeployed to III Corps. On the nineteenth Truong returned to Saigon to brief Thieu on his two contingency withdrawal plans, one predicated on the ARVN keeping control of Highway 1, and the other if the PAVN had taken the highway. According to the first plan, the highway would be used for two simultaneous withdrawals from Hue and Chu Lai headed to Da Nang. Under the second plan, Southern forces would gather in three enclaves, one each in Hue, Da Nang, and Chu Lai, with the troops at Hue and Chu Lai then sealifted to Da Nang by the South Vietnamese Navy. There was a brief pause before Thieu explained to Truong that he had misinterpreted his previous orders and Hue was not to be abandoned. In addition, the general's Marine Division was to be redeployed to III Corps.[48]

Given the circumstances in late March, Truong's second plan was the only realistic option because any phased withdrawal along Highway 1 had become impossible. Faced with amplified PAVN pressure, ARVN troops were holding on to the route by their fingernails. With this crisis facing him, Truong begged for permission to withdraw his forces into the three enclaves as planned and for the retention of the marines. Thieu ordered him to "hold onto any territory he could with whatever forces he now had, including the Marine Division."[49]

Truong returned to Da Nang the same day, only to discover the PAVN had initiated an all-out assault in I Corps Zone and had already breached the ARVN's northern defense line at the Thach Han River. That afternoon, in a nationwide radio broadcast, Thieu declared Hue would be held "at all costs." To carry out this proclamation, Truong ordered a retreat to a new defense line at the My Chanh River, thereby ceding all of Quang Tri Province to the North Vietnamese. Despite this loss, the general truly believed his forces could hold Hue. Once again, however, Thieu changed course. He now informed Truong "because of the inability to simultaneously defend all three enclaves, the I Corps commander was free . . . to redeploy his forces for the defense of Da Nang only." As word of this order leaked out to the populace, tens of thousands of panic-stricken civilians in Quang Tri City and Hue fled toward Da Nang.[50]

As Northern forces gradually ground down the ARVN north and south of Da Nang, General Dung decided to attack the Southern perimeter simultaneously from the west, north, and south and push them back into Da Nang, where they could be destroyed. On 22 March, after savage fighting, the communists cut the highway between Hue and Da Nang near Phu Loc. South of Da Nang, the ARVN 2nd Division barely managed to contain a PAVN thrust toward Tam Ky and the coastal plain. But this ARVN success lasted only two days. Early on 24 March, the PAVN 711th Division, supported by armored elements, captured Tam Ky. Thousands more refugees streamed north toward Da Nang. In turn, PAVN forces seized key parts of Highway 1 between Quang Ngai and Chu Lai from the 2nd Division.[51]

Now, virtually surrounded, the South Vietnamese troops fought their way from Quang Ngai northward to Chu Lai. Most of them never made it. In only forty-eight hours the situation in I Corps Zone had deteriorated into utter desperation and despair. The withdrawal into the three enclaves had been accomplished at a fearful cost. Truong issued orders for the 1st Division and other units near Hue to withdraw overland toward Da Nang while the marine elements were to be picked up from Hue by South Vietnamese ships. In turn, 7,000 members of the 2nd Division, 3,000 of their dependents, and the remnants of the Quang Ngai sector forces were withdrawn by sea to Re Island, twenty miles offshore from Chu Lai.[52]

By 26 March, command and control had collapsed, and no discipline existed within the ranks of the 1st Division. That same day its commander told his men: "We've been betrayed. . . . It is now *sauve qui peu* (every man for himself). . . . See you in Da Nang."[53] As the panicked mob fled toward Da Nang, what order was left disintegrated in a hail of PAVN artillery fire. As the remnants of these forces reached city, most of the soldiers, instead of preparing defensive positions, went in search of their surviving family and relatives; few were found. Meantime in Hue, slightly more than a single regiment of the 1st Division, about 600 marines, and 7,700 civilians were still alive to be rescued by the navy. At the end, just as Hue was about to be overrun, the five marine battalion commanders bid farewell to their soldiers and committed suicide rather than be taken by the enemy.[54]

As four PAVN divisions, supported by armor and artillery, surrounded Da Nang, anarchy and chaos broke out inside the city. On 28 March, with the collapse of the city eminent, Truong asked Thieu for permission to evacuate by sea. In response, the president, by now thoroughly overwhelmed by the rush of events, refused to commit to a clear-cut decision. Truong, on his own authority, ordered a naval withdrawal to start the following morning. As the ships neared shore, they could not come as close as they wanted due to low tides. Panic soon set in as thousands of soldiers and civilians made a mad dash for the sea. Hundreds drowned trying to swim out to the ships, and thousands more died from the unrelenting PAVN artillery barrage. In the end, as the communists poured into the city, of the four ARVN infantry divisions, four ranger groups, the armored brigade, an air-mobile division, and thousands of territorial, support, and staff personnel, only around 16,000 men were saved. Of the 2,000,000 civilians squeezed into Da Nang, only 50,000 were evacuated. In turn, 70,000 South Vietnamese troops were taken prisoner. South Vietnamese forces also abandoned thirty-three undamaged RVNAF A-37 jet fighters at Da Nang and nearly sixty more aircraft at Phu Cat Air Base. The fall of Da Nang came after no pitched battles, and few ARVN troops had even fired their rifles.[55] Quang Ngai fell on 24 March, followed by Qui Nhon and Nha Trang on 1 April and Cam Ranh Bay on 3 April. As Arnold Isaacs put it, all along the southern coast, centers of resistance "fell like a row of porcelain vases sliding off a shelf."[56]

The Last Desperate Action—the Ho Chi Minh
Campaign and the Battle of Xuan Loc

By the first week of April 1975, North Vietnam's military forces had swept through the northern provinces of South Vietnam as ARVN units crumbled due to poor strategic leadership and planning. In the Central Highlands the II Corps Tactical Zone was completely destroyed as the South Vietnamese attempted to escape encirclement in the Mekong delta. In Hue and Da Nang terrified ARVN soldiers failed to put up much of a fight. The devastating defeats suffered by the ARVN prompted the National Assembly to

Figure 9.1. Brig. Gen. Le Minh Dao, commander of the ARVN 18th Division at Xuan Loc

question Thieu's management of the war, with many members pressuring him to resign.[57]

On 4 April, in a speech televised throughout South Vietnam, a disheartened Thieu, rather than accept any blame for these defeats, denounced his generals, his troops, and a lack of support by his allies—particularly the United States. He declared if aid from America did not increase, "we will lose our land gradually to the North Vietnamese communists until the day when we lose it all." He then concluded, "I hope that the American people and Congress now will see clearly the real situation . . . and the consequences of their actions over the past two years and that they will assist us in more practical, more rapid, more efficient and a more adequate manner so that we can defend our remaining territory."[58]

Faced with total defeat, Thieu directed his last military units, the ARVN 18th Infantry Division, known as "The Super Men," to occupy and hold Xuan Loc at all cost. In turn, the PAVN's IV Army Corps was instructed to seize the city to open the gateway to Saigon.[59] At first this may seem to contradict the original plans made by the Politburo at the end of the previous year. But by 25 March, North Vietnamese leaders, buoyed by the success of their troops in the field, no longer believed it necessary to wait until 1976 to start their final offensive against Saigon. They directed General Dung to abandon the doctrine of meticulous planning and methodical preparation of the battlefield in order to defeat what they called the "puppet" regime. The major impediment to this proved to be moving his victorious northern forces 370 miles and his reserve divisions (still in North Vietnam) 1,000 miles south to make the final push on the Southern capital. In what many experts believe was one of the most complicated logistical feats of the war, Dung quickly positioned his forces for the final assault.[60]

What the PAVN did not realize was they were up against the best the ARVN had to offer. While US officers had believed the 18th Infantry Division, a key part of the ARVN III Corps, was often undisciplined and acted with a "cowboy" attitude, these troops proved to be brave and determined fighters. During the last stand they were about to make, they would have to live up to their motto, "God Arrow—Defending the Fatherland." In the aftermath of Xuan Loc, many historians and experts have compared their defense of this last position to the desperate stand by the Greeks at Thermopylae. Commanded by the brilliant and passionate Brigadier General Dao, these confirmed their sobriquet "The Super Men" at Xuan Loc.[61]

North Vietnamese Forces

Since the IV Army Corps was the first PAVN unit to arrive near Xuan Loc, the Central Military Committee decided it would lead the assault. This corps comprised the 6th, 7th, and 341st Infantry Divisions, supported by the 71st Antiaircraft Regiment, the 24th and 25th Engineering Regiments, the 26th Communications Regiment, two armored battalions, two artillery battalions, and two Long Khanh provincial infantry battalions.[62]

By 3 April 1975, corps leaders had formulated two plans of attack. The first called for PAVN forces to seize all the outlying ARVN defenses in order to surround and isolate the town. In turn, if the opportunity arose, they were to launch a full-scale frontal assault and overrun all of Xuan Loc. The other plan assumed the ARVN were so weak at this point the PAVN units could strike Xuan Loc directly with infantry, armor, and artillery.[63]

By the time the battle began, PAVN forces outnumbered the18th Division more than seven to one, and yet these elite ARVN troops remained defiant throughout their apocalyptic defense of their nation. But things continued to go badly for the Republic of Vietnam, even before the communists attacked. Throughout this time, President Thieu had his life threatened by attempted assassinations and coups. On 4 April an RVNAF pilot, 1st Lt. Nguyen Thanh Trung, flying his F-5E Tiger II fighter, attacked the Independence Palace in an apparent coup attempt; subsequent evidence reveled that Trung had been a VC agent since 1969. Thus, when the desperate last stand began, Thieu did not trust any of his own officers and military commanders. It was a bad position from which to make one last frantic effort to save South Vietnam.[64]

Philip Davidson noted, "The ARVN forces defending Saigon were disposed to cover the five main roads leading into Saigon." To the north of the capital, the 5th Division guarded Highway 13, while "to the northeast of the capital, the 18th ARVN Division held Xuan Loc covering Highway 1 and the city and air base of Bien Hoa." Southeast of Saigon, two airborne brigades and a ranger group, all at roughly 50-percent strength, defended Highway 15. To the southwest, "the reactivated and refitted 22nd ARVN Division sat astride Highway 4, the main route from the Mekong Delta to Saigon." Finally, to the northwest, the 25th Division held Route 1 leading in from Tay Ninh.[65]

ARVN leaders placed all of these outlying defenses seventeen to thirty miles from the outskirts of Saigon. General Truong, who after his evacuation from Da Nang became deputy chief of the JGS, was placed in charge of defending the capital. He immediately realized there was no way to establish any real defensive line around the city since the perimeter was too large and there were not enough troops. Yet to constrict the defensive circle meant surrendering valuable real estate and large US-built cantonments at Bien Hoa, Cu Chi, and Lai Khe. Further, he recognized it was essential to hold the main ARVN logistic base at Long Binh as well as the airbase at Bien Hoa. Finally, if they retracted the defense lines too close to Saigon, it exposed the city to lethal artillery fire from the PAVN's 130-mm guns.[66]

The Preliminaries

As noted earlier, in March 1975 the PAVN III Army Corps attacked Ban Me Thuot in the Central Highlands, while their IV Army Corps assaulted Tay Ninh and Binh Duong in the western regions of South Vietnam. The ARVN defenses in those locations were weaker than in the past due to the lack of manpower and resources. While Tay Ninh and Binh Duong did not play a vital role in saving South Vietnam, large numbers of ARVN troops fled to these areas following the 1975 defeats. Tay Ninh became a refuge for members of the 25th Infantry Division, four armored brigades, and two ranger battalions, while Binh Duong sheltered the 5th Infantry Division, one ranger battalion, and one armored brigade. To stop South Vietnamese military units from regrouping at either place, the PAVN decided to seize these enclaves.[67]

The initial IV Army Corps target was Dau Tieng–Chon Thanh, the weakest point in the ARVN's northwestern defenses, held by 2,600 soldiers, one armored brigade, and ten 105-mm artillery guns. The communist assault units were from the 9th Infantry Division, supported by the 16th Infantry Regiment, the 22nd Armored Battalion, one artillery battalion, and one air-defense battalion. The attack began 11 March against the artillery positions in Rung Nan, Bau Don, and Cha La. That afternoon ARVN general Le Nguyen Khang ordered the 345th Armored Squadron to relieve the Dau Tieng military zone. Within a few hours, the unit had been forced to retreat to its staging area. Concurrently, the South Vietnamese artillery units were overrun, and two days later the PAVN had complete control of Dau Tieng.

In addition, communist units took ARVN positions at Vuon Chuoi, Nga Ba Sac, Cau Tau, and Ben Cui. The ARVN 3rd Brigade made plans to retake Dau Tieng with elements of the 5th Infantry Division, but Thieu ordered them to withdraw and defend Truong Mit, Bau Don, and Tay Ninh.[68]

On 24 March two regiments from the PAVN 9th Infantry Division attacked Chon Thanh, only to be repulsed several times. Communist reinforcements joined the fight on 31 March, and by 2 April, the PAVN had seized Chon Thanh, having killed 2,134 ARVN soldiers and capturing 472 others. With all of Binh Long occupied, North Vietnamese leaders now focused on their last great obstacle, Xuan Loc.[69] On 2 April, even as Chon Thanh fell, the Senate of the Republic of Vietnam called for the creation of a new government, with Nguyen Ba Can as the new prime minister. The sitting prime minister, Tran Thien Kiem, resigned. Thieu accepted Kiem's resignation and then swore in Can. Two days later Thieu announced the shakeup and also demanded the arrest of General Phu for the debacle in the Central Highlands, General Pham for his failure to hold Nha Trang, and General Dong for the loss of Phuoc Long; General Truong was spared as he was undergoing medical treatment. There followed a period of finger pointing in an effort to find scapegoats for the president's own tactical and strategic mistakes.[70]

The previous day Thieu had met with General Weyand to lay out his final strategy, declaring Xuan Loc would be the linchpin in his final defensive position, with Tay Ninh and Phan Rang flanking this vital city. At one point in the discussion, Thieu took out a letter he had received from former president Nixon, which promised military retaliation against North Vietnam if they violated the terms of the Paris Peace Accords. After a number of excuses from Weyand, the meeting broke up when Thieu accused the United States of selling out his country the moment they signed the agreements with the DRV.[71] One communist document recorded the event as follows: "Weyand, the US Army Chief of Staff, was in Saigon to urge the puppets on. General Le Minh Dao regarded as one of the best officers of Saigon was put in command of Xuan Loc, swore to defend it to the death."[72]

In Hanoi Northern leaders were very optimistic that victory was near. By 8 April 1975, PAVN forces had captured all the provinces in the I and II Corps Tactical Zones as well as Phuoc Long Province. In addition, the ARVN was disintegrating at every point. Two PAVN army corps were now prepared to attack the outnumbered defenders at Xuan Loc. The 4th Army

Corps approached Xuan Loc from the northeast following its conquest of Tay Ninh, Binh Long, and Long Khanh. Concurrently, the III Army Corps moved in from the northwest, following its victory in the Central Highlands. The stage was set for the last great battle for the future of Vietnam.[73]

The PAVN's Plan of Attack on Saigon

The communist plan to take Saigon called for a concentric five-pronged offensive against the South Vietnamese capital. This would be their greatest prize, and it was one General Dung was determined to take intact if possible. He recalled how, during the Tet Offensive of 1968, much of the city had been damaged, and he wanted to prevent a reoccurrence. More importantly, he wanted to avoid constricting ARVN troops into a small pocket inside Saigon. As a result, his plan called for his five corps to assume a specific axis of advance. Dung also directed each corps to encircle and annihilate the ARVN defenders in their outermost defensive positions to prevent a last-ditch defense in the city itself. In turn, the general designated five critical targets in Saigon for his troops to take. These included the Independence Palace, the headquarters of the JGS near Tan Son Nhut Air Base, the airbase itself, the National Police headquarters, and the headquarters of the Capitol Zone, whose commander controlled troops in and around Saigon. Dung reasoned if these installations were captured quickly before serious fighting in the city began, the battle for Saigon would be over. North Vietnamese leaders also added a caveat to the plan, calling for a "Great Uprising in Saigon" to accompany the "Great Offensive," even though the uprising was unnecessary. None of the previous uprisings, including those in 1968 and 1972, had succeeded, but of course, uprisings were part of communist dogma. Nevertheless, it was an elaborate plan, calling for a political "dau tranh" involving a "dich van" program among the population of South Vietnam and a "binh van" program, or troop proselytizing, aimed at the RVNAF. Instead of an uprising, though, thousands of Saigon's residents were trying to flee the country.[74]

On 7 April Le Duc Tho arrived at Dung's headquarters near Loc Ninh as the Politburo's representative to oversee the final battles. As noted, the initial move called for the IV Corps to capture Xuan Loc, the capital of Long Khanh Province and "the gateway to Saigon." Victory here would open the way to Bien Hoa, where 60 percent of ARVN's remaining ordnance was located. Tactical command of this assault was given to Brigadier General

Tan, the "conqueror of Da Nang." To divert Saigon's attention and prevent reinforcements being sent to Xuan Loc, the recently activated 223rd Tactical Group was to cut off Route 4, severing Saigon from the Mekong delta. The III Corps planned a diversionary operation around Tay Ninh. But Xuan Loc was the main objective since it anchored the eastern end of the outer defenses of Saigon; oversaw traffic along the roads from the east to Saigon, Bien Hoa, and Vung Tau; and covered the two big airbases at Bien Hoa and Tan Son Nhut. Both sides viewed the city as the key to the defense of Saigon. In what General Dung designated the Ho Chi Minh Campaign, the final outcome of the Vietnam War would be decided.[75]

Making the Last Stand

Following the seizure of all the key defenses around Xuan Loc in Long Khanh Province, PAVN commanders spent four days preparing for the final assault against the ARVN 18th Infantry Division, with General Cam assuming personal control of the operation. He decided to make a full-frontal assault on Xuan Loc from the north-northwest, employing his

Figure 9.2. South Vietnamese soldiers posing with captured enemy flags

infantry, tanks, and artillery. Col. Bui Cat Vu, deputy commander of the PAVN IV Army Corps, was to support the main attack with an assault from the east. In turn, Brigadier General Dao and the chief of Long Khanh Province, Col. Nguyen Van Phuc, had positioned their own forces to withstand the upcoming onslaught. Facing overwhelming odds did not seem to faze Dao, who told the foreign media: "I am determined to hold Xuan Loc. I don't care how many divisions the communists will send against me, I will smash them all! The world shall see the strength and skill of the Army of the Republic of Vietnam."[76]

On 9 April at 0540, the IV Army Corps initiated an extensive artillery barrage against ARVN positions all around Xuan Loc. The communists expended 20,000 rounds of artillery and rocket fire. From the north, General Cam sent the 341st Infantry Division headlong into the ARVN defenses. After an hour of fierce fighting, they took the communications center and the police station. PAVN units probing from the north were stopped cold by a counterattack from elements of the ARVN 52nd Task Force. Dao's troops fought fiercely, often hand to hand, rather than surrender. Concurrently, the PAVN 7th Infantry Division attacked ARVN positions from the east without tank support and suffered grievous loses. At 0800 IV Army Corps leadership deployed eight tanks to support the 7th Infantry Division. Three were destroyed almost immediately by entrenched ARVN soldiers.[77]

In a communique from the US embassy in Saigon to the JCS, American officers on the scene reported the battle had begun at the "vital road junction of QL-1 and QL-20 and the province capital at Xuan Loc on April 9, 1975." They went on to record "the enemy ran the ARVN out of city supported by 3,000 rounds of rockets, mortars, and artillery . . . , [but] the ARVN took it back." The report continued by saying the "enemy had committed three divisions by the third day," and "a conservative count indicates 1,200 enemy killed and 30 tanks destroyed." The message concluded: "The valor and aggressiveness of the GVN troops, especially the Long Khanh regional forces, is and properly led, are man for man, vastly superior to their adversaries. The battle for Xuan Loc appears to settle for the time being the question, 'will the ARVN fight?'"[78]

Ambassador Martin, in a subsequent telegram describing the overall situation, declared: "Despite the journalistic reports, what has happened here was a planned withdrawal of military force from Military Regions I and II to more defensible lines. The plan, deemed strategically sound by

Weyand, was poorly executed. Nevertheless, military equation in remainder of country, roughly old Cochin China, is now reasonably stable."[79]

Despite this optimistic appraisal, by noon on the ninth, the PAVN's 209th and 270th Infantry Regiments had wrested control of the 18th Division's headquarters and the governor's residence away from the ARVN 43rd and 48th Infantry Regiments. To the south, the PAVN's 6th Infantry Division engaged the ARVN 332 Armored Brigade, defending Highway 1 from Hung Nghia to Me Bong Con. The South Vietnamese lost eighteen tanks in these encounters. Each time the enemy advanced, the 18th Division counterattacked, forcing a PAVN retreat.[80]

During the night, both sides regrouped and tried to rest for the next day's fighting. On 10 and 11 April, the PAVN 7th Division again ploughed into the 18th Division, the 52nd Task Force, and the 5th Armored Cavalry. Each time it was repelled by ARVN counterattacks on the flanks. To the northwest, the PAVN's 226th and 270th Infantry Regiments, of the 341st Infantry Division, faced the same tactic employed by the ARVN 43rd Infantry Regiment and the 322nd Armored Brigade. For two days, RVNAF fighter-bombers of the 5th Air Force Division flew more than two hundred CAS sorties in support of the 18th Division. On the night of April 11, Dao relocated the 18th's headquarters to the Tan Phong military zone, and Col. Pham Van Phuc moved his headquarters to Nui Thi Vai to continue the struggle.[81]

On 12 April, with the battle going relatively well, the ARVN General Staff decided to reinforce their forces at Xuan Loc with units from the general reserve. In short order the ARVN 1st Airborne Brigade arrived at the Bao Dinh rubber plantation, while two marine battalions moved into place to defend the eastern corridor leading to Bien Hoa. The 33rd Ranger Battalion, 8th Regiment of the 5th Infantry Division, 8th Artillery Battalion as well as the 315th, 318th, and 322nd Armored Brigades deployed to Tan Phong and Dau Giay. In support, RVNAF aircraft flew 80–120 CAS sorties per day to support the defenders at Xuan Loc. Around 1400 on 12 April, a RVNAF C-130 Hercules dropped two 750-pound CBU-55 FAE (Fuel Air Explosive) bombs on PAVN troops in the town of Xuan Vinh, close to Xuan Loc, creating a four-mile-wide crater and killing more than 250 enemy soldiers and about twenty-five civilians. One of the most lethal nonnuclear weapons ever created, this was the only time the CBU-55 was used during the war.[82]

The events of 12 April seemed to encourage the Americans in Saigon. The following morning at 0700 Ambassador Martin sent a communique to

Gen. Brent Scowcroft: "Some of our friends in the Pentagon who, at times, are more influenced by press reporting than by the facts may not have passed on to you our running reports on the Xuan Loc fighting. I am quite well aware that 'one swallow does not make a summer' but whether, in the end, they win or are overwhelmed, recent RVNAF action should put to rest the most devastating argument against us on the Hill—that the RVNAF have lost 'the will to fight.'"[83]

That same day General Tra arrived at the headquarters of the IV Army Corps. After discussions with the PAVN commanders present, he convinced them to change their operational plan. The 6th Infantry Division and elements of the 341st Infantry Division would attack Dau Giay, the weakest point in the defensive line around Xuan Loc, and establish a blocking position along Highway 2, leading to Ba Ria and Vung Tau, and Highway 1 between Xuan Loc and Bien Hoa. The 95B Infantry Regiment of the II Army Corps then would link up with the IV Army Corps and continue the attacks on Xuan Loc. Ironically, even as the enemy forces initiated their new tactics, Thieu announced the 18th had repulsed the "communist attack" on Xuan Loc and "recovered its fighting ability." In fact, the division had only withstood the initial assault—there was much more to come.[84]

At this point the South Vietnamese had committed roughly 25,000–30,000 troops from the 18th Division, the 8th Regiment, the 3rd Armored Brigade, the 81st Airborne Ranger Group, and two ranger and two artillery battalions. In total this was nearly one-third of the remainder of their reserve forces. For the first time since the onset of the North Vietnamese offensive, the RVNAF had provided effective CAS to the defenders. Even General Dung grudgingly acknowledged "the stubbornness of the enemy" in what he described as a "meat grinder." It was a situation the communists had not experienced in the long and successful series of offensives they had undertaken since December 1974. Both sides now wondered if the outcome of this battle might alter the conclusion of the war in general.[85]

In his summation to the State Department, Ambassador Martin reported: "Forty miles away at Xuan Loc, one division of the ARVN, with supporting units, is not only holding but inflicting enormous damage on elements of three PAVN divisions. Given the fact that two of these PAVN divisions are green and have a large preponderance of young teenagers the accomplishment of the ARVN as of this morning is nonetheless remarkable. It at least should completely dispel the canard circulated all over Washington that the

Vietnamese have 'no will to fight.'"[86] He concluded: "On the political front, we cannot exclude continuing difficulties, including the possibility of the departure of President Thieu. Whatever the result, we detect no inclination on the part of any significant political faction to surrender."[87]

As if Dung did not have enough on his plate, on 14 April he received a gratuitous message from Hanoi, declaring, "We must be in Saigon to celebrate Ho Chi Minh's birthday." They gave him a 19 May deadline in which to overrun Xuan Loc and seize Saigon.[88] Given his circumstances, the general decided to circumvent the ARVN forces at Xuan Loc and begin a concerted shelling of Bien Hoa Air Base, which essentially ended RVNAF air support. He also stopped his tactic of direct assaults against the town and instead focused on the destruction of the outposts around Xuan Loc in order to cut off reinforcements to the 18th Division.[89]

The plan worked. On 15 April the PAVN stopped shelling Xuan Loc and began battering Bien Hoa. As a result, nearly all 3rd Air Force Division flight operations ended. In an effort to ameliorate this situation, RVNAF leaders mobilized the 4th Air Force Division, based at Tra Noc, to fly CAS for the defenders of Xuan Loc. While this seemed to stabilize things temporarily, that afternoon the PAVN 6th Infantry Division and the 95B Infantry Regiment defeated a combined ARVN formation that included the 52nd Task Force and the 13th Armored Squadron west of Xuan Loc, further shrinking the South Vietnamese perimeter. These same communist troops also repelled the ARVN 8th Task Force and 3rd Armored Brigade when they tried to retake the Dau Giay military zone. The ARVN 43rd and 48th Infantry Regiments, as well as the 1st Airborne Brigade, took heavy casualties in the attempt. Still, the PAVN were unable to finish them off.[90]

On 16 April yet another airborne superweapon was deployed. This was the 15,000-pound BLU-82 "Daisy Cutter." The US military had built 225 of these massive bombs, mainly to blast helicopter LZs in one explosion. In this particular case an RVNAF C-130 released the ordnance on a concentration of communist troops outside Xuan Loc. In an intercepted radio message, the ARVN discovered the bomb had killed 75 percent of the soldiers near the blast area, including most of the officers in the 341st Division's headquarters.[91]

That same day Thieu sent his personal emissary, Nguyen Tien Hung, to Washington to beg one last time for US aid. He carried letters from Presidents Nixon and Ford swearing to defend South Vietnam and aid it in case

Figure 9.3. Battle
of Xuan Loc

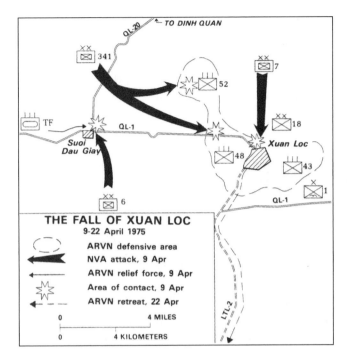

THE FALL OF XUAN LOC
9-22 April 1975
ARVN defensive area
NVA attack, 9 Apr
ARVN relief force, 9 Apr
Area of contact, 9 Apr
ARVN retreat, 22 Apr
0   4 MILES
0   4 KILOMETERS

of crisis. Hung went so far as to ask the president for a $3 billion loan for three years at an interest rate to be determined by Congress. In his letter to Ford, Thieu called this a "freedom loan" designed to allow the South Vietnamese to have a "reasonable chance to survive as a free country." In this regard Thieu hoped he could still hold out in the Mekong delta. The appeal died the next day when the Senate Armed Services Committee voted against approving additional aid to Saigon.[92]

By 18 April, the 18th Division was completely surrounded. While the troops continued to hold on, the next day the ARVN General Staff ordered Dao to evacuate his forces from Xuan Loc in hopes of continuing their resistance elsewhere. On 20 April, under cover of a driving rain, soldiers and civilians began the withdrawal from the beleaguered city in a two-hundred-vehicle convoy. Unlike previous retreats, this one took place in good order, and by the following day, Xuan Loc had been abandoned, with the ARVN 1st Airborne Brigade the last unit to depart. This final battle ended around 1600, when the ARVN 3rd Battalion, 1st Airborne Brigade was defeated at the hamlet of Suoi Ca. As night fell, Xuan Loc was in PAVN hands. The road to Saigon was open.[93]

After three weeks of bitter and bloody combat in which they had suffered 4,000 casualties, the ARVN defenders were now forced to execute a retreat south along Route 2. In turn, they had inflicted 5,000–8,000 casualties on the PAVN, while destroying thirty-seven tanks and tracked vehicles. But despite their heroism, their efforts to save their nation had come to naught. Dao refused to abandon his brave troopers and stood with them until Saigon fell only a few days later, and he was captured. With all of Long Khanh Province in enemy hands, Dung was now free to encircle Saigon with his forces and prepare for the triumphant entry into the great teaming city. The PAVN had won the last great battle of the war, but it had come at a great cost.[94]

The Outcome

With the fall of Xuan Loc, the PAVN controlled roughly two-thirds of South Vietnam. In addition, the ARVN had lost almost every unit from its general reserve. On 18 April Major General Toan had told President Thieu their forces at Xuan Loc were near defeat and the ARVN could only hold out a few more days. According to the official ARVN account of the battle, the South Vietnamese suffered 2,036 soldiers killed or wounded and another 2,731 captured. While the exact numbers of communist casualties is not known, the IV Army Corps reported having lost 460 men killed and 1,428 wounded. Brigadier General Dao reported his forces had killed 50,000 PAVN and destroyed 370 tanks. Estimates by US sources put the communist casualties at 5,000–8,000 troops killed or wounded and 37 tanks destroyed. The reasons for Dao's exaggeration can be only speculated. Later examination, however, suggests he was trying to build up the morale of his men and hoped such numbers might still convince the United States to increase critical aide. Whatever the reason for his excessive numbers, Dao and his forces fought the enemy with great courage and skill.[95] General Westmoreland wrote of Dao, "Never have I known a more admirable man; honest, loyal, reserved, scholarly, and diplomatic."[96] Of all the Southern officers, he was one of the few who fought to the end.

The importance of airpower—or lack thereof—cannot be overlooked in the outcome of the battle. Without US airpower, it fell to the RVNAF to provide CAS for the defenders of Xuan Loc. At first they did an excellent job of devastating PAVN attacking columns. The effective use of special weapons like the "Daisy Cutters" also had a major effect on communist morale.

Ultimately, the extremely accurate PAVN artillery barrages and infantry attacks on Bien Hoa Air Base restricted this effective air support and played a major part in the PAVN victory. When the PAVN turned its attention away from frontal assaults and toward destruction of air assets, they were able to destroy six F-5 fighters and fourteen A-37 fighter-bombers on the ground. Damage to the runways and operational buildings also affected CAS missions. Col. William Le Gro noted in his official account of the war, "The South Vietnamese, already greatly outnumbered, were unable to hold their positions in the absence of effective close air support."[97]

As the military situation degenerated, both houses of the National Assembly debated alternatives. Some advocated that South Vietnam fight to the very end, still convinced the United States eventually would provide enough aid to prevent a communist takeover. Others urged negotiating with the North to avoid a catastrophic defeat. The one thing they all agreed on was that Thieu was responsible for the country's calamitous military and political situation. Nearly every assembly member believed his flawed policies had facilitated the communist breach of South Vietnam's military defenses. As resistance at Xuan Loc crumbled, the pressure on Thieu increased. Finally, on the evening of 21 April 1975, in a tearful televised speech broadcast internationally, he blamed the United States for the fall of his nation, then officially resigned as president of the Republic of Vietnam. A day after Thieu's departure to Taiwan, the assembly appointed Tran Van Huong as the new president, charging him to negotiate peace with North Vietnam at any cost. As for the 18th Division, it eventually surrendered on the afternoon of 30 April. Most Southern political leaders were left in a state of chagrin, having argued things would not have come to this had Thieu resigned earlier and the ARVN had been allowed to defend the nation, not retreat.[98]

Perhaps the best summation of the fall of Indochina comes from Cambodian statesman Sirak Mitak, given just days before his execution at the hands of the Khmer Rouge. He wrote the US ambassador to refuse the American's offer of evacuation:

> I cannot, alas, leave in such a cowardly fashion. As for you and in particular for your great country, I never believed for a moment that you would have this sentiment of abandoning a people who have chosen liberty. . . . You leave and my wish is that you and your country will find

happiness under the sky. But mark it well that, if I shall die here on the spot and in my country that I love, it is too bad because we all are born and must die one day. I have only committed this mistake in believing in you, the Americans.[99]

The Fall of Saigon

For some reason, even when Da Nang fell in March 1975, President Ford and his advisers continued to believe the regime in Saigon would survive. On 10 April Ford asked Congress for $722 million in supplemental military aid to prop up the ARVN and $250 million in economic and refugee aid. His rationale seemed to have changed.[100] Whereas in the past he argued that without aid, South Vietnam would become the first domino to fall in Southeast Asia, now he claimed he feared "if we say 'no more money' Thieu . . . might do something totally irrational."[101] In short, Ford worried the South Vietnamese might turn on the remaining Americans and demand ransom. Congress, influenced by antiwar sentiment throughout the nation and dominated by antiwar Democrats, determined the president was simply overreacting. They concluded he might very well be delaying the evacuation of the remaining US personnel and civilians in Vietnam to force the aid bill through. Congressional debate ended on 17 April. There would be no more funds for Saigon—Xuan Loc was being overrun and resistance was futile.[102]

While the political maneuvering continued, General Toan organized five centers of resistance for the defense of Saigon. The interlocking centers tightly connected to form an arc enveloping the entire area west, north, and east of the capital. The 25th Division defended the Cu Chi front in the northwest, while the 5th Division secured Binh Duong in the north. Remnants of the 18th Division guarded Bien Hoa in the northeast, while the 1st Airborne Brigade and one battalion of the 3rd Division secured Vung Tau and the Route 15 front to the southeast. Finally, the Long An front, for which the Capital Military District Command was responsible, was defended by elements of the reformed 22nd Division. The ARVN defensive forces around Saigon totaled roughly 60,000 troops. Nearly 200,000 additional armed ARVN refugees from Xuan Loc and other disastrous defeats over the past month had made their way into Saigon. While this increased the number of troops on paper, they were spent. Rather than increasing the number of defenders, they only added to the chaos.[103]

Morale in the capitol, which hung by a thread, was further eroded when, on 17 April, the Cambodian capital of Phnom Penh fell to the Khmer Rouge, shortly after the last Americans there departed. On 21 April Thieu resigned as president. In his televised speech he admitted his order to evacuate the Central Highlands and the north had led to the existing disaster. Still, he declared it had been the only course of action open to him, going on to say the plan might still have worked except that his generals had failed him.[104] As noted, Thieu saved his greatest criticism for the United States: "Our great ally . . . , the leader of the free world . . . , [t]he United States has not respected its promises. . . . It is inhuman. It is not trustworthy. It is irresponsible."[105]

The PAVN's Final Attack

At this time General Dung, at his forward command post in Ben Cat, formulated his plans for taking Saigon. He had surrounded the city with four PAVN corps, totaling nineteen divisions, supported by artillery and armored units—around 130,000 men. He hoped to avoid street combat by initially attacking and tying down ARVN forces in their outer defensive positions, then launching five spearheads through them into the city, each of which had a specific target: the Independence Palace, the JGS headquarters, the National Police headquarters, Tan Son Nhut Air Base, and the Special Capital Zone headquarters.[106]

The planned assault began on 26 April, with the PAVN launching an all-out attack on Bien Hoa and the extensive logistical complex at Long Binh from the south and southeast. On 28 April, as its troops squeezed the noose tighter, the PAVN also began its attack on the port city of Vung Tau and against the Cu Chi front. Now the same chaos, lack of leadership, and anarchy that earlier had caused the collapse of ARVN I and II Corps troops during their series of defeats in the Central Highlands spread throughout Saigon. In an effort to curb the lawlessness, officials imposed martial law, but to little effect. The reality that the PAVN would soon seize control of all Vietnam sent shockwaves across the South, leaving citizens petrified with fear and unable to prevent their nation's downfall. In an effort to stimulate some kind of resistance, officials warned that if the communists won, there would follow another massacre like the one in Hue during the 1968 Tet Offensive. The ploy failed; instead of unifying the citizenry, it left them in a state of complete paralysis when the time came to defend the city.[107]

After nibbling away at the flanks of the ARVN defenses during most of the twenty-sixth, the main PAVN assault developed the following day, even as the South Vietnamese National Assembly made General Minh the new president. Sworn in on the twenty-eighth, Minh believed he would be able to attain a ceasefire and reopen negotiations. This was a delusional since the communists had the upper hand on the battlefield and final victory was within reach, regardless of political changes in Saigon. After fighting for thirty years to unify Vietnam under communism, they were not going to be denied absolute victory. They were not going to make the same mistake they had made in the 1950s, when they had accepted the Geneva Accords.[108]

As defeat became more certain with each passing minute, thousands of South Vietnamese sought ways to leave Vietnam. Those Americans still in Saigon had been evacuating since 1 April from Tan Son Nhut Air Base. This route eventually became untenable as the PAVN attacks intensified. It was during this time that two US Marines, LCpl. Darwin Judge and Cpl. Charles McMahon Jr., were killed by an enemy rocket attack while manning the main-gate checkpoint at the airbase. They were the last Americans killed during the Vietnam War.[109]

On 28 April PAVN troops pushed into the outskirts of Saigon. At the Cau Tan Cang, or the Newport, Bridge, roughly three miles from the heart of the city, ARVN forces made a desperate stand against enemy forces trying to cross and cut the capital's last overland connection to the south, gaining access to downtown. That afternoon, even as President Minh was completing his acceptance speech, four captured A-37s, flown by Northern pilots, bombed Tan Son Nhut airport, ending exit flights by Americans and South Vietnamese. Concurrently, Bien Hoa Air Base fell, and General Toan fled to Saigon. In his final report he informed the Southern government nearly all of the top ARVN leadership had virtually resigned themselves to defeat and were seeking ways to escape.[110]

As the attacks expanded on 29 April, chaos broke out everywhere. Military and civilians made a dash to get on any kind of aircraft to escape what they saw as certain death. In one case crewmembers of an overloaded C-130 pushed ARVN soldiers off the rear cargo ramp in order for the plane to gain enough altitude to take off. One C-7 "Caribou" crashed and burned because it was overloaded.[111] James Willbanks later described the scene: "RVNAF pilots manned anything that would fly and took off for Thailand. This symbolized the disintegration of the Vietnamese Air Force; eventually

Figure 9.4. Desperate people climb to the top of the US embassy to take the last chopper out of Saigon during Operation Frequent Wind

132 aircraft were flown to U Tapao Air Base." These included twenty-six F-5 fighters and twenty-seven A-37 fighter-bombers.[112]

Finally, on 29 April at 1051 hours (Vietnamese time), US helicopters commenced Operation Frequent Wind, the aerial evacuation of American military, embassy, and civilian personnel as well as those South Vietnamese deemed at risk of communist reprisal. By the time the exodus had started, forty-two ships of the Seventh Fleet had arrived to recover the choppers and their passengers. All totaled, 1,373 American and 5,595 Vietnamese were flown to the waiting armada. In addition, approximately 60,000 more people were rescued from boats that made their way out to the American vessels.[113] Officially, "the evacuees included 57,507 removed by air and 73,000 by sea." As they final evacuees left, Saigon "descended into pandemonium."[114]

As for the bedraggled ad hoc units of the ARVN, they put up a determined resistance throughout the city, even counterattacking at one point. The PAVN were shocked by the ARVN soldiers who had been abandoned by their officers but continued to fight heroically. Most were certain they were on the communists' execution lists and thus made suicidal strikes at the enemy, hoping for a quick death. The PAVN forces assigned the capture of key buildings and targets also found themselves being attacked by more-disciplined forces commanded by officers who had not been able to escape. These troops used the equipment left behind by their ARVN comrades who had fled to create a perimeter around the city. They fought fanatically. All of their efforts proved to be fruitless, lacking enough resources to resist for long.[115]

By 30 April, nothing was left to stop the PAVN advance into central Saigon. That same day, around 0500, American ambassador Martin, holding a furled US flag under his arm, embarked on a CH-46 for the USS *Blue Ridge* stationed just off the coast in the South China Sea. This was the last helicopter to depart the Saigon embassy. Five and a half hours later, President Minh directed all ARVN forces to cease fighting, a useless order since the army had already ceased to exist. Soon after, Minh made his way to a nearby radio station and announced the unconditional surrender of his government.[116] Clark Dougan and his colleagues described the Republic of Vietnam's final moments: "Around noon, a PAVN tank, number 390,

Figure 9.5. A Soviet-built NVA tank breaks through the gates of Independence Palace in Saigon

crashed through the gates of the Independence Palace. A crewman from the 843, which rammed into the side gate and got stuck, jumped out, ran up the steps, carrying the flag of the Provisional Revolutionary Government. A Western reporter on the scene asked the soldier his name and the man replied, 'Nguyen Van Thieu.' On that ironic note the Vietnam War came to an end."[117]

Even with this, the war was not completely over. Brig. Gen. Le Van Hung's ARVN forces in the Mekong delta were still intact and apparently ready to continue the fight. His plan was to assemble what he called a "secret section" that would exploit the abundance of the delta's agricultural resources and form a resistance. The plan never came to fruition because the VC thwarted it. Most Americans and South Vietnamese believed the VC had been all but destroyed by the Phoenix Program, designed to assassinate NLF leaders. Phoenix proved to be less successful than thought, and long-hidden VC sympathizers fought these last ARVN soldiers. Ultimately, the ARVN IV Corps was isolated from Saigon or any other important city. Soon General Hung was killed, and with him died the "secret plan" and the IV Corps.[118]

Conclusion

In the aftermath of the Vietnam War, there have been many heated exchanges in the United States regarding who lost Vietnam. There have been those, such as President Thieu, who have argued the Paris Accords were the main reason for the defeat since they allowed the PAVN to keep 100,000 troops inside South Vietnam after taking effect. Not only had the United States negotiated and signed this agreement without the presence or approval to its South Vietnamese ally but, in permitting the communists to maintain robust forces in the South, had all but doomed the ceasefire. Of course, President Nixon had promised to take military action if the need arose—specifically, a reintroduction of airpower if necessary. In the end Congress refused to take military action in the face of communist violations of the agreement. Advocates of such action still contend South Vietnam could have been saved by another Linebacker-style bombing campaign. The problem with this notion is that the tension between the Nixon, then Ford, administration and Congress had grown since Linebacker II in late 1972. By 1975, there was no inclination among legislators or the public for a new aerial campaign.

Assuming Ford could have honored Nixon's pledge and initiated such an bombing operation, one must consider what other issues might have arisen. What kind of aircraft would the United States have used? How long would the bombing have lasted? What would the targets have been? How long would it have taken to prepare to start the campaign? How would the Americans have measured success or failure? How many new prisoners of war would have been taken, and how would the United States have recovered them? After all, the previous return of POWs had not been easy—and issues with those missing in action persist even in the early twenty-first century.

Years later Nixon condemned a "Congress which refused to fulfill our obligations," saying legislators were "solely to blame" for what he called a "tragic and irresponsible action."[119] General Vien pointed to cutbacks in US military and materiel aid as having "accelerated the whole process and made defeat inevitable."[120] While shortages probably explain why the Central Highlands had to be evacuated, they do not account for the departure of senior ARVN leaders and generals that led to the complete collapse at the end. Historian Arnold Isaacs, who was present in South Vietnam during its last days, has maintained: "The psychological damage of the aid cuts was almost certainly greater than the real damage. Even with the full amounts requested by the executive, South Vietnam could not have done any more than preserve the battlefield deadlock for another year, after which, the whole exhausting debate would have to be replayed yet again—and in a presidential election year."[121]

Still other analysts have claimed Nixon's Vietnamization program was at the heart of the final collapse. They believe, beginning in 1969, the abrupt and fast-tracked downsizing of American forces left the ARVN ill equipped to continue to fight the same kind of war they had up to that point. In short, the withdrawals happened more quickly than the South Vietnamese expected and left them groping to build up their own forces.[122] Maj. Gen. Nguyen Duy Hinh believed this about the Vietnamization process: "While the troop increases [by the ARVN] could be achieved fairly rapidly, it was almost impossible to improve the quality and technical capabilities . . . within the span of a few years."[123]

In 1974 Gen. Douglas Kinnard conducted a survey of US Army general officers who had served in Southeast Asia and found 73 percent believed the Vietnamization program should have been initiated, in earnest, years earlier. In short, it had come too late, and by the time it began its positive effect proved minimal.[124] In summation, historian Gabriel Kolko contended, "For seven years, the American military had molded South Vietnamese forces into a facsimile of itself, yet it ended up with a system that had all of the liabilities of American military technology and few of its assets."[125]

One cannot examine the final defeat without placing some blame at the feet of the South Vietnamese themselves. President Thieu, as it turned out, was a poor military leader and strategist. Beginning in early 1973, as the initial cuts in US aid were happening, neither he nor his General Staff even entertained strategic, doctrinal, organizational, or training alterations to compensate for the inevitability of further aid reductions. On top of this, Thieu denied subordinates, especially his battlefield commanders, any strategic or tactical flexibility. This contributed greatly to the defeat. To top this off, throughout his tenure as president, Thieu's government and military were rife with corruption and ineptitude within the officer corps itself. Willbanks commented, "Early defeats during the final campaign were compounded not by a lack of will or ability on the part of the enlisted men, but by the cowardice and failing morale of the officers."[126] Isaacs echoed this: "The army did not collapse in its foxholes or for lack of supplies. It disintegrated when its senior officers . . . deserted it."[127]

Years after the American Civil War, Maj. Gen. George Pickett, who led the infamous infantry attack on the Union center on the third day of the Battle of Gettysburg, was asked why the attack had failed and why the South had lost the battle. He replied, "I've always thought the Yankees had something to do with it."[128] In a very real sense, the same can be said for the fall of South Vietnam. The skill of the officers and men of the highly motivated and newly modernized PAVN cannot be overlooked. For the first time in the war, they were not confronted with American airpower and were free from the restraints of nonsensical Marxist combat doctrine. As leaders in Hanoi realized the possibility for victory was at hand, they afforded battlefield commanders more flexibility, which increased the tempo of operations and allowed them to swiftly employ intense pressure against key strategic targets. These successes were also made possible by better weapons, tactical coordination, modern communications, and increased transport and logistical capability. As a result, PAVN commanders attained the goal of all leaders, the rapid application of overwhelming force leading to the utter defeat of the enemy at little cost to their own forces. Throughout the final weeks of the war, the communists suffered relatively few casualties, except at Xuan Loc. General Dung later declared, "The numbers killed and wounded was very small in proportion to the victories won, and the expenditure in terms of weapons and ammunition was negligible."[129]

One last point must be made. While the PAVN outperformed the ARVN in many ways, the South's Achilles heel was the resupply of military aid. This lay at the core of the fall of Saigon. In one memorandum report drawn up by the CIA and Defense Intelligence Agency in late 1974, the authors stated: "Communist aid to North Vietnam from 1970 to 1974 is estimated at $5.6 billion. Total communist military and economic aid was higher in 1974 than in any previous year." The high point came in 1972, with other communist states, primarily the Soviet Union, sending $1.2 billion in military and economic aid to replace the losses experienced during the failed PAVN Spring Offensive. In late 1973, as the United States withdrew, so did communist aid, slipping to $935 million. Once the PAVN reinitiated their major military actions in 1974, aid increased again to more than $1.5 billion. All totaled, this was significantly more than what the South Vietnamese were getting from the Americans at this time. Over a three-year period, this discrepancy built up to make a critical difference.[130]

The North seldom had to worry about having more and better weapons. Not only were they being resupplied with a seemingly endless torrent of military and economic supplies from the Soviet Union and China, but they were also clever enough to employ captured US materiel as they marched south. On the other hand, the reduction in aid from the United States to the South Vietnamese proved significant in terms of both morale and combat capability.

While it was as much a Northern victory as a Southern defeat, the concluding battle for Vietnam mirrored a failure in leadership and policy in both the United States and South Vietnam that had been planted at the very beginning of the 1960s. It was at Xuan Loc where the heroism of the ARVN was best demonstrated, but the heroic defense had come far too late.

Conclusion

Some Personal and Factual Observations

Like so many people my age, the war in Southeast Asia constituted a core aspect of our youth and a formative event in our lives. When I first heard about the war, it was 1962, and I was listening to the *Huntley-Brinkley Report* on NBC. We were visiting my parents' families in the small south Alabama college town of Troy. It was a family routine we performed with great joy every year I can remember, since my sister and I grew up in Miami, Florida. We would pile in the old 1952 Plymouth—later a 1963 Plymouth—and spend the better part of two days, later just one day, traversing Florida on our way to LA—Lower Alabama. My parents made it great fun. We played games, sang songs, and generally imitated *Father Knows Best* about as well as any 1950s and 1960s nuclear American family ever did.

That year 1962 was not a Vietnam year—yet! That summer the news was filled with President Kennedy's efforts to avoid war and a communist take-over in Laos as well as integration and civil rights. In October we experienced the chilling possibility of a nuclear war over missiles in Cuba, only ninety miles from where we lived. Eventually, these concerns were replaced by the assassination of our handsome, young, and beloved president on 22 November 1963 and the subsequent landslide election of Lyndon Baines Johnson the following year. Being labor Democrats, my parents, while born in the Deep South, believed in things like human rights and income equality. Besides, Florida's Dade County and Miami were not really Southern. North Florida was conservative, while the southeastern part was progressive. So, we mostly voted Democrat.

In August 1964 I heard about the Gulf of Tonkin. Congressional debates received a lot of attention on television, and it seemed to me we were going to go to war against some "very bad people" who had attacked our ships. Until I graduated from Coral Gables High School in June 1967, that was what I believed. I figured our side was right and would, ultimately, win since those in the "right" always won! The politics and complexities of the war in Vietnam became clearer once I made it to college, first at Miami-Dade Junior College, near home, then Florida State University. It was at the latter where the war on the other side of the world became more complex and my questions about "our leaders" and "our side" began to multiply. When Bobby Kennedy ran for the Democratic presidential nomination in 1968, I gradually became convinced he was right. Friends of mine had gone to war, and some had not come back; it began to seem like a waste. But Bobby was murdered, and Richard Nixon became president.

When Nixon changed the recruitment process and each of us had our birth dates numbered to see who would be drafted first, it became extremely personal. My number was 176. I remember dozens of us gathered around a radio in our dorm, holding our breath. A couple of guys got low numbers and decided to enlist rather than wait to be drafted, hoping to get a stateside job in the army or air force. One person I knew fled to Canada; I never heard from him again.

I stayed and gambled that I would not have to go. Just before I graduated in June 1971, I went to a concert at Doak Campbell football stadium on campus. One of the acts was Country Joe and the Fish. For those who remember them, their most famous song was "The 'Fish' Cheer" or "I-Feel-Like-I'm-Fixin'-to-Die Rag." They had made it famous at Woodstock 1969. They began by supposedly spelling out "F-I-S-H." Instead, the crowd cried out "F-U-C-K." The words to the antiwar song were:

> And it's one, two, three, four what the hell are we fighting for?
> Don't ask me I don't give a damn,
> Next stop is Vietnam.
> And it's five, six, seven, eight open up the pearly gates,

Well there ain't no time to wonder why,
Whoopie! We're all gonna die!

All of us laughed like crazy. Later I realized it was black humor, and they were singing about a very serious matter that was costing so many people their lives.

While I was in graduate school at the University of Miami, America's role in the war ended. I had made it through without going to Southeast Asia. On the one hand, I was relieved. I would get to live out my dreams of an education, a good job, and a great family. On the other hand, I felt guilty since so many other Americans would not. For that matter, millions of Vietnamese, Laotians, Cambodians, and others would not either. Their families were torn apart, their lives ruined. In many ways those who survived suffered worst of all. One person I knew spent two years in and out of hospitals and clinics, trying to overcome what today we call posttraumatic stress disorder (PTSD). Another was sprayed with Agent Orange. He had served his country and won several of his nation's highest decorations. His reward was to die before he was fifty.

When I first became a professional historian, I studied modern US diplomacy in Asia. I often encountered books or articles about Vietnam. I read many of them, but it was not my field of study, so that was where it ended. When I went to work for the USAF as an historian, my attention turned to airpower and air-force history. I found dozens of original sources, such as Corona Harvest and CHECO publications, all of which examined America's involvement in Vietnam. The more I studied and published, the more I wanted to write a book focused specifically on the bitter struggle that came to an end nearly fifty years ago. Finally, with this book, I have done what I set out to do. I have shed naïve, vague notions about the war in Vietnam. I have dug deeply into archives, books, and articles to grasp a complete and thorough understanding of what composed America's Vietnam War.

Again, Why These Battles?

This work has focused on ground and air combat, mostly from an American viewpoint, but its purpose is to be factual and analytical, encompassing the views of all involved. Each event had a major influence on the course and outcome of the conflict. In addition, each battle became a part of my own personal history. I remember the banana-shaped helicopters from Ap Bac. I remember Mike Wallace's documentary on Ia Drang and the myriad of reporters broadcasting from Khe Sanh and various parts of Vietnam during Tet. I remember the news clips of the aerial bombing and the counting of the dead during the Battle of Hamburger Hill and the Easter Offensive. I also recall that the Paris Peace Accords seemed to be a victory, one we could point to with pride. And just two years later, I was shocked by the images of PAVN tanks rolling onto the grounds of the Independence Palace in Saigon. All I could think was, "How had this happened?"

Looking back, Ap Bac, which took place on 2 January 1963 before US troops had been sent in large numbers, was supposed to be a demonstration of the superiority of the ARVN and their ability to defeat the VC, thus securing their nation without outside intervention. Instead, a smaller, less-well-armed group of antigovernment guerrilla fighters bloodied the ARVN to such an extent it convinced US advisers, such as John Paul Vann, that the Southern leaders then in place could not defeat their communist enemies. This conviction filtered through the Kennedy administration and caused the president's foreign-policy team to reconsider their attitudes toward President Diem and the Republic of Vietnam.

Reforms or possibilities of repairing the ARVN and the Southern government soon evaporated, first with the deaths of both presidents in 1963, and later with the minor attack by Northern gunboats on US naval assets in the Gulf of Tonkin in 1964. Late that summer, on 7 August, the Gulf of Tonkin Resolution passed management of the US role in the Southeast Asian conflict to the administration of the new president, Lyndon Johnson. On 1 November, two days before the US presidential election, VC units shelled Bien Hoa Air Base, near Saigon, with mortar rounds, killing four and wounding seventy-six Americans. They also destroyed five B-57 bombers and damaged fifteen more. It was the first of many hit-and-run attacks to come. This would lead Johnson to take steps to force the DRV—to him the "real" source of the conflagration in Vietnam—to negotiate a peace settlement.

Concerned he might antagonize the Soviet Union and China into a wider war, the president initially rejected the advice of his military leaders to take an aggressive posture toward the North Vietnamese. On 2 March 1965 he launched Operation Rolling Thunder, a haphazard bombing campaign against the major cities and infrastructure of the DRV. Implemented in fits and spurts to slowly raise the quotient of pain on Hanoi, it was supposed to cause enemy leaders to fear what might be coming next. Instead, it was an air campaign limited to such an absurd degree that it was not effective in causing fear among Northern leaders nor in discouraging them from taking bold moves to overrun South Vietnam. At first, targets were limited to insignificant ones in the southern part of the DRV. Only later did American aircraft go farther north. Those targets selected had to go through an arduous process that concluded only when President Johnson approved them. Rolling Thunder lasted until 1 November 1968. While the bombing wrought considerable damage on the DRV's industry, infrastructure, and economy, this simply did not matter. Their infrastructure and industry was limited, in the first place, and the vast majority of their military supplies and equipment was coming in from the Soviet Union and China, much of it through the extensive POL pipelines that stretched from China—eventually even into South Vietnam. These pipelines were off limits to American fighter-bombers for fear of killing Soviet or Chinese personnel. The North also employed a vast infiltration route into South Vietnam known as the Ho Chi Minh Trail, which was only targeted as Rolling Thunder slowed to a halt.

Dr. Earl H. Tilford Jr., in his thought-provoking book *Setup: What the Air Force Did in Vietnam and Why*, asks, "How could one of the longest bombing campaigns in the history of aerial warfare, during which a million sorties were flown and around three quarters of a million tons of bombs dropped, fail so totally?" He provides two major reasons. "First, in their pride, American civilian and military planners did not, probably could not imagine that North Vietnam would endure American aerial attacks." Second, he notes, military leaders were married to the efficacy of the superiority of firepower and the application of military power. Civilian policymakers failed to grasp airpower well enough to employ it properly. Tilford argues that "military leaders failed to develop and purpose a strategy appropriate to the war at hand." Then he makes this final observation: "Bombing strategic targets in the North and the unconventional war going on in the South had little direct interconnection. Furthermore, even when they realized that the constraints imposed by civilian policymakers would not be totally removed, the generals and admirals never devised a strategy applicable to the war as it was defined for them."[1]

When Rolling Thunder ended, it had not stopped the expansion of the war in the South nor had it initiated peace talks; in fact, it led to Johnson's decision not to run for reelection. Meantime, in November 1965, with US troop numbers increasing, the US Army and PAVN regulars met in combat for the first time at the Battle of Ia Drang Valley. This engagements demonstrated the skills of both sides, including the excellence of American battlefield commanders, such as Lt. Col. Hal Moore, and the power of tactics and firepower when properly applied. Enemy leadership was also good, and the dedication of communist troops was impressive. In the end Gen. William Westmoreland believed Ia Drang Valley had validated his belief that search-and-destroy tactics were working and should be expanded. It was the wrong lesson to learn, one that would turn the guerrilla struggle between Southern factions into a full-blown war between the US military and the PAVN, costing tens of thousands of lives and lasting another ten years.

In early 1968, the same year Rolling Thunder ended, search-and-destroy tactics as well as Washington's public-relations campaign to convince the American people victory was at hand exploded with two iconic battles that ultimately helped bring down Johnson and led American civilians and political leaders to rethink their support for the war. The PAVN siege of Khe Sanh, the USMC outpost on the Laotian border, and, concurrently, the massive communist Tet Offensive of 1968 were arguably the turning point of America's role in the war. While enemy forces suffered terrible battlefield casualties, and, tactically, the US and ARVN forces subdued the communists and won major victories, the political outcome proved disastrous. South Vietnamese ambassador to the United States Bui Diem understood this, recalling: "Even though [President Johnson] assured me that he would do his best to resupply needed weapons and promised continued support, his gray and melancholy appearance made it clear to me that Tet had meant the beginning of the end of American commitment to South Vietnam."[2]

Along with the land battles, several air campaigns took place in the skies over Vietnam, Laos, and Cambodia following Rolling Thunder. The first and most persistent were the Arc Light raids, from 18 June 1965 until 17 August 1973. These B-52 missions began as CAS sorties and mostly concluded with the Christmas Bombings of 1972, the largest strategic air operations carried out by these strategic air weapons. Beginning in 1968 after Johnson announced he would not run for office, the seven Commando Hunt campaigns aimed at stemming the tide of men and materiel pouring into South

Vietnam from the North to support communist military operations there. While these day and night raids employed everything from jets and bombers to fixed-wing gunships and did a lot of damage, they could not stop the enemy buildup in the South. The last of the Commando Hunt operations ended just before the Nguyen Hue (Easter) Offensive began on 30 March 1972, the very type of communist campaign they were designed to prevent.

Apart from Arc Light operations, B-52s flew bombing raids on enemy sanctuaries in Cambodia under the codename Menu. These missions against infiltration routes and staging areas in the supposedly neutral country were approved by Nixon and flown anonymously by pilots sworn to secrecy. Menu was only a partial success and ultimately failed to stop NVA resupply efforts.

The final major air campaigns were the two Linebacker operations. Linebacker I sent aircraft north again as Rolling Thunder had. Lifting many of the earlier restrictions present in the earlier operation, though, Linebacker I enjoyed greater effectiveness and helped halt the Easter Offensive and temporarily reduce the enemy's logistics flow. Linebacker II, lasting ten days from 18 to 29 December 1972, was designed to be an offensive flown mostly by B-52s that inflicted such shock, fear, and destruction on the North that leaders in Hanoi returned to the Paris peace talks without conditions. Despite sizable early losses, the B-52s eventually reduced Hanoi and Haiphong to rubble. To avoid further destruction, Northern negotiators did return to the talks, signing the Paris Peace Accords on 27 January 1973.

The great controversy over the use of US airpower arose after Linebacker II, when some retired military and then-serving political leaders argued that, had the civilian leadership in the mid-1960s had the moral courage to employ B-52s against North Vietnam, the United States could have won the war then. Of course, the circumstances in 1965 were very different from those in 1972. In 1965, at a time when the Soviet Union and China were not very friendly toward the United States, President Johnson was deeply concerned about keeping a lid on the US commitment in Southeast Asia and avoiding the expansion of the war at all costs. By 1972, America was withdrawing from the war, and all its leaders really wanted was to get the communists back to negotiations so the two sides could produce an official document allowing the United States to leave and save face at the same time. This was possible due to President Nixon and Dr. Kissinger's peace overtures toward both the Soviet Union and China. With DRV leaders fearful they might lose Sino-Soviet support, they finally acted to end the war. This way they could bide their time and wait for the Americans to leave, then concentrate on rebuilding their own forces, much of which was already in South Vietnam. By 1974–75, with circumstances completely different, the communists could, and would, launch their last offensive and finally win the war.

While the air campaigns continued, the fighting never stopped on the ground—and seemed to be getting worse. The Battle of "Hamburger Hill" in many ways was one of the most heroic conventional ground campaigns carried out by the US Army. To quote from chapter 7: "As one military study has said: 'The Vietnam conflict wore many faces. It was at once an insurrection by indigenous guerrilla forces and an invasion by the regular army of a neighboring regime.' So it was, but for the most part (until the Spring Offensive of 1972), it was not a conventional war with set-piece battles like those in the World Wars and Korea. There were some exceptions, however, the Battle of Hamburger Hill being one of those 'big battles' for which the post–World War II US Army had trained and expected to fight on the open plains of Europe."[3]

As a result, the casualties were significant. When this became public, there arose an outcry criticizing the Nixon administration for sacrificing so many American lives for what seemed to be an obscure pile of rocks in the middle of nowhere (and abandoned shortly after the fighting there ceased). This bloodbath had happened even though the president had come to power promising to transfer combat operations to the ARVN and withdraw US forces as soon as possible. While the peace movement in the United States was already deeply entrenched, this battle outraged many middle-class Americans and politicians, including powerful members of Congress like Sen. Edward Kennedy. It was Hamburger Hill that convinced Nixon the time had come to begin to implement his Vietnamization policy in earnest and to set dates and numbers for the withdrawal of US troops, especially before the midterm elections. In short, Hamburger Hill, while a classic conventional ground operation, wound up being the beginning of the end of America's presence in Vietnam.

The Nguyen Hue (Easter) Offensive began as a great success for the NVA as they caught the ARVN off guard. But the campaign soon bogged down, and by early summer, it was stalemated. In due course the combination of American airpower and the ARVN's tenacity rolled back the communists. One great irony was the role US advisers played in the battles. As if to give symmetry to America's role in the war, John Paul Vann played a key role in winning this victory. This time, however, he was a civilian and he would die just after the combat began to subside. In short, he came on stage at Ap Bac and left during the Easter Offensive, much as the United States had as a whole.

Both sides were beaten and bloodied, but the communists had achieved a few of their goals, despite having paid a heavy price in lives and materiel losses. For the time being, it appeared South Vietnam had been saved and could now rebuild for the long term. Yet this was not the case. Thousands of PAVN soldiers were still in the South, and during the lull in fighting following Nguyen Hue, Linebacker II, and the Paris Peace Accords, they took the opportunity to expand their infiltration roads and pipelines in preparation for a day when the Americans would be gone (and not wish to return) and circumstances would favor them.

The final phase of the war was a two-year campaign that ended in the communists' defeating a badly led ARVN force that fought bravely and patriotically to the bitter end. The last great fight was the defense of Xuan Loc, which blocked the PAVN from a direct assault on Saigon. Facing the communists were many of the best and most dedicated ARVN troops available, men many Americans earlier in the war had described as having an undisciplined "cowboy" attitude. But during these last months of fighting, the soldiers of the 18th Infantry Division demonstrated incredible bravery and dogged determination under the leadership of their commander, Brig. Gen. Le Minh Dao. During the last stand at Xuan Loc, they lived up to not only their unit motto, "God Arrow—Defending the Fatherland," but also their sobriquet, "The Super Men."[4]

The 18th Division's tenacious defense was so effective some in America and Saigon believed there might still be hope of saving the Republic of Vietnam. But saving a country was too much for one division, even the best. On 30 April 1975 Saigon fell to PAVN units, and the war was over. What most of my generation remembers are the helicopters on top of the US embassy evacuating the desperate South Vietnamese trying to escape the communist takeover and possibly death. But on the grounds of the

Presidential Palace in another part of the defeated nation's capital, a PAVN soldier ran up the steps of the building with the Provisional Revolutionary Government's flag in his hands. When a Western reporter asked for his name, this man who had helped bring the Saigon regime to defeat replied "Nguyen Van Thieu."[5] His ironic response inadvertently spoke to a fundamental truth about the war: From the Battle of An Bac to the Battle of Xuan Loc, it was the Vietnamese themselves who ultimately determined the fate of South Vietnam.

Some Final Thoughts

Many of these images are seared into my brain, and when the war ended, I was able to go on with my life. But a great number of my friends who were veterans could not. These men and women remain haunted by their experiences and still wonder why they were sent to a far-off land to fight and die. Perhaps some readers will remember the epic movie *The Sand Pebbles*. At the very end Steve McQueen's character, Machinist's Mate 1st Class Jake Holman, is part of a small rescue party sent to save the local missionary and his beautiful daughter, Shirley Eckert, played by Candice Bergen. They are attacked by nationalist Chinese trying to force the Westerners to leave their country. In the firefight at the end, Eckert resists returning to the American ship without Holman. She only leaves with two sailors after Holman assures her he will be along shortly, leaving him alone in the dark mission school. In the ensuing shootout, Holman kills several soldiers before he is fatally wounded just as he is about to escape and join the others. As he lies dying, he thinks to himself, "I was home . . . what happened . . . what the hell happened?" In this last moment he sums up the futility of the mission of the *San Pablo* (his vessel) and his own life. Eckert and the two remaining sailors reach the ship, which then steams away, leaving a shipmate, having made the ultimate sacrifice, in a faraway land—and for exactly what?

This thinly veiled antiwar movie from 1966 used a story by Richard McKenna in his 1962 novel of the same name, about an American gunboat on the Yangtze River in 1926 and its futile mission. The theme resonated throughout movie theaters in America and still does today. The one thing many Vietnam-era veterans and nonveterans took from this film was the same thing they took from their experiences in Southeast Asia: "What the hell happened?" And yet, as the years passed and we learned more about the realities of Vietnam, the one comforting thought many of us retained was: at least we will never make those mistakes again. We were certain—despite the uncertainties of, the reasons for, and the good or bad of the Vietnam War—it was so full of complexities, both in terms of the combat and the political realities, that it obviously would necessitate intellectual dexterity in the future from military and civilian leaders.

Given the protracted nature of the US commitment to Iraq and Afghanistan and its apparent failures, Americans did not learn the lessons of Vietnam, nor did we make sure to live up to our promises to our veterans or soldiers, sailors, marines, and airmen. So, perhaps the only way to make sure we have some kind of a blueprint that draws us a picture of what the hell happened in Vietnam is to avoid wasting our best and brightest—our most precious resources—when forced to resort to war. It would, at least, be an attempt to pass this gift on from my generation to our children's and grandchildren's generations.

Notes

Abbreviations Used in Notes

7AF	Seventh Air Force
AFB	Air Force Base
AFHRA	Air Force Historical Research Agency, Maxwell AFB, AL
CH	Corona Harvest
CINCPAC	Commander in chief, Pacific
COMUSMACV	Commander, US Military Assistance Command, Vietnam
CSAF	Chief of staff, USAF
EOTA	End-of-Tour-Report
FRUS	US Department of State, Office of the Historian, *Foreign Relations of the United States*
HQ	Headquarters
JCS	Joint Chiefs of Staff, USAF
PACAF	Pacific Air Forces
VCA	The Vietnam Center and Archive, Texas Tech University, Lubbock

Introduction

1. Email to William Head, "Statistical Survey by the Vietnam Veterans Memorial Fund, Washington, DC," n.d.

2. Email to Head, "Statistical Survey by the Vietnam Veterans Memorial Fund."

3. Hirschman et al., "Vietnam Casualties during the American War,," 783–812; Lewy, *America in Vietnam*, 450–53; Wiesner, *Victims and Survivors*, 310.

Chapter 1

1. *FRUS, 1961–1963*, vol. 3, *Vietnam: January–August 1963*, doc. 1, "Editorial Note," Historical Documents, Office of the Historian, Dept. of State, https://history.state.gov/historicaldocuments/frus1961–63v03/d1 [hereafter *FRUS, 1961–1963*, vol. 3, doc. 1].

2. Moyar, *Triumph Forsaken*, 164.

3. For more on the early history of the Vietnam War, see Fitzgerald, *Fire in the Lake*, 99–137, 237–74; Karnow, *Vietnam*, 101–38, 222–57; and Herring, *America's Longest War*, 4th ed., 46–79.

4. Moyar, *Triumph Forsaken*, 164.

5. Moyar, *Triumph Forsaken*, 166, 169; Toczek, *Battle of Ap Bac*, 46. Not all "advisers" were from Special Forces units.

6. Moyar, *Triumph Forsaken*, 170. For more on Lieutenant Colonel Vann, see the bestselling and controversial Sheehan, *Bright Shining Lie*, 35–126. Vann's overt attitude, caustic wit, and clever sarcasm kept his career on the slow track. But despite his unmilitary characteristics, he was much admired by many in the US hierarchy. The forty-seven-year-old Vann was killed in early June 1972, soon after the Battle of Kontum ended, when his helicopter crashed.

7. Moyar, *Triumph Forsaken*, 174–75.

8. Moyar, *Triumph Forsaken*, 174–76; Toczek, *Battle of Ap Bac*, 44–48; Sheehan, *Bright Shining Lie*, 127–200; Halberstam, *Making of a Quagmire*, 80–81.

9. Halberstam, *Making of a Quagmire*, 80–81; Sheehan, *Bright Shining Lie*, 138–99; "Memorandum for the Record by the Director of the Bureau of Intelligence and Research (Hilsman)," 2 Jan. 1963, *FRUS, 1961–1963*, vol. 3, *Vietnam, January–August 1963*, doc. 5, https://history.state.gov/historicaldocuments/frus1961–63v03/d5 [hereafter *FRUS, 1961–1963*, vol. 3, doc. 5].

10. *FRUS, 1961–1963*, vol. 3, doc. 5. The Military Assistance and Advisory Group became MACV on 15 May 1964.

11. *FRUS, 1961–1963*, vol. 3, doc. 5.

12. Elliott, *Vietnamese War*, 180; Toczek, *Battle of Ap Bac*, 71; Truong, *Vietnam War*, 350.

13. *FRUS, 1961–1963*, vol. 3, doc. 5; Toczek, *Battle of Ap Bac*, 72; Moyar, *Triumph Forsaken*, 187; Truong, *Vietnam War*, 351. For more on the UH-1, see Guilmartin and O'Leary, *Helicopters*; McGowan, *Helicopters*; and Mesko, *Airmobile*.

14. Toczek, *Battle of Ap Bac*, 72.

15. MACV, *Ap Bac Battle, 2 January 1963: Translation of VC Document*, 20 Apr. 1963, C0043021, 7 [hereafter *VC Document*].

16. US MACV, *VC Document*, 8; *FRUS, 1961–1963*, vol. 3, doc. 5; Elliott, *Vietnamese War*, 182–83; Truong, *Vietnam War*, 350–52.

17. *FRUS, 1961–1963*, vol. 3, doc. 5; Truong, *Vietnam War*, 355–56; Berman, *Perfect Spy*, 134–43. For more on An, see Bass, *Spy Who Loved Us*.

18. Truong, *Vietnam War*, 356; Elliott, *Vietnamese War*, 182–83; US MACV, *VC Document*, 7–11. For more on the diplomatic and political aspects of the Vietnam War between 1961 and 1963, see Herring, *America's Longest War*, 4th ed., 80–119.

19. *FRUS, 1961–1963*, vol. 3, doc. 5; Truong, *Vietnam War*, 355–57; Duiker, *Sacred War*, 156–58; Sheehan, *Bright Shining Lie*, 212–15. For more on the Battle of Ap Bac, see Karnow, *Vietnam*, 260–63; Halberstam, *Making of a Quagmire*, 77–92; and Berman, *Perfect Spy*, 135–54.

20. Moyar, *Triumph Forsaken*, 187; Kirkpatrick, "Battle at Ap Bac."

21. Truong, *Vietnam War*, 358–59; Kirkpatrick, "Battle at Ap Bac."

22. Truong, *Vietnam War*, 359–61; Kirkpatrick, "Battle at Ap Bac"; Moyar, *Triumph Forsaken*, 187–88; Sheehan, *Bright Shining Lie*, 226–42.

23. Truong, *Vietnam War*, 361; Sheehan, *Bright Shining Lie*, 214–28. Sheehan's book, based on Vann's own memories, gives a detailed but pro-Vann account of the entire battle.

24. Sheehan, *Bright Shining Lie*, 220–44; Kirkpatrick, "Battle at Ap Bac."

25. Kirkpatrick, "Battle at Ap Bac"; Truong, *Vietnam War*, 360–61, 368, 370–72; Moyar, *Triumph Forsaken*, 188–89; Sheehan, *Bright Shining Lie*, 226–59.

26. *FRUS, 1961–1963*, vol. 3, doc. 5; Truong, *Vietnam War*, 374; Starry, *Armored Combat in Vietnam*, 27; Sheehan, *Bright Shining Lie*, 224–46.

27. *FRUS, 1961–1963*, vol. 3, doc. 5; Truong, *Vietnam War*, 377; Moyar, *Triumph Forsaken*, 190–91; Sheehan, *Bright Shining Lie*, 227–36; Elliott, *Vietnamese War*, 182–83.

28. *FRUS, 1961–1963*, vol. 3, doc. 5; Truong, *Vietnam War*, 377–78; Moyar, *Triumph Forsaken*, 190–91; Sheehan, *Bright Shining Lie*, 238–57; Jacobs, *Cold War Mandarin*, 141.

29. *FRUS, 1961–1963*, vol. 3, doc. 5; Elliott, *Vietnamese War*, 182–83; Sheehan, *Bright Shining Lie*, 238–67.

30. *FRUS, 1961–1963*, vol. 3, doc. 5; Jacobs, *Cold War Mandarin*, 141–42; Truong, *Vietnam War*, 404–5; Starry, *Armored Combat in Vietnam*, 27–29.

31. *FRUS, 1961–1963*, vol. 3, doc. 5; Jacobs, *Cold War Mandarin*, 141–42; Truong, *Vietnam War*, 407; Sheehan, *Bright Shining Lie*, 243–67.

32. *FRUS, 1961–1963*, vol. 3, doc. 5; Kirkpatrick, "Battle at Ap Bac"; Truong, *Vietnam War*, 407; Sheehan, *Bright Shining Lie*, 254–55.

33. Truong, *Vietnam War*, 396; Sheehan, *Bright Shining Lie*, 227–37.

34. Truong, *Vietnam War*, 412–13; Moyar, *Triumph Forsaken*, 192–93.

35. Truong, *Vietnam War*, 413; Moyar, *Triumph Forsaken*, 193; Sheehan, *Bright Shining Lie*, 254–69.

36. Truong, *Vietnam War*, 416–17; Moyar, *Triumph Forsaken*, 194; Sheehan, *Bright Shining Lie*, 258–64; US MACV, *VC Document*, 16–27.

37. Truong, *Vietnam War*, 416–19; Moyar, *Triumph Forsaken*, 194; Sheehan, *Bright Shining Lie*, 258–64; US MACV, *VC Document*, 21–27.

38. Truong, *Vietnam War*, 417–21; Sheehan, *Bright Shining Lie*, 241–64.

39. The *FRUS, 1961–1963*, vol. 2, *Vietnam, 1962*, 1–2; Duiker, *Sacred War*, 157.

40. Duiker, *Sacred War*, 158; *FRUS, 1961–1963*, vol. 3, doc. 1; Gen. Paul D. Harkins, oral history interview, 10 Nov. 1981, Gen. Paul D. Harkins Papers, Lyndon Baines Johnson Presidential Library, Austin, TX.

41. Sheehan, *Bright Shining Lie*, 260–61, 311. Sheehan goes so far as to claim that, due to the VC success at Ap Bac, the communists easily recruited new soldiers over the next several months.

42. Karnow, *Vietnam*, 262; Sheehan, *Bright Shining Lie*, 259–67.

43. *Washington Post*, 7 Jan. 1963; *FRUS, 1961–1963*, vol. 3, doc. 1.

44. Duiker, *Sacred War*, 157–58.

45. Nagle, *Counterinsurgency Lessons*, 133–34.

46. Karnow, *Vietnam*, 262; Sheehan, *Bright Shining Lie*, 259–67.

47. Moyar, *Triumph Forsaken*, 194–95.

48. *FRUS, 1961–1963*, vol. 3, doc. 5; Nagle, *Counterinsurgency Lessons*, 134–36; Moyar, *Triumph Forsaken*, 194–95.

49. Wyatt, *Paper Soldiers*, 100–110.

50. Karnow, *Vietnam*, 262.

51. Truong, *Vietnam War*, 419; *FRUS, 1961–1963*, vol. 3, doc. 5.

52. Truong, *Vietnam War*, 419.

53. Fitzgerald, *Fire in the Lake*, 200.

54. Truong, *Vietnam War*, 419.

55. Elliott, *Vietnamese War*, 183–84.

56. Diem, *In the Jaws of History*, 142. See also Diem, "Reflections on the Vietnam War," 241–48.

Chapter 2

1. Nalty, *"Operation Rolling Thunder."*

2. Karnow, *Vietnam*, 237–39; Tilford, *Setup*, 1–88; Spector, *Advice and Support*, 275–373; US State Department, *Aggression from the North*, 60–62.

3. Gillespie, "Joint Chiefs of Staff and the Escalation of the Vietnam Conflict," 63; *Pentagon Papers*, Senator Gravel edition, 3:17–20.

4. Drew, *Rolling Thunder*.

5. Drew, *Rolling Thunder*. Drew's main sources come from *United States–Vietnam Relations, 1945–1967* (Washington, DC: Government Printing Office, 1971), the Defense Department–assembled documents better known as the Pentagon Papers. He also used the documents and reporting that appeared in the *New York Times*. See Sheehan et al., *Pentagon Papers as Published by the New York Times*.

6. Drew, *Rolling Thunder*.

7. Drew, *Rolling Thunder*.

8. Drew, *Rolling Thunder*.

9. Drew, *Rolling Thunder*.

10. Drew, *Rolling Thunder*. See also McGeorge Bundy, "A Policy of Sustained Reprisal," Annex A (7 Feb. 1965), in *United States–Vietnam Relations*, pt. 4, C.3:35. For more on the campaign's design, see Clodfelter, *Limits of Air Power*, 76–84.

11. Drew, *Rolling Thunder*.

12. Drew, *Rolling Thunder*.

13. Drew, *Rolling Thunder*.

14. Drew, *Rolling Thunder*; [Goodwin], *Lyndon Johnson and the American Dream*, 264–65.

15. Drew, *Rolling Thunder*.

16. Drew, *Rolling Thunder*; Tilford, *Crosswinds*, 68.

17. Drew, *Rolling Thunder*.

18. Drew, *Rolling Thunder*.

19. Drew, *Rolling Thunder*.

20. Drew, *Rolling Thunder*.

21. Drew, *Rolling Thunder*.

22. Drew, *Rolling Thunder*.

23. Speech, Pres. Lyndon B. Johnson, "The Bombing of North Vietnam," 28 July 1965, Lyndon Baines Johnson Presidential Library, Austin, TX; "Lyndon Johnson Approves Operation Rolling Thunder," 16 Nov. 2009, History.com, http://www.history.com/this-day-in-history/johnson-approves-operation-rolling-thunder; Tilford, *Crosswinds*, 62.

24. "Johnson Approves Operation Rolling Thunder"; Karnow, *Vietnam*, 415, 454, 682; Correll, "Rolling Thunder," 1.

25. Correll, "Rolling Thunder."

26. Gillespie, "Joint Chiefs of Staff and the Escalation of the Vietnam Conflict," 63; *Pentagon Papers*, Senator Gravel edition, 3:17–20.

27. Tilford, *Crosswinds*, 62–64; [Goodwin], *Lyndon Johnson and the American Dream*, 264–65.

28. Tilford, *Crosswinds*, 59–68; Tilford, *Setup*, 89–102; Schlight, *War in South Vietnam*, 30–33.

29. Simkin, "Operation Rolling Thunder."

30. Simkin, "Operation Rolling Thunder."

31. Tilford, *Setup*, 92; Gillespie, "Joint Chiefs of Staff and the Escalation of the Vietnam Conflict," 60–70; Kahin, *Intervention*, 272.

32. Gillespie, "Joint Chiefs of Staff and the Escalation of the Vietnam Conflict," 70; Johnson, *Vantage Point*, 66–67; Clodfelter, *Limits of Airpower*, 47. For details on the Gulf of Tonkin incident, see Moise, *Tonkin Gulf and the Escalation of the Vietnam War*.

33. Tilford, *Setup*, 93; Gillespie, "Joint Chiefs of Staff and the Escalation of the Vietnam Conflict," 71; Van Staaveren, *Gradual Failure*, 46; McMaster, *Dereliction of Duty*, 218–22.

34. McMaster, *Dereliction of Duty*, 226.

35. Van Staaveren, *Gradual Failure*, 86; Schlight, *A War too Long*, 46; Morocco, *Thunder from Above*, 40–41. See also McNamara, *In Retrospect*, 171–77.

36. Morocco, *Thunder from Above*, 40.

37. Morocco, *Thunder from Above*, 54–55; Van Staaveren, *Gradual Failure*, 86–87; Tilford, *Crosswinds*, 69.

38. [Goodwin], *Lyndon Johnson and the American Dream*, 252.

39. [Goodwin], *Lyndon Johnson and the American Dream*, 263; Tilford, *Crosswinds*, 69.

40. Drew, *Rolling Thunder*. For more on Admiral Sharp's divergent views, see Sharp, *Strategy for Defeat*.

41. Drew, *Rolling Thunder*; Tilford, *Crosswinds*, 70.

42. Drew, *Rolling Thunder*; Tilford, *Crosswinds*, 73.

43. Drew, *Rolling Thunder*.

44. Drew, *Rolling Thunder*.

45. See Tilford, *Crosswinds*; and Drew, *Rolling Thunder*.

46. Fuller, Smith, and Atkins, "'Rolling Thunder' and Bomb Damage to Bridges."

47. Fuller, Smith, and Atkins, "'Rolling Thunder' and Bomb Damage to Bridges."

48. Fuller, Smith, and Atkins, "'Rolling Thunder' and Bomb Damage to Bridges."

49. Fuller, Smith, and Atkins, "'Rolling Thunder' and Bomb Damage to Bridges."

50. Fuller, Smith, and Atkins, "'Rolling Thunder' and Bomb Damage to Bridges."

51. Fuller, Smith, and Atkins, "'Rolling Thunder' and Bomb Damage to Bridges."

52. Fuller, Smith, and Atkins, "'Rolling Thunder' and Bomb Damage to Bridges."

53. Fuller, Smith, and Atkins, "'Rolling Thunder' and Bomb Damage to Bridges"; History (S), by 388th TFW (since declassified), "*Rolling Thunder* Digest (CINCPAC) Edition Five," July–Sept. 1967; CIA intelligence cable, "Bombing of the Cau Long Bien Bridge in Hanoi on 11 August and the Effect of the Closing of the Bridge on Transportation in Hanoi," 1 Sept. 1967, Document ESDN: 0000505896, .

54. Morocco, *Thunder from Above*, 55.

55. Tilford, *Setup*, 109.

56. Morocco, *Thunder from Above*, 57.

57. Thompson, *Hanoi and Back*, 80.

58. Thompson, *Hanoi and Back*, 26–30; Morocco, *Thunder from Above*, 57–60.

59. Thompson, *Hanoi and Back*, 26; Morocco, *Thunder from Above*, 58–61.

60. Morocco, *Thunder from Above*, 62–63; Tilford, *Setup*, 108; Tilford, *Crosswinds*, 72.

61. Tilford, *Setup*, 115; Sheehan et al., *Pentagon Papers as Published by the New York Times*, 442–43; Karnow, *Vietnam*, 415.

62. Morocco, *Thunder from Above*, 62. For two official accounts of how Rolling Thunder unfolded, see Van Staaveren, "Rolling Thunder," 69–79; and Schlight, *War in South Vietnam*, 18, 22–27, 30–33.

63. Drew, *Rolling Thunder*.

64. Drew, *Rolling Thunder*.

65. Drew, *Rolling Thunder*.

66. Drew, *Rolling Thunder*; Tilford, *Crosswinds*, 77–78; "Appraisal of the Bombing of North Vietnam," 22 Dec. 1965, Document 01398 (declassified 12 Jan. 1996), CIA Documents on the Vietnam War, University of Saskatchewan, Saskatoon.

67. Hobson, *Vietnam Air Losses*, 10–166; Van Staaveren, *Gradual Failure*, 316.

68. Morocco, *Thunder from Above*, 107–9; Tilford, *Crosswinds*, 81–82.

69. Morocco, *Thunder from Above*, 130–31; Tilford, *Crosswinds*, 80–81. For more on the pipelines, see Head, *War from above the Clouds*, 45–46, 60. See also Mark, *Aerial Interdiction*, 389–90.

70. Thompson, *Hanoi and Back*, 14; Schlight, *War in South Vietnam*, 24–25.

71. Thompson, *Hanoi and Back*, 15–18. For a detailed account of command and control in Vietnam, see Momyer, *Air Power in Three Wars*, 65–110.

72. For more on USAF theory and doctrine regarding this issue, see Mellinger, *Ten Propositions Regarding Air Power*, 49–55.

73. Tilford, *Crosswinds*, 72–73; Van Staaveren, *Gradual Failure*, 72–76.

74. Thompson, *Hanoi and Back*, 64, 91; Tilford, *Setup*, 113; Tilford, *Crosswinds*, 84.

75. Morocco, *Thunder from Above*, 84–85; Head, *War from above the Clouds*, 23–24. Among airmen, the last letter in the acronym "BUF" typically stood for another, cruder word beginning with "F."

76. Head, *War from above the Clouds*, 19–21.

77. Michel, *Clashes*, 163–64.

78. Michel, *Clashes*, 163–64.

79. Head, *War from above the Clouds*, 29.

80. Michel, *Clashes*, 168.

81. For an example, see Head, *War from above the Clouds*, 44–45.

82. Tilford, *Crosswinds*, 89.

83. Head, *War from above the Clouds*, 45; Tilford, "Bombing Our Way Back Home," 123–44.

84. Van Staaveren, *Gradual Failure*, 83.

85. Morocco, *Thunder from Above*, 96, 137.

86. Morocco, *Thunder from Above*, 100–102; Thompson, *Hanoi and Back*, 40, 311; Head, *War from above the Clouds*, 44–48. For a detailed examination of the Northern air defenses, see Douglas Pike, "North Vietnamese Air Defenses during the Vietnam War," in Head and Grinter, *Looking Back on the Vietnam War*, 160–72. See also Clodfelter, *Limits of Air Power*, 131–32.

87. Morocco, *Thunder from Above*, 102.

88. Morocco, *Thunder from Above*, 142; Thompson, *Hanoi and Back*, 35. For useful primary sources focused on the second half of 1966, see "Analysis of the Communists' Strengths, Capabilities, and Will to Persist in Their Present Strategy in Vietnam, Summary Discussion," 26 Aug. 1966, Document 01182 (declassified); "Appraisal of the Bombing of North Vietnam (through 12 September 1966)," Sept. 1966, Document 00224 (declassified 13 Apr. 1976); "Appraisal of the Effects of the First Year Bombing in North Vietnam," 1 June 1966, Document 01238 (declassified 15 Oct. 1992); and "Appraisal of the Bombing of North Vietnam (through 14 June)," 20 June 1966, Document 00404 (declassified 25 Nov. 25, 1977), Declassified CIA Documents on the Vietnam War, University of Saskatchewan, Saskatoon.

89. Morocco, *Thunder from Above*, 148.

90. Morocco, *Thunder from Above*, 135–39.

91. Tilford, *Setup*, 112.

92. Morocco, *Thunder from Above*, 98, 100.

93. Thompson, *Hanoi and Back*, 40, 50.

94. Thompson, *Hanoi and Back*, 40–41; Hobson, *Vietnam Air Losses*, 15–166. For an original source, see "Appraisal of the Bombing of North Vietnam (through 31 December 1967)," Document 00796 (declassified Oct. 1987), Declassified CIA Documents on the Vietnam War, University of Saskatchewan, Saskatoon.

95. Tilford, *Crosswinds*, 84–86; Mark, *Aerial Interdiction*, 378–79.

96. Tilford, *Crosswinds*, 86; Enthoven and Smith, *How Much Is Enough?*, 304; Lewy, *American in Vietnam*, 395; Tilford, *United States Air Force Search and Rescue Operations*, 121.

97. Hobson, *Vietnam Air Losses*, 15–166; Van Staaveren, *Gradual Failure*, 147–50, 187.

98. Thompson, *Hanoi and Back*, 17.

99. Momyer, *Air Power in Three Wars*, 145–46; Schlight, *A War too Long*, 51–52.

100. See note 88.

101. Morocco, *Thunder from Above*, 159.

102. Dougan, Weiss, et al., *Nineteen Sixty-Eight*, 66–70.

103. Thompson, *Hanoi and Back*, 124–25. For more about Johnson's decision to end the bombing and not seek reelection, see Jacobsen, "President Johnson and the Decision to Curtail Rolling Thunder," 215–29; and Buzzanco, "Myth of Tet," 231–57.

104. McNamara, *In Retrospect*, 265–77; Morocco, *Thunder from Above*, 153–54.

105. Morocco, *Thunder from Above*, 153; Tilford, *Setup*, 120, 138.

106. McNamara, *In Retrospect*, 284–91; Morocco, *Thunder from Above*, 154–56; Thompson, *Hanoi and Back*, 81–82.

107. Morocco, *Thunder from Above*, 156.

108. Tilford, *Setup*, 149–50; Karnow, *Vietnam*, 454; Thompson, *Hanoi and Back*, 135–36.

109. Thompson, *Hanoi and Back*, 136–39; Morocco, *Thunder from Above*, 183–84. See also Buzzanco, "Myth of Tet," 231–57.

110. Thompson, *Hanoi and Back*, 141–45. See also Jacobsen, "Johnson and the Decision to Curtail Rolling Thunder," 215–29.

111. Thompson, *Hanoi and Back*, 151–52; Tilford, *Crosswinds*, 98–103. For an original source on the end of Rolling Thunder, see Joint CIA/DIA Report, "Appraisal of the Bombing of North Vietnam (1 April–30 June 1968)," 30 June 1968, Document 00798, (declassified 1 Nov. 1987), Declassified CIA Documents on the Vietnam War, University of Saskatchewan, Saskatoon.

112. Drew, *Rolling Thunder; United States–Vietnam Relations*, pt. 4, C.7(a):11–15; Lewy, *America in Vietnam*, 390; Thompson, *Hanoi and Back*, 303; Berger, *United States Air Force in Southeast Asia*, 366.

113. Hobson, *Vietnam Air Losses*, 15–166; Schlight, *A War too Long*, 53; Marolda, *By Sea, Air, and Land*, 82. See also "Appraisal of the Bombing of North Vietnam, through 1 January 1968," Vietnam Virtual Archive, Texas Tech University, 32.

114. Tilford, *Crosswinds*, 102.

115. Tilford, *Setup*, 106–7, 132, 155; Head, *War from above the Clouds*, 37.

116. Hallion, "Air Force Fighter Acquisition since 1945"; Bennett, *Weapons of War*, 5, 83.

117. For more on these training schools, see Garner, *Top Gun*; and Nellis AFB Flying Operations, "Exercises and Flight Operations: Red Flag High-Intensity Air-to-Air Combat Exercises," accessed 18 April 2015.

Chapter 3

1. Rikhye, "Operation Silver Bayonet," 1, accessed 31 July 2013.

2. McKay, "Valley of Death," accessed 7 Aug. 2013.

3. Safer, *Battle of Ia Drang Valley*, accessed 7 Aug. 2013.

4. Moore, "After-Action Report, Ia Drang Valley Operation, 1st Battalion, 7th Cavalry," 2 [hereafter Moore, After-Action Report].

5. Moore and Galloway, *We Were Soldiers*, 277, 278; Report, Project CHECO, Southeast Asia, "Special Report, Operation Silver Bayonet," 28 Nov. 1965, K717.0413–2.9 (declassified 26 Dec. 1995).

6. Moore and Galloway, *We Were Soldiers*, 277, 278; Report, Project CHECO, Southeast Asia, "Special Report, Operation Silver Bayonet," 28 Nov. 1965, K717.0413–2.9 (declassified 26 Dec. 1995). See also Banks, *1st Cavalry Division*.

7. Diem, *In the Jaws of History*, 100–105; Moyar, *Triumph Forsaken*, 286–90.

8. Diem, *In the Jaws of History*, 100–105; Moyar, *Triumph Forsaken*, 286–90.

9. Moyar, *Triumph Forsaken*, 286.

10. Moise, *Tonkin Gulf and the Escalation of the Vietnam War*, 50, 78, 82, 158.

11. Galloway, "Vietnam Story"; Moore, "After-Action Report," 3–4; Hanyok, "SIGNT and Battle of the Ia Drang Valley" [hereafter Hanyok, "SIGNT and Ia Drang"].

12. Galloway, "Vietnam Story."

13. Moore and Galloway, *We Were Soldiers*, 276–77.

14. For a detailed account of the history of the NVA from the communist Vietnamese point of view, see Military History Institute of Vietnam, *Victory in Vietnam*.

15. Military History Institute of Vietnam, *Victory in Vietnam*, 277–78; Galloway, "Vietnam Story."

16. Moore, "After-Action Report," 4; Galloway, "Vietnam Story."

17. See Galloway, "Vietnam Story." Lieutenant Marm's Medal of Honor citation reads:

> For conspicuous gallantry and intrepidity at the risk of life above and beyond the call of duty. As a platoon leader in the 1st Cavalry Division (Airmobile), Lieutenant Marm demonstrated indomitable courage during a combat operation. His company was moving through the valley to relieve a friendly unit surrounded by an enemy force of estimated regimental size. Lieutenant Marm led his platoon through withering fire until they were finally forced to take cover. Realizing that his platoon could not hold very long, and see-

ing four enemy soldiers moving into his position, he moved quickly under heavy fire and annihilated all 4. Then, seeing that his platoon was receiving intense fire from a concealed machine gun, he deliberately exposed himself to draw its fire. Thus locating its position, he attempted to destroy it with an antitank weapon. Although he inflicted casualties, the weapon did not silence the enemy fire. Quickly, disregarding the intense fire directed on him and his platoon, he charged 30 meters across open ground, and hurled grenades into the enemy position, killing some of the eight insurgents manning it. Although severely wounded, when his grenades were expended, armed with only a rifle, he continued the momentum of his assault on the position and killed the remainder of the enemy. Lieutenant Marm's selfless actions reduced the fire on his platoon, broke the enemy assault, and rallied his unit to continue toward the accomplishment of this mission. Lieutenant Marm's gallantry on the battlefield and his extraordinary intrepidity at the risk of his life are in the highest traditions of the U.S. Army and reflect great credit upon himself and the Armed Forces of his country.

"Marm, Walter Joseph, Jr.," Vietnam (M–Z Index), Full-Text Citations, Recipients, Medal of Honor, US Army, https://www.army.mil/medalofhonor/citations26.html.

18. Moore, "After-Action Report," 11–12.

19. Porter, "Silver Bayonet," 2–3.

20. Moore and Galloway, *We Were Soldiers*, 117–18.

21. Moore and Galloway, *We Were Soldiers*, 168.

22. Moore and Galloway, *We Were Soldiers*, 133.

23. Moore and Galloway, *We Were Soldiers*, 133.

24. Moore and Galloway, *We Were Soldiers*, 133.

25. Moore and Galloway, *We Were Soldiers*, 133–35; Thompson, "Bruce Crandall," accessed 31 July 2013.

26. Moore and Galloway, *We Were Soldiers*, 133–37, 215–17. See also Galloway, "Reporter's Journal from Hell," pt. 4:1–8; and Thackeray, "Valley of Death."

27. Moore and Galloway, *We Were Soldiers*, 135–38.

28. Moore, "After-Action Report," 13–14; Porter, "Silver Bayonet," 3.

29. Galloway, "Reporter's Journal from Hell," pt. 4.

30. Moore and Galloway, *We Were Soldiers*, 221.

31. Moore, "After-Action Report," 14.

32. Moore, "After-Action Report," 15.

33. Moore, "After-Action Report," 15–16.

34. Moore, "After-Action Report," 16–17.

35. Galloway, "Vietnam Story."

36. Moore and Galloway, *We Were Soldiers*, 285–87.

37. Moore and Galloway, *We Were Soldiers*, 285–87.

38. Moore and Galloway, *We Were Soldiers*, 286–88; Galloway, "Vietnam Story"; Hanyok, "SIGNT and Ia Drang."

39. Galloway, "Vietnam Story"; Moore and Galloway, *We Were Soldiers*, 288–89; Porter, "Silver Bayonet," 5; Hanyok, "SIGNT and Ia Drang."

40. Moore and Galloway, *We Were Soldiers*, 289–90.

41. Moore and Galloway, *We Were Soldiers*, 292, 293.

42. Moore and Galloway, *We Were Soldiers*, 292, 293; Galloway, "Vietnam Story"; Porter, "Silver Bayonet," 5; Hanyok, "SIGNT and Ia Drang."

43. Moore and Galloway, *We Were Soldiers*, 293–95; Galloway, "Vietnam Story"; Porter, "Silver Bayonet," 5. For firsthand account of most of the ground combat from LZ X-Ray to Albany, see Smith, "Death in the Ia Drang Valley," accessed 7 Aug. 2013.

44. Porter, "Silver Bayonet," 5.

45. Moore and Galloway, *We Were Soldiers*, 300–305.

46. Moore and Galloway, *We Were Soldiers*, 309; Porter, "Silver Bayonet," 5–6.

47. Porter, "Silver Bayonet," 6.

48. Moore and Galloway, *We Were Soldiers*, 339–40; Galloway, "Vietnam Story." Buse Tully, later promoted to major, was killed in March 1969.

49. Moore and Galloway, *We Were Soldiers*, 341–43; Galloway, "Vietnam Story."

50. Moore and Galloway, *We Were Soldiers*, 369.

51. Moore and Galloway, *We Were Soldiers*, 352–54.

52. Porter, "Silver Bayonet," 6–7.

53. Porter, "Silver Bayonet," 8–9.

54. Porter, "Silver Bayonet," 10; Safer, *Battle of Ia Drang Valley*.

55. Porter, "Silver Bayonet," 11.

56. Moore and Galloway, *We Were Soldiers*, 416; Galloway, "Vietnam Story."

57. McKay, "Valley of Death." General Moore died on 10 February 2017 in Auburn, Alabama.

58. Grist, "Hal Moore Is More Forgiving Than I Am," accessed 31 July 2013.

59. Galloway, "Ia Drang," accessed 7 Aug. 2013.

60. Galloway, "Ia Drang."

61. Galloway, "Ia Drang."

62. Memorandum, Secretary of Defense McNamara to President Johnson, Washington, 30 Nov. 1965. *FRUS, 1964–1968*, vol. 3, *Vietnam: June–December 1965* (Washington, DC: GPO, 1996), 591–93. Also available online at Historical Documents, Office of the Historian, Dept. of State, https://history.state.gov/historicaldocuments/frus1964–68v03/d212 (document 212); the source note online reads "Johnson [Presidential] Library, National Security File, Country File, Vietnam, 2EE, Primarily McNamara's Recommendations re Strategic Actions. Top Secret [since Declassified]. There is an indication on the source text that the President saw the memorandum."

63. "Excepts from Memorandum," in Galloway, "Ia Drang."

64. "Excepts from Memorandum," in Galloway, "Ia Drang."

65. "Excepts from Memorandum," in Galloway, "Ia Drang."

66. "Excepts from Memorandum," in Galloway, "Ia Drang."

67. Galloway, "Ia Drang."

68. Galloway, "Ia Drang."

69. Galloway, "Ia Drang."

70. Galloway, "Ia Drang."

71. Moore and Galloway, *We Were Soldiers*, 369.

72. Hanyok, "SIGNT and Ia Drang"; Rikhye, "Operation Silver Bayonet," 1.

73. Galloway, "Ia Drang."

74. Hanyok, "SIGNT and Ia Drang."

75. Hanyok, "SIGNT and Ia Drang."

Chapter 4

1. Brush, "Khe Sanh, 1968," 191.

2. Brush, "Khe Sanh, 1968," 191.

3. For a recent focused study on Hue, see Bowden, *Hue.*

4. Oberdorfer, *Tet!*, 250–51; Braestrup, *Big Story*, 493.

5. Davidson, *Vietnam at War*, 486.

6. Olson and Roberts, *Where the Dominos Fell*, 187.

7. Diem, "My Recollections of the Tet Offensive," 133.

8. For details on Tet Mau Thanh campaign, see Brush, "Khe Sanh, 1968," 191–213; Braestrup, *Big Story*; Oberdorfer, *Tet!*; Long, *Tet Offensive and Its Aftermath*; Tra, *Concluding the 30-Year War*; and Pisor, *End of the Line.*

9. For details on Khe Sanh, see Head and Grinter, *Looking Back on the Vietnam War*; and Prados and Stubbe, *Valley of Decision.*

10. Stanton, *Rise and Fall of an American Army*, 35–48.

11. Pisor, *End of the Line*, 15–16.

12. Brush, "Khe Sanh, 1968," 191–92; Tilford, "Bombing Our Way Back Home," 123–44; Head, "Playing Hide and Seek with the 'Trail,'" 101–15.

13. Brush, "Khe Sanh, 1968," 192; Prados and Stubbe, *Valley of Decision*, 1324.

14. Brush, "Khe Sanh, 1968," 192.

15. Brush, "Khe Sanh, 1968," 192.

16. Military Assistance Command, Vietnam, *Command History 1965, Annex N*, 18; Prados and Stubbe, *Valley of Decision*, 140–46; Dougan, Weiss, et al., *Nineteen Sixty-Eight*, 42.

17. Military Assistance Command, Vietnam, *Command History 1965*, 18–19.

18. Schulimson et al., *U.S. Marines in Vietnam*, 60; Telfer, Rogers, and Fleming, *U.S. Marines in Vietnam*, 129–31.

19. Maitland and McInerney, *Contagion of War*, 164–65, 183; Stanton, *Rise and Fall of an American Army*, 160–70. For a detailed account of the Battle of Dak To, see Murphy, *Dak To*, 3–10.

20. Palmer, *Summons of the Trumpet*, 213–15; Dougan, Weiss, et al., *Nineteen Sixty-Eight*, 432.

21. Pearson, *War in the Northern Provinces*, 6; Brush, "Khe Sanh, 1968," 193; Shore, *Battle for Khe Sanh*, 5–6, 11.

22. Shore, *Battle for Khe Sanh*, 17; Prados and Stubbe, *Valley of Decision*, 155. For specifics on the "Hill Fights," see Telfer, Rogers, and Fleming, *U.S. Marines in Vietnam*, chap. 4; and Murphy, *Hill Fights*.

23. Brush, "Khe Sanh, 1968," 193.

24. Brush, "Khe Sanh, 1968," 193–94; Prados and Stubbe, *Valley of Decision*, 27071; McDonald, *Giap*, 279.

25. Pisor, *End of the Line*, 112.

26. Westmoreland, *Soldier Reports*, 128; Sheehan et al., *Pentagon Papers as Published by the New York Times*, 61617.

27. Shore, *Battle for Khe Sanh*, 47.

28. Dougan, Weiss, et al., *Nineteen Sixty-Eight*, 42–43.

29. Military Institute of Vietnam, *Victory in Vietnam*, 216.

30. Prados and Stubbe, *Valley of Decision*, 215.

31. Schulimson et al., *U.S. Marines in Vietnam*, 72, 258–59; Shore, *Battle for Khe Sanh*, 30–31.

32. Dougan, Weiss, et al., *Nineteen Sixty-Eight*, 44.

33. Prados, "Khe Sanh."

34. Prados, "Khe Sanh"; Schulimson et al., *U.S. Marines in Vietnam*, 269.

35. Prados and Stubbe, *Valley of Decision*, 286; Pisor, *End of the Line*, 152.

36. Prados and Stubbe, *Valley of Decision*, 319–20, 329.

37. Schulimson et al., *U.S. Marines in Vietnam*, 276.

38. For details of these actions, see Shore, *Battle for Khe Sanh*, 53–71; and debriefing interview, Col. D. E. Lownds by Col. R. H. Mample, 29 July 1968, Item 992AU0696, VCA [hereafter Lownds interview].

39. Many of the details about these events are from the personal memories of Peter Brush, who has spoken and written extensively on the subject. See Brush, "Khe Sanh, 1968," 194–95; and Shore, *Battle for Khe Sanh*, 33–42.

40. Military Assistance Command, Vietnam, *Command History 1966, Annex M* (Saigon, 1967), 60; Van Staaveren, *Interdiction in Southern Laos*, 230, 290; Schulimson et al., *U.S. Marines in Vietnam*, 67.

41. Lownds interview; Schulimson et al., *U.S. Marines in Vietnam*, 67–68.

42. Shore, *Battle for Khe Sanh*, 53–71; Lownds interview.

43. Shore, *Battle for Khe Sanh*, 42–45; Prados and Stubbe, *Valley of Decision*, 251–55; *New York Times*, 24 Jan. 1968, 1, 3; Brush, "Khe Sanh, 1968," 195.

44. Prados and Stubbe, *Valley of Decision*, 159.

45. Westmoreland, *Soldier Reports*, 236.

46. For validation of the fact that North Vietnamese leaders feared an invasion, see Military Institute of Vietnam, *Victory in Vietnam*.

47. Shore, *Battle for Khe Sanh*, 47.

48. Dougan, Weiss, et al., *Nineteen Sixty-Eight*, 42. For details of the battle, see Clarke, *Expendable Warriors*; Van Staaveren, *Interdiction in Southern Laos*; Rottman, *Khe Sanh*; and Warren, "Mystery of Khe Sanh."

49. Westmoreland, *Soldier Reports*, 316.

50. Davidson, *Vietnam at War*, 55253.

51. Davidson, *Vietnam at War*, 553; Westmoreland, *Soldier Reports*, 102; Pisor, *End of the Line*, 235–36.

52. Pisor, *End of the Line*, 86.

53. For more on Chosen and General Puller, see Martin Russ, *Breakout—The Chosen Reservoir Campaign, Korea, 1950* (New York: Penguin Books, 1999), 230.

54. Pisor, *End of the Line*, 72, 78; Brush, "Khe Sanh, 1968," 196.

55. For more on this point, see Cecil Currey, *Victory at Any Cost: The Genius of Viet Nam's Gen. Vo Nguyen Giap* (Lincoln: University of Nebraska Press, 1997).

56. Oberdorfer, *Tet!*, 12627; Brush, "Khe Sanh, 1968," 196–97.

57. Davidson, *Vietnam at War*, 56769.

58. Head, *War from above the Clouds*, 17–27.

59. Head, *War from above the Clouds*, 17–27.

60. Head, *War from above the Clouds*, 17–27.

61. For more on the air war and Arc Light, see Hopkins and Goldberg, *Development of the Strategic Air Command*; Office of History, SAC, "Activity Input to Project Corona Harvest, ARC LIGHT Operations, "; Berger, *United States Air Force in Southeast Asia*; Tilford, *Setup*; Schlight, *War in South Vietnam*; Nalty, *Air Power and the Fight for Khe Sanh*; and Morocco, *Thunder from Above*.

62. Brush, "Khe Sanh, 1968," 197; Willbanks, *Tet Offensive*, 23.

63. Prados and Stubbe, *Valley of Decision*, 23133.

64. Prados and Stubbe, *Valley of Decision*, 23133.

65. Prados and Stubbe, *Valley of Decision*, 23133. For a detailed analysis of the siege of Dien Bien Phu, see Head, "Significance of Dien Bien Phu."

66. Davidson, *Vietnam at War*, 562; Dickson, *Electronic Battlefield*, 74; Brush, "Khe Sanh, 1968," 198–99; Head, "Significance of Dien Bien Phu."

67. Davidson, *Vietnam at War*, 562; Brush, "Khe Sanh, 1968," 199; Head, "Significance of Dien Bien Phu."

68. Davidson, *Vietnam at War*, 563; McDonald, *Giap*, 282; O'Neill, *General Giap*, 195–96.

69. Davidson, *Vietnam at War*, 567–69; Porter, "1968 'Hue Massacre,'" 8.

70. Prados and Stubbe, *Valley of Decision*, 397; Brush, "Khe Sanh, 1968," 201; Head, "Significance of Dien Bien Phu."

71. Brush, "Khe Sanh, 1968," 201.

72. Brush, "Khe Sanh, 1968," 201–2; Davidson, *Vietnam at War*, 56465. For an examination of the potential use of tactical nuclear weapons at Khe Sanh, see Prados and Stubbe, *Valley of Decision*, 29193; and Pisor, *End of the Line*, 26162.

73. Ehrlich, "US's Secret Plan to Nuke Vietnam, Laos."

74. Robert McNamara, Secretary of Defense, to Pres. Lyndon B. Johnson, 19 Feb. 1968, Khe Sanh Declassified Documents, Raymond P. Anderson Jr. Personal Collection, Ballinger, Tex. Anderson served with the 109th Quartermaster Corps in Vietnam.

He collected numerous formally classified and unclassified materials concerning the unit.

75. Gelb and Betts, *Irony of Vietnam*, 26465.

76. Gelb and Betts, *Irony of Vietnam*, 26465; Head, "Significance of Dien Bien Phu"; Brush, "Khe Sanh, 1968," 202.

77. Prados and Stubbe, *Valley of Decision*, 399.

78. Brush, "Khe Sanh, 1968," 202.

79. Davidson, *Vietnam at War*, 567; Oberdorfer, *Tet!*, 268–69.

80. Cubbage, review of *The Tet Offensive*, 7879.

81. Cubbage, review of *The Tet Offensive*, 7879; Brush, "Khe Sanh, 1968," 202–3.

82. Shore, *Battle for Khe Sanh*, 90.

83. Dougan, Weiss, et al., *Nineteen Sixty-Eight*, 49. For a detailed account of tactical airlift during the Vietnam War, especially at Khe Sanh, see Berger, *United States Air Force in Southeast Asia*, 169–86; and Schlight, *War in South Vietnam*, 276–87.

84. Shore, *Battle for Khe Sanh*, 79.

85. Shore, *Battle for Khe Sanh*, 79; Schulimson et al., *U.S. Marines in Vietnam*, 283.

86. "Khe Sanh," *Time*, 9 Feb. 1968, 16.

87. Prados and Stubbe, *Valley of Decision*, 289–90; Shore, *Battle for Khe Sanh*, 93; Brush, "Khe Sanh, 1968," 203.

88. Shore, *Battle for Khe Sanh*, 74; Brush, "Khe Sanh, 1968," 203.

89. Shore, *Battle for Khe Sanh*, 79; Brush, "Khe Sanh, 1968," 203; Head, "Significance of Dien Bien Phu."

90. Brush, "Khe Sanh, 1968," 204; Prados and Stubbe, *Valley of Decision*, 282, 306. Pisor, *End of the Line*, 188, 199. In the case of Brush's article, much of what he wrote about was the deprivations the marines experienced came from his personal recollections.

91. Brush, "Khe Sanh, 1968," 204; Shore, *Battle for Khe Sanh*, 199.

92. Brush, "Khe Sanh, 1968," 204–5. This description of how the marines received water is based on a diary entry by Ray W. Stubbe, a Lutheran chaplain with the 1st Battalion, 26th Marines at Khe Sanh.

93. Brush, "Khe Sanh, 1968," 205; Davidson, *Vietnam at War*, 56870.

94. Prados and Stubbe, *Valley of Decision*, 364; Pisor, *End of the Line*, 202; Davidson, *Vietnam at War*, 569.

95. Prados and Stubbe, *Valley of Decision*, 373, 374, 375, 390.

96. Prados and Stubbe, *Valley of Decision*, 381, 382, 391; Brush, "Khe Sanh, 1968," 205–6.

97. *Staff Officers' Field Manual, Organizational, Technical, and Logistical Data Planning Factors*, 2–8, 2–9. See also Brush, "Khe Sanh, 1968," 206.

98. Schulimson et al., *U.S. Marines in Vietnam*, 277; Prados and Stubbe, *Valley of Decision*, 348.

99. Schulimson et al., *U.S. Marines in Vietnam*, 279; Col. Carlton Meyer, "Lost Battles of the Vietnam War," 2011, G2mil.com, http://www.g2mil.com/lost_vietnam.htm.

100. Schulimson et al., *U.S. Marines in Vietnam*, 281–82.

101. Schulimson et al., *U.S. Marines in Vietnam*, 282–83.

102. Schulimson et al., *U.S. Marines in Vietnam*, 283; Dougan, Weiss, et al., *Nineteen Sixty-Eight*, 55; Shore, *Battle for Khe Sanh*, 131.

103. "Lyndon B. Johnson—The Final Days"; Prados and Stubbe, *Valley of Decision*, 418, 420. For further details, see Ankony, *Lurps*.

104. Prados and Stubbe, *Valley of Decision*, 419, 428, 431, 437; Murphy, *Hill Fights*, 239–40; Pisor, *End of the Line*, 108.

105. Schulimson et al., *U.S. Marines in Vietnam*, 286–87.

106. Dougan, Weiss, et al., *Nineteen Sixty-Eight*, 54; Stanton, *Rise and Fall of an American Army*, 246.

107. Peter Brush, "Battle of Khe Sanh: Recounting the Battle Casualties," *Vietnam Magazine*, 26 June 2007, Historynet.com, http://www.historynet.com/battle-of-khe-sanh-recounting-the-battlescasualties.htm [hereafter "Battle Casualties"].

108. Schulimson et al., *U.S. Marines in Vietnam*, 289; Pisor, *End of the Line*, 238–42.

109. Brush, "Battle Casualties"; Peter Brush, "The Withdrawal from Khe Sanh," *Vietnam Magazine*, 12 June 2006, Historynet.com, http://www.historynet.com/the-withdrawal-from-khe-sanh.htm.

110. "Lyndon B. Johnson—The Final Days"; Prados and Stubbe, *Valley of Decision*, 418, 420. For further details, see Ankony, *Lurps*.

111. Military Institute of Vietnam, *Victory in Vietnam*, 223, 229.

112. Military Institute of Vietnam, *Victory in Vietnam*, 229.

113. Military Institute of Vietnam, *Victory in Vietnam*, 229; Rottman, *Khe Sanh*, 90.

114. Murphy, *Hill Fights*, 244.

115. Brush, "Battle Casualties"; Pisor, *End of the Line*, 236–37.

116. Pisor, *End of the Line*, 237; Prados and Stubbe, *Valley of Decision*, 451, 454.

117. Head, "Significance of Dien Bien Phu."

118. Head, "Significance of Dien Bien Phu"; Report of Special US Mission to Indochina, 5 Feb. 1954, quoted in Herring, *America's Longest War* (1972), 28. See also Fall, *Hell in a Very Small Place*, 50; and William Head, "Bernard Fall: The Western Conscience in Indochina" (lecture, Georgia Southwestern University, Americus, 10 Apr. 2013).

119. Gilbert and Head, "Introduction," in Gilbert and Head, *Tet Offensive*, 2–3; Diem, "My Recollections of the Tet Offensive," 125–34.

120. Prados and Stubbe, *Valley of Decision*, 173; Pisor, *End of Line*, 61, 210, 240; Brush, "Khe Sanh, 1968," 206–8.

121. Head, "Significance of Dien Bien Phu."

122. Gelb and Betts, *Irony of Vietnam*, 266.

123. For excellent examinations of the "Riddle of Khe Sanh," see Prados and Stubbe, *Valley of Decision*, 173; Pisor, *End of Line*, 61, 210, 240; Warren, "Mystery of Khe Sanh," 333; Dougan, Weiss, et al., *Nineteen Sixty-Eight*, 38; Schulimson et al., *U.S. Marines in Vietnam*, 67–68; Palmer, *Summons of the Trumpet*, 219; Military Insti-

tute of Vietnam, *Victory in Vietnam*, 216–17; Murphy, *Hill Fights*, 235; and Page and Pimlott, *Nam*, 324.

124. Gelb and Betts, *Irony of Vietnam*, 233–37.

125. Prados and Stubbe, *Valley of Decision*, 453–54.

126. Shore, *Battle for Khe Sanh*, 107.

127. Prados and Stubbe, *Valley of Decision*, 297. See also Head, *War from above the Clouds*, 17–25.

128. Brush, "Khe Sanh, 1968," 207–8.

129. Telephone conversation, author and Peter Brush, 2002.

130. Brush, "Khe Sanh, 1968," 213n.

131. Malcolm W. Browne, "Battlefields of Khe Sanh: Still One Casualty a Day," *New York Times*, 13 May 1994, A1, A6; Brush, "Khe Sanh, 1968," 208.

132. Gelb and Betts, *Irony of Vietnam*, 160; Oberdorfer, *Tet!*, 258.

133. Pisor, *End of the Line*, 205–7.

Chapter 5

1. Clarke, "Foreword," in Villard, *1968 Tet Offensive Battles of Quang Tri City and Hue*, v.

2. BACM Research, "Vietnam War: Tet Offensive."

3. BACM Research, "Vietnam War: Tet Offensive."

4. BACM Research, "Vietnam War: Tet Offensive."

5. Memo, JCS to Secretary of Defense, "Holiday Stand-downs in Vietnam," 23 Oct. 1967.

6. BACM Research, "Vietnam War: Tet Offensive."

7. BACM Research, "Vietnam War: Tet Offensive."

8. BACM Research, "Vietnam War: Tet Offensive."; Lung, *General Offensives*, 10; Dougan, Weiss, et al., *Nineteen Sixty-Eight*, 184.

9. Oberdorfer, *Tet!*, 9–10.

10. Oberdorfer, *Tet!*, 11–13.

11. Oberdorfer, *Tet!*, 12–13.

12. Oberdorfer, *Tet!*, 14, 23–24.

13. Oberdorfer, *Tet!*, 9–10, 22–23.

14. Oberdorfer, *Tet!*, 23–24; BACM Research, "Vietnam War: Tet Offensive.."

15. Oberdorfer, *Tet!*, 25–30; BACM Research, "Vietnam War: Tet Offensive"; Memo, CIA to Walter W. Rostow, "Telephone Conversation with Saigon Station," 31 Jan. 1968, Item 0240915008, Record 146025, Larry Berman Collection, VCA.

16. Westmoreland, *Soldier Reports*, 322. See also Summers, *On Strategy: A Critical Analysis of the Vietnam War*, 133; and Gelb and Betts, *Irony of Vietnam*, 333–34.

17. Wirtz, *Tet Offensive: Intelligence Failure in War*, 18 [hereafter *Intelligence Failure*].

18. See Karnow, *Vietnam*, 537; Sharp, *Strategy for Defeat*, 214; McGarvey, *Visions of Victory*; and Wirtz, *Intelligence Failure*, 60.

19. Dougan, Weiss, et al., *Nineteen Sixty-Eight*, 21–3; BACM Research, "Vietnam War: Tet Offensive."

20. Dougan, Weiss, et al., *Nineteen Sixty-Eight*, 22.

21. Dougan, Weiss, et al., *Nineteen Sixty-Eight*, 22; BACM Research, "Vietnam War: Tet Offensive"; Hammond, *United States Army in Vietnam*, 326.

22. Hammond, *United States Army in Vietnam*, 326–27; Dougan, Weiss, et al., *Nineteen Sixty-Eight*, 23; CBS News, *Uncounted Enemy*.

23. Dougan, Weiss, et al., *Nineteen Sixty-Eight*, 68; Karnow, *Vietnam*, 545–46.

24. Sorley, *Better War*, 6.

25. Sheehan et al., *Pentagon Papers as Published by the New York Times*, 592.

26. Karnow, *Vietnam*, 546.

27. Dougan, Weiss, et al., *Nineteen Sixty-Eight*, 66.

28. Schmitz, *Tet Offensive*, 56–58.

29. Dougan, Weiss, et al., *Nineteen Sixty-Eight*, 66.

30. Dougan, Weiss, et al., *Nineteen Sixty-Eight*, 67–69.

31. Karnow, *Vietnam*, 514.

32. Elliott, *Vietnamese War* (2003), 1005; Nguyen, "War Politburo," 4, 15–20; Wirtz, *Intelligence Failure*, 30–50.

33. Wirtz, *Intelligence Failure*, 20; Nguyen, "War Politburo," 22; Doyle et al., *The North*, 55.

34. Wirtz, *Intelligence Failure*, 36–49; Doyle et al., *The North*, 56; Lung, *General Offensives*, 14–16.

35. Lung, *General Offensives*, 16.

36. Nguyen, "War Politburo," 18–20.

37. Nguyen, "War Politburo," 24–27.

38. Military History Institute of Vietnam, *Victory in Vietnam*, 371–80.

39. Lung, *General Offensives*, 24–25; Guan, "Decision-Making Leading to the Tet Offensive," 352.

40. Nguyen, "War Politburo," 24.

41. Ang, "Decision-Making Leading to the Tet Offensive," 352; Doyle et al., *The North*, 56.

42. Hoang, *General Offensives*, 110; Doyle et al., *The North*, 56–58; Nguyen, "War Politburo," 34; Duiker, *Communist Road to Power*, 288.

43. Hoang, *General Offensives*, 22–26; Duiker, *Communist Road to Power*, 289, 299–300; Doyle et al., *The North*, 56–59; Karnow, *Vietnam*, 537; Clifford, *Counsel to the President*, 475.

44. Tra, "Tet," 40.

45. Doyle et al., *The North*, 46–47; Military Institute of Vietnam, *Victory in Vietnam*, 208; Dougan, Weiss, et al., *Nineteen Sixty-Eight*, 10.

46. Hoang, *General Offensives*, 10–11.

47. For a rightwing view, see Hayward, "Tet Offensive."

48. Dougan, Weiss, et al., *Nineteen Sixty-Eight*, 11.

49. Hoang, *General Offensives*, 39.

50. Dougan, Weiss, et al., *Nineteen Sixty-Eight*, 10–11.

51. Shore, *Battle of Khe Sanh*, 17; Morocco, *Thunder from Above*, 174–76; Willbanks, *Tet Offensive*, 16.

52. Willbanks, *Tet Offensive*, 16–17; Hoang, *General Offensives*, 9–10; Maitland and McInerney, *Contagion of War*, 160–85.

53. Palmer, *Summons of the Trumpet*, 229–33.

54. Palmer, *Summons of the Trumpet*, 235; Dougan, Weiss, et al., *Nineteen Sixty-Eight*, 8.

55. Dougan, Weiss, et al., *Nineteen Sixty-Eight*, 124; Willbanks, *Tet Offensive*, 7; Stanton, *Rise and Fall of an American Army*, 195.

56. Dougan, Weiss, et al., *Nineteen Sixty-Eight*, 12.

57. Hoang, *General Offensives*, 35; Sheehan et al., *Pentagon Papers as Published by the New York Times*, 778.

58. Zaffiri, *Westmoreland*, 280.

59. Zaffiri, *Westmoreland*, 280; Hammond, *United States Army in Vietnam*, 342.

60. "Crack the sky, shake the earth" was the code message sent to communist forces, who were also told that they were "about to inaugurate the greatest battle in the history of our country." Dougan, Weiss, et al., *Nineteen Sixty-Eight*, 10.

61. Stanton, *Rise and Fall of an American Army*, 209; Westmoreland, *Soldier Reports*, 323.

62. Westmoreland, *Soldier Reports*, 328; Palmer, *Summons of the Trumpet*, 238. It should be noted that Palmer provides a smaller number of enemy forces—somewhere around 70,000.

63. CIA intelligence memo, "Communist Tet Offensive," 31 Jan. 1968, (top secret, declassified 16 July 1996), Reference Location 1997–3038, University Library at Saskatchewan, Saskatoon.

64. Westmoreland, *Soldier Reports*, 328–32.

65. Karnow, *Vietnam*, 549.

66. Clifford, *Counsel to the President*, 474. For a detailed examination of the intelligence misinterpretations and shock among allied leaders, see CIA report, "Intelligence Failures in Vietnam, Suggestions for Reform," 24 Jan. 1969, D080.5C, Folder 149, Box 11, CIA Repository, VCA.

67. Clifford, *Counsel to the President*, 476; Zaffiri, *Westmoreland*, 283.

68. Braestrup, *Big Story*, 108.

69. Willbanks, *Tet Offensive*, 31–32; Wiest, *Vietnam War*, 41.

70. Stanton, *Rise and Fall of an American Army*, 215. See also Nolan, *Battle of Saigon, Tet 1968*.

71. Willbanks, *Tet Offensive*, 32–36; Westmoreland, *Soldier Reports*, 326.

72. Willbanks, *Tet Offensive*, 34–37.

73. Willbanks, *Tet Offensive*, 36. For a detailed account, see Obituary, "Nguyen Ngoc Loan, 67 Dies; Executed Viet Cong Prisoner," *New York Times*, 16 July 1998.

74. Willbanks, *Tet Offensive*, 37–39; Hoang, *General Offensives*, 40.

75. Willbanks, *Tet Offensive*, 32–39.

76. Karnow, *Vietnam*, 534; Palmer, *Summons of the Trumpet*, 254; Oberdorfer, *Tet!*, 261.

77. Westmoreland, *Soldier Reports*, 332; BACM Research, "Vietnam War: Tet Offensive"; Department of Defense, *Combat Area Casualties*.

78. Villard, *Battles of Quang Tri City and Hue*, 26 [hereafter *Battles of Quang Tri City and Hue*]. Hue is in central Vietnam, adjacent to the Perfume River just a few miles inland from the East Sea, and about 430 miles south of Hanoi and about 680 miles north of Saigon (now Ho Chi Minh City).

79. Villard, *Battles of Quang Tri City and Hue*, 26; Cooling, "Hue City 1968."

80. Villard, *Battles of Quang Tri City and Hue*, 25.

81. Villard, *Battles of Quang Tri City and Hue*, 27.

82. Villard, *Battles of Quang Tri City and Hue*, 29; Tong Ho Trinh, *Huong Tien Cong va Noi Day Tet Mau Than o Tri-Thien-Hue, 1968* [The 1968 Tet Offensive and uprising in the Tri-Thien-Hue Theater], 53.

83. Villard, *Battles of Quang Tri City and Hue*, 30; Trinh, *Huong Tien Cong va Noi Day Tet Mau Than o Tri-Thien-Hue*, 13–23, 28.

84. Villard, *Battles of Quang Tri City and Hue*, 31–32; Smith, *Siege at Hue*, 13–14.

85. Cooling, "Hue City 1968"; Willbanks, *Tet Offensive*, 43–47; Villard, *Battles of Quang Tri City and Hue*, 34.

86. Villard, *Battles of Quang Tri City and Hue*, 28–29; Smith, *Siege at Hue*, 20; Krohn, *Lost Battalion*, 52.

87. Cooling, "Hue City 1968"; Willbanks, *Tet Offensive*, 46; BACM Research, "Vietnam War: Tet Offensive"; MACV Command History, 1968, Vol. 1, After Action Report, "The Battle of Hue, 2–26 February 1968, DOD Files, Washington, DC.

88. Willbanks, *Tet Offensive*, 48–49, 54; Palmer, *Summons of the Trumpet*, 245.

89. Schulimson et al., *U.S. Marines in Vietnam*, 175. See also Nolan, *Battle for Hue, Tet 1968*.

90. Cooling, "Hue City 1968"; Willbanks, *Tet Offensive*, 48–53.

91. Cooling, "Hue City 1968"; Schulimson et al., *U.S. Marines in Vietnam*, 172–77; Villard, *Battles of Quang Tri City and Hue*, 40.

92. Cooling, "Hue City 1968"; Schulimson et al., *U.S. Marines in Vietnam*, 172–77; Villard, *Battles of Quang Tri City and Hue*, 40.

93. Cooling, "Hue City 1968"; Schulimson et al., *U.S. Marines in Vietnam*, 172–77; Villard, *Battles of Quang Tri City and Hue*, 40.

94. Villard, *Battles of Quang Tri City and Hue*, 42–43.

95. Schulimson et al., *U.S. Marines in Vietnam*, 175–77; Warr, *Phase Line Green*, 54–64.

96. Schulimson et al., *U.S. Marines in Vietnam*, 172; Cooling, "Hue City 1968"; Warr, *Phase Line Green*, 65–82.

97. Schulimson et al., *U.S. Marines in Vietnam*, 176.

98. Schulimson et al., *U.S. Marines in Vietnam*, 176. Tropospheric scatter, or tro-

poscatter, is a microwave radio-communication method that can send signals over considerable distances—up to 200 miles. Normally, signals in the microwave frequency range use roughly two GHz and travel in straight lines and so are limited to line-of-sight applications in which the receiver can be seen by the transmitter; the visual horizon thus limits communication distances to around 30–40 miles. Troposcatter allows microwave communication beyond the horizon. It exploits a phenomenon by which radio waves at particular frequencies are randomly scattered as they pass through the upper layers of the troposphere. Radio signals are transmitted in a tight beam aimed at the tropopause midway between the transmitter and receiver sites. As they pass through the troposphere, some of the energy is scattered back toward the ground, allowing the receiver station to pick up the signal. A related system is meteor-burst communications, which uses the ionized trails of meteors to improve the strength of the scattering.

99. Schulimson et al., *U.S. Marines in Vietnam*, 177.

100. Schulimson et al., *U.S. Marines in Vietnam*, 177; Villard, *Battles of Quang Tri City and Hue*, 56. The Ontos (Greek for "thing") was officially designated as the Rifle, Multiple 106-mm, Self-propelled M50. It was a light armored, tracked antitank vehicle developed in the 1950s to be a fast tank killer for airborne forces. The Ontos mounted six M40 106-mm recoilless rifles as its main armament, which could be fired in rapid succession against single targets. It was produced in limited numbers for the USMC after the US Army lost interest. The marines reported excellent results when they used the Ontos for direct fire support against infantry during the Vietnam War. The US stock of Ontos was largely expended by the end of the war, and it was removed from service in 1969.

101. Villard, *Battles of Quang Tri City and Hue*, 65–76.

102. William Tuohy, "Marines Are Taking Hue Wall by Wall," *Washington Post*, 9 Feb. 1968; Peter Brasestrup, "Weather and Thin Ranks Slow Marines' Tough Fight in Hue," *Washington Post*, 12 Feb. 1968; "Battle of Hue," *Time*, 16 Feb. 1968.

103. "Fight for a Citadel," *Time*, 1 Mar. 1968. For a detailed account of the fight for the Citadel, see Villard, *Battles of Quang Tri City and Hue*, 56–61.

104. Villard, *Battles of Quang Tri City and Hue*, 76–77.

105. "Fight for a Citadel," *Time*, 1 Mar. 1968.

106. Villard, *Battles of Quang Tri City and Hue*, 78.

107. Young, *Vietnam Wars*, 223; Kolko, *Anatomy of a War*, 308–9.

108. Karnow, *Vietnam*, 534.

109. Willbanks, *Tet Offensive*, 55, 99–103; Dougan, Weiss, et al., *Nineteen Sixty-Eight*, 35.

110. Willbanks, *Tet Offensive*, 55, 99–103; Dougan, Weiss, et al., *Nineteen Sixty-Eight*, 35. For details, see Pike, *Viet Cong Strategy of Terror*.

111. Lewy, *America in Vietnam*, 274.

112. Tin, *From Enemy to Friend*, 67.

113. Hoang, *General Offensives*, 82; Hosmer, "Viet Cong Repression," 71–78.

114. Jackson, "Hue: The Massacre the Left Wants Us to Forget"; Anderson, *Columbia Guide to the Vietnam War*, 98–99; "List of Civilians Massacred by the Communists during 'Tet Mau Than'"; Kendrick, *My Lai Massacre*, 27; Manley, *Saigon Salvation*, 364.

115. Willbanks, *Tet Offensive*, 101–2; Oberdorfer, *Tet!*, 232–33.

116. Willbanks, "Tet—What Really Happened at Hue" [hereafter "What Really Happened at Hue"]; Laderman, "They Set About Revenging Themselves on the Population," 1–4 (later published as Laderman, *Tours of Vietnam*).

117. "The Study of the Hue Massacre," Mar. 1968, Douglas Pike Collection, Unit 05, National Liberation Front, D012, Folder 14, Box 13, VCA, 28–30. For other publications that mention these order to the VC cadres, see Laderman, "They Set About Revenging Themselves on the Population," 1–4; Porter, "1968 'Hue Massacre,'" 11; and "Communist Document Tells of Civilian Massacre at Hue," Vietnam Virtual Archive, Texas Tech University, Lubbock.

118. "Study of the Hue Massacre," 29–32.

119. "Study of the Hue Massacre," 113.

120. "Study of the Hue Massacre," 193–95.

121. Oberdorfer, "Hue Red Report Found," 2, 10.

122. Oberdorfer, "Hue Red Report Found," 10.

123. Nguyen Minh Cong, video interview on WGBHTV, Boston, n.d.

124. Willbanks, "What Really Happened at Hue"; Robbins, *This Time We Win*, 201.

125. Willbanks, "What Really Happened at Hue"; Robbins, *This Time We Win*, 201–3.

126. "The Massacre at Hue," *Time*, 31 Oct. 1969; "Wire Led to Discovery of Massacre," *Dallas Morning News*, 20 Mar. 1969, 2.

127. Hosmer, "Viet Cong Repression," 72–78.

128. Vennema, *Viet Cong Massacre at Hue*, 191–92.

129. Hosmer, "Viet Cong Repression," 73.

130. K. B. Richburg, "20 Years after Hue, Vietnamese Admit 'Mistake,'" *Washington Post*, 2 Feb. 1988, 8A.

131. Tin, *From Enemy to Friend*, 67.

132. Tin, *From Enemy to Friend*, 67; Willbanks, "What Really Happened at Hue."

133. Willbanks, "What Really Happened at Hue"; Laderman, *Tours of Vietnam*, 94.

134. Tsang, "Vietnam Today," 464.

135. Villard, *Battles of Quang Tri City and Hue*, 80–81.

136. Willbanks, *Tet Offensive*, 101–2; Willbanks, "What Really Happened at Hue."

137. Schulimson et al., *U.S. Marines in Vietnam*, 307; Dougan, Weiss, et al., *Nineteen Sixty-Eight*, 145.

138. Hoang, *General Offensives*, 98.

139. Spector, *After Tet*, 166–75. See also Gropman, *Air Power and the Airlift Evacuation of Kham Duc*, chap. 4.

140. Spector, *After Tet*, 163–65, 319; Hoang, *General Offensives*, 101.

141. Spector, *After Tet*, 235; Hoang, *General Offensives*, 110.

142. Dougan, Weiss, et al., *Nineteen Sixty-Eight*, 152; Spector, *After Tet*, 240.

143. Lung, *General Offensives*, 118.

144. Karnow, *Vietnam*, 544–45; Doyle et al., *The North*, 118–20; Tran, "Tet," 49–50.

145. Villard, *Battles of Quang Tri City and Hue*, 82.

146. Willbanks, *Tet Offensive*, 80.

147. Tra, *Concluding the 30-Year War*, 35. Despite earlier rumors that Tran had been punished for such statements, he was not. The general spent much of his life after the war speaking and writing while touring the world, including the United States.

148. Schmitz, *Tet Offensive*, 106–9.

149. Duiker, *Communist Road to Power*, 296.

150. Duiker, *Communist Road to Power*, 303.

151. Karnow, *Vietnam*, 534; Arnold, *Tet Offensive*, 86–90.

152. Karnow, *Vietnam*, 536.

153. Arnold, *Tet Offensive*, 86–87; Nguyen, "War Politburo," 35.

154. Doyle et al., *The North*, 126–27.

155. Dougan, Weiss, et al., *Nineteen Sixty-Eight*, 118.

156. Dougan, Weiss, et al., *Nineteen Sixty-Eight*, 116; Arnold, *Tet Offensive*, 88–90.

157. Arnold, *Tet Offensive*, 90.

158. Young, *Vietnam Wars*, 223.

159. Dougan, Weiss, et al., *Nineteen Sixty-Eight*, 119–20; Hoang, *General Offensives*, 135–36; Zaffiri, *Westmoreland*, 293.

160. Dougan, Weiss, et al., *Nineteen Sixty-Eight*, 126.

161. Dougan, Weiss, et al., *Nineteen Sixty-Eight*, 127–28; Hoang, *General Offensives*, 147.

162. Clifford, *Counsel to the President*, 47–55, 479.

163. Willbanks, *Tet Offensive*, 147–50; Zaffiri, *Westmoreland*, 304; Palmer, *Summons of the Trumpet*, 258.

164. Westmoreland, *Soldier Reports*, 355.

165. Sheehan et al., *Pentagon Papers as Published by the New York Times*, 594.

166. Westmoreland, *Soldier Reports*, 356; Karnow, *Vietnam*, 549.

167. Schmitz, *Tet Offensive*, 105.

168. Dougan, Weiss, et al., *Nineteen Sixty-Eight*, 72; Zaffiri, *Westmoreland*, 305–9; Clifford, *Counsel to the President*, 482.

169. Johnson, *Vantage Point*, 389–92. For an excellent book on Johnson, see [Goodwin], *Lyndon Johnson and the American Dream*.

170. Clifford, *Counsel to the President*, 485.

171. Sheehan et al., *Pentagon Papers as Published by the New York Times*, 597.

172. Sheehan et al., *Pentagon Papers as Published by the New York Times*, 600–604.

173. Clifford, *Counsel to the President*, 402.

174. Davidson, *Vietnam at War*, 525.

175. Johnson, *Vantage Point*, 399–400; Sheehan et al., *Pentagon Papers as Published by the New York Times*, 623.

176. Oberdorfer, *Tet!*, 269.

177. Oberdorfer, *Tet!*, 265–70; Schandler, *Lyndon Johnson and Vietnam*, 202–5.

178. Oberdorfer, *Tet!*, 250–51; Braestrup, *Big Story*, 493.

179. Buzzanco, "Myth of Tet," 231.

180. Braestrup, *Big Story*, 679, 687nn; Bret Stephens, "American Honor," *Wall Street Journal*, 22 Jan. 2008, 18.

181. Johnson, *Vantage Point*, 400, 415.

182. Clifford, *Counsel to the President*, 507; Karnow, *Vietnam*, 562.

183. Clifford, *Counsel to the President*, 516.

184. Sheehan et al., *Pentagon Papers as Published by the New York Times*, 609–10.

185. B. Drummond Ayers Jr., "As 1968 Joins the Centuries, McCarthy Goes On," *New York Times*, 14 Mar. 1993, http://www.nytimes.com/1993/03/14/us/as-1968-joins-the-centuries-mccarthy-goes-on.html.

186. Clifford, *Counsel to the President*, 520.

187. Buzzanco, "Myth of Tet," 247–48.

188. Westmoreland, *Soldier Reports*, 361–62; Zaffiri, *Westmoreland*, 315–16.

189. Sorley, *Better War*, 18. For more on Commando Hunt operations, see Head, "Playing Hide-and-seek with the 'Trail,'" 101–15.

190. Willbanks, *Tet Offensive*, 52–55, 154; Schulimson et al., *U.S. Marines in Vietnam*, 213–16; Wiest, *Vietnam War*, 42.

Chapter 6

1. For general information on Arc Light, see Guilmartin, "Arc Light," 48. For details on Arc Light operations, see Hopkins and Goldberg, *Development of the Strategic Air Command*; Office of History, SAC, "Activity Input to Project Corona Harvest, Arc Light Operations"; Berger, *United States Air Force in Southeast Asia*; and Schlight, *War in South Vietnam*.

2. *The Joint Chiefs of Staff and the War in Vietnam, 1960–1968*, pt. 2, 24–1, 2; History, "Strategic Air Command (SAC)," Jan.–June 1965, 1:198 [hereafter SAC Hist.]; Schlight, *War in South Vietnam*, 49.

3. *The Joint Chiefs of Staff and the War in Vietnam, 1960–1968*, pt.2, 24–1, 2; SAC Hist., Jan.–June 1965, 1:198; Schlight, *War in South Vietnam*, 49.

4. Office of History, SAC, "Activity Input to Project Corona Harvest, Arc Light Operation," 2:2; SAC Hist., Jan.–June 1964, HA-1093; Msg., COMUSMACV to CINCPAC, "Use of SAC in RVN (Arc Light)," 140805Z May 1965; Schlight, *War in South Vietnam*, 50; Cable, *Unholy Grail*, 98–100, 109.

5. Office of History, SAC, "Activity Input to Project Corona Harvest, Arc Light Operation," 2:2–3, 5–9, 12–13; Hist., "3rd Air Division, Jan–Jun 1967," 134; CINCPAC, "Command History, 1967," 2:711; CH, *Chronology of Important Airpower Events in Southeast Asia, 1950–1968*, 222 [hereafter *Chronology SEA 50–68*]; Director of Operations, DCS, Plans and Operations, HQ USAF, "Analysis of B-52 Conventional Operations in SEA," 29 Oct. 1965.

6. Msg., COMUSMACV to JCS, "Utilization of Arc Light B-52s," 190330Z Mar. 1965; Msg., JCS to CINCPAC, 292147Z Apr. 1965; Schlight, *War in South Vietnam*, 50; SAC Hist., July–Dec. 1965, 2:267.

7. Schlight, *War in South Vietnam*, 51–52; Msg., COMUSMACV to JCS, "Request for Execution of Arc Light Mission," 150305Z June 1965; Memo, AFXOPJ to CSAF, "Changes in Planning and Execution of Arc Light I," 24 June 1965.

8. Schlight, *War in South Vietnam*, 51–52.

9. Schlight, *War in South Vietnam*, 52–53; Hopkins and Goldberg, *Development of the Strategic Air Command*, 131; Msg., JCS to DIRNSA [Director, National Security Agency], "NMCC Opsum, 141–165," 181004Z June 1965; CH, *Chronology SEA 50–68*, 103.

10. Hist., MACV, 1965, 191–92 [hereafter MACV Hist.]; Schlight, *War in South Vietnam*, 53–54; CH, *Chronology SEA 50–68*, 104.

11. CH, *Chronology SEA 50–68*, 114; Schlight, *War in South Vietnam*, 54–55, 82–83; SAC Hist., July–Dec. 1965, 2:270–71; Msg., Zippo 08–225, 7BS to AIG 673, "Commander's Progress Report/Birch Bark," 02/1255Z Aug. 1965; MACV Hist., 1965, 166–67. For details on every major ground operation and their Arc Light and air-support components, see Cable, *Unholy Grail*, 41–47, 98–99, 109, 191–92.

12. For details, see Momyer, *Air Power in Three Wars*, 283–88; PACAF, CH, *Command and Control*, bk. 2, pt. 2, 4–20; PACAF, CH, *Out-Country Report*, bk. 1, 31, 83, bk. 2, 60; Berger, *United States Air Force in Southeast Asia*, 150; SAC Hist., July–Dec. 1965, 279–86.

13. For details, see Patchin, *B-52 Log*, 1, 2, 22–92; Office of History, SAC, "Activity Input to Project Corona Harvest, Arc Light Operation," 2:10–11; Knaack, *Bombers*, 245–47, 257–59; *Pedigree*, 50–51; OCNAO to OCPWA, "External Navy Mine Carriage," 2 Aug. 1966.

14. Office of History, SAC, "Activity Input to Project Corona Harvest, Arc Light Operation," 2:16–18; Study, by RAND Corporation, "Air Interdiction in Southeast Asia, 1966," iii.

15. CH, *Chronology SEA 50–68*, 167; Office of History, SAC, "Activity Input to Project Corona Harvest, Arc Light Operation," 2:16–17; Msg., Zippo 0731, SAC to JCS, "High Reach Charlie Report," 15/1445Z Mar. 1966. For more on *Rolling Thunder* and interservice rivalries, see Tilford, *Crosswinds*; and Cable, "Operation Was a Success, but the Patient Died," 109–58.

16. Ibid., 149; Memo, 7AF to PACAF, "B-52 Operations," 061234Z Oct. 1966; Momyer, *Air Power in Three Wars*, 97–102; Gen. William W. Momyer, "End of Tour Report, Seventh Air Force," 9 [hereafter Momyer, EOTR].

17. Momyer, *Air Power in Three Wars*, 99–102; Schlight, *War in South Vietnam*, 149. Momyer laid out these issues in a memo: Momyer to Maj. Oakah L. Jones, PACAF, "B-52 Concept," 7 Aug. 1966.

18. Futrell, *Ideas, Concepts, Doctrine*, 301–2.

19. Futrell, *Ideas, Concepts, Doctrine*, 302–3.

20. Futrell, *Ideas, Concepts, Doctrine*, 190–91.

21. Futrell, *Ideas, Concepts, Doctrine*, 287–88.

22. Futrell, *Ideas, Concepts, Doctrine*, 298–99.

23. Futrell, *Ideas, Concepts, Doctrine*, 303.

24. Corona Harvest Project, *In-Country Air Strikes Operations, Southeast Asia, 1 Jan 65–31 Mar 68* (Washington, DC: AFHO, 1971); Momyer, *Air Power in Three Wars*, 101–3; Momyer, EOTR, 9; Memo, Momyer to McConnell, 11 Nov. 1966; Msg., 7AF to PACAF, "Arc Light Forces," 22 Sept. 1966; Schlight, *War in South Vietnam*, 149–50.

25. Futrell, *Ideas, Concepts, Doctrine*, 283.

26. Futrell, *Ideas, Concepts, Doctrine*, 284–85; Kinnard, *War Managers*, 62.

27. SAC Hist., Jan.–June 1966, 138; CH, *Chronology SEA 50–68*, 177–82, 186; Msg., COMUSMACV to DIA [Defense Intelligence Agency], "Arc Light Strike Results," 12/2331Z May 1966; Hist., "3d Air Division, Jan-Jun 66," 1:xi; Msg., 12571, COMUS-MACV to CINCPAC, "Use of Arc Light Force," 11/1359Z Apr. 1966; Msg., AMEMBAS-SY [US embassy] Vientiane to CINCPAC, n.s., 12/0600Z Apr. 1966; Msg., Zippo 0496, 4133 BWP to AIG 673, "Commander's Immediate Report, Long Beck I and Jug Head I, II, III, IV," 14/0316Z Apr. 1966; Msg., 13067, COMUSMACV to CINCPAC, "Use of Arc Light Force," 15/1303Z Apr. 1966.

28. CH, *Chronology SEA 50–68*, 185–86; Msg., CINCPAC to COMUSMACV, "Arc Light," 13/0952A May 1966.

29. Schlight, *War in South Vietnam*, 153, 213; SAC Hist., Jan.–June 1966, 106, 138; Hopkins, *SAC Bomber Operations in the Southeast Asia War*, 168; Memo, Deputy SECDEF to CJCA, 1 Sept 1966.

30. CH, *Chronology SEA 50–68*, 197–99; Msg., 0478 3d Air Division to HQ SAC, "Quick Reaction," 30/04482 June 1966; Berger, *United States Air Force in Southeast Asia*, 151; SAC Hist., Jan.–June 1966, 139.

31. Office of History, SAC, "Activity Input to Project Corona Harvest, ARC LIGHT Operation," 3:1, 15, 49; CINCSAC to CSAF, n.s., 26 Aug. 1967.

32. CH, *Chronology SEA 50–68*, 221.

33. CH, *Chronology SEA 50–68*, 227, 231; SAC Hist., Jan.–June 1966, 145; SAC Hist., Jan.–June 1967, 131; Msg., AFXOPDO 89449, CSAF to SAC, 02/1942Z Mar. 1967.

34. Berger, *United States Air Force in Southeast Asia*, 151–56; Schlight, *War in South Vietnam*, 250–58; Cable, *Unholy Grail*, 191–93; CH, *Chronology SEA 50–68*, 235, 238; Msg., 07560, SAC to AIG 667 et al., "SAC BRASSO Report 37," 18/2205Z July 1967, 10.

35. Berger, *United States Air Force in Southeast Asia*, 156; CH, *Chronology SEA 50–68*, 252, 254; SAC Hist., July–Dec. 1967, xviii; Hist., "7th Air Force, 1 Jul–31 Dec 67," xxi, [hereafter 7AF Hist.].

36. "Jason Report," *Pentagon Papers*, Senator Gravel edition, 4:227; "The Speech," 275; Tilford, *Crosswinds*, 88, 96, 97.

37. Tilford, *Crosswinds*, 96–97; Korb, *Joint Chiefs of Staff*, 181. For an excellent account of the tense relationship between Johnson and his military leaders, see Col. Herbert Y. Schandler, "The President, the Secretary of Defense, and the Joint Chiefs

of Staff: The Political Direction of the War," unpublished paper presented to the 1996 Vietnam Symposium, Texas Tech University, 18 Apr. 1996. During those fateful days, Schandler, a liaison officer for the secretary of defense, saw many of these events firsthand.

38. PACAF, CH, *Command & Control*, bk. 1, 2:2–25; SAC Hist., July–Dec. 1967, 152–53; CH, *Chronology SEA 50–68*, 261–63, 268; Berger, *United States Air Force in Southeast Asia*, 156–57; Msg., SAC/VC to CINCPAC, "Continuous Arc Light Emergency Capability for Operation Niagara," 10/1830Z Feb. 1968. It should be noted that the Tet Offensive also began in January.

39. CH, *Chronology SEA 50–68*, 273–74; 7AF Hist., 1 Jan.–30 June 1968, xxii; HQ 7AF, "Weekly Air Intelligence Summary," 11 May 1968, Rpt. 6819; Berger, *United States Air Force in Southeast Asia*, 156–57.

40. Schlight, *War in South Vietnam*, 292; Berger, *United States Air Force in Southeast Asia*, 157.

41. CH, *Chronology SEA 50–68*, 276; 7AF Hist., 1 Jan.–30 June 1968, xxiv; Berger, *United States Air Force in Southeast Asia*, 157, 160.

42. Mark, *Aerial Interdiction*, 329. For more on the Viet Minh struggle against the French, see Karnow, *Vietnam*, 128–205. It should be noted that the NLF was not an arm of the Northern government. In fact, many of its members were noncommunists and opposed reunification, even after the United States left Vietnam. Many scholars have noted this fact, including Larry Cable in *Unholy Grail*.

43. Mark, *Aerial Interdiction*, 329–30. For more on Ngo Dinh Diem, see Karnow, *Vietnam*, 206–311.

44. Mark, *Aerial Interdiction*, 330–31. For more on these deepening commitments, see Karnow, *Vietnam*, 319–48 (esp. 330–34, which covers the NVA buildup).

45. Mark, *Aerial Interdiction*, 331–32; MACV Hist., Jan. 1972–Mar. 1973, vol. 1, Annex A, 35–36, 43–44.

46. CH, *Chronology SEA 50–68*, 294.

47. Berger, *United States Air Force in Southeast Asia*, 109–19; Tilford, "Bombing Our Way Back Home," 126–27. For more on gunships, see Ballard, *United States in Southeast Asia: Development and Employment of Fixed-Wing Gunships* [hereafter *Fixed-Wing Gunships*].

48. CH, *Chronology SEA 50–68*, 296; PACAF CH Reports, "United States Air Force Operations in Laos: 1 Jan 70–30 Jun 71," 25; Gibson, *Perfect War*, 396–97.

49. Tilford, "Bombing Our Way Back Home," 127–28.

50. Berger, *United States Air Force in Southeast Asia*, 109–10.

51. Berger, *United States Air Force in Southeast Asia*, 110.

52. Berger, *United States Air Force in Southeast Asia*, 111.

53. Pike, *PAVN*, chap. 1, conclusion; Pike, *Viet Cong*, 85–105.

54. Berger, *United States Air Force in Southeast Asia*, 111–12, 114; Tilford, *Crosswinds*, 114.

55. Berger, *United States Air Force in Southeast Asia*, 114–18.

56. Maj. Gen. Alton D. Slay, "End-of-Tour Report, August 1971–August 1972," File K717.13, AFHRA, 20 [hereafter Slay, EOTR]; Tilford, "Bombing Our Way Back Home," 132–33.

57. Mark, *Aerial Interdiction*, 332–33; 7AF Hist., "Commando Hunt VII," 20, 89.

58. Mark, *Aerial Interdiction*, 333–34; 7AF Hist., "Commando Hunt VII," 20. For an excellent study detailing the communist supply network, see Nalty, *Interdiction in Southern Laos*, 223–32.

59. Mark, *Aerial Interdiction*, 334–35; Nalty, *Interdiction in Southern Laos*, 234–48.

60. Berger, *United States Air Force in Southeast Asia*, 118; Mark, *Aerial Interdiction*, 344; 7AF Hist., "Commando Hunt VII," 14–17.

61. Berger, *United States Air Force in Southeast Asia*, 118; Mark, *Aerial Interdiction*, 344; 7AF Hist., "Commando Hunt VII," 14.

62. Mark, *Aerial Interdiction*, 345–46; 7AF Hist., "Commando Hunt VII," 23–27.

63. Mark, *Aerial Interdiction*, 346; 7AF Hist., "Commando Hunt VII," 30–33.

64. Berger, *United States Air Force in Southeast Asia*, 118; Tilford, *Crosswinds*, 138; Mark, *Aerial Interdiction*, 344–45; 7AF Hist., "Commando Hunt VII," 14–17, 22–24.

65. 7AF Hist., "Commando Hunt VII," 48–49, 118–27.

66. Berger, *United States Air Force in Southeast Asia*, 119; Mark, *Aerial Interdiction*, 345; 7AF Hist., "Commando Hunt VII," 22–23.

67. Mark, *Aerial Interdiction*, 357–58.

68. 7AF Hist., "Commando Hunt VII," 61, 80; Slay, EOTR, 30.

69. Mark, *Aerial Interdiction*, 358.

70. Mark, *Aerial Interdiction*, 358; Berger, *United States Air Force in Southeast Asia*, 119; Tilford, *Crosswinds*, 138–39, 140.

71. Tilford, "Bombing Our Way Back Home," 127–28; PACAF CH Reports, "United States Air Force Operations in Laos," 76–79; Ballard, *Fixed-Wing Gunships*, 173.

72. Mark, *Aerial Interdiction*, 358–59; 7AF Hist., "Commando Hunt VII," 80; Nalty, *Interdiction in Southern Laos*, 250–51. For details on Commando Hunt V, see 7AF Hist., "Commando Hunt V," 56–57.

73. Col. D. L. Evans, director of intelligence, Task Force Alpha, End-of-Tour Report, 6 July 1972, File 10015110, AFHRA, 30 [hereafter Evans, EOTR]; Mark, *Aerial Interdiction*, 360.

74. Evans, EOTR, 16; Mark, *Aerial Interdiction*, 361–62.

75. Nalty, *Interdiction in Southern Laos*, 148; Mark, *Aerial Interdiction*, 362–63; Slay, EOTR, 26.

76. Mark, *Aerial Interdiction*, 335, 347; Berger, *United States Air Force in Southeast Asia*, 119; Tilford, *Crosswinds*, 138–39; Evans, EOTR, 44, 59; Slay, EOTR, 26.

77. Mark, *Aerial Interdiction*, 335; Nalty, *Interdiction in Southern Laos*, 228–30.

78. Mark, *Aerial Interdiction*, 348–49; 7AF Hist., "Commando Hunt VII," 66–67.

79. Mark, *Aerial Interdiction*, 349–50; Slay EOTR, 23–24. For details on the sensors, see Horrocks, *Air Force in Southeast Asia: The Sensor War*, 17–19.

80. Mark, *Aerial Interdiction*, 350; Slay, EOTR, 28–29; 7AF Hist., "Commando Hunt VII," 47, 133.

81. Mark, *Aerial Interdiction*, 355; 7AF Hist., "Commando Hunt VII," 89–93; Evans, EOTR, 47–48.

82. Mark, *Aerial Interdiction*, 346–47, 355–56; 7AF Hist., "Commando Hunt VII," 33–40, 140–41, 231.

83. Mark, *Aerial Interdiction*, 355–56; 7AF Hist., "Commando Hunt VII," 139–41.

84. Mark, *Aerial Interdiction*, 348; 7AF Hist., "Commando Hunt VII," 39–44.

85. Mark, *Aerial Interdiction*, 356–57; 7AF Hist., "Commando Hunt VII," 21–22, 51–58, 132–42; Evans, EOTR, 48.

86. Mark, *Aerial Interdiction*, 336; Ballard, *Fixed-Wing Gunships*, 77–175.

87. 7AF Hist., "Commando Hunt VII," 67, 80–82; Mark, *Aerial Interdiction*, 353.

88. Berger, *United States Air Force in Southeast Asia*, 119; Tilford, *Crosswinds*, 139.

89. Mark, *Aerial Interdiction*, 329–34; Berger, *United States Air Force in Southeast Asia*, 109–19; Tilford, "Bombing Our Way Back Home," 126–33; Slay, EOTR, 20; 7AF Hist., "Commando Hunt VII," 14, 20, 89. See also Nalty, *Interdiction in Southern Laos*, 234–48.

90. Mark, *Aerial Interdiction*, 358–60; Berger, *United States Air Force in Southeast Asia*, 119; Tilford, *Crosswinds*, 138–40; 7AF Hist., "Commando Hunt VII," 80; Nalty, *Interdiction in Southern Laos*, 250–51; Futrell, *Ideas, Concepts, Doctrine*, 266–67. For details on Commando Hunt V, see 7AF Hist., "Commando Hunt V," 56–57; Tilford, "Bombing Our Way Back Home," 127–28; Ballard, *Fixed-Wing Gunships*, 173; and Evans, EOTR, 30.

91. Nixon, *RN*, 2:79, 259; Nixon, *In the Arena*, 335–37.

92. Tilford, *Crosswinds*, 143; Clodfelter, *Limits of Air Power*, 152–53; Mark, *Aerial Interdiction*, 365–66; Futrell, *Ideas, Concepts, Doctrine*, 267–68.

93. Truong, *Vietcong Memoir*, 200–202, 210–23.

94. Kissinger, *White House Years*, 1109; Clodfelter, *Limits of Air Power*, 153.

95. Palmer, "US Intelligence and Vietnam," 91; Mark, *Aerial Interdiction*, 368.

96. Nicholson, *USAF Response to the Spring 1972 NVN Offensive*, 21; Tilford, *Crosswinds*, 143.

97. About 30,000 other troops involved in the offensive were VC guerilla units. Mann, *1972 Invasion of Military Region I*, 13–52; Liebchen, "Kontum," 28–44; Ringenbach and Melly, *Battle for An Loc*, 1–16.

98. Tilford, *Crosswinds*, 146; Slay, EOTR, 51, 156; Futrell, *Ideas, Concepts, Doctrine*, 275. For details, see Lavalle, *Air Power and the 1972 Spring Offensive*, 58, 98.

99. Nicholson, *USAF Response to the Spring 1972 NVN Offensive*, 38, 67; Mark, *Aerial Interdiction*, 373; 7AF Hist., 1 July 1971–30 June 1972, 273–77; Clodfelter, "Nixon and the Air Weapon," 169; McCarthy and Allison, *Linebacker II*, 11. See also McCarthy and Allison, *Linebacker II* (Revised).

100. Nicholson, *USAF Response to the Spring 1972 NVN Offensive*, 67; Mark, *Aerial Interdiction*, 373; Hist., "PACAF, 1 Jul 71–30 Jun 72," 1:121–22; Clodfelter, "Nixon and

the Air Weapon," 169; Tilford, *Crosswinds*, 145; Hist., "7AF History of Linebacker Operations, 10 May—23 October 1972," 1973, File K740.04-24, AFHRA, 3–5 [hereafter 7AF Hist., *Linebacker*].

101. Nicholson, *USAF Response to the Spring 1972 NVN Offensive*, 123–24; Mark, *Aerial Interdiction*, 373; Clodfelter, "Nixon and the Air Weapon," 169.

102. Nixon, *RN*, 2:606; Clodfelter, "Nixon and the Air Weapon," 172; Hersh, *Price of Power*, 506; Porter, *Linebacker*, 14–15.

103. Mark, *Aerial Interdiction*, 375; Clodfelter, "Nixon and the Air Weapon," 170; Nixon, *RN*, 2:64–65; CH, PACAF, *USAF Air Operations against NVN, 1 Jul 71–30 Jun 72*, 1973), 52–61, [hereafter *Air Ops vs NVN*].

104. Hersh, *Price of Power*, 568; Kissinger, *White House Years*, 1118, 1176; Clodfelter, "Nixon and the Air Weapon," 170–71; Mark, *Aerial Interdiction*, 375–76; Nixon, *RN*, 2:81.

105. PACAF CH, *Air Ops vs NVN*, 90–91; Momyer, *Air Power in Three Wars*, 33; Tilford, *Crosswinds*, 149–50; PACAF CH, *Command and Control*, bk. 1, 1–24. Specifically, the report determined that Linebacker I's goal was to "1) restrict resupply of North Vietnam from external sources; 2) destroy internal stockpiles of military supplies and equipment; and 3) restrict flow of forces and supplies to the battlefield."

106. Porter, *Linebacker*, 16–17; Clodfelter, "Nixon and the Air Weapon," 171.

107. Nixon, *RN*, 2:79–80; Clodfelter, "Nixon and the Air Weapon," 171.

108. Mark, *Aerial Interdiction*, 378–79; PACAF CH, *Air Ops vs NVN*, 65, 121–31; PACAF, SEA Rpt., "*Air Operations Summary*, April, May, and June 1972," File K717.3063, AFHRA [hereafter Air Ops Summary].

109. PACAF CH, *Air Ops vs NVN*, 131.

110. Mark, *Aerial Interdiction*, 379.

111. PACAF CH, *Air Ops vs NVN*, 132–36; 7AF Hist., *Linebacker*, 51–52.

112. PACAF, "North Vietnamese Current Assessment."

113. Mark, *Aerial Interdiction*, 382.

114. PACAF CH, *Air Ops vs NVN*, 91–95; Momyer, *Air Power in Three Wars*, 174–75, 183–96.

115. Mark, *Aerial Interdiction*, 385–86; PACAF CH, *Air Ops vs NVN*, 98–103; Clodfelter, "Nixon and the Air Weapon," 172.

116. Mark, *Aerial Interdiction*, 386–88; PACAF CH, *Air Ops vs NVN*, 103–4.

117. Porter, *Linebacker*, 25; PACAF CH, *Air Ops vs NVN*, 111–17.

118. PACAF CH, *Air Ops vs NVN*, 109–17.

119. Palmer, "US Intelligence and Vietnam," 97–98.

120. Mark, Aerial *Interdiction*, 392–95; SAC Hist., 1 July 1971–30 June 1972, 461–67; PACAF SEA, "Air Ops Summaries," Apr.–Aug. 1972.

121. Mark, Aerial *Interdiction*, 395–97.

122. Clodfelter, *Limits of Air Power*, 166, 173.

123. Palmer, "US Intelligence and Vietnam," 98–99.

124. MACV Hist., Jan. 1972–Mar. 1973, 53, 74, 79.

125. Mark, *Aerial Interdiction*, 399, 408.

126. Clodfelter, "Nixon and the Air Weapon," 172; Clodfelter, *Limits of Air Power*, 159–60; Kissinger, *White House Years*, 1102; Hist., HQ Eighth Air Force, "History of the Eighth Air Force," vol. 1, "Narrative," 148–49.

127. Clodfelter, *Limits of Air Power*, 159–61.

128. Clodfelter, *Limits of Air Power*, 161–62.

129. Clodfelter, *Limits of Air Power*, 165; Clodfelter, "Nixon and the Air Weapon," 172; Tilford, *Crosswinds*, 153.

130. Tilford, *Crosswinds*, 148.

131. Nixon, *RN*, 2:188–93; Szulc, *Illusion of Peace*, 629.

132. Kissinger, *White House Years*, 1397, 1409–10; Hersh, *Price of Power*, 604.

133. Clodfelter, "Nixon and the Air Weapon," 173–74; Nixon, *RN*, 2:222–27, 230; Kissinger, *White House Years*, 1411–12, 1416; Clodfelter, *Limits of Air Power*, 177–79.

134. Clodfelter, *Limits of Air Power*, 179–82; Clodfelter, "Nixon and the Air Weapon," 174–77; Nixon, *RN*, 2:224–31, 234–42; Kissinger, *White House Years*, 1420–47; Hersh, *Price of Power*, 619.

135. Clodfelter, *Limits of Air Power*, 182–83; Truong, *Vietcong Memoir*, 168.

136. Nixon, *RN*, 2:242; Clodfelter, "Nixon and the Air Weapon," 177; Clodfelter, *Limits of Air Power*, 183–84; McCarthy and Allison, *Linebacker II*, 39; McCarthy and Allison, *Linebacker II* (Revised), 39–40.

137. Futrell, *Ideas, Concepts, Doctrine*, 296.

138. Futrell, *Ideas, Concepts, Doctrine*, 296. For more details on this issue, see US Senate, *DOD Appropriations for FY75: Hearings before a Subcommittee of the Committee on Appropriations*, 93rd Cong., 2nd sess., 1974, pt. 1, 101.

139. Ibid.; Clodfelter, "Nixon and the Air Weapon," 178.

140. Futrell, *Ideas, Concepts, Doctrine*, 296–97.

141. Clodfelter, "Nixon and the Air Weapon," 178. Clodfelter obtained most of this information from interviews with Col. Clyde E. Bodenheimer on 7 January 1983 and from interviews with members of General Meyer's staff, as well as an internal interview of Lt. Gen. Gerald W. Johnson.

142. Clodfelter, *Limits of Air Power*, 184; McCarthy and Allison, *Linebacker II* (Revised), 41.

143. Tilford, *Crosswinds*, 165–66; Morocco, *Rain of Fire*, 149; Clodfelter, *Limits of Air Power*, 186; McCarthy and Allison, *Linebacker II* (Revised), 50–64; Office of History, SAC, *Chronology of SAC Participation in Linebacker II*, 95–96 [hereafter *SAC Participation in Linebacker II*].

144. Nixon, *RN*, 2:242–46.

145. Clodfelter, "Nixon and the Air Weapon," 179; *SAC Participation in Linebacker II*, 106, 109–11, 121, 140–43; McCarthy and Allison, *Linebacker II*, 41–44, 77, 89, 96; McCarthy and Allison, *Linebacker II* (Revised), 64–89.

146. Clodfelter, "Nixon and the Air Weapon," 179; McCarthy and Allison, *Linebacker II*, 121.

147. Berger, *United States Air Force in Southeast Asia*, 166–67.

148. Futrell, *Ideas, Concepts, Doctrine*, 297.

149. Futrell, *Ideas, Concepts, Doctrine*, 297–98.

150. Clodfelter, *Limits of Air Power*, 187; *SAC Participation in Linebacker II*, 153–59, 185–86; McCarthy and Allison, *Linebacker II* (Revised), 91–98.

151. McCarthy and Allison, *Linebacker II* (Revised), 99–123; *SAC Participation in Linebacker II*, 170–75, 187–90, 202–5, 223–27, 230; Clodfelter, *Limits of Air Power*, 188.

152. McCarthy and Allison, *Linebacker II*, 121–39; McCarthy and Allison, *Linebacker II* (Revised), 126–44; *SAC Participation in Linebacker II*, 122; Tilford, *Crosswinds*, 168–69; Clodfelter, *Limits of Air Power*, 188–89; Clodfelter, "Nixon and the Air Weapon," 179–80.

153. McCarthy and Allison, *Linebacker II*, 145–53; McCarthy and Allison, *Linebacker II* (Revised), 155–66; *SAC Participation in Linebacker II*, 277, 322; Clodfelter, "Nixon and the Air Weapon," 180; Clodfelter, *Limits of Air Power*, 189.

154. Clodfelter, *Limits of Air Power*, 191–95; McCarthy and Allison, *Linebacker II* (Revised), 171–75; PACAF, *Linebacker II Air Force Bombing Survey*, 37; Berger, *United States Air Force in Southeast Asia*, 167. Note that the Seventh Air Force alone flew 613 tactical-combat sorties and 2,066 support sorties, losing one aircraft to a SAM, three to AAA, and two to MiGs. The fifteen B-52s downed meant that, based on the 729 sorties, the SAMs had a 1.7-to-1 kill rate and a 2.06-percent sortie loss rate. For more, see Futrell, *Ideas, Concepts, Doctrine*, 297–98.

155. Clodfelter, "Nixon and the Air Weapon," 180; Truong, *Vietcong Memoirs*, 226; Davidson, *Vietnam at War*, 728.

156. The original Vietnamese version of this quote is in Tra, *Concluding the 30-Year War*, 33. The English translation of this is also in Kolko, *Anatomy of a War*, 444–45. See also Clodfelter, *Limits of Air Power*, 196; and Clodfelter, "Nixon and the Air Weapon," 181.

157. Clodfelter, "Nixon and the Air Weapon," 181.

158. Clodfelter, "Nixon and the Air Weapon," 181.

159. Clodfelter, "Nixon and the Air Weapon," 182–83.

160. The main proponent of this argument was Adm. U. S. G. Sharp. See Sharp, *Strategy for Defeat*.

161. Head and Grinter, *Looking Back on the Vietnam War*, 119; Berger, *United States Air Force in Southeast Asia*, 167; Tilford, *Crosswinds*, 178–80; Thayer, *War without Fronts*, 26, 37.

162. Clodfelter, *Limits of Airpower*, 209; Rice, *Wars of the Third Kind*; Drew, "Vietnam, 'Wars of the Third Kind,' and Air Force Doctrine."

Chapter 7

1. Scalard, "Battle of Hamburger Hill: Battle Command in Difficult Terrain against a Determined Enemy," accessed 17 Sept. 2013 [hereafter "Hamburger Hill: Battle Command"].

2. Scalard, "Hamburger Hill: Battle Command"; Sheet 6441-IV, Series L7014, Defense Mapping Agency, 2070; Zaffiri, *Hamburger Hill*, 1. For book-length accounts of the battle, see DiConsiglio, *Vietnam: The Bloodbath at Hamburger Hill*; and Pimlott, *Vietnam: The Decisive Battles*. Among the important archival collections available online, see especially 3rd Brigade, 101st Airborne Division, "Combat Operations After Action Report—Summary Apache Snow," 25 June 1969, Virtual Vietnam Archive, VCA, http://www.virtual.vietnam.ttu.edu/; Tony Mabb, "Vietnam Eagles: Five Days in May," *Screaming Eagle* (Jan.–Feb. 2002): 39–43, Gary Jestes Collection, Virtual Vietnam Archive, VCA, updated 30 Aug. 2013, https://www.vietnam.ttu.edu/reports/images; John J. McGrath, *The Brigade: A History, Its Organization and Employment in the U.S. Army* (Fort Leavenworth, KS: Combat Studies Institute Press, 2004), 69–76, US Army Combined Arms Center, http://usacac.army.mil/CAC2/cgsc/carl/download/csipubs/Brigade-AHistory.pdf; and 101st Airborne Division, "Narrative, Operation 'Apache Snow,'" n.d., Johnson Vietnam Archive Collection, Virtual Vietnam Archive, VCA, updated 23 Aug. 2018, https://www.vietnam.ttu.edu/reports/images.php?img=/images/F0311/F031100081462.pdf; https://www.vietnam.ttu.edu/virtualarchive/.

3. Summers, "Battle of Hamburger Hill," accessed 12 June 2006.

4. Summers, "Battle of Hamburger Hill"; Zaffiri, *Hamburger Hill*, 5–10, 42–46, 47–52, 60–62.

5. Sams, "Fall of A Shau"; Majs. Bernard F. Fisher and Dafford W. Myers and Capts. Jon I. Lucas and Dennes B. Hague, interview by Kenneth Sams, 12 Mar. 1966, .

6. Department of Information, 2nd Air Division, Ken Sams, AFHRA, News Release, 20 Mar. 1966.

7. Boian, "Zais and Hamburger Hill," 25.

8. Boian, "Zais and Hamburger Hill," 25; Scalard, "Hamburger Hill: Battle Command"; Zaffiri, *Hamburger Hill*, 48–50.

9. Boian, "Zais and Hamburger Hill," 26–28; Zaffiri, *Hamburger Hill*, 49–50, 58, 186; "Vietnam Veteran Arthur Wiknik Describing His Experiences during the Battle of Hamburger Hill"; "Battle for Hamburger Hill," *Time*, 30 May 1969, accessed 17 Sept. 2013. The term "Rakkasans" literally means "falling down umbrellas." The 3/187 was activated as a glider airborne unit at Camp Mackall, North Carolina, on 25 February 1943. Since then, it has participated in every major war fought by the United States. Today its headquarters are located at Fort Campbell, Kentucky. The unit was one of the most decorated during the Vietnam War. For details, see Flanagan, *Rakkasans*. The 506th Infantry Regiment was originally formed as the 506th Parachute Infantry Regiment at Camp Toccoa, Georgia, on 10 June 1942. The camp was near Currahee Mountain, so the unit became known as the "Currahees." Today the regiment is headquartered at Fort Campbell, Kentucky. For more on the 506th, see Ambrose, *Band of Brothers*.

10. Boian, "Zais and Hamburger Hill," 29; Willbanks, "Hamburger Hill," 29.

11. Zaffiri, *Hamburger Hill*, 19–36.

12. Scalard, "Hamburger Hill: Battle Command."

13. Scalard, "Hamburger Hill: Battle Command"; Zaffiri, *Hamburger Hill*, 1–10.

14. Scalard, "Hamburger Hill: Battle Command."

15. Scalard, "Hamburger Hill: Battle Command"; Zaffiri, *Hamburger Hill*, 70–74, 90–98, 151.

16. Scalard, "Hamburger Hill: Battle Command"; Zaffiri, *Hamburger Hill*, 83–95; Boian, "Zais and Hamburger Hill," 30.

17. Zaffiri, *Hamburger Hill*, 95–98; Scalard, "Hamburger Hill: Battle Command."

18. Scalard, "Hamburger Hill: Battle Command."

19. Scalard, "Hamburger Hill: Battle Command." For a nonanalytical account by a frontline soldier, see Boccia, *Crouching Beast*.

20. Scalard, "Hamburger Hill: Battle Command"; Zaffiri, *Hamburger Hill*, 193–208.

21. Scalard, "Hamburger Hill: Battle Command."

22. Scalard, "Hamburger Hill: Battle Command."

23. Scalard, "Hamburger Hill: Battle Command"; Zaffiri, *Hamburger Hill*, 173–92.

24. Scalard, "Hamburger Hill: Battle Command"; Zaffiri, *Hamburger Hill*, 173–92.

25. Scalard, "Hamburger Hill: Battle Command"; Zaffiri, *Hamburger Hill*, 207.

26. Scalard, "Hamburger Hill: Battle Command"; Zaffiri, *Hamburger Hill*, 206–8; Boian, "Zais and Hamburger Hill," 32.

27. Scalard, "Hamburger Hill: Battle Command"; Zaffiri, *Hamburger Hill*, 208; Boian, "Zais and Hamburger Hill," 33; Lewy, *America in Vietnam*, 144.

28. Scalard, "Hamburger Hill: Battle Command"; Zaffiri, *Hamburger Hill*, 241–44.

29. Scalard, "Hamburger Hill: Battle Command"; Zaffiri, *Hamburger Hill*, 244; Boian, "Zais and Hamburger Hill," 34.

30. Wiest, *Vietnam's Forgotten Army*, 168.

31. Scalard, "Hamburger Hill: Battle Command"; Zaffiri, *Hamburger Hill*, 244–52; Boian, "Zais and Hamburger Hill," 35.

32. Zaffiri, *Hamburger Hill*, 273–80; "Foe Reported Back on Hamburger Hill," *New York Times*, 18 June 1969.

33. Scalard, "Hamburger Hill: Battle Command"; Zaffiri, *Hamburger Hill*, 204.

34. To read more about Sharbutt and this controversy, see Kirkpatrick, *1969*; and Lamb, "Reporters at Work: Giving a Battle a Name."

35. Lamb, "Reporters at Work: Giving a Battle a Name;" Jay Sharbutt, "U.S. Assault on Viet Mountain Continues, Despite Heavy Toll," *Washington Post*, 20 May 1969; Sharbutt, "Allied Troops Capture Mountain on Eleventh Try in Ten Days," ibid., 21 May 1969. Among the subsequent articles about the battle for Hill 937 were "Allies Operating in Ashau Valley," *New York Times*, 16 May 1969; and "GI's, in 10th Try, Fail to Rout Foe on Peak at Ashau," ibid., 20 May 1969.

36. Fred Farrar, "Army Defends Long Fight for Hill in South Vietnam," *Chicago Tribune*, 9 June 1969; Robert G. Kaiser, "Commanders Say Tactics Save Lives," *Washing-*

ton Post, 8 June 1969; B. Drummond Ayers Jr., "US Aides Defend Ap Bia Peak Battle," *New York Times*, 22 May 1969.

37. "US Troops Abandon 'Hamburger Hill,'" accessed 16 Sept. 2013.

38. Sen. Edward Kennedy, "Military Operations in Vietnam," *Congressional Record* (Washington, DC: Government Printing Office, 1969).

39. Boain, "Zais & Hamburger Hill," 37–38. Original from Maj. Gen. Melvin Zais, interview with Cols. William L. Golden and Richard C. Rice, 1977, Project 77–3, transcript Vol. 3, Senior Officers Oral History Program, US Army Heritage and Education Center, Carlisle Barracks, PA, 582.

40. Boain, "Zais & Hamburger Hill," 37–38.

41. "Battle for Hamburger Hill."

42. "U.S. Troops Abandon Hamburger Hill."

43. "The Faces of the American Dead in Vietnam: One Week's Toll," *Life*, 27 June 1969. For more on the Nixon Doctrine and Vietnamization, see Kissinger, *Ending the Vietnam War*, 81–82.

44. Sheehan, "Ap Bia Mountain."

45. Zaffiri, *Hamburger Hill*, 281–92.

46. Summers, "Battle of Hamburger Hill."

47. Summers, "Battle of Hamburger Hill."

48. Summers, "Battle of Hamburger Hill"; "Faces of the American Dead"; "Kennedy Criticizes the 'Hamburger Hill' Battle," accessed 20 Sept. 2013.

49. Summers, "Battle of Hamburger Hill."

Chapter 8

1. Tilford, *Crosswinds*, 143; Karnow, *Vietnam*, 640; Clodfelter, *Limits of Air Power*, 152–53; Mark, *Aerial Interdiction*, 365–66; Futrell, *Ideas, Concepts, Doctrine*, 267–68; Truong, *Vietcong Memoir*, 200–202, 210–13.

2. Truong, *Vietcong Memoir*, 200–213.

3. Kissinger, *White House Years*, 1109; Clodfelter, *Limits of Air Power*, 153.

4. Karnow, *Vietnam*, 640; Nixon, *RN*, 2:79, 259; Nixon, *In the Arena*, 335–37.

5. Palmer, "US Intelligence and Vietnam," 91; Mark, *Aerial Interdiction*, 368.

6. Nicholson, *USAF Response to the Spring 1972 NVN Offensive*, 21; Tilford, *Crosswinds*, 143.

7. Nicholson, *USAF Response to the Spring 1972 NVN Offensive*, 38, 67; Mark, *Air Interdiction*, 373; 7AF Hist, 1 July 1971–30 June 1972, 273–77; Clodfelter, "Nixon and the Air Weapon," 169; McCarthy and Allison, *Linebacker II*, 11. See also McCarthy and Allison, *Linebacker II* (Revised 1985).

8. Fulghum et al., *South Vietnam on Trial*, 120–22.

9. Fulghum et al., *South Vietnam on Trial*, 122.

10. Fulghum et al., *South Vietnam on Trial*, 122. For more on Linebacker I, see chapter 6 herein.

11. Palmer, *Summons of the Trumpet*, 310–11.

12. Fulghum et al., *South Vietnam on Trial*, 122; Andrade, *Trial by Fire*, 36–37.

13. Fulghum et al., *South Vietnam on Trial*, 122.

14. Andrade, *Trial by Fire*, 43–44.

15. Fulghum et al., *South Vietnam on Trial*, 122.

16. Fulghum et al., *South Vietnam on Trial*, 120–21.

17. Andrade, *Trial by Fire*, 27–28.

18. Andrade, *Trial by Fire*, 28.

19. Nalty, *Air War over South Vietnam, 1968–1975*, 326, 348–49.

20. "The Tet That Wasn't," editorial, *Life*, 24 Mar. 1972, 38.

21. Palmer, *Summons of the Trumpet*, 316.

22. Andrade, *Trial by Fire*, 46–48.

23. Andrade, *Trial by Fire*, 49, 67–68; Truong, *Easter Offensive*, 18.

24. Andrade, *Trial by Fire*, 52; Fulghum et al., *South Vietnam on Trial*, 129; Truong, *Easter Offensive*, 18–20.

25. Truong, *Easter Offensive*, 24–27; Brand, "Airpower and the 1972 Easter Offensive," 1–10.

26. Palmer, *Summons of the Trumpet*, 317.

27. Mann, *1972 Invasion of Military Region I*, 13–52; Liebchen, "Kontum," 28–44; Ringenbach and Melly, *Battle for An Loc*, 1–16.

28. Truong, *Easter Offensive*, 27–30; Andrade, *Trial by Fire*, 94–95.

29. Tilford, *Crosswinds*, 143–45.

30. Truong, *Easter Offensive*, 30–46; Fulghum et al., *South Vietnam on Trial*, 145–47; Andrade, *Trial by Fire*, 150.

31. Truong, *Easter Offensive*, 45–46; Sorley, *Better War*, 329–30.

32. Fulghum et al., *South Vietnam on Trial*, 150; Andrade, *Trial by Fire*, 171; Truong, *Easter Offensive*, 62, 166; Brand, "Airpower and the 1972 Easter Offensive," 10–11, 44–55.

33. Andrade, *Trial by Fire*, 181–87; Truong, *Easter Offensive*, 49–50.

34. Andrade, *Trial by Fire*, 187–90; Truong, *Easter Offensive*, 55–57; Brand, "Airpower and the 1972 Easter Offensive," 44–55.

35. Andrade, *Trial by Fire*, 190, 198; Truong, *Easter Offensive*, 57, 60.

36. Lavalle, *Air Power and the 1972 Spring Offensive*, 56–58.

37. Andrade, *Trial by Fire*, 176.

38. Truong, *Easter Offensive*, 65–67; Nalty, *Air War over South Vietnam*, 391.

39. Truong, *Easter Offensive*, 65–67, 89.

40. Truong, *Easter Offensive*, 70–71; Andrade, *Trial by Fire*, 211–13; Fulghum et al., *South Vietnam on Trial*, 178–80.

41. Fulghum et al., *South Vietnam on Trial*, 178–80.

42. For details of the air war during this period, see chapter 6.

43. Andrade, *Trial by Fire*, 212, 226.

44. Truong, *Easter Offensive*, 114–16; Andrade, *Trial by Fire*, 373.

45. Truong, *Easter Offensive*, 115–16.

46. Andrade, *Trial by Fire*, 439.

47. For more details on General Hung, see chapter 9.

48. Truong, *Easter Offensive*, 119; Fulghum et al., *South Vietnam on Trial*, 153.

49. Lavalle, *Air Power and the 1972 Spring Offensive*, 86; Momyer, *Vietnamese Air Force*, 50.

50. *Paris Match*, N12/13/15 aout 1972/3F (5 July 1972).

51. Andrade, *Trial by Fire*, 472; Momyer, *Vietnamese Air Force*, 47.

52. Tilford, *Crosswinds*, 146; Futrell, *Ideas, Concepts, Doctrine*, 275. For details, see Lavalle, *Air Power and the 1972 Spring Offensive*, 58, 98; Brand, "Airpower and the 1972 Easter Offensive," 12, 63–72; and Head, *Night Hunters*, 144–46.

53. Fulghum et al., *South Vietnam on Trial*, 154.

54. Lavalle, *Air Power and the 1972 Spring Offensive*, 104; Andrade, *Trial by Fire*, 499–500.

55. Andrade, *Trial by Fire*, 241.

56. Andrade, *Trial by Fire*, 241, 252.

57. Andrade, *Trial by Fire*, 252; Sheehan, *Bright Shining Lie*, 749.

58. Fulghum et al., *South Vietnam on Trial*, 156.

59. Sheehan, *Bright Shining Lie*, 759.

60. Sheehan, *Bright Shining Lie*, 783; Andrade, *Trial by Fire*, 286.

61. Andrade, *Trial by Fire*, 322; Tilford, *Crosswinds*, 146. For more details on the B-52 operations in and around Kontum, see chapter 6 herein. For more on Vann's role, see Sheehan, *Bright Shining Lie*, 783. For more details on the aerial combat at Kontum, see Brand, "Airpower and the 1972 Easter Offensive," 11, 56–62.

62. Andrade, *Trial by Fire*, 313.

63. Andrade, *Trial by Fire*, 318. The TOWs were first produced by Hughes Aircraft in 1970. For more on the TOW, see Gunston, *Illustrated Guide to Modern Missiles*, 155–58.

64. Andrade, *Trial by Fire*, 356; Liebchen, "Kontum," 88–89.

65. Andrade, *Trial by Fire*, 356–58, 363; Sheehan, *Bright Shining Lie*, 786.

66. Nalty, *Air War over South Vietnam*, 358. For more on LORAN, see William T. Dickinson, *Engineering Evaluation of the LORANC*; Jerry Proc, *LORANA, Hyperbolic Radionavigation Systems* (Etobicoke, ON, 2012).

67. Tilford, *Setup*, 223–24; Morocco, *Rain of Fire*, 169–70; Davidson, *Vietnam at War*, 673, 701–2; Special Study, "History of Linebacker Operations," 10 May 1972–23 October 1972, HQ PACAF, 1973, K740.04, U.S. Air Force Historic Research Center, Maxwell AFB, AL, 3–5.

68. Lavalle, *Air Power and the 1972 Spring Offensive*, 17–27; Tilford, *Setup*, 224; Nalty, *Air War over South Vietnam*, 333; Head, *Night Hunters*, 131–42; Brand, "Airpower and the 1972 Easter Offensive," 77–98. For studies of the AC-119G/K fixed-wing gunships, see Head, *Shadow and Stinger*.

69. Lavalle, *Air Power and the 1972 Spring Offensive*, 34–35. For details on air operations during Freedom Train and Linebacker I, see chapter 6 herein.

70. Lavalle, *Air Power and the 1972 Spring Offensive*, 44–46; Sorley, *Better War*, 326.

71. Nalty, *Air War over South Vietnam*, 369–70.

72. Tilford, *Setup*, 228; Mark, *Aerial Interdiction*, 374–75.

73. Tilford, *Setup*, 227–29; Mark, *Aerial Interdiction*, 375–76; Head, *War from above the Clouds*, 65–67.

74. Tilford, *Setup*, 244–45. For a detailed account of Linebacker I and II, see ibid., 227–48; Head, *War from above the Clouds*, 65–86; and Mark, *Aerial Interdiction*, 377–98. See also chapter 6 herein.

75. Palmer, *Summons of the Trumpet*, 324.

76. Truong, *Easter Offensive*, 158.

77. Tilford, *Crosswinds*, 160–63. For details on the lead in to Linebacker II and the Paris peace talks, see chapters 6 and 9 herein.

78. Tilford, *Crosswinds*, 163; Mark, *Aerial Interdiction*, 399.

79. Andrade, *Trial by Fire*, 529–31.

80. Truong, *Easter Offensive*, 536.

81. Fulghum et al., *South Vietnam on Trial*, 183.

82. Tilford, *Crosswinds*, 163–72; Head, *War from above the Clouds*, 72–87. For a detailed account of Linebacker II, see chapter 6 herein.

Chapter 9

1. For a detailed account of the last days of the Republic of Vietnam, see Butler, *Fall of Saigon*.

2. Pribbenow and Vieth, "Fighting Is an Art," 191–200.

3. For details on these matters, see Lipsman, Weiss, et al., *False Peace*, 37; and Vien, *Final Collapse*, 11. Cao Van Vien was the defense minister of South Vietnam.

4. Snepp, *Decent Interval*, 91–93.

5. Le Gro, *Vietnam from Cease Fire to Capitulation*, 96–122; Willbanks, *Abandoning Vietnam*, 192, 210.

6. Willbanks, *Abandoning Vietnam*, 193; Willbanks, "Last 55 Days," 1–3.

7. For more on aid, see Joes, *War for South Vietnam*, 125.

8. Khuyen, *RVNAF*, 387.

9. Willbanks, *Abandoning Vietnam*, 199.

10. Dougan, Fulghum, et al., *Fall of the South*, 11.

11. Dougan, Fulghum, et al., *Fall of the South*, 11; Dung, *Our Great Spring Victory*, 12; Willbanks, *Abandoning Vietnam*, 221.

12. Dougan, Fulghum, et al., *Fall of the South*, 17; Tran, *Concluding the 30-Year War*, 166–93. See also the Combined Studies Institute version of Tran's memoir, published as Southeast Asia Report 1247 on 2 February 1983.

13. Vien, *Final Collapse*, 23; Le Gro, *Vietnam from Cease Fire to Capitulation*, 28; Willbanks, *Abandoning Vietnam*, 190.

14. Willbanks, *Abandoning Vietnam*, 205; Dougan, Fulghum, et al., *Fall of the South*, 26.

15. Dougan, Fulghum, et al., *Fall of the South*, 48; Le Gro, *Vietnam from Cease Fire to Capitulation*, 80–89.

16. Willbanks, *Abandoning Vietnam*, 232; Marc Leepson, ed., *Webster's New World Dictionary of the Vietnam War*, with Helen Hannaford (New York: Simon & Schuster, 1999), 522–24; Report, by CIA, "Communist Military and Economic Aid to North Vietnam, 1970–1974 (declassified in 2005).

17. Prados, *Blood Road*, 371–73. For a pro-PAVN view of the Ho Chi Minh Trail, see Morris and Hill, *History of the Ho Chi Minh Trail*.

18. Momyer, *Vietnamese Air Force*, 70–71.

19. Momyer, *Vietnamese Air Force*, 55–56.

20. Willbanks, *Abandoning Vietnam*, 189–94.

21. Head, "Significance of Dien Bien Phu," 23–24.

22. Isaacs, *Without Honor*, 333–35; Thai, *Liberation of South Vietnam*, 36–37, 73. Thai's book was published after the general's death in 1986. For an anticommunist view of this period, see Sarin and Dvoretsky, *Alien Wars*; and Veith, *Black April* (published by a press with a very conservative leaning).

23. Pribbenow, "North Vietnam's Final Offensive," 58–71.

24. Willbanks, *Abandoning Vietnam*, 225; Vien, *Memoirs*, 58–60.

25. Willbanks, *Abandoning Vietnam*, 224–26.

26. Vien, *Final Collapse*, 63–65; Le Gro, *Vietnam from Cease Fire to Capitulation*, 136–37; Willbanks, "Last 55 Days," 2–3.

27. Vien, *Final Collapse*, 68; Willbanks, "Last 55 Days," 3–4.

28. Military Institute of Vietnam, *Victory in Vietnam*, 360; Willbanks, "Last 55 Days," 4–5.

29. Khuyen, *RVNAF*, 27. This specific account is recounted in Tra, *Concluding the 30-Year War*, 136–38. For specifics on the lead up to Xuan Loc, see ibid., 136–65; and Willbanks, "Last 55 Days," 5–6.

30. Vien, *Final Collapse*, 30–32; Military Institute of Vietnam, *Victory in Vietnam*, 364; Willbanks, "Last 55 Days," 6.

31. Vien, *Final Collapse*, 69–70.

32. Vien, *Final Collapse*, 72.

33. Isaacs, *Without Honor*, 314–15.

34. Isaacs, *Without Honor*, 320.

35. Wallbanks, *Abandoning Vietnam*, 229; Willbanks, "Last 55 Days," 6–7.

36. Vien, *Final Collapse*, 78.

37. Vien, *Final Collapse*, 76.

38. Vien, *Final Collapse*, 78.

39. Vien, *Final Collapse*, 80–82.

40. Dawson, *55 Days*, 58; Willbanks, "Last 55 Days," 7–9.

41. Dougan, Fulghum, et al., *Fall of the South*, 52; Willbanks, "Last 55 Days," 8–10.

42. Dougan, Fulghum, et al., *Fall of the South*, 54–55; Vien, *Mamoirs*, 94; Willbanks, "Last 55 Days," 11–13.

43. Willbanks, "Last 55 Days," 13–16; Dung, *Our Great Spring Victory*, 95.

44. Dougan, Fulghum, et al., *Fall of the South*, 59–60; Hosmer, Kellen, and Jenkins, *Fall of South Vietnam*, 95; Olson and Roberts, *Where the Last Domino Fell*, 251.

45. Willbanks, "Last 55 Days," 15; Olson and Roberts, *Where the Last Domino Fell*, 259.

46. Vien, *Memoirs*, 75–76, 118; Le Gro, *Vietnam from Cease Fire to Capitulation*, 160–62.

47. Dougan, Fulghum, et al., *Fall of the South*, 68–69. Da Nang is the largest city in central Vietnam and one of its important ports. With mountains on one side and the South China Sea on the other, it is 472 miles south of Hanoi and 600 miles north of Saigon (now Ho Chi Minh City).

48. Dougan, Fulghum, et al., *Fall of the South*, 68–69.

49. Vien, *Final Collapse*, 102.

50. Vien, *Final Collapse*, 104; Dougan, Fulghum, et al., *Fall of the South*, 70.

51. Dougan, Fulghum, et al., *Fall of the South*, 70–71.

52. Dougan, Fulghum, et al., *Fall of the South*, 73–74; Willbanks, "Last 55 Days," 16–19.

53. Hosmer, Kellen, and Jenkins, *Fall of South Vietnam*, 109.

54. Vien, *Final Collapse*, 109.

55. Vien, *Final Collapse*, 108–13; Willbanks, *Abandoning Vietnam*, 251–53; Willbanks, "Last 55 Days," 19–22; Dougan, Fulghum, et al., *Fall of the South*, 83. For more on South Vietnamese airpower, see Momyer, *Vietnamese Air Force*, 76.

56. Isaacs, *Without Honor*, 380.

57. Willbanks, *Abandoning Vietnam*, 251; Willbanks, "Last 55 Days," 22–27; Dawson, *55 Days*, 66, 234, 238, 239.

58. Willbanks, "Last 55 Days," 27; Isaacs, *Without Honor*, 414–15.

59. Dawson, *55 Days*, 59; Thach and Khang, *War of Resistance*, 372–76.

60. Tra, *Concluding the 30-Year War*, 166–93; Dung, *Our Great Spring Victory*, 134–37.

61. Dawson, *55 Days*, 238.

62. Willbanks, "Last 55 Days," 27–28; Dai, *4th Army Corps*, 112. For more details, see Bieu, *Army at the Tây Nguyên Front—3rd Army Corps*.

63. Thach and Khang, *War of Resistance*, 381.

64. Willbanks, "Last 55 Days," 27; Hao, *Tragic Chapter*, 208.

65. Davidson, *Vietnam at War*, 767–94.

66. Davidson, *Vietnam at War*, 767–94.

67. Hao, *Tragic Chapter*, 219.

68. Dai, *4th Army Corps*, 102; Thien and Linh, *Battles on the Doorstep of Saigon*, 3–5.

69. Dai, *4th Army Corps*, 104–5; Davidson, *Vietnam at War*, 780–88.

70. Dawson, *55 Days*, 63; Snepp, *Disastrous Retreat*, 75.

71. Hao, *Tragic Chapter*, 208; Dawson, *55 Days*, 59.

72. Czechoslovakian Committee for Solidarity with Afro-Asian Countries, Printed by Ruch Liberec, 43 Item 2390811003, File, Vietnam: The Collapse of the Neo-Colonial Regime, Doug Pike Collection, Unit 11 Monographs, 43–47, Xuan Loc and fall of Saigon, VCA.

73. Thach and Khang, *War of Resistance*, 372–76.

74. Snepp, *Decent Interval*, 275.

75. Dougan, Fulghum, et al., *Fall of the South*, 113; Dung, *Our Great Spring Victory*, 160.

76. Hao, *Tragic Chapter*, 228–29; Cam, *Journey of Ten Thousand Days*, 168.

77. Willbanks, "Last 55 Days," 28; Ban, *7th Infantry Division*, 146.

78. Message, Defense Attaché, US Embassy in Saigon, Gen. Smith to Gen. Brown, CJCS, "The Battle of Long Khanh [Xuan Loc]," 130351Z Apr. 1975, Box 8, "Saigon to Washington, April 9–28, 1975 (1)," NSA, Saigon Embassy Files of Amb. Graham Martin, Gerald R. Ford Presidential Library, Grand Rapids, MI.

79. Telegram, Amb. Graham Martin, Saigon, to American Embassy, Jidda, Saudi Arabia, 9 Apr. 1975, Box 8 "Saigon to Washington, April 9–28, 1975 (1)," NSA, Saigon Embassy Files of Amb. Graham Martin, Ford Presidential Library.

80. Ban, *7th Infantry Division*, 146; Thach and Khang, *War of Resistance*, 382; Cam, *Journey of Ten Thousand Days*, 172.

81. Willbanks, "Last 55 Days," 28; Dai, *4th Army Corps*, 135.

82. Dai, *4th Army Corps*, 136–37; Thach and Khang, *War of Resistance*, 384. The CBU-55 was an FAE cluster bomb developed during the Vietnam War by the US Army; it was used only once. Unlike most incendiaries, which contained napalm or phosphorus, the 750-pound CBU-55 was fueled primarily by propane. It was one of the more powerful conventional weapons used in Vietnam. The CBU-55 had three main compartments, with propane, a blend of other gases to act as an oxidizing agent, and an explosive. There were two variations. The CBU-55/B consisted of three BLU-73A/B FAE submunitions in a SUU-49/B Tactical Munitions Dispenser, while the CBU-55A/B had three BLU-73A/B submunitions in a SUU-49A/B dispenser. The SUU-49/B dispenser could be carried only by helicopters or low-speed aircraft, whereas the SUU-49A/B was redesigned with a strong back and folding tailfins so that it could be delivered by high-speed aircraft too.

83. Message, Amb. Graham Martin to Gen. Brent Scowcroft, 0700 Saigon time, 13 Apr. 1975, (declassified 21 Sept. 1994, NARA), Box 8, "Saigon to Washington, April 9–28, 1975 (1)," NSA, Saigon Embassy Files of Amb. Graham Martin, Ford Presidential Library.

84. Dai, *4th Army Corps*, 138–89.

85. Dung, *Our Great Spring Victory*, 167; Le Gro, *Vietnam from Cease Fire to Capitulation*, 173.

86. Telegram, Amb. Graham Martin to State Dept. and NSC 4884, 13 Apr. 1975, (declassified, 24 Aug. 1994, NARA), Box 8, "Saigon to Washington, April 9–28, 1975 (1)," NSA, Saigon Embassy Files of Amb. Graham Martin, Ford Presidential Library.

87. Telegram, Amb. Graham Martin to State Dept. and NSC 4884, 13 Apr. 1975.

88. Dougan, Fulghum, et al., *Fall of the South*, 130.

89. Dung, *Our Great Spring Victory*, 167–68.

90. Hosmer, Kellen, and Jenkins, *Fall of South Vietnam*, 133; Kiet, *Narratives of Saigon Generals*, 181–82.

91. Duong, *Tragedy of the Vietnam War*, 206; Fricker, "Crosswind," 120.

92. Willbanks, "Last 55 Days," 30. Original in Letter, Pres. Nguyen Van Thieu to Pres. Gerald R. Ford, in Hung and Schecter, *Palace File*, 320–27.

93. Kiet, *Narratives of Saigon Generals*, 181–83; Thach and Khang, *War of Resistance*, 369, 392–93.

94. Willbanks, "Last 55 Days," 30–32; Le Gro, *Vietnam from Cease Fire to Capitulation*, 173; Willbanks, *Abandoning Vietnam*, 400–406.

95. Snepp, *Decent Interval*, 99; Thach and Khang, *War of Resistance*, 369, 392–93; Vien, *Final Collapse*, 132.

96. Westmoreland, *Soldier Reports*, 242.

97. Le Gro, *Vietnam from Cease Fire to Capitulation*, 173.

98. Dawson, *55 Days*, 66; Hao, *Tragic Chapter*, 241–42; Dai, *4th Army Corps*, 138–89; Willbanks, "Last 55 Days," 30–32.

99. Summers, "America's Bitter End in Vietnam," accessed 28 Mar. 2013.

100. Willbanks, *Abandoning Vietnam*, 255, 402–8.

101. Isaacs, *Without Honor*, 408.

102. Dougan, Fulghum, et al., *Fall of the South*, 127.

103. Willbanks, *Abandoning Vietnam*, 257.

104. Dougan, Fulghum, et al., *Fall of the South*, 100; Vien, *Final Collapse*, 142.

105. Dougan, Fulghum, et al., *Fall of the South*, 139.

106. Willbanks, *Abandoning Vietnam*, 271; Dung, *Our Great Spring Victory*, 184–87.

107. Willbanks, *Abandoning Vietnam*, 257–59; Vien, *Final Collapse*, 135–38.

108. Willbanks, *Abandoning Vietnam*, 258; Dougan, Fulghum, et al., *Fall of the South*, 102–3, 142–44; Vien, *Final Collapse*, 146; Isaacs, *Without Honor*, 433–39.

109. Willbanks, "Last 55 Days," 32–33; Dougan, Fulghum, et al., *Fall of the South*, 158; Tobin, Lehr, and Hilgenberg, *Last Flight from Saigon*, 21–22.

110. Willbanks, *Abandoning Vietnam*, 275; Willbanks, "Last 55 Days," 34–36.

111. Willbanks, "Last 55 Days," 37.

112. Willbanks, "Last 55 Days," 37; Momyer, *Vietnamese Air Force*, 79.

113. Dougan, Fulghum, et al., *Fall of the South*, 172.

114. Tobin, Lehr, and Hilgenberg, *Last Flight from Saigon*, 122.

115. Willbanks, "Last 55 Days," 38; Isaacs, *Without Honor*, 467.

116. Willbanks, "Last 55 Days," 38.

117. Dougan, Fulghum, et al., *Fall of the South*, 175.

118. McNamara, *Escape with Honor*, 129–49.

119. Isaacs, *Without Honor*, 500.

120. Vien, *Final Collapse*, 7.

121. Isaacs, *Without Honor*, 502.

122. Willbanks, *Abandoning Vietnam*, 278.

123. Hinh, *Vietnamization and the Cease-Fire*, 190.

124. Kinnard, *War Managers*, 145.

125. Kolko, *Anatomy of a War*, 380.

126. Willbanks, *Abandoning Vietnam*, 278.

127. Isaacs, *Without Honor*, 502.

128. Gabor Boritt, ed., *Why the Confederacy Lost* (New York: Oxford University Press, 1992), 19.

129. Dung, *Our Great Spring Victory*, 62.

130. CIA/DIA, "Communist Military and Economic Aid to North Vietnam, 1970–1974," 1–7.

Conclusion

1. Tilford, *Setup*, 154–55. Tilford was one of only a handful of officers who served in the war to write about it while still on active duty.

2. Diem, "My Recollections of the Tet Offensive," 131–32.

3. Scalard, "Battle of Hamburger Hill: Battle Command," accessed 17 Sept. 2013.

4. Dawson, *55 Days*, 238.

5. Dougan, Fulghum, et al., *Fall of the South*, 175.

Bibliography

The following is a composite of the major works and sources used by the author.

Archival and Library Sources

Rather than include each detailed archival item used in this work, the reader should note that the majority of primary materials used in this work are located at the 78th Air Base Wing History Archives, Robins Air Force Base, Georgia. This repository contains a large number of Vietnam-era holdings, particularly Warner Robins Air Materiel Area and SAC documents, histories, and studies. Among the other sources used were messages, letters, and memos between key political and military players involved in the Vietnam War. These also include military situation reports; end-of-tour reports; site-team reports; mission reports; background reports; Air Force Material Command, Service (Army, Navy, United States Air Force, etc.), Interviews, Briefings; and statements before Congress and other government agencies. Many of these primary sources are found in the files of various government agencies, including the Departments of State, Defense, Air Force, Army, and Navy as well as the JCS and the US Senate and House of Representatives, including the Committees on Foreign Affairs and Armed Services. Other documents came from the National Archives in College Park, Maryland; the Kennedy, Johnson, Nixon, Ford, and Carter Presidential Libraries; the archival holdings at the Air Force Historical Research Agency at Maxwell Air Force Base, Alabama (AFHRA); and the Navy War College in Newport, Rhode Island. I used documents and reports (all declassified) from the CIA, the Defense Intelligence Agency, and other government intelligence agencies. Of equal value was finding original documents at multiple and various internet sites. Specific documents and sources may be found in each chapter's endnotes.

Secondary Sources

These include books; journal, magazine, and newspaper articles; government publications; monographs; theses and dissertations; published interviews; and chapters in edited anthologies. Government publications are defined as published reports by government agencies as well as institutions or individuals contracted by the US government. Also included are official histories such as special studies, pamphlets, monographs, special publications, periodic and annual histories, CHECO reports, and Corona Harvest studies.

Ambrose, Stephen. *Band of Brothers: E Company, 506th Regiment, 101st Airborne from Normandy to Hitler's Eagles Nest.* New York: Simon and Schuster, 2001.

Anderson, David L. *The Columbia Guide to the Vietnam War.* New York: Columbia University Press, 2004.

Andrade, Dale. *Trial by Fire: The 1972 Easter Offensive, America's Last Vietnam Battle.* New York: Hippocrene Books, 1994.

Ankony, Robert C. *Lurps: A Ranger's Diary of Tet, Khe Sanh, A Shau, and Quang Tri.* Rev. ed. Lanham, MD: Rowman and Littlefield, 2009.

Arnold, James R. *The Tet Offensive, 1968.* Westport, CT: Praeger, 1990.

BACM Research. "Vietnam War: Tet Offensive." (Downloadable collection of CIA, Defense Department, and State Department documents; a South Vietnamese Army history of Tet; and photographs by the US Army and ARVN.) PaperlessArchives.com. http://www.paperlessarchives.com/vw_tet_offensive.html. Downloaded 25 June 2014.

Ballard, Jack S. *The United States Air Force in Southeast Asia: Development and Employment of Fixed Wing Gunships, 1962–1972.* Washington, DC: Office of Air Force History, 1982.

Ban, Tran Xuan. *History of the 7th Infantry Division.* Hanoi: People's Army Publishing House, 2006.

Banks, Herbert C. *1st Cavalry Division: A Spur Ride through the 20th Century "From Horses to the Digital Battlefield."* Atlanta: Turner, 2003.

Bass, Thomas. *The Spy Who Loved Us: The Vietnam War and the Life of Pham Xuan An.* New York: Perseus Books, 2009.

"The Battle for Hamburger Hill." *Time*, 30 May 1969. http://content.time .com/time/magazine/article/0,9171,840113,00.html.

"Battle of Hue." *Time*, 16 February 1968.

Bennett, James, ed. *Weapons of War: Jet Fighters Inside and Out*. New York: Rosen, 2011.

Berger, Carl, ed. *The United States Air Force in Southeast Asia, 1961–1973: An Illustrated Account*. Washington, DC: Office of Air Force History, 1984.

Berman, Larry. *Perfect Spy: The Incredible Double Life of Pham Xuan An*. New York: Harper Collins, 2007.

Bieu, Nguyen Van. *The Army at the Tây Nguyên Front—3rd Army Corps*. Hanoi: People's Army Publishing House, 2005.

Boccia, Frank. *The Crouching Beast: A United States Army Lieutenant's Account of the Battle for Hamburger Hill, May 1969*. Jefferson, NC: McFarland, 2013.

Boettcher, Thomas D. *Vietnam: The Valor and the Sorrow*. Boston: Little, Brown, 1985.

Boian, Maj. Kelly. "Major General Melvin Zais and Hamburger Hill." School of Advanced Military Studies Monograph. US Army Command and General Staff College, Fort Leavenworth, Kansas, 2012.

Boritt, Gabor, ed. *Why the Confederacy Lost*. New York: Oxford University Press, 1992.

Bowden, Mark. *Hue*. New York: Grove, 2017.

Braestrup, Peter. *Big Story: How the American Press and Television Reported and Interpreted the Crisis of Tet in Vietnam and Washington*. New Haven, CT: Yale University Press, 1983.

Brand, Lt. Col. Matthew C. "Airpower and the 1972 Easter Offensive." Master's thesis, US Army Command and General Staff College, Webster University, Saint Louis, Missouri, 1997. Ft. Leavenworth, Kansas, 2007. https://apps.dtic.mil/dtic/tr/fulltext/u2/a471201.pdf.

Brown, Harold. SECAF Policy Statement. "Supplement to Air Force Policy Letter for Commanders, No. 3–68." March 1966.

Brush, Peter. "The Battle of Khe Sanh, 1968." In Gilbert and Head, *Tet Offensive*, 191–214.

Bundy, McGeorge. "A Policy of Sustained Reprisal." Annex A (7 February 1965). In *United States-Vietnam Relations, 1945–1967*. Washington, DC: Government Printing Office, 1971.

Bundy, William. "Draft Position Paper on Southeast Asia." 29 November 1964. In *Pentagon Papers*, Senator Gravel edition, 3:677–83.

Butler, David. *The Fall of Saigon: Scenes from the Sudden End of a Long War.* New York: Simon and Schuster, 1985.

Buzzanco, Robert. "The Myth of Tet: American Failure and the Politics of War." In Gilbert and Head, *Tet Offensive,* 231–58.

Cable, Larry. *Conflicts of Myths: The Development of American Counterinsurgency Doctrine and the Vietnam War.* New York: New York University Press, 1986.

———. "Don't Bother Me with the Facts; I've Made Up My Mind: The Tet Offensive in the Context of Intelligence and US Strategy." In Gilbert and Head, *Tet Offensive,* 167–80.

———. "Everything Is Perfect and Getting Better: The Myths and Measures of the American Ground War in Indochina, 1965–1968." In Head and Grinter, *Looking Back on the Vietnam War.*

———. "The Operation Was a Success, but the Patient Died: The Air War in Vietnam, 1964–1969." In Showalter and Albert, *American Dilemma,* 109–58.

———. "Playing in the Sandbox: Doctrine, Combat, and Outcome on the Ground." In *The Eagle in the Desert: Looking Back on US Involvement in the Persian Gulf War,* edited by William P. Head and Earl H. Tilford, Jr., 175–200. Westport, CT: Praeger, 1996.

———. *Unholy Grail: The US and the Wars in Vietnam, 1965–1968.* London: Routledge, 1991.

Cam, Hoang. *Journey of Ten Thousand Days.* Hanoi: People's Army Publishing House, 2001,

CBS News. *The Uncounted Enemy: A Vietnam Deception.* Aired 23 January 1982.

CIA report. "Communist Military & Economic Aid to NVN, 1970–1974." Declassified 2005.

CIA/DIA. "Communist Military and Economic Aid to North Vietnam, 1970–1974." Memo/Report. Washington, DC: Bureau of Intelligence and Research, Department of State, 1975.

CHECO Project report. Southeast Asia. "Special Report, Operation Silver Bayonet." K717.0413–2.9. 28 November 1965. Declassified 26 December 1995.

Clarke, Bruce B. G. *Expendable Warriors—The Battle of Khe Sanh and the Vietnam War.* Westport, CT: Praeger International Security, 2007.

Clarke, Jeffrey J. "Foreword." In Villard, *Tet Offensive Battles of Quang Tri City and Hue,* v.

Clarke, Jeffrey J. Chief of Military History, US Army Center of Military History. "Foreword." In Villard, *Tet Offensive Battles of Quang Tri City and Hue*. Ft. Leslie J. McNair, DC: US Army Center of Military History (CMH). 9 February 2008, v.

Clifford, Clark. *Counsel to the President: A Memoir.* With Richard Holbrooke. New York: Random House, 1991.

Clodfelter, Mark. *The Limits of Air Power: The American Bombing of North Vietnam.* New York: Free Press, 1989.

———. "Nixon and the Air Weapon." In Showalter and Albert, *American Dilemma.*

Cole, James Lawrence. "Fixed-Wing Gunships in Southeast Asia." CHECO/Corona Harvest Division, CHECO Project. July 1969-June 1971.

Cole, Marvin. "Fixed-Wing Gunships in SEA (July 1969-July 1971)." Hickam AFB, HI: Headquarters, Pacific Air Forces Directorate of Operations Analysis, 1971.

Cong, Nguyen Minh. Video interview on WGBHTV, Boston. 1968.

Cooling, Norman L. "Hue City 1968: Winning a Battle while Losing a War." *Marine Corps Gazette.* July 2001. USMC Association and Foundation. https://www.mca-marines.org/gazette/hue-city-1968-winning-battle-while-losing-war. Page removed.

Corgan, Michael T. "Clausewitz's *On War* and the Gulf War." In *The Eagle in the Desert: Looking Back on US Involvement in the Persian Gulf War*, edited by William P. Head and Earl H. Tilford Jr., 269–89. Westport, CT: Praeger, 1996.

Corona Harvest Project, PACAF. "United States Air Force Operations in Laos, 1 Jan 70–30 Jun 71." Maxwell AFB, AL, 1971.

Corona Harvest Project, PACAF. "USAF Air Operations against NVN, 1 Jul 71–30 Jun 72." Maxwell AFB, AL, 1973.

Corona Harvest Project. "A Chronology of Important Airpower Events in Southeast Asia, 1950–1968." Maxwell AFB, AL: Aerospace Studies Institute, Air University, 1 May 1969.

Correll, John T. "Rolling Thunder." *Air Force Magazine* 88, no. 3 (March 2005): 1.

Cross, Brig. Gen. Richard G. "End-of-Tour Report." 22 January 1973. File K740.131.2. AFHRA.

Cubbage, Thomas L., II. Review of *The Tet Offensive: Intelligence Failure in War*, by James J. Wirtz. *Conflict Quarterly* 13, no. 3 (Summer 1993): 7879.

Czechoslovakian Committee for Solidarity with Afro-Asian Countries. Printed by Ruch Liberec. Item 2390811003. File, Vietnam: The Collapse of the Neo-Colonial Regime, Unit 11 Monographs, Doug Pike Collection. Vietnam Center and Archive, Texas Tech University, Lubbock, Texas.

Dai, Ho Son. *History of the 4th Army Corps—Cuu Long Corps*. Hanoi: People's Army Publishing, 2004.

Davidson, Philip B. *Vietnam at War: The History, 1946–1975*. Novato, CA: Presidio, 1988. Reprint, New York: Oxford University Press, 1991.

Dawson, Alan. *55 Days: The Fall of South Vietnam*. Englewood Cliffs, NJ: Prentice-Hall, 1977.

Dean, Lt. Col. David J. *The Air Force Role in Low-Intensity Conflict*. Maxwell AFB, AL: Air University Press, 1986.

Department of Defense. *Combat Area Casualties Current File: Combat Area, Southeast Asian*. Washington, DC: National Archives, 1993.

Dickson, Paul. *The Electronic Battlefield*. Bloomington: Indiana University Press, 1976.

Dickinson, William T. *Engineering Evaluation of the LORANC Navigation System*. Washington, DC: Jansky and Bailey for the US Coast Guard, 1959.

DiConsiglio, John. *Vietnam: The Bloodbath at Hamburger Hill*. New York: Franklin Watts, 2010.

Diem, Bui. *In the Jaws of History*. With David Chanoff. Boston: Houghton Mifflin, 1987.

———. "My Recollections of the Tet Offensive." In Gilbert and Head, *Tet Offensive*, 125–34.

———. "Reflections on the Vietnam War: The Views of a Vietnamese on Vietnamese-American Misconceptions." In Head and Grinter, *Looking Back on the Vietnam War*, 241–48.

Dougan, Clark, David Fulghum, et al. *The Fall of the South*. The Vietnam Experience. Boston: Boston Publishing, 1985.

Dougan, Clark, Stephen Weiss, et al. *Nineteen Sixty-Eight*. The Vietnam Experience. Boston: Boston Publishing, 1983.

Doyle, Edward, Samuel Lipsman, Terrance Maitland, et al. *The North*. The Vietnam Experience. Boston: Boston Publishing, 1986.

Drew, Dennis. *Rolling Thunder 1965: Anatomy of a Failure*. Report AUAR-ICP-86-3. 1986. Abridged. Air University. http://www.au.af.mil/au/awc/awcgate/readings/drew2.htm.

———. "Vietnam, 'Wars of the Third Kind,' and Air Force Doctrine." Paper presented at Seminar on the Vietnam War, Center for the Study of the Vietnam Conflict, Texas Tech University, Lubbock, 18–21 April 1996.

Duiker, William J. *The Communist Road to Power in Vietnam.* Boulder, CO: Westview, 1996.

———. *Sacred War: Nationalism and Revolution in a Divided Vietnam.* New York: McGraw-Hill, 1995.

Dung, Van Tien. *Our Great Spring Victory: An Account of the Liberation of South Vietnam.* Translated by John Spragens Jr. New York: Monthly Review Press, 1977.

Dunham, George R. *U.S. Marines in Vietnam: The Bitter End, 1973–1975.* Marine Corps Vietnam Operational Historical Series. Quantico, VA: USMC Association, 1990.

Duong, Van Nguyen. *The Tragedy of the Vietnam War: A South Vietnamese Officer's Analysis.* Jefferson, NC: McFarland, 2008.

Duong, Hao. *A Tragic Chapter.* Hanoi: People's Army Publishing House, 1980.

Ehrlich, Richard S. "America's Secret Plan to Nuke Vietnam & Laos." 17 April 2008. http://www.scoop.co.nz/stories/HL0804/S00228/americas-secret-plan-to-nuke-vietnam-laos.htm.

Elliott, David W. P. *The Vietnamese War: Revolution and Social Change in the Mekong Delta, 1930–1975.* 2 vols. Armonk, NY: M. E. Sharp, 2003; concise ed., 2007.

Enthoven, Alain C., and Wayne K. Smith. *How Much Is Enough? Shaping the Defense Program, 1961–1969.* New York: Harper and Row, 1971.

Evans, Col. D. L., director of intelligence. "Task Force Alpha, End-of-Tour Report." 6 July 1972. File 10015110. AFHRA.

"The Faces of the American Dead in Vietnam: One Week's Toll." *Life,* 27 June 1969.

Fall, Bernard. *Hell in a Very Small Place.* Philadelphia: Lippincott, 1967.

Farrar, Fred. "Army Defends Long Fight for Hill in South Vietnam." *Chicago Tribune,* 9 June 1969.

"Fight for a Citadel." *Time,* 1 March 1968.

Fitzgerald, Frances. *Fire in the Lake: The Vietnamese and the Americans in Vietnam.* New York: Vintage Books, 1972.

Flanagan, E. M., Jr. *Rakkasans.* Novato, CA: Presidio, 1997.

Fletcher, Elton "Larry." *Shadows of Saigon: Air Commandos in Southeast Asia.* Philadelphia: Xlibris, 2001.

Frankum, Ronald. *Like Rolling Thunder: The Air War in Vietnam, 1964–1975*. Lanham, MD: Rowan and Littlefield, 2005.

Fricker, John. "Crosswind." *Aeroplane* 34, no. 10 (October 2006): 120.

Fulghum, David, et al. *South Vietnam on Trial: Mid-1970 to 1972*. Boston: Boston Publishing, 1984.

Fuller, Kenneth C., Bruce Smith, and Merle Atkins. "'Rolling Thunder' and Bomb Damage to Bridges." CIA Analysis. Declassified 2 July 1996. CIA Center for the Study of Intelligence. Last updated 4 August 2011. https://www.cia.gov/library/center-for-the-study-of-intelligence/kent-csi/v0113n04/html/v13i4a01p_0001.htm.

Futrell, Robert Frank. *Ideas, Concepts, Doctrine: Basic Thinking in the United States Air Force 1907–1960*. Vol. 2. Maxwell AFB, AL: Air University Press, 1989.

Galloway, Joseph L. "Ia Drang—The Battle That Convinced Ho Chi Minh He Could Win." *Vietnam Magazine*, 18 October 2010. Historynet.com. http://www.historynet.com/ia-drang-where-battlefield-losses-convinced-ho-giap-and-mcnamara-the-u-s-could-never-win.htm.

———. "Joe Galloway." *Huffington Post*, 29 September 2009.

———. "A Reporter's Journal from Hell." *Digital Journalist* (Spring 2002): pt. 4:1–8.

———. "Vietnam Story: The Word Was the Ia Drang Would Be a Walk. The Word Was Wrong." 29 October 1990. USNews.com, https://www.usnews.com/news/national/articles/2008/05/16/vietnam-story.

Garner, Dean. *Top Gun: Miramar*. Oxford, UK: Osprey, 1992.

Gelb, Leslie H., and Richard K. Betts. *The Irony of Vietnam: The System Worked*. Washington, DC: Brookings Institute, 1979.

Gibson, J. William. *The Perfect War: Technowar in Vietnam*. Boston: Atlantic Monthly Press, 1986.

Gilbert, Marc Jason, and William Head, eds. *The Tet Offensive*. Westport, CT: Praeger, 1996.

Gillespie, Robert M. "The Joint Chiefs of Staff and the Escalation of the Vietnam Conflict, 1964–1965." Master's thesis, Clemson University, 1994.

Gilster, Herman L. *The Air War in Southeast Asia*. Maxwell AFB, AL: Air University Press, 1993.

Gomez, Ian. "Vietnam Pilot to Receive Medal of Honor." *USA Today*, 22 February 2007.

[Goodwin], Doris Kearns. *Lyndon Johnson and the American Dream.* New York: Harper and Row, 1976.

Goodwin, Doris Kearns. *Lyndon Johnson and the American Dream: The Most Revealing Portrait of a President and Presidential Power Ever Written.* Rev. ed. New York: St. Martin's, 1991.

Gravel, Sen. Mike, ed. *The Pentagon Papers.* Boston: Beacon, 1971. Vol. 3. NARA Pentagon Papers, "Rolling Thunder."

Grist, Charles M. "Hal Moore Is More Forgiving Than I Am—My Problem, Not His." *American Ranger* (blog), 27 May 2008. http://americanranger.blogspot.com/2008/05/hal-moore-is-better-man-than-me.html.

Gropman, Lt. Col. Alan. *Air Power and the Airlift Evacuation of Kham Duc.* Washington, DC: Office of Air Force History, 1985.

Guan, Ang Cheng. "Decision-Making Leading to the Tet Offensive (1968): The Vietnamese Communist Perspective." *Journal of Contemporary History* 33, no. 3 (July 1998): 341–53.

Guilmartin, John F., Jr. "Arc Light." In *Encyclopedia of the Vietnam War*, edited by Stanley I. Kutler. New York: Charles Scribner's Sons, 1996.

———. *A Very Short War: The Mayaguez and the Battle of Koh Tang.* College Station: Texas A&M University Press, 1995.

Guilmartin, John F., Jr., and Michael O'Leary. *Helicopters.* Vol. 11 of *The Illustrated History of the Vietnam War.* New York: Bantam Books, 1988.

Gunston, Bill. *An Illustrated Guide to Modern Missiles.* London: Salamander Books, 1983.

Halberstam, David. *The Making of a Quagmire: America and Vietnam during the Kennedy Era.* Rev. ed. Baltimore: Rowman and Littlefield, 2008.

Hallion, Richard P. "Air Force Fighter Acquisition since 1945." *Air Power Journal* (Winter 1990).

Hammond, William H. *The United States Army in Vietnam, Public Affairs: The Military and the Media, 1962–1968.* Washington, DC: US Army Center of Military History, 1988.

Hanyok, Robert J. "SIGNT and Battle of the Ia Drang Valley, November 1965." Center for Cryptologic History, 24 February 1998.

Hartsock, Elizabeth H. *The Air Force in Southeast Asia: The Role of Air Power Grows.* Washington, DC: Office of Air Force History, 1972.

Hartsock, Elizabeth H. *The United States Air Force in Southeast Asia: Shield for Vietnamization, 1971.* CHECO Report. May 1974.

Hayward, Steven F. "The Tet Offensive." 1 April 2004. *Dialogues*. Ashbrook Center. https://ashbrook.org/publications/dialogue-hayward-tet/.

Head, William P. "Introduction." In *The Eagle in the Desert: Looking Back on US Involvement in the Persian Gulf War*, edited by William P. Head and Earl H. Tilford Jr., 1–15. Westport, CT: Praeger, 1996.

———. *Night Hunters: The AC-130s and Their Role in US Airpower*. College Station: Texas A&M University Press, 2014.

———. "Playing Hide-and-Seek with the 'Trail': Operation Commando Hunt, 1968–1972." *Journal of Third World Studies* 19, no. 1 (Spring 2002): 101–15.

———. *Shadow and Stinger: Developing the AC-119G/K Gunships in the Vietnam War*. College Station: Texas A&M University Press, 2007.

———. "The Significance of Dien Bien Phu and the End of the First Indochina War, 1953–1954." *Virginia Review of Asian Studies* 10, no. 1 (Spring 2012): 18–43. http://www.virginiareviewofasianstudies.com/archived-issues/2012-2/.

———. "Vietnam and Its Wars: A Historical Overview of US Involvement." In Head and Grinter, *Looking Back on the Vietnam War*.

———. *War from above the Clouds: B-52 Operations during the Second Indochina War and the Effects of the Air War on Theory and Doctrine*. Maxwell AFB, AL: Air University Press, 2002.

Head, William P., and Lawrence E. Grinter, eds. *Looking Back on the Vietnam War: A 1990s Perspective on Decision, Combat, and Legacies*. Westport, CT: Praeger, 1993.

Head, William P., and David R. Mets, eds. *Plotting a True Course: Reflections on USAF Strategic Attack Theory and Doctrine, the Post–World War II Experience*. Westport, CT: Praeger, 2003.

Herring, George C. *America's Longest War: The United States and Vietnam, 19501975*. New York: Alfred A. Knopf, 1979.

———. *America's Longest War: The United States and Vietnam, 1950–1975*. 4th ed. New York: McGraw-Hill, 2001.

———. "The Johnson Administration's Conduct of Limited War in Vietnam." In Head and Grinter, *Looking Back on the Vietnam War*.

Hersh, Seymour M. *The Price of Power: Kissinger in the Nixon White House*. New York: Summit Books, 1983.

Hinh, Maj. Gen. Nguyen Duy. *Vietnamization and the Cease-Fire*. Washington, DC: US Army Center of Military History, 1980.

Hirschman, Charles, et al. "Vietnam Casualties during the American War: A New Estimate," Population Development Review, *JSTOR* 21, no. 4 (December 1995): 783–812.

History. Seventh Air Force. Semiannual histories and chronology: July–December 1965; January–June 1966; July–December 1967, vol. 1; 1 July 1971–30 June 1972.

History. Seventh Air Force. "Historical Study—Commando Hunt V." May 1971.

History. Seventh Air Force. "History of Linebacker Operations." 10 May 1972–23 October 1972. Special study, HQ PACAF, 1973. K740.04, US Air Force Historic Research Center, Maxwell AFB, AL.

History. Seventh Air Force. "Commando Hunt VII." CHECO Project. June 1972.

History. Pacific Air Forces. Annual histories. Narrative and document vols.: 1 July 1971–30 June 1972. Hickam AFB, HI.

History, Pacific Command. Commander-in-Chief Pacific Command (CINCPAC). "Command History, 1967." Vol. 2.

History, Strategic Air Command. "Activity Input to Project Corona Harvest, ARC LIGHT Operations, 1 January 1965–31 March 1968." 3 vols. Offutt AFB, NE: SAC/HO, 1970.

History, Strategic Air Command. *Chronology of SAC Participation in Linebacker II*. Offutt AFB, NE: SAC/HO, 12 August 1973.

History. Tactical Air Command. July 1969–June 1970. Vol. 1, "Narrative."

History. 8th Tactical Fighter Wing. 1 October–31 December 1968; 1 April–30 June 1969, vol. 3; January–May 1969, vol. 1; 1 October–31 December 1969; Chronology; 16 SOS, 1 January–31 March 1970; 1 January–31 March 1970; 1 July–30 September 1970.

Hobson, Chris. *Vietnam Air Losses: US Air Force, Navy, and Marine Corps Fixed-Wing Aircraft Losses in Southeast Asia, 1961–1973*. Hinkley, UK: Midlands, 2001.

Hopkins, Charles K. *SAC Bomber Operations in the Southeast Asia War*. Vol. 1. Study 204. Offutt AFB, NE: SAC/HO, 1985.

Hopkins, J. C., and Sheldon A. Goldberg. *The Development of the Strategic Air Command, 1946–1986*. Offutt AFB, NE: SAC/HO, 1986.

Horrocks, Michael. *The Air Force in Southeast Asia: The Sensor War, 1966–1971*. Washington, DC: USAF History Office, 1985.

Hosmer, Stephen T. "Viet Cong Repression and its Implications for the Future." Report. Santa Monica, CA: RAND, 1970.

Hosmer, Stephen T., Konrad Kellen, and Brian M. Jenkins. *The Fall of South Vietnam: Statements by Vietnamese Civilian Leaders*. Santa Monica, CA: RAND, 1978.

Hung, Nguyen Tien, and Jerrold L. Schecter. *The Palace File*. New York: Harper and Row, 1986.

"Interview by Lt. Col. Robert G. Zimmerman with Lt. Col. Stephen J. Opitz, July 18, 1975." Oral history interview. IRIS Document 01016327, Document K239.0512–846. Historic Research Center, Air University, Maxwell AFB, AL.

Isaacs, Arnold R. *Without Honor: Defeat in Vietnam and Cambodia*. Baltimore: Johns Hopkins University Press, 1982.

Jackson, Gerald. "Hue: The Massacre the Left Wants Us to Forget." *New Australian*, 16–22 February 1998.

Jacobs, Seth. *Cold War Mandarin: Ngo Dinh Diem and the Origins of America's War in Vietnam, 1950–1963*. Lanham, MD: Rowman and Litterfield, 2006.

Jacobsen, Mark. "President Johnson and the Decision to Curtail Rolling Thunder." In Gilbert and Head, *Tet Offensive*, 215–30.

"Jason Report." *Pentagon Papers: Department of Defense History of Decision Making in Vietnam*, Senator Mike Gravel Edition. Vol. IV. Boston: Beacon, 1971.

Joes, Anthony J. *The War for South Vietnam, 1954–1975*. New York: Praeger, 1989.

Johnson, Maj. Calvin R. HQ PACAF, Project CHECO. *Linebacker Operations, September–December 1972*. Washington, DC: Office of Air Force History, 1974.

Johnson, Lyndon B. *The Vantage Point: Perspectives of the Presidency, 1963–1969*. New York: Holt, Rinehart, and Winston, 1971.

Kahin, George M. *Intervention: How America Became Involved in Vietnam*. New York: Knopf, 1986.

Kahin, George M., and John W. Lewis. *The United States in Vietnam*. New York: Dell, 1969.

Karnow, Stanley. *Vietnam: A History*. New York: Viking, 1983.

Kendrick, Oliver. *My Lai Massacre in American History and Memory*. Manchester, UK: Manchester University Press, 2006.

"Kennedy Criticizes the 'Hamburger Hill' Battle." 16 November 2009. This Day in History. History.com. http://www.history.com/this-day-in-history/kennedy-criticizes-the-hamburger-hill-battle.

Khuyen, Dong Van. *The RVNAF*. Indochina Monographs. Washington, DC: Center for Military History, 1979.

Kiet, Le Anh Dai. *The Narratives of Saigon Generals*. Hanoi: People's Police Publishing, 2003.

Kinnard, Douglas. *The War Managers*. Hanover, NH: University of Vermont Press, 1977.

Kinney, Gen. William A. "TACAIR Vietnam." *Airman* 12, no. 7 (July 1968): 40–41.

Kirkpatrick, Charles E. "The Battle at Ap Bac Changed America's View of the Vietnam War." *Vietnam Magazine*, June 1990. Historynet.com, 25 July 2006. http://www.historynet.com/the-battle-at-ap-bac-changed-americas-view-of-the-vietnam-war.htm.

Kirpatrick, Rob. *1969: The Year That Everything Changed*. New York: Skyhorse, 2011.

Kissinger, Henry. *Ending the Vietnam War: A History of America's Involvement and Extrication from the Vietnam War*. New York: Simon and Schuster, 2003.

———. *The White House Years*. Boston: Little, Brown, 1979.

———. *Years of Renewal*. Boston: Little, Brown, 1980.

Kohn, Richard, and Joseph P. Harahan, eds. *Air Superiority in World War II and Korea: An Interview with General James Ferguson, General Robert M. Lee, General William Momyer, and Lt Gen Elwood R. Quesada*. Washington, DC: USAF History Office, 1983.

Kolko, Gabriel. *Anatomy of a War: Vietnam the United States, and the Modern Historical Experience*. New York: Pantheon, 1985.

Korb, Lawrence J. *The Joint Chiefs of Staff: The First Twenty-Five Years*. Bloomington: University of Indiana Press, 1976.

Kott. Maj. Richard F. *The Role of United States Air Force Gunships in Southeast Asia (SEASIA)*. CHECO Project. Hickam AFB, HI: HQ PACAF, 30 August 1969.

Krohn, Charles A. *The Lost Battalion: Controversy and Casualties in the Battle of Hue*. Westport, CT: Praeger, 1993.

Kutler, Stanley I., ed. *Encyclopedia of the Vietnam War*. New York: Charles Scribner's Sons, 1996.

Laderman, Scott. "They Set about Revenging Themselves on the Population: The 'Hue Massacre,' Travel Guidebooks, and the Shaping of Historical Consciousness in Vietnam." MacArthur Scholar, Department of American Studies, University of Minnesota, 2002.

————. *Tours of Vietnam: War, Travel Guides, and Memory*. Durham, NC: Duke University Press, 2009.

Lake, John. *Stratofortress Units in Combat, 1955–1973*. Oxford, UK: Osprey, 2004.

Lamb, David. "Reporters at Work: Giving a Battle a Name." *About Editing and Writing* (blog), 4 September 2012. http://jacklimpert.com/ 2012/09/04/.

Lavalle, Maj. A. J. C., ed. *Air Power and the 1972 Spring Offensive*. USAF Monograph Series, vol. 2. Washington, DC: CPO, 1977.

Le Gro, William E. *Vietnam from Cease Fire to Capitulation*. Publication 90–29. Washington, DC: US Army Center of Military History, 1981, 1985, 2001. Also Honolulu, HI: University of the Pacific Press, 2006.

Leonard, Steven M. US Army Center of Military History. "Forward Support in the Ia Drang Valley." *Army Logistician* (March–April 2006).

Lewy, Gunter. *America in Vietnam*. New York: Oxford University Press, 1978.

Liebchen, Capt. Peter A. W. "Kontum: Battle for the Central Highlands, 30 March–10 June 1972." CHECO Division, Project CHECO Southeast Asia Report. Hickam AFB, HI: HQ PACAF, 7AF/DOAC, 27 October 1972. Accession ADA487009.

Lipsman, Samuel, Stephen Weiss, et al. *The False Peace*. Boston: Boston Publishing, 1985.

"List of Civilians Massacred by the Communists during 'Tet Mau Than' in Thua Thien Province and Hue City." Report by Republic of Vietnam, 1969.

Littauer, Raphael, and Norman Uphoff, eds. *The Air War in Indochina*. Boston: Beacon, 1972.

Long, Ngo Vinh. *The Tet Offensive and Its Aftermath*. Ithaca, NY: Cornell University Press, 1993.

————. "The Tet Offensive and Its Aftermath." In Gilbert and Head, *Tet Offensive*, 89–124.

Loye, Col. J. F., Jr., et al. "Lom Son 719: The South Vietnamese Incursion into Laos, 30 January–24 March 1971." CHECO Project. Hickam AFB, HI: HQ PACAF, 24 March 1971.

Lung, Hoang Ngoc. *The General Offensives of 1968–1969*. McLean, VA: General Research, 1978.

"Lyndon B. Johnson—The Final Days." Profiles of US Presidents. http:// www.presidentprofiles.com/Kennedy-Bush/Lyndon-B-Johnson-The-final-days.html.

Maintenance Division, Aircraft Testing Unit. "PACAF Capability Study." DPL/TSC-65–240. 12 March 1965.

Maitland, Terrance, and John McInerney. *A Contagion of War*. Boston: Boston Publishing, 1983.

Manley, Jacqueline. *Saigon Salvation*. Maitland, FL: Xulon, 2010.

Mann, Capt. David K. *The 1972 Invasion of Military Region I: Fall of Quang Tri and Defense of Hue*. CHECO Project. Saigon: 7 AF/CDC, 15 March 1973.

Mark, Eduard. *Aerial Interdiction: Air Power and the Land Battle in Three American Wars*. Washington, DC: Center for Air Force History, 1994.

Marolda, Edward J. *By Sea, Air, and Land: An Illustrated History of the US Navy and the War in Southeast Asia*. Washington, DC: Naval Historical Center, 1994.

"The Massacre at Hue." *Time*, 31 October 1969.

McCarthy, Brig. Gen. James R., and Lt. Col. George B. Allison. *Linebacker II: A View from the Rock*. Maxwell AFB, AL: Air War College, Airpower Research Institute, 1979.

McCarthy, Brig. Gen. James R., and Lt. Col. George B. Allison. *Linebacker II: A View from the Rock*. Rev. ed. USAF Southeast Asia Monograph Series, vol. 6, monograph 8. Washington, DC: USAF History Office, 1985.

McDonald, Peter. *Giap: The Victor in Vietnam*. New York: W. W. Norton, 1993.

McGarvey, Patrick. *Visions of Victory*. Stanford, CA: Stanford University Press, 1969.

McGowan, Stanley S. *Helicopters: An Illustrated History of Their Impact*. Santa Barbara, CA: ABCCLIO, 2005.

McKay, Mary-Jayne. "Valley of Death: Vietnam Vet on Movie Set." 6 March 2002. CBSNews.com. http://www.cbsnews.com/2100–500164_162–503 144.html.

McMaster, H. R. *Dereliction of Duty: Lyndon Johnson, Robert McNamara, and the Joint Chiefs of Staff and the Lies That Led to Vietnam*. New York: Harper and Collins, 1997.

McNamara, Francis Terry. *Escape with Honor: My Last Hours in Vietnam*. With Adrian Hill. Dulles, VA: Brassey's, 1997.

McNamara, Robert. *In Retrospect: The Tragedy and Lessons of Vietnam*. New York: Times Books, 1995.

Mellinger, Col. Philip. *Ten Propositions Regarding Air Power*. Washington, DC: Air Force History and Museum Program, 1995.

Mesko, Jim. *Airmobile: The Helicopter War in Vietnam*. Carrollton, TX: Squadron/Signal, 1984.

Michel, Marshall L. *Clashes: Air Combat over North Vietnam, 1965–1972*. Annapolis, MD: Naval Institute Press, 1997.

Military Assistance Command, Vietnam. *Ap Bac Battle, 2 January 1963: Translation of VC Document*. 20 April 1963. C0043021, .

———. "Linebacker Study." 20 January 1973. Unofficial/Uncoordinated draft report. File K712.041–19. AFHRA.

Military Assistance Command. Semiannual, periodic, and annual histories. Narrative and document vols. 1965, January 1972–March 1973. 15 July 1973, Saigon.

Military Assistance Command, Vietnam. Annual Histories. Vol. 2, 1967; 1970, Vol. 1, Annex A; January 1972–March 1973. Vol. 1, Annex A.

Military Assistance Command, Vietnam. *Command History 1965, Annex N*. Saigon, 1966.

Military History Institute of Vietnam. *Victory in Vietnam: The Official History of the People's Army of Vietnam, 1954–1975*. Translated by Merle L. Pribbenow. Lawrence: University Press of Kansas, 2002.

Moise, Edwin E. *Tonkin Gulf and the Escalation of the Vietnam War*. Chapel Hill: University of North Carolina Press, 1996.

Momyer, Gen. William W. *Air Power in Three Wars*. Washington, DC: Government Printing Office, 1978.

———. *The Vietnamese Air Force, 1951–1975: An Analysis of Its Role in Combat*. Washington, DC: Office of Air Force History. Rev. ed. Maxwell AFB, AL: Air University Press, 1985.

Moore, Lt. Col. Harold G., Commander, 1st Battalion, 7th Cavalry. "After Action Report, Ia Drang Valley Operation, 1st Battalion, 7th Cavalry, 14–16 November 1965." 9 December 1965.

Moore, Harold G., and Joseph L. Galloway. *We Were Soldiers Once . . . and Young*. New York: Harper Torch/Random House, 1992.

Morocco, John. *Rain of Fire: Air War, 1969–1973*. The Vietnam Experience. Boston: Boston Publishing, 1984.

———. *Thunder from Above: Air War, 1941–1968*. The Vietnam Experience. Boston: Boston Publishing, 1984.

Morris, Virginia, and Clive Hill. *A History of the Ho Chi Minh Trail: The Road to Freedom*. Bangkok: Orchid, 2006.

Moyar, Mark. *Triumph Forsaken: The Vietnam War, 1954–1965*. New York: Cambridge University Press, 2006.

Mrozek, Donald J. "The Limits of Innovation: Aspects of Air Power in Vietnam." Center for Aerospace Doctrine Research and Education (CADRE). Maxwell AFB, AL, 1985.

Murphy, Edward F. *Dak To*. New York: Pocket Books, 1995.

———. *The Hill Fights: the First Battle of Khe Sanh*. New York: Presidio, 2004.

Nagle, John. *Counterinsurgency Lessons from Malaya to Vietnam: Learning to Eat Soup with a Knife*. Westport, CT: Praeger, 2002.

Nalty, Bernard C. *Air Power and the Fight for Khe Sanh*. Washington, DC: Office of Air Force History, 1986.

———. *The Air War over South Vietnam, 1968–1975*. Washington, DC: Air Force History and Museum Program, 2000.

———. *Interdiction in Southern Laos*. Washington, DC: Office of Air Force History, 1988.

———. *"Operation Rolling Thunder," an Uncommon War: The US Air Force in Southeast Asia*. Fact sheet. Washington, DC: USAF History Support Office, 1994.

———. "Post-Vietnam." In *Winged Shield, Winged Sword: A History of the United States Air Force*. Vol. 2, *1950–1997*. Bolling AFB, DC: Air Force Museum and History Program, 1997.

Nellis AFB Flying Operations. "Exercises and Flight Operations: Red Flag High-Intensity Air-to-Air Combat Exercises." http://www.nellis.af.mil/library/flyingoperations.asp. Page removed.

Nicholson, Capt. Charles A. *The United States Air Force Response to the Spring 1972 North Vietnamese Offensive: Situation and Redeployment*. CHECO Project. Saigon: 7 AF DOAC, 1972.

Nguyen, Lien-Hang T. "The War Politburo: North Vietnam's Diplomatic and Political Road to the Tet Offensive." *Journal of Vietnamese Studies* 1, nos. 1–2 (February/August 2006): 4–58.

Nixon, Richard M. *In the Arena: A Memoir of Victory, Defeat, and Renewal*. New York: Simon and Schuster, 1990.

———. *RN: The Memoirs of Richard Nixon*. 2 vols. New York: Warner Books, 1978.

Nolan, Keith W. *Battle for Hue, Tet 1968*. Novato, CA: Presidio, 1983.

———. *The Battle of Saigon, Tet 1968*. New York: Pocket Books, 1996.

Oberdorfer, Donald. "Hue Red Report Found." *Milwaukee Sentinel*, 8 December 1969.

———. *Tet!* 1971. Reprint, Garden City, NY: Doubleday, 1984.

Office of the Press Secretary. News Release. "President Bush Presents the Medal of Honor to Lieutenant Colonel Bruce Crandall." 26 February 2007. www.whitehouse.gov.

Olson, James S., and Roberts, Randy. *Where the Domino Fell: America and Vietnam, 1945–1990*. New York: St. Martin's, 1991.

O'Neill, Robert J. *General Giap*. North Melbourne, Australia: Cassell, 1969.

Pacific Air Forces. *Linebacker II Air Force Bombing Survey*. Hickam AFB, HI, 1973.

Pacific Air Forces. "North Vietnamese Current Assessment." Vol. 7. *US Air Force Operations in Defense of RVN*. CHECO Project. Hickam AFB, HI: HQ PACAF, 1 June 1972. Document Collection. File K717.03–219. AFHRA.

Pacific Air Forces. Southeast Asia Report, *Air Operations Summary, April, May, and June 1972*. File K717.3063. AFHRA.

Pacific Air Forces. *US Air Operations against NVN, 1 July–30 June 1972*. CHECO Project. Hickam AFB, HI: HQ PACAF, 1973.

Page, Tim, and John Pimlott, eds. *Nam—The Vietnam Experience*. New York: Orbis, 1995.

Palmer, Bruce Jr., ed. *US Intelligence and Vietnam*. CIA Studies in Intelligence. Special Issue, June, 1984. Declassified 2007.

Palmer, Bruce, ed. *Grand Strategy for the 1980s*. Washington, DC: American Enterprises Institute for Public Policy Research, 1978.

Palmer, Dave Richard. *Summons of the Trumpet: The History of the Vietnam War from a Military Man's Viewpoint*. New York: Ballentine, 1978. https://www.cia.gov/library/readingroom/document/0001433692

Pearson, Gen. Willard. *The War in the Northern Provinces, 19661968*. Washington, DC: Department of the Army, 1975.

Pentagon Papers: The Defense Department History of United States Decisionmaking on Vietnam. Senator Gravel edition. 5 vols. Boston: Beacon, 1971–72.

Pike, Douglas. *PAVN: People's Army of North Vietnam*. Novato, CA: Presidio, 1986.

———. *Viet Cong: The Organization and Techniques of the National Liberation Front of South Vietnam*. Cambridge, MA: MIT Press, 1966.

———. *The Viet Cong Strategy of Terror.* Saigon: US Mission, US State Department, February 1970. http://www.faculty.virginia.edu/jnmoore/vietnam/vietcongstrat.pdf.

Pimlott, John. *Vietnam: The Decisive Battles.* New York: Macmillan, 1990.

Pisor, Robert. *The End of the Line: The Siege of Khe Sanh.* New York: Norton, 1982.

Poglione, John A., et al. *Air Power and the 1972 Spring Invasion.* Air Force SEA Monograph Series, vol. 3. Hickam AFB, HI: HQ PACAF, 1976.

Porter, Melvin F. *Linebacker: Overview of the First 120 Days.* Project CHECO. Saigon: 7AF/DOA, 1973.

Porter, Melvin F. "Silver Bayonet." 28 February 1966. CHECO Project report. USAF, HRA, Archive Item K717.0413-2, 9–28 Nov 1965. Declassified 26 December 1995.

Porter, D. Gareth. "The 1968 'Hue Massacre.'" *Indochina Chronicle.* Vol. 3 (24 June 1974). https://msuweb.montclair.edu/~furrg/Vietnam/porter hueic74.pdf.

———, ed. *Vietnam: The Definitive Documentary of Human Decisions.* 2 vols. Sanfordville, NY: Earl M. Coleman, 1979. https://msuweb.montclair.edu/

Prados, John. *The Blood Road: The Ho Chi Minh Trail and the Vietnam War.* New York: John Wiley and Sons, 1998.

———. "Khe Sanh: The Other Side of the Hill." *Veteran* (July/August 2007). Vietnam Veterans of America. http://archive.vva.org/archive/TheVet eran/0807/khesanh.html.

Prados, John, and Ray W. Stubbe. *Valley of Decision.* Boston: Houghton Mifflin, 1991.

Pribbenow, Merle L. "North Vietnam's Final Offensive: Strategic Endgame Nonpareil." *Parameters: US Army War College Quarterly* (Winter 1999–2000): 58–71.

Pribbenow, Merle L., and George J. Vieth. "Fighting Is an Art: The Army of the Republic of Vietnam's Defense of Xuan Loc, 9–21 April 1975." *Journal of Military History* 68, no. 1 (January 2004): 191–200. https://muse.jhu.edu/article/50686.

Rice, Edward E. *Wars of the Third Kind: Conflict in Underdeveloped Countries.* Berkeley: University of California Press, 1988.

Richburg, K. B. "20 years after Hue, Vietnamese admit 'mistake.'" *Washington Post*, 2 February 1988, 8A.

Rikhye, Ravi. "Operation Silver Bayonet: The Battle of the Ia Drang, 1965." 19 February 2003, p. 1.

Ringenbach, Maj. Paul T., and Capt. Peter J. Melly. *The Battle for An Loc, 5 April—26 June 1972*. Project CHECO. Hickam AFB, HI: HQ PACAF, 31 January 1973.

Robbins, James. *This Time We Win: Revisiting the Tet Offensive*. New York: Encounter, 2010.

Rottman, Gordon L. *Khe Sanh 1967–68*. Oxford, UK: Osprey, 2005.

Safer, Morley. *The Battle of Ia Drang Valley, 1965*. CBS News Special Report. National Archives, LI 265.2408. https://www.c-span.org/video/?c4683027/battle-ia-drang-valley.

Sams, Kenneth.. *First Test and Combat Use of the AC-47*. Project CHECO. Hickam AFB, HI: HQ PACAF, December 1965.

Sams, Kenneth. "The Fall of A Shau." SE Asia Team Project CHECO Report. Hickam AFB, HI: HQ PACAF, 18 April 1966.

———. "The Fall of A Shau." SE Asia Team Project CHECO Report. Hickam AFB, HI: HQ PACAF, 18 April 1966.

Sarin, Oleg, and Lev Dvoretsky. *Alien Wars: The Soviet Union's Aggression against the World, 1919 to 1989*. Novato, CA: Presidio, 1996.

Scalard, Lt. Col. Douglas P. "The Battle of Hamburger Hill: Battle Command in Difficult Terrain against a Determined Enemy." Studies in Battle Command: By the Faculty Combat Studies Institute, US Army. E-History Archives. Ohio State University. https://ehistory.osu.edu/articles/studies-battle-command.

Schandler, Herbert Y. *Lyndon Johnson and Vietnam: The Unmaking of a President*. Princeton, NJ: Princeton University Press, 1977.

Schlight, Col. John. *The War in South Vietnam: The Years of the Offensive, 1965–1968*. The United States Air Force in Southeast Asia. Washington, DC: Office of Air Force History, 1988.

———. *A War too Long: The USAF in Southeast Asia, 1961–1973*. Washington, DC: Government Printing Office, 1996.

Schmitz, David F. *The Tet Offensive: Politics, War, and Public Opinion*. Westport, CT: Praeger, 2004.

Schulimson, Jack, Leonard Blaisol, Charles R. Smith, and David Dawson. *The U.S. Marines in Vietnam: 1968, the Decisive Year*. Washington DC: History and Museums Division, USMC, 1997.

Seig, Louis. *Impact of Geography on Air Operations in Southeast Asia.* CHECO Project. Hickam AFB, HI: HQ PACAF, 11 July 1970.

Sharp, Adm. U. S. G. *Strategy for Defeat: Vietnam in Retrospect.* 1978. Reprint, Novato, CA: Presidio, 1986.

Sheehan, Neil. "Ap Bia Mountain (Vietnam), Battle of 1969: Letters from Hamburger Hill." *Harper's Weekly*, November 1969. http://harpers.org/archive/1969/11/letters-from-hamburger-hill/.

———. *A Bright Shining Lie: John Paul Vann and America in Vietnam.* New York: Random House, 1988.

Sheehan, Neil, Hedrick Smith, E. W. Kenworthy, and Fox Butterworth. *The Pentagon Papers as Published by the New York Times.* New York: Bantam Inc., 1971.

Shore, Capt. Moyers S., II. *The Battle for Khe Sanh.* Washington, DC: History and Museums Division, USMC, 1969.

Showalter, Dennis E., and John G. Albert, eds. *An American Dilemma: Vietnam, 1964–1973.* Chicago: Imprint, 1993.

Simkin, John. "Operation Rolling Thunder." Spartacus Educational. Last updated August 2014. http://spartacus-educational.com/VNrollingthunder.htm.

Slay, Maj. Gen. Alton D. "End-of-Tour Report, August 1971–August 1972." File K717.13, AFHRA.

Smith, George W. *The Siege at Hue.* Boulder, CO: Lynne Rienner, 1999.

Smith, Pfc. Jack P. "Death in the Ia Drang Valley, November 13–18, 1965." *Saturday Evening Post*, 28 January 1967. *Vietnam Veterans Association.* http://www.vietnamwall.org/news.php?id=1.

Snepp, Frank. *Decent Interval: An Insider's Account of Saigon's Indecent End Told by the CIA's Chief Strategy Analyst in Vietnam.* Rev. ed. Lawrence: University Press of Kansas, 2002.

———. *A Disastrous Retreat.* Ho Chi Minh City: Ho Chi Minh City Publishing, 2001.

Sorley, Lewis. *A Better War: The Unexamined Victories and Final Tragedy of America's Last Years in Vietnam.* New York: Harvest Books, 1999.

Spector, Ronald H. *Advice and Support.* Washington, DC: US Center for Military History, 1983.

———. *After Tet: The Bloodiest Year in Vietnam.* New York: Free Press, 1993.

Staff Officers' Field Manual, Organizational, Technical, and Logistical Data

Planning Factors. Vol. 2. Field Manual 101–10–1-1/2. Washington, DC: Headquarters, Department of the Army, 1987.

Stanton, Shelby L. *The Rise and Fall of an American Army: US Ground Forces in Vietnam, 1965–1973.* New York: Dell, 1985.

Starry, Don A. *Armored Combat in Vietnam.* North Stratford, CT: Avro, 1980.

"The Study of the Hue Massacre." March 1968. Douglas Pike Collection. Unit 05, National Liberation Front, D012, Folder 14, Box 13. Vietnam Center and Archive, Texas Tech University, Lubbock.

Summers, Col. Harry G., Jr. "America's Bitter End in Vietnam," *Vietnam Magazine,* April 1995. http://www.historynet.com/americas-bitter-end-in-vietnam.htm.

———. "Battle of Hamburger Hill during the Vietnam War." *Vietnam Magazine,* June 1999. Historynet.com. http://www.historynet.com/battle-for-hamburger-hill-during-the-vietnam-war.htm.

———. *On Strategy: A Critical Analysis of the Vietnam War.* Novato, CA: Presidio, 1982.

———. *On Strategy: The Vietnam War in Context.* Carlisle Barracks, PA: Army War College, 1981.

Szulc, Ted. *The Illusion of Peace: Foreign Policy in the Nixon Years.* New York: Viking, 1978.

Telfer, Maj. Gary L., Lt. Col. Lane Rogers, and V. Keith Fleming. *U.S. Marines in Vietnam: 1967, Fighting the North Vietnamese.* Washington, DC: History and Museums Division, USMC, 1984.

"The Tet That Wasn't." Editorial. *Life,* 24 March 1972, p. 38.

Thach, Pham Ngoc, and Ho Khang. *History of the War of Resistance against America.* 8th ed. Hanoi: National Politics Publishing, 2008.

Thackeray, Lorna. "The Valley of Death." *Billings (MT) Gazette,* 30 March 2002.

Thai, Hoang Van. *The Liberation of South Vietnam, Memoirs.* Hanoi: Gioi, 1992.

Thayer, Thomas C. *War without Fronts: The American Experience in Vietnam.* Boulder, CO: Westview, 1985.

Thien, Dinh Van, and Do Phuong Linh. *Battles on the Doorstep of Saigon.* Hanoi: People's Army Publishing, 2005.

Thompson, Ben. "Bruce Crandall." *Badass of the Week.* http://www.badassoftheweek.com/crandall.html.

Thompson, Wayne. *To Hanoi and Back: The U.S. Air Force and North Vietnam, 1966–1973*, Washington, DC: Smithsonian Institution Press, 2002.

Tilford, Earl H., Jr. "Bombing Our Way Back Home: The 'Commando Hunt' 'Menu' Campaigns of 1969–1973." In Head and Grinter, *Looking Back on the Vietnam War*, 123–44.

———. *Crosswinds: The Air Force's Set Up in Vietnam*. College Station: Texas A&M University Press, 1993.

———. *Setup: What the Air Force Did in Vietnam and Why*. Maxwell AFB, AL: Air University Press, 1991.

———. *United States Air Force Search and Rescue Operations in Southeast Asia, 1961–1975*. Washington, DC: Office of Air Force History, 1980.

Till, Gerald J., and James C. Thomas. *Pave Aegis Weapon System (AC-130E Gunship)*. CHECO Project. Hickam AFB, HI: HQ PACAF, 30 July 1973.

Tin, Bui. *From Enemy to Friend: A North Vietnamese Perspective on the War*. Annapolis, MD: Naval Institute Press, 2002.

———. *Memiors*. 2 vols. English ed. Irvine, CA: Nhan Quyen Editeur, 1991–93.

Tobin, Thomas G., Arthur E. Lehr, and John F. Hilgenberg. *Last Flight from Saigon*. Maxwell AFB, AL: Air University Press, 1979.

Toczek, David M. *The Battle of Ap Bac: They Did Everything but Learn from It*. Westport, CT: Greenwood, 2001.

Tra, Tran Van. *Concluding the 30-Year War*. Vol. 5 of *Viet Nam: History Bulwark B-2 Theatre*. Ho Chi Minh City: Van Nghe, 1983. English ed. Arlington, VA: Joint Publications Research Service, 1983.

———. "Tet: The 1968 General Offensive and General Uprising." In *The Vietnam War: Vietnamese and American Perspectives*, edited by Jayne S. Warner and Luu Doan Huynh. Armonk, NY: M. E. Sharpe, 1994.

Trinh, Tong Ho. *Huong Tien Cong va Noi Day Tet Mau Than o Tri-Thien-Hue, 1968* [The 1968 Tet Offensive and uprising in the Tri-Thien-Hue Theater]. Hanoi: Vien Lich Su Quan Su Viet Nam [Vietnamese Institute for Military History], 1968.

Truong, Lt. Gen. Ngo Quang. *The Easter Offensive of 1972*. Indochina Monographs. Washington, DC: US Army Center of Military History, 1980.

Truong, Nhu Tang. *A Vietcong Memoir: An Inside Account of the Vietnam War and Its Aftermath*. With David Chanoff and Doan Van Toai. New York: Harcourt, Brace, and Jovanovich, 1985.

Truong, Vinh Van. *Vietnam War: The New Legion*. Vol. 1. Victoria, BC: Trafford, 2010.

Tsang, Daniel C. "Vietnam Today, Ngo Vinh Long, Interview with Daniel C. Tsang." *Critical Asian Studies* 34, no. 3 (September 2002).

Tuohy, William. "Marines Are Taking Hue Wall by Wall." *Washington Post*. February 9, 1968, p. 1A.

United States–Vietnam Relations, 1945–1967. 12 vols. Washington, DC: Government Printing Office, 1971.

US State Department. *Aggression from the North*. Washington, DC: Government Printing Office, 1965.

"US Troops Abandon 'Hamburger Hill.'" 16 November 2009. This Day in History. History.com. https://www.history.com/this-day-in-history/us-troops-abandon-hamburger-hill.

Van Staaveren, Jacob. *Gradual Failure: The Air War over North Vietnam, 1965–1966*. Washington, DC: Air Force History and Museum Program, 2002.

———. *Interdiction in Southern Laos, 1961–1968*. Washington, DC: Center for Air Force History, 1993.

———. "Rolling Thunder." In Berger, *United States Air Force in Southeast Asia*.

Veith, George J. *Black April: The Fall of South Vietnam, 1973–1975*. New York: Encounter Books, 2012.

Vennema, Alje. *The Viet Cong Massacre at Hue*. New York: Vantage, 1976.

Vien, Cao Van. *The Final Collapse*. Washington, DC: US Army Center of Military History, 1985.

"Vietnam Veteran Arthur Wiknik Describing His Experiences during the Battle of Hamburger Hill." Oral history interview. Veterans History Project, Central Connecticut State University, New Britain, 1985

Villard, Erik. *The 1968 Tet Offensive Battles of Quang Tri City and Hue*. Ft. Leslie J. McNair, DC: US Army Center of Military History, 9 February 2008.

Warr, Nicholas. *Phase Line Green: The Battle for Hue, 1968*. Annapolis, MD: Naval Institute Press, 1997.

Warren, James. "The Mystery of Khe Sanh." In *The Cold War: A Military History*, edited by Robert Cowley. New York: Random House, 2005.

Weiss, George. "TAC Air: Present and Future Lessons, Problems, and Needs." *Armed Forces Journal*. September 1971.

Westmoreland, William C. *A Soldier Reports*. Garden City, NY: Doubleday, 1976.

Wiesner, Louis. *Victims and Survivors: Displaced Persons and Other War Victims in Vietnam.* New York: Greenwood, 1988.

Wiest, Andrew. *Vietnam's Forgotten Army: Heroism and Betrayal in the ARVN.* New York: NYU Press, 2007.

———. *The Vietnam War, 1956–1975.* Oxford, UK: Osprey, 2002.

Willbanks, James H. *Abandoning Vietnam: How America Left and South Vietnam Lost Its War.* Lawrence: University Press of Kansas, 2004.

———. "Hell or Hamburger Hill." *Vietnam* (June 2009). https://www.history net.com/hell-on-hamburger-hill.htm.

———. "The Last 55 Days." Paper delivered at the Third Triennial Vietnam Symposium, Vietnam Center, Texas Tech University, Lubbock, 15–17 April 1999.

———. "Tet—What Really Happened at Hue." Historynet.com, 25 January 2011. http://www.historynet.com/tet-what-really-happened-at-hue.htm.

———. *The Tet Offensive: A Concise History.* New York: Columbia University Press, 2007.

Wirtz, James J. *The Tet Offensive: Intelligence Failure in War.* Ithaca, NY: Cornell University Press, 1991.

Wyatt, Clarence. *Paper Soldiers: The American Press and the Vietnam War.* Chicago: University of Chicago Press, 1995.

Young, Marilyn. *The Vietnam Wars, 1945–1990.* New York: Harper Perennial, 1991.

Zaffiri, Samuel. *Hamburger Hill: The Brutal Battle for Dong Ap Bia, May 11–May 20, 1969.* Novato, CA: Presidio, 1988.

———. *Westmoreland.* New York: William Morrow, 1994.

Zais, Maj. Gen. Melvin. "Interview with Colonels Golden, William L. and Rice, Richard C." 1977. Project 77–3. Transcript vol. 3, Senior Officers Oral History Program. US Army Heritage and Education Center, Carlisle Barracks, PA.

Index